The Encyclopedia of Mental Health Trainings, Certifications, & Credentials

A Professional's Guide
to Becoming a Highly Qualified Mental Health Practitioner

EDITORS

BILL OWENBY
EdD, MC, FAAETS, DAAETS, DCMHS, LPC, LAAC, NCC, CCMHC, ACS
AAETS FELLOW, AAETS DIPLOMATE, AMHCA DIPLOMATE

KATHERINE CAMPBELL
MAED, LPC, LAAC, NCC

It is not legal to reproduce, duplicate, or transmit any part of this document in either electronic means or printed format without the permission of the author, available by directly purchasing this manual or through correspondence. Recording or copying of this publication is strictly prohibited.

By purchasing this copy, you assume all ethical, clinical, legal, medical, financial, boards of health, malpractice, and any other forms of liability and cannot hold the publisher, authors, or editors liable or responsible for the buyer's actions, intent, or outcomes obtained from using this manual within own personal or professional practice. This manual is designed for individuals with professional degree training and accomplishments in order to either deliver such a modality or determine the clinical ability to do so in their own practices. Individuals who may be reading this and who are not professionally trained or with malintent of using such information could be considered outside of their scope of practice and doing so may indicate negative outcomes and representation of their respective field and profession. If you continue to read, pursue, and seek out further training, you do so at your own risk, and thereby withhold any legal, ethical, medical, financial, and other forms of liability and cannot hold the author liable or responsible for any legal, board, or employment pursuits.

This book does not meet minimal training requirements or certification standards for any modality, therefore, it is not legally binding, malpractice liability exempt or boards of medical/nursing/behavioral health approved. The user of these recommendations assumes all liability, intent, and responsibility for their practice, their scope of practice, malpractice insurance requirements, and restrictions. By using this/these recommendations appropriately or not, you assume all liability and automatically deny any legal, financial, clinical, or ethical responsibility upon the creator/authors of this book and ONBLLC. Any derivation from this manual is at the risk of the reader/clinician and in no way holds the authors or editors liable.

Materials included in this book and by extension websites may include recommendations and or interventions that are beyond your authorized scope of practice. As the consumer of this material and professional in your field, you are responsible for reviewing your abilities, scopes of practice, and or supervision needs in order to practice within your boundaries in accordance with your legal boards and ethical standards.

Table of Contents
Volume 4: G-L

Geek Therapy

SARAH STILLWELL, PHD, LPC-SUPERVISOR, NCC

RUBY CRAMER, MS

Geek Therapy is an innovative approach to therapy that integrates elements of geek culture, such as video games, comics, and other interests, into therapeutic practices. The idea is to use these shared interests to build rapport and create a comfortable environment for clients, helping them to open up and explore their thoughts and feelings more easily (*Geek Therapy*, 2024). It's a way to meet clients where they are and use their passions to help them work through challenges.

Geek Therapy was invented by Josué Cardona in 2011 (*Geek Therapy*, 2024). The idea came about when Josué, who was working as a mental health counseling intern, asked his supervisor if he could use video games with his clients. His supervisor said no, so Josué went home and created a website to collect research and stories about the positive applications of geek culture. He called it Geek Therapy. Josué was inspired by the work of mental health professionals like Lawrence Rubin, Robin Rosenberg, and Patrick O'Connor, who were already exploring the intersection of geek culture and mental health. He also drew from his Rational Emotive Behavior Therapy clinical training at the Albert Ellis Institute in New York City. Since its inception, Geek Therapy has grown into a nonprofit organization that advocates for the effective use of popular media in therapy, education, and community practice. It has expanded to include mediums like comics, video games, anime, and more. The core components of Geek Therapy are affinity, resonance, and understanding (*Geek Therapy*, 2024):

Affinity identifies the client's interests and passions within geek culture. This could include video games, comics, anime, tabletop games, science fiction, fantasy, and more. By recognizing these interests, therapists can build trust and rapport with the client. The idea is that when clients talk about something they're passionate about, they feel more comfortable and engaged in the therapeutic process.

Resonance involves finding connections between the client's interests and personal experiences or challenges. For example, a therapist might explore how a client relates to a particular superhero's struggles or how they feel empowered by a character in a video game. By drawing parallels between these fictional narratives and the client's real-life experiences, therapists can help clients gain new perspectives and insights into their lives.

Understanding uses the insights gained from affinity and resonance to facilitate personal growth and change. Therapists use the client's geek culture interests as a bridge to discuss deeper emotional and psychological issues. This can help clients develop coping strategies, improve their self-esteem, and work through trauma in a way that feels accessible and relevant to them.

CERTIFICATIONS, TRAINING, AND LICENSURE REQUIREMENTS

Geek Therapy is accredited by the National Board for Certified Counselors (NBCC) as an Approved Continuing Education Provider (ACEP) (*Geek Therapy*, 2024). Geek Therapy's learning platform, Geek Therapy U, provides educational courses every two to three months regarding implementing popular geek media in therapeutic practice. To practice as a certified Geek Therapist, one must complete a two-hour, live online course, which results in two continuing education (CE) credits. Certification courses serve to acquaint professionals with the Geek Therapy model and prepare them to practice Geek Therapy ethically and informally. Upon completion, participants are added to Geek Therapy's client referral list of certified practitioners. Given that this model can be integrated into many different therapeutic approaches and practiced by various clinicians, no prerequisite credentials are required to take an online course or obtain certification in Geek Therapy (*Geek Therapy*, 2024).

In addition to offering certification courses, the Geek Therapy website provides several open-access resources (e.g., podcast episodes, blog posts, research library, consultation opportunities, online library of therapeutic materials, Discord server) that help foster an environment of learning and community. These resources help professionals stay on the pulse of innovations, updates, and events pertinent to the Geek Therapy model (*Geek Therapy*, 2024).

General Cost

Geek Therapy certification courses operate on a donation system, meaning the cost is relative to each participant, and there is no universal cost. The payment amount is entirely determined by individuals. Additionally, neither consultation appointments nor office hours attendance require payment (*Geek Therapy*, 2024). By reducing barriers related to duration and cost, Geek Therapy effectively endeavors to make the certification process more financially accessible to individuals of varying degrees of scheduling availability and financial circumstances.

The Geek Therapy website houses a free-access library of nerdy content for clinicians, though clinicians may purchase supplemental books or materials from other sources. Given that there are no CE requirements for the upkeep of Geek Therapy certification, ongoing expenses are minimal for clinicians. The core certification of Geek Therapy is affordable. Payment is left to individual discretion, but professionals have the option to engage in conferences, events, or other supplemental CE activities that may entail registration, attendance, or video recording access fees, such as Therapeutic and Applied Geek and Gaming Summits (TAGGS) (*Geek Therapy*, 2024).

CURRENT RESEARCH ON MODALITY

As Geek Therapy is an emerging practice, researchers and professionals are establishing a framework of evidentiary support for this modality. While the Affinity + Resonance = Understanding (A+R=U) model is an emerging therapeutic approach that requires further research and testing, the existing body of literature on integrating nerd culture into therapy informs the overarching themes and concepts in Geek Therapy.

Certification Available/Required/Recommended

At present, Geek Therapy offers one certification program. After completing an online Geek Therapy course, participants are credentialed as Geek Therapy Certified and may market themselves as such. Certification status lasts indefinitely and does not entail any renewal requirements. Although there are no specifications for CE, Geek Therapy Certified professionals are encouraged to engage in ongoing development and utilize opportunities for professional growth. Without renewal requirements, professionals are also expected to maintain compliance and stay current with Geek Therapy guidelines and ethical standards (*Geek Therapy,* 2024).

Degree Requirements

Geek Therapy does not require specific educational or professional prerequisites (*Geek Therapy*, 2024). Geek Therapy certification is accessible to clinicians, educators, and community leaders interested in integrating this model into their work, regardless of the nature of their educational or professional backgrounds. Due to this therapeutic model's flexibility and adaptability, Geek Therapy can be applied in many different contexts and cases.

ETHICAL CONSIDERATIONS AND LIMITATIONS

While innovative and engaging, Geek therapy has several limitations, including issues related to escapism, accessibility, misunderstandings, over-reliance on pop culture, and cultural relevance (NeuroLaunch, 2024). One concern is that it might encourage clients to escape from real-world issues rather than address them directly. Regarding accessibility, not all therapists are well-versed in geek culture, which can limit the availability of this therapeutic approach. Additionally, clients' and therapists' lack of understanding or acceptance of geek culture may impede the therapeutic process. There is also a risk of over-reliance on pop culture references, which might not always provide practical solutions for real-life problems. Furthermore, geek culture may not resonate with all clients, particularly those from different cultural or age groups (ACA Standard B.1.a).

Geek Therapy should be practiced responsibly and ethically, with integrity and honesty (ACA, 2014). Practitioners must be transparent about their qualifications, experience, and limitations (ACA Standard C.2.a). Counselors should be adequately trained and competent in the use of Geek therapy. They should only use techniques and interpretations that they are knowledgeable of and skilled in. Providing accurate information and acknowledging the inherent subjectivity of this therapeutic modality is critical. Counselors must ensure that the use of Geek Therapy does not cause harm to the client (ACA Standard A.4.a). This includes being mindful of potential emotional or psychological impacts and providing appropriate support.

WHAT TYPES OF PROFESSIONALS WOULD DO WELL WITH THIS MODALITY?

Several types of mental health professionals can effectively incorporate Geek Therapy into their practice, especially those open to integrating clients' interests into therapeutic work. Ultimately, any mental health professional who is open-minded, adaptable, and willing to explore non-traditional therapeutic techniques can thrive with Geek Therapy. It's all about meeting clients where they are and leveraging their passions to foster healing and growth. Here are some examples:

Clinical Psychologists: Clinical psychologists with a flexible and creative approach to therapy can use Geek Therapy techniques to engage clients, particularly those who might not respond well to traditional methods (Ceranoglu, 2009; Ceranoglu, 2010). Their training in various therapeutic modalities allows them to adapt Geek Therapy strategies to suit different clients' needs.

Counselors and Therapists: Licensed Professional Counselors (LPCs) and Marriage and Family Therapists (MFTs) can effectively incorporate Geek Therapy into their practice, especially when working with young adults, adolescents, and families (Annema et al., 2010; Smedley & Croffie, 2023). Their focus on client-centered approaches aligns well with the principles of Geek Therapy.

Social Workers: Licensed Clinical Social Workers (LCSWs) often work with diverse populations, including individuals dealing with trauma, social anxiety, and other challenges (Sorbring et al., 2015). Geek therapy techniques can enhance their training in building rapport and understanding clients' contexts.

School Counselors: School counselors can utilize Geek Therapy to connect with students personally, using shared interests in video games, comics, or other aspects of geek culture to address academic, social, and emotional challenges (Asrowi et al., 2019).

Art Therapists: Art therapists can integrate Geek Therapy into their practice by using clients' interests in geek culture to inspire creative projects (Bryan, 2022). This can help clients express themselves and work through issues safely and enjoyably.

Career Counselors: Career Counselors can use Geek Therapy strategies to help clients develop social skills, discover transferable job skills from leisure activities, explore vocational personality types, and increase motivation for achievement (Rochat & Armengol, 2020).

Play Therapists: Play therapists working with children and adolescents can incorporate elements of Geek Therapy, such as role-playing games and character narratives, to create therapeutic play experiences that resonate with their young clients (Coyle & Doherty, 2009).

WHAT KIND OF CLIENTELE WOULD DO WELL IN THIS MODEL?

Geek Therapy can be particularly effective for individuals who might feel alienated or misunderstood in more traditional therapeutic settings. It embraces the client's unique interests and uses them as a powerful tool for healing and growth. This modality can be effective for various clients, especially those interested in geek culture. Here are some types of clients who might respond well to Geek Therapy:

Young Adults and Adolescents: Many young adults and adolescents deeply connect with video games, comics, anime, and other geek culture elements. Geek Therapy can engage them in a relevant and interesting way, making it easier for them to be open about their thoughts and feelings. One typical example of a young adult or adolescent's connection to geek culture is their involvement with video games (Annema et al., 2010; Ceranoglu, 2019; Ceranoglu, 2010; Kowal et al., 2021). Let's consider a hypothetical scenario:

Case Study: Jake and His Journey with Video Games

Jake is a 15-year-old high school student who has always been passionate about video games, particularly role-playing games (RPGs) like "The Legend of Zelda" and "Final Fantasy." These games provide him with entertainment and offer a sense of adventure, achievement, and escape from the stresses of daily life.

Affinity: Jake's therapist recognizes his deep interest in RPGs and starts building rapport by discussing his favorite games, characters, and storylines. This helps Jake feel understood and valued, creating a safe space to open up.

Resonance: The therapist identifies game themes that resonate with Jake's experiences. For example, Jake might relate to the protagonist's journey of overcoming obstacles and finding inner strength. The therapist uses these connections to discuss Jake's challenges, such as dealing with school pressures or navigating friendships.

Understanding: Jake sees parallels between the game's narratives and his life through these discussions. He gains insights into his coping mechanisms and develops new strategies for dealing with stress and building resilience. The therapist might suggest game-related activities, like creating his game character or story, to explore his emotions and goals further.

Geek Therapy uses Jake's passion for video games to create an engaging therapeutic experience that fosters self-reflection, personal growth, and better mental health.

Neurodivergent Individuals

Clients with autism spectrum disorder (ASD), attention-deficit hyperactive disorder (ADHD), or other neurodivergent conditions often have specific interests and hobbies that can be leveraged in Geek Therapy. This approach can provide comfort and familiarity, making therapeutic discussions more accessible. Let's explore how a neurodivergent individual might connect with geek culture through their passion for comics and superheroes ("Doctors and Therapists Are Turning to Comic Books," 2022; Mazowita, 2022).

Case Study: Emily and Her Connection to Superheroes

Emily is a 12-year-old girl with autism spectrum disorder (ASD). She is deeply fascinated with superheroes, particularly those from Marvel and DC Comics. Superhero stories provide her with a structured and predictable narrative, which she finds comforting and engaging.

Affinity: Emily's therapist recognizes her passion for superheroes and starts sessions by discussing her favorite characters and storylines. This creates a sense of trust and rapport, as Emily feels understood and respected for her interests.

Resonance: The therapist identifies themes in superhero stories that resonate with Emily's experiences. For instance, Emily might connect with Spider-Man's journey of balancing his responsibilities as a superhero with his daily life as Peter Parker. The therapist uses this connection to discuss Emily's challenges in balancing school, social interactions, and personal interests.

Understanding: Through these discussions, Emily begins to see similarities between her life and the lives of her favorite superheroes. She learns to draw strength from their stories, finding courage and resilience in her challenges. The therapist might also use superhero narratives to teach social skills and coping mechanisms, making the lessons more relatable and engaging for Emily.

Geek Therapy uses Emily's interest in superheroes to provide a therapeutic experience that aids her emotional and social development.

Individuals with Social Anxiety or Introversion

People who experience social anxiety or are naturally introverted might find traditional therapy settings intimidating. Geek Therapy can create a more relaxed and engaging environment by incorporating familiar and enjoyable topics. The following case study looks at how geek culture can help individuals with social anxiety or introversion by using tabletop role-playing games (RPGs) as an example (Arenas, 2022; Baker et al., 2023; Otani et al., 2024)

Case Study: Alex and His Connection to Tabletop RPGs

Alex is a 20-year-old college student who experiences significant social anxiety. He finds social situations overwhelming and often struggles to make new friends. However, Alex has a strong passion for tabletop RPGs, like Dungeons & Dragons, where he enjoys creating characters and immersing himself in imaginative worlds.

Affinity: Alex's therapist recognizes his interest in tabletop RPGs and starts building rapport by discussing his favorite campaigns, characters, and game sessions. This helps Alex feel more comfortable and understood.

Resonance: The therapist identifies elements of the RPGs that resonate with Alex's personal experiences. For instance, they might explore how Alex's characters face challenges and work together with others in the game. This can be a gateway to discussing Alex's social challenges and anxieties.

Understanding: Alex begins to see parallels between his in-game experiences and real-life situations through these discussions. The therapist might use RPG scenarios to practice social skills like teamwork, communication, and problem-solving. Alex can experiment with different social interactions in the safe and structured environment of the game, gaining confidence and insight into his social behavior.

By utilizing Alex's interest in tabletop RPGs, Geek Therapy provides a therapeutic experience designed to address his social anxiety and enhance his social skills.

Trauma Survivors

Using narratives and characters from geek culture, therapists can help trauma survivors explore their experiences and develop coping strategies. Relating to resilient characters or powerful story arcs can be empowering and healing. This modality can support trauma survivors by using the connection to comic book characters as an example ("Doctors and Therapists Are Turning to Comic Books," 2022; Mazowita, 2022).

Case Study: Jasmine and Her Connection to Comic Book Characters

Jasmine is a 25-year-old woman who has experienced significant trauma in her past. She finds comfort and strength in reading comic books, particularly those featuring strong, resilient characters like Wonder Woman and Batman. These characters' stories of overcoming adversity and fighting for justice resonate deeply with her.

Affinity: Jasmine's therapist recognizes her passion for comic books and begins their sessions by discussing her favorite characters and storylines. This helps build trust and rapport, as Jasmine feels seen and respected for her interests.

Resonance: The therapist identifies themes in the comic book stories that resonate with Jasmine's experiences. For instance, Wonder Woman's journey of resilience and empowerment might mirror Jasmine's struggles and her efforts to rebuild her life. The therapist uses these connections to explore Jasmine's feelings, strengths, and coping mechanisms.

Understanding: Through these discussions, Jasmine parallels the superheroes' narratives with her life. She starts to see herself as a survivor with inner strength, much like her favorite characters. The therapist might encourage Jasmine to think about her "superpowers" or unique strengths that have helped her navigate difficult times. This can foster a sense of empowerment and self-compassion.

Geek Therapy uses Jasmine's interest in comic book characters to create a therapeutic environment that aids in addressing her trauma and improving her self-image.

Sexual and Gender Minority Community

Geek Therapy can also benefit clients within the sexual and gender minority community. Many find representation and acceptance in geek culture, which can be a supportive framework for exploring identity and experiences in therapy. Geek culture can support LGBTQ+ individuals by focusing on their connection to inclusive and diverse TV shows or movies (Philip & Cherian, 2020; Smedley & Croffie, 2023).

Case Study: Ryan and His Connection to LGBTQ+ Inclusive Media

Ryan is a 22-year-old who identifies as gay. Growing up, he struggled with acceptance and finding role models who reflected his identity. However, Ryan found solace and inspiration in LGBTQ+ inclusive media, such as TV shows like "Pose" and movies like "Love, Simon." These stories of LGBTQ+ characters navigating their lives authentically and resilient deeply resonate with him.

Affinity: Ryan's therapist acknowledges his passion for these inclusive media representations and initiates discussions about his favorite characters and storylines. This establishes trust and rapport, as Ryan feels seen and respected for his interests.

Resonance: The therapist identifies themes in the media that resonate with Ryan's personal experiences. For instance, Ryan might relate to the characters' struggles in "Pose" as they seek acceptance and build their chosen families. The therapist uses these connections to explore Ryan's journey of self-acceptance and his experiences with family and community.

Understanding: Through these discussions, Ryan begins to draw parallels between the narratives of the LGBTQ+ characters and his own life. He starts to see himself as part of a larger community with shared experiences and challenges. The therapist might use these stories to discuss coping strategies, resilience, and the importance of finding supportive communities.

Through Ryan's link to LGBTQ+ inclusive media, Geek Therapy offers relatable and empowering therapeutic support, aiding him in exploring his identity and fostering a positive self-image.

General Population

Even clients who do not fit into the above categories might find Geek Therapy appealing if they have a passion for geek culture. It offers a unique, personalized therapy approach that can be more engaging and effective. Ultimately, Geek Therapy's strength lies in its ability to connect with clients through their passions and interests, making the therapeutic process more enjoyable and relatable.

SUMMARY

Therapy modalities are various methods aimed at promoting human well-being. Though there may be dragons involved, Geek therapy follows the same principle. These approaches have been associated with reduced anxiety, decreased depressive symptoms, improved self-esteem, richer interpersonal interactions, greater social and school engagement, and enhanced social skills and problem-solving abilities. They are used to enhance overall psychological well-being across all age groups, as well as address specific needs of targeted populations, such as individuals with learning and developmental disorders, trauma, and mood and anxiety disorders. Geek therapy combines pop culture and psychology elements, offering a unique mental health and personal development approach. Using stories and characters that resonate deeply with individuals provides a pathway to self-discovery and healing that is both effective and engaging. As research into geek therapy progresses, new methods to utilize imagination and storytelling for mental health are being discovered. This emerging area in treatment aims to make mental health support more accessible and tailored to individual interests.

Sarah is an Assistant Professor at Loyola University- New Orleans, where they teach a variety of courses and are developing an Affirmative Therapy Specialization. They have a specialization in Affirmative therapy for sexual orientation and gender identity minorities (SOGI) from Southern Methodist University and a PhD from Texas A&M University-Commerce, where they researched competencies for working with sexual and gender minorities. They also have a part-time clinical practice and provide affirmative supervision for provisionally licensed counselors. Sarah is a gender-affirming mental health provider who offers assessments for letters of support for medical and legal gender transitions. Additionally, they have expertise in counseling for Ethical non-monogamous (ENM) individuals and relationships, and they are kink-aware. Sarah has been a volunteer leader and an advocate for various professional boards and committees related to SOGI and gender and equity issues in counseling.

sjstillw@loyno.edu

Sarah Stillwell | College of Nursing and Health

Ruby is a candidate for an M.S. degree in Clinical Mental Health Counseling at Loyola University New Orleans. They are a clinical intern at a nonprofit mental health clinic where they work with individuals and families across the life span, as well as specialize in case management for sexual and gender minorities. They approach counseling with a relational-cultural perspective and have previously founded and facilitated a relational-cultural theory reading group.
recramer@my.loyno.edu

Ruby Cramer | College of Nursing and Health

REFERENCES

American Counseling Association. (2014). *2014 ACA code of ethics.*
    https://www.counseling.org/knowledge-center/ethics

Annema, J. H., Verstraete, M., Abeele, V. V., Desmet, S., Geerts, D. (2010). Video games in therapy: A
    therapist's perspective. *International Journal of Arts and Technology, Conference Paper.*
    https://doi.org/10.1145/1823818.1823828

Arenas, D. L., Viduani, A., & Araujo, R. B. (2022). Therapeutic Use of Role-Playing Game (RPG) in Mental
    Health: A Scoping Review. *Simulation & Gaming, 53*(3), 285–311. https://doi-
    org.loyno.idm.oclc.org/10.1177/10468781211073720

Asrowi, Gunarhadi, & Hanif, M. (2019). The Power of Role-Playing in Counseling Children with Learning
    Difficulties in Inclusive Schools of Indonesia. *International Journal of Education and Practice, 7*(4), 324–
    333. https://doi-org.loyno.idm.oclc.org/10.18488/journal.61.2019.74.324.333

Baker, I. S., Turner, I. J., & Kotera, Y. (2023). Role-play Games (RPGs) for Mental Health (Why Not?): Roll
    for Initiative. *International Journal of Mental Health & Addiction, 21*(6), 3901–3909. https://doi-
    org.loyno.idm.oclc.org/10.1007/s11469-022-00832-y

Bean, A. M. (2020, August 21). Geek therapy for professionals. *Psychology Today.*
    https://www.psychologytoday.com/us/blog/geek-therapy-professionals/202008/geek-
    therapy-professionals

Bryan, C. (2022). *How Geek Therapy Plays Into Expressive Arts Therapy: A Literature Review* (Master's thesis).
    Lesley University. https://digitalcommons.lesley.edu/expressive_theses/622/

Ceranoglu, T. A. (2009). Star Wars in psychotherapy: Video games in the office. *Academic Psychiatry, 34*(3),
    233-236. https://doi.org/10.1176/appi.ap.34.3.233

Ceranoglu, T. A. (2010). Video games in psychotherapy. *Review of General Psychology, 14*(2), 141-146.
    https://doi.org/10.1037/a0019439

Coyle, D. & Doherty, G. (2009). An evaluation of a solution focused computer game in adolescent
    interventions. *Clinical Child Psychology and Psychiatry, 14*(3), 345-360.
    https://doi.org/10.1177/1359104508100884

Doctors and therapists are turning to comic books. (2022, May 19). *The Economist*, NA. https://link-gale-
    com.loyno.idm.oclc.org/apps/doc/A762141900/BIC?u=lln_aluno&sid=ebsco&xid=9758adc
    5

Eckardt, J. P. (2024). Therapeutic uses of gaming in mental health: An untapped potential. *JMIR Serious
    Games, 12*(1), e57714. https://doi.org/10.2196/57714

Geek Therapy. (2024, October 1). https://geektherapy.org/

Kerr, D. J. R., Deane, F. P., & Crowe, T. P. (2019). Narrative identity reconstruction as adaptive growth
    during mental health recovery: A narrative coaching boardgame approach. *Frontiers in Psychology, 10*,
    Article 994. https://doi.org/10.3389/fpsyg.2019.00994

Kowal, M., Conroy, E., Ramsbottom, N., Smithies, T., Toth, A., & Campbell, M. (2021). Gaming your mental
    health: A narrative review on mitigating symptoms of depression and anxiety using commercial video
    games. *JMIR Serious Games, 9*(2), e26575. https://doi.org/10.2196/26575

Leyline Education (2020). Geek therapy 101: What is geek therapy and who is it for? [webpage]. https://www.geektherapeutics.com/geek-therapy-101/

Mazowita, A., (2022) "Graphic Communities: Comics as Visual and Virtual Resources for Self and Collective Care", *The Comics Grid: Journal of Comics Scholarship* 12(1). doi: https://doi.org/10.16995/cg.6493

NeuroLaunch. (2024, October 1). Geek therapy. https://neurolaunch.com/geek-therapy/#google_vignette

Otani, V. H. O., Novaes, R. A. C. B., Pedron, J., Nabhan, P. C., Rodrigues, T. M., Chiba, R., Guedes, J. V. C., Marques, L. M., & Vissoci, J. R. N. (2024). Framework proposal for Role-Playing Games as mental health intervention: the Critical Skills methodology. *Frontiers in Psychiatry, 15*. https://doi-org.loyno.idm.oclc.org/10.3389/fpsyt.2024.1297332

Philip, J., & Cherian, V. (2020). Psychiatry and "pop" culture: millennials for mental health – Psychiatry in music. *British Journal of Psychiatry, 217*(6), 678. https://doi-org.loyno.idm.oclc.org/10.1192/bjp.2020.203

Rochat, S., & Armengol, J. (2020). Career Counseling Interventions for Video Game Players. *Journal of Career Development, 47*(2), 207–219. https://doi-org.loyno.idm.oclc.org/10.1177/0894845318793537

Smedley, D. & Croffie, A. L. (2023). The power of vulnerability: Connecting families using Spider-man: Into the Spider-Verse. *Journal of Creativity in Mental Health, 18*(2), 277–287. https://doi-org.loyno.idm.oclc.org/10.1080/15401383.2021.1960667

Sorbring, E., Bolin, A., & Ryding, J. (2015). Game-Based Intervention-A Technical Tool for Social Workers to Combat Adolescent Dating Violence. *Advances in Social Work, 16*(1), 125–139.

Vita-Barrull, N., March-Llanes, J., Guzmán, N., Estrada-Plana, V., Mayoral, M., & Moya-Higueras, J. (2022). The Cognitive Processes Behind Commercialized Board Games for Intervening in Mental Health and Education: A Committee of Experts. *Games for Health Journal.* https://doi-org.loyno.idm.oclc.org/10.1089/g4h.2022.0109

Gestalt Equine Facilitated Psychotherapy Certification (GEP)

DUEY FREEMAN, MA, LPC, GEP

JOAN RIEGER, MA, LPC, GEP

IOANA MARCUS, PhD, LPC, GEP

CO-FOUNDERS OF GESTALT EQUINE PSYCHOTHERAPY

HISTORY AND BACKGROUND OF THE CERTIFICATION PROGRAM

Founded in 2008 by two Gestalt trained therapists, Duey Freeman and Joan Rieger, The Gestalt Equine Institute of the Rockies provides the most comprehensive equine-assisted training program available. Duey Freeman was a former instructor at Naropa University for thirty-one years, and Joan Rieger is currently The Gestalt Institute of the Rockies director. Duey and Joan wanted to create an opportunity for new and practicing therapists to experience the fullness that a relational approach to equine therapy had to offer. The Gestalt Institute of the Rockies now has four faculty members that co-teach with Duey.

Relationship, awareness, exploration, and creativity are at the core of Gestalt Equine Psychotherapy™ (GEP). "Gestalt Therapy", is defined as the process of exploring our experience in and of relationship while in relationship. Holding 'I-Thou' with the utmost respect, working to support growth in relationships, deepening contact, and inspiring creative choice are core tenets of this therapy.

Obtaining/Achieving a unique certification in GEP, participants gain an understanding of the therapeutic relationships between therapist-horse-client, and competency in the essential theoretical concepts and experiential process of Gestalt Therapy and relational horsemanship methods. GEIR provides extensive training in Gestalt Theory and Practice as well as human development, attachment, somatic therapy, family therapy and ethics.

"Gestalt Therapy is defined as the process of exploring our experience in and of relationship while in relationship. Holding 'I-Thou 'with the utmost respect, working to support growth in relationships, deepening contact, and inspiring creative choice are core tenants of this therapy. GEP holds the above definition as fundamental as we integrate horses, and therefore nature, into the therapeutic process. Horses bring desire for relationship without prejudice, seeking contact and congruence as the only criteria for the creation of emotional intimacy."

The program has been hosted at the Happy Dog Ranch in Littleton, CO, an animal sanctuary where animals are treated with utmost respect for their sentience, a value shared with GEIR.

As summarized in Freeman & Rose:

"nature exemplifies awareness and presence, providing an opening for us to move into contact and connection in the way in which we are designed - unburdened by layers of familial, societal, and systemic introjects. Horses and nature therefore allow the opportunity to re-create our original attachment with ourselves, the environment, and others when we have experienced emotional injury, relational rupture and/or loss. GEP is our journey into land/nature/equine- based relationships which provide the foundation to heal the nature of our being." (Freeman, D. & Rose K., 2020).

The core of the program consists of eight training intensives, or modules. Each of these intensive courses is four days long. Students are required to complete eight intensive courses for a certificate. The program takes two years to complete when modules are completed consecutively. However, the program is designed so that students can complete the eight intensives at their own pace.

The topics include, but are not limited to, the following: an introduction to Gestalt and GEP; a thorough understanding of contact boundaries for humans and horses; the therapeutic circle and Gestalt experiment; developmental theory and process for humans and horses; nature and equine applications to therapy and facilitation; somatic processes in humans, horses and earth; working with families and groups, and ethics in facilitation and working with horses in equine facilitated psychotherapy.

Content of the Modules and Training

- Gestalt theory, practice, history, and community building
- Gestalt equine therapy, theory, and practice
- Emotional developmental theory and practice and how to integrate this with Gestalt Equine Psychotherapy (GEP)™
- Experiential practice therapy sessions with the other students and the horses either in the group or dyads
- Nature awareness, principles, knowledge and interventions blend with equine therapy.
- Relational horsemanship, horse knowledge and care
- Special knowledge: such as Horse nutrition, Vet care, Farrier work
- Ground and mounted work

Supervision

For certification you are required to meet with Duey Freeman and other instructors/faculty for 16 hours of supervision, including assessing and honing equine skills, discussing your clients/students, consulting on the application of equine and nature therapy to its specific context, deepening your understanding of Gestalt therapy and/or to help you apply this work.

The certification requires the completion of the modules, supervision, a final project and two assessments, focused on Gestalt theory assessment, and equine and relational horsemanship assessment.

The final project consists of a project on an equine facilitated topic of the student's choice and needs to be presented to the group. It is intended to help the student deepen this work in an area of interest to them, and to help take the Gestalt EFP work out into the world. Examples include applications of Gestalt equine facilitated psychotherapy to clinical areas of practice, such as eating disorders.

Cost: $995/ intensive

EXPERIENCES AND IMPRESSIONS WITH GEIR GEP TRAINING

As a former student of GEIR between 2013-2017, Dr. Ioana Marcus wanted to invite Duey Freeman and Joan Rieger to collaborate on this textbook chapter project. Ioana completed the program and while reflecting on her experience, she believes it has been the most significant, powerful and empowering training experience received, in a non-academic training environment. Initially, Ioana struggled to make the leap from the academic and cognitive based knowledge to the experiential nature of the GEIR program. During her first intensive, however, she discovered the journey to transformative connections between horses and humans and has learned throughout the intensives, to authentically related to herself and others. She contends that learning Gestalt and connecting with the horses became an authentic lifestyle choice that she carries with her, long time after graduating from the program.

She remembers, most intensives were profoundly eye-opening, both professionally but also personally. No aspect of us as Gestalt therapists remains unturned and unexplored throughout this process. It leads to a deeper understanding of ourselves as humans, our growth and our ways of relating to others, as taught by the horses. Ioana has made life-long friends and trusted colleagues, she continues consulting with them to this day. She found a community in which real connection, collaboration, and honest feedback/challenging can co-exist to support growth and transformation. The horses and the people, the shared moments of real relational growth are unparalleled.

Gestalt Equine Institute of the Rockies: http://www.gestaltequineinstitute.com/about-geir.htm

Duey Freeman is a sought-after teacher, trainer, licensed therapist, and equine professional around the world. He has travelled to teach professionally in over 8 countries, has developed a practical attachment theory and human development theory that is taught to thousands of university students, has over 60,000 direct client hours, and co-founded both the Gestalt Equine Institute and the Gestalt Institute of the Rockies. He provides supervision to therapists and graduate students, does business and land consultations for new equine therapy sites, and models being a life-long student to your passions. Gestalt and Relational Horsemanship are not just approaches to Duey; they are how he walks through the world. He embodies both tenderness and strength in all his relations and work. His quality of contact and relationship with others is authentic and unique and has many people coming from around the country and world to study with him. He has worked incredibly hard to master his arts and finds great joy in teaching 'honest students'.

Joan Rieger, MA, LPC is a licensed psychotherapist with her Masters in Counseling from Naropa University (2001) and undergrad from the University of Michigan (1990). She is currently in private practice in Wheat Ridge, CO specializing in trauma resolution, attachment issues, couples counseling, depression, anxiety, and grief. She also offers equine assisted psychotherapy to clients at Happy Dog Ranch in Littleton, CO. Along with being the current Director at the Gestalt Institute of the Rockies, Joan co-founded the Gestalt Equine Institute of the Rockies with Duey Freeman, MA, LPC. Joan taught the masters level Gestalt class for several years as an adjunct faculty member for Naropa University and was the clinical supervisor for the Medicine Horse Program in Boulder, CO. Joan is certified as a Gestalt therapist from the Gestalt Institute of the Rockies (2002), and trained in Level 1 Somatic Experiencing.

Dr. Ioana Marcus is a licensed professional counselor in private practice integrating equine facilitated psychotherapy in her work with clients with trauma, eating disorders, anxiety, grief and life transitions. She graduated with her doctorate in Counselor Education and Supervision with The University of Texas at San Antonio, and has trained extensively in Gestalt equine facilitated psychotherapy, Equilateral (EA-EMDR), EMDR, Animal Assisted Play Therapy and more. After more than a decade in the academia with numerous publications and conference presentations, she is grateful to focus her energy on clinical work with clients and supervision of residents towards licensure. She shares her life and adventures with amazing animal teachers and friends, her two thoroughbreds, her German Shepherd and cat.

REFERENCES

Freeman, D. (2022, October). Interview regarding Gestalt equine facilitated psychotherapy.

Gestalt Therapy

MONIQUE N. RODRÍGUEZ, PH.D., LPCC

ANSEL L. WOLDT, ED.D., LICENSED PSYCHOLOGIST, LPCC

INTRODUCTION TO GESTALT THERAPY

Gestalt therapy is a humanistic, experiential, and process-oriented approach to psychotherapy that emphasizes awareness, personal responsibility, and the client's present experience. It focuses on the individual's unique perception of reality and how they make meaning of their current situations. The goal is to assist clients in developing a realistic awareness of their realities by attending to their present, here-and-now experiences and environmental contexts.

Fritz and Laura Perls founded Gestalt therapy in the 1940s and 1950s. Fritz was a physician who incorporated neuroscience principles into enhancing living. Laura earned her PhD in neuropsychology. Together, they began seeing clients face-to-face, focusing on present life experiences, a significant departure from traditional psychoanalysis.

The philosophical underpinnings of Gestalt therapy are existential, dialectical, phenomenological, and experiential. Key concepts include awareness, existential knowing, phenomenological experiencing, dialogical attitude, empathy, perception, experience, the paradoxical theory of change, context, and self-awareness.

The theoretical foundations of Gestalt therapy draw from various disciplines, including Gestalt psychology, psychoanalysis, existentialism, and field theory. The Gestalt approach emphasizes the importance of the client-therapist relationship and the use of experiential techniques to promote awareness and facilitate change. Gestalt therapists view individuals as whole, integrated beings who are constantly interacting with their environment. The goal of gestalt therapy is to help clients develop a more authentic and satisfying way of being in the world by increasing their awareness of their thoughts, feelings, behaviors, and the impact of their environment.

CERTIFICATION, TRAINING, AND LICENSURE REQUIREMENTS

Most Gestalt therapy training is conducted in Gestalt institutes worldwide as post-graduate work. In the United States, licensure as a mental health professional (e.g., psychologist, counselor, social worker) is regulated by state boards for each profession. While Gestalt therapy training is not typically required for licensure, it provides specialized skills and can enhance a practitioner's effectiveness and marketability.

The Gestalt Institute of Cleveland (GIC), founded in the 1960s, is a premier institution for Gestalt therapy training. GIC offers a comprehensive range of programs for both personal growth and professional development:

1. Gestalt Experience Workshop (GEW): This 13-hour workshop is an introductory prerequisite for more advanced training. It provides an experiential introduction to Gestalt principles and methods.

2. Gestalt Training Program (GTP): GIC's flagship 18-month program consists of ten 4-day weekends. It provides a thorough grounding in Gestalt theory and practice. The program includes: 227.50 continuing education (CE) contact hours. A requirement of at least 25 hours of individual therapy with an approved Gestalt-oriented psychotherapist. Tuition of $10,500 (with early registration and payment plan options available)

3. Advanced Training Programs: GIC offers various advanced training options for those who have completed the GTP, such as advanced workshops in Working With Physical Process.

4. Professional Development Workshops: These shorter programs cover specific topics or skills within Gestalt therapy, allowing practitioners to refine and expand their expertise continually.

5. Coaching Certification Program: This program integrates Gestalt principles into coaching practice.

The Gestalt Institute of Cleveland is approved by the Ohio Psychological Association to offer continuing education to psychologists. Continuing Education approved by OPA is accepted by The Ohio Counselor, Social Worker & Marriage and Family Therapist Board under OAC Rule 4757-9-05. Additionally, GIC is an approved provider for the National Board for Certified Counselors (NBCC). This NBCC approval ensures that the institute's programs meet rigorous standards for continuing education in the counseling profession. The wide range of approvals allows professionals from various mental health disciplines to earn continuing education credits through GIC's programs, enhancing the interdisciplinary appeal of their Gestalt therapy training offerings.

For individuals interested in incorporating Gestalt therapy into their practice, the recommended path typically involves:

1. Attending a Gestalt Experience Workshop (GEW) or similar introductory program

2. Completing a comprehensive training program like the Gestalt Training Program (GTP)

3. Engaging in personal Gestalt therapy

4. Pursuing advanced training or specialization as desired

5. Continuing professional development through workshops and seminars

While the Gestalt Institute of Cleveland provides a comprehensive example of Gestalt therapy training, it's important to note that there are numerous other reputable institutes throughout the United States and internationally that offer Gestalt therapy training and certification. Some notable examples include:

1. The New York Institute for Gestalt Therapy: Founded by Fritz and Laura Perls, this is the oldest Gestalt therapy institute in the world. It offers training programs, workshops, and a certification track.

2. Pacific Gestalt Institute (Los Angeles, CA): Provides training programs, workshops, and seminars in Gestalt therapy, with a focus on relational Gestalt therapy.

3. Gestalt Training Institute of Philadelphia: Offers a comprehensive three-year training program in Gestalt therapy, as well as workshops and continuing education opportunities.

4. Gestalt Associates for Psychotherapy (New York, NY): Provides a four-year training program in Gestalt therapy, along with workshops and seminars.

5. Gestalt Institute of Toronto: Offers a range of training programs, including a five-year clinical training program in Gestalt therapy.

Each institute may have its own unique approach, emphasis, and training structure within the broader framework of Gestalt therapy. Prospective trainees are encouraged to research various institutes to find a program that best aligns with their professional goals and learning styles.

International training opportunities are also available, with Gestalt institutes and training programs in many countries worldwide. This global presence speaks to the widespread recognition and application of Gestalt therapy principles across diverse cultural contexts.

Certification in Gestalt therapy is available through various Gestalt institutes upon completing their training programs. While certification is not typically required for licensure, it is recommended for those seeking to specialize in this approach. Certification requirements vary by institute but generally involve a combination of coursework, supervised clinical practice, and personal therapy.

It's important to note that while Gestalt therapy training enhances one's therapeutic skills, it does not replace the need for appropriate licensure in one's professional field. Practitioners should always work within the scope of their professional license and seek additional supervision or consultation when incorporating new therapeutic approaches into their practice.

General Cost

The cost of Gestalt therapy training varies depending on the institute and the specific program. More detailed cost information can be obtained from individual training institutes. Gestalt therapy training programs can range from short workshops to multi-year programs. The cost of training can vary widely depending on factors such as the length of the program, the location, and the institute's reputation. Short workshops may cost a few hundred dollars, while comprehensive training programs can cost several thousand dollars. Some institutes offer scholarships or financial assistance to help offset the cost of training.

While Gestalt therapy may not be explicitly labeled as a "gold standard" or "evidence-based practice" by official governing bodies, it has a long history of clinical application. It has been subjected to numerous research studies that support its effectiveness. Meta-analyses and systematic reviews have examined the efficacy of Gestalt therapy for various mental health concerns. For example, a meta-analysis by Roubal et al. (2016) found that Gestalt therapy was effective in treating a range of psychological problems, including anxiety, depression, and interpersonal difficulties. The authors concluded that Gestalt therapy could be considered an evidence-based treatment. Another systematic review by Elliot et al. (2013) examined the effectiveness of humanistic therapies, including Gestalt therapy, for depression. The review found that these approaches were associated with large pre-post effect sizes and were comparable in effectiveness to other established treatments, such as cognitive-behavioral therapy (CBT).

In addition to these research findings, Gestalt therapy has been recognized by professional organizations as a legitimate and valuable approach to psychotherapy. For instance, the American Psychological Association (APA) includes Gestalt therapy as a recognized theoretical orientation in Division 29 (Society for the Advancement of Psychotherapy).

While more research is needed to establish Gestalt therapy as an "evidence-based" treatment for specific mental health conditions, the existing evidence suggests that it is a well-established, effective, and respected approach in the field of psychotherapy.

Certification Available/Required/Recommended

Various Gestalt institutes offer certification in Gestalt therapy upon completing their training programs. While certification is not typically required for licensure, it is recommended for those seeking to specialize in this approach. Certification in Gestalt therapy demonstrates that a practitioner has completed a comprehensive training program and has met the standards set by the certifying organization. Certification requirements vary by institute but generally involve a combination of coursework, supervised clinical practice, and personal therapy. Some institutes offer different levels of certification, such as basic, intermediate, and advanced, to reflect the depth and breadth of a practitioner's training and experience.

Pursuing certification in Gestalt therapy can enhance a practitioner's credibility and marketability. It demonstrates a commitment to ongoing professional development and a high level of competence in the approach. Certification can also provide opportunities for networking and collaboration with other Gestalt therapists.

Degree Requirements

Most Gestalt therapy training programs require a graduate degree in a mental health field, such as psychology, counseling, or social work. Some Gestalt institutes offer training programs for graduate students or individuals completing their graduate degrees. These programs may be structured differently than those intended for post-graduate professionals, but they still provide a comprehensive introduction to Gestalt therapy theory and practice.

Some Gestalt therapy training programs may require a graduate degree in addition to other prerequisites, such as a certain number of years of clinical experience or completion of specific coursework. Prospective trainees should carefully review the requirements of individual programs to ensure that they meet the necessary qualifications.

CAUTIONS OR LIMITATIONS

As with all therapeutic approaches, practitioners must adhere to legal and ethical guidelines related to their professional licenses. Gestalt therapists should be aware of the potential for intense emotional experiences during therapy and be prepared to manage these situations appropriately.

Gestalt therapy's emphasis on experiential techniques and exploring present-moment experiences can lead to powerful emotional reactions in clients. Therapists must be skilled in creating a safe and supportive therapeutic environment and be prepared to help clients process and integrate these experiences. Gestalt therapists should also be aware of their own limitations and seek consultation or supervision when needed.

Another potential limitation of Gestalt therapy is that it may not be suitable for all clients or all presenting problems. For example, clients who are in crisis or who have severe mental health conditions may require a more structured or directive approach. Gestalt therapists should be able to assess the appropriateness of the approach for each client and make referrals when necessary.

Ethically, Gestalt therapists must maintain appropriate boundaries with clients and avoid dual relationships that could compromise the therapeutic alliance. They must also be mindful of cultural differences and adapt the approach as needed to ensure that it is culturally sensitive and relevant to the client's experiences.

SCOPE OF PRACTICE ISSUES

Gestalt therapy can be applied to individuals, couples, families, groups, and organizations. It is particularly effective for those suffering from post-traumatic stress disorder (PTSD), anxiety, depression, and personality disorders.

Gestalt therapists work with a wide range of populations and presenting problems. The approach has been successfully adapted for children, adolescents, adults, and older adults. Gestalt therapy has also been applied in various settings, including mental health clinics, hospitals, schools, and the workplace.

While Gestalt therapy can be effective for many clients, practitioners must understand the limits of their scope of practice and work within the boundaries of their professional licenses. For example, a Gestalt therapist who is licensed as a counselor may not be able to provide certain services that are restricted to psychologists or psychiatrists, such as psychological testing or medication management.

Gestalt therapists should also be aware of the specific scope of practice issues related to their geographic location or professional organization. Some states or countries may have specific regulations or guidelines that limit the types of services that different mental health professionals can provide.

Individuals who are open to experiential learning, self-exploration, and personal growth may be particularly well-suited to Gestalt therapy, both as clients and as practitioners. Gestalt therapy requires a willingness to engage actively in the therapeutic process and to explore one's thoughts, feelings, and behaviors in the present moment. Clients who are motivated to develop greater self-awareness and who are open to trying new experiences may find Gestalt therapy to be a good fit.

Similarly, individuals who are interested in becoming Gestalt therapists should be comfortable with self-disclosure and be willing to engage in their own personal growth work. Gestalt therapists must be able to model authenticity and vulnerability in their interactions with clients, and this requires a high level of self-awareness and emotional maturity.

Other characteristics that may be well-suited to Gestalt therapy include:

Creativity and spontaneity

Comfort with ambiguity and uncertainty

Ability to tolerate intense emotions

Interest in holistic approaches to wellbeing

Willingness to take responsibility for one's choices and actions

Ultimately, the key to success in Gestalt therapy, whether as a client or practitioner, is a commitment to ongoing self-discovery and growth. Those who are willing to embrace this process may find Gestalt therapy to be a deeply rewarding and transformative experience.

SUMMARY

Gestalt therapy is a powerful and transformative approach emphasizing awareness, personal responsibility, and the client's present experience. Training in this approach requires personal therapy, authentic involvement, self-disclosure, and full participation in various learning activities.

Gestalt therapy training is a rigorous and immersive experience that involves a significant investment of time, energy, and resources. Trainees are expected to engage in their own personal growth work in individual therapy and group settings. This self-exploration is considered essential for developing the self-awareness and authenticity needed to be an effective Gestalt therapist.

Training programs typically combine didactic instruction, experiential exercises, and supervised clinical practice. Trainees learn about the theoretical foundations of Gestalt therapy and the specific techniques and interventions used in the approach. They also have opportunities to practice their skills with clients under the guidance of experienced supervisors.

One unique aspect of Gestalt therapy training is the emphasis on the trainee's own process of self-discovery and growth. Trainees are encouraged to explore their own thoughts, feelings, and behaviors in the present moment and to use this awareness to inform their work with clients. This focus on personal growth and self-awareness can be challenging but is ultimately seen as a necessary part of becoming an effective Gestalt therapist.

Overall, Gestalt therapy training is a transformative experience that requires a significant commitment from trainees. However, for those who are willing to engage fully in the process, the rewards can be significant, both personally and professionally.

Dr. Monique Rodríguez, Ph.D., LPCC, NCC, is an Assistant Professor of Counselor Education at the University of New Mexico and a Licensed Professional Clinical Counselor. She is also a Gestalt therapist and faculty member at the Gestalt Institute of Cleveland, further enriching her diverse expertise. Dr. Rodríguez's research focuses on enhancing self-awareness and embodiment in counselor training, substance use, and emotional well-being to deepen the impact of counseling practices on client outcomes. Her work is instrumental in advancing our understanding of how counselor self-awareness and embodiment contribute to effective therapeutic relationships and client progress. By integrating her roles as an educator, researcher, and Gestalt practitioner, Dr. Rodríguez brings a unique and comprehensive perspective to counseling.

www.drmoniquerodriguez.com

www.sanarlab.unm.edu

mnrodriguez@unm.edu; monique@drmoniquerodriguez.com

Ansel Woldt, Ed.D., Emeritus Professor, Kent State University, where he mentored doctoral and master's degree students to become counselors and psychotherapists. He is notorious for his 50 years of experiential Gestalt pedagogy. He directed over 100 PhD dissertations and MA theses, many on Gestalt therapy topics, while creating a Gestalt Therapy Research Collection in the Kent State University Library and developing the *Gestalt Inventory of Resistance Loadings (GIRL)* and companion **Qualtrics GIRL Inventory** that measures 7 Gestalt styles of resistance. He graduated in 1973 from the Gestalt Institute of Cleveland 3-yr. Post-Doctoral Program where he is on the faculty as a specialist in Gestalt group therapy. Ansel was the principal co-founder and architect of AAGT, now the **International Association for the Advancement of Gestalt Therapy** (IAAGT), serving on the Board of Directors and Gestalt Archivist. He is co-editor with Sarah Toman of the textbook *Gestalt Therapy: History, Theory and Practice*, translated into Spanish and now Japanese. Ansel has maintained a private practice as a counseling psychologist at his residence in Kent. Ohio since 1970 and still sees clients weekly. He has 3 adult sons whose mother died very young from cancer. He was a farmer/rancher in South Dakota growing up, an interior decorator, a high school teacher, a guidance counselor, and an educational grant writer before becoming a professor and therapist. Ansel and Nancy have been happily married 30 years and enjoy their family gatherings, including 5 grandchildren and 8 great-grandchildren. Ansel suffered a closed-head injury as a child causing severe brain damage and loss of his Left Frontal Lobe, contributing significantly to his career decisions. He is handicapped with acute hearing impairment, which may not be evident in his international teaching, writing, and speaking engagements.

Practice in Psychology & Counseling

511 Beryl Drive, Kent, OH 44240

Office: 330-673-8729; Cell: 330-414-4917

nanselw@aol.com; awoldt1@kent.edu

REFERENCES

Elliot, R., Watson, J., Greenberg, L. S., Timulak, L., & Freire, E. (2013). Research on humanistic-experiential psychotherapies. In M. J. Lambert (Ed.), *Bergin & Garfield's Handbook of Psychotherapy and Behavior Change* (6th ed., pp. 495-538). Hoboken, NJ: Wiley.

Jung, C. G. (1933). *Modern man in search of his soul.*

Perls, F., Hefferline, R., & Goodman, P. (1951). *Gestalt therapy: Excitement and growth in the human personality.*

Roubal, J., Francesetti, G., & Gecele, M. (2016). Gestalt therapy approach to psychopathology. In J. Roubal (Ed.), *Gestalt Therapy in Clinical Practice: From Psychopathology to the Aesthetics of Contact* (pp. 27-47). Siracusa, Italy: Istituto di Gestalt HCC.

Gifted People

AMY L. DOAR, MS, LPC- S

So, you want to work with the GT (Gifted & Talented) population? Chances are you already see clients who fall into this category. Unless you were identified gifted as a child, you may be unaware of the differences between the gifted person and everyone else. Let's get a few of the misconceptions out of the way. For starters, being gifted does not always mean that a person made better grades than everyone else in school. It also doesn't mean that someone was at the top of their class, or that things in school or adulthood have been easy for them. Often you will find a gifted student in a scenario like this: Acing calculus and Chemistry, failing English, and playing violin in a youth orchestra. You also might see them making C's in all their classes but entering a national art competition and winning. A gifted adult may have dropped out of college but ended up as the Vice President of a company, and they don't quite know how they got there. Don't get me wrong, sometimes you will find a straight A student, who sailed through a coveted university on a full scholarship and has a stellar career. Then you may be looking at a gifted person who is also a *high achieving* person! So, what's the difference? Let's take a look.

We start with understanding the basic definitions of the gifted person and the high achieving person. The National Association for Gifted Children (NAGC.org) states:

> "Students with gifts and talents perform—or have the capability to perform—at higher levels compared to others of the same age, experience, and environment in one or more domains. They require modification(s) to their educational experience(s) to learn and realize their potential. Student with gifts and talents:

- Come from all racial, ethnic, and cultural populations, as well as all economic strata.

- Require sufficient access to appropriate learning opportunities to realize their potential.

- Can have learning and processing disorders that require specialized intervention and accommodation.
- Need support and guidance to develop socially and emotionally as well as in their areas of talent."

Davidson Gifted (DavidsonGifted.org) adds this:

"…While no two gifted children are the same, many share common gifted characteristics and traits, such as:

- Advanced thinking and comprehension above their age peers
- Emotional intensity at a young age
- Heightened sense of self awareness
- Highly developed curiosity
- Excellent memory"

Compare this to the High Achiever, which Frisco Independent School District (FriscoISD.org) just north of Dallas, TX states beautifully:

"At school, high achievers are motivated extrinsically by making good grades and pleasing their teachers. They typically succeed, for they show interest in assignments, learn and understand easily, are talented memorizers, and thrive on knowing the answers. Because of their desire to please and stand out, high achievers prefer detailed and concrete instructions to follow for assignments, sometimes including the font type and size and if they should put a cover on their project. They want to know exactly what to do to turn in an exemplary product, and they work hard to produce one."

Now we see that gifted persons are motivated intrinsically, and high achievers are motivated extrinsically. These are major differences in the way they perceive the world around them. Let us explore this intrinsic world.

Gifted children will often have a high IQ, and an emotional EQ that is somewhat delayed. You will find more gifted children struggling socially when they seem to have little problem with subject matter. They will have high emotional intensities, where their senses about everything around them (taste, smell, vision, hearing, imagination) are heightened, and this can lead to a lower distress tolerance with peers. Once they enter adulthood, the EQ has often caught up with the IQ, but in the cases where it has not, you will find more people seeking therapy.

Another term you will want to be familiar with is Twice Exceptional or 2E. A twice exceptional person is one who is identified gifted, but also has a recognized disability. This could range from Autism Spectrum Disorder, to ADHD and dyslexia – all neurodiverse. Many 2E persons find themselves in counseling, often starting as children and many times again as adults, which can add nuanced layers to your therapy.

When a gifted person is in your office, you will notice after a few conversations that they have a colorful and rich inner world and are interested in a wide variety of topics and ideas – far beyond the average person. They may be a multipotentialite who has many hobbies and an interesting job, or who has had several jobs over the course of their lifetime. They may also express feeling stuck and like a stranger to themselves, not believing they are as talented as everyone says they are. I have noted that every single gifted person who has been in my office has also experienced Existential Depression in some form or fashion. Existential Depression centers around inner conflicts which may feel as if a person's life has little meaning. This can also lead to personal identity confusion.

If you are interested in reading how it relates to gifted people, I highly recommend the article on "Existential Depression and Gifted Children" by Dr. James T. Webb, which can be found on Seng.org. It is wonderful for both teens and adults to read. I assign each of my gifted patients this article for homework. They then return the next session and reflect on what they have experienced. The reactions are astounding, beautiful, sad, multilayered, and deep. Many have tears in their eyes when they say, "Finally somebody understands me!" I often seem to be the first person to recognize that their giftedness plays a major role in everything they do. It does not go away, it does not hide, and they never grow out of it. They are amazed to find out that this is a powerful thing and can be one of their biggest assets.

Working with gifted people means supporting their curious minds. Often, as therapists, we find ourselves helping people work to achieve their dreams. We can function as much of a career counselor as a therapist! When they realize that many of the ideas they have been ruminating about all their lives are simply a facet of their gifted brain, suddenly the ruminations can lighten and their ability to see future goals is attainable. It is important to help the gifted person parse through mistaken beliefs about themselves and find their truth. They are usually ready to dig deep, and they often make excellent processors. If you take the time to support these beautiful minds, they will reward you with some of the most incredible sessions you could ever hope to have as a therapist.

While it does not take special certifications to work with this population, there are training courses to be found through Seng.org, Johns Hopkins, and many of your local universities. A foundational book for anyone working with this population is "A Parent's Guide to Gifted Children" by James T. Webb, Janet L. Gore, Edward R. Amend, and Arlene Devries. Reading this will give you incredible insight into the gifted mind, whether you are a parent or practitioner. It was one of the most helpful books I have read as an adult, and the parent of a gifted child, and my #1 recommended book for parents!

A former IT recruiter with over 13 years in private practice at Community Counseling Associates (CCA), Amy equally enjoys therapy with older teens, adults, senior citizens, & veterans. She has worked in private and community counseling clinics, churches, and public schools in Allen, Wylie, Plano, San Antonio, Schertz-Cibolo, and DeSoto, Texas. She has presented at churches, school districts, conferences, and private gatherings, and is a frequent speaker for Allen Gifted, AISD, SAGE, and the United Methodist Church. She is a Supervisor working with both Practicum students and Associates at CCA, which is a training facility. Amy has trained extensively in multiple treatment modalities, including Cognitive Behavioral Therapy (CBT), DBT, Gifted and Talented, Brief Solution-Focused Therapy, Psychoanalysis, Gestalt, Grief & Loss Therapy, Marriage & Family Therapy, Trauma/PTSD Therapies, LGBTQ+ issues, and Group Therapy. Her next adventure will be EMDR, which she started in 2022.

Adults, Gifted, Veterans & Active Duty, LGBTQIA, & Telehealth

Community Counseling Associates

amy@communitycounselingassociates.com

Community Counseling Associates – Allen, TX (a Dallas suburb)

www.communitycounselingassociates.com

Global Career Development Facilitator (GCDF)

JENNIFER WILLS MOORE, PHD, LPC, CERTIFIED SCHOOL COUNSELOR

The Global Career Development Facilitator (GCDF) certification is offered to individuals in varying fields across the globe that work with clients to facilitate their understanding of knowledge, the labor market, and employability skills. Although it is not specified, the GCDF certification is not simply for individuals in the helping professions. The term facilitator was intentionally used to provide an open door to various professionals that worked with clients in need of employability skills and labor market information (Heibert et al., 2014; Hinkle, 2011).

The certification consists of a minimum 120 hours of training in 12 core competency areas with flexibility in curriculum to fit the needs of the country that the training and certification are being utilized (Heibert et al., 2014; Hinkle, 2011; Normandale Community College, 2025; University of Wisconsin-Madison, 2025). Individuals with the GCDF certification are considered career service providers that are skilled in work placement decisions and knowledgeable about the advances in technology as it relates to the world of work (Hinkle, 2011).

Originally developed in the mid-1990s by the National Career Development Association (NCDA), the National Occupational Information Coordinating Committee (NOICC), and the Center for Credentialing & Education ([CCE], 2025), the purpose of the certification was to provide training and insights to professionals in a number of fields as they navigated the ever-changing environments of work in the United States. In response to a needs assessment completed by NOICC and the Career Development Training Institute (CDTI), the Career Development Facilitator (CDF) certification was officially launched in 1997 (CCE, 2025; Heibert et al., 2014; Hinkle, 2011).

As the certification and training developed around the world, the need for certification portability arose. In 2001, CDF certification was officially renamed the GCDF certification in 2001 to better align with the curriculum and professionals around the world that had adopted the certification (CCE, 2025; Central Carolina Technical College, 2024; Furbish et al., 2009; Heibert et al., 2014; Hinkle, 2011). Over the years since its creation, the GCDF certification has grown to be one of the largest career development certifications in the world with the flexibility to adapt to the needs of clients in various countries (European Board for Certified Counselors [EBCC], 2025).

CERTIFICATIONS, TRAININGS, AND LICENSURE REQUIREMENTS FOR GCDF

General Cost

$1300-$2000 (on avg. ~$1350) for GCDF training administered by a CCE Registered Credential Training Provider (RCTP)

$100 USA initial fee to for certification & $40 annual fee to maintain certification with an Ethics Attestation requirement every 5 years

Training Required

The CCE requires a minimum of 120 hours of comprehensive training that is offered by one of the CCE's RCTP that is listed on their website (CCE, 2025c). The training must include the following topics: helping skills, labor market information/resources, diverse populations, ethical and legal issues, career development models, employability skills, training clients/peers, program management/implementation, promotion/public relations, technology, and consultation.

In order to maintain the GCDF certification, a total of 75 continuing education hours must be completed over the course of 5 years (CCE, 2025a). The courses must be aligned in terms of competency area and activity type in order to gain continuing education credit towards maintaining the GCDF certification.

Training Recommended

The comprehensive training course stated above is the only required training for the GCDF certification, and continuing education credits are required to maintain certification (CCE, 2025c). As such, the CCE provides recommended training to earn continuing education credit on their website. Additionally, any continuing education course is recommended as long as it meets the requirements regarding the competency area and activity type (CCE, 2025a).

Certification Required

In order to practice as a Global Career Development Facilitator, the certification requirements for training, adherence to the CCE's *GCDF Code of Ethics* (CCE Board of Directors, 2015), and experience based on the highest level of education (CCE, 2025c) must be met.

Degree Requirements

Although the CCE does not outline specific degree requirements for GCDF certification, there is a requirement for work experience based on the highest level of degree earned based on the country the certification is being pursued. Below is the minimum number of experience hours required in most countries based on the highest level of education:

- 1,400 hours for those with a graduate degree (master or doctoral)
- 2,800 for those with a bachelor's degree
- 4,200 for those with an associate degree
- 5,600 for those with a high school diploma

There are some countries that are limited by access to training. As a result, the requirements for the number of experience hours can vary depending on the country (Hinkle, 2011).

Instructor Certification
General Cost

One of the requirements to be a certified GCDF Instructor is to maintain GCDF certification, so all costs listed above for certification and maintenance of certification would need to be considered for the GCDF Instructor certification.

As part of the costs for this certification, the GCDF Instructor must pay an initial $150 application fee (CCE, 2025c). Additionally, there is a $50 Instructor designation fee when applying for certification status with the National Board of Certified Counselors (NBCC).

Training Required

The GCDF Instructor needs to complete all of the required training for the GCDF certification along with a GCDF Instructor training which can be outlined when contacting one of the CCE's RCTP for the initial GCDF training (CCE, 2025c).

Training Recommended

There is no additional training recommended for the GCDF Instructor certification.

Certification Required

In order to facilitate GCDF training either online or hybrid, the GCDF Instructor and GCDF certification is required in addition to an approved RCTP (CCE, 2025c).

Degree Requirements

There are no additional requirements to be an GCDF Instructor (CCE, 2025c).

SCOPE OF PRACTICE ISSUES

All GCDFs must complete the required training, maintain their certification, and attest to their adherence to CCE's *GCDF Code of Ethics* (CCE Board of Directors, 2015). Although the GCDF certification is recognized worldwide, only certain states in the United States recognize the GCDF certification for professional advancement and employment, including Maryland, North Carolina, Tennessee, Michigan, South Carolina, & Wisconsin (CCE, 2025). Due to a lack of understanding and despite ongoing advocacy efforts, it is speculated that policymakers view career development professionals as lacking a true professional identity; therefore, there is little guidance regarding scope of practice implications aside from abiding by the *GCDF Code of Ethics* (Heibert et al., 2014).

SUMMARY

With close to 30 years of development, the GCDF certification has adapted and evolved to meet the needs of professionals in various fields of practice that work with clients to develop a better understanding of employability skills and the impact of the labor market (Heibert et al., 2014; Hinkle, 2011). Launched in the United States in 1997 as the Career Development Facilitator (CDF) certification, the GCDF now serves 14 countries and offers certification portability spanning the globe (CCE, 2025). Additionally, the GCDF certification is at this time recognized by six states in the United States as contributing to professional career development and employability.

For facilitators to become certified, a GCDF training program approved by the CCE and consisting of a minimum of 120 hours across 12 core competencies must be completed (CCE, 2025c). Additionally, the practitioner must have a minimum number of experience hours based on their highest degree and that can vary depending on the country depending on the availability of training opportunities (CCE, 2025a; CCE, 2025b). Additionally, to maintain the GCDF certification, a minimum of 75 continuing education hours that are aligned in both competency area and activity type are required along with an attestation to adhere to the CCE's *GCDF Code of Ethics* (CCE Board of Directors, 2015).

Although there is a lack of research regarding the practice of individuals utilizing GCDF certification, the continuing interest and growth across the globe highlight the need for career development support around the world and in varying fields of practice. The flexibility and portability of the GCDF certification as it is recognized in at least 14 countries provides facilitators with the knowledge, skills, and competencies to work with clients in development of their understanding of the ever-changing world of work and career development (CCE, 2025; Heibert et al., 2014; Hinkle, 2011; Furbish et al., 2009).

Jennifer Moore has a background in the field of education and counseling. Previously serving as a school counselor at the high school level in the State of Texas and a school-based therapist at the elementary level, Jennifer now works as an Assistant Professor and School Counseling Certification Program Coordinator at Texas A&M University - Central Texas in Killeen, TX. Additionally, she continues her work as an LPC through her private practice. Her research interests include school counseling, trauma counseling, and education of new counselors.

drjenn@mooretolifecounseling.net.

REFERENCES

CCE Board of Directors.(2015, February 7). *GCDF code of Ethics - cce-global.org*. GCDF Code of Ethics. https://www.cce-global.org/Assets/Ethics/GCDFcodeofethics.pdf

Center for Credentialing & Education.(2025). *GCDF global career development facilitator*. Global Career Development Facilitator GCDF. https://www.cce-global.org/credentialing/gcdf

Center for Credentialing & Education.(2025a). *United States Continuing Education*. Continuing Education US GCDF. https://www.cce-global.org/credentialing/gcdf/us/ce

Center for Credentialing & Education.(2025b). *United States maintaining your credential*. Maintain US GCDF. https://www.cce-global.org/credentialing/gcdf/us/maintain

Center for Credentialing & Education.(2025c). *United States required training*. Requirements US GCDF. https://www.cce-global.org/credentialing/gcdf/us/requirements

Central Carolina Technical College. (2024, January 9). *Global Career Development Facilitator (GCDF)*. Central Carolina Technical College. https://www.cctech.edu/course/global-career-development-facilitator-gcdf/

European Board for Certified Counselors. (2025). *Global Career Development Facilitator (GCDF): European Board for Certified Counselors*. Home. https://www.europeanbcc.eu/Programs/GCDF-Certification

Furbish, D., Neault, R. A., & Pickerell, D. (2009). The global career development facilitator credential: An international perspective. *Journal of Employment Counseling, 46*(4), 187–189. https://doi-org.tamuct.idm.oclc.org/10.1002/j.2161-1920.2009.tb00083.x

Hiebert, B., Neault, R., Leong, F. T. L., Bakshi, A. J., Arulmani, G., & Watts, A. G. (2014). Career Counselor Competencies and Standards: Differences and Similarities across Countries. In *Handbook of Career Development* (pp. 689–707). Springer New York.

Hinkle, S. (2009). Global career development facilitator: An international certification. *Career Planning and Adult Development Journal, 24*(4), 83-87.

Normandale Community College. (2025). *Global Career Development Facilitator CERT Program*. Global Career Development Facilitator Cert Program - Normandale Community College - Continuing Education & Customized Training. https://normandale.augusoft.net/index.cfm?method=ClassInfo.ClassInformation&int_class_id=66650

University of Wisconsin-Madison. (2025). *Professional development: Facilitating career development (FCD)*. Counseling Psychology. https://counselingpsych.education.wisc.edu/clinic-and-outreach/facilitating-career-development-fcd/professional-development-facilitating-career-development-fcd/

Good Lives Model (GLM)

DAVID S. PRESCOTT, LCSW, LICSW

TONY WARD, PHD, MA, DIPCLINPSYC (CANTY), FRSNZ
DEVELOPER OF GOOD LIVES MODEL

GWENDA M. WILLIS, PHD, PGDIPCLINPSYC

The Good Lives Model (GLM) is a strengths-based practice framework of rehabilitation developed and elaborated on by Tony Ward and colleagues from the early 2000s (Ward, 2002; Ward & Maruna, 2007; Ward & Stewart, 2003). It is primarily used with people who have engaged in behaviors that are illegal and/or harmful to others. The GLM first emerged in response to the shortcomings of treatment programs that focused almost exclusively on risk reduction. This included difficulties ensuring that clients were motivated and engaged in treatment programs, especially when those programs' methods and goals did not necessarily align with the client's values and priorities. The GLM adopts the dual aims of risk reduction alongside helping clients to develop and implement a prosocial "good life plan" underpinned by the client's core values, priorities, and strengths. Ultimately, the goal is to help clients build on their strengths so that they can develop a lifestyle that is incompatible with offending, one in which harming others is undesirable and unnecessary.

UNDERLYING THEORETICAL ASSUMPTION OF GLM

The GLM accommodates the principles of risk, need, and responsivity (Andrews & Bonta, 2017). In GLM practice, criminogenic needs are conceptualized as signaling problems with capacity to achieve *primary human goods* (actions, experiences, or states of being that people seek for their own sake such as relationships, experiences of competence and mastery, inner peace, and autonomy) in prosocial ways. In this way, "risk factors," also known as criminogenic needs represent impairments in the internal and/or external conditions necessary to achieve valued goals; that is, they are impairments of agency. Criminogenic needs are thus addressed in the broader pursuit of strengthening a client's capacity to achieve valued goods (versus addressing criminogenic needs with the sole aim of reducing risk) by way of the acquisition of internal (e.g., skills, knowledge) and external resources (e.g., social supports, vocational training). A core underlying theoretical assumption of the GLM is that human beings are naturally inclined to desire a range of primary goods, formulate plans to achieve them and to enact these plans in their day to day lives. The GLM has been embraced by treatment providers in a wide range of settings and in countries all over the world (e.g., The USA and Canada,- McGrath et al., 2010).

Properly implemented, GLM case formulations and treatment sessions focus on acquiring valued primary goods through Good Life goals as well as managing risk factors. In implementation, a focus on approaching/acquiring primary goods is clear in each session, with the focus for each client reflecting their prioritized primary human goods. All primary goods are included in some way, even though they may be prioritized differently. In other words, no goods are left out of the treatment process entirely. The primary good most heavily weighted by an individual is closely connected with their conception of personal identity, and therefore, what is considered to be a meaningful and worthwhile life. The therapist is ready, willing, and able to help the client talk about relevant and meaningful goals and develop an understanding of how the client's own goals relate to the GLM primary goods. For example, if the client's only goal is to be able to run a marathon, the therapist can explore underlying primary goods such as "excellence at work and play" and "living and surviving".

The GLM is concerned with more than simply living a good life. It also involves understanding how the pursuit of good life goals was implicated in an individual's offending and in their associated psychological and social problems. In other words, the GLM proposes that underlying even the most egregious behaviors are primary goods that are common to all human beings in one form or another. For example, the primary good of "relationships and friendships" is implicated in a crime where a person sexually abuses children while believing that they have a "special" relationship with them. The goal of having a relationship is central to being human. Pursuing sexual relationships with children, however, poses an unacceptable risk to the child, their loved ones, and the individual seeking the relationship.

TRAINING, LICENSURE, AND EDUCATIONAL REQUIREMENTS

The GLM should be practiced by professionals with specific training in providing therapeutic treatment to clients who have caused harm to others. While there is no specific licensure requirements, possession of a terminal degree (such as a doctoral degree in psychology or Master's in Clinical Social Work or Counseling), alongside an applicable license, and participating in training specific to the GLM are highly recommended. Ultimately, while professional training is important, the clinician's ability to remain warm, empathic, rewarding, and directive are critical components, as is the ability to seek out client feedback (Marshall, 2005; Prescott et al., 2017; Prescott et al., this volume).

FURTHER TRAINING OPPORTUNITIES

There are live and on-demand trainings for the GLM available, as well as a fidelity monitoring tool (Prescott et al., 2022). A recent paper reviewed lessons learned from international implementations (Prescott & Willis, 2021).

Tony is a clinical psychologist by training and has been working in the clinical and forensic field since 1987. He was formerly Director of the Kia Marama Sexual Offenders' Unit at Rolleston Prison in New Zealand, and has taught both clinical and forensic psychology at Victoria, Deakin, Canterbury, and Melbourne Universities. He is affiliated with the Swinburne University of Technology, and is currently Professor of Forensic Clinical Psychology at Victoria University of Wellington. Tony is a Fellow of the Royal Society of New Zealand. His current research projects include: (a) explanation and inquiry in research and practice. This includes the nature of psychopathology and crime related problems such as symptoms and dynamic risk factors; (b) normative issues in clinical practice; and (c) change processes in the psychopathology and forensic/correctional domains. Tony has published over 440 academic papers and books, and is currently working on book project with the provisional title of "Science informed practice in clinical psychology". He is the creator of the Good Lives Model of correctional rehabilitation and the Self-regulation Model of sexual offending.

A mental health practitioner of 39 years, David Prescott is the Director of the Safer Society Continuing Education Center. He is the author and editor of 25 books in the areas of understanding and improving services to at-risk clients. He is best known for his work in the areas of understanding, assessing, and treating sexual violence and trauma. Mr. Prescott is the recipient of the 2014 Distinguished Contribution award from the Association for the Treatment and Prevention of Sexual Abuse (ATSA), the 2018 recipient of the National Adolescent Perpetration Network's C. Henry Kempe Lifetime Achievement award, and the 2022 recipient of the Fay Honey Knopp Award from the New York State Alliance for the Prevention of Sexual Abuse and New York State ATSA. He also served as ATSA President in 2008-09. Mr. Prescott currently trains and lectures around the world. His published work has been translated into Japanese, Korean, German, French, Polish, and Dutch. He has served on the editorial boards of four scholarly journals.

Gwenda is a Clinical Psychologist with expertise in forensic/correctional psychology research and practice. She joined the School of Psychology at The University of Auckland in 2013. Her research and clinical work focus on strengths-based approaches to psychological assessment and treatment, trauma-informed care and sexual abuse prevention. Gwenda is an Editorial Board member for Sexual Abuse and the Journal of Sexual Aggression (JSA). Gwenda has received numerous awards and accolades for her research, including the 2012 New Zealand Psychological Society Early Career Goddard Award – Applied Psychology. In 2015, Gwen was awarded a Rutherford Discovery Fellowship.

REFERENCES

Andrews, D. A., & Bonta, J. (2017). The psychology of criminal conduct (6th ed.). Cincinnati, OH: Anderson Publishing.

Marshall, W. L. (2005). Therapist Style in Sexual Offender Treatment: Influence on Indices of Change. *Sexual Abuse: Journal of Research and Treatment, 17*(2), 109-116. **https://doi.org/10.1177/107906320501700202**

McGrath, R., Cumming, G., Burchard, B., Zeoli, S., & Ellerby, L. (2010). *Current Practices and Emerging Trends in Sexual Abuser Management: The Safer Society 2009 North American Survey.* Brandon, Vermont: Safer Society Press.

Prescott, D.S., Maeschalck, C., & Miller, S.D. (2017). Feedback-Informed Treatment in Clinical Practice: Reaching for Excellence, 2017. Washington, DC: American Psychological Association Press.

Prescott, D. S., Maeschalck, C. M., & Miller, S. D. (2022). Feedback-Informed Treatment. In R. Fulmer (Ed.), Counseling and psychotherapy: Theory and beyond. San Diego, CA: Cognella.

Prescott, D. S., & Willis, G. M. (2021). Using the good lives model (GLM) in clinical practice: Lessons learned from international implementation projects. Aggression and Violent Behavior. https://doi.org/10.1016/j.avb.2021.101717

Prescott, D., Willis, G., & Ward, T. (2022). Monitoring Therapist Fidelity to the Good Lives Model (GLM). International Journal of Offender Therapy and Comparative Criminology. DOI: 10.1177/0306624X221086572.

Ward, T. (2002). Good lives and the rehabilitation of offenders: Promises and problems. *Aggression and Violent Behavior, 7*(5), 513–528. https://doi.org/10.1016/S1359-1789(01)00076-3

Ward, T., & Maruna, S. (2007). *Rehabilitation: Beyond the risk assessment paradigm.* London, UK: Routledge.

Ward, T., & Stewart, C. A. (2003). The treatment of sex offenders: Risk management and good lives. *Professional Psychology: Research and Practice, 34,* 353-360.

Gottman Method Couples Therapy (GMCT)

CARRIE COLE, PHD, LPC-S, LMHC

CERTIFIED GOTTMAN THERAPIST

GOTTMAN THERAPY MASTER TRAINER

GOTTMAN METHOD COUPLES THERAPY

Gottman Method Couples Therapy was developed by Drs. John and Julie Gottman based on more than 40 years of scientific research on couple relationships. Through their careful observations and analyses of couple relationships, both those who were successful and those that ended, the Gottmans learned which behaviors best predicted relationship satisfaction and which ones predicted relationship dissolution. This form of couples therapy is grounded in science and informed by science. While it is beyond the scope of this chapter to include all the scientific research that informed Gottman Method Couples Therapy, some findings are important to help ground the clinician in the underpinnings of the therapy. There were significant findings about couples' interactions which included behaviors, affect, physiology, and perceptions of their history. Some interactions are more destructive than others. Four of these behaviors, which we later came to know "The Four Horsemen of the Apocalypse," are criticism, defensiveness, contempt, and stonewalling (Cook et al., 1995; Gottman, 1993, p. 62; Gottman & Gottman, 2017, p. 13). Longitudinal research that was conducted over the course of 6 years indicated that these behaviors destroyed relationships. Interestingly, another behavior influenced whether couples were happy or not. That behavior was the ability to accept influence. In heterosexual relationships, failure of the male partner to accept influence from the female partner also predicted relationship breakup (Gottman, 1993; Gottman et al., 1998).

Another important research finding was the importance of emotions. How couples express affect in their conversations with each other impacts the quality of their relationship. Gottman and colleagues discovered that divorce could be accurately predicted 93% of the time based on the amount of time that couples spent in positivity versus negativity (Gottman, 1993; Gottman et al., 1998; Gottman & Gottman, 2017). Couples who stayed together had a positive to negative affect ratio of 5 to 1 during conflicts and a positive to negative affect ratio of 20 to 1 during non-conflict conversations (Gottman, 1994). Distressed couples displayed a positive to negative affect ratio of .8 to 1 (Gottman, 1993; Levenson & Gottman, 1983). In addition, unhappy couples entered a negative emotional state that became all-consuming, and once that absorbing state of negativity was entered, it was almost impossible to escape. Healthy couples also expressed negative affect during conflicts. However, they quickly made repairs to escape the negativity (Gottman & Gottman, 2017).

Affect was also proven to be at the core of the demand-withdraw pattern found in couple relationships. A demand-withdraw pattern refers to a pattern in which one partner demands something of the other partner by complaining, criticizing, or nagging and the other partner withdraws by avoiding or terminating the interaction in some way (Baucom et al., 2010). How individuals feel about having certain emotions will determine whether they are emotion-accepting or emotion-dismissing. When one person is emotion-accepting, and the other is emotion-dismissing, the demand-withdraw pattern emerges (Gottman & Gottman, 2018).

Affect impacts an individual's physiology. When having conversations in the Gottman Love Lab, some individuals' heart rates increased to the point that stress hormones were released, and they entered into a state of diffuse physiological arousal (DPA), which meant they could not process information. Researchers found that negative communication, such as the expression of anger and stonewalling, also predicted poor health as it negatively affected cardiovascular and musculoskeletal systems (Gottman & Gottman, 2017; Haase et al., 2016). Relationship dissatisfaction was also related to mental disorders, such as depression and anxiety (Gottman et al., 2020; Lebow et al., 2012). These scientific findings and many others led to the development of the sound relationship house theory (Gottman & Gottman, 2017).

THE SOUND RELATIONSHIP HOUSE THEORY

Gottman method couples therapy is based on the sound relationship house theory. There are three systems that need to be healthy according to this theory. They are the friendship system, the conflict management system, and the shared meaning system. Each of these systems will be discussed.

Friendship System

The friendship system has three main parts: Love maps, fondness and admiration, turning towards bids, and a positive perspective. Every couple begins their relationship by getting to know each other. They learn about their partner's favorite foods, how they take their coffee, when their birthday is, what stresses they struggle with currently, and countless other little bits of information that are unique to that person. This knowledge of the other's inner world is called Love Maps. Sometimes, once something is known about the other, it is known for life. However, some information will change over time, like favorite songs, or their sources of stress, so partners need to continually update their knowledge about the other's inner world, or those love maps can be out of date (Gottman & Gottman, 2017; 2018).

Another part of the friendship system is partners' fondness and admiration for one another. When relationships are new, chances are that the couple are letting one another know what they like and appreciate about the other. They express nice, sweet comments to the other to let them know their feelings about them. They say things like "I love the way you leave sweet, random notes for me to find." Those expressions of fondness and appreciation help deepen the connection of the relationship. The more specific those words, the better. For example, it's nice to hear "You're wonderful!" but what does that really mean? It's a little different to hear "I was so impressed with the way you handled our disgruntled neighbor. You have some great communication skills!" When couples stop expressing their fondness and admiration for each other, the relationship can begin to grow distant.

A third part of the friendship system is turning towards bids. Couples often attempt to get one another's attention as a way of beginning a conversation or as a way of connecting in a small moment. These attempts are called bids for connection or "bids" for short. There are three response options to bids: turn towards, turn away and turn against. Turning towards is responding to the bid by engaging in the conversation, or something like, "Uh huh." When couples turn toward each other they are building an emotional bank account that serves to buffer them from negativity (Gottman & Gottman, 2017). Turning away is a lack of response to the bid. It is not mean-spirited, but it is thoughtless and neglectful. Turning against is mean-spirited. It is responding nastily, such as "Not now!" or "I don't care." How bids are responded to impact the bidding partner's heart and the relationship long term. If the bid is turned toward, it has a calming, soothing effect on the person who made the bid and that person's heart rate goes down and they feel a sense of connection with their partner. If the bid is turned away from or turned against, the bidder's heart rate goes up and they feel a sense of disconnection. They crumple a little within and it usually takes them a long time to risk making another bid (Gottman & Gottman, 2017).

If the couple's friendship system is going well, then they are likely in a positive perspective. They think and feel positively about their partner and their relationship. They maximize the good parts of their partner and minimize any challenges. They give their partner the benefit of the doubt and attribute good intentions to their partner. That positive perspective can easily slip down into a negative perspective. Once in a negative perspective, partners are sensitive to slights, put-downs, and hear things as negative that were not intended to be negative. They seem to be on the lookout for things that do not go well so that they can comment on their disappointment in the partner. This slide into negativity can slowly culminate over the course of many years of putting everything else before the relationship, or it can take a quick nosedive if there has been a betrayal of any kind.

Conflict Management System

Research has shown that only 31% of couples' problems are solvable. That means that 69% of all couples' problems are perpetual. The goal of Gottman method couples therapy is not to eliminate conflict. Conflict is a natural part of relationships and can contribute to greater emotional intimacy between partners. However, some negative behaviors during conflict are destructive to relationships. The key is to manage conflict effectively and help the couple stay in respectful dialogue about the issue. There are several parts to the conflict management system: harsh startups, four horsemen, flooding, accepting influence, repair attempts, gridlock, and compromise (Gottman & Gottman, 2015; 2017). Each of these will be discussed.

Harsh startups occur within the first 3 minutes of a conflict conversation. When a person brings up an issue negatively and begins to define the partner or criticize the partner for what has gone wrong, the startup of that conversation is considered harsh. Those first 3 minutes predict how the rest of the conversation will go, and how the relationship will go if there is no intervention (Gottman, 1993).

As stated above, there are four behaviors that are so destructive that they predict relationship dissolution. Gottman method refers to them as the "Four Horsemen of the Apocalypse". They are criticism, defensiveness, contempt, and stonewalling. Criticism is attacking and blaming the other person for the problem. It often begins with "You always" or "You never". It is pointing the finger at the other person. Defensiveness is denying any responsibility for the problem ("No I didn't"), the innocent victim ("It's not my fault") or a counterattack ("You do it too!"). Contempt is the worst of the killers of the relationship. It is any way that one gives their partner the message that they are superior to them. Some examples are name-calling, facial expressions, such as rolling one's eyes or smirking, sarcasm, and correcting the other person's grammar. The last of these killers is stonewalling. Stonewalling is giving refusing to respond. It is giving one's partner the silent treatment. It feels like a punishment.

Sometimes during conflicts an individual's heart rate can increase to the point that the person goes into diffuse physiological arousal (DPA). This occurs at about 100 beats per minute for the average person. Once this happens it causes stress hormones to be released within the body. These stress hormones cause the frontal lobes of the brain to shut down and throws the person into the fight, flight, or freeze response. The experience of the person in DPA is that there is a traffic jam in their brain, they can't get their point across, and they just want to get away from the situation. The Gottmans refer to this experience as being "Flooded". The person is overwhelmed with emotions and either leaves (flight), stops talking (freeze), or begins to really escalate and repeat themselves (fight). It takes about 20-30 minutes to calm back down from this state, but that is 20-30 minutes of not dwelling on the situation.

Another important concept to the management of conflict is the ability of partners to accept influence from one another (Gottman, 1998). Accepting influence means taking in the other person's perspective as valid. It is giving one's partner the message that they make sense, or that they have a good point. The alternative, rejecting influence is giving the other person the message that they are crazy, they do not know what they are talking about, or that they got the facts wrong. To be influential in a relationship, one must first be willing to accept the influence of others. Otherwise, it becomes a power struggle where there must be a winner and a loser.

Couples are miscommunicating with each other over 75% of the time according to the research. That means that couples are going to need to repair those miscommunications. Sometimes a simple apology will suffice ("I'm sorry I was so grumpy."). These attempts to correct the course are called repair attempts. The research indicated that happy couples repaired quickly and allowed those repair attempts to be successful. Unhappy couples tended to hold on to grudges.

Perpetual problems can become gridlocked for couples if not managed carefully. When problems are gridlocked, the couple either shuts down or escalates every time that issue comes up. Each partner becomes entrenched in their own position and digs their heels in. They often feel misunderstood or that their feelings do not matter to their partner. At the heart of gridlocked issues are deeper longings and symbolic meaning. On the surface, these problems seem to have simple solutions. For example, many couples argue about finances. One person might want to enjoy life while they have the ability to do so, which means spending money to have nice things and go on vacations. The other person may want to save money, so they have money in case of emergencies, or enough money to see them through retirement. Which person is right? At first blush it would seem that these problems are easily solvable, yet many couples struggle with these kinds of issues for years. When couples are gridlocked, there are deeper underlying symbolic meanings at the core of the problem that stem from their beliefs, values, ethics, and early family history that relate to their feelings and the reason that it is so important to them. There is an underlying core need at the heart of the matter for each individual (Gottman & Gottman, 2017). The meaning of money alone can have multiple meanings, such as safety, security, a sense of freedom, a sense of belonging, or power.

A successful component to managing conflict is a couple's ability to compromise with one another. There is an art to compromise. To begin with, it must be conceptualized as temporary. If agreements made feel like they are written in stone, one simply cannot commit to the compromise because the spirit of compromise is giving something up. Sometimes, in the spirit of compromise, people give up too much. Therefore, they need to be able to go back to the drawing board and forge out something that will work for both parties. To be successful, each person needs to understand what their core need around the particular issue is. If it is a need, they cannot be flexible around it. Take the example of money. If security is at the heart of the matter for one partner, they cannot compromise on spending money on new cars or vacations until their need for financial security is met. Questions then need to be asked and answered about what financial security means, how much money is required to feel financially secure, and how can they be flexible so that their partner can get their needs around money met.

At the core of the gridlocked issues are life dreams, and how to make those life dreams come true. Every individual has a dream about what they want to do in life – including what they want to accomplish. One person may have always wanted to be a parent. Another person may be a real adventurer and wants to explore the entire world. If these two individuals form a partnership, their life dreams may be at odds with each other. How they talk about these dreams and manage their differences will be important. To be successful together, they will need to develop a compromise around these dreams that is satisfactory to both individuals (Gottman & Gottman, 2017).

Shared Meaning System

The shared meaning system has 4 parts. It includes the couple's rituals, goals, roles and symbols. There are no right or wrongs to these, and they can be very different for different people. Rituals are the couple's traditions and the way in which they go through time. It includes their everyday routines, like sharing meals together, going to bed, leaving and coming home, as well as the way they celebrate important events, such as birthdays, anniversaries, and holidays. Another part of the shared meaning system are goals. This includes shared goals and individual goals. How similar are their goals? How supportive are they of each individual's goals? Similarly, how supportive are they around the various roles that each person has in life? The last component of the shared meaning system is symbols. Symbols are one's values, beliefs, and philosophy of life. For example, a home is a symbol of the relationship. What does each person want that home to be like? One person may want it to be like Grand Central Station – the place where everyone gathers, and all are welcome. Another person may want their home to be a quiet, peaceful retreat, free from intrusion. If these two individuals commit to one another, they will have to manage their differing values and beliefs about what a home should be like (Gottman & Gottman, 2018).

Trust and Commitment

The sound relationship house is held up by two walls: trust and commitment. The first wall is trust. Trust is believing that one's partner will be present and supportive when needed. It means that each partner will have the other's back, and each can count on that. They will stand up for each other even with friends or family members. The second wall is commitment. Commitment is the belief that the partner one has chosen is their best life option and they are dedicated to their partner for life. Committed partners are loyal to the relationship that they have and are not interested in other alternatives (Gottman & Gottman, 2018).

INTRODUCTION TO GOTTMAN METHOD

Gottman method couples therapy (GMCT) is an affectively based therapy. That means that emotion is at the core of the therapeutic work. The therapist is listening for emotion and helps the individual partners identify with their own emotions, name those emotions, and convey them to their partner. GMCT has 3 phases. These are the assessment phase, the active treatment phase, and the relapse prevention phase. The gold standard for GMCT is a 90-minute session. Each of these phases will be discussed.

Assessment

GMCT always begins with a thorough assessment. This phase can be difficult for empathetic therapists when transitioning to GMCT. It is tempting to want to jump in and immediately try to help struggling couples. However, this would be the equivalent of a surgeon pulling out a scalpel and operating on a patient without doing an MRI or any testing. Before a therapist begins cutting into a relationship, they need to be aware of what they are cutting into.

Assessment has 3 main parts and requires a minimum of 3 sessions. Assessment involves interviewing the couple together, interviewing each individual separately, and providing feedback to the couple, which includes a treatment plan. Each part of these assessments will be discussed.

In the first session the therapist gets the couple's narrative, asks them about the history of their relationship, gets a sample of a conflict discussion, and has the couple fill out questionnaires. A narrative is what brings the couple in for treatment. It is learning about the issues that they currently struggle with. The narrative should take about 10-15 minutes at the beginning of the first session. The therapist then transitions into the history of the couple's relationship. The therapist asks questions from the Oral History Interview. This extensive interview asks questions about how the couple met and got together, first impressions of one another, as well as questions about major life transitions. Toward the end of the first session the therapist will ask the couple to dyadically discuss an ongoing conflict for 10 minutes. This conflict discussion will be video recorded and reviewed later by the therapist to listen and watch for conflict management struggles including the four horsemen. At the end of the session the therapist will ask the couple to fill out the Gottman questionnaires, which can either be taken online and automatically scored, or by pen and paper and hand scored by the therapist.

The next part of the assessment process is to interview each partner individually. This can be done in 1 90-minute session where one partner waits in the waiting room while the other is interviewed for about 45 minutes, or it can be divided up into 2 different 45-minute sessions. The therapist does not keep secrets, and this should be stated in the first session and again at the beginning of the individual session with each partner. The partners should have filled out their questionnaires prior to their individual session so that the therapist can review and ask about anything that stands out in the individual questionnaire responses. In addition, each partner is asked questions about their family of origin, such as what their parents were like, what their parent's relationship was like, and how their parents handled emotions. The therapist also finds out what life was like for this person growing up. A psychological history is also collected on each individual including any individual diagnoses, history of suicide, history of abuse, and substance use. This is also a time when the individual can bring up any concerns or struggles about the relationship that they would like to work on in therapy. The therapist should ask if there has been any instance of domestic violence or intimate partner aggression, as well as if there have been any history emotional or sexual affairs.

If the therapist discovers that there has been an affair, it is important to know if the betrayed partner is aware of the affair. If the affair is either ongoing or unknown by the other person, couples therapy is contra-indicated. If the therapist discovers that there has been characterological domestic violence and one partner is afraid of the other partner, couples therapy is also contra-indicated. In either of these cases, the couple is not yet ready for couples therapy and these individuals need to be referred to individual therapy.

The third session (or fourth if individual sessions were broken up) is the feedback and treatment planning session. The therapist has synthesized all the information collected throughout the assessment process and shares with the couple an analysis of their relationship based on the sound relationship house levels and any co-morbidities that the relationship may be struggling with. It is important to refrain from singling any individual out as being the problem. These are relationship issues. It is also important to give the couple hope during this feedback process. Identifying the problem is half the battle. Once the problem is understood there are tools that can be used and skills that can be developed to help manage the problem. The treatment goals emerge from the struggles identified through the assessment process. For example, if conflict management is a problem, and the couple is arguing, the therapist will help the couple process the arguments using a tool called The Aftermath of a Fight or Regrettable Incident.

Active Treatment Phase

There are three therapeutic domains that need to be addressed during the treatment phase of therapy: The couple's conflict, their friendship, and their shared meaning system. The treatment begins with the issue that the couple struggles with the most. The therapist encourages the couple to engage in the conversations dyadically. This means that the couple talks directly to each other rather than the therapist. The therapist interrupts the couple when their conversations go off track and guides them to use more effective strategies. Couples are taught relationship skills and given tools to help navigate difficult conversations. They are taught to recognize their own contribution to the struggles in their relationship, including their use of the four horsemen. Therapy is guided by the results of the assessment. Quite often the place that couples therapy needs to begin is with the conflict management system.

Conflict Management System

Some couples come to treatment because of an attachment injury. Others are struggling with small, seemingly meaningless, arguments and/or they have ongoing perpetual or gridlocked issues that have not been managed well. If a partner has felt betrayed in any way, that betrayal can create an attachment injury. Betrayals can come in the form of sexual betrayals, financial betrayals, betrayals of confidence, a failure to be there for a partner, or taking someone else's side instead of one's partner's side. If there has been an injury that has wounded one partner so badly that it has created a rift in their attachment to one another, then that is where treatment begins in GMCT.

Couples need to be able to repair after fights so that they can reconnect to one another. Fights or arguments need to be fully processed, or else they keep coming back up and infect each new argument. When processing an argument, it is important to stick to that one specific argument and not allow other arguments to get thrown into the mix. In addition, couples often argue about an ongoing perpetual or gridlocked issue. After the argument is processed, there may be more work that needs to be done to explore the underlying meaning around the ongoing issue for each partner. Each of these types of conflicts requires the use of different tools.

Friendship System

It is important to attend to the couple's friendship system in addition to helping them improve their conflict discussions. Couples regain a sense of connection by feeling known, admired, and respected by one another. They also need to believe that their partner is interested in them and will turn toward them in small and large ways. This part of the therapy can be enjoyable for all parties. Couples are encouraged to be curious about each other. They are to ask questions and remember the answers. They learn to tune into each other's emotional world on a day-to-day basis.

Shared Meaning System

Finally, it is important to help the couple develop a sense of shared meaning. Happy couples are the ones who have a lot of rituals that connect them. Those rituals of connection can be created and designed by the couple, such as having a cup of coffee together before the start of the day, cooking meals together, or debriefing out on the deck at the end of a workday. The couple also needs to have a way of having safe conversations about their life dreams as well as values, beliefs, and philosophy of life. The couple needs to develop a sense of "we-ness" that makes their relationship unique and special to them. In addition to rituals, couples also need to talk about their goals and their roles in life. How similar are their goals? How supportive are they of one another's goals? Are they supportive of one another's roles in life? The couple also needs to share their values and beliefs with one another and feel that this relationship is a safe place to express those deeper parts of themselves.

Relapse Prevention Phase

GMCT masses therapy in the beginning and phases out over time to prevent relapse. After the couple has learned the tools to repair and have safer discussions about their areas of conflict, the therapy sessions are spaced further apart. The couple is given the opportunity to try it on their own for a period of time and then checks back in with the therapist. The most effective relapse prevention technique is to have a check-in appointment with the couple once every 6 months for 18-24 months. If the couple begins to slide back into some unproductive habits, they can be corrected quickly and get back on course through these follow up appointments.

CERTIFICATIONS, TRAININGS, LICENSURE REQUIREMENTS FOR GMCT

There are multiple requirements to become a certified Gottman method therapist. The first is licensure. The second is going through 3 levels of training. The third requirement is to go through a consultation process. The fourth requirement is to submit four videos of the therapist's work with real couples using Gottman interventions. Each of these will be discussed.

Licensure

GMCT requires that the therapist be licensed to conduct couples therapy in whatever state, province, or country in which they are performing these services. Licensure requires that the therapist have formal education and an advanced degree in psychology with some specialization in counseling. Following the counseling degree program there is usually an internship in which the beginning therapist is supervised until they have met some prerequisite number of hours and proficiency in therapy. Eligible therapists can be licensed mental health counselors, licensed professional counselors, licensed clinical social workers, and licensed clinical psychologists.

Trainings

There are three levels of training in GMCT. Level 1 Clinical Training: Bridging the Couple Chasm is the first level of training. In this 2-day training the therapist is introduced to the research on which the therapy is based, the therapist learns what makes relationships work and what contributes to their failure. The therapist also learns how to assess couple relationships and why assessment is needed. The procedure and the tools for assessment are taught in this first training. The therapist is introduced to the sound relationship house theory in this training. The therapist learns to identify specific problems in couple relationships through this theory, which helps them determine when and where to intervene to help strengthen specific struggles. The goals of the therapy are taught as well. This first training is an introduction to the basic Gottman interventions. These interventions are used to help couples manage conflict, build friendship, and build shared meaning (Gottman & Gottman, 2018).

The second training, Level 2: Assessment, Intervention, and Co-Morbidities is a 3-day training that goes deeper into assessment, teaches more Gottman interventions, and informs the therapist how to work with couples who struggle with co-morbidities, such as addiction, affairs, and domestic violence. The basics of human observation, as well as how to watch for bids and turning toward behaviors, are added to the assessment process in this training. The therapist watches videos of the application of specific interventions during this training and is given an opportunity to gain some experience using the interventions through role play. The format is to listen to the underlying rationale for the use of the intervention, observe a video of the use of the intervention, and then to break into small groups to practice using the intervention. When taking this training in-person, the therapist has the opportunity to receive personal coaching from the trainer. In addition, therapists are also taught how to and whether to treat couples who struggle with co-morbidities, such as substance abuse and addiction, sexual and emotional affairs, and domestic violence (Gottman & Gottman, 2014a).

The third training, Level 3: Practicum is also a 3-day training. Therapists are asked to bring in video recordings of couple interactions that are therapeutically problematic. This training is to help therapists gain more practice using specific interventions, as well as learn how to manage difficult cases. The training class watches a video of a problematic couple that one of the trainees brought into the class. The Gottman trainer gets a little background about the couple, and then role-plays how to manage that particular issue using an appropriate Gottman intervention. The training class then breaks into small groups and practices using the intervention with the same issue. There are times when a GMCT will need to use an intervention within an intervention. This process is demonstrated in this advanced training (Gottman & Gottman, 2014b).

Once all three levels of training have been completed, the therapist is eligible to enter the certification track to become a certified GMCT. The therapist has 2 years to enter the certification track from the date of their Level 3 training. Once they enter the certification track, they have 2 years to complete the process.

The process of certification requires that the therapist have an approved consultant who guides them through certification. The consultant must be recognized as a consultant through The Gottman Institute, and most consultants are master trainers. The therapist meets with their consultant for a minimum of 8 sessions individually, or for a minimum of 12 sessions if going through consultation with a group of therapists. While this is a minimum requirement, most therapists meet with their consultants for much longer. The consultation process is where most GMCTs learn how to be effective Gottman therapists. The therapist will video record their couple sessions and share those videos with their consultant. The consultant observes the videos with the therapist and gently guides the therapist in ways to conceptualize the case as a Gottman therapist, and how to effectively use Gottman interventions. The therapist must show competency in four interventions: stopping the four horsemen, intervening when one person is physiologically flooded, the use of the dreams within conflict intervention, and the use of compromise ovals. When the therapist has 4 videos that adequately show the use of these specific interventions, the therapist will submit those videos for review.

The therapist submits their videos to the training department of The Gottman Institute. The videos are sent to a video reviewer who critiques each video based on benchmarks of proficiency. If the benchmarks are met, then the video passes. If all videos pass, then the therapist is certified. If any of the intervention videos do not pass, then the therapist is asked to submit another video of that intervention. The therapist is allowed to submit a video(s) 3 times. If, on the third attempt the video still does not pass, then the therapist is asked to take Level 3 training again. In addition, the therapist has 2 years to submit their videos for review. If they have not submitted their videos within that 2-year time frame, they will need to take Level 3 training again.

Cost, Gold standard & EBP

Gottman method couples therapy is grounded in science and developed through experimental research; therefore, it is scientifically based, which is considered an evidence-based practice. The gold standard is to conduct therapy based on evidence-based scientifically tested treatment procedures.

Gottman method training requires considerable time and financial commitment from the therapist. The three levels of training can be accomplished relatively quickly as the time to complete all levels of training is 8 days. However, the actual process requires a considerable amount of time. The first two trainings can be taken online or in person at a live event. The third level is usually taken in person. There have been concessions with the onset of the pandemic. Therapists who have rushed through these trainings without spending some time between each training to practice this method are usually at a disadvantage when it comes to consultation, and the length of time spent in consultation is usually longer.

At the time of this writing the cost of all three levels of training is around $2000. Each trainer sets their own pricing for each event, so this is an estimated cost. There are additional costs. There is a cost, under $1000, to register for the certification track, which is paid directly to The Gottman Institute. This registration cost covers administrative costs, a HIPAA compliant box.com account, and the video reviewer fees. Consultation fees are also an additional cost. These fees are paid directly to the consultant, and there can be some variation in consultation fees as they are set by the consultant. The fees are often the consultant's normal therapy session rate.

Other Trainings Offered

The Gottman Institute offers additional training programs. Two of these programs are specifically for therapists and those in helping professions. Treating Affairs and Trauma is designed to help the therapist navigate affairs and trauma. The other, Couples and Addiction Recovery is designed to help the therapist treat couples recovering from substance addiction. There are two additional workshops for anyone who wants to help couples have better relationships and include Bringing Baby Home and Seven Principles Leader Training. One workshop, The Art and Science of Love is specifically for couples. Each of these will be discussed.

Treating Affairs and Trauma

The Treating Affairs and Trauma is a training program for therapists, clergy, chaplains, coaches, students, and other professionals who work with couples. Sexual and emotional betrayals often create trauma within the betrayed partner. Therefore, therapists need to learn to manage and help couples heal from affairs and PTSD. This program introduces the Atone, Attune, Attach model for treating affairs based on the science of trust. This training teaches attendees how to recognize the signs of trauma and assess the impact it has on the relationship. Through this program the clinician also learns how to assess the impact of an affair on the relationship, help the couple rebuild trust, and insulate the relationship from future betrayals. Level 1 training is a prerequisite for those who are interested in taking this course. Seventeen hours of continuing education credits are available for this course.

Couples and Addiction Recovery

This training is also for therapists, counselors, and professionals who work with couples who struggle with addictions. This training was created by and based on the addiction recovery research of Dr. Robert Navarra. The training provides tools and interventions to help the person struggling with addiction, the partner, and the couple's relationship as all are impacted by the addiction. Those who attend this training will learn to identify addiction, break through denial, manage the challenges that occur through the recovery process, help the couple improve conflict and communication skills, and set boundaries. This training helps clinicians understand how to support each individual's independent recovery as well as move toward a healthy relationship together. While there are no prerequisites for this course, it would be beneficial to have taken Level 1 before attending this training. Eight hours of continuing education are available for this course.

Bringing Baby Home

Research on relationships showed that within the first three years of the birth of a child, about two-thirds of couples will suffer a decline in relationship satisfaction. This training was created to teach professionals in the medical and mental health field how to help couples manage this transition into parenthood and strengthen their relationship in the process. It is appropriate for nurses, childbirth educators, midwives, doulas, coaches, clergy, and mental health care professionals. Once trained, those who have taken this course can teach Bringing Baby Home Workshops to couples. They may consider themselves Bringing Baby Home educators.

Seven Principles Leader Training

This training was based on the book *The Seven Principles for Making Marriage Work,* written by Dr. John Gottman. This training was designed to teach others how to be trainers of the Seven Principles Workshop for Couples. It is an appropriate training for anyone who is interested in helping couples have better relationships. Those who take this training will be able to teach the *Seven Principles* workshop. This workshop consists of lectures, video presentations, interactive exercises using card decks, as well as through role-plays and discussions. In addition to providing information about how to teach couples ways to strengthen their relationship, this training also helps the trainer plan, budget, and advertise the workshop to potential couples.

Art and Science of Love Workshop

The *Art* and *Science of Love* workshop was created by Drs. John and Julie Gottman to directly provide help to couples. It is appropriate for any committed couple relationship. The couple learns how to strengthen their friendship system through lectures, role plays and the use of interactive interventions that the couple does on their own. This workshop is taught by certified GMCTs who have been trained to present the workshop. Couples learn to strengthen their friendship, manage conflict productively, develop temporary compromises and build a sense of shared meaning with one another. Couples can attend a live workshop in person, they can attend a live event virtually, or they can purchase a pre-recorded workshop from The Gottman Institute and watch it on demand.

Gottman et al. (2020) examined relationships in over 40,000 couples and discovered that couples who come into therapy are much more distressed than couples who have been studied in academic settings and on which most couple treatment programs are designed to treat. Gottman method couples therapy is appropriate for all couple issues where couples therapy is the appropriate modality of treatment. A recent study provided support that GMCT is an appropriate modality to treat gay and lesbian couples (Garanzini et al., 2017). Certified therapists have been trained to work with couples who have suffered serious relationship betrayals, such as sexual and emotional affairs. It is appropriate for those on the brink of divorce, as well as couples who feel relatively stable, yet need some assistance managing conflicts constructively. This method is also appropriate for couples who are in new relationships that want to begin their relationship on the right track. Couples therapy is not appropriate when there is an ongoing sexual or emotional affair. Couples therapy is also inappropriate when there is characterological domestic violence with a clear perpetrator and victim and fear and domination are means to control one partner. Some clinicians trained in this method have extended its principles to help people with their friendships, their workplace relationships, and parent-child relationships, however there is no scientific data to provide proof of the effectiveness of the Gottman method in these relationships.

OVERALL RECOMMENDATIONS AND IMPRESSIONS OF MODALITY TRAINING

There are almost 500 certified Gottman method couple therapists around the world, and countless therapists who have been trained in at least one level of Gottman training. Most of these therapists indicated that the training helped them conceptualize and understand couple relationships through a scientifically based theory. The interventions were also very helpful to them in the treatment of couples.

Pros:

There are several pros to this therapy. This type of therapy is based on observational and experimental science. This means that couple relationships are assessed scientifically through scales that have been found to be scientifically valid and reliable. This therapy modality provides a roadmap and treatment goals for the therapist based on the couple's assessment. The therapy modality provides interventions to help the couple have more productive conversations and heal past injuries. There are interventions to help couples create more emotional intimacy, and a meaningful shared life experience.

Cons:

There are cons for this type of therapy as well. It takes time and commitment to go through the training process. The certification process can take up to two or more years. Most CGTs take between 5 to 24 months to complete the process. The certification process can be costly when considering the consultant fees for 2 or more years. This type of therapy requires that the therapist keep the couple as dyadic as possible, especially during interventions, which is a shift from having the partners talk directly to the therapist. This type of therapy also requires that the therapist be attuned to the couple's affect and to explore affect within the dyad. This can be a challenge for some therapists. The certification process also requires that therapists submit videos of their work with couples. This means that they must be able to use video equipment, such as an iPhone, a computer, or an electronic tablet, and at times edit those videos. In addition to the ability to use this technology, submitting videos means that someone is observing and critiquing their work. This may create a great deal of anxiety for some therapists.

SUMMARY AND BRIEF OVERVIEW OF TRAINING, PROCESS OF CERTIFICATION AND CREDENTIAL

Gottman method couples therapy requires rigorous training. It requires that the clinician understand the research that guided the sound relationship house theory. Gottman therapy requires a thorough assessment of the relationship before beginning treatment. There are three systems that need to be healthy in couple relationships. The treatment phase of therapy is primarily dyadic. The therapist guides and coaches the couple in more effective communication skills. The therapist also helps the couple explore emotion and underlying symbolic meaning around their ongoing conflicts. The therapist also helps the couple become more emotionally connected to each other through building their friendship system and their shared meaning system. Therapy is massed and faded over time to give the couple support as they begin to navigate newly acquired communication skills.

The certification process can be lengthy and costly. However, certification means that the therapist has gone through a rigorous process, their work with couples examined, and displayed a proficient level of competency when using Gottman interventions. This method of couples therapy has been transformational both for the clinician and for the couples. Couples want and need guidance. They need to trust that their therapist is confident and has a plan. Gottman method training provides the therapist with tools to help the couple, the knowledge to know when and how to use those tools, and a roadmap to strengthen couple relationships.

Dr. Carrie Cole is the Love Lab Director and Research Director for The Gottman Institute. She is also a licensed professional counselor and an approved LPC supervisor. Carrie holds a master's degree in Counseling Psychology, and a PhD. in psychology with a specialization in research, her work with couples includes couples therapy, workshops, seminars, and intensive marathon sessions.

Carrie's passion for working with couples led her to found the Center for Relationship Wellness together with her husband, Dr. Don Cole. She has always had a profound interest in using a scientific approach to psychotherapy. Having discovered the research of Dr. John Gottman in graduate school, Carrie became a Certified Gottman Therapist and Certified Gottman Workshop Leader in 2007.

Carrie is a Master Trainer for The Gottman Institute and trains other therapists in Gottman Method Couples Therapy. She is also a consultant and a video reviewer for the certification program. She has led The Art and Science of Love weekend workshop for couples multiple times a year since 2008. In addition to leading workshops and training other therapists, Carrie has authored and co-authored several peer-reviewed journal articles and book chapters.

She has been interviewed and quoted in several newspapers and magazines including Business Insider, The Chicago Tribune, Cosmopolitan, Redbook, Real Simple, Women's Health, Woman's World, and Verily.

https://centerforrelationshipwellness.com/
https://www.gottman.com/participate-in-research/

Baucom, B. R., McFarland, P. T., & Christensen, A. (2010). Gender, topic, and time in observed demand-withdraw interaction in cross- and same-sex couples. *Journal of Family Psychology, 24*(3), 233-242. http://doi.org/10.1037/a0019717

Cook, J., Tyson, R., White, J., Rushe, R., Gottman, J., & Murray, J. (1995). Mathematics of marital conflict: Qualitative dynamic mathematical modeling of marital interaction. *Journal of Family Psychology, 9*(2), 110-130. http://doi.org/10.1037/0893-3200.9.2.110

Garanzini, S., Yee, A., Gottman, J., Gottman, J., Cole, C., Preciado, M., & Jasculca, C. (2017). Results of Gottman method couples therapy with gay and lesbian couples. *Journal of Marital and Family therapy, 43*(4), 674-684. https://doi.org/10.1111/jmft.12276

Gottman, J., & Gottman, J. (2017). The natural principles of love. *Journal of Family Theory and Review, 9*(1), 7-26. http://doi.org/10.1111/jftr.12182

Gottman, J., & Gottman, J. S. (2018). *Level 1 Clinical Training Gottman method couples therapy: Bridging the couple chasm.* The Gottman Institute.

Gottman, J., & Gottman, J. S. (2014). *Level 2 Clinical Training Gottman method couples therapy: Assessment, Intervention, and Co-Morbidities.* The Gottman Institute.

Gottman, J., & Gottman, J. S. (2014). *Level 3 Clinical Training Gottman Method Couples Therapy: Practicum Training.* The Gottman Institute.

Gottman, J. M. (1993). A theory of marital dissolution and stability. *Journal of Family Psychology, 7*(1), 57-75. http://doi.org/10.1037/0893-3200.7.1.57

Gottman, J. M. (1994). *What predicts divorce? The relationship between marital processes and marital outcomes.* Lawrence Erlbaum Associates, Inc.

Gottman, J. M., Coan, J., Carrere, S., & Swanson, C. (1998). Predicting marital happiness and stability from newlywed interactions. *Journal of Marriage and Family, 60*(1), 5-22. http://doi.org/10.2307/353438

Gottman, J. M., & Gottman, J. S. (2015). Gottman couple therapy. In Gurman, A. S., Lebow, J. L., & Snyder, D. K. (Eds.), *Clinical Handbook of Couple Therapy* (5th ed.). (pp.129-157). Guilford Press.

Gottman, J. M., & Gottman, J. S. (2018). *The science of couples and family therapy: Behind the scenes at the love lab.* W. W. Norton & Co.

Gottman, J. M., Gottman, J. S., Cole, C., & Preciado, M. (2020). Gay, lesbian, and heterosexual couples about to begin couples therapy: An online relationship assessment of 40,681 couples. *Journal of Marital and Family Therapy, 46*(2), 218-239. http://doi.org/10.1111/jmft.12395

Gottman, J. M., & Levenson, R. W. (1985). A valid procedure for obtaining self-report of affect in marital interaction. *Journal of Consulting and Clinical Psychology, 53*(2), 151-160. http://doi.org/10.1037/0022-006X.53.2.151

Gottman, J. M., & Tabares, A. (2018). The effects of briefly interrupting marital conflict. *Journal of Marital and Family Therapy, 44*(1), 61-72. http://doi.org/10.111/jmft.12243

Haase, C. M., Holley, S. R., Bloch, L., Verstaen, A., & Levenson, R. W. (2016). Interpersonal emotional behaviors and physical health: A 20-year longitudinal study of long-term married couples. *Emotion 16*(7), 965-977. http://doi.org/10.1037/a0042039

Lebow, J. L., Chambers, A. L., Christensen, A., & Johnson, S. M. (2012). Research on the treatment of couple distress. *Journal of Marital and Family Therapy, 38*(1), 145-168. http://doi.org/10.1111/j.1752-0606.2011.00249.x

Levenson, R. W., & Gottman, J. M. (1983). Marital interaction: Physiological linkage and affect exchange. *Journal of Personality and Social Psychology, 45*(3), 587-597. http://doi.org/10.1037/0022-3514.45.3.587

Grief Yoga

BILL OWENBY, EdD, MC, FAAETS, DAAETS, DCMHS, LPC, LAAC, NCC, CCMHC, ACS, DIPLOMATE, FELLOW

Grief Yoga, developed by Paul Denniston, is a compassionate practice that combines movement, breath, and sound to help individuals process grief and loss. This therapeutic approach encourages the expression and release of pain, facilitating a journey toward healing and empowerment. Grief Yoga is accessible to all, regardless of yoga experience, and serves as a valuable tool for mental health professionals, life coaches, and wellness practitioners seeking to support clients through bereavement.

Grief Yoga integrates principles from various therapeutic frameworks:

- **Somatic Therapy**: Recognizes the connection between mind and body, using physical movement to process and release stored emotions associated with grief.
- **Mindfulness-Based Stress Reduction (MBSR)**: Encourages present-moment awareness to acknowledge and accept grief without judgment.
- **Expressive Arts Therapy**: Utilizes creative expression through movement and sound to facilitate emotional release and healing.

CERTIFICATIONS, TRAININGS, AND LICENSURE REQUIREMENTS

Grief Yoga offers a range of training programs designed to equip individuals and professionals with the skills to integrate this modality into personal practices or professional settings. Below are the primary certifications available:

1. **Grief Movement Training**
   o **Overview**: Teaches participants how to use movement, breath, and sound to transform grief into healing and empowerment. Ideal for individuals or professionals who want to understand the core principles of Grief Yoga without pursuing full teacher certification.
   o **Cost**: $299 for the self-paced online course.
   o **Time Commitment**: Approximately 8–10 hours of content, completed at your own pace.
   o **Prerequisites**: No prior yoga experience is required. Open to anyone interested in exploring Grief Yoga for personal growth or as a supportive tool in professional settings.
2. **Grief Yoga Teacher Training**
   o **Overview**: A comprehensive program designed for yoga teachers, therapists, and wellness professionals who want to incorporate Grief Yoga into their practice.
   o **Cost**: $499 for the online course. Additional costs may apply for live workshops if offered.
   o **Time Commitment**: Approximately 25–30 hours, completed online with optional live training components.
   o **Prerequisites**: Participants are encouraged to have some prior yoga experience or certification, although it is not strictly required. A background in mental health or wellness coaching is also beneficial.
3. **Chakra Energy Flow Training**
   o **Overview**: Focuses on working with the body's energy centers to support balance and healing. Integrates Grief Yoga principles with chakra-focused movement and breathwork.

- o **Cost**: $199 for the online course.
- o **Time Commitment**: Approximately 6–8 hours of instruction, self-paced.
- o **Prerequisites**: Suitable for all levels, including those with no prior yoga experience.
4. **Live Workshops and Retreats**
    - o **Overview**: Occasional live workshops and retreats provide in-depth, hands-on training in a supportive group environment. These events complement the online courses, offering participants the opportunity to practice techniques in real-time.
    - o **Cost**: Typically ranges from $200 to $1,000, depending on the duration and location of the event.
    - o **Time Commitment**: 1–5 days, depending on the specific workshop or retreat.
    - o **Prerequisites**: Open to all levels, although familiarity with Grief Yoga concepts is recommended.
5. **Grief Yoga Certification Path**
    - o **Steps to Certification**:
        1. Complete the Grief Yoga Teacher Training.
        2. Submit a short teaching video demonstrating understanding of Grief Yoga principles.
        3. Engage in continuing education by attending live workshops or completing additional online courses.
    - o **Maintenance Requirements**: Continuing education credits or participation in ongoing workshops may be required to maintain certification.

General Cost

Training costs vary depending on the program. For the most current pricing and available discounts, visit the official Grief Yoga website at griefyoga.com.

IDENTIFIED AS GOLD STANDARD, BEST PRACTICE, EMERGING PRACTICE, OR EVIDENCE-BASED PRACTICE

Grief Yoga is considered an emerging practice in the field of grief therapy. While empirical research is ongoing, anecdotal evidence and practitioner testimonials suggest its effectiveness in helping individuals process grief through embodied movement and mindfulness.

Certification Available/Required/Recommended

- **Available**: Certifications are available upon completion of specific training programs.
- **Recommended**: Certification is highly recommended for professionals intending to incorporate Grief Yoga into their practice to ensure a comprehensive understanding of the methodology.

Degree Requirements

No formal degree is required to participate in Grief Yoga training programs. However, a background in mental health, coaching, or yoga instruction may enhance the application of the techniques learned.

CAUTIONS OR LIMITATIONS

- **Emotional Intensity**: Engaging in Grief Yoga can evoke strong emotions. Participants should approach the practice with readiness to explore deep feelings and may benefit from additional support.
- **Physical Considerations**: Individuals with physical limitations should consult with a healthcare provider before participating and may need to modify certain movements.

Practitioners should operate within their professional scope when integrating Grief Yoga. Mental health professionals can incorporate it as a therapeutic tool, while yoga instructors should refrain from offering psychological counseling unless appropriately licensed.

WHAT KIND OF PERSON WOULD DO WELL IN THIS MODEL?

Grief Yoga is suitable for individuals who:

- Are experiencing grief or loss and seek a holistic approach to healing.
- Prefer expressive and movement-based therapeutic modalities.
- Are open to exploring the mind-body connection in their healing journey.

SUMMARY

Grief Yoga offers a unique and compassionate approach to navigating the complexities of grief. By combining movement, breath, and sound, it facilitates emotional expression and release, guiding individuals toward healing and empowerment. Whether practiced personally or integrated into professional services, Grief Yoga serves as a valuable resource for those seeking to transform loss into a pathway of growth and resilience.

For more information, training opportunities, and resources, visit griefyoga.com. Additionally, Paul Denniston's book, *Healing Through Yoga: Transform Loss into Empowerment*, provides further insights and practices for those interested in this approach.

I hold two independent licenses in the states of Arizona and Ohio, supervisory status in Arizona, along with a substance abuse license in Arizona. I am board certified as a Diplomate and Clinical Mental Health Specialist, an Approved Clinical Supervisor, Nationally Certified Counselor, a Certified Clinical Mental Health Counselor, NeuroLinguistic Programming Practitioner, and a Clinical Trauma Specialist for Individuals and Family including EMDR Therapy and NET. I completed my training in Animal-Assisted Therapy and Pet Handlers certification in order to evaluate and incorporate the human-animal bond in therapy. I am the sole author and creator of the SxC Model of ESA Evaluation. My research interests surround post-traumatic growth, resiliency, strengths-based therapy, positive psychology, mindfulness, Animal-Assisted Therapy, Sandtray Therapy, Creative approaches in therapy, and martial arts in mental health. I have presented at local, state, regional, national, and international levels on various topics including personality traits, licensure reciprocity challenges, Sandtray and supervision, and Animal-Assisted Therapy within supervision. eonbllc@gmail.com

Group Counseling

Joseph Campbell, Ph.D., LMHC, ACS, NCC

Group work is an exciting treatment modality that empowers group members to engage in self-and-other awareness, to learn, change, develop, and heal. It continues to grow due to its efficacy in treating a variety of issues, cost effectiveness for the client, and clinical resources (Paturel, 2012). Group counseling is a primary intervention informed by theory, used in multiple settings, for different purposes, and treatment of a variety of presenting issues.

The American Psychological Association Division of Society of Clinical Psychology supports the efficacy of group therapy to treat major depressive disorder, bipolar disorder, panic disorder, post-traumatic stress disorder, social phobia, obsessive-compulsive disorder, bulimia nervosa, binge-eating disorder, substance use disorder, schizophrenia, and borderline personality disorder (Paturel, 2012). Groups can be designed around different theoretical models including cognitive-behavioral theory, person-centered theory, solution-focused theory, or other theories. Additionally, groups can be focused on development, coping skills, issues of anger management, divorce, or stress. There are also groups in school settings focused on social emotional learning, bullying and friendship, and employment and college preparation programs. Groups also are used for different populations such as counseling groups for children, adolescents, college students, older adults, parents, and other populations.

Corey (2015) described five different types of groups: group psychotherapy, counseling groups, psychoeducation groups, task groups, and self-help groups. The major differences between a psychotherapy and counseling group are that counseling groups focus on growth, development, self-awareness, and prevention; psychotherapy groups focus on remediation, treatment, personality reconstruction, the unconscious and conscious, and of the present and past. Psychoeducation groups are used in a variety of settings and focus on providing education, support, and are structured with specific content or themes. For example, in a substance use psychoeducation group, content could include triggers for use, relapse prevention, and coping skills. Task groups are generally formed by organizations that include committees, planning groups, and study groups. Self-help groups include organizations such as Alcoholics Anonymous, Adult Children of Alcoholics, or Overeaters Anonymous.

Group development theory (Tuckman, 1965; Tuckman & Jensen, 1977) identified five stages of group development: forming, storming, norming, performing, and adjourning that groups progress through. Prior to the stages of development, the pre-group phase is when the group leader focuses on group membership selection and planning. Group leaders interview prospective group members to discuss the purpose of the group, assess motivation, readiness for change, goals, and discuss the group process. Additionally, Yalom and Leszcz (2020) describe 11 therapeutic and curative factors of group work: instillation of hope, universality, imparting information, altruism, the corrective recapitulation of the primary family group, development of socializing techniques, imitative behavior, interpersonal learning, group cohesiveness, catharsis, and existential factors. These factors are present in groups and different factors have different significance depending on the type of group and group development stage.

There are benefits and limitations to group work. Some benefits include members learning from each other, building a support network and socialization opportunities, a place to explore personal issues of concern, feelings of unity, and cost effectiveness. Two major limitations include issues regarding confidentiality and less individualized treatment focus.

EDUCATION IN GROUP WORK

Education and training in group work begins at the undergraduate level. Many social work, human services, behavior analysist, and similar undergraduate programs include a group skills course as part of the curriculum. Further training in groups continues at the master's level and social work, counseling, psychology, and other related programs require students to complete a group course. Some professional programs require students to gain group facilitation leadership experience prior to graduation through coursework and internships. Upon graduation with a master's degree, clinicians have group counseling skills and use the modality in practice. Additional clinical training in group work, as well as group supervision training, are parts of doctoral level course work and internships, providing clinicians and supervisors advancement in group work theory, practice, and expertise.

CERTIFICATION IN GROUP WORK

The American Group Psychotherapy Association (AGPA), through the International Board for Certification in Group Psychotherapists (IBCGP), credentials clinicians as Certified Group Psychotherapist (CGP). The CGP requires a graduate degree and the highest state clinical license to practice independently. The general cost is from $295-$420, depending on membership in AGPA.

According to the IBCGP (https://agpa.org/cgp-certification/), the CGP credential has required group psychotherapy knowledge, experience, and supervision requirements:

- Knowledge: 15 clock hours of study in group psychotherapy theory and practicing that includes: historical, contemporary, and cultural perspectives; group dynamics and development; leadership tasks and skills; and ethics, neuroscience, and personal style. The IBCGP recommends the training curriculum include *Core principles of group psychotherapy: An integrated theory, research, and practice training manual* (Kaklauskas & Greene, 2019) and the AGPA and affiliates offers educational training to meet the required content knowledge areas.

- Experience: 300 hours of group psychotherapy experience as a leader or co-leader accrued during or following clinical graduate training. To qualify the experience must be for the purposes of providing psychotherapy serves to client populations with a DSM-5 diagnosis. This does not include peer group, self-help groups, or training groups.

- Supervision: 75 hours of group psychotherapy supervision accrued during or following clinical graduate training with an approved group psychotherapy supervisor in individual or group format and must involve regular presentation of group psychotherapy clinical material.

All applicants submit two references with the application, one reference from the supervisor and other from a colleague, current professional liability insurance certificate, and a copy of license.

The CGP credential requires recertification every two years and include: maintenance of the active credential/license for independent practice and liability insurance. Continuing education requirements include 20 hours every two years with a minimum of three hours on diversity, equity, and inclusion related to group work. Additionally, a minimum of 12 hours must be formal learning activities through accrediting bodies (e.g., attend a professional conference of the American Psychological Association or the National Board of Certified Counselors) and a maximum of 8 hours can be informational (e.g., study groups, peer supervision, preparation of articles and books on group psychotherapy). Recertification fees required: $180-$270 every two years, depending on membership in AGPA.

PROFESSIONAL DEVELOPMENT IN GROUP WORK

In addition to the CGP credential, clinicians can join professional associations and organizations and engage in ongoing training and development around treatment and leadership in groups. The following organizations provide additional educational and training opportunities to further clinical skills and knowledge related to group work: the Association for Specialists in Group Work, the International Association for Social Work with Groups, and the American Board of Group Psychology.

Joseph Campbell is an Associate Professor of Counseling and Human Services at Indiana University South Bend, a licensed mental health counselor (IN), an Approved Clinical Supervisor (ACS), and a National Certified Counselor (NCC). He teaches core and clinical mental health counseling courses, supervises field experiences, and his research agenda focuses on counselor practice, human sexuality, and teaching and learning in counselor education.

josacamp@iusb.edu

REFERENCES

Corey, G. (2015). *Theory and practice of group counseling* (9th ed.). CENGAGE Learning Custom Publishing.

International Board for Certification of Group Psychotherapists (n.d.). How to apply. Retrieved from: https://agpa.org/cgp-certification/how-to-apply

Kaklauskas, F. J. and Greene, L. R. (2019). Core principles of group psychotherapy: An integrated theory, research, and practice training manual. Routledge Taylor and Francis Group

Paturel, A. (2012). Power in numbers: Research is pinpointing the factors that make group therapy successful. Monitor on Psychology, 11. American Psychological Association. Retrieved from: https://www.apa.org/monitor/2012/11/power

Tuckman, B. W. (1965). Development sequence in small groups. *Psychological Bulletin, 63*(6), 384-399

Tuckman, B. W., & Jensen, M. C. (1977). Stages of small-group development revised. *Group & Organization Studies, 2*(4), 419-427.

Yalom, I. D., & Leszcz, M. (2020). The theory and practice of group psychotherapy (6th ed.). Basic Books: New York, NY

Habit Reversal Therapy for Tics (HRT)

ARIELLE ASHKENASE, MA IN MENTAL HEALTH COUNSELING EXPECTED 2026), BA

DANIELLE BAGDASAROV, MA IN MENTAL HEALTH COUNSELING EXPECTED 2026, BA

NATHANIEL DANIEL, MA IN MENTAL HEALTH COUNSELING EXPECTED 2025

DEVORA FREUNDLICH, MA IN MENTAL HEALTH COUNSELING EXPECTED 2025, BA

STEFANIE HERSHFIELD, MA IN MENTAL HEALTH COUNSELING EXPECTED 2025, MA HEALTH PSYCHOLOGY 2023

RASHEL PAULA, MA IN MENTAL HEALTH COUNSELING EXPECTED 2025, BS

STELLA KIM HANSEN, PHD, LMHC

Diagnoses that fall under the umbrella of tic-related disorders are noted as significant stressors in individuals' lives as they may impede their daily functioning. A well-developed psychotherapeutic intervention would be essential to improving the quality of life for people with tic-related disorders. Habit Reversal Therapy (HRT), also knowing as Habit Reversal Training, is a specific intervention that has demonstrated significant promise in reducing repetitive behaviors and tics (Skurya et al., 2020). When used to treat repetitious conduct, HRT is an effective clinical procedure in which a strategy for behavior change is developed (Varrasi et al., 2022).

HRT was developed in the 1970s through a research group led by Azrin & Nunn to develop a clinical treatment for nervous habits, as none were shown to be generally effective at the time (1973). Early developments of HRT focused on the treatments of nervous habits such as nail biting, hair pulling, lip biting, and stuttering (Varrasi et al., 2022). The intention was to build a competent method to intervene in multiple forms of repetitive and unwanted behaviors that interfered with the quality of life of the individual with the habit disorder (Varrasi et al., 2022). The procedure was found to help manage the persistence of behaviors that resulted from tic-related disorders, as researchers found that habits persisted because of response chaining, limited awareness, excessive practice, and social tolerance (Azrin & Nunn, 1973).

A method was devised to counteract the influences of these tic habits by making participants aware of each instance of the habit and then differentiating them from their usual response chain, which was followed by positive reinforcement by social approval for each effort to inhibit the replacement habit (Azrin & Nunn, 1973). The procedure assessed diverse tic behaviors, including nail-biting, thumb-sucking, eyelash picking, head jerking, shoulder jerking, tongue pushing, and lisping (Azrin & Nunn, 1973). Within a single trial session, the 12 participants with diverse tic habits had their behaviors virtually eliminated (Azrin & Nunn, 1973). The tic habits did not return for 11 of the 12 clients during the extended follow-up, as they were the ones who followed the instructions (Azrin & Nunn, 1973). HRT broke away from other approaches of its time because the intervention conceptualized these habits according to the construct of operant conditioning, which defined the procedure as a way to reduce the tension through avoidance learning (Varrasi et al., 2022).

Given HRT's emphasis on behavioral interventions to reduce tic habits, there are several core components to the approach within its implementation. The first of these core components is the awareness training phase, in which a patient becomes cognizant of their tic habit (Skurya et al., 2020). In this phase, the patient must define their habit and acknowledge it, thus becoming fully aware of their repetitive behaviors and any activities that may cause such behaviors to occur (Skurya et al., 2020). Implemented in this initial stage are the self-monitoring components of HRT, in which the patient is responsible for recording their repetitive behaviors (Teng et al., 2006). Once the patient is aware of their habit, they additionally become aware of certain variables that may trigger a tic (Teng et al., 2006). This brings us to the next component of HRT, which is the stimulus control phase, where the patient works to decrease the stimuli that cause the tic habit (Teng et al., 2006).

An additional way to reduce the urge to engage in the tic habit is through the relaxation component of HRT, as stress is often a major contributor to the development and progression of many repetitive and maladaptive behaviors (Dunbar et al., 2018). Through relaxation training, a patient would be able to change their behaviors that they may not be fully conscious of, thus preventing the occurrence of repetitive behavior (Dunbar et al., 2018). The next crucial component in HRT for tic disorders is the competing response phase, where patients are taught to practice alternative responses to events that trigger repetitive behaviors (Farhat et al., 2020). Methods and strategies involved in the competing response phase are diverse and depend on the specific tic habit but are ideally formed as discrete and harmless responses (Farhat et al., 2020).

Along with the established components of HRT for tic disorders during treatment come components that prevent the relapse of the reversed behaviors. Despite the efficacy of HRT, clinicians must help patients understand that relapses are a normal part of the process (Jafferany & Patel, 2019). Understanding why a relapse occurred is crucial to deter future relapses and develop plans to implement changes (Jafferany & Patel, 2019). This component entails the clinician emphasizing the progress made and the knowledge gained about the tic habit (Jafferany & Patel, 2019). The relapse prevention phase coincides with the problem-solving components of HRT for tic disorder, where the clinician helps develop new techniques to reduce unwanted behaviors (Skurya et al., 2020). During the relapse prevention component, HRT undergoes a collaborative process in which any issues with self-monitoring are addressed and viable solutions are found to manage the tic habits (Skurya et al., 2020).

GENERAL GOAL OF HABIT REVERSAL TRAINING

When implemented to treat tic disorders, several goals are involved in this behavioral intervention that satisfies different realms of the disorder. It is well established that HRT's main goal is to limit tics' frequency and duration through a functional analysis of tic relaxation techniques and psychosocial support activities (Plessen, 2013). That being said, a more specific goal of HRT is to make the patient cognizant of their tics as they occur and to promote their self-awareness to regulate these behaviors (Jafferany & Patel, 2019). Another goal of HRT is empowering the individual to develop long-term skills to manage their tics independently. Self-help strategies from HRT are empirically affirmed to be effective in maintaining the exhibition of tics; thus, patients can be active participants in their treatment (Moritz et al., 2012). Furthermore, another goal of HRT for tic therapy is managing any co-occurring behavioral or emotional difficulties. HRT can further help to treat comorbidities with tic disorders, including Attention Deficit Hyperactivity Disorder (ADHD), Obsessive Compulsive Disorder (OCD), substance use disorders, and depressive disorders (American Psychological Association, 2013).

PHILOSOPHIES OF HABIT REVERSAL TRAINING

HRT is invaluable in empowering individuals to develop control over their behaviors through structured learning. Since habits are repetitive behaviors that frequently occur outside the awareness of the affected individual and are automatically reinforced (Heinicke et al., 2020), behavioral training replaced unwanted behaviors with more desired outcomes. B.F. Skinner acknowledged the significance of behavior analysis and how individuals' life challenges are exacerbated by their own behavior (Skinner, 1971). Increasing one's awareness of a habit and acknowledging the premonitory urge that leads up to the habit play vital roles in HRT.

These social supports also remind the individual to practice their awareness training and competing responses when appropriate (Heinicke et al., 2020). This collaborative approach can be highly beneficial in promoting sustained compliance in different environments. It is essential that caregivers understand the importance of remaining quietly supportive and patient with the process. When family and friends become overly involved with interventions, it can put undue pressure on the affected individual and ultimately lead to adverse effects.

Self-acceptance is a primary step in successful behavioral treatment. Due to shame and embarrassment, the affected individuals may resist help because they do not feel they deserve it (Eapen et al., 2016). They may believe something fundamentally wrong with them and that they cannot be "fixed." Common dialogues that can hinder compliance include:

- I do not need treatment. I can stop on my own.
- I can't be helped. I am not strong enough.
- I should not need to seek help for a problem I am bringing on myself.
- Therapy will uncover something I do not want to find out about myself.
- Treatment will bring more awareness to the behavior and make it worse.
- I've tried lots of treatments, and nothing has helped thus far, so I, therefore, can't be helped.
- I need this behavior to cope with my emotions.
- I will feel worse if I do not have this behavior/coping mechanism to fall back on.
- I do not want to put work into treatment if the outcome is not guaranteed.

Through cognitive reframing, individuals can modify their maladaptive patterns, adopt a more positive narrative, and ultimately comply with and succeed in the therapeutic practice (Espil & Houghton, 2018). In addition, cognitive reframing and psychoeducation about the neurological and genetic underpinnings of tics and related behaviors can be an effective way to reduce shame and promote self-acceptance and treatment compliance. It can be useful for the individual to understand that there is a difference between brain functioning and genetics of people with tic-related disorders versus healthy controls. People can accept that biology is not their fault by highlighting how these patterned behaviors are more than merely bad habits (National Institute of Neurological Disorders and Stroke, 2024). In turn, they can accept that reaching out to a therapist for assistance can be beneficial.

There has been an emphasis on using practical tools to manage tics without reliance on pharmacological interventions. Utilizing these practical tools through HRT can help individuals with tic disorder build confidence in their ability and autonomy. Those with tic-like behaviors can receive education on the condition and engage in behavioral therapy centered on tics and, if necessary, comorbidities (Billnitzer et al., 2020). HRT could be used to accompany Cognitive Behavioral Therapy techniques to assist with compulsions more efficiently (Lee et al., 2019).

CERTIFICATIONS AND LICENSURE REQUIREMENTS FOR HABIT REVERSAL TRAINING

Although no specific degree is required to practice this form of CBT, it should be practiced by licensed counselors, clinicians, and therapists. When it comes to HRT, there is no nationally recognized overarching certification; however, clinicians can become certified in Comprehensive Behavioral Intervention for Tics (CBIT) which is a comprehensive intervention combining HRT with additional tic management strategies (TAA, 2024). The Tourette Association of America's (TAA) Tourette Syndrome Behavior Therapy Institute (TS-BTI) offers in-person training for the CBIT certification at various locations across the country at different times of the year. The Possibilities Clinic also offers the CBIT certification, but through a virtual training option.

https://tourette.org/research-medical/behavioral-therapy-institute-cbit-trainings/

https://possibilitiesclinic.com/comprehensive-behavioural-intervention-for-tics-training-cbit/

Time Commitment

Both of these CBIT certifications are two-day training programs, and participants must attend both days of training.

Costs

Programs and workshops range in price depending on the intensity and institution providing the training. The cost for TS-BTI's certification in CBIT is $899 which includes two days of training and all materials and resources needed for the completion of the training. This cost does not include travel, lodging, or meals (TAA, 2024). The cost for Possibilities Clinic's certification is $700, plus textbooks. There are no additional costs, as the training is virtual (Possibilities Clinic, 2024).

Requirements

Following the two-day training, TS-BTI's CBIT certification requires attendees to complete three to five follow-up phone calls/consultation sessions with a designated TS-BTI faculty member (TAA, 2024). Similarly, Possibilities Clinic's CBIT training program requires three 15-minute phone calls to complete formal CBIT certification.

Continuing Education on Habit Reversal Training

Ongoing education in HRT is fundamental for clinicians specializing in treating tic disorders and BFRBs. While no formal certification is required to practice HRT, pursuing specialized training can significantly enhance a mental health professional's proficiency. This commitment to continuous learning can ultimately lead to better outcomes for clients. Associations like the Tourette Association of America (TAA) offer free introductory workshops that introduce clinicians to CBIT and HRT. https://tourette.org/research-medical/cbit-for-practitioners/

Other organizations, such as the International OCD Foundation (IOCDF), BFRB Changemakers Academy, Cognitive Behavior Institute (CBI), and the Center for the Treatment and Study of Anxiety (CTSA), offer workshops on HRT specifically for BFRBs (IOCDF, 2024; BFRB Changemakers Academy, 2024; Cognitive Behavior Institute, 2023; University of Pennsylvania, 2022). These workshops provide CEUs for clinicians wanting to specialize and refine their skills in BFRB. https://iocdf.org/event/treating-body-focused-repetitive-behaviors-utilizing-awareness-compassion-and-evidence-based-practices/ https://bfrbchangemakers.org/pages/bfrb-changemakers-training-academy https://cbicenterforeducation.com/courses https://www.med.upenn.edu/ctsa/training_opportunities.html

Costs

The CE courses offered through CBI range in price from $15 to $1,395 based on the length and intensity of training. The BFRB Changemakers Academy workshop is $130 with an option to join a four session consultation group following the training at no additional cost. A three-hour webinar for HRT through the CBI is $39.99. A CSTA workshop costs $450 but provides scholarships to clinicians who cannot pay the total (University of Pennsylvania, 2022).

The IOCDF holds annual conferences, including a dedicated training track on BFRBs, covering HRT techniques, clinical challenges, and therapeutic innovations in this field (International OCD Foundation, 2024). Registration for the IOCDF conferences is typically priced between $100- $300, with early registration discounts available for members and reduced rates for students and early-career professionals. These conferences enable clinicians to participate in CE-accredited workshops and facilitate networking with other experts, which enhances professional growth and fosters collaboration in advancing HRT practices (IOCDF, 2024).

Time Commitment

The trainings all vary in duration and intensity. The workshop offered by BFRB Changemakers is a six-hour interactive training. The training course offered by the CBI is a three-hour live interactive webinar (CBI, 2023). UPenn's training is offered on Zoom and is an eight hour course (University of Pennsylvania, 2024). The IOCDF annual conference spans four days, and attendees are able to attend workshops and trainings during the duration of the event.

Requirements

Generally, workshops for HRT are open to mental health professionals, graduate students, and licensed healthcare workers who work in treating individuals with Tourette Syndrome, tic disorders, and BRFBs. In terms of training for clinicians, HRT requires an understanding of awareness training, competing response training, and intensive training in order to be considered the gold standard. Awareness training is used to guide clients toward noticing specific urges. Competing response training is to identify a different response to the tic. Intensive training helps patients rely on family and friends' support to reinforce competing behaviors. Some articles also discuss "Relaxation Training" as beneficial in HRT (Liu et al., 2020). Relaxation training aims to teach patients to decrease their sympathetic nervous system arousal. (Morris et al., 2013).

According to multiple journal articles, HRT has been found to be beneficial for those with Tourette's (Himle et al., 2006), Trichotillomania (Morris et al., 2013), tic disorders (Liu et al., 2020), and OCD (Sulkowski et al., 2013) with certain physical manifestations. Due to the significant amount of evidence-based practice supporting HRT as a modality, it has become the gold standard for body-focused repetitive behaviors (Anxiety and Depression Association of America, n.d.).

WHO WOULD BE A GOOD PROFESSIONAL IN THIS MODALITY?

Mental health professionals with training and experience in Cognitive Behavioral Therapy may be a good fit for this modality. Cognitive Behavioral Therapy's underlying principles of goal oriented work, collaboration, and being present all lend themselves to effectively executed HRT (Morand-Beaulieu et al., 2015). Cognitive Behavioral Practitioners who incorporate Acceptance and Commitment Therapy and mindfulness-based strategies may also be well suited to HRT. ACT can be combined with HRT, using mindfulness and acceptance to recognize tic urges and replace them with a competing response (Franklin et al., 2011).

LIMITATIONS

There are limitations to the use of HRT for tic disorder reflected in the research done on its efficacy. Individuals with additional cognitive impairments, emotional and behavioral difficulties, and obsessive-compulsive symptoms have not been broadly considered (Liu et al., 2020). Premonitory urges have likewise been neglected. Further research should include the above elements as well as more of a focus on the use of HRT in children and adolescents (Nissen et al., 2021).

SUMMARY

HRT was developed to address repetitive and unwanted behaviors in an individual and has proved beneficial for those struggling with tic-related disorders and Body-Focused Repetitive Behaviors. HRT has five key stages that each emphasize behavior modification, self-monitoring, and relapse management. The primary goal of HRT is to reduce the duration and frequency of these repetitive behaviors through different techniques, such as enhancing the patient's self-awareness and regulation. Helping patients become cognizant of their tics allows them to foster the skills necessary for long-term management. HRT recognizes that tic-related disorders are unconscious acts and focuses on empowering individuals to gain control over their behaviors. Although HRT is very effective, clinicians must help patients understand that relapses are a normal part of the process. Planning for future relapses aids in developing a plan to prepare better for implementing changes. It has a strong emphasis on support from family members and friends. While there is no standardized national certification for HRT, clinicians can obtain training through various workshops and programs. There are also various workshops for continuing education that allow professionals to improve their proficiency when practicing this modality. These ongoing education opportunities equip professionals with specialized skills, peer support, and recent research on treating tic-related disorders and BFRBs.

Arielle Ashkenase is a Mental Health Counseling graduate student at Yeshiva University's Ferkauf Graduate School of Psychology in New York. She has a B.A. in Sociology from the University of Maryland, College Park where she gained experience working with high-performing athletes in an intensive atmosphere. Since leaving College Park, she has focused on acquiring the necessary skills to aid adolescent girls as they develop and strives to be a voice that empowers women. Over the past five years, she has dedicated her time working as a Division Head where she is responsible for the mental and physical well-being of thirty teenage girls. She is driven to gain more specialized knowledge in eating disorders, body dysmorphia, and other disciplines that affect young women.

aashken3@mail.yu.edu

Danielle Bagdasarov is a Mental Health Counseling graduate student at Yeshiva University's Ferkauf Graduate School of Psychology in New York, where she combines academic training with a commitment to holistic mental health care. With a B.A. in Psychology from Binghamton University, she brings a strong foundation in psychological principles, enriched by her travels and hands-on experience with diverse cultures, enhancing her multicultural understanding and empathy. Passionate about the brain-gut connection and preventative care, she aspires to pursue a PhD in neuroscience to blend evidence-based practices with herbal and holistic approaches, making mental wellness accessible and personalized across various populations.

dbagdasa@mail.yu.edu

Nathaniel is a Master of Arts candidate in Mental Health Counseling at Yeshiva University's Ferkauf Graduate School of Psychology. With a diverse range of experience in both academic and clinical settings, Nathaniel brings a unique blend of teaching, clinical, and research skills to his graduate studies. Nathaniel has supported individuals with trauma-related disorders through his clinical work at Post Tour Processing, a non-profit organization that serves first responders who have undergone traumatic experiences. His prior work as a behavioral service provider with Proud Moments ABA involved direct support for children with intellectual and developmental disorders to promote skills and adaptive behaviors. Through his diverse research experiences, Nathaniel has contributed to the effectiveness of multimodal therapeutic practices in diverse populations. Driven by a commitment to culturally responsive care, Nathaniel aspires to continue working within mental health and forensic settings for underserved populations and advancing his trauma-informed care.

ndaniel2@mail.yu.edu

Devora Freundlich is a Mental Health Counseling graduate student at Yeshiva University's Ferkauf Graduate School of Psychology in New York. She has a BA in Psychology from Yeshiva University's Stern College for Women, and experience working in educational, research, clinical, and administrative positions. At Ferkauf, Devora is a founding member of The Jewish Affinity Group and a representative of The Organization of Psychology Students. She is drawn to advocacy, and intends to work in a hospital setting post-graduation. Devora believes in accessible mental healthcare and is invested in working with underserved populations.

devorafreundlich@gmail.com

Stefanie Hershfield earned her undergraduate degree from the University of Miami, and graduated Suma Cum Laude from Touro University with a Master's Degree in Health Psychology. She earned her second masters in Mental Health Counseling from the Ferkauf Graduate School of Psychology at Yeshiva University on the Albert Einstein College of Medicine campus.

Stefanie is a former WTA-ranked tennis player and is currently a professional tennis coach for both adolescents and adults. She has and continues to serve as co-captain for the Mental Health Volunteers at the New York City Marathon.

Stefanie helps individuals maximize their peak performance by addressing insecurities, promoting mindfulness and providing them with the necessary tools to overcome challenges as effectively and efficiently as possible. Her focus includes cognitive behavior therapy (CBT) to assist individuals with general anxiety, performance anxiety, and emotion regulation. Stefanie is an avid learner who resides in New York with her family.

Stefanie.hershfield@mail.yu.edu

Rashel Paula is a Mental Health Counseling graduate student at Yeshiva University's Ferkauf Graduate School of Psychology in New York. She has a B.S. in Applied Psychology from New York University and spent a few years as a research assistant at the RISE lab. Since graduating, Rashel hasgained clinical experience in in-patient and residential settings with the unrepresented population with various acuity. She is also the student ambassador for the New York Mental Health Counselors Association to encourage other students to be more involved with the field. Her future goals are to pursue a PhD in counseling psychology and provide awareness and mental health treatment to the minority population.

rpaula@mail.yu.edu

Dr. Stella Kim Hansen is a Clinical Assistant Professor and Director of the Mental Health Counseling program at Yeshiva University's Ferkauf School of Psychology. She completed her Master's degree at Pace University, and completed her Master's internship at The Center for Cognitive-Behavioral Psychotherapy, a group private practice specializing in the treatment of Obsessive-Compulsive Disorder (OCD). She received her doctorate from Oregon State University. Her dissertation was a corpus linguistics study of the autogenous and reactive forms of OCD. She has also worked on NIMH genetic studies where she led efforts to collect phenotypic data about Schizophrenia, Bipolar Disorder, and OCD. She is passionate about educating more clinicians to be able to provide Exposure and Response Therapy (ERP) to individuals diagnosed with OCD.

https://www.yu.edu/ferkauf

stella.kimhansen@yu.edu

REFERENCES

Anxiety and Depression Association of America. (n.d.). *Body-focused repetitive behaviors*. Retrieved December 4, 2024, from https://adaa.org/understanding-anxiety/co-occurring-disorders/body-focused-repetitive-behaviors#:~:text=How%20are%20BFRBs%20Treated?,aid%20in%20recovery%20with%20BFRBs

American Psychiatric Association. (2022). *Diagnostic and statistical manual of mental disorders* (5th ed., text rev.). https://doi.org/10.1176/appi.books.9780890425787

Azrin, N. H., & Nunn, R. G. (1973). Habit-reversal: A method of eliminating nervous habits and tics. *Behaviour Research and Therapy, 11* (4), 619–628. https://doi.org/10.1016/0005-7967(73)90119-8

Billnitzer, A., & Jankovic, J. (2020, August 27). Current management of tics and Tourette syndrome: Behavioral, pharmacologic, and surgical. *Neurotherapeutics*, 1681-1693. https://pmc.ncbi.nlm.nih.gov/articles/PMC7851278/

BFRB Changemakers NFP. (2024). DAY 1: Contemporary practices in the treatment of body-focused repetitive behaviors (BFRB) training. *International OCD Foundation*. https://iocdf.org/event/day-1-contemporary-practices-in-the-treatment-of-body-focused-repetitive-behaviors-bfrb-training/

Campbell, C. (2024). Behavioral therapy institute - CBIT trainings. *Tourette Association of America*. https://tourette.org/research-medical/behavioral-therapy-institute-cbit-trainings/

Cognitive Behavior Institute. (2023). Habit reversal training for skin-picking and hair-pulling behaviors. Retrieved [11/05/24], from https://cbicenterforeducation.com/courses/habit-reversal-training-for-skin-picking-hair-pulling-november-2023

Dunbar, A. B., Magid, M., & Reichenberg, J. S. (2018). Habit reversal training for body-focused repetitive behaviors: A practical guide for the dermatologist. *Giornale Italiano di Dermatologia e Venereologia, 153*(4), 557–566. https://doi.org/10.23736/S0392-0488.18.05949-7

Eapen, V., Cavanna, A. E., & Robertson, M. M. (2016). Comorbidities, social impact, and quality of life in Tourette syndrome. *Frontiers in Psychiatry, 7*, 97. https://pmc.ncbi.nlm.nih.gov/articles/PMC4893483/

Espil, F. M., & Houghton, D. C. (2018). Cognitive restructuring about tics. In J. F. McGuire, T. K. Murphy, J. Piacentini, & E. A. Storch (Eds.). *The clinician's guide to treatment and management of youth with Tourette syndrome and tic disorder* (pp. 101–119). Elsevier Academic Press. https://doi.org/10.1016/B978-0-12-811980-8.00005-4

Farhat, L. C., Olfson, E., Nasir, M., Levine, J. L. S., Li, F., Miguel, E. C., & Bloch, M. H. (2020). Pharmacological and behavioral treatment for trichotillomania: An updated systematic review with meta-analysis. *Depression and Anxiety, 37* (8), 715–727. https://doi.org/10.1002/da.23028

Franklin, M. E., Best, S. H., Wilson, M. A., Loew, B., & Compton, S. N. (2011). Habit reversal training and acceptance and commitment therapy for Tourette syndrome: A pilot project. Journal of Developmental and Physical Disabilities, 23, 49-60.

Heinicke, M. R., Stiede, J. T., Miltenberger, R. G., & Woods, D. W. (2020, July 20). Reducing risky behavior with habit reversal: A review of behavioral strategies to reduce habitual hand-to-head behavior. *Journal of Applied Behavior Analysis, 53* (3), 1225-1236. https://doi.org/10.1002/jaba.745

Himle, M. B., Woods, D. W., Piacentini, J. C., & Walkup, J. T. (2006). Brief review of habit reversal training for Tourette syndrome. *Journal of Child Neurology, 21*(8), 719–725. https://doi.org/10.2310/7010.2006.00158

Jafferany, M., & Patel, A. (2019). Skin-picking disorder: A guide to diagnosis and management. *CNS Drugs, 33* (4), 337–346. https://doi.org/10.1007/s40263-019-00621-7

Lee, M. T., Mpavaenda, D. N., & Fineberg, N. A. (2019). Habit reversal therapy in obsessive-compulsive related disorders: A systematic review of the evidence and CONSORT evaluation of randomized controlled trials. *Frontiers in Behavioral Neuroscience, 13*, 79.

Liu, S., Li, Y., & Cui, Y. (2020). Review of habit reversal training for tic disorders. *Pediatric Investigation, 4* (2), 127–132. https://doi.org/10.1002/ped4.12190

Morand-Beaulieu, S., O'Connor, K. P., Sauvé, G., Blanchet, P. J., & Lavoie, M. E. (2015). Cognitive-behavioral therapy induces sensorimotor and specific electrocortical changes in chronic tic and Tourette's disorder. Neuropsychologia, 79, 310-321.

Moritz, S., Fricke, S., Treszl, A., & Wittekind, C. E. (2012). Do it yourself! Evaluation of self-help habit reversal training versus decoupling in pathological skin picking: A pilot study. *Journal of Obsessive-Compulsive and Related Disorders, 1* (1), 41–47. https://doi.org/10.1016/j.jocrd.2011.11.001

Morris, S. H., Zickgraf, H. F., Dingfelder, H. E., & Franklin, M. E. (2013). Habit reversal training in trichotillomania: Guide for the clinician. *Expert Review of Neurotherapeutics, 13* (9), 1069–1077. https://doi.org/10.1007/s10608-022-10334-9

National Institute of Neurological Disorders and Stroke. (2024, July 19). Tourette syndrome. https://www.ninds.nih.gov/health-information/disorders/tourette-syndrome

Nissen, J. B., Carlsen, A. H., & Thomsen, P. H. (2021). One-year outcome of manualised behavior therapy of chronic tic disorders in children and adolescents. Child and Adolescent Psychiatry and Mental Health, 15, 1-10.

Plessen, K. J. (2013). Tic disorders and Tourette's syndrome. *European Child & Adolescent Psychiatry, 22* (Suppl 1), S55–S60. https://doi.org/10.1007/s00787-012-0362-x

Skinner, B. F. (1971). *Beyond freedom and dignity.* Knopf/Random House.

Sulkowski, M. L., Jacob, M. L., & Storch, E. A. (2013). Exposure and response prevention and habit reversal training: Commonalities, differential use, and combined applications. *Journal of Contemporary Psychotherapy, 43*(3), 179–185. https://doi.org/10.1007/s10879-013-9234-z

Tourette Association of America. (2024, October 15). Comprehensive behavioral intervention for tics (CBIT) - National Institute of Health study. *Tourette Association of America.* https://tourette.org/cbit-nih-study/

Teng, E. J., Woods, D. W., & Twohig, M. P. (2006). Habit reversal as a treatment for chronic skin picking: A pilot investigation. *Behavior Modification, 30*(4), 411–422. https://doi.org/10.1177/0145445504265707

University of Pennsylvania. (2022). CTSA workshop scholarship opportunities. *Center for the Treatment and Study of Anxiety.* https://www.med.upenn.edu/ctsa/CTSA_Workshop_Scholarship_Opportunities.html

University of Pennsylvania. (2024, October 17). Habit reversal training for trichotillomania and excoriation [Zoom workshop]. *Center for the Treatment and Study of Anxiety.* https://www.med.upenn.edu/ctsa/Habit_Reversal_Training_for_Trichotillomania_and_Excoriation.html

Varrasi, S., Castellano, S., Platania, G. A., Guerrera, C. S., Caponnetto, P., & Pirrone, C. (2022). "Don't touch your face!" The contribution of habit reversal in the COVID-19 pandemic. *Health Psychology Research, 10*(4), 39650. https://doi.org/10.52965/001c.39650

Hakomi Mindful Somatic Therapy

LORENA MONDA, MS, OMD, LPCC, DOM, CHT

DONNA ROY, MS, LPC, CHT

CO-DEVELOPER OF PRIMARY ATTACHMENT THERAPY

More than three decades before mindfulness and somatics in psychotherapy went viral, Ron Kurtz and a core group of trainers developed Hakomi Mindful Somatic Psychotherapy (HMSP)—a comprehensive and uniquely effective approach to depth psychotherapy actively rooted in mindfulness and the body. It remains the gold standard for the clinical application of mindfulness.

Hakomi MSP integrates the perennial wisdom of Eastern mindfulness practices with current research on how the brain changes through experience. Clinically applied mindfulness is a central aspect of Hakomi MSP, not just an adjunct to therapy. Working throughout the session in mindful awareness allows clients to notice how they organize their experience in the present moment—sensations, habitual postures and tensions, emotions, thoughts, images, attitudes, beliefs—and how these are shaped by templates created from early family, social, and cultural experiences. These formative experiences are often unconscious, stored in the neural networks of implicit memory, and can be brought to consciousness through supported mindful exploration of what is arising right here, right now.

ORIGINS OF HAKOMI

Hakomi Mindful Somatic Psychotherapy was developed in the USA by Ron Kurtz and a group of colleagues in the mid 1970s. The name "Hakomi" comes from the indigenous Hopi language and means "How do you stand in relation to these many realms?" or "Who are you?" This word came through a dream of one of the early developers, who, through linguistic research, found its meaning in a Hopi lexicon. Later, Hopi Elder, Grandfather David Monongye, gave counsel on the dream and the word *hakomi*. He confirmed its meaning and gave his blessing for the newly forming institute to use the name.

Today, the Hakomi Institute and community are actively engaged in a deep discernment process about the use, as nonindigenous people, of this indigenous word as our name. Three years ago, the Hakomi Institute board charged a Name Committee with exploring, sorting, and recommending a path forward related to the impact of "Hakomi" as the public face of our work. Two years ago, two members of our sister organization, Hakomi Education Network (HEN), joined the committee holding aligned intentions. With the help of Indigenous consultants, the committee members continue to face and educate themselves. The ultimate intention is to support a broad commitment to examine our history and actions, centering Hopi people in our discernment process, being open and responsive to what we discover, and making changes based on self-awareness, cultural sensitivity, and humility. At the same time, the two Hakomi-centered organizations are finding ways to understand and support our shared history and methodology.

The Hakomi Institute (HI) was founded in 1981 to codify and promote the teaching of Hakomi MSP internationally. The ultimate goal of HI trainings is to foster high quality, caring therapists who are as dedicated to their own development as they are to the evolution of others. We further support students in discovering their own style, creativity, and unique application of Hakomi MSP. Hakomi integrates well with many therapeutic modalities, and is effective for both brief and long-term therapy in a wide range of applications and populations, including work with individuals, couples, and groups.

FOUNDATIONAL THEORETICAL CONCEPTS

Gregory Bateson (1979) and systems theory view humans as self-organizing, self-directing, and self-correcting systems. This perspective strongly influenced Hakomi MSP's founders and helped codify their commitment to collaborative, non-coercive engagement; inclusivity; living systems thinking; and trust in natural processes. This resulted in the articulation of the following Five Principles which still guide all Hakomi work:

Unity

The Unity principle assumes that, as people, we are living, organic systems that are integral wholes, composed of parts, which also participate in larger systems. We acknowledge the interdependency of all levels of the human system, including the physical/metabolic, intrapsychic, interpersonal, family, cultural, global, and spiritual.

Organicity

The organicity principle assumes that when all the parts are communicating within the whole, a living system is self-directing and self-correcting and has an inner wisdom of its own. In Hakomi, we support our client's organic unfolding toward wholeness, and trust that this is the direction that their system will naturally seek. Rather than imposing our own agenda, the therapist works cooperatively with the client's natural unfolding.

Body-Mind Holism

This principle affirms the interconnectedness of mind and body, and how they jointly manifest and reflect beliefs we hold about ourselves, others, and the world. This embodied expression of self arises from our life experiences, and in turn influences how we perceive and participate in life. Hakomi has many ways of exploring the mind-body connection to help bring awareness to core beliefs and the experiences that generate them. Hakomi faculty have spent close to fifty years developing a deep understanding of what embodiment really means and how to apply it in a psychotherapeutic process.

Nonviolence

The nonviolence principle promotes safe, non-forceful, cooperative exploration through honoring the signs and signals of our organic processes, especially those that manifest as what is often called "resistance." In contrast to confronting or overpowering a client's so-called defenses, the Hakomi methodology respects and literally supports them, allowing protective impulses to be befriended for the wisdom they contain. Nonviolence in Hakomi work does not mean passively following. As therapists we use our leadership to gently guide the process into territory that may be difficult for the client to face, while always being responsive to clients pacing, capacity, and organicity.

Applied Mindfulness

This powerful, aware state of consciousness is both a principle and a clinical intervention used throughout Hakomi sessions. It allows therapists to be radically present and clients to study the organization of their experience with openness, acceptance, and non-judgement. Mindfulness is an exploratory, relaxed, alert witnessing (though non-hypnotic) state of consciousness. It allows movement beyond normal, habitual thoughts and actions to the often richly non-verbal unfolding of deeper states of consciousness. The process also supports the mobilization of the client's essential or core self, which has a presence, centeredness, compassion, and wisdom that transcends the limitations of personal and collective history.

Loving Presence and the Therapeutic Relationship in Hakomi

Loving presence is another foundational tenet that is woven into all aspects of Hakomi MSP. The Hakomi therapist is responsible for creating and nurturing a loving, compassionate, accepting therapeutic relationship. In alignment with the Common Factors theory, Hakomi sees the therapeutic relationship as foundational to deep change. The therapist learns to embody a state of loving presence and attunement that supports the safety needed for the client to tolerate and benefit from Depth Psychotherapy. The quality of such an attuned relationship directly impacts client healing and change. To create the most attuned container, Hakomi therapists not only learn to operate from an implicitly and explicitly loving state of being, but they also hone their observational and empathy skills, learn to hold an attitude of "resting in non-violence" (Kurtz, 1990), and commit to an ongoing path of self-awareness.

How Hakomi Approaches Change

In Hakomi ". . . [deep] change requires exquisite attention to safety issues that foster the willingness to be vulnerable and the courage to move forward in spite of danger, uncertainty, and past traumas. It requires the existence of a protected and caring environment for the journey and the presence of an honest, supporting loving therapist willing to wait and call forth what is true. "(Kurtz, 1990). It also "supports change unfolding in life affirming ways, trusts that change wants to happen, happens in the present, and occurs when the principles are honored." (Roy, 2007).

As Hakomi MSP therapists and educators, we see that early unconscious shaping is foundational to the development of beliefs we hold and to our related daily patterns of behavior. However, clinical experience tells us that insight alone does not create change—clients often have keen insights about the hows and whys of the issues that they bring to therapy, without being able to make needed and satisfactory change. In Hakomi MSP, what we call core transformation requires the creation, support, and reinforcement of new neural networks. This is achieved with remarkable efficiency through mindful explorations of new and often unimagined possibilities. Through direct in-the-moment explorations clients can recognize how they avoid nourishing choices and discover new possibilities. Within the session, they can then practice taking in novel, psychologically nourishing (corrective or missing) experiences. Over time, this allows integration of new beliefs and behaviors into their lives.

LEVELS OF TRAINING

Hakomi Mindful Somatic Psychotherapy is successfully used by counselors, psychotherapists, social workers, coaches, group therapists, and professionals in related healing arts fields.

The Hakomi Institute offers a range of trainings serving the various needs of healing arts professionals. Today, Hakomi trainings and workshops are presented throughout the world, including in North America, Latin America, Europe, Israel, Japan, China, Australia and New Zealand. Each region has unique approaches to their training formats based on local cultural and professional norms, although a common foundational curriculum is taught in every training. In addition, Hakomi faculty share an understanding of what makes an inspirational and safe learning container for adults committed to personal and professional development and integrate this wisdom into how we implement trainings.

Hakomi workshops are generally introductions to Hakomi MSP and may be organized around a particular theme or aspect of the work.

- Level One trainings are designed to give students fundamental skills, theory, practice, and self-development in HMSP.
- Level Two trainings offer deepening and integration of basic skills, and introduction of relevant clinical maps focusing on therapeutic thinking, application, and the personhood of the therapist.
- Other specialty trainings are available in the areas of trauma, attachment, interpersonal neurobiology, personal growth; new training topics continue to be added.

Certification

After completing a Hakomi Training, students may either integrate their learnings into their existing scope of practice and allow this to be the completion of their explicit Hakomi training, choose to take additional trainings, or pursue certification as a Hakomi Therapist or Practitioner. A person who gets certified in Hakomi may call themself a Certified Hakomi Therapist (CHT) or a Certified Hakomi Practitioner (CHP) and is entitled to practice and advertise using the appropriate title. CHTs are expected to be bona fide credentialed professionals in the helping fields. CHPs are graduates who meet all other certification requirements but who offer alternative services such as coaching, etc. Once certified, they may use the Hakomi logo and may be listed on the Hakomi Institute website.

The certification process itself is rigorous and experiential and not based on "seat time." It is typically multiyear and always performance based. It requires two international trainers to approve of the candidate's knowledge, skills, and personal capacity for effective embodiment of this gentle yet powerful modality. The certification candidate works with their certification mentors over time, either submitting tapes for review or working live with a volunteer partner, with the goal of showing their professional and personal integration of the Hakomi body of work.

SCOPE OF PRACTICE AND CREDENTIALING

Use of Hakomi as psychotherapy is governed by the jurisdiction in which the therapist practices (e.g., State Counseling and Therapy Licensing Boards, etc.) and since Hakomi MSP is an experiential and mindfulness-based approach to change, clinicians need to be clear about both its potential for deep healing and its capacity for uncovering intense unconscious material. In Hakomi, a little mindfulness can go a long way, opening up windows to the unconscious that may seem new, scary, or even dangerous to the client. Clinicians need to be ready to respond appropriately, skillfully, and with great care, always placing the client's highest good at the forefront. This requires adequate clinical assessment skills, advanced clinical thinking, and sufficient breadth of experience in the role of professional helper—including the ability to assess for signs of traumatic activation, underdeveloped psychological structures, or significant clinical disorders for which working in prolonged mindfulness might be contraindicated. The Hakomi Institute is currently in the process of examining who and what we teach and considering offering specific training tracks for professionals holding different scopes of practice.

Diversity, Equity, & Inclusion

Social, cultural, and global contexts outside of our families of origin also shape our core beliefs. We know the individual and family are embedded in larger systems and take their cues from them. Consequently, we cannot ignore that these larger systems contribute to how core material operates at a personal level—affecting individual, societal, and planetary wellbeing.

The Hakomi Institute is an organization whose leadership has been predominantly represented by people with dominant culture identities (white, cisgender, able bodied, heterosexual). Recognizing the implications of this are broad and deep, we are committed to actively and humbly doing our part in unraveling harmful beliefs and behaviors embedded within the dominant cultural context. With the goal of creating a more generative and supportive organizational culture for people of all identities, and in alignment with the practice of loving presence and our core principles and values, the Hakomi Institute Diversity, Equity and Inclusion Action Group was formed. Through the work of this group, the Hakomi Institute faculty and staff are actively educating ourselves. Our intent is to openly examine our curriculum, teaching methods, policies, and leadership structure and to uproot attitudes and behaviors which uphold dominant culture systems that result in marginalization and oppression.

SUMMARY

Learning and developing mastery in Hakomi MSP is a significant commitment of time, energy, and money, as the entire process—from initial training through certification—can take 3-5 years. Those who stick with it, however, find deep satisfaction in this gentle and powerful method and within the vibrant professional Hakomi community. As Hakomi trainers, both authors consider Hakomi our home base. Its principles, as founder, Ron Kurtz, used to say, are what we always "lean back into." Its interventions are sophisticated and effective and leave room for therapist creativity. The emphasis on loving presence, practitioner personhood, and inclusivity of the multiplicity of human experience make it an approach that can itself evolve and nourish both therapist and client. Those of us called to support others in deep change processes and who recognize the importance of lifelong learning often find Hakomi to be both science and art. Both seasoned and developing clinicians who seek authentic mindful and embodied therapeutic engagement can find a "home base" in this method.

Donna Roy, MS, LPC, CHT is a Certified Trainer for the Hakomi Institute and psychotherapist in private practice. Donna practices out of Portland, Oregon. Though she is in the process of retiring, she continues to see some clients, teaches in Hakomi trainings locally, offers Hakomi-informed Primary Attachment Therapy internationally, and supports Hakomi graduates in their certification processes.

Lorena Monda, MS, OMD, LPCC, DOM, CHT is a Certified Trainer for the Hakomi Institute and psychotherapist in private practice. Lorena lives in Santa Fe, New Mexico. She teaches in Hakomi in the US and Japan and offers Hakomi consultation and certification support for graduates. She has recently retired from private practice after 40 years. She is the author of *The Practice of Wholeness: Spiritual Transformation in Everyday Life*, and a co-editor of the Hakomi textbook, *Hakomi Mindfulness-Centered Somatic Psychotherapy: A Comprehensive Guide to Theory and Practice*. The Hakomi Institute is a non-profit, professional organization providing training in Hakomi Mindful Somatic Psychotherapy worldwide.

www.HakomiInstitute.com

REFERENCES

Books

Bateson, G. (1979) *Mind and nature: A necessary unity.* New York: L E.P. Dutton.

Benz, D. & Weiss, H. (1989) *To the core of your experience.* Luminas Press.

Cole, J. D. & Ladas-Gaskin, C. (2007) Mindfulness Centered Therapies: An Integrative Approach. Seattle, WA: Silver Birch Press.

Fisher, R. (2002) *Experiential psychotherapy with couples: A guide for the creative oragmatist.* Phoenix, AZ: Zeig, Tucker & Theisen.

Johanson, G. & Kurtz, R. (1991) *Grace unfolding: Psychotherapy in the spirit of the Tao-te Ching.* New York: Bell Tower.

Kurtz, R. (1990) *Body-centered psychotherapy: The hakomi method.* Mendocino: LifeRhythm.

Kurtz, R. & Martin, D. (2019) *The practice of loving presence: A mindful guide to open-hearted relating.* Stone's Throw Publications.

Kurtz, R. & Prestera, H. (1976) *The body reveals: An illustrated guide to the psychology of the body.* New York: Harper Row/Quicksilver Books.

Monda, L. (2000) The practice of wholeness: Spiritual transformation in everyday life. Golden Flower Publications.

Weiss, H. Johanson, G. & Monda, L. eds. (2015) *Hakomi mindfulness-centered Somatic psychotherapy: A comprehensive guide to theory and practice.* New York:. Norton.

Chapters

Kurtz, R & Minton, K. (1997) Essentials of Hakomi body-centered psychotherapy. In C. Caldwell (Ed.), *Getting in touch: The guide to new body-centered therapies* (pp. 45-60). Wheaton: Quest Books.

Ogden, P. (1997) Hakomi integrative somatics: Hands-on psychotherapy. In C. Caldwell (Ed.), *Getting in touch: The guide to new body-centered therapies* (pp. 153-178). Wheaton: Quest Books.

Roy, D. M. (2007) Body-centered counseling and psychotherapy. In D. Capuzzi & D. Gross (Eds.) *Counseling and Psychotherapy: Theories and Interventions.* (4th ed. pp. 360-389). Upper Saddle River, NJ: Merrill Prentice Hall.

Professional Journal

Hakomi forum. https://hakomiinstitute.com/resources/professional-journal

Harm Reduction

KONJA KLEPPER, PH.D., LPCC, LAADAC, NCC, CCMHCE, ICAADC

WESTON EDWARDS, PH.D. PH.D., LP

The harm reduction model is a public health framework aimed at minimizing the negative consequences associated with certain behaviors, particularly substance use, without requiring complete cessation (National Harm Reduction Coalition, 2024). Rooted in the principles of pragmatism, public health, and human rights, this model adopts a non-judgmental approach that prioritizes harm reduction over abstinence. Recognizing that behaviors such as drug use are integral to human society, the model provides practical interventions to reduce associated risks. It also acknowledges that abstinence may not be a feasible or desirable goal for all individuals, offering alternative strategies to improve health outcomes while respecting personal choices.

From a public health perspective, harm reduction emphasizes interventions designed to mitigate adverse health, social, and legal consequences associated with high-risk behaviors. Strategies such as needle exchange programs, supervised consumption sites, and naloxone distribution are evidence-based approaches reducing the transmission of infectious diseases, preventing overdose deaths, and addressing other health-related harms. These interventions are integrated into broader public health initiatives, focusing on immediate and long-term health outcomes for individuals and communities (National Harm Reduction Coalition, 2024).

The harm reduction model is also grounded in human rights principles, emphasizing respect for individual dignity, autonomy, and informed decision-making. By meeting individuals "where they are," harm reduction fosters a supportive environment that empowers individuals to take control of their health without coercion or stigma (Marlatt, 1996). This approach balances the need for practical health solutions with a commitment to social justice, making harm reduction a key framework for addressing complex health behaviors in an equitable and compassionate manner (National Harm Reduction Coalition, 2024).

CERTIFICATIONS, TRAININGS, AND LICENSURE REQUIREMENTS

No certifications or licensure requirements exist to engage in harm reduction. Numerous short trainings are available (ranging from one hour to two days). Many of these trainings are available for continuing education credits for individuals who need them. Harm reduction specialists positions often require a high school diploma or equivalent. Training such as "Harm Reduction Specialist" is one example of training (https://harmreductionspecialist.com).

General Cost

Workshops are available online and in person. Costs are consistent with workshop prices. The referenced Harm Reduction Specialist costs $295 for 21 hours of training. Some trainings are offered free of charge (supported by federal or state grants). Check with your local or state Department of Health regarding available training.

IDENTIFIED AS GOLD STANDARD, BEST PRACTICE, EMERGING PRACTICE, OR EBP

While there is no single standard in harm reduction, the National Harm Reduction Coalition created in 1982 is one of the earliest training coalitions to promote harm reduction (SAMSHA, 2023). This organization reflects the development of the primary principles of Harm Reduction.

Certification available/required/recommended

No certification is available or required. Professional development and training via workshops are recommended.

Degree Requirements

Supporting individuals within the harm reduction model requires a combination of formal education, specialized training, and practical experience. Professionals working in harm reduction typically hold degrees in fields such as social work, psychology, sociology, public health, or related disciplines. While a bachelor's degree is often the minimum educational requirement, a master's degree is preferred for roles involving mental health practice, leadership, or policy development. Higher education in these fields provides foundational knowledge in human behavior, public health principles, and evidence-based interventions, all of which are critical for implementing harm reduction strategies.

In addition to formal education, specialized training in harm reduction principles and practices is essential. Certifications such as the Harm Reduction Specialist (HRS) credential, offered by organizations like the International Certification & Reciprocity Consortium (IC&RC), provide focused education on harm reduction methodologies and their application in recovery and public health contexts. Similarly, training programs offered by credentialing boards, such as the Missouri Credentialing Board, equip professionals with the skills necessary to effectively apply harm reduction frameworks in practice (Missouri Credentialing Board. n.d.). These certifications and training programs enhance competency and ensure adherence to best practices.

Practical experience is a critical component of supporting harm reduction initiatives. Professionals often gain experience through internships, volunteer work, or employment in settings that implement harm reduction strategies, such as needle exchange programs, supervised consumption sites, or outreach services. This hands-on experience, combined with formal education and specialized training, equips professionals with the knowledge, skills, and empathy required to address the complex health and social challenges faced by individuals engaging in high-risk behaviors. Such preparation ensures that harm reduction practitioners can deliver effective, evidence-based support within this compassionate and inclusive framework.

CAUTIONS OR LIMITATIONS

As with any helping relationship, providers applying harm reduction skills need to engage in self-reflection to assess the unconscious biases they might portray toward people who use drugs (PWUD). A foundation of harm reduction is the non-judgmental respect and acknowledgement of a person's autonomy regarding their choice to continue using drugs. Inherent conflict and bias can exist between the provider's beliefs and the individual's choice.

SCOPE OF PRACTICE ISSUES

Harm reduction practices, while effective and widely recognized for their public health benefits, often face challenges related to scope of practice. These issues arise when professionals or organizations operate beyond their defined roles or boundaries, raising concerns about safety, ethical standards, and legal compliance (Canadian Centre on Substance Use and Addiction [CCSA], 2021).

A significant area of concern involves professional training and boundaries. Harm reduction encompasses a range of services, including needle exchange programs, supervised consumption sites, and educational outreach, each requiring specific expertise. For example, a public health professional may not be adequately qualified to address complex psychological conditions or perform medical interventions. Without proper training and certification, practitioners risk exceeding their professional competencies, potentially jeopardizing the safety and well-being of clients (Harm Reduction International, 2020; Substance Abuse and Mental Health Services Administration [SAMHSA], 2020).

Legal and regulatory frameworks further complicate harm reduction efforts. In certain jurisdictions, practices such as the distribution of sterile needles or the operation of supervised consumption facilities may conflict with existing laws. Practitioners must navigate these legal constraints to ensure compliance, creating potential tensions between harm reduction objectives and legal mandates (United Nations Office on Drugs and Crime [UNODC], 2017).

To highlight the ethical section, ethical considerations also present challenges within harm reduction practice. Practitioners may face conflicts when balancing harm reduction principles with organizational expectations, such as those of abstinence-based recovery programs. These situations require careful adherence to ethical guidelines to maintain professional integrity while meeting the diverse needs of clients (Harm Reduction International, 2020).

Collaboration across disciplines introduces additional scope of practice complexities. Harm reduction frequently involves multidisciplinary teams, including public health professionals, social workers, and medical providers. Without clear communication and defined responsibilities, practitioners may inadvertently encroach upon areas outside their expertise, potentially compromising the effectiveness of care and client outcomes (IHRA, n.d.; SAMHSA, 2020).

Policy and funding constraints exacerbate these challenges. Limited resources may pressure harm reduction practitioners to assume responsibilities beyond their formal training, resulting in overextension and reduced quality of care. These limitations underscore the need for adequate support and infrastructure to sustain harm reduction initiatives (CCSA, 2021; IHRA, n.d.).

Addressing scope of practice concerns requires clear delineation of roles, comprehensive training programs, and adherence to professional standards. Advocacy for supportive policies and legal protections is essential to align harm reduction practices with regulatory frameworks and public health goals. By addressing these challenges, harm reduction initiatives can maintain their commitment to providing safe, ethical, and effective care within defined professional boundaries (UNODC, 2017).

WHAT KIND OF PERSON WOULD DO WELL IN HARM REDUCTION

Individuals who excel in implementing the harm reduction model possess a unique combination of personal traits, professional skills, and core values. This approach requires practitioners to engage with people who face complex health and social challenges, often stemming from substance use or other stigmatized behaviors. A key quality for success in this field is empathy and a non-judgmental attitude. Practitioners must provide care and support without imposing moral judgments, creating a safe and trusting environment for individuals to seek help and make informed decisions. You might recognize these qualities as consistent with the person-centered approach advocated by Carl Rogers, which emphasizes unconditional positive regard, empathy, and authenticity as central to building meaningful therapeutic relationships (Harm Reduction International, 2023; Rogers, 1951; SAMHSA, 2020).

Cultural competence is another essential trait for harm reduction professionals. Understanding and respecting the diverse backgrounds, identities, and experiences of the individuals they support is crucial to delivering inclusive and accessible services. This includes sensitivity to factors such as race, ethnicity, gender, socioeconomic status, and sexual orientation. Alongside this, strong communication skills are vital. Practitioners must be able to convey information clearly, actively listen, and establish meaningful rapport with individuals who may be hesitant or distrustful of traditional healthcare systems (CCSA, 2021; IHRA, n.d.).

Working in harm reduction also requires resilience and patience. Practitioners often face emotionally demanding situations where progress is slow, or setbacks occur. Maintaining a consistent and supportive presence despite these challenges is essential for fostering long-term positive outcomes. Additionally, a commitment to evidence-based practices ensures that harm reduction professionals are equipped with the most effective tools and interventions, such as naloxone distribution, safe consumption strategies, and needle exchange programs (Harvard T.H. Chan School of Public Health, n.d.; Harm Reduction International, 2023).

Flexibility and adaptability further define successful harm reduction practitioners. Every individual's circumstances are unique, and practitioners must tailor their approaches to meet specific needs. This requires creativity, problem-solving, and a willingness to adjust methods as needed. Advocacy skills are also critical, as harm reduction often intersects with broader systemic issues such as healthcare access, public policy, and human rights. Professionals in this field frequently engage in efforts to reduce stigma, promote equitable care, and drive systemic change (CCSA, 2021; SAMHSA, 2020).

By embodying these traits and skills, harm reduction practitioners create a compassionate and inclusive framework for addressing complex challenges. Their work not only supports individuals in improving their health and well-being but also contributes to broader societal efforts to address stigma and promote justice (IHRA, n.d.; Harvard T.H. Chan School of Public Health, n.d.).

SUMMARY

The harm reduction model has evolved significantly in recent years to address emerging public health challenges and adapt to shifting societal perspectives on substance use. One major advancement has been the integration of harm-reduction strategies into medical settings. This approach aims to bridge the gap between substance use interventions and traditional healthcare by offering services such as safe consumption sites and expanded access to medications for opioid use disorder. These initiatives not only reduce immediate health risks but also engage individuals with substance use disorders in comprehensive medical care, fostering long-term health improvements (Harvard T.H. Chan School of Public Health, n.d.).

Globally, harm reduction has also benefited from progressive policy shifts. International organizations, including the United Nations Office of the High Commissioner for Human Rights, have called for drug policies that prioritize human rights (UNODC, 2017). This paradigm shift reflects a growing recognition of the need to balance public health priorities with individual dignity and autonomy. By treating substance use as a health issue rather than solely a criminal matter, these policy changes pave the way for more humane and effective harm reduction strategies (Harm Reduction International, 2023).

The harm reduction model has expanded beyond drug-related interventions to address other substances, such as alcohol. Recent research has highlighted strategies to mitigate the health and social harms associated with regular alcohol consumption. These targeted interventions mark a broader application of harm reduction principles, demonstrating the model's adaptability to various public health contexts and its potential to address diverse behavioral health issues (Harm Reduction Journal, 2024).

These developments reflect the dynamic evolution of the harm reduction model. By incorporating innovative practices, adapting to diverse contexts, and fostering community engagement, harm reduction continues to offer an inclusive and practical framework for addressing complex substance use challenges. The ongoing integration of harm reduction strategies into medical and public health systems, coupled with supportive policy changes, underscores the model's relevance and effectiveness in contemporary health care (CCSA, 2021).

With over a decade of experience as a counselor educator in higher education and more than two decades as a professional counselor and clinical supervisor, Konja Klepper brings a wealth of expertise to her roles. A Reiki master, Dr. Klepper's extensive background encompasses a focus on Doctoral Research, Holistic Health and Wellness, and Spirituality and Counseling. She is dedicated to preparing counselors and counselor educators to become advocates for human development, social justice, and positive change. Currently serving as an Associate Professor at Capella University, Dr. Klepper holds licenses in three states, covering both professional counseling and substance abuse. Her commitment to the holistic well-being of individuals is evident in her multifaceted professional journey.

Konja.Klepper@Capella.edu

Dr. Edwards is a licensed psychologist in MN and Nevada. He has a PhD from the University of Minnesota in an APA-accredited Counseling Psychology program (2004) and a second PhD from Capella University in a CACREP-accredited Counselor Education and Supervision (2023) program. He has 30 years of experience working in human sexuality including HIV prevention, sex offender treatment, LGBQT+, alternative sexuality, and culturally specific chemical dependency treatment. He has worked in clinical practice since 1993 at the inpatient, outpatient, and intensive outpatient levels of care. He has been a clinical supervisor for bachelor's, master's, and doctoral students. He currently works as a faculty member at Capella University in the School of Psychology.

Weston.edwards@capella.edu

REFERENCES

Canadian Centre on Substance Use and Addiction (CCSA). (2021). *Harm reduction: Policies and practices.* Retrieved from https://www.ccsa.ca/harm-reduction-policies-and-practices

Harm Reduction International. (2020). *Harm reduction policy and legal frameworks.* Retrieved from https://www.hri.global/policy

Harm Reduction Journal. (2024). *Alcohol harm reduction: Interventions to mitigate health and social harms.* Retrieved from https://harmreductionjournal.biomedcentral.com/articles/10.1186/s12954-024-01105-8

Harvard T.H. Chan School of Public Health. (n.d.). *Overdose prevention: New strategies for harm reduction.* Retrieved from https://hsph.harvard.edu/news/overdose-prevention-new-strategies-for-harm-reduction/

International Certification & Reciprocity Consortium (IC&RC). (n.d.). *Harm Reduction Specialist Certification.* Retrieved from https://www.internationalcredentialing.com/Harm-Reduction-Certification

International Harm Reduction Association (IHRA). (n.d.). *What is harm reduction?* Retrieved from https://www.hri.global/what-is-harm-reduction

Marlatt, G. A. (1996). Harm reduction: Come as you are. *Addictive behaviors, 21(6),* 779-788.

Missouri Credentialing Board. (n.d.). *Harm Reduction Specialist (HRS) Training.* Retrieved from https://missouricb.com/harm-reduction-specialist-hrs-training

Rogers, C. (1951). *Client-centered therapy.* Boston: Houghton Mifflin.

Substance Abuse and Mental Health Services Administration (SAMHSA). (2020). *Harm reduction framework.* Retrieved from https://www.samhsa.gov/harm-reduction

United Nations Office on Drugs and Crime (UNODC). (2017). *A comprehensive approach to harm reduction.* Retrieved from https://www.unodc.org

Harmony Therapy

BILL OWENBY, EDD, MC, FAAETS, DAAETS, DCMHS, LPC, LAAC, NCC, CCMHC, ACS, DIPLOMATE, FELLOW

Harmony Therapy is a holistic therapeutic approach that integrates emotional, cognitive, physical, and spiritual elements to promote well-being and balance. Drawing from mindfulness, energy healing, and cognitive-behavioral techniques, Harmony Therapy seeks to align individuals with their authentic selves, fostering self-awareness, emotional resilience, and deep inner peace.

OVERVIEW OF HARMONY THERAPY

Harmony Therapy is based on the premise that healing occurs when individuals align their mental, emotional, and physical states. It emphasizes self-regulation, emotional balance, and body-mind integration through guided interventions that address trauma, stress, and personal growth.

Core Principles of Harmony Therapy

1. **Holistic Integration**
   o Recognizes the interconnectedness of mental, physical, and emotional health.
   o Uses techniques that engage all aspects of self for deep healing.
2. **Balance and Alignment**
   o Encourages individuals to harmonize their emotions and thoughts to create inner peace.
   o Promotes self-acceptance and emotional resilience.
3. **Self-Regulation and Empowerment**
   o Clients learn to take charge of their well-being through guided exercises.
   o Emphasizes self-awareness, mindfulness, and personal responsibility.
4. **Emotional and Cognitive Processing**
   o Utilizes therapeutic conversations, mindfulness practices, and guided visualizations to resolve emotional imbalances.
   o Addresses limiting beliefs and emotional blockages to promote transformation.

APPLICATIONS OF HARMONY THERAPY

Mental Health and Emotional Well-Being

- Supports individuals struggling with anxiety, depression, and emotional dysregulation.
- Helps manage stress and promote self-compassion.

Trauma Recovery

- Offers a safe, structured approach to processing past trauma.
- Integrates grounding techniques and somatic awareness to facilitate healing.

Physical Health and Wellness

- Promotes relaxation and stress reduction to improve overall health.
- Encourages body awareness and self-care practices.

Spiritual and Personal Growth

- Helps individuals explore their life purpose and personal development.
- Encourages mindfulness and meditation to cultivate inner peace.

Key Techniques in Harmony Therapy

1. **Mindfulness and Meditation**
   - Incorporates breathwork, guided imagery, and meditation to enhance self-awareness.
   - Supports emotional regulation and stress reduction.
2. **Cognitive Restructuring**
   - Identifies and challenges negative thought patterns.
   - Promotes positive thinking and cognitive flexibility.
3. **Energy Healing and Somatic Awareness**
   - Utilizes body-centered approaches to release stored emotional tension.
   - Encourages movement, relaxation, and grounding exercises.
4. **Expressive Arts and Creative Therapies**
   - Incorporates music, art, and movement to facilitate emotional expression.
   - Supports clients in exploring feelings in a non-verbal manner.

TRAINING AND CERTIFICATION IN HARMONY THERAPY

Educational Pathways

1. **Foundational Knowledge**
   - Requires a background in psychology, counseling, or holistic health practices.
   - Many programs offer introductory courses in mindfulness, somatic therapy, and energy healing.
2. **Advanced Training Programs**
   - Specialized certification programs provide in-depth training in Harmony Therapy techniques.
   - Training may include coursework in meditation, energy balancing, and trauma-informed care.

Certification Requirements

1. **Eligibility**
   - Open to mental health professionals, holistic practitioners, and wellness coaches.
   - Some programs require prior experience in counseling or bodywork.
2. **Core Training Components**
   - Completion of a structured training program (typically 6 months to 2 years).
   - Supervised practice hours and case study presentations.
3. **Accredited Training Organizations**
   - Holistic Therapy Certification Institute
   - International Association for Holistic Mental Health
   - Mind-Body Healing Institute
4. **Time and Cost Commitments**
   - Training programs range from $1,000–$5,000 depending on depth and certification level.
   - Some programs offer weekend intensives, while others require long-term study.

Benefits

- **Comprehensive Healing:** Addresses mind, body, and spirit for holistic well-being.
- **Customizable Approach:** Adaptable to individual needs and treatment goals.
- **Encourages Self-Growth:** Clients develop skills to sustain emotional balance.

Limitations

- **Not a Replacement for Clinical Treatment:** Best used in conjunction with traditional psychotherapy for severe disorders.
- **Limited Scientific Validation:** While many principles are supported by research, the holistic nature of the therapy lacks extensive empirical validation.
- **Accessibility:** Not widely available in all locations, requiring travel or online learning for certification.

ETHICAL CONSIDERATIONS

1. **Informed Consent**
   - Clients must understand the holistic nature of the therapy and any potential limitations.
2. **Scope of Practice**
   - Practitioners must operate within their training and refer clients to other professionals when necessary.
3. **Cultural Sensitivity**
   - Therapists should tailor interventions to align with clients' cultural and spiritual beliefs.

SUMMARY

Harmony Therapy provides a unique and integrative approach to emotional healing, fostering self-awareness, balance, and resilience. By blending mindfulness, cognitive restructuring, and body-based techniques, this modality empowers individuals to cultivate inner harmony and well-being. For professionals seeking to incorporate holistic healing methods into their practice, training in Harmony Therapy offers valuable tools for supporting clients on their journey toward healing.

I hold two independent licenses in the states of Arizona and Ohio, supervisory status in Arizona, along with a substance abuse license in Arizona. I am board certified as a Diplomate and Clinical Mental Health Specialist, an Approved Clinical Supervisor, Nationally Certified Counselor, a Certified Clinical Mental Health Counselor, NeuroLinguistic Programming Practitioner, and a Clinical Trauma Specialist for Individuals and Family including EMDR Therapy and NET. I completed my training in Animal-Assisted Therapy and Pet Handlers certification in order to evaluate and incorporate the human-animal bond in therapy. I am the sole author and creator of the SxC Model of ESA Evaluation. My research interests surround post-traumatic growth, resiliency, strengths-based therapy, positive psychology, mindfulness, Animal-Assisted Therapy, Sandtray Therapy, Creative approaches in therapy, and martial arts in mental health. I have presented at local, state, regional, national, and international levels on various topics including personality traits, licensure reciprocity challenges, Sandtray and supervision, and Animal-Assisted Therapy within supervision. eonbllc@gmail.com

REFERENCES

Siegel, D. J. (2012). The Mindful Brain: Reflection and Attunement in the Cultivation of Well-Being. W. W. Norton & Company.

Porges, S. W. (2011). The Polyvagal Theory: Neurophysiological Foundations of Emotions, Attachment, Communication, and Self-Regulation. W. W. Norton & Company.

Levine, P. A. (2010). In an Unspoken Voice: How the Body Releases Trauma and Restores Goodness. North Atlantic Books.

Recommended Resources

- **International Association for Holistic Mental Health**: https://www.iahmh.org
- **Mind-Body Healing Institute**: https://www.mindbodyhealinginstitute.org
- **The Holistic Therapy Certification Institute**: https://www.holistictherapycertification.com

Havening Technique

ALYSON POMPEO-FARGNOLI, PH.D., LPC, SAC, NCC

BENJAMIN PERSKY, MA, BA

The Havening Technique is a form of psychosensory therapy with a goal of healing to help individuals overcome past trauma and distress. Havening uses the sensory touch of stroking arms gently, as well as hands and face. There are two types of havening- Facilitative Havening and Self Havening. Facilitative Havening involves assistance from a certified practitioner, who will implement the technique onto the client. The second type of Havening is called Self Havening which is completed by the individual themselves, and may include following an instructional video. Havening has shown to be equally effective online as it is in person. Both of these methods can support the goal of self-healing and overcoming problems which are the result of anxiety based disorders. Some of the anxiety-based issues and disorders that Havening has been shown to successful in treating are phobias, distressing memories, stress, anger, grief, panic attacks, PTSD, etc. (Havening.org, 2022). In fact, one study showed that just a single-session of the Havening had a positive impact on depression, anxiety, and work and social adjustment (Gursimran, et al., 2015).

HAVENING TECHNIQUES WITHIN THE SESSION

Havening was created by Dr. Ronal Ruden, an American medical practitioner and theorist. Early on he was introduced to the practice of Thought Field Therapy (TFT) and Emotional Freedom Technique (EFT) which utilizes tapping to encourage emotional healing (Beck, 2023). Ruden observed that through gentle touch, certain eye-movements, and distracting techniques, clients could experience relief from distressing and traumatic memories. This phenomenon was coined an "Event Havening" and led to the start of the Havening Technique theory. It was proposed that through these Havening Techniques, there was the potential to eliminate problematic receptors within the brain's amygdala; thus, disconnecting the recalled memory from its emotional content and emotionally detaching the individual from the memory of the traumatic event (Sumich et al., 2022). An increase in the neurotransmitter, serotonin, has also been observed during this process (Ruden, 2005).

Event Havening consists of three main components that are used by practitioners with the client. The first one being activation of an emotional event by recall, in which the client recalls an event as the practitioner directs them to rate this event on the Subjective Units of Distress Scale (SUDS) which ranges from 0 (absolutely relaxed) to 10 (worst distress) (Molin, 2020). After declaring and rating event on SUDS, the second step is using Havening touch, which is applied to the arms, hands, and face. The third and final step is using distraction techniques, such as visualizing and counting. The purpose of these three steps is to positively alter brain waves, specifically, delta brain waves. It has been shown that these delta brain wave gives off an electroceutical effect which leads to the de-encoding of the traumatic event that has been recalled (Ruden, 2019).

Following the technique, the client will reevaluate their identified traumatic event via the SUDS. The goal of the session is for the client's SUDS score to positively improve (decrease in its level of stress). A major takeaway from using Havening Techniques is that this process can be applied to client issues that may not have been dealt with using talking therapy or pharmacological intervention. Havening may also be used in conjunction with existing therapies (Pickersgill, 2014).

REQUIRED TRAINING AND CERTIFICATION

No matter what the therapy is, practitioners must understand and know how to properly use the techniques and in an ethical manner. To accomplish such competency, required trainings are available for Havening Techniques. The best resource for this and more information is the official website, Havening.com. This website offers a free introduction to havening training. Following this initial introduction, should practitioners be interested in gaining the Havening certification, the site also offers registration of multi-day certification trainings. While individuals may gain information about Havening via online searches, and even online instructional videos, the formal trainings and certifications are recommended for all practitioners. (Havening.org, 2022).

THE HAVENING TECHNIQUES PRACTITIONER

In order to become a certified Havening Techniques practitioner, there are two required steps. First, practitioners must attend a training which is an accredited training, given by one of the Havening Techniques trainers. These trainings include lectures, demonstrations, and practice that provide an overall comprehension of the neuroscience behind the Havening Techniques. Most of the trainings consist of one to three days of in person or virtual participation, can vary in cost. Many of the training times vary because they all offer different things, but must be attend in order to proceed to the second step (Havening.org, 2022).

Following completion of the first step, one may officially enter the certification process (step two). The second step consists of six different parts which must be completed, including all practical work with clients. The first step out of the six is to complete a science review and pass an exam that is provided by the Havening Techniques official website. The second step varies based on where one resides. If within the United States, an ethics course online is required. If practicing outside of the United States, one simply needs to agree to and sign the Written Acknowledgement of Receipt of Havening Techniques Ethics & Conduct Policy. The third step is solely for the practitioners in the United States since after completing the ethics course they will then have to agree to and sign the Written Acknowledgement of Receipt of Havening Techniques Ethics & Conduct Policy. The fourth step is to submit an application along with the application fee. The fifth step requires submission of 30 case studies using Havening Techniques, plus a submission of two video sessions using Havening Techniques, with two different clients in each video. The videos have a minimum requirement of 15 minutes and a maximum of 60 minutes. Along with the video submissions, the applicant must upload the two signed permission to video agreements from the clients. The sixth and final step is to complete all account details including full name for the future certificate. Once all of the six sub steps of the overarching second and final step have been completed, applicants will submit everything and wait for application review (Havening.org, 2022).

Final approval will result in certification as a Havening Techniques practitioner. As per the Havening Techniques official website, certified practitioners are given access to the organization's resource library which contains official presentations, logos, and training videos which are exclusive to being a practitioner. In addition, a yearly accreditation fee is required to maintain certification (Havening.org, 2022).

Education & Degree Requirements

Currently, there is no educational and degree requirements that are officially listed in order to become an official certified Havening Techniques practitioner. The training and certification process is open to a wide audience including therapists, educators, physicians, coaches, hypnotists, etc. All in all, Havening Techniques incorporates easily into many different methods of practice (Ericksonian.com, 2023).

Certification Limitations for Students

Students may apply and receive a one year membership to a closed page provided by the official Havening Techniques website that will provide content from the doctors that developed the Havening Techniques, trainers, and accredited practitioners from around the world. After the one year has passed, students can either take another training class or become officially certified to maintain their membership in the private group (Havening.org, 2022).

Havening Techniques is a new alternative therapy and is considered part of the field of Complementary and Alternative Medicine (CAM). CAM practices may not always based on research and evidence. Some other practices that are part of CAM include acupuncture, tai chi, massage, and yoga. Even though Havening has very promising mental, emotional, and physical health benefits, the Havening Techniques have yet to be completely researched and studied by academics, medical, and psychological associations. With that being said, Havening is still considered experimental, and its effectiveness and benefits, along with its risks, are not fully known yet. Regarding the touch technique of Havening, it must be noted that clients should be made fully aware of this, and approve of it. However, if the client or the practitioner is uncomfortable about touching, the client may self-apply Havening Touch and follow along with the practitioner or watch along in the videos that are provided online (Havening.org, 2022).

CONCLUSION

Overall, Havening Techniques are an alternative therapy practice that can have promising results in a short amount of time. Havening can be used as a tool for a wide range of concerns, from reducing minor anxiety to deep rooted trauma. Havening is a relatively simple process that anyone can perform. In conclusion, Havening Techniques can provide an alternative or supplemental therapeutic technique to utilize on one's self or with clients.

Dr. Alyson Pompeo-Fargnoli is an Associate Professor and Program Director in the department of Educational Counseling & Leadership at Monmouth University, in West Long Branch, NJ— on the beautiful Jersey Shore. She holds a PhD in Counselor Education & Supervision, is a licensed professional counselor (LPC), a nationally certified counselor (NCC), and holds a Substance Abuse and Addictions Counseling Certification practice experience, including as a Director of a college counseling center. Her research and Covid-19 and the mental health impacts, college counseling, first generation college students, and mental health stigma. She has over 10 years of clinical publications span the areas of counseling theories, the mental health/physical health connection, and mental health stigma. Her work includes 25 published articles and book chapters, and 45 professional presentations. Yet, her greatest accomplishments are that of her and her husband: their two young children, Julia and Matthew.

Benjamin Persky is a second year graduate student at Monmouth University originally from Fair Lawn, New Jersey. He has a Bachelor of Arts in history and a Master of Arts in Teaching from Quinnipiac University. He is currently on track to receive his second master's degree, a Master of Science in Education in School Counseling. After the completion of his second master's, Benjamin will also be receiving his certificate to become a Student Assistance Coordinator (SAC). He is a member of the American Counseling Association (ACA), the American School Counseling Association (ASCA), the New Jersey School Counselor Association (NJSCA), the Bergen County School Counseling Association (BCSCA), and the Association of Student Assistance Professionals of New Jersey (ASAP-NJ). Benjamin would like to start working towards completing the requirements in order to become a Licensed Professional Counselor (LPC) after he has graduated.

REFERENCES

Beck, D (2023). "EFT and Thought Field Therapy." *Health-Success.Co.Uk*, www.health-success.co.uk/eft-and-tft/#:~:text=The%20techniques%20aim%20to%20bring,work%20in%20the%20same%20way. Accessed 2023.

Dal Molin, L. (2023). "A User Guide to: Using the SUDS Scale to Measure the Intensity of Feelings." *InnerActions.Com*, www.inneractions.com.au/res_articles.php. Accessed 2023.

Gursimran, T., Deborah, T., Matthew, G., Paul, M., & Neil, G. (2015). Impact of a single-session of havening. *Health Science Journal, 9(5),* 1-5. Retrieved from https://ezproxy.monmouth.edu/login?url=https://www.proquest.com/scholarly-journals/impact-single-session-havening/docview/1734309131/se-2

"Havening Techniques - Better Living through Neuroscience." *Havening Techniques Official Website*, havening.org/. Accessed 2023.

Pickersgill, G. (2014). "Havening: A New Way to Heal." *Article - Havening: A New Way To Heal*, Jan. 2014, www.positivehealth.com/article/nlp/havening-a-new-way-to-heal/.

Ruden, R. A. (2019). Harnessing Electroceuticals to Treat Disorders Arising From Traumatic Stress: Theoretical Considerations Using A Psychosensory Model. *Explore-the Journal of Science and Healing, 15*(3), 222–229. https://doi.org/10.1016/j.explore.2018.05.005

Ruden, R. (2023). "Havening Techniques® Certification Training - Ericksonian." *Ericksonian*, ericksonian.com/training/havening-techniques-certification-training. Accessed 2023.

Ruden R. (2005) A neurological basis for the observed peripheral sensory modulation of emotional responses. *Traumatology 11:* 145-158.

Sumich, A., Heym, N., Sarkar, M., Burgess, T., French, J., Hatch, L., & Hunter, K. (2022). The power of touch: The effects of havening touch on subjective distress, mood, brain function, and psychological health. *Psychology & Neuroscience, 15*(4), 332–346. https://doi-org.ezproxy.monmouth.edu/10.1037/pne0000288

111

Health & Wellness Coach

Lorrie-Anne Monte, PhD, MPH, CHES, NCC, LPC, PCS, BC-TMH

Real Balance Global Wellness Services Certified Wellness & Health Coach

Integrative Nutrition Health Coach

Robbins-Madanes Trained Coach

*Health is a state of complete physical, mental, and social well-being
and not merely the absence of disease or infirmity.*
-World Health Organization

*Wellness is an active process through which people become aware of,
and make choices toward, a more successful existence.*
-National Wellness Institute

The lifestyle choices that people make every day significantly impact their health and wellness for better or worse. Many diseases and chronic conditions, such as coronary heart disease, high cholesterol, diabetes, and hypertension are lifestyle related (Moore & Jackson, 2018). By eating nutritious meals, engaging in physical activity on a regular basis, getting enough sleep, developing social connections, managing stress, and avoiding smoking and excessive alcohol consumption, people's health and wellness can be greatly increased (American College of Lifestyle Medicine, 2022). Many people want to live heathier lives; however, change is hard, and they might need some help and encouragement to make and sustain the changes they want to. This is where health and wellness coaches can help.

THE ROLE OF A HEALTH & WELLNESS COACH

Health and wellness coaches accept people where they are in their desire to change and help them discover what they would like to accomplish. Coaches help their clients to increase their self-awareness and to reflect on various facets of themselves and their lives, such as values and priorities. Together, the coach and client co-create a plan that sets the focus for the journey ahead. Health and wellness coaches champion their clients' successes and are supportive and encouraging as the difficulties and challenges of change emerge. They help clients to persevere, understand themselves more, and continue moving forward until the goals are accomplished and permanent changes have been made (Arloski, 2009).

If you are interested in becoming a health and wellness coach, there are many programs available to choose from. Some programs offer certificates of completion while others offer certification. Every health and wellness coach training program is different with regards to modality of learning (in-person or online), hours required, cost, practical skills assessments, examinations, annual fees, and continuing education requirements.

It is extremely important to thoroughly research any health and wellness coach training program that you are interested in to ensure that you are choosing a high-quality program. Also, you should research what certifications they offer or what advanced certifications you can pursue if you complete their program. Certification is an important consideration since the profession of health and wellness coaching is progressing rapidly and plans for the reimbursement of health and wellness coaching services through insurance companies has already begun (National Commission for Health Education Credentialing, Inc., 2022).

In recent years, the National Board for Health & Wellness Coaches (NBHWC) has emerged as the go-to organization for health and wellness coaching professional standards and certification. They also offer a board certification examination which leads to the National Board Certified Health & Wellness Coach (NBC-HWC) credential. To qualify for the examination, a NBHWC approved coach training program must be completed. A list of NBHWC approved coach training programs can be found on their website (NBHWC, 2022).

Some health and wellness coach training programs also provide opportunities for their graduates to become certified with the International Coach Federation (ICF). ICF is the largest coaching organization worldwide (ICF, 2022a). The ICF has specific accrediting requirements for coach training programs, and they offer three coaching credentials: Associate Certified Coach (ACC), Professional Certified Coach (PCC), and Master Certified Coach (MCC). Each credential has its own requirements regarding examination, evaluation, coaching training, and client coaching hours. A list of ICF approved coach training programs can be found on their website (ICF, 2022b).

SUMMARY

Health and wellness coaching is uplifting and transformational. It is about helping people to be clearer and more intentional about their choices. It is about helping people live healthier and more fulfilling lives. If this work interests to you, then you might want to become a health and wellness coach.

When I was in graduate school, I stumbled across the wheel of wellness counseling by Myers, Sweeney, and Witmer (2000) and I fell in love. I already had a Master of Science in Counseling with School Counselor Certification and was working as a full-time high school counselor, but that wheel inspired me and eventually led me into the world of health and wellness coach training programs. After extensive research, I chose to complete the Wellcoaches Health Coach & Wellness Coach Training program. The training was excellent, and the core textbook, *Coaching Psychology Manual* (2010) by Margaret Moore and Bob Tschannen-Moran was one of the best books that I have ever read. The experience taught me about coaching psychology, behavior change, appreciative inquiry, nonviolent communication, motivational interviewing, and so much more. It was truly a phenomenal experience.

My second coach training program was the Real Balance Global Wellness Services Wellness Mapping 360 Wellness and Health Coach Training. After reading the book, *Wellness Coaching for Lasting Lifestyle Change* (2009) by Michael Arloski, I had to complete his training program. Dr. Arloski is an exquisite writer, and the book was a masterpiece on wellness coaching. Dr. Arloski is a licensed psychologist and a professional certified coach who has been involved in the wellness field for decades. Through his book and training, I learned about the influence of psychology and the wellness field in the creation of wellness and health coaching, the core principles of high-quality coaching, and how to help others create lasting lifestyle change. His book is a must read for anyone interested in wellness coaching and the training program was excellent.

My third coach training program was the Institute for Integrative Nutrition Health Coach Training Program. The program was amazing because it provided an opportunity to learn from many experts in nutrition, wellness, personal development, functional medicine, and coaching. It also provided exceptional training in marketing and business skills. The health and wellness coach training programs that I completed have helped me to learn, grow, and improve as a person, as a school counselor, and as a counselor educator.

Dr. Lorrie-Anne Monte is an Assistant Professor and the Fieldwork Coordinator in Counselor Education at Western Connecticut State University. Prior to that she was a high school counselor for over 18 years. She has a Bachelor of Science in Human Development and Family Relations from the University of Connecticut (UCONN). She also has a Master of Science in Counseling and a Master of Public Health from Southern Connecticut State University. She completed her 092 Educational Leadership coursework at Sacred Heart University. She also has a PhD in Educational Psychology: Counselor Education and Counseling Psychology from UCONN. Lorrie-Anne loves to learn, and constant personal and professional development is the air that she breathes. She is a Certified Health Education Specialist, a Real Balance Global Wellness Services Certified Wellness & Health Coach, an Integrative Nutrition Health Coach, a Robbins-Madanes Trained Coach, a National Certified Counselor, a Licensed Professional Counselor, a Pastoral Care Specialist, and a Board Certified-TeleMental Health Provider. Lorrie-Anne also strongly believes in being of service to others. montel@wcsu.edu

REFERENCES

American College of Lifestyle Medicine. (2022). *6 pillars of lifestyle medicine.* https://lifestylemedicine.org/

Arloski, M. (2009). *Wellness coaching for lasting lifestyle change.* Whole Person Associates.

International Coaching Federation. (2022a, January 24). *International Coaching Federation surpasses 50,000 ICF members worldwide.* https://www.prnewswire.com/news-releases/international-coaching-federation-surpasses-50-000-icf-members-worldwide-301465699.html

International Coaching Federation. (2022b). *What is an ICF credential?* https://coachingfederation.org/credentials-and-standards

Moore, M., & Jackson, E. (2018). Health and wellness coaching. In E. Cox, T. Bachkirova, & D. Clutterbuck, (Eds.), *The complete handbook of coaching* (3rd ed.) (pp. 345-362). Sage.

Moore, M., & Tschannen-Moran, B. (2010). *Coaching psychology manual.* Wolters Kluwer Health/Lippincott, Williams & Wilkins.

Myers, J. E., Sweeney, T. J., & Witmer, J. M. (2000). The wheel of wellness counseling for wellness: A holistic model for treatment planning. JOURNAL OF COUNSELING & DEVELOPMENT, 78(3), 251–266. https://libres.uncg.edu/ir/uncg/f/J_Myers_Wheel_2000.pdf

National Board for Health & Wellness Coaching. (2022). *Find an approved health & wellness coach training program.* https://nbhwc.org/

National Commission for Health Education Credentialing. (2022). *NCHEC, NBHWC, and UC San Diego announce a collaborative project to advance reimbursement for health & wellness coaching services in healthcare.* https://www.nchec.org/news/posts/reimbursementupdate

Health at Every Size® (HAES®)

HEIDI L. HENRY, PHD, LPC

INTRODUCTION TO HEALTH AT EVERY SIZE® (HAES®)

The Health at Every Size (HAES®) approach is a framework for healthcare and fitness providers, such as doctors, nurses, dietitians, therapists, and fitness coaches, that promotes inclusive, compassionate care free from anti-fat bias and supports healthcare as a human right for people of all sizes. It emphasizes patient autonomy, informed consent, and the need for healthcare providers to critically evaluate weight-related medical practices and address both personal and systemic biases. The HAES® framework also encourages health goals focused on wellbeing rather than weight loss, striving for an equitable healthcare environment for all.

To best understand the conceptual framework of Health at Every Size® (HAES®), it is important to examine the historical events that led to its development. The HAES® framework emerged from the body liberation and feminist movements of the 1960s and 1970s. In the 1960s, Lew Louderback, a fat activist married to a fat person, published an article titled *More people should be FAT* (Bruno, 2013). This is often recognized as the first mainstream defense of fat people to ever appear in the media; it was published in 1967 in the *Saturday Evening Post* (Kight, 2014). Bill Fabrey, an engineer who preferred larger women, read Louderback's article, they connected, and this led Fabrey to found the National Association to Aid Fat Americans in 1969, which is known today as the National Association to Advance Fat Acceptance (NAAFA). This was the start of the size acceptance movement (Bruno, 2013a).

In the 1970s, the Fat Underground (radical therapists and feminists) emerged and started advocating for broader definitions of beauty, which would encourage self-acceptance and an inclusive view of all body sizes and shapes, especially fat bodies (Simic, 2015). Some prominent members of the Fat Underground were members of the NAAFA, and they published articles in radical therapy journals (Bruno, 2013b).

In the 1980s and 1990s there was an increase in diet culture, which led to an increase in weight-based discrimination (Bruno, 2013c). Researchers and activists began challenging diet culture by examining the psychological and physical harm caused by dieting and weight stigma. They emphasized that many of the health conditions that were associated with obesity, such as heart disease and diabetes, could also occur in individuals across a variety of body sizes. The significance of this emphasis was that it led to the conclusion that weight loss may not be the most effective solution; instead, prioritizing healthy behaviors was a more beneficial approach (Bruno, 2014d).

During this same time in the late 1990s, aerobics instructors in the San Francisco Bay Area opened the Women of Substance Health Spa and hosted Think Tank meetings. Think Tank members, along with nutritionists Frances Berg and Joanne Ikeda, and members on a 'showmethedata' listserv discussed and debated terms for the burgeoning movement as "health at every size" and "health at any size." Both phrases continued to be used (Bruno, 2014e).

In the early 2000s, Linda Bacon, a researcher, author, and advocate, developed the HAES® framework, emphasizing that health should be defined by a combination of behaviors and well-being rather than solely by weight or size. Bacon's book *Health at Every Size: The Surprising Truth about your Weight (2008)* popularized the HAES® approach. (Bruno, 2013f). The HAES® approach emphasizes health-promoting behaviors, such as intuitive eating, pleasurable physical activity, and prioritizing mental health. Researchers began publishing studies demonstrating that weight loss often had limited long-term success and could even contribute to negative outcomes like disordered eating and weight cycling (e.g., Mann et al., 2007), while simultaneously studies related to using the HAES® approach were published and produced positive outcomes (e.g., Bacon & Aphramor, 2011). The HAES® movement continued growing and expanded beyond academia and research to popular culture, including social media. Health professionals, including dietitians, doctors, and therapists, began integrating HAES® principles into their practices.

In 2003, the Association for Size Diversity and Health (ASDAH) formed and published their first version of HAES® principles. They were revised in 2013 and 2024, and in 2024 they also published a Framework of Care (ASDAH, 2024a). The most recent revisions were developed out of critiques that the HAES® approach was an assimilationist versus liberationist approach, meaning that HAES® "ascribe to ideas that fail to question the morality of healthful discourse" (Williams, 2017, p. 2). Additionally, ASDAH (2024b) acknowledged that their HAES® trademark guidelines and principles needed significant updating, and the guidelines prior to the 2024 revisions were criticized for: (a) neglecting perspectives from Black, fat, and disabled communities; (b) not addressing recent critiques about fatphobia; and (c) failing to prevent "thin-washing" and white-centric approaches. They shared that ASDAH (2024b) recognized that the HAES® movement, particularly among white providers, needed to evolve beyond a white-centric perspective; therefore, they aimed to refocus their efforts on supporting those most affected by anti-fat medical bias, especially superfat+, Black, BIPOC, and disabled individuals, rather than primarily serving thin white people's interests. Examining the history was essential to showing that the 2024 HAES® principles and framework are grounded in fat liberation and Black liberation movements, emphasizing the destigmatization of fat and fat acceptance.

The HAES® (ASDAH, 2024a) principles include: (a): healthcare is a human right for people of all sizes, including those at the highest end of the size spectrum; (b) wellbeing, care, and healing are resources that are both collective and deeply personal; (c) care is fully provided only when free from anti-fat bias and offered with people of all sizes in mind; and (d) health is a sociopolitical construct that reflects the values of society. The HAES® Framework of Care (ASDAH, 2024a) serves as a guide for healthcare providers to become HAES®-aligned. The elements outlined in the framework of care are equally necessary and all need to be incorporated in order to provide HAES®-aligned care.

Those core elements include the following:

1. Grounding in liberatory frameworks: HAES® acknowledges it is not a standalone liberation movement, but rather aims to support broader social justice movements (i.e., Black, fat, disability, queer liberation, womanism, intersectional feminism, etc.) to avoid benefiting only privileged groups while marginalizing others.

2. Patient Bodily Autonomy: HAES® emphasizes that patient autonomy extends beyond just the right to refuse treatment. It includes the right to choose between treatment options after being fully informed of risks and benefits. The practice of restricting healthcare based on Body Mass Index (BMI) or requiring weight loss before treatment typically violates patient autonomy. HAES® providers aim to maximize patient choice in treatment decisions whenever ethically possible.

3. Informed Consent: HAES® emphasizes that true informed consent requires disclosing both known and unknown information, including knowledge gaps due to BMI-based exclusions in medical research. They argue that fatphobia and healthism often bias treatment recommendations and information sharing. True informed consent should be unbiased and support patient autonomy in decision-making.

4. Compassionate Care: HAES® providers aim to develop genuine empathy (not pity) by learning about diverse life experiences and how they affect people's health and healthcare relationships. They actively seek out different perspectives to provide more compassionate, understanding care.

5. Critical analysis, application, and execution of research and medical recommendations related to weight: HAES® originated partly from the Fat Underground activists who challenged medical advice after finding discrepancies between research and healthcare recommendations regarding weight and health. HAES® emphasizes that anti-fat bias continues to influence medical research, clinical training, and healthcare policy, requiring providers to critically examine how weight bias affects their practice and understanding.

6. Skills and equipment to provide compassionate and comprehensive care for fat people's bodies: HAES® providers must develop practical skills and equipment for treating larger bodies effectively. This includes learning appropriate protocols for weight discussions, physical examinations, and treatments that typical medical training may not address.

7. Provider Roles and Responsibilities: HAES® providers use ethical and liberation-focused frameworks to guide their care decisions, particularly given their role as gatekeepers in the medical system. They also focus on harm reduction strategies to help patients navigate a weight-biased healthcare environment.

8. Tools that support wellbeing and healing with contributing to oppression: HAES® providers focus on supporting health goals without emphasis on weight loss. They reclaim tools like nutrition and physical activity from the diet industry, help patients develop healthier relationships with food and movement, and offer treatment options for various health conditions that do not depend on weight loss.

9. Addressing Your Anti-Fat Bias: HAES® requires all providers to recognize and address their internalized and external weight biases, beliefs, attitudes, and practices since they can impact their practice and patient care.

10. Addressing Systemic Anti-Fat Bias: HAES® providers commit to fighting systemic anti-fat bias through challenging the BMI system, reforming the Medical Industrial Complex, and advocating for conditions so that all people have access to equitable, comprehensive care.

In conclusion, the Health at Every Size® (HAES®) approach has evolved through a history of activism, research, and critical reflection on the harm caused by weight stigma and diet culture. Emerging from the body liberation and feminist movements, HAES® challenges traditional views of health by shifting the focus away from weight and weight loss and toward behaviors that support overall well-being. The 2024 revisions to the HAES® principles and framework support a deeper commitment to fat liberation and acknowledging and affirming populations most impacted by anti-fat medical bias, including superfat+, Black, BIPOC, and disabled individuals. By rejecting the BMI system and working to dismantle the Medical Industrial Complex (i.e., network of institutions, businesses, and organizations, driven by profit that shapes the production, delivery, and regulation of healthcare; Relman, 1980), HAES-aligned providers are helping to create a healthcare environment that values patient autonomy, combats discrimination, and supports health at every size. The goal is to ensure that all individuals, especially those in larger bodies from intersectional identities, have access to the care, respect, and resources they need to live fulfilling lives.

CERTIFICATIONS, TRAININGS, AND LICENSURE AND DEGREE REQUIREMENTS

There is no standardized training, certification, nor accreditation endorsed by ASDAH for healthcare providers to become HAES®-aligned; however, they declare on their website that they are currently developing a curriculum (ASDAH, 2024c). They also host a biannual virtual conference, trainings, and events to "deepen our understanding of health equity, improving access to healthcare, and abolishing weight-centric care" (ASDAH, 2024d, para 1). Information can be found on their website. Some of these trainings and events are only available for paying members of ASDAH, while others are open to community members.

The HAES® Framework of Care can be used by dietitians, nutritionists, mental health professionals, medical doctors, nurses and nurse practitioners, physical therapists, personal trainers, fitness instructors, and health coaches. Many of these professions require advanced training, degrees, and licensure or certification to practice; however, there is currently no required training or special certification to become a HAES®-aligned provider. However, ASDAH (2024c) is currently working on a HAES® Healthcare Provider database, but the timeline and details are evolving to ensure providers and professionals are thoroughly vetted.

One of the major scope of practice issues is related to the lack of required training, certification, or licensure to become a HAES®-aligned provider. HAES-aligned providers are typically healthcare providers, mental healthcare practitioners, or physical and fitness related providers. The lack of required formalized training opens the doors for anyone to provide HAES® training or call themselves a HAES®-aligned practitioner. Practically, that means that a person who advertises themselves as a "coach" could use the HAES-approach without any degree or certification. It does appear that ASDAH (2024b) is working to address this by enforcing trademark guidelines and by creating an application for HAES®-aligned providers to be officially recognized on their provider list. They also offer trainings and events, but there is no formalized training one can take to become a HAES®-aligned provider. It is essentially the opposite, i.e., train yourselves to become HAES®-aligned by implementing our principles and framework of care, and then we will let you know if you qualify to be on our list.

HAES®-aligned practitioners will not help clients reach their goals of losing weight. The HAES® framework is based in liberation frameworks, which means that rather than telling a client their weight is a problem, HAES®-aligned providers work to dismantle the oppressive systems that continue to marginalize fat people (ASDAH, 2024a). HAES®-aligned practitioners believe "that any focus on weight loss is harmful and unethical" (Millner, n.d., para. 3). Healthcare providers and mental health professionals work to promote the well-being of their clients and avoid harming their clients; this is written into many of their ethical codes (e.g., ACA Code of Ethics, 2014, Preamble, A.1.a).

General Cost

There is no cost associated with becoming a HAES®-aligned provider because there is no required formalized training, degree, certification, or licensure; however, ASDAH (2024e) does offer membership for those who support the mission, vision, and values of ASDAH and those whose profession or advocacy aligns with the HAES principles. There are webinars and events that are only available for ASDAH paying members (ASDAH 2024d).

EVIDENCE-INFORMED APPROACH

There is a decent body of research supporting the use of HAES® as an approach for promoting the health of individuals, including fat individuals, suggesting it is an "evidence-informed approach" (Gao & Raffoul, 2024, p. 306). Mensinger et al. (2016) studied the implementation of the HAES® approach versus a weight-loss program and found at post-intervention that the HAES® group had greater improvements in their LDL cholesterol and intuitive eating; whereas, the weight-loss group had greater reductions in BMI, weight, and temporary decreases in dietary risk. They concluded that health benefits can be achieved and sustained without focusing on weight loss. Clarke et al. (2024) conducted a metanalysis of 128 studies using the HAES® approach and found that HAES® interventions produced similar results to weight-based interventions on anthropometric (e.g., BMI, waist-to-hip ratio) and cardiometabolic (e.g. blood pressure, lipids, glucose) outcomes. Berman et al. (2022) studied the use of a HAES®/ACT treatment known as Accept Yourself (AY)! compared to Weight Watchers (WW) on depression, eating disorder symptoms, and weight gain. Participants in both groups improved in both self-reported and clinician-rated depression, but the reduction of self-reported depression in the AY group was greater than the WW group. Neither group showed improvement in fitness, and group members in the WW group increased in eating disorder symptoms and weight gain. Additionally, practitioners, such as dietitians, who use the HAES® framework are less likely to engage in stigmatizing behaviors towards their clients, such as weight blaming (Wijayatung et al., 2024).

CAUTIONS AND LIMITATIONS

Although the HAES®-approach offers a transformative, weight-inclusive framework that prioritizes health-promoting behaviors over body size, it also presents a range of ethical considerations for practitioners. These considerations involve questions about the role of medical interventions, client autonomy, navigating societal pressures related to body image and health, and practitioner bias. HAES®-aligned providers do not promote weight loss, but there may be times an individual's medical doctor necessitates weight loss for medical-related reasons. For example, there are BMI restrictions on medical interventions, such as In Vitro Fertilization (IVF; Boots et al., 2024). This creates an ethical dilemma for HAES®-providers: How can they promote client autonomy and holistic well-being while not focusing on weight loss required by a medical professional? First, the practitioner should advocate to the medical provider for a change in this requirement, but if this is unsuccessful, then they will need to decide whether to adjust their approach to meet their clients' needs or if referring them to another provider would be more beneficial.

Many clients might seek treatment from healthcare providers with an expectation they must lose weight to achieve better health. This expectation is driven by societal norms and pervasive diet culture. HAES®-aligned providers might feel compelled to educate their clients about the harms to diet culture and urge them to adopt a weight inclusive, fat positive approach. If a client is not wanting this, then this can hurt the relationship or ultimately cause the client to withdraw from treatment with that provider. Practitioners must be mindful of the ethical responsibility to challenge harmful cultural narratives that equate health with thinness, while at the same time recognizing that some clients may not be ready to embrace HAES® principles. This will present an ethical dilemma, requiring a decision on whether the provider should make adjustments to accommodate the client's needs or if referring them to another provider would be more helpful.

All healthcare and mental health providers have biases they must address to provide culturally sensitive care (Merino et al., 2018). Practitioners adopting the HAES®-approach are not immune to their own implicit biases, including weight bias. Internalized weight stigma or assumptions about a client's health based on their body size can unknowingly affect treatment recommendations and interactions with clients (Byrd et al., 2023). Practitioners have an ethical responsibility to be aware of how their personal biases may influence their practice and take measures to address these biases and ensure they do not impede client care. Engaging in ongoing cultural sensitivity and bias training, supervision, and consultation can help practitioners to continue to address their biases.

QUALITIES AND VALUES NECESSARY FOR HAES® PROVIDERS

Implementing the HAES®-framework requires a unique blend of personal and professional qualities that align with its core values of body diversity, weight inclusivity, and social justice. To successfully integrate HAES® principles into practice, healthcare providers and professionals need to cultivate specific mindsets, skills, and values that support an environment of compassion, affirmation, and holistic care for individuals of all body sizes. There are several qualities that contribute to success in implementing the HAES® approach. Open-mindedness and ongoing self-reflection are necessary, because HAES®-aligned providers must possess an openness to rethinking traditional health paradigms and a willingness to challenge deeply ingrained assumptions about weight, health, and body size. They must also possess an awareness of anti-fat bias and how societal attitudes toward fatness influence their treatment of clients and be committed to challenging these biases at every level—personal, professional, and institutional. An ongoing commitment to cultural humility is also an essential value for a HAES®-aligned provider. HAES®-aligned practitioners must recognize that experiences of body image, health, and wellness are shaped by cultural, racial, socioeconomic, and disability factors. This includes understanding that the effects of weight stigma are not the same for everyone and are more detrimental for marginalized groups such as Black, Indigenous, and People of Color (BIPOC), as well as people with disabilities. Practitioners should develop cultural humility and be open to learning from clients about their lived experiences. This involves actively seeking knowledge about the intersectional impacts of fatphobia, racism, ableism, and other forms of discrimination, as well as adapting care to be more inclusive and equitable.

SUMMARY

In conclusion, the Health at Every Size® (HAES®) approach offers a transformative shift in how we conceptualize health, emphasizing well-being and self-care over weight loss and body size. Rooted in the body liberation and feminist movements, HAES® challenges the harmful impact of diet culture and weight-based discrimination, promoting a more inclusive and compassionate healthcare model for individuals of all body sizes. The recent revisions to the HAES® principles and framework reflect a deeper commitment to addressing the needs of marginalized communities, including those impacted by fatphobia, racism, and ableism. By aligning with HAES®, healthcare providers embrace a holistic, client-centered approach that prioritizes bodily autonomy, compassion, and the deconstruction of oppressive systems. Although there are challenges to fully integrating HAES® principles, such as overcoming biases and navigating cultural expectations, the ultimate goal remains clear: to foster an environment where all individuals, especially fat people, from historically marginalized groups, receive the care, dignity, and support they deserve, regardless of size or shape.

Dr. Heidi L. Henry (she/her) is an Assistant Professor at St. Bonaventure University, where she teaches in the fully online CACREP-accredited School and Clinical Mental Health (CMH) counseling programs. She holds a PhD in Counselor Education from Sam Houston State University and a Master's degree in Community Counseling from Louisiana State University. Since January 2018, Dr. Henry has been a counselor educator and is a Licensed Professional Counselor in both Texas and Pennsylvania. Her professional counseling experience spans both school and clinical settings. Her research focuses on addressing mental health and educational disparities among diverse and historically marginalized communities, with a particular emphasis on issues related to body size and fatness.

hhenry@sbu.edu

REFERENCES

American Counseling Association. (2014). *ACA code of ethics*. Author. https://www.counseling.org/docs/default-source/ethics/2014-aca-code-of-ethics.pdf

Association for Size Diversity and Health. (2024a). *Health At Every Size® principles*. https://asdah.org/haes/

Association for Size Diversity and Health. (2024b). *Trademark guidelines*. https://asdah.org/trademark-guidelines/

Association for Size Diversity and Health. (2024c). *Contact ASDAH*. https://asdah.org/contact/

Association for Size Diversity and Health. (2024d). *Events*. https://asdah.org/events/

Association for Size Diversity and Health. (2024e). *Membership*. https://asdah.org/join/

Bacon, L., & Aphramor, L. (2011). Weight science: Evaluating the evidence for a paradigm shift. *Nutrition Journal, 10*, Article 9. https://doi.org/10.1186/1475-2891-10-9

Berman, M. I., Park, J., Kragenbrink, M. E., & Hegel, M. T. (2022). Accept yourself! A pilot randomized controlled trial of a self-acceptance-based treatment for large-bodied women with depression. *Behavior Therapy, 53*(5), 913-926. https://doi.org/10.1016/j.beth.2022.03.002

Boots, C. E., Gloff, M., Lustik, S. J., & Vitek, W. (2024). Addressing weight bias in reproductive medicine: A call to revisit body mass index restrictions for in vitro fertilization treatment. *Fertility & Sterility, 122*(2), 204-210. https://doi.org/10.1016/j.fertnstert.2024.05.140

Bruno, B. A. (2013a). *History of the Health At Every Size® movement, part 1*. https://asdah.org/history-of-the-health-at-every-size-movement-part-1/

Bruno, B. A. (2013b). *History of the Health At Every Size® movement--the 1970s and 80s (part 2)*. https://asdah.org/history-of-the-health-at-every-size-movement-the-1970s-and-80s-part-2/

Bruno, B. A. (2013c). *History of the Health At Every Size® movement--the early 1990s (part 3)*. https://asdah.org/history-of-the-health-at-every-size-movement-the-early-1990s-part-3/

Bruno, B. A. (2013d). *History of the Health At Every Size® movement--the mid-to late 1990s (part 4)*. https://asdah.org/history-of-the-health-at-every-size-movement-the-mid-to-late-1990s-part-4/

Bruno, B. A. (2013e). *History of the Health At Every Size® movement--early 21st century (part 5)*. https://asdah.org/history-of-the-health-at-every-size-movement-late-1990s-part-5/

Bruno, B. A. (2013f). *History of the Health At Every Size® movement--early 21st century (part 7)*. https://asdah.org/history-of-the-health-at-every-size-movement-early-21st-century-part-7/

Byrd, R., Dolbier, C., Whited, M., & Carels, R. A. (2023). The role of weight stigma in health care avoidance and mistrust among pregnant women. *Stigma and Health*. Advance online publication. http://dx.doi.org/10.1037/sah0000481

Clarke, E. D., Stanford, J., Gomez-Martin, M., & Collins, C. E. (2024). Revising the impact of Health at Every Size® interventions on health and cardiometabolic related outcomes: An updated systematic review with meta-analysis. *Nutrition & Dietetics, 81*(3), 261-282. https://doi.org/10.1111/1747-0080.12869

Gao, C., & Raffoul, A. (2024). Incorporating a Health at Every Size approach in Canadian medicine. *British Columbia Medical Journal, 66*(8), 306-309. https://bcmj.org/articles/incorporating-health-every-size-approach-canadian-medicine

Kight, D. (2014). *Uncovering the history of fat acceptance: Lew Louderback's 1967 article.* https://powerfulhunger.com/powerful_hunger_blog/history-of-fat-acceptance-lew-louderback-1967-article/

Mann, T., Tomiyama, A. J., Westling, E., Lew, A.-M., Samuels, B., & Chatman, J. (2007). Medicare's search for effective obesity treatments: Diets are not the answer. *American Psychologist, 62*(3), 220-233. https://doi.org/10.1037/0003-066x.62.3.220

Mensinger, J., L., Calogero, R. M., Stranges, S., & Tylka, T. L. (2016). A weight-neutral versus weight-loss approach for health promotion in women with high BMI: A randomized-controlled trial. *Appetite, 105*(1), 364-374. http://dx.doi.org/10.1016/j.appet.2016.06.006

Merino, Y., Adams, L., & Hall, W. J. (2018). Implicit bias and mental health professionals: Priorities and directions for research. *Psychiatric Services, 69*(6), 723-725. https://doi.org/10.1176/appi.ps.201700294

Millner, R. (n. d.) *Health at Every Size® weight inclusive care.* https://rachelmillnertherapy.com/haes/

Relman, A. S. (1980). The new medical-industrial complex. *The New England Journal of Medicine, 303*(17), 963-970. https://doi.org/10.1056/NEJM198010233031703

Simic, Z. (2015). Fat as a feminist issue: A history. In H. Hester & C. Walters (Eds.), *Fat sex: New directions in theory and activism* (pp. 15–35). Ashgate.

Wijayatung, N. N., Bailey, D., Klobodu, S. S., Donatello, R., Knight, K. & Dhurandhar, E. J. (2024). Alignment with Health at Every Size may be associated with lower weight blaming among registered dietitians in the United States. *Topics in Clinical Nutrition, 39*(3), 238-247. https://www.doi.org/10.1097/TIN.0000000000000371

Williams, A. A. (2017). Fat people of color: Emergent intersectional discourse online. *Social Sciences, 6*(15), 1-16. https://doi.org/10.3390/socsci6010015

Heart Assisted Therapy (HAT)

BILL OWENBY, EDD, MC, FAAETS, DAAETS, DCMHS, LPC, LAAC, NCC, CCMHC, ACS, DIPLOMATE, FELLOW

Heart Assisted Therapy (HAT) is an integrative, trauma-informed psychotherapeutic method that combines somatic awareness, mindfulness, and heart-focused techniques to facilitate emotional healing and resolution of psychological distress. Developed by Dr. John Hartung, HAT is designed to access core emotional experiences stored in the body and heart center, integrating those experiences with cognitive and behavioral insights. It is rooted in the belief that healing comes from connecting to and processing emotions through the heart, supported by intentional breathing, body-based awareness, and guided dialogue.

HISTORICAL BACKGROUND

Heart Assisted Therapy was developed in the early 2000s by Dr. John Hartung as a structured yet flexible clinical tool to address trauma and emotional dysregulation. Drawing from the fields of neuroscience, somatic psychology, energy psychology, and transpersonal therapy, Dr. Hartung sought to create a therapy that addressed the physiological, emotional, cognitive, and spiritual aspects of healing. Clinical application of HAT has been documented since 2009, with practitioners using the method in individual, group, and trauma therapy settings. The development of HAT aligns with contemporary findings in psychophysiology, particularly in relation to heart-brain coherence and autonomic nervous system regulation.

IDEAL CLIENT POPULATIONS

HAT is suitable for clients who:

- Are seeking trauma resolution or have a history of PTSD, CPTSD, or complex trauma.
- Struggle with emotional dysregulation, anxiety, depression, or grief.
- Are open to somatic or body-based psychotherapy approaches.
- Are interested in mind-body integration, spirituality, or heart-centered practices.
- Have not fully responded to traditional cognitive-behavioral or talk therapy modalities.

HAT is often used with adolescents, adults, and older adults, but can be adapted for use with children through developmentally appropriate modifications.

IDEAL PROFESSIONAL FOR TRAINING

HAT training is best suited for:

- Licensed mental health counselors, psychologists, and clinical social workers.
- Trauma specialists and EMDR-certified professionals seeking integrative methods.
- Body-based therapists, including somatic experiencing practitioners.
- Integrative and holistic mental health providers.
- Clinicians comfortable with mindfulness, emotional processing, and energy psychology.

THEORETICAL FOUNDATIONS

HAT integrates multiple theoretical perspectives:

- **Polyvagal Theory:** HAT emphasizes autonomic regulation through breath and heart connection, promoting vagal tone and nervous system safety.
- **Somatic Psychology:** The use of body awareness and positioning enhances emotion identification and processing.
- **Attachment Theory:** HAT supports reprocessing of attachment wounds through heart-centered connection and corrective emotional experiences.
- **Mindfulness and Compassion Practices:** Clients are guided to access inner stillness and self-compassion during emotional recall.
- **Energy Psychology:** Incorporates subtle energetic awareness of heart coherence and emotional flow.

Core Techniques and Interventions

- **Heart Focusing:** Centering attention on the heart area to ground, soothe, and access emotional material.
- **Somatic Tracking:** Clients are invited to notice sensations and shifts in body awareness as they process.
- **Emotional Unburdening:** A structured process helps clients release trapped emotional energy linked to trauma.
- **Mindful Inquiry and Dialogue:** Therapists use open-ended questions to support reflection and integration.
- **Resource Anchoring:** Positive internal states and memories are accessed to support safety and regulation.
- **Coherent Breathing:** Breathwork is used to align physiological and emotional states.

TRAINING, CERTIFICATION, AND REQUIREMENTS

HAT is taught through the Heart Assisted Therapy Institute under the direction of Dr. John Hartung.

1. **Introductory Training (HAT Level I)**
   - Time Commitment: 3 days (24 CE hours)
   - Format: In-person or online
   - Cost: $595–$695
   - Prerequisites: Master's-level mental health professional or currently licensed clinician
   - Website: https://heartassistedtherapy.net
2. **Advanced Training (HAT Level II and Consultation)**
   - Additional 3-day course + case consultation
   - Focus on deepening clinical application and adapting for specific populations
   - Required for HAT Certification
3. **Certification Requirements**
   - Completion of Level I and II
   - Supervised case review or written reflection
   - Ongoing education recommended every 2 years
4. **Continuing Education Credit**
   - HAT training is approved by NBCC for continuing education for LPCs and LMFTs

Scope of Practice Considerations

- HAT is appropriate for licensed clinicians within their scope of practice.

- Best used in trauma treatment, emotional regulation, and integrative therapy settings.
- Not a substitute for crisis intervention or medication for acute psychiatric conditions.
- Ethical informed consent and discussion of somatic/introspective work are essential.
- HAT should be offered in alignment with client preferences and treatment goals.

CAUTIONS AND LIMITATIONS

- Not appropriate for clients with dissociation or active psychosis unless modified and used with caution.
- Requires careful pacing for clients with complex trauma.
- Should be facilitated only by trained clinicians familiar with trauma reactions and somatic processing.
- Must be integrated with evidence-based practices when treating severe mental illness.

RESEARCH AND CLINICAL EVIDENCE

Clinical studies conducted through the Heart Assisted Therapy Institute have shown promising results:

- Clients reported significant reductions in anxiety, trauma symptoms, and emotional reactivity after 6–10 sessions.
- Qualitative feedback highlighted feelings of peace, integration, and emotional release.
- Preliminary findings suggest efficacy in both group and individual therapy settings.
- Ongoing research efforts continue to validate outcomes for diverse clinical populations.
- See: https://heartassistedtherapy.net/hat-clinical-research

SUMMARY

Heart Assisted Therapy is a trauma-informed, heart-centered, and body-aware therapy modality that empowers clients to reconnect with their emotional core in a safe and supportive way. By combining somatic processing, mindfulness, and heart-based techniques, HAT provides mental health professionals with a compassionate and effective tool for treating trauma and emotional dysregulation. For clinicians seeking integrative methods grounded in contemporary science and timeless wisdom, HAT offers a unique and transformative approach to healing.

I hold two independent licenses in the states of Arizona and Ohio, supervisory status in Arizona, along with a substance abuse license in Arizona. I am board certified as a Diplomate and Clinical Mental Health Specialist, an Approved Clinical Supervisor, Nationally Certified Counselor, a Certified Clinical Mental Health Counselor, NeuroLinguistic Programming Practitioner, and a Clinical Trauma Specialist for Individuals and Family including EMDR Therapy and NET. I completed my training in Animal-Assisted Therapy and Pet Handlers certification in order to evaluate and incorporate the human-animal bond in therapy. I am the sole author and creator of the SxC Model of ESA Evaluation. My research interests surround post-traumatic growth, resiliency, strengths-based therapy, positive psychology, mindfulness, Animal-Assisted Therapy, Sandtray Therapy, Creative approaches in therapy, and martial arts in mental health. I have presented at local, state, regional, national, and international levels on various topics including personality traits, licensure reciprocity challenges, Sandtray and supervision, and Animal-Assisted Therapy within supervision. eonbllc@gmail.com

References

Hartung, J. (2024). Heart Assisted Therapy: A Clinical Manual. Heart Assisted Therapy Institute.

Heart Assisted Therapy Institute. (2024). HAT Clinical Research. https://heartassistedtherapy.net/hat-clinical-research

Porges, S. W. (2011). The polyvagal theory: Neurophysiological foundations of emotions, attachment, communication, and self-regulation.

Norton. Ogden, P., Minton, K., & Pain, C. (2006). Trauma and the body: A sensorimotor approach to psychotherapy.

Norton. Schore, A. N. (2012). The science of the art of psychotherapy.

Norton. Siegel, D. J. (2010). Mindsight: The new science of personal transformation. Bantam.

Heart Rate Variability

LINCOLN STOLLER, PHD, CHT, CCPCPR

Your pulse is not a simple, regular heartbeat varying only with exertion. While we feel our heartbeat's dominant rhythm, it has many harmonics of which we're unaware. Some of these harmonics reflect the passage of blood through our tissues, and others act as responsive metronomes that coordinate systems in our body.

The vagus nerve establishes a connection between the brain and the organs in the body. Most of the signals in the vagus travel from the organs to the brain to inform and maintain homeostasis. While we identify our personalities as controlling our functions, the central nervous system tells another story: our body plays a major role in regulating our moods and, perhaps, defining our personality.

While it keeps an even tempo, the rhythms of the heart are not simple or regular. The flow of blood through our bodies is a combination of laminar and chaotic. These flow patterns are indicators of the health of many bodily systems, and the more aware we are of these rhythms the more we can coordinate their functions. Surprisingly, we can train better cardiac rhythms to improve both physiological and psychological health.

RHYTHMS

Heart rhythms range from fast atrial oscillations of a hundredth of a second, to slow circadian rhythms varying over twenty-four hours. These rhythms coordinate arousal, response, blood chemistry, gut activity, emotional balance, neurological coordination, hormone production, diurnal activity, the immune system, and probably everything else!

Rhythm is measured as the time between repeating structures. This also involves the shape of the pulse which reflects the pulse's harmonic components. Focusing on beats and the structures they contain measures rhythm in what's called the time domain. This is what is easiest for us to sense and control because the time domain is sequential and specific, which is consonant with our awareness. Rhythm in the time domain is given by the pulse—which we can count—and correlates with our breath, level of arousal, and sense of time.

The harmonics in the pulse measure the pulse's rhythms in the frequency domain. This is measured as average patterns over time. Measuring these patterns requires their recording, averaging, comparing, and tabulation. Our awareness of harmonic patterns is poor.

We can hear auditory harmonics, and we can feel harmonics in our body as moods, comfort levels, and our ability to focus. Our temporal control affects our ability to rationalize, intellectualize, predict, and speak. We can slow ourselves down or speed ourselves up. We can be more or less reflective or reactive, and we can create more or less emotional environments.

We are more aware of ourselves and our heart rhythms in the time domain because we think in sequential terms. We are more aware of how we control ourselves in terms of cause and effect. While we are less aware of our cardiopulmonary and cognitive frequencies, we have some awareness of and control over them.

The shape of our pulse is a qualitative measure that combines rhythm and structure. A changing rhythm, which is what variability amounts to, requires changes in the dominant frequencies. Higher frequencies contribute to the pulses' small-scale structure.

A completely smooth, oscillating pulse requires the organization of all frequencies. We can see this in smoothly oscillating waves of change in heartbeat, blood oxygenation, blood pressure, and muscle tone.

We experience frequency control as a state of body and mind. Descriptions such as agitation, vigilance, relaxation, and flow-state describe dominant mind-body frequencies. We have varying degrees of psychological control over them. Psychologically impaired people typically have less control over these frequencies. The frequencies over which a person lacks control can be specific to their impairment (Montano et al. 2009; Forte 2019).

Something similar appears to be described by Traditional Chinese Medicine and its Theory of Pulses, which uses 28 qualitative, poetic descriptions of the pulse taken manually (Al-Shura 2014). Our Western theory of the pulse is based on blood flow and the vascular system. The Eastern theory of pulses is based on life energy, or chi, and energetic centers in the body.

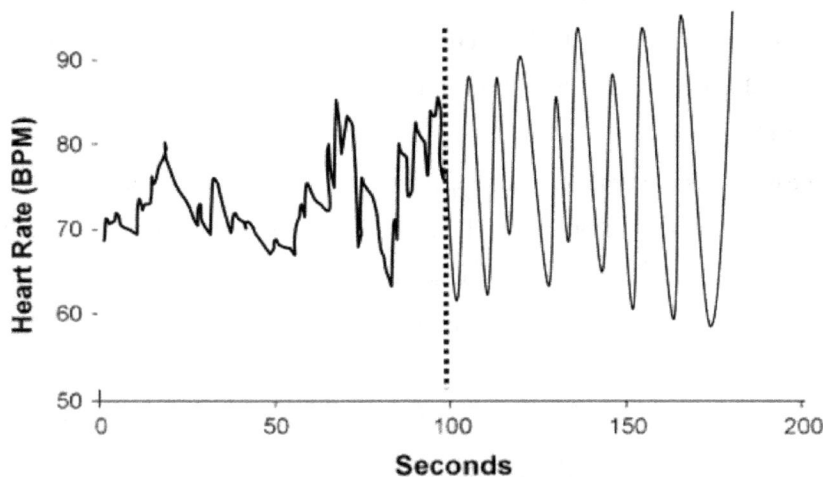

"Figure 1: Heart rate variability pattern for an individual participating in a deep breathing session: prior to initiating the deep breathing technique (left of the dotted line) and after starting with the technique (right of the dotted line). A change in emotional stress correlates with the shift from an erratic and disordered heart rhythm pattern (low coherence) to a sine wave-like (high coherence) pattern." From Aritzeta et al. (2017)

The body-mind connection is the key to understanding the importance of the heart's rhythms. The degree to which these pulse frequencies reflect and adapt is termed heart rate variability (HRV). The term is not precise because it includes all rhythms and responses, so we have to discriminate which of the body's systems we're talking about.

Microsecond heart rhythm changes are internal to the heart's coordinated function. Changes over periods from 2.5 to 7 seconds correlate with respiration and are called the high-frequency band. Variability in this range is associated with emotional lability.

Changes over time spans of 7 to 25 seconds correlate with blood pressure and vascular elasticity. This is the time scale over which we control our general blood pressure. Decreased rhythmic variability in what's called the low-frequency range correlates with age, morbidity, and impaired baroreflex function. Higher HRV has been correlated with lower diastolic blood pressure (Yugar et al. 2023).

The very-low frequency band describes variations in the heart's rhythm over periods from 25 to 300 seconds. These changes indicate a person's ability to modulate arousal. A lack of very-low frequency variability is typical of people with chronic tension, such as post-traumatic stress (McCraty 2015).

A healthy personality responds to arousing and sedating situations, and a healthy heart and circulatory system responds similarly. And because of the extensive connections between the circulatory system and the mind, mental variability is reflected in heart rate variability. These variabilities differ according to the time and frequency ranges over which they're measured and encouraged.

Just as a healthy mind responds smoothly and appropriately, the circulatory system should too. We can see the mind's health in the heart's rhythms, and we can improve the mind's health by improving the heart's rhythms. This can be done with psychotherapy, physiotherapy, and biofeedback.

"Heart rate variability reflects the capability of an organism to adapt and recover. Patients with reduced heart rate variability might need additional psychotherapeutic sessions to achieve the same symptom improvements than patients with retained heart rate variability. (The degree to which) psychotherapy might increase vagal activity can be indexed non-invasively by measuring heart rate and calculating interbeat variability, i.e., heart rate variability."

"High variability means greater opportunity for the organism to adapt to internal and external challenges. Consequently, reduced HRV is a predictor of disease risk, e.g., higher inflammatory state, morbidity, myocardial infarction, and mortality. HRV was found to be reduced in depression and anxiety disorders." (Balint et al. 2023)

CARDIO-PULMONARY RHYTHM

Most of the heart's energy is expended in pumping blood through the lungs, not the body. The heart and lung collaborate in perfusion of gasses into and out of the blood. The absorption of oxygen is enhanced by an increase in blood pressure, while improved release of carbon dioxide correlates with lower blood pressure. A healthy heart facilitates these exchanges by beating more rapidly on the inhale and more slowly on the exhale (Yugar et al. 2023). This difference is only a few percent of the pulse rate and is not cognitively obvious, but it's easily trained using a pulse sensor driving a graphical display of HRV.

"Respiratory Sinus Arrhythmia (RSA) is the variation in heart rate (HR) that accompanies breathing, such that HR increases during inhalation and decreases during exhalation... It is mediated by the vagus nerve, a major parasympathetic nerve, such that it is stimulated in periods of calmness and relaxation and depressed during periods of stress. The amount of RSA can be quantified by the amplitude of peak-to-trough excursions in heart rate that occur with each breath. The amplitude of changes (in beats per minute) tends to be greater in healthy people than in sick people, in younger people than in older people, and in people who are aerobically more fit... those with major social deficits, particularly autism, have very low levels of RSA. Among married couples, those with good marriages tend to have high levels of RSA while interacting, while those with bad marriages tend to have less. Although little research has been done yet on effects of heart rate variability biofeedback on sociability, this is a potential application." (Lehrer et al. 2020)

Since you have control of your breathing rate, it's easy to train a person to coordinate breathing with their pulse when the pulse is displayed using a biofeedback device. People with responsive cardiopulmonary and neuropsychological systems are able to quickly improve their heart rate variability, often dramatically in my experience. People with poor cardiopulmonary or neuropsychological health have more difficulty, but improvement will be more important for their health.

"Cardiac coherence refers to a stable state of increased synchrony between the rhythms of different oscillatory systems, typically heart rate, respiration, and blood pressure. In practice, this coherent state is reflected by a more ordered and sine wave-like Heart Rate Variability waveform, oscillating at a frequency approximating 0.1 Hz, the frequency at which the phase synchrony of heart rate and respiration occurs." (Pham et al. 2021)

BIOFEEDBACK AND PSYCHOTHERAPY

Some studies claim the effectiveness of psychotherapy can be measured by its effect on HRV (Balint et al. 2023; Kiema et al. 2014). While interesting, it's unclear how therapists can make use of this.

More efficacious is the combined application of heart rate variability biofeedback (HRVB) and psychotherapy to improve outcome measures in both physiological and psychological tone. Healthy people can quickly improve their HRV through inexpensive, noninvasive biofeedback. Those with ailments also improve, and while it would be reasonable to expect that greater effort would be required, the benefits would also be greater.

"Studies have found that HRVB does, in fact, produce improvement in a variety of physical and emotional conditions including anxiety, depression, hypertension, asthma, and pain, as well as improvement in various kinds of human performance including mental concentration and agility, athletics, dance, and music. The technique is easily learned and can be trained using inexpensive equipment, including several free smart phone applications. HRVB has been proposed as a psychotherapy component that specifically targets the neurovegetative components of emotional problems and may improve treatment effectiveness. Most people can achieve high-amplitude oscillations in HR after just a few minutes of training, and almost everyone can master the technique within one to four sessions of coaching." (Lehrer et al. 2020)

Lehrer et al. (2020) compared the results of 58 controlled studies of HRVB targeting various biological and psychological measures of health. Ten studies show HRVB yielded improvements at a 95% certainty, 41 showed HRVB yielded improvements at less than 95% certainty, and 3 showed no improvement. In 10 studies, the control group showed more improvement than the training group, but with less than 95% certainty. In no study did the control group outperform the training group with 95% or greater certainty.

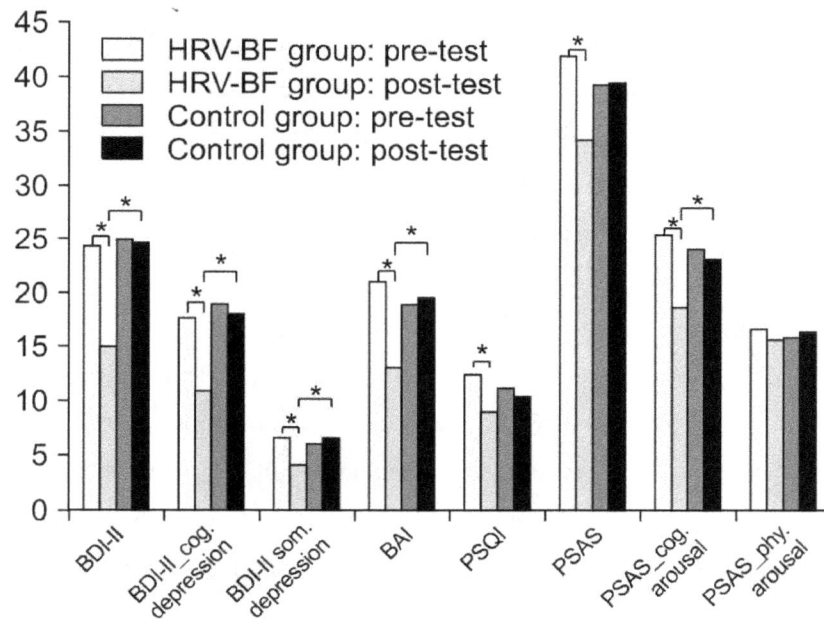

"The psychological questionnaires at pre- and post-tests for the heart rate variability biofeedback (HRVB) and control groups. BDI-II, Beck Depression Inventory-II; cog., cognitive; som., somatic; BAI, Beck Anxiety Inventory; PSQI, Pittsburgh Sleep Quality Index; PSAS, Pre-Sleep Arousal Scale; phy., physical. (* indicates p<0.05)." Fig. 1 from Lin et al. 2019.

Referring to their study of 20 subjects with major depressive disorder (MDD) who did or did not receive psychotherapy combined with HRVB training, compared to controls who either did or did not receive HRVB, Caldwell and Steffen (2018) report:

"It appears that combining heart rate variability biofeedback training with psychotherapy has the potential to significantly improve therapy outcomes."

TRAINING HRV

Biofeedback training involves presenting the user with a real-time display of their physiological states so that they can either adjust their state or recognize the actions that affect it. HRV training can be done using inexpensive, noninvasive equipment at home or in a clinician's office. Clinic-based training has the benefit of more careful training and data analysis.

Most HRV feedback data is collected using a finger monitor or ear clip that records the intensity of light transmitted through the tissues. These devices, called photo plethysmographs or PPGs, appear in pulse oximeters integrated into rings, wrist watches, and wrist and body sensors. They are accurate during relaxation and mild stress, but are prone to large errors during any form of exercise. (Singstad et al. 2021). They are useful for biofeedback training when used judiciously.

Biofeedback's salutary effect depends on multiple, simultaneous, real-time indicators presented in an integrated manner and with little or no intellectual instruction. Training requires the feedback, through sight or sound in real time, of information that is otherwise difficult to sense or cannot be sensed at all. The feedback enables the trainee to gain an awareness of which of their actions have a controlling effect.

Reward and inhibition cues are added to the feedback to encourage the trainee to do more or less of whatever is changing the display. Typical rewards include more vibrant colors and clearer sounds, while typical inhibits include faded colors and muted sounds. These cues help teach trainees to control systems in ways that they are otherwise unaware. They can see how they're performing, sense what they're doing to cause the changes in feedback, and get a summary of their performance.

Supervised training ensures the training is regular and effective. Training can also be done at home. When done carefully with an effective tool, training can generate semi-permanent improvements in HRV after a half dozen, 10-minute sessions. With regard to the training of HRV, significant improvements have been reported after a single session of training (Prinsloo 2013). Improvement can be anything from enduring to evanescent depending partly on outside mechanical, medical, behavioral, or situation sources of dysregulation. Clearly, old habits can work against improvements learned through biofeedback.

Here are four HRV biofeedback devices that generate HRV scores based on the shape of the pulse and not just the time between heartbeats. This is a more effective measure of HRV.

Cell Phone Apps

Many cell phone apps are available at little or no cost that offer HRV measurements. They use the smart phone's flashlight to illuminate circulation through the user's finger, and the smart phone's video camera to record the variance of the transmitted light.

These require correct, static placement of the user's finger, and a tonic state of muscles of one's hand to retain correct contact with the phone. As such, they cannot be used during exercise, and they interfere with one's ability to relax. In addition, there is no calibration between the software running on the phone's operating system and the light source and photo sensors of the phone itself.

Cell phone based HRV programs provide an attractive starting point for learning about HRV, but they are a poor option for serious biofeedback training.

Journey to the Wild Divine, Wild Divine, and Healing Rhythms

Variously titled, this game was originally released for desk and laptop Windows-based computers in 2001. While the product is sometimes hard to find, it is inexpensive and has more features than most of the higher priced biofeedback products.

The original Wild Divine combined finger sensors used in various challenges in a fantasy environment. The sensors combined the measurement of Galvanic Skin Response (GSR) with photo plethysmography allowing for feedback based on the combination of emotional arousal and heart rhythm.

Current versions (as of 2023) use a PPG-only sensor incompatible with the original hardware component. The product is now supported by Wild Divine Inc. (https://wilddivine.com/) and runs on Windows, Mac, iOS, and Android operating systems.

Older versions can still be found for sale as used products. The older software will not run on Windows 10 or more recent operating systems in normal mode, but they can be launched in "compatibility mode." This is an option in recent Windows systems that allows the use of software written for older versions of the operating system.

The game element complicates the software beyond a simple training tool, and the variety of graphical challenges train the low frequency components of HRV. In my experience, this combination allows one to improve HRV more quickly than the devices that use only a PPG, or the versions of Wild Divine that rely only on the PPG sensor.

Alive

Closely related to the Wild Divine products, the Alive Personal Biofeedback Software (https://www.somaticvision.com/) originally used the same GSR+PPG combined sensor hardware. Its latest version supports a wide variety of sensors and up to four sensors combined, through the addition of skin temperature and breath monitoring.

Alive provides more choices of audio-visual feedback that are both game-like and involve the control of abstract visual and auditory patterns. It also provides clinical support to train and track multiple training clients using an internet connection.

The advent of ubiquitous mobile technology and virtual reality environments is leading to new feedback displays capable of training more biological metrics. The extent to which biological control can be trained or learned is an open question (Kerr 2023, Stoller 2020). The new forms of biofeedback being developed will open new research questions and create new personal training products.

HeartMath Inner Balance™ Coherence Plus

This 3-module device combines an earlobe PPG sensor wired to a wearable recording device connected by Bluetooth to a cell phone app. Some real-time feedback is provided through the cellphone-based application. Beats per minute is graphically displayed in real time, but the HRV score is delayed until the end of each breath cycle.

The feedback emphasizes the combination of regular breathing and smooth variability in the heartbeat. The cellphone application provides visual feedback for pacing one's breath. Effective HRV training depends on finding one's optimal rate, as this is the rate at which the heart resonates. Optimal pace differs between individuals and the user can adjust this breathing rate, but the setting of the rate is not automatic and relies on the user's adjustment.

HeartMath Emwave2

The Emwave2 is a self-contained, handheld device that records data using a PPG and links to a computer program that can display real-time HRV or historical training results. Its session-generated data is delayed by a few seconds as it displays a HRV score during each breath cycle.

Other Devices

Many wearable training devices that claim to train HRV are recording devices, not training devices. This includes smartwatches, headbands, armbands, and rings that provide downloadable, recorded data. These are monitoring, not training tools. Monitoring can help in discerning the effects of your daily habits, but they do not train your autonomic nervous system.

SUMMARY

All of the devices that purport to provide real-time feedback differ in their responsiveness, sensitivity, accuracy, and data presentation. Delayed feedback makes training less efficient (Whited 2014), and this applies to all devices. The delays programmed into HeartMath's Inner Balance and Emwave devices are minimal.

New devices, algorithms, applications, and combinations are being developed. The optimal device is the one that provides the most accurate, real-time feedback with the least distraction and the most convenience. More can be done in the analysis, combination, and presentation of data. Prices of consumer wearables will continue to drop.

Studies of Heart Rate Variability quickly descend into physiological measures and computational complexity. From a training perspective, this all ignores the simple and startling fact that it is one's mood that affects one's HRV more than any other action or intention.

HRV training is essentially mood training. It is plausible but unproven that training to improve one's HRV can permanently improve one's mood. "Heart rate oscillations can enhance emotion by entraining brain rhythms in ways that enhance regulatory brain networks (Mather and Thayer 2018)."

"HRV was positively associated with positive hedonic tone (cheerfulness) and positive tense arousal (calmness), and these effects were completely mediated by the habitual use of executive emotion regulation strategies." — Geisler et al. (2010)

Learning to regulate one's autonomic nervous system through biofeedback is playing an increasingly important role in psychotherapy. Therapists should inform their clients of the potential benefits of biofeedback training. Psychotherapists who remain uninformed of the value of autonomic nervous system training are under-serving their clients.

Dr. Stoller's research in astronomy, quantum physics, and computation led to work in data management, business automation, and software design. His interest in neurology led to his mentoring with inventors of EEG biofeedback and his expertise as a neurofeedback therapist. Expanding on his interests in altered states and psychopathy, he is certified as a hypnotherapist and clinical counselor. He writes on topics of neuropsychology, and practices as a coach and therapist in British Columbia, Canada.

https://www.mindstrengthbalance.com
https://mindstrengthbalance.substack.com

REFERENCES

Al-Shura, A. N. (2014). Significance of cardiovascular symptoms, Chapter 4 in Integrative Cardiovascular Chinese Medicine, Elsevier. ttps://doi.org/10.1016/B978-0-12-420014-2.00032-6

Aritzeta, A., Soroa, G., Balluerka, N., Muela, A., Gorostiaga, A., and Aliri, J. (2017 Sep). Reducing anxiety and improving academic performance through a biofeedback relaxation training program, *Applied Psychophysiology and Biofeedback, 43* (3):193-202. https://doi.org/10.1007/s10484-017-9367-z

Balint, E. M., et al. (2023). Heart rate variability predicts outcome of short-term psychotherapy at the workplace. *Psychophysiology, 60*:e14150, https://doi.org/10.1111/psyp.14150

Caldwell, Y. T., Steffen, P. R. (2018). Adding HRV biofeedback to psychotherapy increases heart rate variability and improves the treatment of major depressive disorder, *International Journal of Psychophysiology, 131*:96-101. https://doi.org/10.1016/j.ijpsycho.2018.01.001

Geisler, F. C. M., Vennewald, N., Kubiak, T., and Weber, H. (2010 Nov). The impact of heart rate variability on subjective well-being is mediated by emotion regulation, *Personality and Individual Differences 49*: 723-28. https://doi.org/10.1016/j.paid.2010.06.015

Giuseppe Forte, G., Favieri, F., Casagrande, M. (2019 Jul 9). Heart rate variability and cognitive function: A systematic review, Frontiers of. Neuroscience, 13. https://doi.org/10.3389/fnins.2019.00710

Kerr, J. I.; Weibel, R. P., Naegelin, M., Ferrario, A., Schinazi, V. R., La Marca, R., Hoelscher, C., Nater, U. M., von Wangenheim, F. (2023). The effectiveness and user experience of a biofeedback intervention program for stress management supported by virtual reality and mobile technology: a randomized controlled study. *BMC Digital Health, 1*:42. https://doi.org/10.1186/s44247-023-00042-z

Kiema, H, Rantanen, A., Laukka, S., Siipo, A., and Soini, H. (2014). The connection between skilled counseling and client's heart rate variability. *Procedia – Social and Behavioral Sciences, 159*: 802-07. https://doi.org/10.1016/j.sbspro.2014.12.452

Lehrer, P., Kaur, K., Sharma, A., Shah, K., Huseby, R., Bhavsar, J., and Zhang, Y. (2020 May 8). Heart rate variability biofeedback improves emotional and physical health and performance: A systematic review and meta analysis, *Applied Psychophysiology and Biofeedback, 45*:109-125. https://doi.org/10.1007/s10484-020-09466-z

Lin, I-M., Fan, S-Y., Yen, C-F., Yeh, Y-C., Tang, T-C., Huang, M-F., Liu, T-L., Wang, P-W., Lin, H-C., Tsai, H-Y., and Tsai, Y-C. (2019 May 31). Heart rate variability biofeedback increased autonomic activation and improved symptoms of depression and insomnia among patients with Major Depression Disorder, *Clinical Psychopharmacology and Neuroscience, 17* (2):222-32. https://doi.org/10.9758/cpn.2019.17.2.222

Mather, M., and Thayer, J. (2018 Feb). How heart rate variability affects emotion regulation brain networks. *Curr Opin Behav Sci. 19*: 98-104. https://doi.org/10.1016/j.cobeha.2017.12.017

McCraty, R., Shaffer, F. (2015 Jan). Heart rate variability: New perspectives on physiological mechanisms, assessment of self-regulatory capacity, and health risk, *Global Advances in Health and Medicine, 4* (1): 45-61. https://doi.org/10.7453/gahmj.2014.073

Montano, N., Porta, A., Cogliati, C., Costantino, G., Tobaldini, E., Casali, K. R., and Iellamo, F. (2009). Heart rate variability explored in the frequency domain: A tool to investigate the link between heart and behavior, Neuroscience and Behavioral Reviews 33: 71-80. https://doi.org/doi:10.1016/j.neubiorev.2008.07.006

Pham, T., Lau, Z. J., Chen, S. H. A., Makowski, D. (2021 Jun 9). Heart rate variability in psychology: A review of HRV indices and an analysis tutorial, *Sensors, 21*: 3998. https://doi.org/10.3390/s21123998

Prinsloo, G. E., Derman, W. E., Lambert, M. I., and Rauch H. G. L. (2013). The effect of a single episode of short duration heart rate variability biofeedback on measures of anxiety and relaxation states, *International Journal of Stress Management, 20* (4): 391-411. https://doi.org/10.1037/a0034777

Singstad, B., Azulay, N., Bjurstedt, A., Bjørndal, S. S., Drageseth, M. F., Engeset, P., Eriksen, K. Gidey, M. Y., Granum, E. O., Greaker, M. G., Grorud, A. Hewes, S. O., Hou, J., Recha, A. M. L., Matre, C., Seputis, A., Sørensen, A. E., Thøgersen, V., Joten, V. M., Tronstad, C., and Martinsen, O. G. (2021 Jan). Estimation of heart rate variability from finger photoplethysmography during rest, mild exercise and mild mental stress, *Journal of Electrical Bioimpedance, 12* (1): 89-102. https://doi.org/10.2478/joeb-2021-0012

Stoller, L. (2020). Covid-19: Illness and Illumination: A hypnotic exploration. Mind Strength Books. https://www.mindstrengthbalance.com/product/covid-19-illness-illumination/

Yugar, L.B.T., Yugar-Toledo, J.C., Dinamarco, N., Sedenho-Prado, L.G., Moreno, B.V.D., Rubio, T.d.A., Fattori, A., Rodrigues, B., Vilela-Martin, J.F., and Moreno, H. (2023 Feb 19). The

Role of Heart Rate Variability (HRV) in Different Hypertensive Syndromes. *Diagnostics 13* (4). https://www.mdpi.com/2075-4418/13/4/785

Whited, A., Larkin, K.T. & Whited, M. (2014 Jun). Effectiveness of *emWave* biofeedback in improving heart rate variability reactivity to and recovery from stress. *Appl Psychophysiol Biofeedback 39*, 75–88. https://doi.org/10.1007/s10484-014-9243-z

HeartMath Therapy

BILL OWENBY, EdD, MC, FAAETS, DAAETS, DCMHS, LPC, LAAC, NCC, CCMHC, ACS, DIPLOMATE, FELLOW

HeartMath Therapy is an evidence-based intervention that combines biofeedback, self-regulation techniques, and heart-brain coherence strategies to reduce stress, improve emotional balance, and enhance overall well-being. Developed by the HeartMath Institute, this therapy integrates research on heart rhythm variability (HRV) and the physiological impact of emotions, empowering individuals to cultivate resilience and inner balance through scientifically backed techniques.

OVERVIEW OF HEARTMATH THERAPY

HeartMath Therapy is based on the principle that the heart plays a vital role in emotional regulation and cognitive function. By achieving heart coherence—a physiological state where heart rhythms synchronize with the brain and body—individuals can reduce stress, enhance decision-making, and improve physical and mental health outcomes.

Core Principles of HeartMath Therapy

1. **Heart-Brain Coherence**
   o Encourages synchronization between heart rhythms and brain function to improve emotional regulation.
   o Enhances clarity, focus, and stress resilience.
2. **Emotional Self-Regulation**
   o Teaches individuals to recognize and shift emotional states using breathing and visualization techniques.
   o Reduces emotional reactivity and enhances cognitive flexibility.
3. **HRV Biofeedback Training**
   o Utilizes heart rate variability (HRV) monitoring to assess and improve autonomic nervous system balance.
   o Teaches individuals to shift from stress-based physiological patterns to coherence-based states.
4. **Resilience and Well-Being**
   o Empowers individuals with techniques to sustain emotional equilibrium.
   o Strengthens adaptability to life's challenges through heart-centered awareness.

Applications of HeartMath Therapy

Stress and Anxiety Management
- Reduces symptoms of anxiety and chronic stress by improving physiological regulation.
- Enhances relaxation response through controlled breathing and cognitive restructuring.

Trauma and PTSD Treatment
- Supports nervous system regulation for trauma survivors.
- Provides tools for emotional stabilization and resilience-building.

Cardiovascular Health and Wellness
- Reduces hypertension and heart disease risks by improving autonomic nervous system balance.
- Promotes healthier heart rhythms and stress responses.

Cognitive Performance and Focus
- Enhances cognitive function and memory by optimizing heart-brain coherence.
- Improves academic and workplace performance through emotional self-regulation.

Peak Performance and Personal Growth
- Applied in sports psychology, executive coaching, and creative professions.
- Enhances mental clarity, creativity, and intuitive decision-making.

Key Techniques in HeartMath Therapy
1. **Quick Coherence Technique**
   - Involves focused breathing while generating a positive emotional state to shift into heart coherence.
   - Can be practiced anytime to reduce stress and regain focus.
2. **Heart-Focused Breathing**
   - Teaches individuals to slow their breathing and direct attention to the heart area.
   - Helps regulate emotions and enhance autonomic balance.
3. **Freeze-Frame Technique**
   - A cognitive-emotional reframing tool that helps individuals shift from reactive emotions to a state of clarity.
   - Encourages problem-solving through heart-centered awareness.
4. **HRV Biofeedback Training**
   - Uses biofeedback devices such as Inner Balance™ and emWave® to track heart rhythm patterns.
   - Helps individuals practice and sustain optimal coherence states.

TRAINING AND CERTIFICATION IN HEARTMATH THERAPY

Educational Pathways
1. **Foundational Knowledge**
   - Requires an understanding of psychophysiology, stress management, and HRV biofeedback.
   - Mental health professionals, healthcare providers, and wellness coaches are ideal candidates.
2. **HeartMath Institute Training Programs**
   - Offers specialized training for therapists, educators, and healthcare practitioners.
   - Training includes self-paced modules, live webinars, and hands-on practice.

Certification Requirements
1. **Eligibility**
   - Open to licensed mental health professionals, healthcare providers, and coaches.
   - No prior experience in biofeedback required, but knowledge of somatic therapies is beneficial.
2. **Core Training Components**
   - Completion of a HeartMath Certified Practitioner or Coach training program (typically 3–6 months).
   - Supervised practice and submission of case studies.
3. **Accrediting Organizations**
   - **HeartMath Institute**: Primary provider of official HeartMath certification.
   - **Biofeedback Certification International Alliance (BCIA)**: Recognizes HRV biofeedback as a professional intervention.
4. **Time and Cost Commitments**
   - Certification programs range from $995 to $3,000, depending on the level of training.
   - Some programs offer in-person intensives, while others are fully online.

BENEFITS AND LIMITATIONS OF HEARTMATH THERAPY

Benefits

- **Scientifically Validated:** Backed by over 30 years of research on HRV and heart-brain coherence.
- **Immediate Practical Application:** Techniques are simple, effective, and easy to integrate into daily life.
- **Non-Invasive and Accessible:** Suitable for individuals of all ages and backgrounds.

Limitations

- **Not a Standalone Treatment:** Works best when combined with traditional psychotherapy and medical care.
- **Requires Consistency:** Benefits are maximized through regular practice and engagement.
- **Biofeedback Equipment Costs:** HRV monitoring devices require an additional investment.

ETHICAL CONSIDERATIONS

1. **Informed Consent**
   o Clients must understand the nature of HRV biofeedback and its intended applications.
2. **Scope of Practice**
   o Practitioners should integrate HeartMath techniques within their licensed profession's guidelines.
   o Not a replacement for trauma-focused therapies in severe cases.
3. **Cultural Sensitivity**
   o Heart-centered techniques must be adapted to diverse cultural and spiritual beliefs.

SUMMARY

HeartMath Therapy provides a powerful, evidence-based approach to emotional regulation, stress reduction, and physiological balance. By utilizing heart-brain coherence techniques, individuals can enhance resilience, improve health outcomes, and optimize cognitive performance. With structured training and certification, practitioners can integrate HeartMath into their practice, offering clients practical tools to navigate life's challenges with greater ease and clarity.

I hold two independent licenses in the states of Arizona and Ohio, supervisory status in Arizona, along with a substance abuse license in Arizona. I am board certified as a Diplomate and Clinical Mental Health Specialist, an Approved Clinical Supervisor, Nationally Certified Counselor, a Certified Clinical Mental Health Counselor, NeuroLinguistic Programming Practitioner, and a Clinical Trauma Specialist for Individuals and Family including EMDR Therapy and NET. I completed my training in Animal-Assisted Therapy and Pet Handlers certification in order to evaluate and incorporate the human-animal bond in therapy. I am the sole author and creator of the SxC Model of ESA Evaluation. My research interests surround post-traumatic growth, resiliency, strengths-based therapy, positive psychology, mindfulness, Animal-Assisted Therapy, Sandtray Therapy, Creative approaches in therapy, and martial arts in mental health. I have presented at local, state, regional, national, and international levels on various topics including personality traits, licensure reciprocity challenges, Sandtray and supervision, and Animal-Assisted Therapy within supervision. eonbllc@gmail.com

Heimler Model of Social Functioning (HSF)

HANNAH L. BUTTON, B.A.

WILLIAM H. SNOW, PH.D.

Dr. Eugene Heimler developed the Heimler Method of Social Functioning (HSF) in the 1950's following his release from the World War II concentration camps (Heimler International, n.d.). In one of these camps, an SS Commandant conducted a "mental health experiment" that aimed to break the prisoners' will to live by making them do meaningless work (Heimler, 1975). Unlike many of the other participants, Heimler survived this experiment, and he found himself spending years after his release contemplating what it was that enabled him to continue wanting to live, in spite of the odds. He came to believe that the answer to this question was that he had a sense of meaning.

THE HEIMLER METHOD

This insight led Heimler to consider the impact of *satisfactions* and *frustrations* on an individual's sense of meaning in life. *Satisfactions* refer to meaningful or satisfying experiences, like the positive recollections from his childhood that Heimler drew on for strength in the concentration camps. These satisfactions give a sense that one is living up to their potential, whereas *frustrations* refer to the factors that an individual believes are preventing them from achieving that potential (Marx, 1977). While working with the unemployed as a psychiatric social worker after the war, Heimler (1975) came to believe that it was the balance between these two factors that produced direction in life; this was the foundation of what is now known as The Heimler Method of Human Social Functioning.

He observed that many of the people he served had lost sight of their satisfactions because they focused too much energy on their frustrations. Heimler's clients were unable to distance themselves from their problems enough to identify their true issue or begin to take positive action. The method aims to integrate these frustrating experiences as something that can be useful in the moment by helping the client to gain perspective on their problem and harness their innate creativity to help them explore possible solutions (Heimler, 2017). Heimler suggested that once someone can see their problems written out more clearly, they can often find a solution on their own, and the sense of self-efficacy this can provide is a key element of the success of this method (Heimler, 1975). So his goal was to encourage the client to become their own therapist by helping them to externalize the problem in order to gain a more objective view of their ability to act in response to it.

THE HEIMLER SCALE

The Heimler Scale of Social Functioning (HSSF) is derived from HSF principles and is an integral element of the overall Heimler method. This scale measures the balance of satisfactions and frustrations in an individual's life in order to assess how well a person feels that they are coping and functioning in society. It is a diagnostic and therapeutic tool that identifies the specific areas where a client is living up to their potential and those where they are experiencing the most frustration or getting "stuck" (M. Heimler, n.d.). This component of HSF stands out from other theories because it is designed as a self-help tool for clients to both independently assess their own problems and also to enhance their sharing with their therapist (Heimler, 1975). This improves a client's ability to identify growth areas and explore alternative courses of action to promote their inner potential.

The HSSF is a 55 questionnaire, broken down into 25 questions about satisfactions, 25 questions about frustrations, and five measuring an individual's overall outlook, or *synthesis*. *Synthesis* questions assess the individual's feelings regarding their past, present, and future aspirations. Each of the two major 25-item question sections is further broken down into five subscales addressing the areas of life in which Heimler believed satisfactions or frustrations were most likely to manifest themselves. The satisfactions subscales consist of work and interests, financial security, friends, family life, and sexual satisfaction. The frustrations subscales consist of activity, health, influences, moods, and escape behaviors. Clients can answer with three possible choices of "Yes," "Perhaps," and "No." Heimler posited that by examining the relationship between a client's frustration and satisfaction scores, a counselor could determine if a client had the capacity to cope effectively (Marx et al., 1977).

The results of the HSSF and the various subscales provide clients with a wealth of information to assess where they may lack satisfaction and feel overwhelmed as well as areas of strength where they experience more satisfaction. The feedback gained can help clients develop their own solutions to promote their mental health and overall personal growth.

CERTIFICATIONS, TRAINING, AND LICENSURE REQUIREMENTS

Heimler International (https://www.heimler-international.com/) is the only advertised source of HFS education and training. As of July 2022, the Heimler International website listed five trainers. This list includes therapist and lecturer Miriam Bracha Heimler, the wife of Eugene Heimler. She is still attempting to keep HSF alive today and supports professionals attempting to learn about Heimler's legacy, theories, and tools. When she passes on it is not clear if anyone is left to keep the memory of the Heimler method alive.

HSF training was designed to be highly experiential. It required the trainee to receive clinical supervision from a trained HSF practitioner on all phases of the process (Heimler International, n.d.). In his 1975 book, *Constructive Use of Destructive Forces,* Heimler outlined four "levels of competency," the first being the Certificate-to-Use level. Upon completion of the first phase of training, practitioners would receive a certificate from Heimler International designating them as "Practitioner in the Heimler Method of Social Functioning." The second, third, and fourth levels required advanced training and experience.

SUMMARY

In the 1960s Heimler's model of Social Functioning (HSF) would have been considered an emerging and promising tool. Unfortunately, the development of the model stalled and it has an uncertain future. Training opportunities in the United States are now rare and will soon become non-existent as the last of the aging HSF practitioners end their careers. The Heimler method has all but faded into history in this country and its role as a free-standing therapeutic method is nearing its end of life. Even if one could obtain HSF training, the certification would hold limited value as few would understand or appreciate its worth. Given its current state of affairs, HSF as a certification is not recommended.

The Heimler Scale of Social Functioning (HSSF) holds value separate from HSF. Unfortunately, for the last 60 years, it has been under copyright protection and not freely available. This has made it difficult to scrutinize the instrument and has slowed efforts to establish its efficacy. The Eugene Heimler Literary Trust (EHLT) still requires written permission to use the HSSF for research and completion of training in the Heimler method if used by practitioners. The EHLT would be wise to lift the restrictions on HSSF use or risk that instrument fading into obscurity as well.

In summary, Heimler's insights on social functioning and treatment are still worth studying but not as a standalone therapeutic model. If any early professionals are looking to learn more about HSF without having to invest in seeking out training opportunities, a great resource is Heimler's *Constructive Use of Destructive Forces* (1975). This book outlines the use of both the scale as well as Heimler's overall theoretical approach, and while it may be somewhat outdated, it provides ideas and techniques that all counselors could learn from and integrate into their practice. Additionally, the Heimler Scale of Social Functioning (HSSF) appears useful for research and clinical practice and maybe even as a viable tool if/when the Eugene Heimler Literary Trust lifts the use restrictions in the future.

Hannah L. Button, B.A. is a student at Palo Alto University, pursuing their Masters in Clinical Mental Health Counseling with an emphasis in Marriage and Family Counseling. They completed their BA in communication, psychology, and a minor in sociocultural anthropology, which they use to develop an integrative perspective as a counselor. Hannah has over 15 years of experience working with nonprofits, fundraising for health care needs such as breast cancer research and treatment for children with HIV/AIDS, as well as environmental and social causes. They are currently working with seniors and at-risk youth, and have special interests in ADHD and autism, end-of-life care, and holistic or integrative therapeutic modalities. Recently, Hannah has been working as a research assistant, in admissions as a student interviewer, and assisting end-of-life doulas with clients pursuing medical aid in dying.

William H. Snow, Ph.D. is a Professor of Counseling at Palo Alto University. He has over 40 years of experience working in the fields of counseling, mental health, military behavioral medicine, and higher education. Dr. Snow is currently focused on training the next generation of counselors and clinicians by exploring best practices in counselor education in residential and online settings. These research studies include distance and residential learning pedagogy, educational cohort dynamics, methods to measure cohort organizational climates, and strategies to optimize educational cohort group processes and functioning. Most recently Dr. Snow is working with the University Latinx Task Force to research the need for a Spanish language and cultural pedagogy in counselor education.

REFERENCES

Heimler, E. (1975). Constructive Use of Destructive Forces: An Innovative Approach to Overcoming Obstacles. The Literary Trust of Eugene Heimler.

Heimler International. (n.d.). https://www.heimler-international.com/

Heimler, M. B. (2017). Eugene Heimler: A hero of the twentieth century. European Judaism, 50(2), 67–73. https://doi.org/10.3167/ej.2017.500210

Heimler, M. B. (n.d.). Heimler method of social functioning. Miriam's Healing Well. http://www.miriamshealingwell.com/heimler-method-of-social-functioning.html

Marx, M. B., Garrity, T. F., & Somes, G. W. (1977). The effect of imbalance in life satisfactions and frustrations upon illness behavior in college students. Journal of Psychosomatic Research, 21(6), 423–427. https://doi.org/10.1016/0022-3999(77)90064-2

Herbalist

BILL OWENBY, EdD, MC, FAAETS, DAAETS, DCMHS, LPC, LAAC, NCC, CCMHC, ACS, DIPLOMATE, FELLOW

Herbal medicine has been used for thousands of years as a natural healing approach, addressing physical, emotional, and psychological well-being. Today, herbalism is experiencing a resurgence, with many mental health professionals and holistic practitioners integrating botanical medicine into their treatment plans. Herbalist training and certification provide individuals with the necessary knowledge and skills to safely and effectively use herbs for therapeutic purposes.

CORE PRINCIPLES OF HERBALISM

Herbal medicine operates on the belief that plants contain medicinal properties that can support healing processes in the body and mind. The key principles of herbalism include:

1. Holistic Healing
    o   Herbalism focuses on treating the whole person, not just symptoms.
    o   It considers diet, lifestyle, emotional state, and environmental factors in treatment.
2. Individualized Care
    o   Treatment plans are tailored to the unique needs of each client.
    o   Herbs are selected based on a person's constitution, symptoms, and imbalances.
3. Synergy of Plant Compounds
    o   Herbs contain multiple active compounds that work together to promote healing.
    o   This differs from pharmaceutical drugs, which typically isolate a single active ingredient.
4. Preventative and Restorative Medicine
    o   Herbal medicine is used for both preventative health and treatment of chronic conditions.
    o   Many herbalists focus on strengthening the immune, nervous, and digestive systems to support long-term well-being.

APPLICATIONS OF HERBALISM IN MENTAL HEALTH

Herbal medicine has a growing role in mental health care, complementing psychotherapy, nutrition, and mind-body practices. Common applications include:

1. Anxiety and Stress Management

-   Adaptogens (e.g., ashwagandha, rhodiola, holy basil) help the body regulate stress and maintain balance.
-   Nervine herbs (e.g., chamomile, passionflower, valerian root) promote relaxation and improve sleep.

2. Depression and Mood Disorders

-   St. John's Wort is commonly used for mild to moderate depression.
-   Saffron and lemon balm have shown promise in mood stabilization.

3. Cognitive Support and ADHD

- Ginkgo biloba and bacopa are used to enhance focus, memory, and cognitive function.
- L-theanine (found in green tea) promotes calm focus and stress reduction.

4. Sleep Disorders

- Valerian root, skullcap, and lavender support better sleep quality and relaxation.
- Magnesium-rich herbs like oat straw aid in nervous system regulation.

5. Gut-Brain Connection and Mental Health

- Herbal remedies targeting gut health (e.g., peppermint, ginger, dandelion) can reduce symptoms of anxiety and depression linked to digestive imbalances.

TRAINING AND CERTIFICATION IN HERBALISM

Aspiring herbalists can pursue training through schools and certification programs that focus on botanical medicine, holistic healing, and clinical herbalism. Below are some of the most reputable training options.

Levels of Herbalist Training

There are three primary levels of herbalist training, each with distinct educational requirements and scope of practice:

1. Community Herbalist
   - Focuses on self-care, family care, and basic herbal remedies.
   - Typically completes introductory or intermediate herbalist courses.
   - No formal certification is required, but foundational education is beneficial.
2. Clinical Herbalist
   - Works with clients in a professional setting, offering herbal consultations and health support.
   - Requires formal training in herbal medicine, anatomy, physiology, and holistic health.
   - Certification through organizations like the American Herbalists Guild (AHG) is recommended.
3. Medical Herbalist
   - Trained at the highest level, often holding degrees in botanical medicine, naturopathy, or integrative health.
   - Requires extensive clinical training, scientific research, and case studies.
   - Works in clinical settings, hospitals, or integrative health practices.

Herbalist Training Pathways and Requirements

Aspiring herbalists can choose from various training programs depending on their education level, career goals, and clinical aspirations. Below are some of the most recognized training programs and their requirements.

American Herbalists Guild (AHG) – Registered Herbalist (RH) Credential

- Overview:
  The AHG offers the Registered Herbalist (RH) credential, a widely respected certification for clinical herbalists.
- Requirements:

- o   Minimum of 400 hours of formal herbal education from an approved school or program.
- o   500 hours of clinical experience, including supervised herbal consultations.
- o   Completion of case studies demonstrating practical knowledge.
- o   Submission of two professional recommendation letters.
- o   Membership in the AHG organization.
- Prerequisites:
  - o   A high school diploma or equivalent is required, though many applicants hold bachelor's degrees in health sciences, nutrition, or holistic medicine.
  - o   No medical license is required, but applicants must show competence in botanical medicine.
- Time Commitment:
  - o   Training duration varies, typically 2–4 years depending on prior experience.
- Cost:
  - o   Application fee: $150
  - o   Annual membership: $100–$200
  - o   Course fees vary by program (ranging from $3,000–$15,000 for comprehensive training).
- More Information: https://www.americanherbalistsguild.com

Maryland University of Integrative Health (MUIH) – Master's in Clinical Herbal Medicine

- Overview:
  MUIH offers a Master of Science (MS) in Clinical Herbal Medicine, designed for professionals seeking advanced botanical medicine training.
- Prerequisites:
  - o   Bachelor's degree in health sciences, nutrition, biology, or a related field.
  - o   Science prerequisites in biology, anatomy, or chemistry may be required.
- Curriculum Includes:
  - o   Botanical pharmacology
  - o   Herbal formulation and compounding
  - o   Pathophysiology and herbal treatment strategies
  - o   Clinical internship and case study research
- Time Commitment:
  - o   2–3 years of coursework (full-time or part-time options).
- Cost:
  - o   Tuition: $30,000–$45,000
  - o   Financial aid and scholarships available.
- More Information: https://muih.edu

Bastyr University – Herbal Sciences Degree

- Overview:
  Bastyr University offers undergraduate and graduate programs in herbal sciences and botanical medicine.
- Prerequisites:
  - o   High school diploma (for bachelor's degree) or bachelor's degree (for master's program).
  - o   Background in chemistry, biology, or nutrition is recommended.
- Courses Cover:
  - o   Phytochemistry and plant pharmacology
  - o   Clinical herbal practice and patient care
  - o   Western and Eastern herbal traditions
- Time Commitment:
  - o   Bachelor's program: 4 years
  - o   Master's program: 2 years
- Cost:
  - o   Tuition: $15,000–$40,000 per year (depending on the degree level).

- More Information: https://bastyr.edu

Herbal Academy – Clinical Herbalist Pathway

- Overview:
  Offers self-paced online courses leading to clinical herbalist certification.
- Prerequisites:
  o Open to all learners; no prior education required.
- Curriculum Includes:
  o Introductory, Intermediate, and Advanced Clinical Herbalism courses.
  o Hands-on herbal formulation and case study training.
- Time Commitment:
  o 6 months to 2 years, depending on the student's pace.
- Cost:
  o $495 – $1,600 per course.
- More Information: https://theherbalacademy.com

The School of Evolutionary Herbalism – Vitalist Herbal Practitioner Training

- Overview:
  Focuses on energetic herbalism, traditional medicine, and clinical herbalism.
- Prerequisites:
  o No formal education required, but background knowledge in holistic medicine is beneficial.
- Time Commitment:
  o 9–18 months (self-paced).
- Cost:
  o $2,000 – $5,000.
- More Information: https://www.evolutionaryherbalism.com

SCOPE OF PRACTICE FOR HERBALISTS

Herbalism is an unregulated profession in many countries, meaning there is no universal licensure. However, herbalists must:

- Work within state and federal regulations regarding herbal medicine recommendations.
- Avoid diagnosing or prescribing medication unless also licensed as a medical professional.
- Use ethical informed consent when recommending herbs.
- Collaborate with integrative medicine providers, naturopaths, and mental health professionals.

CAUTIONS AND LIMITATIONS OF HERBAL MEDICINE

While herbalism is safe when practiced correctly, there are some key cautions and limitations:

- Drug-Herb Interactions: Some herbs (e.g., St. John's Wort, ginseng) can interact with prescription medications.
- Allergic Reactions: Certain plant compounds can trigger sensitivities.
- Lack of Standardization: Herbal products vary in potency and quality.
- Legal Restrictions: Some states have limitations on herbal consultations unless the practitioner holds a recognized health license.

SUMMARY

Herbalist training and certification provide a structured pathway for individuals seeking to integrate botanical medicine into holistic health care. Herbalism is widely used to support mental health conditions, stress management, cognitive function, and sleep disorders. Training programs range from introductory courses to master's degrees, with certification options through organizations like the American Herbalists Guild (AHG).

Herbal medicine, when used responsibly and ethically, can be a powerful tool in integrative mental health care, offering natural, holistic support for emotional well-being. However, practitioners must remain aware of legal restrictions, client safety, and ethical considerations when incorporating herbal remedies into clinical practice.

I hold two independent licenses in the states of Arizona and Ohio, supervisory status in Arizona, along with a substance abuse license in Arizona. I am board certified as a Diplomate and Clinical Mental Health Specialist, an Approved Clinical Supervisor, Nationally Certified Counselor, a Certified Clinical Mental Health Counselor, NeuroLinguistic Programming Practitioner, and a Clinical Trauma Specialist for Individuals and Family including EMDR Therapy and NET. I completed my training in Animal-Assisted Therapy and Pet Handlers certification in order to evaluate and incorporate the human-animal bond in therapy. I am the sole author and creator of the SxC Model of ESA Evaluation. My research interests surround post-traumatic growth, resiliency, strengths-based therapy, positive psychology, mindfulness, Animal-Assisted Therapy, Sandtray Therapy, Creative approaches in therapy, and martial arts in mental health. I have presented at local, state, regional, national, and international levels on various topics including personality traits, licensure reciprocity challenges, Sandtray and supervision, and Animal-Assisted Therapy within supervision.

conbllc@gmail.com

REFERENCES

American Herbalists Guild. (2024). *Registered Herbalist Credential Requirements*. Retrieved from
https://www.americanherbalistsguild.com

Bone, K., & Mills, S. (2013). *Principles and Practice of Phytotherapy: Modern Herbal Medicine*. Elsevier.

Winston, D., & Maimes, S. (2007). *Adaptogens: Herbs for Strength, Stamina, and Stress Relief*. Healing Arts Press.

Maryland University of Integrative Health. (2024). *Master's in Clinical Herbal Medicine Program Overview*.
Retrieved from https://muih.edu

Hip-Hop Therapy

MEGAN PICKENS, PH.D., LPC-S

In the ever-evolving landscape of therapeutic interventions, hip-hop therapy emerges as a dynamic and culturally resonant approach that deeply connects with individuals seeking healing and self-discovery (Tyson, 2012). Rooted in the vibrant tapestry of hip-hop culture, this innovative therapeutic modality harnesses the expressive power of music, dance, and poetry to facilitate emotional release, personal growth, and transformation (Crenshaw & Roberson, 2006). Its efficacy is underscored by a growing body of research and its increasing recognition as a valuable tool in the mental health profession (Stewart et al., 2015).

EXPANDING THE THERAPEUTIC LANDSCAPE

This chapter embarks on a comprehensive exploration of the captivating realm of hip-hop therapy, endeavoring to uncover the nuances of its methodology, its profound impact on mental well-being, and its seamless integration into contemporary therapeutic practice (Snyder, 2011). Through this exploration, we gain invaluable insights into hip-hop therapy's potential to address a broad spectrum of mental health issues, ranging from anxiety and depression to trauma recovery and identity exploration (Chang, 2005; Rose, 2008).

The Heartbeat of Hip-Hop

Guided by the heartbeat of hip-hop culture, we navigate the intricate rhythms and lyrical storytelling that constitute its essence (Strobach & Avila, 2018). This journey reveals the dynamic interplay between spoken word, rhythmic movement, and creative expression, highlighting how each element serves as a conduit for emotions that may elude conventional forms of communication (Snyder, 2011). Furthermore, we trace the evolution of hip-hop therapy from its grassroots origins to its current status as an established and respected therapeutic modality, acknowledging the substantial body of research supporting its efficacy and transformative potential (Chang, 2005).

Implementing Hip-Hop Therapy Ethically

Throughout this chapter, we shed light on the ways in which mental health professionals can thoughtfully and ethically incorporate hip-hop therapy into their clinical practices. A key focus lies on fostering cultural sensitivity, collaborative therapeutic relationships, and ethical considerations (American Psychological Association, 2017). From recognizing the historical significance of hip-hop within marginalized communities to creating a safe and empowering therapeutic environment for clients, we unveil a blueprint for effective implementation.

A Journey into Human Expression

In this exploration of hip-hop therapy, we embark on a profound journey into the realm of human expression (Tyson, 2012). This chapter extends an invitation to witness the fusion of healing and artistry, inviting readers to comprehend the transformative potential of cultural resonance (Kitwana, 2002). It encourages the embrace of a therapeutic approach that harmoniously bridges the gap between tradition and innovation (Stewart et al., 2015). As we turn these pages, we uncover the tangible benefits of hip-hop therapy and its underlying philosophy, one that steadfastly affirms the healing power of self-expression in all its diverse and authentic forms.

THE HISTORY OF HIP-HOP THERAPY

Hip-hop therapy's roots in the early days of hip-hop culture are intertwined with its emergence as a powerful cultural movement in New York City during the 1970s (Chang, 2005; Rose, 2008). This cultural phenomenon was primarily centered around the artistic expressions of music, dance, and visual art, providing a unique platform for marginalized communities to creatively voice their experiences and address pressing social and political issues that affected their lives. The birth of hip-hop culture marked a transformative moment in history, enabling individuals to channel their emotions, frustrations, and aspirations into a vibrant artistic narrative.

As hip-hop culture continued to evolve throughout the subsequent decades, it transcended geographical and cultural boundaries, becoming a global phenomenon that resonated profoundly with youth culture worldwide (Kitwana, 2002; Neal, 2006). Hip-hop artists harnessed the power of their music to confront a spectrum of social and political challenges, from poverty and violence to racism and drug abuse. This musical genre evolved into a compelling vehicle for social commentary, offering a platform for artists to advocate for change and amplify the voices of marginalized communities.

In the early 2000s, a pioneering group of therapists and educators recognized the therapeutic potential inherent in hip-hop culture (Tyson, 2012). They observed that hip-hop had the capacity to engage young people in a manner that allowed them to authentically and meaningfully express their emotions, experiences, and aspirations. This realization sparked the formal development of hip-hop therapy as a structured therapeutic approach designed to harness the core elements of hip-hop culture for healing and self-discovery.

Hip-hop therapy embraces these core elements as therapeutic tools, each offering a unique avenue for individuals to engage in creative and authentic self-expression (Crenshaw & Roberson, 2006; Snyder, 2011; Tsai, 2012; Strobach & Avila, 2018):

Rap Music: Writing and performing rap lyrics provide individuals with a therapeutic channel to express their thoughts, emotions, and life experiences creatively and authentically. This medium allows them to craft their narratives, fostering self-reflection and emotional release.

Graffiti Art: Creating graffiti art enables individuals to communicate visually, developing their artistic skills while expressing their feelings, stories, and perspectives. It serves as a powerful outlet for those who resonate with visual forms of self-expression.

Breakdancing: Learning and practicing breakdancing moves not only enhance physical coordination but also offer a unique mode of self-expression through movement. Breakdancing fosters a sense of empowerment as individuals master intricate routines and develop their unique dance style.

DJing: The art of DJing involves the selection and manipulation of music, providing a therapeutic avenue for individuals deeply connected to music. DJs express themselves through their song choices and mixing techniques, offering a creative outlet that resonates with those who find solace and creativity in music.

Hip-hop therapy continues to evolve and gain recognition as a culturally responsive and effective approach to mental health and personal development, particularly for youth and individuals from diverse backgrounds (Stewart et al., 2015). Researchers and practitioners are actively exploring its applications in various therapeutic settings and documenting its profound impact on individuals' well-being, self-discovery, and empowerment (Strobach & Avila, 2018).

Understanding Hip-hop Culture

Hip-hop culture is an intricate and multifaceted tapestry that has woven together creativity, resilience, and social commentary over the decades. This cultural phenomenon transcends continents and generations, representing a multi-dimensional force that has captivated audiences worldwide (Chang, 2005; Forman & Neal, 2004). At its core, hip-hop celebrates individuality while embodying shared experiences, creating a vibrant mosaic of artistic and cultural expressions that have resonated across time and geography.

The Essence of Hip-Hop Culture

Diving deeper into the essence of hip-hop culture reveals a dynamic canvas defined by self-expression, creativity, and community (Rose, 1994). While it has global reach, hip-hop's roots can be traced back to neighborhoods marked by socio-economic challenges, inequality, and systemic injustice, primarily within African American and Latinx communities (Kitwana, 2002; Neal, 2005). In response to adversity, hip-hop emerged as a potent mode of expression—a medium through which stories of triumph, resilience, and the raw realities of life could be laid bare.

More Than Entertainment

At its core, hip-hop transcends mere entertainment; it serves as a vehicle for catharsis and connection (Neal, 2006). The music's intricate melodies and poetic lyrics capture the essence of experiences that words alone struggle to convey. Hip-hop's rhythm, flow, and lyrical finesse provide an outlet through which personal tales of love, loss, joy, pain, and aspiration intertwine, creating a tapestry of relatability that transcends cultures and generations.

The Language of Dance

Dance, another cornerstone of hip-hop culture, transforms movement into a visual language of emotion and unity (LaBoskey, 2012). Whether it's breakdancing or street dance, each style communicates a unique story that speaks to individuality and the shared human experience. The fluidity of motion in hip-hop dance encapsulates the essence of vulnerability and strength, offering participants a channel to communicate the unspeakable and express the ineffable.

The Power of Poetry

Poetry, often celebrated as the heartbeat of hip-hop, allows individuals to encapsulate their stories within verses that resonate with rhythm and eloquence (Krims, 2001). Spoken word and rap become platforms for self-reflection and social commentary, magnifying the profound impact of personal narratives on collective consciousness.

A Global Phenomenon

While hip-hop's roots lie within marginalized communities, its influence and reach have transcended continents and cultural barriers (Kitwana, 2002). The global prevalence of hip-hop underscores its universal appeal and the timeless allure of its creative expressions. This evolution reflects the potency of its themes and their capacity to create bridges of understanding between people of diverse backgrounds. As a global phenomenon, hip-hop embodies the power of culture to transcend boundaries, fostering connections that transcend race, ethnicity, and nationality.

A Tale of Resilience and Unity

In exploring the profound depths of hip-hop culture, we unearth a narrative of creativity, empowerment, and communal resilience (Chang, 2005). It is a tale of individuals who transform pain into power, adversity into art, and isolation into unity. As we delve further into the potential of hip-hop therapy, we must acknowledge the cultural roots from which it springs and the indelible impact it continues to make on the human experience.

GENERAL GOAL OF TREATMENT AND PHILOSOPHY

Hip-hop therapy, as a unique and innovative therapeutic model, is guided by a philosophy deeply rooted in the transformative power of hip-hop culture (Tyson, 2012). It seeks to facilitate healing, self-expression, and personal growth, with the overarching goal of providing individuals with a platform for creative self-expression, emotional release, and empowerment while fostering a sense of belonging and connection within a supportive community.

At the heart of hip-hop therapy lies the belief that the elements of hip-hop culture—music, dance, and poetry—can serve as potent tools for emotional catharsis and self-discovery (Crenshaw & Roberson, 2006). The model's philosophy recognizes that individuals possess an innate capacity to translate their lived experiences, emotions, and challenges into artistic expressions that resonate with others who share similar struggles.

Hip-hop therapy aims to create a safe and inclusive space where individuals can harness the power of hip-hop's artistic forms to explore their thoughts and emotions (Tyson, 2012). Through music production, dance movements, and poetic narratives, participants are encouraged to voice their innermost feelings and experiences, ultimately promoting a deeper understanding of themselves and their unique narratives.

In alignment with the philosophy of hip-hop therapy, the general goal of treatment is to enable individuals to (Crenshaw & Roberson, 2006):

Express Emotions: Hip-hop therapy seeks to provide individuals with a creative outlet to express complex emotions that may be difficult to convey through traditional communication. Music, dance, and poetry channel feelings of joy, pain, anger, and vulnerability.

Build Self-Esteem: Individuals can cultivate a sense of accomplishment and heightened self-esteem by creating and sharing artistic expressions. As they witness the impact of their creations on others, they gain confidence in their ability to effect change through their unique voice.

Promote Connection: Hip-hop therapy emphasizes the importance of community and connection. By participating in group activities and sharing their artistry, individuals develop a sense of belonging and forge relationships with peers who share similar experiences.

Foster Resilience: The creative process inherent in hip-hop therapy encourages individuals to confront challenges and setbacks, transforming them into opportunities for growth and resilience. This shift in perspective empowers individuals to view obstacles as catalysts for personal transformation.

Encourage Authenticity: The philosophy of hip-hop therapy values authenticity and encourages individuals to explore their identities, vulnerabilities, and strengths. This exploration fosters a deeper understanding of oneself and paves the way for genuine self-expression.

In essence, the general goal of hip-hop therapy aligns with its philosophy of using the creative elements of hip-hop culture to promote healing and growth (Tyson, 2012; Crenshaw & Roberson, 2006). Hip-hop therapy offers individuals a pathway toward emotional well-being and empowerment by providing a platform for self-expression, fostering a sense of community, and encouraging the exploration of emotions and personal narratives. Through the lens of this dynamic model, the journey from struggle to triumph becomes a collaborative narrative of transformation and artistic resilience.

BENEFITS OF HIP-HOP THERAPY

Hip-hop therapy offers several benefits for mental health professionals and their clients, aligning with a philosophy that emphasizes creative expression, emotional processing, and personal growth (Crenshaw & Roberson, 2006). For one, it provides a creative outlet for individuals to express themselves and process their emotions, which can be especially helpful for those with difficulty articulating their feelings or feeling isolated and disconnected from others (Tyson, 2012). Hip-hop therapy also helps individuals build self-esteem and confidence by providing a platform to showcase their talents and abilities within a supportive community (Crenshaw & Roberson, 2006).

Furthermore, hip-hop therapy has demonstrated its effectiveness in addressing a wide range of emotional, mental, and behavioral challenges (Tyson, 2012). These include:

Depression and anxiety: Writing and performing rap lyrics can help individuals express their emotions and improve their mood (Crenshaw & Roberson, 2006).

Substance abuse: Hip-hop therapy can assist individuals in developing a sense of self-worth and purpose, reducing their reliance on drugs and alcohol (Tyson, 2012).

Trauma: Hip-hop therapy can be a valuable tool for helping individuals process traumatic experiences and develop coping skills (Crenshaw & Roberson, 2006).

Relationship problems: Hip-hop therapy can facilitate the development of communication and conflict resolution skills, enhancing individuals' ability to navigate interpersonal challenges (Tyson, 2012).

Another noteworthy benefit of hip-hop therapy is its capacity to facilitate relationship-building and connections among participants (Crenshaw & Roberson, 2006). Many hip-hop therapy programs are designed to be group-based, allowing individuals to share their experiences and provide mutual support. This group dynamic can be particularly advantageous for those struggling with social anxiety or experiencing difficulties in forming and maintaining relationships.

In addition to these benefits, research has shown that hip-hop therapy effectively treats various mental health issues, including depression, anxiety, and PTSD (Crenshaw & Roberson, 2006). Hip-hop music's rhythmic and repetitive nature can have a calming effect on the brain, aiding individuals in regulating their emotions (Tyson, 2012).

For mental health professionals interested in incorporating hip-hop therapy into their practice, a crucial starting point is familiarizing themselves with the culture and its various expressions (Kitwana, 2002). This may involve attending hip-hop concerts, actively listening to hip-hop music, or observing hip-hop dance performances.

Once mental health professionals have a solid understanding of hip-hop culture, they can begin incorporating its elements into their therapy sessions (Tyson, 2012). This could entail using hip-hop music as a tool for relaxation or incorporating hip-hop dance and poetry into therapy sessions, tailored to individual client preferences and therapeutic goals.

Importantly, mental health professionals should continually assess their clients' needs and preferences before introducing hip-hop therapy into their treatment plan (Crenshaw & Roberson, 2006). While it can be a powerful tool for healing and self-expression, it may not be suitable for everyone, underscoring the importance of a client-centered approach in mental health practice.

TRAINING AND CERTIFICATION

Hip-hop therapy is a specialized and dynamic field that necessitates specific training and certification for mental health professionals seeking to incorporate this innovative approach into their practice (Tyson, 2012). To embark on a career in hip-hop therapy, individuals should commence their journey by obtaining a degree in counseling, psychology, or social work. This foundational education provides the essential knowledge and skills required to excel in the field of mental health therapy.

Upon completing their formal education, mental health professionals can further specialize in hip-hop therapy by pursuing specialized training and certification programs. Several reputable organizations offer comprehensive training and certification in hip-hop therapy, ensuring that practitioners are well-equipped to provide effective and culturally sensitive care. Notable institutions in this domain include the Hip-hop Therapy Institute and the Global Hip-hop Collective, both of which offer a range of training options, including online courses, workshops, and, in some instances, in-person programs (Crenshaw & Roberson, 2006).

Incorporating hip-hop therapy into clinical practice demands adherence to specific best practices that align with the philosophy of this therapeutic approach. Here are some fundamental principles that mental health professionals should keep in mind when practicing hip-hop therapy (Crenshaw & Roberson, 2006):

Cultural Sensitivity: Mental health professionals should approach hip-hop therapy with an acute awareness of the cultural significance of hip-hop and its various expressions. They should demonstrate cultural sensitivity and respect for the origins and history of hip-hop culture, recognizing its roots in African American and Latinx communities (Kitwana, 2002).

Empowerment: Hip-hop therapy should serve as a tool for empowering individuals, aiding them in building self-esteem and confidence (Tyson, 2012). Practitioners should strive to create an environment where clients feel empowered to express themselves creatively and authentically.

Collaboration: Hip-hop therapy is most effective when it operates as a collaborative process between the therapist and the client (Crenshaw & Roberson, 2006). Mental health professionals should engage in a partnership with their clients, working together to identify therapeutic goals and develop a treatment plan tailored to each client's unique needs and aspirations.

Safety: Prioritizing the safety and well-being of clients is paramount in hip-hop therapy (Tyson, 2012). Mental health professionals should ensure that the therapeutic environment is safe, welcoming, and comfortable. Clients should feel supported and validated throughout their therapeutic journey.

Ethical Considerations: Mental health professionals must adhere to ethical guidelines and standards of practice when incorporating hip-hop therapy into their clinical work (American Psychological Association, 2017). This includes maintaining client confidentiality, respecting boundaries, and upholding the highest standards of professional conduct.

In summary, hip-hop therapy is a specialized therapeutic approach that requires specific training and certification for mental health professionals. By following best practices rooted in cultural sensitivity, empowerment, collaboration, safety, and ethical considerations, practitioners can effectively harness the power of hip-hop culture to facilitate healing and personal growth in their clients.

Training and Certification Details
- Healing Young People Thru Empowerment (H.Y.P.E.)

   The Original Hip Hop Therapy Certification

   Hip Hop Therapy Certified Facilitator Training Package

   1-day Intensive training

   $500

   www.Letsgethype.com

- Sankofa Healing Studio

   Mind, Body and Rhyme: Using EMDR Hip Hop Therapy to Foster Creativity

   $333

   2-day training

www.Sankofahealingstudio.org

- Rhythm & Truth

  14 CMTEs for Music Therapists

  12 NBCC for counselors, social workers and MFTs

  2-day training

  www.Rhythmandtruth.org

Hip-hop therapy stands as an innovative and potent form of therapeutic intervention with the capacity to aid individuals in processing emotions, fostering relationships, and cultivating self-esteem and confidence (Crenshaw & Roberson, 2006). This dynamic approach has garnered attention within the realm of mental health therapy, offering mental health professionals a creative and engaging tool to address a diverse array of emotional and psychological challenges.

Mental health professionals aspiring to embark on a journey in the field of hip-hop therapy must first acquire the requisite training and certification (Tyson, 2012). This journey typically commences with a foundational education in counseling, psychology, or social work, laying the groundwork for the core competencies needed in the field of mental health therapy. Subsequently, mental health professionals can pursue specialized training programs to immerse themselves in the principles and practices of hip-hop therapy.

Several esteemed organizations, such as the Hip-hop Therapy Institute and the Global Hip-hop Collective, offer comprehensive training and certification programs tailored to the needs of mental health professionals (Crenshaw & Roberson, 2006). These programs encompass a range of training modalities, including online courses, workshops, and, in some instances, in-person training sessions. By obtaining the necessary training and certification, mental health professionals can equip themselves with the knowledge and skills required to effectively implement hip-hop therapy in their practice.

Dr. Megan Pickens, hailing originally from Kansas City, Kansas, has firmly planted her roots in Arlington, Texas, where she has carved out an enviable reputation as a serial entrepreneur and a vanguard in counseling. Her flagship venture, The Volition Collective Counseling and Wellness Center, is where she exercises her expertise as a Licensed Professional Counselor Supervisor. Her focus areas include life enrichment, women's empowerment, and the cultivation of healthy relationships. Renowned for her unfiltered, straight-shooting style, Dr. Pickens is adept at spurring her clients toward actionable life changes. As an LPC Supervisor, she also imparts invaluable knowledge and mentorship to newcomers and students in the counseling field.

Branching out further, Dr. Pickens inaugurated Private Practice Revolution, a consultancy designed to guide other behavioral health professionals in assimilating new technologies into their practices. This innovative service addresses an extensive list of topics, ranging from practice expansion and health insurance intricacies to website development and effective use of social media. Alongside a colleague, she co-founded the Multicultural Behavioral Health Provider Networking Group (MBHPN), aiming to tackle the unique mental health issues prevalent in multicultural communities.

A member of the American Counseling Association and the Texas Counseling Association, Dr. Pickens has previously served as the President of TACES, a subdivision of the Texas Counseling Association, and also as the President and currently as the Alternate Senator of the Texas Association for Multicultural Counseling and Development. Her affiliation with Delta Sigma Theta Sorority Inc. further attests to her commitment to professional and community organizations.

As an articulate public speaker, Dr. Pickens has enriched various platforms as a panelist including associations, nonprofits, and private and religious events. Acknowledged as an expert in relationships and mental health, she has also participated as an internet radio commentator and in live-streaming events. Her public speaking engagements, seminars, and workshops delve into various issues such as personal development, personality assessments, and women empowerment, focusing on de-stigmatizing mental health issues within the Black family, church, and the wider community.

On the personal front, Dr. Pickens is an empty-nest parent of an adult daughter. She is fervently involved in her local church and engages with a ministry focused on empowering women and enhancing mental health education within the community. She completed her Ph.D. in the Marriage & Family Therapy Department at Texas Wesleyan University, specializing in research topics that intersect emotional abuse, high-achieving Black women, and the Black community. Her contributions to academia include a published chapter on Rational Emotional Behavioral Therapy in the second edition of "Marriage and Family Therapy: A Practice-Oriented Approach."

Her personal predilections span an eclectic range, from her passion for documentary and independent films to her enjoyment of music and dance for physical fitness. Politically engaged at the local level, Dr. Pickens is a vociferous advocate for the positive representation of Black individuals in the media. Travel also figures prominently among her diverse interests.

In summary, Dr. Megan Pickens has wielded a profound influence across multiple sectors through her myriad professional activities and personal commitments. Her work consistently champions empowerment, education, and the mental health of the communities she serves.

Megan Pickens, Ph.D., LPC-S

The Volition Collective Counseling and Wellness Center

(817) 617-2638 Office

www.thevococo.com

REFERENCES

American Psychological Association. (2017). Ethical principles of psychologists and code of conduct. https://www.apa.org/ethics/code

Campbell, C., & Connolly, M. (2007). Hip-hop therapy: An exploratory study of a rap music intervention with at-risk and delinquent youth. Journal of child and adolescent psychiatric nursing, 20(5), 299-306.

Chang, J. (2005). Can't Stop Won't Stop: A History of the Hip-Hop Generation. St. Martin's Press.

Crenshaw, D. A., & Roberson, L. M. (2006). The Therapeutic Potential of Hip-Hop and Rap. Journal of Adolescent Research, 21(3), 269-298.

Daniels, J. (2012). The therapeutic potential of hip-hop culture. Journal of humanistic psychology, 52(2), 210-233.

Forman, M. & Neal, M. A. (Eds.). (2004). That's the Joint!: The Hip-Hop Studies Reader. Routledge.

Kitwana, B. (2002). The Hip Hop Generation: Young Blacks and the Crisis in African American Culture. Basic Civitas Books.

Kivel, P. (2010). Healing through hip-hop. Social Work Today, 10(3), 18-19.

Krims, A. (2001). Rap Music and the Poetics of Identity. Cambridge University Press.

LaBoskey, S. B. (2012). Hip Hop Dance as an Urban Locus of Learning. Urban Education, 47(4), 807-827.

Neal, M. A. (2005). New Black Man: Rethinking Black Masculinity. Routledge.

Neal, M. A. (2006). The Hip Hop Wars: What We Talk About When We Talk About Hip Hop—and Why It Matters. Basic Civitas Books.

Rose, T. (2008). The Hip Hop Wars: What We Talk About When We Talk About Hip Hop—and Why It Matters. Basic Civitas Books.

Snyder, G. J. (2011). Graffiti Lives: Beyond the Tag in New York's Urban Underground. NYU Press.

Strobach, G. M., & Avila, T. (2018). Therapeutic DJing: Enhancing Emotional Expression and Connection Through Music. Arts in Psychotherapy, 59, 20-27.

Sweeney, A., Filippou, D., & Jones, C. (2013). Hip-hop and therapeutic practice with young people. British Journal of Occupational Therapy, 76(11), 503-506.

Tsai, J. (2012). Breaking Down Barriers: Hip-Hop Dance as a Therapeutic Intervention. American Journal of Dance Therapy, 34(2), 98-117.

Tyson, E. H. (2012). Hip Hop Therapy: An Exploratory Study. Journal of Human Behavior in the Social Environment, 22(3), 211-219.

Williams, T. J., & Morton, D. J. (2008). Music

Hoarding Disorder Certificates

Audrey Zatopek, Ph.D., M.A., LPC-S, LCDC

Popularized by shows like *Hoarders* (Chan et al., 2009–2024) and *Hoarding: Buried Alive* (Kane, 2010–2014), hoarding disorder is classified as an obsessive-compulsive and related disorder and is characterized "by persistent difficulty discarding or parting with possessions, regardless of their actual value, as a result of a strong perceived need to save the items and distress associated with discarding them" (American Psychiatric Association [APA], 2022, p. 265). Compared to normative collecting, hoarding disorder involves the accumulation of objects that lead to a cluttering of and congestion in the living space that compromises its intended use (Tolin et al., 2025). For example, accumulation of clutter could "interfere with the resident's functioning in the home, including ability to move around the home, prepare and eat food, sleep comfortably or use basic items like the sofa, refrigerator, kitchen sink, bathtub, or toilet" (Ayers et al., 2010, as cited in Bedi & Woody, 2025, p. 1).

In cases of excessive acquisition of objects (which make up approximately 80% to 90% of hoarding disorder cases), individuals may engage in "collecting, buying, or stealing of items that are not needed or for which there is no available space" (APA, 2022, p. 265). Items hoarded may include clothing, trash, artwork, furniture, electronics, animals, and/or any other type of possession, and hoarding disorder has been documented worldwide. As an important consideration, mental health professionals need to be sure to rule out obsessive-compulsive disorder, as "Some individuals also have difficulties discarding and accumulate objects as a consequence of typical obsessions and compulsions (e.g., fears of harming others)" (pp. 266-267). A healthy and normative amount of collecting "does not produce the clutter, distress, or impairment typical of hoarding disorder" (p. 278). In cases involving poor insight, the individuals may not endorse experiencing distress and their impairment may only be apparent to their social circle. When working with hoarding disorder clinically, it is important to attend to an individual's level of insight and whether there are any delusional beliefs perpetuating the hoarding behavior. Despite lack of insight, attempts made by their social circle to clean, clear, or discard the hoarding person's possessions will result in high levels of distress.

Other common features associated with hoarding disorder include "indecisiveness, perfectionism, avoidance, procrastination, difficulty planning and organizing tasks, and distractibility," and some may "live in unsanitary conditions that may be a logical consequence of severely cluttered spaces and/or that are related to planning and organizing difficulties" (APA, 2022, p. 280). In some cases, the unsanitary conditions may be resultant of animal hoarding. If you are interested in learning more about certificates for treating animal hoarding, there is another chapter in this text dedicated to this topic (see Chapter on Animal Hoarding Certificate). In the treatment of any type of hoarding, it will also be important for a mental health professional to attend to any grief, trauma, attachment, or other kinds of woundings that may have preceded and led to the start of hoarding behavior (Guerra et al., 2025).

CERTIFICATION, CERTIFICATE, DEGREE, AND LICENSURE REQUIREMENTS

Although there is not a single, universally recognized "certification" for the treatment of hoarding, there are a few specialized training, certificate, and certification opportunities related to understanding and treating hoarding disorder available. Located in New York, USA, the Institute for Challenging Disorganization (ICD, 2025f) "provides five levels of certificates and certification all focused on chronic disorganization (CD), and a holistic approach to working with organizing and productivity clients" (para. 3). Though primarily geared toward professional organizers, mental health professionals of diverse backgrounds may benefit from completing the first two levels of certificates offered by the ICD, as levels three and above are for professional organizer certification, mentoring, and becoming a trainer in the ICD program. In fact, if a mental health professional wanted to add the skills of the last three levels to their repertoire then this program could be a great fit. To participate in any of the courses, it is required to pay an initial fee to be an ICD® Premium subscriber, which is also an annual fee. Fee-related information associated with this certification will be provided in the costs section of this chapter.

Prior to accessing the five levels of ICD certification, it is required for an individual to first complete a "Foundation Certificate of Study in Chronic Disorganization" (ICD, 2025e). All classes are completed through the ICD's online Learning Management System and certificates awarded are available in the transcript of an individual's Learning Management System profile. Classes for the foundational certificate cover several topics, including: the conditions that may lead to an individual struggling with CD; "strategies, techniques and resources to help clients address their organizational and productivity challenges;" "ethical, boundary and safety issues;" and the five areas of study that include "[Attention-Deficit/Hyperactivity Disorder], Hoarding Behavior, Aging Issues, and Time Management and Productivity" (ICD, 2025e, paras. 2-3). The five levels that follow must be completed sequentially, with a requirement for maintained subscribership throughout completion. As for the five levels, participants can expect to learn the following during each level.

- **Level I: Certificate of Study in Understanding Hoarding Behavior (HRD).** "This certificate covers the specialized needs and issues with working with clients with hoarding behaviors. The classes completed for this certificate include information about symptoms, presentations, and co-existing conditions of Hoarding Behavior and Hoarding Disorder" (ICD, 2025b, paras. 1-2). Furthermore, "Subscribers who complete this certificate understand treatments for Hoarding Disorder and know strategies, techniques, and resources to help clients address their organizational and productivity challenges" (para. 2). Those who complete this certificate will also "understand the definition of hoarding disorder, the characteristics of clients with hoarding behavior, and the likelihood of co-morbid conditions" with the ability to "identify resources available to help in hoarding situations, [be] keenly aware of safety issues, and [identify] their own limits in working with clients displaying hoarding behavior" (para. 3). After completing the required six classes, a certificate will automatically be awarded.

- **Level II: Specialist Certificates in Chronic Disorganization, Attention-Deficit/Hyperactivity Disorder (ADHD), Aging, Hoarding, and Time Management and Productivity.** Upon completion of a specialized area of study, an ICD subscriber will add to the depth and breadth of their knowledge of hoarding. Each specialization has selected required readings and exam that must be passed upon completion of the chosen course. Each specialization requires the completion of six classes and the passing of a specialization-specific exam. Learners are able to obtain each Specialist certificate through meeting the 6-class, payment, and exam requirements (ICD, 2025i).

- **Level III: Certified Professional Organizer in Chronic Disorganization® (CPO-CD®).** Starting in January of each year, a learner may start working towards a certification as "A Level III Certified Professional Organizer in Chronic Disorganization (CPO-CD) [who] is a professional organizer who has been educated in depth on the issues of chronic disorganization. The CPO-CD student spends 17-20 months of intensive time studying and applying this learning in practical application with current clients. The purpose of the ICD CPO-CD program is to develop a professional organizer's skills and knowledge by utilizing a mentor-style relationship. This program provides the intermediate and advanced professional organizer an environment and forum to discuss client issues, problems and challenges. Participation in the CPO-CD program develops professional integrity and improves an organizer's communication skills. The CPO-CD® program is specifically geared to improve the quality of service, techniques and knowledge professional organizers provide to their clients affected by CD. Recertification is required every three years." (ICD, 2025j, para. 1)

- **Level IV: Communication Mentor.** Starting in the month of November in a given year and lasting for 10 to 11 months, "The objective of the ICD® Level IV Communication Mentor Program is to develop an organizer's skills and knowledge in the areas of training, coaching, motivating, communicating and leadership. This program allows intermediate and advanced organizers to work independently and with peers and, in the process, expand and improve their training and communication skills. This development process will also assist the candidates with their own current and future client work. In addition, this program requires publishing and presenting of material to further individual and group knowledge." (ICD, 2025d, para. 1)

- **Level V: Master Trainer.** Lasting for 22 months and starting in January of each year, "The objective of the ICD® Master Trainer Program is to develop and acknowledge an organizer's skills and knowledge in the areas of training, coaching, motivating, communicating and leadership. This program allows intermediate and advanced organizers to work independently and with peers and, in the process, expand and improve their training and communication skills. This development process will also assist the candidates with their own current and future client work. The purpose of the ICD® Master Trainer certificate is to develop and acknowledge leadership, publication, training, service, and commitment to the field of study and exploration of Chronic Disorganization and Organization. This is the ICD® certificate and certification program's highest level of achievement." (ICD, 2025h, para. 1)

Classes offered by the ICD may be attended live by any person with interest in the topic(s) presented, and up to 40 classes per year are offered (ICD, 2025c). While receiving class credits is required for the ICD Certification program, pursuit of certification is not required to attend classes. Live classes are 1 hour long on Zoom and typically take place at 8:00 pm Eastern Time on Mondays from January to March, on Tuesdays April to June, on Wednesdays July to September, and Thursdays October to December. Class presenters include ICD subscribers, authors, medical professionals, psychiatrists, psychologists, researchers, people with lived experience, and "other experts across many disciplines" (para. 5).

To remain current, there is a required recertification every three years for CPO-CD®, Communication Mentors, and ICD Master Trainers (ICD, 2025k). For the Level III CPO-CD® certification, "graduates must participate in twenty-seven (27) hours of continuing education in the field of [CD]. A portion of the education requirements (nine hours) may be replaced by volunteer service to ICD or the population affected by CD" (para. 2). For those recertifying for the Level IV Communication Mentor and Level V ICD Master Trainer, "graduates must participate in eighteen (18) hours of continuing education in the field of [CD] plus demonstrate leadership in the community" (para. 3). Additionally, to keep the highest level of ICD credentialing that has been achieved, recertification must meet that level's requirements or, to regain the highest credential, all higher levels will have to be repeated that follow the lower level of recertification chosen.

As another option for learning about and getting certificates related to hoarding disorder, the Center for Hoarding and Clutter (CHC, 2018) offers two self-paced certificate courses online. The first course is a 1-hour course titled "Understanding Hoarding Behavior: A Brief Overview," and the course's objectives are for participants to increase their knowledge of mental health features of hoarding disorder, to be familiarized with assessment tools for hoarding disorder, and to learn how motivation and outcomes may impact value-based goals (CHC, 2021). Participants will learn about eight topics and take a quiz to get the certificate. The second course offered is a 9-hour course titled "Safety Day: An Application of Disaster Psychology to Hoarding Clean-outs – Certificate of Completion Course." The overall objectives for the course are for participants to increase their knowledge of mental health features of hoarding disorder, to be introduced to and learn about how to apply Disaster Psychology to severe hoarding, and "learn how to develop and implement a person-centered collaborative Safety Day plan to address severe hoarding" (CHC, 2020, para. 6). As final educational options to consider, there are several organizations that offer on-demand online continuing education on hoarding for free or for a low cost, but none of them offer a certificate or certification. Some organizations found by this author at the time of this writing include Hoarding Cleanup, Hoarding UK, the International Obsessive-Compulsive Disorder Foundation, and the NOCD Academy.

General Costs

The ICD Certificate program costs vary by certificate and subscribership choice (ICD, 2025a). A premium subscribership is $400 but a subscribership with the cost of the foundation certificate is $450. Level I certificates of study are $110 each and the coupled cost of the Level II exam and each specialist certificate is $219. The cost of the Level III CPO-CD® is $3,400, a price for which there is a payment plan available, and the CPO-CD® peer-review is $133. For Levels IV and V, entrance and completion fees are listed as required payments, but their amounts are not listed. Lastly, recertification for Levels III, IV, and V is $200 every three years. The certificate courses offered by the CHC (2018) are priced at $20 for the 1-hour course and $120 for the 9-hour course, and there is no required recertification or payment to maintain the certificates once earned.

EFFECTIVENESS OF THE TRAININGS

Presently, the trainings offered by the CHC (2018) and the ICD (2025f) do not provide information about whether their teachings are in alignment with any therapeutic or evidence-based practices. However, pertinent mental health topics are sprinkled into the descriptions and the ICD program invites various types of experts in working with hoarding disorder to present in classes, suggesting that they will have value to complete. As such, the effectiveness of the trainings by the CHC (2018) and the ICD (2025f) was ambiguous at the time of this chapter's writing based upon information provided on their websites.

CAUTIONS & LIMITATIONS

A primary limitation of the ICD certificates and certification is that they are not geared towards mental health professionals, so their value may be limited for mental health professionals. As a separate caution, issues related to insight and delusional beliefs may present when treating hoarding disorder. Therefore, it is important that mental health professionals are educated about how to construct treatment goals and interventions alongside these issues. Mental health professionals also need to be prepared for the reality that hoarding disorder may not be something easily overcome by their clients. Research has suggested that "Recidivism [for hoarding] is almost 100%, showing the inefficacy of the intervention[s], the lack of follow-up, and the failure to respond to the mental health component of the hoarders" (Chartered Institute of Environmental Health, 2008; Ockenden et al., 2014; Patronek, 1999, Patronek et al., 2006; Saldarriaga-Cantillo & Nieto, 2015; Strong et al., 2019, as cited in Guerra et al., 2020, p. 9). So, treatment for hoarding disorder is likely to be long-term and perhaps ongoing. Another concern is the potential for grief and trauma to have an impact on the attachment style of someone with hoarding disorder, making attachment and trauma interventions important skills for mental health professionals working with the disorder to possess.

Legal issues related to hoarding are an added concern for mental health professionals working with the disorder, as some clients may be at risk of losing their homes, pets, children, and/or freedom depending upon the protective services or legal authorities a professional may need to contact as a mandated reporter. In some cases, mental health professionals may enter the homes of those suffering from hoarding disorder and therefore it is important that informed consent takes this into consideration, documentation notates this intervention, Health Insurance Portability and Accountability Act limitations are clear for the client, professional liability insurance covers this activity, training has been completed and/or supervision has been received for such community interventions, that licensure is held for the state in which the property is located, and safety measures are put into place to prevent the injury of the professional and client if entering into a hoarded space. When entering a hoarded space, it is important for professionals and their clients to be cautious of the damages caused by the hoarding behavior, e.g., damaged home structure, toxic air quality, and/or toxic waste from humans and/or animals. Finally, ongoing consultation and supervision is recommended for working with the complex issues of this niche population.

SCOPE OF PRACTICE ISSUES

Hoarding disorder often presents as a complex issue for those who are managing it due to financial, hygienic, interpersonal, legal, comorbid mental health, and/or health issues that may be present, among other issues. Because of the potential for hoarding disorder's complexity, it is crucial for mental health professional to stay within their scope of practice to reduce the chances for client harm. In severe cases of hoarding for which extreme cleaning may be needed and a mental health professional has expertise as an organizer, it is important to prevent dual relationship issues and have an accessible list of professional organizing and cleaning services ready to use. Furthermore, the potential need for a team approach (e.g., including a psychiatrist, cleaning team, law enforcement) highlights the importance of a mental health professional being skilled in a team-based approach to treatment when working with severe cases of hoarding disorder.

WHAT KIND OF PERSON WOULD DO WELL IN COMPLETING TRAININGS

The ICD Certification program (ICD, 2025f) and certificates from the CHC (2018) are for anyone who has clients struggling with and affected by hoarding and CD. Good candidates for these certificate trainings are individuals who are motivated to learn about hoarding disorder and are disciplined in completing required assignments, classes, and readings. Because cognitive behavioral therapy is considered a primary treatment for hoarding disorder (Guerra et al., 2020; Tolin et al., 2025), mental health professionals skilled in its application may have an increased likelihood for success with clients when combined with knowledge gained from the trainings described here.

SUMMARY

Hoarding disorder is a complex mental health condition and as such requires specialized knowledge to treat as a mental health professional. The ICD (2025f) and CHC (2018) offer mental health professionals the opportunity to increase their knowledge about hoarding disorder, and the ICD (2025f) also offers a certification for becoming a professional organizer with a specialty in hoarding. Although the ICD program is expensive and the CHC offers courses at cheaper rates compared to the ICD, there are organizations that offer free of low-cost webinars and on-demand courses on the therapeutic treatment of hoarding disorder. To conclude, there are various scope of practice, ethical, legal, mandated reporting, dual relationship, and safety considerations that are important to understand and know when doing work with hoarding disorder.

Dr. Audrey Zatopek, Ph.D., M.A., LPC-S, LCDC has been a licensed counselor in Texas since 2016 and earned a Ph.D. in Counselor Education from Texas Tech University in May 2024. As a counselor educator, she has taught at several institutions and is currently an Adjunct Professor for master's level counseling programs as needed. As a counselor, she is trained in Brainspotting (BSP), Eye Movement Desensitization and Reprocessing (EMDR), Hypnosis, Parts and Memory Therapy (P&MT), Revisioning, and Sensorimotor Psychotherapy (SP). As specializations, Dr. Zatopek has expertise in working with trauma, dissociation, addiction, chronic illness, mood disorders, psychosis, self-harm, and suicidality.

Mental Health Institute, PLLC

Audrey@mentalhealthinstitute.com

https://mentalhealthinstitute.com

Phone: (832) 585-2874

REFERENCES

Bedi, S., & Woody, S. R. (2025). Social networks in the context of hoarding disorder: A cross-sectional study. *Journal of Obsessive-Compulsive and Related Disorders*, *45*, 100949. https://doi.org/10.1016/j.jocrd.2025.100949

Chan, M., Severson, D., Flynn, J., (Executive producers), Sharenow, R., Berg, A., (Executive producers for A&E), Butts, G., & Barnes, P. (Producers). (2009–2024). *Hoarders* [TV series]. TLG Motion Pictures; A&E Productions.

Guerra, S., Sousa, L., & Ribeiro, O. (2021). Report practices in the field of animal hoarding: A scoping study of the literature. *Journal of Mental Health*, *30*(5), 646–659. https://doi.org/10.1080/09638237.2020.1844872

Institute for Challenging Disorganization. (2025a). *Certificate costs FY 2025*. https://www.challengingdisorganization.org/wp-content/uploads/2024/08/Certificate-Costs-FY-2025.pdf

Institute for Challenging Disorganization. (2025b). *Certificate of study in understanding hoarding behavior (HRD)*. https://www.challengingdisorganization.org/certificates/level-i/hoarding/

Institute for Challenging Disorganization. (2025c). *Classes*. https://www.challengingdisorganization.org/education-and-events/classes/

Institute for Challenging Disorganization. (2025d). *Communication mentor*. https://icdorg.memberclicks.net/level-iv-communication-mentor

Institute for Challenging Disorganization. (2025e). *Foundation certificate*. https://www.challengingdisorganization.org/certificates/

Institute for Challenging Disorganization. (2025f). *ICD® certificate and certification overview*. https://www.challengingdisorganization.org/certificates/

Institute for Challenging Disorganization. (2025g). *ICD® classes*. https://www.challengingdisorganization.org/education-and-events/classes/

Institute for Challenging Disorganization. (2025h). *ICD® master trainer*. https://www.challengingdisorganization.org/certificates/level-v/

Institute for Challenging Disorganization. (2025i). *Level II specialist certificates*. https://www.challengingdisorganization.org/certificates/level-ii/

Institute for Challenging Disorganization. (2025j). *Level III Certified Professional Organizer in Chronic Disorganization® CPO-CD®*. https://www.challengingdisorganization.org/certificates/level-iii/

Institute for Challenging Disorganization. (2025k). *Recertification for CPO-CD®, communication mentors and ICD master trainers*. https://www.challengingdisorganization.org/certificates/recertification/

Kane, M. (Executive producer). (2010–2014). *Hoarding: Buried alive* [TV series]. Discovery Studios; A&E Productions.

The Center for Hoarding and Clutter. (2018). *Certificate courses*. https://www.centerforhoardingandcluttering.com/certificate-courses/

The Center for Hoarding and Clutter. (2020). *Safety day: An application of disaster psychology to hoarding clean-outs – certificate of completion course.* https://www.centerforhoardingandcluttering.com/courses/safety-day-an-application-of-disaster-psychology-to-hoarding-clean-outs-2/

The Center for Hoarding and Clutter. (2021). *Understanding hoarding behavior: A brief overview.* https://www.centerforhoardingandcluttering.com/courses/understanding-hoarding-behavior-a-brief-overview/

Tolin, D. F., Worden, B. L., & Levy, H. C. (2025). State of the science: Hoarding disorder and its treatment. *Behavior Therapy*, (In Press, Journal Pre-proof). https://doi.org/10.1016/j.beth.2025.03.002

Hospice Therapy

Bill Owenby, EdD, MC, FAAETS, DAAETS, DCMHS, LPC, LAAC, NCC, CCMHC, ACS, Diplomate, Fellow

Hospice therapy focuses on providing compassionate, holistic care to individuals with terminal illnesses and their families. By addressing physical, emotional, social, and spiritual needs, hospice therapy supports patients and loved ones during the end-of-life journey. For mental health professionals, integrating hospice principles into therapy can enhance their ability to provide comfort, acceptance, and resilience-building for clients facing mortality or grief.

Overview of Hospice Therapy

Hospice therapy emphasizes quality of life rather than curative treatments, recognizing the multifaceted challenges of terminal illness. Key components include:

1. **Patient-Centered Care:**
   o Focuses on the patient's goals, comfort, and dignity.
2. **Family Support:**
   o Provides education, counseling, and respite care to family members.
3. **Interdisciplinary Collaboration:**
   o Combines the expertise of healthcare professionals, counselors, spiritual advisors, and volunteers.
4. **Grief and Bereavement Support:**
   o Offers ongoing counseling to loved ones before and after the patient's death.

The Role of Mental Health Professionals in Hospice

1. **Psychosocial Support:**
   o Addressing fears, anxiety, and emotional distress for patients and families.
2. **End-of-Life Counseling:**
   o Guiding clients through existential questions, unresolved conflicts, and acceptance of mortality.
3. **Grief Counseling:**
   o Providing tools for coping with anticipatory grief and the loss of a loved one.
4. **Cultural and Spiritual Sensitivity:**
   o Honoring diverse beliefs and practices related to death and dying.

Integrating Hospice into Therapy

1. **Therapeutic Modalities:**
   o **Existential Therapy:**
      ▪ Explores meaning, purpose, and mortality to foster acceptance and peace.
   o **Cognitive Behavioral Therapy (CBT):**
      ▪ Helps patients and families reframe negative thought patterns and reduce anxiety.
   o **Narrative Therapy:**
      ▪ Encourages clients to reflect on their life stories and create a legacy.
   o **Mindfulness and Relaxation Techniques:**

- Supports emotional regulation and stress reduction.
2. **Family Systems Approach:**
   - Addresses dynamics within the family to promote communication and shared understanding.
3. **Art and Music Therapy:**
   - Offers creative outlets for expressing emotions and connecting with others.

TRAINING AND CERTIFICATION FOR HOSPICE THERAPY

1. **Eligibility:**
   - Licensed counselors, social workers, psychologists, and chaplains can pursue hospice-related training.
2. **Certifications:**
   - **Certified Hospice and Palliative Care Counselor (CHPCC):**
     - Offered by organizations like the National Board for Certified Counselors (NBCC).
   - **Advanced Certified Hospice and Palliative Social Worker (ACHP-SW):**
     - Provided by the National Association of Social Workers (NASW), this credential recognizes expertise in hospice care and requires a master's degree, experience, and continuing education.
   - **End-of-Life Counseling Certifications:**
     - Programs tailored to grief counseling and existential support, such as those offered by the American Academy of Grief Counseling.
3. **Continuing Education:**
   - Hospice-focused workshops, webinars, and conferences provide ongoing professional development. Online platforms such as Counseling Schools offer resources to explore these pathways.
4. **Cost and Time Commitment:**
   - Training programs range from $500 to $3,000, depending on certification level.
   - Certification may require 20-60 hours of coursework and supervised practice.

APPLICATIONS IN MENTAL HEALTH PRACTICE

1. **Individual Therapy:**
   - Helping terminally ill clients navigate emotional and existential challenges.
2. **Family Counseling:**
   - Supporting families in preparing for loss and fostering connection.
3. **Group Therapy:**
   - Facilitating bereavement groups for shared healing and mutual support.
4. **Community Outreach:**
   - Partnering with hospice organizations to provide workshops and resources.

ETHICAL CONSIDERATIONS

1. **Informed Consent:**
   - Clearly communicating the goals and scope of hospice therapy to clients and families.
2. **Boundaries:**
   - Maintaining professional boundaries while providing empathetic care.
3. **Cultural Competence:**
   - Understanding and respecting diverse beliefs about death and dying.

Case Example

Jane's Story:

- Jane, a 55-year-old woman with terminal cancer, expressed fears about leaving her family unprepared. Through hospice therapy:
    - She engaged in narrative therapy to reflect on her life and create a memory book for her children.
    - Mindfulness practices helped her manage anxiety and find moments of peace.
    - Family counseling sessions facilitated open conversations, reducing emotional strain for everyone involved.

BENEFITS OF INTEGRATING HOSPICE PRINCIPLES

1. **Holistic Care:**
    - Addresses the full spectrum of physical, emotional, and spiritual needs.
2. **Enhanced Resilience:**
    - Empowers clients and families to navigate the end-of-life process with grace and strength.
3. **Professional Growth:**
    - Expands the mental health professional's scope and understanding of complex human experiences.

SUMMARY

Hospice therapy offers a compassionate and comprehensive framework for addressing the emotional and spiritual challenges of terminal illness. By integrating hospice principles into mental health practice, professionals can provide meaningful support to clients and their families during one of life's most profound transitions. This work not only fosters healing and acceptance but also strengthens the bond between loved ones, leaving a legacy of connection and care.

I hold two independent licenses in the states of Arizona and Ohio, supervisory status in Arizona, along with a substance abuse license in Arizona. I am board certified as a Diplomate and Clinical Mental Health Specialist, an Approved Clinical Supervisor, Nationally Certified Counselor, a Certified Clinical Mental Health Counselor, NeuroLinguistic Programming Practitioner, and a Clinical Trauma Specialist for Individuals and Family including EMDR Therapy and NET. I completed my training in Animal-Assisted Therapy and Pet Handlers certification in order to evaluate and incorporate the human-animal bond in therapy. I am the sole author and creator of the SxC Model of ESA Evaluation. My research interests surround post-traumatic growth, resiliency, strengths-based therapy, positive psychology, mindfulness, Animal-Assisted Therapy, Sandtray Therapy, Creative approaches in therapy, and martial arts in mental health. I have presented at local, state, regional, national, and international levels on various topics including personality traits, licensure reciprocity challenges, Sandtray and supervision, and Animal-Assisted Therapy within supervision. eonbllc@gmail.com

REFERENCES

National Hospice and Palliative Care Organization. (2023). *Guidelines for Hospice Care.*

Neimeyer, R. A. (2012). *Techniques of Grief Therapy: Creative Practices for Counseling the Bereaved.*

American Counseling Association. (2023). *Ethical Standards for End-of-Life Counseling.*

Recommended Online Resources

National Hospice and Palliative Care Organization
American Academy of Grief Counseling
National Board for Certified Counselors

Human Givens Therapy (HGT)

DEREK X. SEWARD, PhD, LMHC, NCC, ACS

BRITTANY WILLIAMS, PhD, LCPC, NCC

Human Givens Therapy (HGT) is a short-term, solution-oriented therapeutic approach focused on helping individuals alleviate their mental health distress and promote wellness (Welsted, 2022). HGT has been applied to a range of mental health concerns including depression (Karamiboldaji et al., 2021) and post-traumatic stress disorder (Adams & Allen, 2019; Burdett & Greenberg, 2019). Scholars have noted its effectiveness with youth (Yates, 2011) and adults (Burdett & Greenberg, 2019). Co-developed by Joe Griffin and Ivan Tyrrell, HGT is based on the theory that humans have innate needs or "givens" that when met allow for the achievement and maintenance of healthy emotional well-being. Psychological distress can emerge when an individual's innate needs are not met. HGT focuses on helping clients identify and address their unmet innate needs.

Central to HGT is the theoretical understanding that humans' innate needs are emotional and physical. The emotional needs that must be met for humans to live healthily include (a) a sense of security and safety; (b) giving and receiving attention; a sense of autonomy and control; (c) a sense of privacy; (d) being connected to a community beyond immediate family; (e) a sense of intimacy with others; (f) a sense of social status within social groupings; (g) a sense of competence and achievement; and (h) a sense of meaning and purpose (Griffin & Tyrrell, 2013). The physical needs required for humans include but are not limited to air, water, food, and a safe environment (Griffin & Tyrrell, 2013).

To help meet their needs, HGT posits that humans have innate resources. These resources or tools allow humans to make sense of and engage with their environment. Innate human resources include (a) possessing emotions and instincts that help in making sense of the environment; (b) the ability to develop complex long term memory which supports learning; (c) the ability to build rapport and empathize with others; (d) possessing imagination that can be used for creative problem solving; having intuition or the ability to understand the world unconsciously through pattern matching; (e) being able to check out emotions, analyze, and plan; (f) awareness or the ability to step back to be objective; and the ability to dream which allows the brain to decompress in preparation for the next day (Welsted, 2022). HGT aims to help clients identify and utilize their resources to meet their emotional needs.

HGT's treatment philosophy is rooted in neuropsychology research on how the human brain functions (see, LeDoux, 1998). Griffin and Tyrrell (2013) identified three key principles related to brain functioning that are essential to facilitate therapeutic change. First, the brain uses a complex, unconscious pattern-making process that entails making sense of stimuli via our innate and learned reality templates (i.e., perceptions). Second, emotions precede thoughts with all thoughts and perceptions being associated with emotions. Third, the higher a person's emotional arousal, the more primitive the emotional and mental pattern that is engaged. In essence, thinking in extremes (i.e., black and white thinking) can result from hyper-emotional arousal, which may not be advantageous for healthy pattern-matching. These key principles serve as the foundation for HGT treatment which is best understood via the APET Model.

Griffin and Tyrell (2013) presented the APET Model to help practitioners conceptualize how to approach human givens treatment. APET is an acronym for (A) activating event, (P) pattern matching, (E) emotions, and (T) thoughts. This framework explains the process of how the brain pairs stimuli with emotions in healthy and unhealthy ways. Essentially, it is an activating event or environmental stimulus that triggers the pattern matching process through which perceptions (i.e. meaning) are associated with the stimuli followed by emotions being attached or 'tagged' to the perceptions. Thoughts may emerge at the end of this process if the person is not overly emotionally aroused.

For Human Givens (HG) practitioners, the APET model is advantageous because treatment can be centered around any of the specific stages in the model (Yates, 2011). For instance, if a client is struggling with the chaotic nature of their work environment (which is the activating event), the HG practitioner might help the client explore various options such as speaking with supervisors, exploring other roles within the company that are less activating, changing their company, or changing their job. At the pattern matching level, practitioners might help the client to alter their perception of their work environment. Practitioners might help the client learn relaxation techniques to deal with their feelings if intervening at the emotions level. At the thought level, cognitive restructuring or reframing might be used by practitioners with clients to promote healthy, productive thoughts about their job.

HGT is present and future-oriented in its treatment approach. Less emphasis is placed on past experiences as here and now aspects are considered important to helping clients identify and address their unmet needs. Practitioners assume a collaborative relationship with clients as they work together to identify innate and environmental resources that can be leveraged in treatment. HGT utilizes a range of techniques from various therapeutic traditions to help clients meet their emotional needs more effectively. Techniques can include guided imagery, relaxation, reframing, metaphors, and cognitive behavioral interventions. Unique to HGT is the rewind technique which is a trauma-exposure treatment that has received increased attention as an effective treatment for traumas including post-traumatic stress disorder (Adams & Allan, 2019; Uçar, 2022).

The HG treatment process involves practitioners following specific treatment phases as delineated by the acronym RIGAAR (Griffin & Tyrrell, 2013). Rapport building (R) starts the treatment process as practitioners work to develop a positive working alliance with clients. Information gathering (I) occurs next as practitioners learn about the client's problems including onset, duration, and contextual factors. Goal setting (G) is the next treatment phase. Practitioners collaboratively work with clients to establish clear, specific, and measurable goals which are used to evaluate treatment progress. Practitioners then engage in accessing a strategy (A), which involves identifying at what APET level(s) treatment will focus. Also, intervention strategies are identified. The next phase, accessing resources (A), involves helping clients to identify their strengths, achievements, and successes that can be used to highlight client capacity for overcoming challenges. Although practitioners are attentive to resources in this phrase, they seek to learn about the client's innate and environmental resources throughout the treatment process. Rehearsal (R) is the final treatment phase. It involves helping clients imagine using learned skills and resources to cope with their challenges using techniques such as guided imagery and metaphorical reframing.

CERTIFICATIONS, TRAININGS, AND LICENSURE REQUIREMENTS FOR HUMAN GIVENS THERAPY

To become a qualified human givens practitioner, an individual must earn a Human Givens Practitioner Level Diploma (HG.Dip.P). Pursuit of this diploma begins with training offered through the Human Givens College (HGC, **www.humangivens.com/college/**), which provides instruction online and in-person in the United Kingdom. It is expected to take between 1.5-3 years to complete the full Human Givens Diploma program to practitioner level, however, since the trainee can go at their own pace completion times will vary (Human Givens College, n.d.). HGC also provides workshops and professional development for mental health professionals interested in HGT but not seeking to obtain a degree.

HGC degree training is divided into 3 sequential components (Human Givens College, n.d.). Part 1 consists of a series of 17 in-person workshops and online courses that can be completed at a trainee's own pace. Home study that includes a reading list is also required. Part 2 includes two weeks of intensive training in which the trainee engages with therapy demonstrations by the tutors, skills development, trainee practice sessions, a 2-hour written examination, and competency-based assessments. Upon successful completion of part 1 and 2 tasks, trainees earn the Human Givens Diploma (HG.Dip.), which affords them eligibility to be considered a Human Givens Practitioner Trainee. Graduate-level membership in the Human Givens Institute (HGI), the professional organization that promotes the human givens approach, is required to work as a practitioner trainee. Prior to starting part 3, practitioner trainees must work with a minimum of 10 different clients under the supervision of an HGI-approved supervisor to develop their clinical competency. Supervisors determine when trainees can advance to the final training part based on the trainee's demonstrated competence. Part 3 requires trainees to engage in an intensive weeklong training that requires them to practice and demonstrate their clinical skills. Trainees must successfully pass the evaluation of a written case study of their clinical work and demonstrate human givens techniques (i.e., the rewind technique, counter-conditioning) to receive their Human Givens Practitioner Level Diploma. With their diploma, individuals can practice as fully qualified HG practitioners as determined by the HGI.

Cost: The general costs were at minimum 9,827 Pounds, which converted to about $12,265 USD and vary based on the availability and offering of workshops and courses at each part of the diploma process.

SCOPE OF PRACTICE ISSUES

The Human Givens Diploma (HG.Dip) is primarily for professionals in mental health, social services, or education who want to enhance their knowledge, skills, and effectiveness. Other professionals who pursue HG training include counselors, psychiatric nurses, midwives, chaplains, human resources professionals, physicians, and community development consultants. HG training provides information in an accessible manner whereby various professionals - even those without a mental health background - can benefit from learning about HG psychological understandings and interventions. The Human Givens Practitioner Level Diploma (HG.Dip.P) allows an individual to fully practice as an HG counselor or therapist. Also, Practitioner Level graduates are eligible to be listed on the Human Givens Institute's Therapist Register, which is the official international register of fully qualified HG practitioners (Human Givens Institute, n.d.).

The Human Givens Institute (HGI) is the professional organization that promotes the HG approach. Central to its mission is advocacy, education and training, support for HG practice, support for scholarly inquiry, public access to a registry of fully qualified HG practitioners and serving as a hub for HG publications. Specific to HG therapeutic practice, HGI provides information on professional standards, continuing professional development requirements, and professional ethics. HGI encourages professionals, trainees, and individuals interested in HG to join the organization at one of the various membership levels (e.g., registered member, graduate-level member, associate member).

SUMMARY

Human Givens Therapy represents a unique approach to mental health treatment and wellness. The key premise of HGT is that psychological distress and mental health problems arise when an individual's innate needs are inadequately met or unfulfilled. HGT focuses on helping individuals identify and address their unmet needs so they can achieve emotional health and wellness. Various therapeutic interventions are used to help clients meet their emotional needs including guided imagery, relaxation techniques, cognitive restructuring, and rewind - which is unique to HGT. The treatment approach is practical and solution-focused with practitioners partnering with clients to focus on here-and-now aspects to help clients fulfill their emotional needs.

Derek Xavier Seward is a counselor educator in the School of Education at Syracuse University. Dr. Seward's scholarly interests focus on multicultural and social justice counselor education. He is a Licensed Mental Health Counselor in New York State, National Certified Counselor, and Approved Clinical Supervisor.

https://soe.syr.edu/
315-443-9623
dxseward@syr.edu

Brittany A. Williams is an assistant teaching professor in the School of Education at Syracuse University. Dr. Williams's scholarly interests include multicultural competence in counseling populations of color and training counselors and supervisors with minoritized identities. Dr. Williams is also a licensed clinical professional counselor (LCPC) in Maryland and is invested in fostering alternative environments to assist people with mental health concerns, and who have had traumatic life experiences.

Website: https://soe.syr.edu/
315-443-9655
bawill05@syr.edu

REFERENCES

Adams, S., & Allan, S. (2019). The effectiveness of Human Givens Rewind treatment for trauma. *Mental Health Review Journal, 24*, 228-242. doi: 10.1108/MHRJ-10-2018-0033

Burdett, H., & Greenberg, N. (2019). Service evaluation of a Human Givens Therapy service for veterans. *Occupational medicine, 69*, 586–592. doi: 10.1093/occmed/kqz045

Griffin, J., & Tyrrell, I. (2013). Human givens: The new approach to emotional health and clear thinking. HG Publishing.

Human Givens College. (n.d.). The stages of qualification and registration as a human givens therapist. https://www.hgi.org.uk/stages-qualification-and-registration-human-givens-therapist

Karamiboldaji, R., Zarei, E., Fallahchai, S. R., & Sadeghifard, M. (2021). Comparison of the Effectiveness of Human Givens Therapy (HGT) and Rational-Emotive-Behavior Therapy (REBT) on Reducing Irrational Beliefs of Divorced Women. *Journal of Applied Psychological Research, 12*, 1-18. doi: 10.22059/japr.2021.307264.643595

LeDoux, J.E. (1998) The Emotional Brain. New York: Weidenfeld and Nicolson

Uçar, S. (2022). A Systematic Review Study on Human Givens Therapy's Effectiveness. *Psikiyatride Guncel Yaklasimlar, 14*, 276-283.

Welstead, J. (2022). *Human givens: The essentials.* Human Givens College.

Yates, Y. (2011). *Human givens therapy with adolescents: A practical guide for professionals.* Jessica Kingsley Publishers.

Human Services-Board Certified Practitioner (HS-BCP)

BILL OWENBY, EDD, MC, FAAETS, DAAETS, DCMHS, LPC, LAAC, NCC, CCMHC, ACS, DIPLOMATE, FELLOW

The Human Services-Board Certified Practitioner (HS-BCP) credential serves as a professional standard for individuals in the field of human services. This certification demonstrates advanced knowledge, skills, and commitment to ethical practices in supporting diverse populations. For professionals aiming to advance their careers and enhance service delivery, obtaining the HS-BCP credential is a critical step.

WHAT IS THE HS-BCP?

The HS-BCP credential, offered by the Center for Credentialing & Education (CCE), is designed for human services professionals who have completed academic and fieldwork requirements in human services or related fields. It provides a benchmark for competency and ethical practice across various roles and settings.

Key Features

1. **Nationally Recognized**: Provides validation of skills and knowledge applicable across states and organizations.
2. **Ethical Standards**: Requires adherence to the National Organization for Human Services (NOHS) Code of Ethics.
3. **Continuing Education**: Mandates ongoing professional development to maintain the credential.

Eligibility Requirements

To qualify for the HS-BCP, candidates must meet the following criteria:

Educational Background

1. **Associate's Degree:**
   o Minimum of 60 semester hours in human services or a closely related field.
2. **Bachelor's Degree:**
   o Completion of an accredited bachelor's program in human services or related fields such as social work, psychology, or counseling.

Field Experience

1. **Associate's Level:**
   o 4,500 hours of post-degree human services work experience.
2. **Bachelor's Level:**
   o 3,000 hours of post-degree human services work experience.

Supervision

- A portion of field experience must be supervised by a qualified professional.

Examination

- Successful completion of the HS-BCP exam, which assesses knowledge in:
  - Ethical and legal practices.
  - Case management.
  - Assessment and intervention strategies.

BENEFITS OF HS-BCP CERTIFICATION

For Professionals

1. **Career Advancement**:
   - Opens doors to leadership and specialized roles within the human services field.
2. **Credibility**:
   - Demonstrates commitment to high professional standards and ethical practices.
3. **Marketability**:
   - Increases competitiveness in job markets and opportunities for promotions.

For Employers

1. **Assured Competency**:
   - Ensures staff meet a recognized standard of practice.
2. **Reduced Liability**:
   - Credentialed professionals are more likely to adhere to ethical and legal guidelines.
3. **Enhanced Service Delivery**:
   - Clients benefit from high-quality, competent care.

APPLICATIONS OF THE HS-BCP CREDENTIAL

Settings

1. **Nonprofit Organizations**:
   - Roles in case management, advocacy, and program coordination.
2. **Government Agencies**:
   - Positions in child welfare, public health, and community development.
3. **Healthcare Settings**:
   - Support services in hospitals, clinics, and rehabilitation centers.
4. **Educational Institutions**:
   - Career counseling, academic advising, and student support roles.

Specialized Roles

1. **Case Manager**:
   - Coordinates care and resources for individuals and families.
2. **Behavioral Health Specialist**:
   - Provides support in managing mental health and substance use challenges.
3. **Community Outreach Coordinator**:
   - Develops programs to address community needs and improve access to services.

CHALLENGES AND CONSIDERATIONS

Cost

- Initial application and exam fees can range from $200 to $400, depending on eligibility level.
- Continuing education requirements may add financial and time commitments.

Maintaining Certification

- Requires periodic renewal and completion of continuing education units (CEUs).
- Staying updated on evolving ethical and professional standards is essential.

Field Limitations

- Certain advanced roles may require licensure or additional credentials beyond the HS-BCP.

HOW TO OBTAIN THE HS-BCP CREDENTIAL

1. **Educational Preparation:**
   o Enroll in accredited programs focusing on human services, social work, or counseling.
2. **Accumulate Field Experience:**
   o Pursue internships, volunteer roles, or entry-level positions to gain supervised experience.
3. **Prepare for the Exam:**
   o Utilize study guides and practice exams provided by CCE.
4. **Apply for Certification:**
   o Submit proof of education, experience, and supervision through the CCE application portal.
5. **Pass the Exam:**
   o Demonstrate competency in ethical, practical, and theoretical aspects of human services.
6. **Maintain Certification:**
   o Complete required CEUs and adhere to NOHS ethical standards.

THE FUTURE OF HS-BCP IN HUMAN SERVICES

The HS-BCP credential is increasingly recognized as a benchmark for professional excellence. As the field of human services grows in complexity, the need for certified practitioners who can navigate ethical challenges, advocate for clients, and deliver high-quality care will continue to rise. Additionally, technological advancements and policy changes are likely to expand the roles and responsibilities of HS-BCPs in addressing societal needs.

SUMMARY

The Human Services Board Certified Practitioner credential represents a commitment to ethical excellence, professional growth, and high-quality care. By obtaining this certification, professionals not only enhance their careers but also contribute to the betterment of the human services field. For those dedicated to making a difference, the HS-BCP is an invaluable asset.

I hold two independent licenses in the states of Arizona and Ohio, supervisory status in Arizona, along with a substance abuse license in Arizona. I am board certified as a Diplomate and Clinical Mental Health Specialist, an Approved Clinical Supervisor, Nationally Certified Counselor, a Certified Clinical Mental Health Counselor, NeuroLinguistic Programming Practitioner, and a Clinical Trauma Specialist for Individuals and Family including EMDR Therapy and NET. I completed my training in Animal-Assisted Therapy and Pet Handlers certification in order to evaluate and incorporate the human-animal bond in therapy. I am the sole author and creator of the SxC Model of ESA Evaluation. My research interests surround post-traumatic growth, resiliency, strengths-based therapy, positive psychology, mindfulness, Animal-Assisted Therapy, Sandtray Therapy, Creative approaches in therapy, and martial arts in mental health. I have presented at local, state, regional, national, and international levels on various topics including personality traits, licensure reciprocity challenges, Sandtray and supervision, and Animal-Assisted Therapy within supervision. eonbllc@gmail.com

REFERENCES

Center for Credentialing & Education (CCE). (2024). *HS-BCP Credential Handbook*. Retrieved from CCE website.

National Organization for Human Services (NOHS). (2024). *Code of Ethics*. Retrieved from NOHS website.

Smith, J. A. (2023). "Professionalization of Human Services: Trends and Implications." *Journal of Human Services*, 42(3), 12-22.

Recommended Resources

- **National Organization for Human Services (NOHS):** https://www.nationalhumanservices.org
- **Center for Credentialing & Education (CCE):** https://www.cce-global.org
- **Human Services Education Directory:** https://www.humanservicesedu.org

Hypnosis/Hypnotherapy (CCH)

Lauren C. Ostrowski, MA, LPC, NCC, BC-TMH, CCTP, CCH

Imagine a rainbow. When you visualize this, you are actually using your mind's eye to see a division of white light. Upon closer inspection, you'll see that the rainbow is not one stripe of red or orange, for example, as human eyes tend to perceive it. Rather, it's a complete range of a stunningly large number of colors that make up the entire color spectrum, each one gradually and gently fading into the next. This is a very appropriate metaphor for how many options there are for the clinical application of hypnosis. A few clinical examples are below.

When working with a symptom like anxiety, the client may visualize their feelings of anxiety in a color or shape, being able to exhale a lot of the emotion or visualize a symbol for the emotions in front of them so they are then able to see or learn about what it connects to. Perhaps they see that it ties to an argument that they had three days ago with their significant other. In addition to asking the client what they would like to change or learn from what happened, the hypnotherapist may offer techniques such as a dial to lower the emotional intensity to make it easier to examine. Additionally, some clients prefer to look at an event from above so they are slightly dissociated from the emotion and more able to see their role in what happened. Perhaps they would identify what they could possibly do differently during arguments to either have the presence of mind to walk away for a few minutes or to use their voice more effectively.

Maybe the client would choose to imagine themselves surrounded by a calming color or repeat a centering phrase to themselves. Some people even notice that they are bringing content from the past into a current discussion and that this past content does not apply in the present moment. They are then able to adjust that by changing the size of the effect, putting those thoughts aside, or attaching the emotion to the scenario where it was actually useful. In his course on using parts work in hypnosis, Nongard (2022) explains that dissociation is a way that the brain and body manage very overwhelming feelings. While the hypnotherapist must be aware that the client is fully integrated in body and mind prior to the end of the session, some intentional dissociation during the session creates space for examination, learning, and change.

For a topic like sadness or depression, it is possible that a client would be able to identify part of their behaviors in the present that are leading to that feeling. Other clients may more readily identify self-talk that includes limiting beliefs. There was a woman who once said that she really felt she was a good mother to her children when they were very young, but did not know how to shift into being what she felt was an accomplished mother to teenagers. Once she identified what made her feel more secure in mothering her younger children, she was able to also recognize how some of those principles were still part of her parenting as she mothered her teenagers, whereas her teenagers had been practicing patterns that she taught them previously and they were doing so independently. In being able to release some of the way that she defined successful parenting of younger children, she made the space for looking at what else she could add now because she was increasing her understanding as much as her children were growing alongside of her.

While this author uses a lot of techniques and interventions within hypnosis that are topic-specific at the time of the session, most clients also see how the work can be generalized, either through what they experience in the week or two after a hypnotic session or as the hypnotherapist is able to facilitate being able to see those connections.

INTRODUCTION TO TREATMENT MODALITY

Hypnosis was originally developed by Franz Anton Mesmer and it was thought to be animal magnetism. Later, hypnosis was used in the treatment of "hysteria," which is now called anxiety (Calof, 1985). Hypnosis was approved as a treatment modality by the American Medical Association in the 1950s (Calof, 1985).

Hypnosis is a very diverse treatment modality. "[Milton] Erickson believed that trance is a natural phenomenon, that we are always in one state of trance or another" (Nongard & Thomas, 2009, p. 33). Additionally, all hypnosis is self-hypnosis, and the hypnotherapist is a guide throughout the process (Nongard & Thomas, 2009). Consider the automatic relaxation that happens while driving down the highway. The driver can react quickly if needed, but otherwise may find that they have reached their destination much quicker than they expected because their experience of time is a bit distorted. Watching a movie is another example of hypnosis because the person watching may feel enveloped by the world in the film. For this author, most of the hypnosis starts with creating a safe place.

Woods and Gibbons (2017) discuss that a hypnotic induction requires that clients are able to use their imagination and are willing participants in the process. This author adds that having a desire for change is necessary for hypnotic success. While relaxation is often a part of the process, it is not a requirement. All clients will only make changes or utilize skills that they believe are useful or appropriate for them. If a hypnotist makes a suggestion that does not fit for a client, they will either not follow through with the suggestion or forget it completely. This is a very important part of consent for hypnosis so that clients understand that they are in complete control of what is happening. Nongard and Hazlerig (2014) also recommend using an ecology check, which involves the hypnotherapist asking the client if a certain concept or change would be valuable to them and in line with their intentions or desires.

Clinical hypnosis is far different than stage hypnosis. In both types of hypnosis, the client will only follow through with ideas that they find useful or comfortable for them. In clinical hypnosis, the focus is on changing or adding to a particular skill set, understanding, or perhaps looking to separate past patterns from those in the present. In stage hypnosis, it is very likely that participants will do something silly, such as clucking like a chicken, because the whole idea of a stage show is to be funny and spontaneous. Those who participate in a hypnosis stage show are essentially agreeing to do something that is amusing or fun. This contrast is important, as people who are considering using clinical hypnosis will often ask about the phenomena practiced during stage shows.

A booklet compiled by Nongard (n.d.) shows links to more than 100 articles showing that hypnosis is effective. In addition, hypnosis has a tremendous amount of utility in strengthening interventions from any school of thought within psychotherapy. For example, a client may be very receptive to suggestions about recognizing antecedents and consequences for a particular behavior or moving from all-or-nothing thinking into recognizing choices that fall between one end of the spectrum and another, both of which would be hypnotic applications for cognitive behavioral therapy. Hypnosis also offers a unique opportunity for Gestalt modalities of empty chair or two-chair work with intrapsychic splits because of the ability for the client to feel as if they are able to have a dialogue between multiple parts of themselves or to see the perspective of someone else who is important to them. The hypnotic realm magnifies the clients' ability to notice thoughts, feelings, and bodily sensations within the different parts of these processes. Nongard (2022) also discusses using hypnosis to examine parent, adult, and child parts, as recognized in Internal Family Systems. Related to trauma treatment, there is tremendous utility in helping clients to separate the lessons they would benefit from carrying forward into the rest of their lives from those that would be best left in the past. Additionally, this author notes the usefulness of the hypnotic modality for creating or emphasizing calm and comfort or use of other preferred mindfulness or grounding techniques to create more tolerance for stressful situations or therapeutic work that may otherwise have been too distressing.

The positive elements of becoming a certified hypnotherapist or hypnotist are far too many to list here. Explained briefly, connecting with a safe place as part of the hypnotic process creates a space where clients are willing to take risks to look into patterns in thinking, feeling, and behavior in a way that they otherwise may not. Hypnosis opens a lot of creative doors for clients to shift their beliefs or reactions in the ways that are best for them. In addition, hypnotic language patterns are useful in conversation without intentional use of hypnotic trance. For example, being very straightforward, a clinician might say "Relax your body." Someone with training or experience in hypnosis might say "Notice what happens when you allow your body to begin relaxing now." Words or phrases, including "imagine," "consider," "recognize," "become aware of," "give yourself permission," and "empower yourself to," commonly create opportunities for further awareness and change.

The difference between a hypnotist and a hypnotherapist could be described this way: Generally, a hypnotist is a coach or someone with specialized training, while a hypnotherapist is someone who has completed formal education or licensure as a helping professional and also has training as a hypnotist.

- General costs: $50 per month through self-paced course to $300 for foundational coursework; some multi-level courses are much higher in cost

- Hypnosis includes use of evidence-based practices

- Certificates are available; training is required

- Supervision requirements vary depending on certification; continued education or interactions with groups of hypnotists or hypnotherapists is recommended; conferences are available and provide the opportunity to learn different styles after initial training or certification

There are innumerable options for training in hypnosis or hypnotherapy. Here are a few resources:

- The International Certification Board of Clinical Hypnotherapy (ICBCH): https://hypnotherapyboard.com/

- American Society of Clinical Hypnosis (ASCH): https://asch.net/aws/ASCH/pt/sp/home_page

- National Guild of Hypnotists (NGH) directory of possible training options: https://www.ngh.net/ngh-certified-consulting-hypnotist-courses/

SCOPE OF PRACTICE ISSUES

Hypnotherapy has potential to be a useful modality for almost anyone who is committed to a change process that is valuable to them. Scope of practice concerns for a hypnotherapist depend upon client concerns and clinical training. Remembering that hypnosis is a modality that draws from other areas of clinical experience, a therapist should always practice within clinical areas in which they are competent.

Certain clinical issues require additional specialized hypnotherapy training or more specific consent. For example, medical hypnosis is a large subset of clinical treatment using hypnosis. It involves specific consent from treating physicians, so the hypnotist is not suggesting that a client changes a pain response that is being used to determine whether medical treatment is effective. The limitations of hypnosis, related to most issues presented in a clinical therapy setting, rest not in the limits of the modality itself, but rather in limits of the overall competency of the therapist or hypnotherapist.

Additionally, it is within suggested practice to address clinical issues in a way that is has been discussed in training, even if the topic being addressed is different. For example, if a calming color was taught as a method to reduce anxiety or increase calm, this same technique may very easily be applied to other changes in mood. Nongard and Woods (2018) write about the concept of integrating hypnosis into the use of various theoretical models of psychotherapy, which they term "contextual hypnotherapy." Nongard and Woods (2018) further express that hypnotherapists have "the ability to recognize the value of language and language patterns in change work" (p. 9). While hypnosis is based in science and evidence-based modalities are used, the application of hypnosis is an art form.

Some individuals may view the possibility of additional training as a negative idea. There are many options for training in hypnosis and new possibilities are often available. This author believes that continued training is important so that new concepts or ideas can be integrated into the therapist's skill set.

REVIEW OF TRAINING, PROCESS OF CERTIFICATION/CREDENTIAL, AND OVERALL EXPERIENCE

Hypnosis is a modality that creates a unique space for client change. Length of certifications vary and are often available online. The process of hypnosis is typically very enjoyable to clients because it is tailored to both their presenting issues and their strengths. In addition, because all hypnosis is self-hypnosis, clients are able to practice skills or ideas on their own after they have learned from a hypnotist or hypnotherapist. This author enjoys being able to guide clients to create a space where they are able to work toward changes that are best for them. Also, many clients verbalize that they are able to attain goals hypnotically that they had chosen not to address or had not found their desired success through other therapeutic modalities. If a therapist is looking to provide a way for clients to be able to exponentially increase their ability to self-regulate, build trust in their abilities, and expand confidence in their own strengths, hypnosis or hypnotherapy will open those doors.

Lauren Ostrowski is a Licensed Professional Counselor in a group private practice in the greater Philadelphia area. Hypnosis is part of her work almost daily, surrounding many clinical issues, including anxiety reduction, grief and trauma healing, and being able to more completely identify strengths and limitations that increase effectiveness of clinical work. Lauren is also a teaching assistant for the Couples Institute's comprehensive online training program and specializes in working with couples and individuals using the Bader-Pearson Developmental Model of Couples Therapy. Additionally, Lauren enjoys studying the connections between the emotional or mental components of martial arts and therapeutic interactions.

https://www.psychologytoday.com/us/therapists/lauren-c-ostrowski-pottstown-pa/308965
ostrowski.lauren@gmail.com

REFERENCES

American Society of Clinical Hypnosis (n.d.). https://asch.net/aws/ASCH/pt/sp/home_page

Calof, D. (1985). *A short history of hypnosis.* Family Therapy Networker, 9(2), 27.

International Certification Board of Clinical Hypnotherapists (n.d.). *ICBCH professional hypnosis certification and membership.* https://hypnotherapyboard.com/

National Guild of Hypnotists (n.d.). *Find an NGH certified consulting hypnotist instructor.* Https://www.ngh.net/ngh-certified-consulting-hypnotist-courses/

Nongard R. K. & Hazlerig J. (2014). *Speak Ericksonian: Mastering the hypnotic methods of Milton Erickson.* PeachTree Professional Education.

Nongard R. K. & Thomas N. (2009). *Keys to the mind: Learn how to hypnotize anyone and practice hypnosis and hypnotherapy correctly.* PeachTree Professional Education.

Nongard R. K. & Woods, K. T. (2018). *Reframing hypnotherapy: Evidence-based techniques for your next hypnosis session.* PeachTree Professional Education.

Nongard, R. (2022). *The experiential parts therapy workshop.* Expert Hypnosis: The New Subliminal Science Website. https://experthypnosis.com/product/the-experiential-parts-therapy-workshop/

Nongard, R. (n.d.). *101 proofs that hypnosis helps heal faster, recover stronger and works in medical treatment.* International Certification Board of Clinical Hypnotherapy and Subliminal Science, Expert Hypnosis Training & Professional Networking. https://subliminalscience.com/wp-content/uploads/2019/03/101-Proofs-that-Hypnosis-Words-ICBCH-HPTI-Hypnosis.pdf

Woods, K.T. & Gibbons, D.E. (2017). *Virtual reality hypnosis: Adventures in the multiverse.* CreateSpace Independent Publishing Platform.

Ice/Cold Therapy

BILL OWENBY, EdD, MC, FAAETS, DAAETS, DCMHS, LPC, LAAC, NCC, CCMHC, ACS, DIPLOMATE, FELLOW

Ice/Cold Therapy, commonly referred to as cryotherapy, cold water immersion, or cold exposure, involves the application of cold temperatures to the body to promote healing, reduce inflammation, and enhance mental and physical well-being. With roots in ancient healing practices, cold therapy has gained modern recognition for its therapeutic benefits in diverse fields, including sports medicine, mental health, and integrative therapy.

FOUNDATIONS OF ICE/COLD THERAPY

Cryotherapy leverages the body's natural response to cold to stimulate physiological and psychological healing processes. Techniques range from localized cold packs to whole-body immersion in cryogenic chambers.

Core Principles

1. **Vasoconstriction and Vasodilation**:
   o Exposure to cold causes blood vessels to constrict, reducing inflammation, followed by vasodilation, which promotes circulation and healing.
2. **Endorphin Release**:
   o Cold exposure triggers the release of endorphins, enhancing mood and reducing pain perception.
3. **Stress Response Activation**:
   o Stimulates the body's stress-response systems, improving resilience and adaptability.

APPLICATIONS OF ICE/COLD THERAPY

Physical Health

1. **Inflammation Reduction**:
   o Treats conditions such as arthritis, tendonitis, and muscle soreness.
2. **Pain Management**:
   o Alleviates chronic and acute pain through localized cold application.
3. **Improved Recovery**:
   o Accelerates recovery for athletes and individuals undergoing physical rehabilitation.

Mental Health

1. **Anxiety and Depression**:
   o Whole-body cryotherapy has shown promise in alleviating symptoms by modulating stress hormones and increasing endorphin levels.
2. **Stress Reduction**:
   o Cold immersion enhances parasympathetic nervous system activity, promoting relaxation.

Integrative Therapy

- Complements other therapeutic modalities, including physical therapy, trauma recovery, and mindfulness practices.

TECHNIQUES IN ICE/COLD THERAPY

1. Cold Packs and Compresses

- Commonly used for localized pain and swelling.
- Example: Applying a cold pack to an inflamed joint for 15-20 minutes.

2. Cold Water Immersion (CWI)

- Involves submerging the body in cold water, typically between 50-59°F.
- Example: Ice baths used by athletes for recovery after intense physical activity.

3. Whole-Body Cryotherapy (WBC)

- Exposes the body to extremely cold air (below -200°F) in a cryogenic chamber for 2-3 minutes.
- Example: A therapy session at a cryotherapy center for chronic pain management.

4. Ice Massage

- Combines cold application with massage techniques for targeted muscle relief.
- Example: Using an ice ball to massage a sore back or shoulder.

PATHWAYS TO BECOMING A CRYOTHERAPY SPECIALIST

Education Requirements

1. **Background in Healthcare or Fitness:**
   o Professionals often hold degrees in physical therapy, sports medicine, or related fields.
2. **Certification Programs:**
   o Cryotherapy-specific training programs offered by accredited organizations.

Certifications

1. **Certified Cryotherapy Technician (CCT):**
   o Covers the science, safety protocols, and operation of cryotherapy equipment.
2. **Specialized Sports Recovery Training:**
   o Focuses on integrating cryotherapy into athletic recovery programs.

Continuing Education

- Workshops on advancements in cryotherapy technology and evidence-based practices.

ETHICAL AND PRACTICAL CONSIDERATIONS

1. **Client Safety:**
   - Monitoring for adverse reactions, such as frostbite or hypothermia.
2. **Informed Consent:**
   - Ensuring clients understand potential risks and benefits.
3. **Individualized Treatment:**
   - Tailoring therapy to the client's specific needs and health conditions.

BENEFITS OF ICE/COLD THERAPY

For Clients

1. **Enhanced Recovery:**
   - Speeds up healing and reduces downtime for injuries.
2. **Mental Clarity:**
   - Cold exposure has been linked to improved mood and cognitive function.
3. **Resilience Building:**
   - Improves the body's ability to handle stress and adversity.

For Therapists

1. **Versatile Applications:**
   - Complements various therapeutic practices, broadening service offerings.
2. **Client Attraction:**
   - Meets growing demand for innovative wellness solutions.

CHALLENGES IN ICE/COLD THERAPY

1. **Accessibility:**
   - High costs of cryotherapy equipment and facilities may limit availability.
2. **Client Discomfort:**
   - Some individuals find cold exposure intolerable.
3. **Contraindications:**
   - Not suitable for clients with certain medical conditions, such as Raynaud's disease.

SUMMARY

Ice/Cold Therapy is a powerful tool for enhancing mental and physical health. By leveraging the body's natural responses to cold, this modality offers benefits ranging from pain relief and inflammation reduction to improved mood and stress resilience. As interest in holistic and integrative therapies continues to grow, cryotherapy stands out as a versatile and impactful approach to wellness.

I hold two independent licenses in the states of Arizona and Ohio, supervisory status in Arizona, along with a substance abuse license in Arizona. I am board certified as a Diplomate and Clinical Mental Health Specialist, an Approved Clinical Supervisor, Nationally Certified Counselor, a Certified Clinical Mental Health Counselor, NeuroLinguistic Programming Practitioner, and a Clinical Trauma Specialist for Individuals and Family including EMDR Therapy and NET. I completed my training in Animal-Assisted Therapy and Pet Handlers certification in order to evaluate and incorporate the human-animal bond in therapy. I am the sole author and creator of the SxC Model of ESA Evaluation. My research interests surround post-traumatic growth, resiliency, strengths-based therapy, positive psychology, mindfulness, Animal-Assisted Therapy, Sandtray Therapy, Creative approaches in therapy, and martial arts in mental health. I have presented at local, state, regional, national, and international levels on various topics including personality traits, licensure reciprocity challenges, Sandtray and supervision, and Animal-Assisted Therapy within supervision. eonbllc@gmail.com

REFERENCES

Costello, J. T., Baker, P. R., & Minett, G. M. (2015). Whole-body cryotherapy: Empirical evidence and theoretical perspectives. *Sports Medicine, 45*(1), 12-18.

van der Kolk, B. (2015). *The Body Keeps the Score: Brain, Mind, and Body in the Healing of Trauma.* Penguin Books.

Lombardi, G., Ziemann, E., & Banfi, G. (2017). Whole-body cryotherapy in athletes: From therapy to stimulation. *Clinical Journal of Sport Medicine, 27*(5), 601-611.

Recommended Resources

- **Cryotherapy Association:** https://www.cryotherapyassociation.org
- **International Institute for Cryotherapy:** https://www.iicryotherapy.com
- **Sports Medicine Research Journal:** https://www.smrj.org

Identity-oriented Psychotrauma Therapy (IoPT)

Nicole Hurless, PhD, LPC, NCC

Identity-oriented Psychotrauma Therapy (IoPT) or Identity Therapy is a trauma-focused therapeutic approach that is used to help clients heal from attachment wounds in early childhood which have affected their adult life (Center for Healthy Autonomy, 2018). It was developed by Franz Ruppert as a reaction to his experiences in individual and group therapy settings. IoPT draws on holistic frameworks of trauma-informed counseling including Family Constellations (Hellinger et al., 1998), complex relational and developmental trauma, and attachment theory (Ruppert, 2020; Stjernswärd, 2021).

The underlying theory of IoPT posits that psychotraumatic experiences in early relationships (i.e., with our caregivers) can split the psyche into inner parts that struggle to both relive and also avoid the traumatic experience(s) (Green, n.d.). Some practitioners believe that traumatic experiences can begin as early as the conception of the fetus. Theoretically, if the mother experiences stress, ambivalence, fear, or other emotions beyond unconditional acceptance of the child, the child will react and internalize the experience of the unsupportive environment (Vivian Broughton IoPT Videos, 2019). According to Ruppert's model, there are three pieces of the traumatized psyche: a healthy part, a traumatized part containing the memories and emotions of the traumatic event(s), and a survival part which attempts to protect the system from the trauma via various coping mechanisms (Ruppert, 2020). In a process similar to internal family systems (IFS), the counselor and client can acknowledge the wounded parts and strengthen the healthy parts to bring the client to stronger self-regulation and understanding of the holistic self (Broughton, 2014).

IoPT also includes a technique called the "intention method," whereby the client develops a sentence that encapsulates a trauma-related challenge they want to address. For example, a client might choose the sentence "I want to forgive myself." The client writes down this intention to serve as a concrete reminder of the goal. Next, the counselor guides the client to explore the "resonance" or connection between the inner parts of the psyche and the written intention. The resonance can help clients gain insight into unconscious processes and shed light on emotions previously hidden or avoided (Stjernswärd, 2021). During this stage of IoPT, inner parts and their interrelationships are made external and visible through the use of representatives. Inner parts may react with a variety of emotions to the intention, sometimes expressing fear, mistrust, numbing, and other experiences. The resonance exercise can also be done in a group setting, in which other group members can behave as a client's inner parts and embody different elements of the split psyche. In individual sessions, the counselor or various inanimate objects may serve as representatives of the psyche. To conclude the resonance, the counselor makes a statement thanking the part for its energy and bringing attention to the client's holistic self.

RESEARCH LIMITATIONS AND EVIDENCED-BASED EFFICACY

There is currently no research on the efficacy of this approach in the treatment of traumatic stress. In a qualitative study on the experiences of counselors trained to provide IoPT (often called facilitators), participants reported several common themes including understanding the self, the experience of witnessing and being witnessed by others, and transformation through the process ((Stjernswärd, 2021). Participants also noted that IoPT is less cognitive in its approach, and primarily taps into emotional experiences in the body and mind. This can mean that IoPT is more integrative of a person's holistic experiences and may take less time for clients to process trauma. Finally, the participants reported that the facilitation's capacity to hold space for client emotions as well as maintain a strong therapeutic alliance are crucial to the success of this modality. The exact mechanism of reported client changes is unknown at this time.

CERTIFICATIONS, TRAININGS, AND LICENSURE REQUIREMENTS FOR IoPT

There is no required training needed to practice IoPT in the United States. However, for clinicians wanting to integrate this approach into their practice effectively and ethically, training is strongly recommended. IoPT training will be most beneficial for counselors who are already licensed and understand the nuanced of developing a strong therapeutic relationship. Competence in trauma-informed counseling, or some form of trauma-focused counseling (e.g., trauma-focused cognitive behavioral therapy [TF-CBT], eye movement desensitization and reprocessing [EMDR] therapy, or internal family systems [IFS] therapy) is also recommended but not required. At the time this chapter was written, most trainings are available in Europe and may be available in languages other than English. For example, the IoPT organization of Norway offers English and Norwegian classes for certification in IoPT for €550 (Thorsheim, n.d.). Readers should bear in mind that there may be different training requirements to practice IoPT internationally.

Dr. Franz Ruppert, the developer of IoPT, also presents on IoPT to international audiences and his speaking schedule can be found at https://www.franz-ruppert.de/weiterbildungen. Finally, Vivian Broughton is an eminent IoPT psychotrauma practitioner who provides multiple online resources in this modality. She has trained with Dr. Ruppert and has created multiple books, videos, blog posts, and seminars on her experience using IoPT. She offers an online training session lasting three days which costs €240 (Vivian Broughton, n.d.).

The most rigorous forms of IoPT training require the counselor to participate in their own work in resonance and understanding their inner parts. Personal work in IoPT helps the counselor be more open, reliable, and supportive facilitator for clients. This helps the counselor facilitators build capacity for resonating with clients in such a way to not allow their own inner parts to infiltrate a session and affect the client's growth process.

SCOPE OF PRACTICE ISSUES

IoPT should be practiced only by trained mental health professionals and students, given the sensitive nature of client's traumatic experiences and the potential for re-traumatization. Additionally, while practicing IoPT, counselors need to be aware of signs of dissociation and complex trauma in order to support the client most effectively. Following an intention and resonance session, it is often helpful to debrief with the client to allow the client some closure and reflection on the process, rather than leaving their psyche open and emotionally raw. Counselors should also be competent in managing suicidal ideation and other forms of crises in clients, as these challenges may arise while processing intense emotional, traumatic, and disturbing experiences.

SUMMARY

In summary, IoPT or Identity Therapy is trauma sensitive approach grounded in attachment theory and holistic interpretations of how traumatic stress is experienced and processed. IoPT practitioners help clients gain deeper insight and self-regulation through techniques such as the intention method and resonating with inner parts that have split from the healthy element of the psyche due to trauma. Through the process, clients are guided to their own solutions, conclusions, and/or closure surrounding traumatic experiences. This approach is best suited for trained mental health professionals who understand traumatic stress from an integrated lens and want to serve as a guide for clients rather than an expert on healing. Due to the risk of harm to the client, training in IoPT is strongly recommended before attempting this approach.

Nicole Hurless is a counselor educator and nationally certified counselor (NCC) in the state of Texas. She earned her PhD in counselor education and supervision from the University of Missouri St. Louis in 2021. Her clinical work and research focus on applying trauma-informed principles to supervision, counseling, and education. She is a trained EMDR practitioner and primarily provides identity-affirming, trauma-informed counseling to queer young adult clients.

REFERENCES

Broughton, V. (2014). Becoming Your True Self: A Handbook for the Journey from Trauma to Healthy Autonomy. Green Balloon Publishing.

Centre for Healthy Autonomy. (2018, May 14). About identity therapy. Identity Therapy Workshops London & Online. Retrieved January 20, 2023, from https://www.identitytherapy-constellations.co.uk/about-identity-therapy/

Green, M. (n.d.). The basics of IoPT (identity-oriented psychotrauma therapy). Symbiosis & Autonomy. Retrieved January 20, 2023, from https://www.symbiosis-autonomy.com/theory/

Hellinger, B., Weber, G., & Beaumont, H. (1998). LOVE'S HIDDEN SYMMETRY: WHAT MAKES LOVE WORK IN RELATIONSHIPS. Zeig, Tucker & Co.

Ruppert, F. (2020). IoPT, Anliegenmethode und Resonanztechnik. In Praxishandbuch Aufstellungsarbeit (pp. 319-328). Springer, Wiesbaden.

Stjernswärd, S. (2021). Getting to Know the Inner Self. Exploratory Study of Identity Oriented Psychotrauma Therapy—Experiences and Value from Multiple Perspectives. Frontiers in Psychiatry, 773.

Thorsheim, M. (n.d.). Advanced training. IoPT Norge. Retrieved January 20, 2023, from https://www.iopt.no/en/advanced-training/

Vivian Broughton IoPT Videos (2019, May 27). Introduction to IoPT [Video]. YouTube. https://www.youtube.com/watch?v=qrvMV7f8MA8

Vivian Broughton. (n.d.). The IOPT individual session. IoPT Education & Practitioner Events with Vivian Broughton. Retrieved January 20, 2023, from https://www.iopt-practitioner-events.com/practitioner-seminars/

Illness Management and Recovery (IMR)

BILL OWENBY, EdD, MC, FAAETS, DAAETS, DCMHS, LPC, LAAC, NCC, CCMHC, ACS, DIPLOMATE, FELLOW

Illness Management and Recovery (IMR) is an evidence-based, structured therapeutic approach designed to empower individuals with severe mental illnesses (SMI)—such as schizophrenia, bipolar disorder, and major depressive disorder—to take an active role in managing their conditions and achieving personal recovery goals (Mueser et al., 2002). IMR focuses on psychoeducation, skill-building, goal setting, and coping strategies to help individuals reduce symptoms, prevent relapses, and improve overall functioning (SAMHSA, 2021).

IMR is a client-centered model that integrates cognitive-behavioral techniques (CBT), motivational enhancement therapy (MET), and relapse prevention strategies to foster long-term wellness (Beck & Rector, 2005). It provides individuals with practical tools to manage their symptoms, navigate treatment options, and enhance quality of life.

IMPORTANCE OF IMR IN MENTAL HEALTH TREATMENT

The IMR model plays a critical role in recovery-oriented mental health care by shifting the focus from symptom reduction alone to holistic recovery, personal empowerment, and self-management (Mueser et al., 2002). The program helps clients to:

- Understand their mental illness and treatment options.
- Develop self-management strategies to reduce distress and improve daily functioning.
- Build problem-solving and coping skills to handle stress and avoid relapse (Beck & Rector, 2005).
- Strengthen social and community supports.
- Set and achieve personal goals in areas such as employment, relationships, and independent living.

IMR is used in outpatient clinics, psychiatric rehabilitation programs, peer support groups, and integrated mental health services. It is designed for individuals with chronic mental health conditions who need ongoing support to maintain stability and recovery (SAMHSA, 2021).

THEORETICAL FOUNDATIONS OF IMR

IMR is based on several key psychological and therapeutic frameworks, including:

Cognitive-Behavioral Therapy (CBT) for Symptom Management

- Helps clients recognize and modify maladaptive thoughts and behaviors related to their illness.
- Provides structured problem-solving techniques to manage distress and develop adaptive coping strategies (Beck & Rector, 2005).

Motivational Enhancement Therapy (MET) for Treatment Engagement

- Encourages self-motivation and readiness for change (SAMHSA, 2021).
- Uses motivational interviewing to help clients explore and commit to personal recovery goals.

Psychoeducation for Illness Awareness

- Provides structured education about mental illness, treatment options, and wellness strategies (Mueser et al., 2002).
- Enhances treatment adherence and informed decision-making.

Relapse Prevention and Self-Management Strategies

- Identifies early warning signs of relapse and develops personalized relapse prevention plans (Beck & Rector, 2005).
- Strengthens coping skills and crisis intervention techniques.

Recovery-Oriented Care Principles

- Client empowerment and shared decision-making.
- Focus on strengths, capabilities, and personal growth (SAMHSA, 2021).
- Integration of social, vocational, and independent living goals into treatment.

CORE COMPONENTS AND TECHNIQUES IN IMR

Therapist's Role in IMR

- Facilitates structured psychoeducational sessions tailored to the client's needs.
- Guides goal-setting and action planning for illness management and personal recovery.
- Provides motivational support and problem-solving strategies to address treatment barriers (Mueser et al., 2002).
- Encourages self-monitoring and adaptive coping techniques.

Common IMR Techniques

1. **Psychoeducation Modules:**
   o Teaching about mental illness, treatment adherence, and symptom management (SAMHSA, 2021).
2. **Relapse Prevention Planning:**
   o Identifying early warning signs and developing personalized crisis response plans (Beck & Rector, 2005).
3. **Behavioral Activation and Goal Setting:**
   o Encouraging clients to engage in meaningful activities that promote well-being.
4. **Social Skills Training and Communication Techniques:**
   o Building assertiveness, emotional expression, and interpersonal problem-solving skills (Mueser et al., 2002).
5. **Medication and Treatment Adherence Strategies:**
   o Addressing concerns about medication side effects and promoting collaborative treatment planning.
6. **Cognitive Restructuring and Coping Skills Development:**
   o Challenging negative beliefs about illness and recovery.
   o Teaching stress management and relaxation techniques (Beck & Rector, 2005).

Key Training Programs for IMR

1. **Illness Management and Recovery (IMR) Practitioner Training – Substance Abuse and Mental Health Services Administration (SAMHSA)**
   o **Website:** samhsa.gov
   o **Time Commitment:** Varies (self-paced online and workshop formats)
   o **Cost:** Free (for government-funded training)
   o **Prerequisites:** Open to licensed therapists, social workers, case managers, and peer support specialists
   o **Overview:** Covers CBT-based interventions, motivational enhancement techniques, and relapse prevention planning (SAMHSA, 2021).
2. **Recovery-Oriented Cognitive Therapy (CT-R) for IMR – Beck Institute**
   o **Website:** beckinstitute.org
   o **Time Commitment:** 3–6 months
   o **Cost:** $2,000–$5,000
   o **Prerequisites:** Open to licensed clinicians, peer specialists, and social workers
   o **Overview:** Provides advanced training in CBT-based recovery interventions for severe mental illness (Beck & Rector, 2005).

FINAL RECOMMENDATIONS FOR MENTAL HEALTH PROFESSIONALS

- If you work in community mental health or psychiatric rehabilitation, an IMR certification from SAMHSA provides practical training.
- If you are interested in CBT-integrated IMR interventions, Recovery-Oriented CT-R training from the Beck Institute is a valuable option (Beck & Rector, 2005).

SUMMARY

Illness Management and Recovery (IMR) is an evidence-based therapy that equips individuals with severe mental illness with the skills, knowledge, and confidence to manage their conditions and pursue meaningful recovery (Mueser et al., 2002). By integrating psychoeducation, cognitive-behavioral techniques, and self-management strategies, IMR empowers clients to take control of their mental health (SAMHSA, 2021). As training programs expand and IMR gains wider implementation, mental health professionals will have greater opportunities to deliver effective, recovery-oriented care.

I hold two independent licenses in the states of Arizona and Ohio, supervisory status in Arizona, along with a substance abuse license in Arizona. I am board certified as a Diplomate and Clinical Mental Health Specialist, an Approved Clinical Supervisor, Nationally Certified Counselor, a Certified Clinical Mental Health Counselor, NeuroLinguistic Programming Practitioner, and a Clinical Trauma Specialist for Individuals and Family including EMDR Therapy and NET. I completed my training in Animal-Assisted Therapy and Pet Handlers certification in order to evaluate and incorporate the human-animal bond in therapy. I am the sole author and creator of the SxC Model of ESA Evaluation. My research interests surround post-traumatic growth, resiliency, strengths-based therapy, positive psychology, mindfulness, Animal-Assisted Therapy, Sandtray Therapy, Creative approaches in therapy, and martial arts in mental health. I have presented at local, state, regional, national, and international levels on various topics including personality traits, licensure reciprocity challenges, Sandtray and supervision, and Animal-Assisted Therapy within supervision. eonbllc@gmail.com

REFERENCES

Mueser, K. T., Corrigan, P. W., Hilton, D. W., et al. (2002). *Illness management and recovery: A review of the research.* Psychiatric Services, 53(10), 1272-1284.

Substance Abuse and Mental Health Services Administration (SAMHSA). (2021). *Illness Management and Recovery Program Toolkit.* Retrieved from samhsa.gov.

Beck, A. T., & Rector, N. A. (2005). *Cognitive approaches to schizophrenia: Theory and therapy.* Acta Psychiatrica Scandinavica, 111(4), 257-264.

Image Rehearsal Art-Based Therapy (IRT-AT)

TRACI BITONDO, PH.D., LPC, LMHC, LPAT, ATR-BC, ACS, ATCS, NCC

Post-Traumatic Stress Disorder (PTSD) presents a complex and challenging condition that demands comprehensive and innovative therapeutic approaches to achieve effective treatment outcomes. In recent years, Imagery Rehearsal Therapy (IRT), a Cognitive Behavior Technique (CBT), has been integrated with Art Therapy (AT). This approach has garnered increasing attention as a promising intervention for individuals afflicted by trauma-induced nightmares. This chapter explores Imagery Rehearsal Art Therapy (IRT-AT) elements and how art is integrated into the phases of IRT: exposing, rescripting, and rehearsing. Alongside providing an in-depth introductory description of IRT-AT, the chapter also delves into the considerations for integrating this approach into clinical practice; crucial aspects, such as training requirements, credentialing, and scope of practice, are thoroughly examined to ensure a comprehensive understanding of implementing this dynamic therapeutic modality.

The complex is the relationship between PTSD, post-traumatic nightmares, and sleep difficulties. After a traumatic event, nightmares and insomnia can predict the development of PTSD (Belleville et al., 2018; Germain et al., 2008). Insomnia and sleep disturbances can also exacerbate daytime post-traumatic symptoms, thereby perpetuating PTSD (Spoormaker & Montgomery, 2008). Among the intrusion and hyperarousal symptoms of PTSD are disturbing dreams and sleep disturbances (American Psychiatric Association [APA], 2022). The recommended treatment for PTSD is trauma-focused cognitive behavioral therapies (CBTs), such as prolonged exposure therapy, which reduce symptoms and enhance the quality of life (Agency for Healthcare Research and Quality, 2013). However, some patients continue to experience sleep difficulties even after receiving effective treatment for PTSD, necessitating the need for additional therapies to treat these nighttime disturbances (Aurora et al., 2010). In these instances, IRT is used to counteract nightmares and change their underlying premise by rehearsing modified dream scripts during the day, which alters the association between nightmares and sleep (Lancee et al., 2010; Germain, 2013). According to Haeyen and Staal (2020), the utilization of IRT has demonstrated efficacy in addressing PTSD-related nightmares. However, specific individuals may encounter difficulties accessing traumatic memories because those memories are stored in non-verbal, audio, or audiovisual forms. Consequently, integrating art therapy with conventional IRT techniques emerges as a promising approach to treatment.

When integrated with IRT, art therapy arises as an additional, potentially more effective treatment, particularly for patients who are less responsive to or unable to tolerate verbal exposure techniques (Haeyen & Staal, 2020). This is because art therapy is an experiential and non-verbal treatment that makes use of one's creative processes in order to facilitate healing and growth. An alternative to traditional talking therapies, it uses visual means of expression like sketching, sculpting, and painting to access and process traumatic memories (Malchiodi, 2020; Schouten et al., 2014). Making art requires using both the right and left hemispheres of the brain, which has been shown to reduce PTSD-related nightmares and promote feelings of hope and emotional restoration (Perryman et al., 2019). According to research conducted by Morgan and Johnson (1995), clients who engaged in art therapy reported having fewer and milder nightmares. As a whole, the use of art therapy in treating PTSD has been shown to help manage and reduce PTSD symptoms (Campbell et al., 2016; Hass-Cohen et al., 2014; Gantt & Tinnin, 2007), explicitly improving resilience to the effects of trauma-related thoughts and emotions (Lobban & Murphy, 2017; Campbell et al., 2016; Walker et al., 2017), safely and effectively facilitate the processing of traumatic memories (Campbell et al., 2016), foster an integrated sense of identity (Walker et al, 2017), and improve overall quality of life (Lobban, 2014).

TREATMENT OVERVIEW

According to Krakow & Zadra (2010), there are variations in the application of IRT, including its use with children suffering from nightmares. These differences typically relate to the intensity of exposure during therapy sessions and how treatments are used. Regarding IRT-AT, there is no formal manual; rather, artmaking is integrated throughout. Below is an overview of how artmaking is integrated during different aspects of IRT.

Interventions

Similarly to traditional IRT, IRT-AT can be provided both individually or in groups (Haeyen & Staal, 2020). Prior to implementing IRT-AT, steps should be taken to ensure the safety of the client, which includes assessing the client's mental and physical well-being. The therapist should focus on rapport building during the initial sessions to help establish a solid, trusting relationship (Krakow & Zadra, 2010). When discussing their study on IRT-AT, Haeyen, and Stall (2020) emphasize the necessity for a secure connection between client and therapist, which can be elucidated through the conceptual framework of containment. Containment can be conceptualized as a therapeutic process wherein the therapist provides patients with a secure and nurturing environment to express and explore their thoughts, emotions, and lived encounters (Finlay, 2016). The therapist assumes the role of receiving and representing the individual's experiences, with the aim of facilitating their manageability and comprehension. Consequently, this leads to the capacity to regulate levels of arousal. Trauma-focused art therapy employs art materials as a means to provide individuals with a sense of well-being and safety. The art items serve as tangible and visual manifestations of subjective experiences. Consequently, the phenomenon of containment occurs not only within the therapeutic relationship between the therapist and client but also within the interaction between the client and the art materials (Hinz, 2020; Malchiodi, 2020). This containment can help keep the client safe and create the space necessary to conduct IRT-AT effectively.

Imagery Exposure

Imagery Exposure (IE) involves engaging the clients with psychoeducation, using in vivo exposure, imagined exposure, and emotional processing (Kunze et al., 2016; Rauch et al., 2012). During IE, clients are confronted with the content of their nightmares. In traditional IRT, they are typically asked to write their nightmare as a story (Krakow & Zadra, 2010). In IRT-AT, clients might be asked to recreate their nightmares using art materials (Haeyen & Stall, 2020). While artmaking can be used to externalize the imagery in their mind, which is particularly helpful in accessing unconscious content, the art can also serve to help mitigate arousal in the recalling of these stories (Haeyen & Stall, 2020).

Imagery Rescripting

Once a nightmare has been identified and graphically reconstructed, the client is prompted to modify the narrative or script into a more acceptable version through a therapeutic technique known as Imagery Rescripting (Haeyen & Stall, 2020). In a study conducted by Haeyen and Stall (2020), art therapists had clients create comic strips as a means to modify the narrative of nightmares. During this stage, the utilization of comic strips provided a method to modify various aspects of the narrative, such as the topic, storyline, ending, or any other elements that the client wishes to alter, with the intention of shifting the nightmare imagery into a less distressing story.

Imagery Rehearsal

After the client has successfully changed the nightmare story, the concept of rehearsal is introduced. During this stage, clients are asked to rehearse or practice the rescripted imagery throughout the day in prescribed increments (Kunze et al., 2016; Krakow & Zadra, 2010). While in traditional IRT, participants rehearse the imagery by rereading their written story or revisualizing the images in their mind (Krakow & Zadra, 2010), those who engage in IRT-AT can rehearse by looking at the art they created during the rescripting stage or by creating more art about the rescripted story. By utilizing art during the rescripting and rehearsal stage, clients are empowered to physically changes the imagery of their stories, can see their story from different perspectives, and have the ability to change elements and symbols depicted in the art piece (Haeyen & Stall, 2020).

Conclusion

The IRT-AT is a therapeutic approach that incorporates non-verbal and experiential techniques. It utilizes artmaking activities as a means to delve into traumatic memories and emotions, with the goal of addressing traumatic dreams, alleviating symptoms of post-traumatic stress disorder (PTSD) and enhancing sleep quality. The IRT-AT intervention presents a viable option for those who are unable to articulate their traumatic experiences verbally and may have difficulty tolerating exposure-based therapies. With the incorporation of art therapy treatments into established ITR protocols, individuals are able to visually see and actively modify distressing memories, leading to their substitution with empowering and transforming artistic creations. The integration of IRT procedures with art therapy has the potential to enhance outcomes in individuals with trauma-related nightmares in contrast to the utilization of IRT in isolation.

CERTIFICATIONS, TRAININGS, AND LICENSURE REQUIREMENTS

As of this writing, there are currently no standardized trainings or certification specific to using IRT-AT as a treatment intervention with clients other than the relevant state or district licensing and credentialing requirements in the practice of psychotherapy and/or counseling in the state or district the treatment is occurring.

BEST PRACTICES

It is recommended that any practitioners integrating artmaking into their work with clients stays within their scope of practice. Art Therapy is a masters level profession requiring licenses to practice in many states.

Certification Recommended

It is recommended to obtain necessary credentials to practice art therapy in the state or district you plan to practice. Many states have licenses and title protection regarding the practice of art therapy in their state. The American Art Therapy Association keeps a relatively updated list of where to find that information **https://arttherapy.org/credentials-and-licensure/**.

In states without licensure, it is recommended to seek credentialling as an art therapist, to ensure you meet the education and training requirements to engage in the practice. The Art Therapy Credentials Board, Inc (atcb.org) is an example of a credentialing body that issues such credentials. Below are the most common credentials those practicing art therapy receive:

- Provisionally Registered Art Therapist (ATR-P)- Individuals who possess the appropriate graduate-level educational requirements to practice but are completing their post-graduate working hours under the oversight of a qualified supervisor.

- Registered Art Therapist (ATR)- completed educational and supervised post-graduate experience in art therapy.

- Board Certified Art Therapist (ATR-BC)- those ATR's that have received board certification.

Degree Requirements

Minimum of a Graduate Degree in Mental Health Field (i.e., Art Therapy, Expressive Arts Therapy, Counseling, Social Work, etc.)

SUMMARY

The utilization of the IRT-AT method has proven to be a valuable intervention for addressing PTSD associated nightmares. However, it is imperative for practitioners to exercise caution and adhere to the boundaries of their professional expertise while employing this approach. This entails ensuring that one possesses the necessary license and credentials to actively participate in professional practice, as well as possessing the requisite expertise and training to effectively address trauma-related concerns. Moreover, it is imperative to acknowledge that although creativity holds significant value in our role as practitioners, particularly in the context of trauma therapy, it is crucial to exercise caution and fully comprehend the potential hazards involved with employing interventions for which one lacks proper training. For instance, Art therapists undergo comprehensive training in the utilization of art materials, art processes, and the safe and efficacious application of these techniques within the context treating mental health conditions. So be sure that you have the necessary training to integrate artmaking effectively and safely as an intervention in the treatment of PTSD.

Dr. Traci Bitondo is an Assistant Professor and Co-Director of the Center for Teaching and Learning at Caldwell University, as well as a Director on the Board of Directors for the American Art Therapy Association and Immediate Past President of the New Jersey Art Therapy Association. She has received awards from the American Art Therapy Association, including the 2022 Nancy Schoebel Legislative Service Award, and the New Jersey Counseling Association's Edward Stroh LPC Award. Dr. Bitondo regularly presents nationally and internationally on trauma treatment, art therapy innovations, and clinical supervision. She maintains a private practice and is dedicated to mentoring the next generation of counselors and art therapists.

Empoweredheartstherapy.com

Traci@empoweredheartstherapy.com

REFERENCES

Agency for Healthcare Research and Quality. (2017, May 24). *Psychological and pharmacological treatments for adults with posttraumatic stress disorder (PTSD): Systematic review.* https://effectivehealthcare.ahrq.gov/products/ptsd-adult-treatment-update/research-2018

American Psychiatric Association. (2022). *Diagnostic and statistical manual of mental disorders* (5th ed., text rev.). **https://doi.org/10.1176/appi.books.9780890425787**

Aurora, R. N., Zak, R. S., Auerbach, S., Casey, K. R., Chowdhuri, S., Karippot, A., Maganti, R., Ramar, K., Kristo, D. A., Bista, S. R., Lamm, C., Morgenthaler, T. I., & Tracy, S. L. (2010). Best practice Guide for the Treatment of Nightmare Disorder in Adults. *Journal of Clinical Sleep Medicine, 06*(04), 389–401. https://doi.org/10.5664/jcsm.27883

Belleville, G., Dubé-Frenette, M., & Rousseau, A. (2018). Efficacy of imagery rehearsal therapy and cognitive behavioral therapy in sexual assault victims with posttraumatic stress disorder: A randomized controlled trial. *Journal of Traumatic Stress, 31*(4), 591–601. https://doi.org/10.1002/jts.22306

Campbell, M., Decker, K. P., Kruk, K., & Deaver, S. P. (2016). Art therapy and cognitive processing therapy for combat-related PTSD: A randomized controlled trial. *Art Therapy, 33*(4), 169–177. **https://doi-org/10.1080/07421656.2016.1226643**

Finlay, L. (2016). *Relational integrative psychotherapy: Engaging process and theory in practice.* John Wiley & Sons Inc.

Gantt, L., & Tinnin, L. W. (2007). Intensive trauma therapy of PTSD and dissociation: An outcome study. *The Arts in Psychotherapy, 34*(1), 69–80. **https://doi-org /10.1016/j.aip.2006.09.007**

Germain A. (2013). Sleep disturbances as the hallmark of PTSD: where are we now? *American Journal of Psychiatry,* 170(4), 372–382. https://doi.org/10.1176/appi.ajp.2012.12040432

Germain, A., Buysse, D. J., & Nofzinger, E. (2008). Sleep-specific mechanisms underlying posttraumatic stress disorder: Integrative review and Neurobiological Hypotheses. *Sleep Medicine Reviews, 12*(3), 185–195. https://doi.org/10.1016/j.smrv.2007.09.003

Krakow, B., & Zadra, A. (2010). Imagery rehearsal therapy: Principles and practice. *Sleep Medicine Clinics, 5*(2), 289–298. https://doi.org/10.1016/j.jsmc.2010.01.004

Kunze, A., Arntz, A., Morina, N., Kindt, M., & Lancee, J. (2017). Treatment efficacy of imagery rescripting and imaginal exposure for nightmares. evidence from a randomized wait-list controlled trial. *Sleep Medicine, 40.* https://doi.org/10.1016/j.sleep.2017.11.521

Hass-Cohen, N., Clyde Findlay, J., Carr, R., & Vanderlan, J. (2014). 'Check, change what you need to change and/or keep what you want': An art therapy neurobiological-based trauma protocol. *Art Therapy, 31*(2), 69–78. **https://doi-org/10.1080/07421656.2014.903825**

Haeyen, S., & Staal, M. (2021). Imagery Rehearsal Based Art Therapy: Treatment of Post-traumatic Nightmares in Art Therapy. *Frontiers in psychology, 11*, 628717. **https://doi.org/10.3389/fpsyg.2020.628717**

Hinz, L. D. (2020). *Expressive therapies continuum: A framework for using art in therapy.* Routledge.

Lancee, J., Spoormaker, V. I., & van den Bout, J. (2010). Cognitive-behavioral self-help treatment for nightmares: a randomized controlled trial. *Psychotherapy and psychosomatics, 79*(6), 371–377. **https://doi.org/10.1159/000320894**

Lobban, J. (2014). The invisible wound: Veterans' art therapy. *International Journal of Art Therapy*, *19*(1), 3–18. **https://doi-org/10.1080/17454832.2012.725547**

Lobban, J., & Murphy, D. (2017). Using art therapy to overcome avoidance in veterans with chronic post-traumatic stress disorder. *International Journal of Art Therapy*, *23*(3), 99–114. **https://doi-org/10.1080/17454832.2017.1397036**

Malchiodi C. A. (2020). *Trauma and Expressive Arts Therapy: Brain, Body, & Imagination in the Healing Process*. New York, NY: Guilford Press

Morgan, C. A., & Johnson, D. R. (1995). Use of a drawing task in the treatment of nightmares in combat-related post-traumatic stress disorder. *Art Therapy*, *12*(4), 244–247. **https://doi-org/10.1080/07421656.1995.10759172**

Perryman K., Blisard P., Moss R. (2019). Using creative arts in trauma therapy: the neuroscience of healing. *J. Ment. Health Counsel.* 1:80 10.17744/mehc.41.1.07

Rauch, S. A., Eftekhari, A., & Ruzek, J. I. (2012). Review of Exposure Therapy: A gold standard for PTSD treatment. *The Journal of Rehabilitation Research and Development*, *49*(5), 679. https://doi.org/10.1682/jrrd.2011.08.0152

Walker, M. S., Kaimal, G., Gonzaga, A. M., Myers-Coffman, K. A., & DeGraba, T. J. (2017). Active-duty military service members' visual representations of PTSD and TBI in masks. *International Journal of Qualitative Studies on Health and Well-Being*, *12*(1), 1267317. **https://doi-org/10.1080/17482631.2016.1267317**

Yücel, D. E., van Emmerik, A. A., Souama, C., & Lancee, J. (2020). Comparative efficacy of imagery rehearsal therapy and prazosin in the treatment of trauma-related nightmares in adults: a meta-analysis of randomized controlled trials. Sleep medicine reviews, 50, 101248.doi: 10.1016/j.smrv.2019.101248.

Image Rehearsal Therapy (IRT)

Connie Elkins, Ph.D., LPC, NCC

Recurrent nightmares for individuals who have been exposed to a traumatic event can be a frequent symptom of Post-Traumatic Stress Disorder (American Psychiatric Association, 2022). In some studies, 80% percent of PTSD patients report nightmares, and even when many of their symptoms resolve, PTSD-associated nightmares can persist throughout life (Aurora et al., 2010). Image Rehearsal Therapy (IRT) is a trauma-focused Cognitive Behavioral Therapy (CBT) used for the treatment and management of nightmares exhibited in patients with Post Traumatic Stress Disorder (PTSD) as well as idiopathic nightmares. Using cognitive restructuring and imagery education/training, IRT acts to inhibit the original nightmare and provides a cognitive shift that empirically refutes the original premise of the nightmare (Krakow & Zadra, 2010; Aurora et al., 2010). Therapists help patients restructure their perceptions of nightmares as a learned sleep disorder and teach them to use imagery steps to decrease nightmares, and can be delivered through groups or individually.

Meeting standards for evidence-based modalities, IRT has been shown to be an effective treatment for nightmares resulting from a variety of different traumas, including abuse, sexual assault, psychosis, and trauma-affected refugees, to name a few (Casement & Swanson, 2012; Baskaran, et al, 2023; Krakow, et al., 2001; Reeve, et al., 2019; Sandahl, et al., 2017; Seda, et al., 2015) A recent meta-analysis concluded IRT to be comparable in efficacy to current pharmacological treatment (i.e. Prazosin, a recommended for treatment of PTSD-associated nightmares), with moderate effects on nightmare frequency, PTSD stress symptoms, and sleep quality (Yücel, et al., 2020).

OUTLINE OF SESSIONS

IRT has a structured process of 4 sessions (Krakow & Zadra, 2010). Sessions 1 and 2 teach patients to recognize the effect of nightmares on their sleep by showing them how nightmares promote learned insomnia – creating the potential for avoidance of sleep. Sessions 3 and 4 engage the patient in learning about the human imagery system, monitoring how this system operates, appreciating the connections between daytime imagery and dreams, and implementing the specific steps of IRT (i.e., selecting a nightmare, changing the nightmare into a new dream, and rehearsing the new dream).

Krakaw and Zadra (2010) describe topics to be covered within the four-session outline. Session 1 addresses treatment credibility, dissuasion of discussing past trauma or traumatic content of nightmares, linking nightmares with insomnia, and unsuspected benefits or purpose of nightmares. In Session 2, participants explore why nightmares persist after traumatic exposure, concepts of symptom substitution, and principles/application of imagery. Session 3 leads participants to discover imagery as a vehicle of change and how to change nightmare imagery. In Session 4, participants focus on practicing dream rehearsal and change.

The guided practice of IRT is accessible to the general population through published imagery instructions. For instance, Abueng (n.d.) leads individuals through four steps of imagery rehearsal: 1). Write the narrative of the central elements of the bad dream; 2). Rewrite the dream, changing the story to have a positive ending; 3). Before falling asleep, induce the intention to re-dream; and 4). Rejoice in positive re-dreaming.

SCOPE OF PRACTICE

IRT was developed as a Cognitive Behavior Therapy (CBT) treatment, and as such, mental health professionals trained in CBT are readily qualified to employ IRT after relatively brief training. IRT training provides a clear structure of therapy sessions which allows for immediate implementation. It is interesting to note recent research into IRT in combination with Art Therapy (AT) techniques as an effective approach to relief of trauma-related nightmares (Haeyen & Staal, 2021). The potential for AT to break through avoidance and provide more readily gained access to traumatic experiences for clients who benefit least from verbal exposure techniques can add value to IRT. IRT Art Therapy emphasizes the expression of memories to help individuals expose painful memories and to make sense of experiences by putting them into narratives (Malchiodi, 2020). Practitioners of IRT Art Therapy need training in both IRT and AT to provide effective treatment with high fidelity to these modalities.

TRAINING

IRT is a therapeutic modality used by those with specific training in psychotherapeutic techniques. It is widely assumed that licensed mental health professionals are best situated for providing maximum fidelity to established techniques. States may vary in regulations of who can utilize IRT, but professionals qualified to practice CBT require no further certifications or licensing to practice this treatment modality.

Dr. Barry Krakow, a leading innovator and researcher of IRT, offers an introductory video explaining the purpose and protocol for employing imagery techniques. The video includes the main cognitive restructuring themes used by Dr. Krakow to prepare patients for IRT and then concludes with the three main IRT steps. Any mental health professional with advanced skills in CBT will likely find the program sufficient to begin using IRT. The training video is $50. Dr. Krakow also offers a training workbook and a 4-hour audio program, Turning Nightmares Into Dreams, for those with less experience in CBT. The workbook and audio are $100. These training resources can be found at https://barrykrakowmd.com/product/turning-nightmares-into-dreams-digital-download/

Trauma-Based Nightmare Treatment: Rapidly Reduce Frequency and Intensity with Image Rehearsal Therapy is a training from Lillian Gibson, PhD. In this 6-hour digital seminar, Dr. Gibson demonstrates techniques of IRT to help clients confront and change their nightmares and replace their fear and anxiety with feelings of safety and security. Training participants are provided with a step-by-step guide that includes session outlines, scripting, and detailed guidance. Specifically, they learn imagery exercises, techniques to reinforce positive dream scenarios, and ways to help clients manage nightmare anxiety and hyperarousal. The cost of the training is $249.99 and includes a CE certificate with the completion of the test. Purchase of the training is located at https://catalog.pesi.com/item/traumabased-nightmare-treatment-rapidly-reduce-frequency-intensity-image-rehearsal-therapy-123182

SUMMARY

A significant proportion of individuals exposed to a traumatic event experience trauma-related nightmares (Krakow & Zadra, 2010). Through the structured 4 sessions of IRT, patients learn the function of nightmares and how to change them into a new dream through cognitive restructuring and rehearsal techniques. IRT is an effective treatment for nightmares resulting from a variety of different traumas, including abuse, sexual assault, psychosis, and trauma affected refugees, to name a few (Casement & Swanson, 2012; Krakow, et al., 2001; Reeve, et al., 2019; Sandahl, et al., 2017; Seda, et al., 2015; Yücel, et al., 2020). Training is available to mental health professionals through online seminars, videos, and workbooks and can be achieved in 6 hours or less. Mental health professionals with training and experience in CBT techniques will quickly be prepared to implement the sessions of IRT into effective practice.

Connie Elkins, Ph.D., is Assistant Professor for Professional Counseling programs at Lincoln Memorial University. She is a National Certified Counselor and Licensed Professional Counselor. Her curiosity and desire to meet the needs around her have led to years of experience as a school counselor, college counselor, outpatient and in-home counselor, and counselor educator and supervisor. Her current professional passions include training entry-level counselors through student-centered supportive practices and training counseling supervisors and administrators to do the same. She continues to seek expertise in CBT and related practices but is a Person-Centered Counselor at her core.

Connie Elkins [iD] https://orcid.org/0000-0003-0580-1301

connie.elkins@hotmail.com

REFERENCES

Abueg, F. A brief guide to imagery rehearsal therapy (IRT) for nightmare disorders for clinicians and patients. **http://wichitasac.com/wp-content/uploads/2018/10/Reflections-A-Brief-Guide-to-Imagery-Rehearsal-Therapy-for-Nightmares.pdf**

American Psychiatric Association. (2022). Diagnostic and statistical manual of mental disorders (5th ed., text rev.). https://doi.org/10.1176/appi.books.9780890425787

Aurora, R. N., Zak, R. S., Auerbach, S. H., Casey, K. R., Chowdhuri, S., Karippot, A., Maganti, R. K., Ramar, K., Kristo, D. A., Bista, S. R., Lamm, C. I., Morgenthaler, T. I., Standards of Practice Committee, & American Academy of Sleep Medicine (2010). Best practice guide for the treatment of nightmare disorder in adults. Journal of clinical sleep medicine : JCSM : official publication of the American Academy of Sleep Medicine, 6(4), 389–401. PMCID: PMC2919672

Baskaran, A., Marogi, E., Bitar, R., Attarian, H., & Saadi, A. (2023). Improving Sleep Health Among Refugees: A Systematic Review. Neurology: Clinical Practice, 13(2). https://doi.org/10.1212/CPJ.0000000000200139

Casement, M. D., and Swanson, L. M. (2012). A meta-analysis of imagery rehearsal for post-trauma nightmares: effects on nightmare frequency, sleep quality, and posttraumatic stress. Clin. Psychol. Rev. 32, 566–574. doi: 10.1016/j.cpr.2012.06.002

Haeyen, S., & Staal, M. (2021). Imagery rehearsal-based art therapy: treatment of post-traumatic nightmares in art therapy. Frontiers in psychology, 11(6). doi: 10.3389/fpsyg.2020.628717

Krakow, B., Hollifield, M., Johnston, L., Koss, M., Schrader, R., Warner, T. D., ... & Prince, H. (2001). Imagery rehearsal therapy for chronic nightmares in sexual assault survivors with posttraumatic stress disorder: a randomized controlled trial. Jama, 286(5), 537-545. doi:: 10.1001/jama.286.5.537

Krakow, B., and Zadra, A. (2010). Imagery rehearsal therapy: principles and practice. Sleep Med. Clin. 5, 289–298. doi: 10.1016/j.jsmc.2010.01.004

Malchiodi, C. A. (2020). Trauma and Expressive Arts Therapy: Brain, Body, & Imagination in the Healing Process. New York, NY: Guilford Press.

Reeve, S., Sheaves, B., & Freeman, D. (2019). Sleep disorders in early psychosis: incidence, severity, and association with clinical symptoms. Schizophrenia bulletin, 45(2), 287-295. doi: 10.1093/schbul/sby129.

Sandahl, H., Jennum, P., Baandrup, L., Poschmann, I. S., & Carlsson, J. (2017). Treatment of sleep disturbances in trauma-affected refugees: Study protocol for a randomised controlled trial. Trials, 18, 1-13. doi: 10.1186/s13063-017-2260-5.

Seda, G., Sanchez-Ortuno, M. M., Welsh, C. H., Halbower, A. C., & Edinger, J. D. (2015). Comparative meta-analysis of prazosin and imagery rehearsal therapy for nightmare frequency, sleep quality, and posttraumatic stress. Journal of Clinical Sleep Medicine, 11(1), 11-22. doi: 10.5664/jcsm.4354.

Image Rehearsal Therapy for Nightmares (IRT-N)

BILL OWENBY, EdD, MC, FAAETS, DAAETS, DCMHS, LPC, LAAC, NCC, CCMHC, ACS, DIPLOMATE, FELLOW

DEFINITION AND OVERVIEW

Image Rehearsal Therapy for Nightmares (IRT-N) is a cognitive-behavioral treatment specifically designed to address chronic nightmares, particularly those associated with post-traumatic stress disorder (PTSD). It involves guiding individuals through a process of re-imagining and rewriting the narrative of their nightmares in a way that reduces their emotional impact. IRT-N empowers clients to take control over the content of their dreams and facilitates reductions in nightmare frequency, intensity, and associated distress.

HISTORICAL BACKGROUND

IRT was initially developed in the 1980s and gained popularity through the work of Dr. Barry Krakow and others who studied the role of nightmares in trauma and sleep disorders. It was further refined to help those with PTSD-related nightmares, with the technique later being adopted and researched within military and civilian populations. IRT is now included in treatment guidelines for PTSD and chronic nightmares by the American Academy of Sleep Medicine and the U.S. Department of Veterans Affairs.

THEORETICAL FOUNDATIONS

IRT-N is grounded in several cognitive-behavioral theories:

- **Cognitive Theory of Emotion**: Emphasizes that emotional responses are tied to cognitive appraisals. By changing the imagery and narrative associated with nightmares, emotional responses can be altered.
- **Exposure Therapy Principles**: Repeated confrontation with distressing thoughts in a safe, controlled manner leads to reduced anxiety.
- **Memory Reconsolidation Theory**: Suggests that memories can be re-encoded with altered emotional valence when re-imagined in a safe context.

CORE COMPONENTS AND TECHNIQUES

1. **Psychoeducation**: Clients are taught about the nature of nightmares, the sleep cycle, and how trauma can disrupt REM sleep.
2. **Nightmare Recording**: Clients document the content, emotions, and triggers associated with their nightmares.
3. **Imagery Rescripting**: The core technique involves changing the plot or ending of the nightmare to something less distressing or even positive.
4. **Rehearsal Practice**: Clients are instructed to rehearse the rewritten dream imagery during the day for several minutes each day.
5. **Relaxation Training**: Techniques such as diaphragmatic breathing or progressive muscle relaxation are sometimes incorporated.

IDEAL CLIENT POPULATIONS

IRT-N is particularly beneficial for:

- Individuals with PTSD-related nightmares
- Survivors of trauma (military, sexual assault, disasters)
- Clients with chronic nightmare disorder without clear trauma
- Adolescents and adults experiencing frequent, distressing dreams

IDEAL PROFESSIONAL

IRT-N is best suited for:

- Licensed mental health professionals trained in trauma-focused therapies
- Clinicians working with veterans or trauma survivors
- Therapists comfortable with CBT and imaginal exposure work

TRAINING, LICENSURE, AND CERTIFICATION REQUIREMENTS

There is no formal licensure specific to IRT-N, but the following training pathways are commonly used:

- **CBT-I and IRT Certification Programs**: Organizations like PESI and the Veterans Health Administration offer training.
  - Example: Dr. Barry Krakow's Nightmare Treatment training (often in workshop or online format)
  - Time Commitment: 1-2 days
  - Cost: $150-$500
- **Continuing Education Courses**: Offered by the American Academy of Sleep Medicine (AASM) or professional CE platforms
- **Clinical Experience**: Supervised practice or case consultation is recommended for new clinicians

General Cost

IRT training courses typically cost between $150 and $500, depending on the provider and course depth.

Degree Requirements

Mental health clinicians with a master's or doctoral degree in counseling, psychology, social work, or psychiatry are the primary providers of IRT. Familiarity with cognitive-behavioral techniques is recommended.

SCOPE OF PRACTICE

IRT-N is considered a psychotherapeutic intervention and should be implemented by licensed professionals acting within their legal and ethical scope of practice. Paraprofessionals may assist in psychoeducation under supervision but should not conduct rescripting without appropriate credentials.

CAUTIONS AND LIMITATIONS

- IRT may not be appropriate for individuals experiencing acute psychosis or severe cognitive impairment.
- Some clients may initially resist changing the narrative of their nightmares due to fears of forgetting or distorting the memory of a traumatic event.
- Must be used with caution in clients with dissociative symptoms or significant distress triggered by imaginal exposure.

BENEFITS AND OUTCOMES

- Reduces nightmare frequency and severity
- Improves sleep quality and overall mental health
- Enhances a client's sense of control and emotional regulation
- Can be delivered in individual or group formats and is suitable for telehealth

SUMMARY

Image Rehearsal Therapy for Nightmares (IRT-N) is an evidence-based and trauma-informed approach to alleviating the distress caused by recurrent nightmares. With its cognitive-behavioral roots and flexible delivery model, it is an empowering tool for both clients and clinicians. IRT-N helps reframe nightmares into manageable narratives, fostering better sleep and emotional well-being.

I hold two independent licenses in the states of Arizona and Ohio, supervisory status in Arizona, along with a substance abuse license in Arizona. I am board certified as a Diplomate and Clinical Mental Health Specialist, an Approved Clinical Supervisor, Nationally Certified Counselor, a Certified Clinical Mental Health Counselor, NeuroLinguistic Programming Practitioner, and a Clinical Trauma Specialist for Individuals and Family including EMDR Therapy and NET. I completed my training in Animal-Assisted Therapy and Pet Handlers certification in order to evaluate and incorporate the human-animal bond in therapy. I am the sole author and creator of the SxC Model of ESA Evaluation. My research interests surround post-traumatic growth, resiliency, strengths-based therapy, positive psychology, mindfulness, Animal-Assisted Therapy, Sandtray Therapy, Creative approaches in therapy, and martial arts in mental health. I have presented at local, state, regional, national, and international levels on various topics including personality traits, licensure reciprocity challenges, Sandtray and supervision, and Animal-Assisted Therapy within supervision. eonbllc@gmail.com

REFERENCES

American Academy of Sleep Medicine. (2021). Clinical Practice Guidelines for the Treatment of Nightmare Disorder in Adults.

Krakow, B. (2007). *Turning Nightmares into Dreams: A Practical Guide to Nightmare Therapy.* New Harbinger Publications.

Krakow, B., Kellner, C. H., Pathak, D., & Lambert, L. (1995). Imagery rehearsal treatment for chronic nightmares. *Behavior Research and Therapy, 33*(7), 837-843.

Moore, B. A., & Krakow, B. (2010). Imagery Rehearsal Therapy: An Innovative Treatment for PTSD Nightmares. *Cognitive and Behavioral Practice, 17*(4), 405-413.

U.S. Department of Veterans Affairs. (2022). PTSD: National Center for PTSD. Retrieved from https://www.ptsd.va.gov

Imago Relationship Therapy (IRT)

WENDY PALMER PATTERSON, PHD, LCSW, LMFT

SENIOR FACULTY, IMAGO INTERNATIONAL TRAINING INSTITUTE (IITI)

DIRECTOR OF MA AND PH.D. PROGRAM WITH A SPECIALIZATION IN IMAGO RELATIONSHIP THERAPY (IRT)

AT DAYBREAK UNIVERSITY

JESICA EAMES, LCSW, JD

FACULTY, IMAGO INTERNATIONAL TRAINING INSTITUTE (IITI)

ADVANCED IMAGO CLINICIAN

CERTIFIED IMAGO GETTING THE LOVE YOU WANT WORKSHOP PRESENTER

ALLISON DRAGONY, *CERTIFIED IMAGO PROFESSIONAL FACILITATOR*

Imago Relationship Therapy (IRT) is a research-based therapy model and theory that is globally recognized as a premier structured modality for working with couples, individuals, and families. IRT is currently offered by Certified Imago Relationship Therapists in around 60 countries (Hendrix & Hunt, 2021). IRT offers a deeper understanding for clients of the purpose of their relationships and a practical set of tools for doing relationship therapy. With a primary emphasis from the beginning on couples therapy, the modality has expanded to include all relationships. Imago Relationship Theory differentiates itself from other modalities by holding true that "being in a relationship is our primary reality" (Hendrix & Hunt, 2021) and shifts the focus from the self alone to our interconnected relationships.

IRT became widely known in the 80's because of Oprah Winfrey's engagement with Harville Hendrix, one of the founders and author of best-selling books beginning with Getting the Love You Want: A Guide for Couples written with his partner, Helen LaKelly Hunt (Hendrix & Hunt, 2007, 2021).

UNIQUE PRACTICE ART

Imago Therapy builds on and evolves from the psychological developments of the past century. It focuses on relationships, believing that the human conditions of pain result from ruptured relationships, and healing occurs when relationships are constructive and enhancing. In IRT, we hold the belief that less-than-functional relationships are a result of cultural/societal influences that have not yet leaned into the importance of relating consciously.

The Imago model involves teaching skills such as the Imago Dialogue, enlightening clients to the importance of understanding their brain functioning and unconscious defense systems that create disharmony, and the value of striving for conscious relating by valuing and enhancing the space between people (Hendrix & Hunt, 2021).

While the full healing process using Imago Relationship Therapy takes time, couples and individuals can learn the basic tenets of the dialogue quickly, allowing them to achieve marked success early on in the process. This aspect of IRT is beneficial to therapists using the model because it can give clients improved relationship experiences quickly (Luquet, 2007).

GOALS OF TREATMENT

The IRT model provides a structured experience of skill development to assist relationships in moving and deepening from unconscious relating to conscious relating. In the foreword for *Short Term Couples Therapy*, Harville Hendrix (1996) writes, "In Imago Relationship Therapy, the goal of therapy is to help couples co-create a conscious marriage." Imago therapy helps couples and individuals identify and heal ruptures from early life experiences through restoring connection in their relationships. (Hendrix, 1996). IRT has also been shown to increase empathy and relationship satisfaction in therapy clients and workshop participants (Schmidt & Gelhert, 2015, 2017) (Weigle, 2006).

CERTIFICATIONS, TRAININGS, AND LICENSURE REQUIREMENTS

IRT offers multiple levels of certification for clinicians including a Certified Imago Relationship Therapist, Advanced Imago Therapist, Imago Consultant, Certified Imago Workshop Presenter, and potentially joining the Imago International Training Institute (IITI) Faculty as a Clinical Instructor.

Non-Clinical Trainings and Certifications are also available. The Certification Training for non-therapists is the Imago Professional Facilitator Program.

Training Model

All certified Imago practitioners are extensively trained in the Relational Paradigm that has evolved through Imago's development. Our experience has taught us that it is important to spread the training out over 3 to 6 months, allowing for several months of focused repetition to integrate the materials and skills. It is also important that the training include personal as well as professional opportunities for growth and development.

Imago Clinical Training: Level 1 & 2

Imago trainings build on each other, beginning with the Imago Clinical Training (ICT).

During Level 1 of the ICT, therapists will participate in a twelve-day training program offered in different segments. The training is typically spread out over a 4–12-month experience, depending on the offerings from a faculty member of IITI.

Level 2 of the ICT includes a 6-month period of supervision and submission of a clinical video for evaluation. Completion of all requirements results in certification as a Certified Imago Therapist (CIT) (Imago International Training Institute, 2022) (Imago Relationships North America, 2022).

Cost: $4,500 in the United States that would result (with completion of the requirements) in a Level 2 Certified Imago Relationship Therapist accreditation.

Pre-requisites: Attend Getting the Love You Want or Keeping the Love You Find Workshop.

Degree Requirements: Advanced Degree in a mental health field (M.A., M.S., or PhD) or enrollment in an advanced degree program.

Licensing Requirements: Certification for all levels of clinical training require a recognized and active therapeutic license to practice in the therapist's geographic area.

Supervision: 6 months of supervision is required for certification. Ongoing supervision is recommended.

CEUs: Continuing Education is recommended for Certified Imago Therapists. There is an annual conference each year where therapists can earn CEUs and many advanced Imago training opportunities.

Annual Membership Fees: Certified Imago Therapists are required to join their local Imago Organization (ILO). There is an annual membership fee.

Advanced Imago Therapist: Level 3

Certified Imago Therapists must complete four Advanced Imago courses to achieve status as an Advanced Imago Therapist. Advanced courses are typically offered over a course of 4 days. Several courses are offered throughout the year by Imago Faculty Members worldwide (Imago International Training Institute, 2022).

Imago Workshop Presenter Training: Level 4

This certification training allows Advanced Imago Clinicians to present the Getting the Love You Want and Keeping the Love You Find Workshops. This training is usually presented in 3 modules culminating in a workshop presentation for review by an Imago Consultant or Imago Faculty Member (Imago International Training Institute, 2022).

Requirements: CIT certification for 2 years. Must have Advanced Imago Therapist status or Completion of Characterological Growth and at least 2 other Advanced Trainings.

Certified Imago Consultant or Supervisor: Level 4

Advanced Imago Clinicians can become Imago Consultants or Supervisors after completing the Imago Supervision Training Parts 1 & 2 (Imago International Training Institute, 2022).

Requirements: Must have Advanced Imago Therapist status or Completion of at least 2 Advanced Trainings.

Imago Clinical Instructor / Faculty Member: Level 5

This training path is available to Advanced Imago Therapists who have trained extensively in Imago Relationship Therapy and have completed a detailed apprenticeship with an Imago Faculty member. The training involves assisting at Imago Clinical Trainings with a Faculty Mentor and presenting a Supervised Clinical Training for evaluation. This track takes several years to complete (Imago International Training Institute, 2022).

Imago Professional Facilitator Training: For Non-Therapists

Certification of non-clinician professionals to become Imago Professional Facilitators. This training structure parallels the clinical track, beginning with an Imago Fundamentals training. A Facilitator is expected to take advantage of 3 of 5 advanced modules including: Working with Individuals, Working with Dyads, Working with Groups, Working with Organizations and Imago Presentation Skills. Students participate in PODS for supervision, support, and development of projects highlighting their specialties (Imago International Training Institute, 2021)

Cost: $4,600 - $5,400 in the United States. Completion of all requirements results in Certification as an Imago Professional Facilitator.

Pre-requisites: Attend Getting the Love You Want or Keeping the Love You Find Workshop.

Degree Requirements: There are no degree requirements for this program.

Licensing Requirements: There are no licensing requirements for this program.

Supervision: Supervision is included in the Certification Program as the PODS class. Ongoing supervision is recommended.

CEUs: Imago Professional Facilitators are not required to have continuing education to maintain their certification, however they are encouraged and eligible to take Advanced Imago courses.

Annual Membership Fees: Certified Imago Professional Facilitators are required to join their local Imago Organization (ILO). There is an annual membership fee.

NON-CERTIFIED TRAININGS

Imago trainings are offered in many settings, including community workshops and personal growth workshops. IRT is active in 60 countries around the globe and shares the commitment to teaching couples, parents, individuals and organizations about Imago skills. The workshop systems include Getting the Love You Want, Keeping the Love You Find, Giving the Love that Heals, Start Right and Stay Connected, and Safe Conversations. These workshops offer powerful training in relationship skills. Many Imago practitioners began their Imago journey inspired by having attended one of these workshops.

Requirements: There are no degree or licensing requirements for the non-certified Imago trainings.

SUMMARY

Imago Relationship Therapy is a theory and therapy technique with many avenues of development for therapists, coaches, couples, and individuals. The non-certification trainings and workshops are available globally, and promote relationship consciousness with clear and effective tools. The model has had great success with online and in-person presentations of the materials with participants reporting a sense of hope and preparedness for the future in surveys after completing the trainings and workshops.

The certification process for an Imago Relationship Therapist or Imago Professional Facilitator is a personal and professional journey that enriches not only the clinical knowledge of the trainee, but their relational lives. The experiential nature of Imago training helps clinicians and facilitators apply what they are learning from the beginning of the process. By the end of the training process, Imago trainees have developed in-depth, working knowledge of the skills and techniques of Imago Relationship Theory, and are prepared to take them into practice.

In coordination with the founders, Harville Hendrix and Helen LaKelly Hunt, The Imago International Training Institute continues to create new courses to enrich and develop the Imago process. Pursuing Imago Relationship Therapy as a specialty provides clinicians the opportunity to continue to grow and learn with courses for individual growth and development, as well as specialization courses available for couples, individuals, families, and organizations.

Taking advanced Imago courses allows Certified Imago Therapists to gain additional certifications as an Advanced Imago Therapist, Certified Imago Workshop Presenter, Imago Consultant, and optionally as an IITI Faculty Member.

Imago Relationship Therapy is a perfect fit for therapists or coaches interested in concrete skill building that translates into therapeutic techniques that allow you to create a challenging and constructive environment with a sense of ease between facilitator and client. The focus of Imago Relationship Therapy is to promote healing through conscious relating, and this informs the experience and culture of the global Imago community.

AUTHOR'S EXPERIENCE WITH THE IMAGO PROCESS

For the three of us, Imago Relationship Theory is incorporated into our life and work. In addition to finding professional fulfillment with the Imago process, we each have used Imago Dialogue skills with our own families and relationships to their betterment.

Imago has been a 40-year journey for Wendy, becoming the first to receive a PhD in Counseling with a specialty in Imago Relationship Therapy from Daybreak University. As an Imago Master Trainer and Senior Faculty Member with IITI, Wendy believes in integrating intention with impact. She works diligently teaching the Imago model to couples, individuals, groups, therapists, and professionals. One of Wendy's favorite parts of her Imago work is the process of co-creating change with her clients, students, and colleagues. (Imago Georgia, 2022)

Jesica has been involved with the Imago process for over 20 years, using the techniques in her family before changing careers and becoming a Certified Imago Therapist, Workshop Presenter, and Faculty Member. Through her work, Jesica has come to believe that human beings thrive in connection and often suffer in isolation. Her experience of the training process is one of curiosity, embracing challenges, and helping her students and clients to learn the skills to allow them to create new chapters in their relationships (Imago Georgia, 2022).

Allison has had the privilege to assist many Imago trainings over the last decade with Imago Georgia and has seen the power of the Imago training process in action over and over again. Therapists, coaches, couples and individuals experience great fulfillment when they are able to be truly connected and heard through utilizing the Imago skills and concepts. Through Imago training they advance both their professional skill and personal healing, and in turn, see the same progress with their clients.

Wendy is a Licensed Clinical Social Worker and Licensed Marriage & Family Therapist with more than four decades of experience. She holds a PhD in Counseling with a Specialization in Imago Relationship Therapy. Her focus is relationship consciousness, and she helps couples, individuals, and businesses build more intentional and fulfilling relationships.

Wendy offers counseling for couples, individuals, families, and groups as well as seminars, workshops, and business consultations. As an Imago International Training Institute Faculty Member, and the Director of Imago Relationship Therapy Program at Daybreak University, Wendy trains professionals in all levels of theory and application of Imago Relationship Therapy.

With a PhD in Counseling with a Specialization in Imago Relationship Therapy, Wendy has held leadership roles overseeing addiction counseling services for both public and private organizations. This included training and supervising clinical staff, managing multiple clinics, and leading community awareness programs. She has also served as Director for The Bridge Family Center, Atlanta's first mediation center for family therapy. Wendy's favorite part of her work is co-creating change with her colleagues and clients.

Imago Georgia: www.imagogeorgia.com

Jesica is a Certified Advanced Imago Clinician, a Licensed Clinical Social Worker, a Clinical Instructor/Faculty member with the Imago International Training Institute, and a Certified Imago Workshop Presenter. She specializes in helping couples and individuals strengthen their relationships through Imago Relationship Therapy.

As a faculty member and clinical instructor with the Imago International Training Institute, Jesica also teaches and trains therapists and professionals in Imago Relationship Theory throughout the United States and Internationally.

Jesica consults with businesses using principles of Imago Relationship Therapy. Her work includes consulting with accounting firms, law firms and legal partnerships, family businesses, and more.

Prior to joining Imago Georgia, Jesica served as Senior Litigation Associate on the healthcare team for King & Spalding, LLP. She also clerked for a U.S. Senior District Court Judge and served as Assistant Dean of Admission for Emory University.

Imago Georgia: www.imagogeorgia.com

Allison is a Certified Imago Professional Facilitator. She is the Director of Trainings, Workshops and Practice Development at Imago Georgia. She served as the Administrator for the online Imago Professional Facilitator Training Program from 2020-2023. Allison holds a BFA in Theatre Production and a BA in Ecology and Evolutionary Biology, as well as a certificate in Digital Marketing Science from the University of Arizona. She specializes in writing Imago based articles for Imago Georgia and helping artists and families using Imago principles.

Imago Georgia: www.imagogeorgia.com

REFERENCES

Hendrix, H. (2007) Foreword. Short-term couples therapy: The Imago model in action 2nd ed. Routledge. Taylor and Francis Group.

Hendrix, H. (2007). Getting the Love you Want: A guide for couples. St. Martin's Griffin.

Hendrix, H., & Hunt, H. L. (2021). Doing Imago Relationship Therapy in the Space-Between: A Clinician's Guide. WW Norton & Company.

Imago Georgia. (2022) Meet the Team. https://www.imagogeorgia.com/about

Imago International Training Institute. (2021) The Imago Professional Facilitator Training Online. https://www.imagotraining.info/pft

Imago International Training Institute. (2022) The Imago Professional Path. https://imagocertificationandtraining.com/professional-development

Imago Relationships North America. (2022) Certification Training. https://www.imagorelationshipswork.com/professionals/imago-certification-training

Luquet, W. (2007) Short-term couples therapy: The Imago model in action. 2nd ed. Routledge. Taylor and Francis Group.

Schmidt, C. D., Luquet, W., & Gelhert, N. C. (2015). Evaluating the impact of the Getting the Love You Want Couples workshop on relational satisfaction and communication patterns. Journal of Couple and Relationship Therapy, 15(1), 1-18.

Schmidt, C. D., & Gelhert, N. C. (2017). Couples therapy and empathy: An evaluation of the impact of Imago relationship therapy on partner empathy levels. The Family Journal, 25(1), 23–30. https://doi.org/10.1177/1066480716678621

Weigle, J. B. (2006). The effect of Participating in an Imago Therapy Workshop on Marital Satisfaction [Doctoral dissertation, Walden University].

Immigration Evaluations Training and Certification

Yesenia Teran, DMFT, LMFT

Immigration cases may often involve traumatic experiences and hardships; as such, there is a need for an evaluation from a trained mental health provider to offer a professional opinion through a psychological or psychosocial evaluation. An evaluation can provide a thorough report on the impact of the individual or family's experience. An immigration evaluation provides expert insight that can help the judge or immigration agents and the immigration attorney formulate a case for or against the immigration decision. Immigration evaluations provide the clients with an increased likelihood of receiving a favorable outcome to their immigration case. However, the report does not guarantee the outcome, as it is an unbiased professional evaluation of the client's case.

There are various types of visas that people may submit for, and each has different requirements. Immigration lawyers will work with their clients to inform them of what type of evaluation they need, and that will inform the therapist or psychologist with guidance on the interview they will need to conduct, the assessments that will need to be conducted, and the report that will be written.

EVALUATIONS AND VISAS

Hardship Waiver

A hardship waiver is a step that many families have to take when they are petitioning for their spouse or other family member to be granted a green card which grants an individual permanent legal residency. These waivers allow applicants to remain in or return to the U.S. if they can prove that their removal would cause extreme hardship to a qualifying U.S. citizen or lawful permanent resident (LPR) family member. In these cases, the focus is on the U.S. citizen and not the individual seeking to obtain a visa. The role of mental health professionals in these cases is pivotal, as psychological hardship is a key factor in determining eligibility. A family member of the petitioner can receive a penalty of up to 10 years if they had unlawful presence in the country, a penalty that includes removal from the U.S. or barring the individual from returning to the U.S., and therefore proving the hardship is essential to these types of cases. There are two types of waivers a U.S. citizen can apply for: the I-601 (Application for Waiver of Grounds of Inadmissibility) and the I-601A Provisional Waiver (for unlawful presence).

The I-601 and the I-601A both require proof of psychological, emotional, or other hardship to the U.S. citizen, known as the petitioner, if their family member is not allowed to enter or remain in the U.S. Although a hardship is not defined or specified by the United States Citizenship and Immigration Services (USCIS), there are several hardships that are considered, provided the hardship is beyond typical difficulties. The following information is evaluated and obtained during the clinical interview.

Psychological Hardship: A diagnosable mental health condition, outlined by meeting DSM criteria through clinical assessment and measurement tools. Reliable measurement tools such as the patient-health questionnaire 9 (PHQ9) or general anxiety disorder 7 (GAD7) can be helpful.

Medical Hardship: Need for specialized care, care that cannot be accessed in their family member's home country, or dependency on the family member for medical support. In this case, the clinician will need to review medical records before or after the interview.

Financial Hardship: Economic instability, loss of income, or financial dependence on the family member seeking a visa.

Educational Hardship: Disruption in schooling for children or adults, lack of special education services abroad.

Country Conditions: Political instability, violence, lack of basic resources, cultural and language gaps, and barriers.

Asylum

Asylum provides protection to individuals who have suffered persecution or have a well-founded fear of persecution in their home country due to race, religion, nationality, political opinion, or membership in a particular social group. An additional factor is the government's unwillingness to protect the individual. The refugee or asylum-seeker would likely have experienced past persecution, which allows the belief it will continue in the future, and they have a reasonable fear that they will be persecuted due to their membership of a class or identity. Asylum seekers must prove that their return to their country would result in serious harm or that they have already suffered persecution. Asylum cases require strong evidence about the effects of past persecution and future anticipated persecution if they were to return to their home country. Asylum cases will be presented in front of an immigration judge and the clinician should be prepared to provide expert witness if necessary, however, it is not required that the clinician present to court. The following information is evaluated and obtained during the clinical interview.

- Document trauma, traumatic stress, and other relevant psychological diagnoses related to past persecution.
- Assess the long-term psychological impact of previously experienced torture, sexual violence, threats, or discrimination.
- Demonstrating consistency between the applicant's mental state and their reported experiences will strengthen the credibility.
- Psychological barriers to testifying or presenting their case.

Violence Against Women Act (VAWA)

The Violence Against Women Act (VAWA) allows survivors of all genders of domestic violence, sexual assault, or extreme cruelty to self-petition for lawful status without needing the abuser's cooperation and without having other LPR petition the victim seeking a visa. It applies to people of all genders who are spouses, children, and parents of U.S. citizens or lawful permanent residents (LPRs). Family members who can prove they suffered abuse or extreme cruelty while maintaining a relationship with the abuser are eligible to file for their own petition. VAWA cases do not require cooperation with law enforcement and can lead directly to a green card. The following information is evaluated and obtained during the clinical interview.

- Assess the emotional, psychological, and physical impact of abuse.
- Evaluate coercion, control, isolation, and financial abuse that contributed to the survivor's vulnerability.
- Establish how the abuse has affected mental health, activities of daily living, occupational or academic functioning, parenting, and safety.
- Provide supporting evidence of trauma that aligns with the survivor's legal claim including reviewing police reports and any medical records that document assault.

U Visa (Crime Victim Visa)

The U Visa offers legal protection to victims of serious crimes, such as domestic violence, sexual assault, kidnapping, trafficking, and aggravated assault. Any crime that resulted in substantial mental or physical harm to the victim qualifies for a U-Visa petition. The victim must cooperate with law enforcement in the investigation or prosecution of the crime, and police reports and medical records, if applicable, should be reviewed during the assessment. The investigation does not need to have ended in a conviction for an applicant to be eligible. The requirement is only that there was a crime and the victim cooperated with law enforcement. The following information is evaluated and obtained during the clinical interview.

- Document trauma, traumatic stress, anxiety, depression, and other emotional distress caused by the crime.
- Assess the ongoing psychological impact of victimization, such as fear, isolation, and hypervigilance.
- Explain how the crime disrupted the victim's daily functioning, work, and relationships.
- Demonstrate the necessity of legal stability to recover from trauma and maintain safety.

T Visa (Human Trafficking Visa)

The T Visa is designed for survivors of severe human trafficking, which includes sex trafficking (forced or coerced commercial sex acts), and labor trafficking (forced labor or servitude through coercion or fraud). Applicants can be individuals who were brought to the U.S. through trafficking or were trafficked throughout the U.S. The victims of trafficking must show they were victims of trafficking in the U.S. and must generally cooperate with law enforcement, unless exempt due to trauma-related concerns. The following information is evaluated and obtained during the clinical interview.

- Assess the psychological impact of exploitation, coercion, and forced labor/sex work.
- Evaluate fear, trauma responses, dissociation, PTSD, and long-term mental health effects.
- Provide clinical evidence of abuse, powerlessness, and control tactics used by traffickers.
- Demonstrate the need for continued safety and mental health support in the U.S.

EVALUATION PROCESS AND CLINICAL INTERVIEW

An immigration evaluation is not a therapy session, and it does not establish a long-term therapeutic relationship. The session can be two to three hours and include follow-up sessions for clarification of any missing or mixed information. The evaluation can also be split into multiple 1-hour sessions and include follow-up sessions. An evaluation should include the mental status exam (MSE), formal assessments with measurement tools, and a psychosocial evaluation. The following components should be included in all evaluations:

- Identifying Information – Demographics, country of origin, immigration history.

- Reason for Evaluation – Visa type, purpose, legal basis, and referral source.

- Personal and Family History – Childhood, family structure, relationships, prior trauma.

- Immigration and Trauma History – Reasons for migration

- Mental Health History – Diagnoses, therapy, hospitalizations, and medications

- Trauma-Related Symptoms – If applicable to the case

- Functional Impairment – Impact on occupation, relationships, and daily life.

- Coping Mechanisms & Strengths – Support systems, therapy, resilience, goals.

- Clinical Observations & Testing – Mental status exam (MSE), measurement tools

- Conclusion & Clinical Impression – Summary of findings, impact on the client.

A clinician is not writing a report to advocate for the client's case to reach a specific decision or outcome. The clinician's role is to report the facts. Therefore, in the summary and findings section, the clinician should provide objective information related to the case.

CERTIFICATIONS, TRAININGS, AND LICENSURE REQUIREMENTS

Immigration evaluations must be completed by a licensed mental health clinician who is authorized to practice independently by their state licensing board. This includes licensed psychologists, clinical social workers (LCSWs), marriage and family therapists (LMFTs), and licensed professional clinical counselors (LPCCs). In some cases, such as when neuropsychological testing or the assessment of medical or intellectual disabilities is required, evaluations must be completed by a licensed psychologist. Otherwise, any independently licensed clinician can begin conducting immigration evaluations immediately upon licensure. There is no minimum experience requirement.

Clinicians can draw on many of the core clinical skills developed during their general training. These include clinical interviewing, conducting psychosocial assessments, using diagnostic skills after gathering relevant information, and administering basic assessment tools. Trauma-informed care and cultural competency skills are especially critical in this line of work. Clinicians with experience in documentation and report writing will also find that those skills transfer well to immigration evaluations. In addition, the ability to conduct risk assessments and create safety plans can be an essential part of the evaluation process, depending on the case.

Although formal certification is not required to conduct immigration evaluations, many clinicians pursue it to enhance their credibility and strengthen their skill set. Certification programs are particularly useful for tailoring psychosocial assessments to the specific requirements of each visa type. Each visa—whether for asylum, hardship waivers, or VAWA—requires unique documentation and a specific structure. Certification training prepares clinicians to identify these nuances and apply them appropriately.

Because many clients seeking immigration evaluations have experienced trauma, it is important that clinicians conduct assessments through a trauma-informed lens. Certification programs often include training on trauma assessment and trauma-informed care, offering either new tools or a helpful review of existing knowledge. They also provide guidance on legal and ethical considerations unique to immigration work.

One area where many clinicians may benefit from additional training is report writing. While most are accustomed to writing clinical notes or progress summaries, immigration evaluations require a comprehensive report intended for clients, attorneys, immigration officers, and judges. A quality certification program helps clinicians learn how to organize, write, and present these reports clearly and effectively.

There are a number of certification programs available, each offering slightly different structures and benefits. A good program will provide training in the following areas:

- Understanding the legal context of common visa types
- Conducting thorough, trauma-informed psychosocial assessments
- Writing complete reports suitable for submission to all parties involved
- Providing testimony in immigration court, if necessary
- Marketing services to immigration attorneys

Some widely recognized certification programs include:

PESI, a continuing education provider offering training, certification, and CE credits approved by many licensing boards and professional associations.

> **Name:** Immigration Evaluations for Mental Health Professionals: Must-Have Skills to Conduct Psychological Trauma Assessments, Write Reports & Testify in Court
> **Facilitator:** Marc Sadoff, LCSW
> **CEU and certification:** Six hours of continuing education. The clinician will self-study and receive a certificate to present to their licensing board. There are no additional credentials obtained.
> **Link:** https://catalog.pesi.com/item/immigration-evaluations-mental-health-professionals-conduct-psychological-trauma-assessments-write-reports-refugees-avoid-deportation-146297?_gl=1*qoefpj*_up*MQ..*_gs*MQ..&gclid=Cj0KCQjw2N2_BhCAARIsAK4pEkXyvuTJA_Om-Z5Ixrg-_WEsRx13Nw6z-c1giQQ9GRawF2H6MNX5dZgaAjw_EALw_wcB&gclsrc=aw.ds#tabCredit

The Immigration Evaluation Institute offers a comprehensive certification program with training, resources, a directory, and CE credit.

> **Name:** Immigration psychological evaluation training for therapists to help immigrant families.
> **Facilitator:** Cecilia Racine, LCSW,
> **CEU and certification:** Nine hours of continuing education. The clinician will self-study and receive a certificate to present to their licensing board. The certificate of completion in Comprehensive Immigration Evaluations and the clinician can be designated as an IEI graduate in the directory. There are no additional credentials obtained

Link: https://www.immigrationevaluationinstitute.com/
Immigration Evaluation Training with Georgia King, which provides training materials, certification, and continuing education credit as well.

      Name: Immigration Evaluation Training with Georgia King

      Facilitator: Georgia King, LCSW

      CEU and Certification: Six hours of continuing education. The clinician will self-study and receive a certificate in Advanced Training in Conducting Mental Health Evaluations for Immigration Cases. There are no additional credentials obtained

      Link: https://www.therapistimmigrationtraining.com/about

Clinicians interested in certification should review available programs and choose the one that best fits their learning style, professional goals, and budget. Since there is no regulatory board that mandates certification or sets minimum continuing education requirements for immigration evaluations, clinicians are free to select any training they feel aligns with their needs. However, it's important to consider the reputation and affiliations of the training provider, especially if you plan to use CE credits toward licensure renewal.

General Cost

The cost of obtaining training and certification in immigration evaluations varies depending on the program a clinician selects. In general, the investment can range from a few hundred to several thousand dollars. Most programs include all necessary training materials, so there are no additional costs for supplies or textbooks. Because these trainings are offered virtually, clinicians can also avoid travel-related expenses. Any additional costs that arise are typically related to ongoing marketing efforts tailored to this niche area of practice. Many programs offer flexible payment plans, with total costs typically ranging between $200 and $2,700.

Degree Requirements

Individuals who are conducting psychosocial evaluations for immigration cases must possess, at a minimum, a master's degree. Additionally, the practitioner should be fully licensed, meaning they are able to practice independently without any supervision requirements. In some states, pre-licensed clinicians can conduct immigration evaluations, provided they are supervised by a licensed clinician.

Therapists who engage in conducting immigration evaluations are limited to conducting the evaluations only in the state or states in which the clinician is licensed. Similarly, clinicians should work with language concordant clients, or be able to utilize interpreters during sessions. Immigration evaluations should not lead to a therapeutic relationship that involves therapeutic processing of history or trauma. Per the APA's (American Psychological Association) recommendation and the American Association of Marriage and Family Therapy (AAMFT) code of ethics, Clinicians do not provide therapeutic services to clients for whom they have completed an evaluation. The APA guidelines state that "providing forensic and therapeutic psychological services to the same individual or closely related individuals involves multiple relationships that may impair objectivity and/or cause exploitation or other harm. A relationship in which a therapist conducts a psychological evaluation and engages in therapy services with the patient outside the psychological evaluation is considered a dual relationship. Therefore, if the assessment results conclude that therapy services are recommended in compliance with the above regulations and guidelines, a clinician's ethical obligation is to refer the patient to a qualified clinician who can provide the necessary treatment.

WHAT KIND OF PERSON WOULD DO WELL IN THIS EVALUATIONS

Conducting immigration evaluations is a time-intensive and highly specialized form of clinical work that requires considerable commitment and attention to detail. Clinicians should anticipate spending several hours conducting the evaluation interview alone, during which they must gather comprehensive psychosocial information. Detailed and accurate documentation is essential, and the report-writing process itself can be extensive, requiring far more time than typical clinical note-taking or standard session documentation. Therefore, this work is best suited for providers who are willing and able to devote significantly more time per case than what is typically required in ongoing therapeutic treatment.

Given the nature of immigration cases, clinicians will frequently work with individuals who have limited proficiency in English. It is essential for providers to be prepared to collaborate effectively with professional interpreters to ensure clear, accurate communication. Bilingual and multilingual clinicians may have an advantage in this area, but even they must be prepared to navigate linguistic and cultural nuances with care and professionalism.

Immigration evaluations often require interdisciplinary collaboration. Clinicians must be comfortable communicating and coordinating with attorneys, paralegals, and other legal professionals involved in the case. An understanding of legal processes and the ability to translate psychological findings into legally relevant language is critical to producing an effective and useful report.

Above all, clinicians must approach this work with cultural humility and a deep sense of empathy for the immigrant experience. This includes recognizing the profound emotional, psychological, and systemic challenges faced by individuals navigating the immigration process. Many clients have histories marked by trauma, displacement, loss, and persistent fear related to their legal status. A culturally humble provider does not presume to fully understand these experiences, but rather remains open, curious, and respectful of the client's worldview and lived experiences. Cultural humility involves an ongoing commitment to self-evaluation, acknowledgment of power imbalances, and responsiveness to the unique cultural and contextual needs of each client. Empathy in this context means offering a safe, nonjudgmental space where clients feel seen, heard, and validated—often in ways they may not have experienced elsewhere. Such an approach not only enhances the quality of the evaluation but also honors the dignity and humanity of the individuals served.

SUMMARY

Immigration evaluations are a critical component of the legal process for individuals who were not born in the U.S. but want to live in the U.S. without fear of deportation. These evaluations provide a bridge between professional mental health assessments and immigration law. Immigration evaluations offer a structured and professional assessment of the psychological, emotional, and sometimes physical hardships faced by individuals and families navigating complex immigration procedures. By detailing the impact of trauma, abuse, and persecution, clinicians inform legal decisions and advocate for the well-being of vulnerable populations. Not all visas have a trauma component directly linked to the visa process, such as hardship waiver applications, however, the immigration process itself can be traumatic, and therefore, clinicians should be careful to engage clients in a trauma-informed approach. Especially when working with those seeking asylum visas, U-Visas, T-visas, or VAWA visas. While they each require tailored assessment, evaluation, and reporting, every individual has a history of trauma that clinicians should carefully consider.

Ultimately, the rigorous training and ethical practice standards outlined for clinicians in this field underscore the importance of cultural humility, empathy, and trauma-informed care. As immigration policies and processes continue to evolve, the expertise of these professionals remains essential in ensuring that the psychological dimensions of each case are thoroughly understood and thoughtfully considered. As policies change and shift, the need for immigration evaluations remains, and regardless of the political climate and attitude toward immigrants, clinicians committed to this work should hold on to the values that brought them to this work in the first place. This commitment to ethical and comprehensive evaluation not only supports just legal outcomes but also upholds the dignity and humanity of those seeking a new life.

Dr. Yesenia Teran is a Licensed Marriage and Family Therapist (LMFT) and Doctor of Marriage and Family Therapy (DMFT) with a passion for advancing mental health equity through clinical practice, education, and community-based care. With over four years of experience supporting individuals and families navigating chronic medical conditions, Dr. Teran has a particular focus on serving people living with HIV/AIDS through federally funded programs.

Dr. Teran provides comprehensive psychosocial immigration evaluations for individuals and families navigating the legal immigration process. She offers trauma-informed and culturally sensitive assessments to support individuals facing complex legal and emotional challenges.

Dr. Teran also serves as an adjunct professor, teaching graduate-level courses to future therapists. Her teaching is known for being engaging, reflective, and values-driven—centered on student empowerment and critical thinking.

Tonalli Therapy

www.tonalli-therapy.com

drteran@tonalli_therapy.com

REFERENCES

American Association for Marriage and Family Therapy. (2015). *AAMFT code of ethics.* https://www.aamft.org/Legal_Ethics/Code_of_Ethics.aspx

American Psychological Association. (2017). Ethical principles of psychologists and code of conduct (2002, amended effective June 1, 2010, and January 1, 2017). https://www.apa.org/ethics/code

King, G. (n.d.). Immigration evaluation training with Georgia King [Continuing education course]. Therapist Immigration Training. https://www.therapistimmigrationtraining.com/about

Racine, C. (n.d.). Immigration psychological evaluation training for therapists to help immigrant families [Continuing education course]. Immigration Evaluation Institute. https://www.immigrationevaluationinstitute.com/

Sadoff, M. (n.d.). Immigration evaluations for mental health professionals: Must-have skills to conduct psychological trauma assessments, write reports & testify in court [Continuing education course]. PESI. https://catalog.pesi.com/item/immigration-evaluations-mental-health-professionals-conduct-psychological-trauma-assessments-write-reports-refugees-avoid-deportation-146297

USCIS U.S. Citizenship and Immigration Services. (n.d.). Extreme hardship considerations and factors. U.S. Department of Homeland Security. Retrieved April 6, 2025, from https://www.uscis.gov/policy-manual/volume-9-part-b-chapter-5

USCIS U.S. Citizenship and Immigration Services. (n.d.). Victims of human trafficking: T nonimmigrant status. U.S. Department of Homeland Security. Retrieved April 6, 2025, from https://www.uscis.gov/humanitarian/victims-of-human-trafficking-t-nonimmigrant-status

USCIS U.S. Citizenship and Immigration Services. (n.d.). Victims of criminal activity: U nonimmigrant status. U.S. Department of Homeland Security. Retrieved April 6, 2025, from https://www.uscis.gov/humanitarian/victims-of-criminal-activity-u-nonimmigrant-status

USCIS U.S. Citizenship and Immigration Services. (n.d.). Abused spouses, children, and parents (VAWA). U.S. Department of Homeland Security. Retrieved April 6, 2025, from https://www.uscis.gov/humanitarian/abused-spouses-children-and-parents

USCIS U.S. Citizenship and Immigration Services. (n.d.). Asylum. U.S. Department of Homeland Security. Retrieved April 6, 2025, from https://www.uscis.gov/humanitarian/refugees-and-asylum/asylum

Impact Therapy

CEDAR STAGNER KILE, PHD, LPC, LASAC

Impact Therapy was founded by Ed Jacobs, Ph.D. as "a theory-driven, multi-sensory approach to counseling which recognizes that change or impact comes from not only verbal, but also visual and kinesthetic exchanges" (Impact Therapy Associates, 2023). This approach assists the counselor to help their clients using different ways to reach them since the talk/listen approach does not reach all clients. The brain likes novelty and this approach is a way to help clients remember what they learned in the counseling sessions (E. Jacobs, personal communication, January 16, 2023). It provides the counselor with ways to frame the counseling process and assess the progress of a session (Impact Therapy Associates, 2023). "Impact Therapy is an active, brief form of counseling that is very helpful for school counselors, mental health counselors, social workers, psychologists, and other helping professionals" (Impact Therapy Associates, 2023).

This integrative approach to counseling shows respect for the way clients learn, change, and develop (Impact Therapy Associates, 2023). It is action and insight-oriented, and often resolution-oriented (Impact Therapy Associates, 2023). It emphasizes helping the client as much as possible in each session. The therapist focuses on getting to "the core of the problem by cutting off unnecessary details, irrelevant stories, and unfocused discussions" (Impact Therapy Associates, 2023). The impact therapist sees the goal of any therapy session as creating change or setting in motion the process for change (Impact Therapy Associates, 2023).

Impact Therapy is a form of therapy that combines creative counseling techniques and certain counseling theories. These creative counseling techniques were first presented in CREATIVE COUNSELING TECHNIQUES: AN ILLUSTRATED GUIDE (Jacobs, 1992). "The emphasis is on making counseling clear, concrete, and thought-provoking, rather than vague, abstract, and emotional" (Impact Therapy Associates, 2023). Although it is a type of brief therapy, it is different from the work of Watzlawick, Weakland, and Fisch who have developed a school of therapy called "Brief Therapy" (Impact Therapy Associates, 2023). This unique approach to counseling integrates foundational concepts from existing theories of Rational Emotive Behavior Therapy (REBT), Transactional Analysis (TA), and Gestalt Therapy, such as challenging clients' self-talk, and using analogies, props, movement, and chairs (Impact Therapy Associates, 2023).

"Therapists who subscribe to Systems Theory, Adlerian Counseling, Reality Therapy, and most other theories will find Impact Therapy to be compatible" as it "serves as a solid bridge between theories and techniques and provides a clear way to understand the process and progress of a therapy session" (Impact Therapy Associates, 2023). Impact therapists try to help clients help themselves by getting the clients to think rationally about their issues (Impact Therapy Associates, 2023). "Impact Therapy is an empowering approach to therapy that shows great respect for the client" engaging with the client to be active, thinking, seeing, and experiencing during the session (Impact Therapy Associates, 2023).

Although there is not a specific certification, the Impact Therapy Associates' website offers tools to help counselors become effective in using this modality. This includes their book *Impact Therapy – The Courage to Counsel* ($29), DVD or audio download – *Impact Therapy: Putting Theories into Practice* ($10.95), Impact Therapy audio download ($5), and other tools via audio downloads ($5 each) – *The Counseling Contract, Rapport: Beyond Listening, Creative Counseling,* and *Group Counseling.* There are also YouTube videos on the website. They can be found under Impact Therapy, Ed Jacobs, or Danie Beaulieu. It is important, like with any modality, if counselors are going to state they provide this specific type of therapy, they first need to study it and be able to follow the techniques, which are provided in a very accessible way. Further Dr. Jacobs is willing to work with counselors who want to learn to practice using this modality (E. Jacobs, personal communication, January 16, 2023). It is expected that practitioners have a master's degree in counseling, or related field, and also receive appropriate supervision as would be appropriate to any clinician related to learning a new modality. For specific supervision and consultation related to Impact Therapy you may contact Dr. Jacobs through the website (impacttherapy.com) (E. Jacobs, personal communication, January 16, 2023).

SUMMARY

Even highly skilled and well-trained counselors with knowledge in and experience with many different approaches, they are not always effective with some clients. Or, as Jacobs may say, they do not always have an impact. Many counselors, whether due to their training, comfort level, or both, "use a rather slow process of counseling where much time is spent building rapport and responding with reflections and clarifications" (Impact Therapy Associates, 2023). While this approach is beneficial for some clients, a faster and more active approach to counseling can also be beneficial. Some clients feel frustrated by their therapist because the pace was too slow, not focused, and, most of all, not helpful (Impact Therapy Associates, 2023). Impact Therapy offers a way to accomplish more in a session, while also being creative.

Due to counselors needing to engage the client quickly in certain settings, such as mental health centers, drug and alcohol treatment agencies, and schools, Impact Therapy is an approach that helps the counselor speed up the counseling process by following some basic steps while also using creative, multi-sensory techniques (Impact Therapy Associates, 2023). It gets clients thinking for themselves, promoting confidence and independence (versus dependency) to help them move through process rather than staying stuck (Impact Therapy Associates, 2023).

Dr. Kile is an Assistant Professor at the University of the Cumberlands and is also a Licensed Professional Counselor and Licensed Associate Substance Abuse Counselor in Arizona. Her clinical experience began in 2007 and she still enjoys providing counseling services through her private practice. As a Counselor Educator since 2018, she values helping new counselors learn skills and find their place in this profession.

Better Day Counseling, LLC
www.better-day-counseling.com

REFERENCES

Jacobs, E. (2023, January 16). Impact Therapy Associates. https://impacttherapy.com

Implosion Therapy

La Toya L Patterson PhD, LCPC, NCC

Implosion therapy garnered attention during the 1960s, due to a theoretical paper by Stampfl and Levis (Hackman, 1998). Flooding and implosion techniques derived from classical extinction theory. Implosion therapy, or flooding is a form of therapy that assists clients with imaging situations or participate in real-life situations that they may find extremely frightening for a prolonged period. Teaching relaxation techniques is not a part of this therapy. There must be a significant amount of time allowed for these sessions because brief periods may be ineffective or even harmful. Termination of sessions can be considered once the client has exhibited less anxiety than at the start of the session (Townsend, 2014). The rationale behind the therapy is that when an individual is continuously exposed to anxiety-producing cues, removal of negative reinforcement, the fearful response should reduce and finally extinguish. Implosion therapy focuses on the cues that bring about the conditioned response. Visualization techniques may also be used with implosion interventions as well as in vivo exposure to treat anxiety disorder (Laurent & Potter, 1998).

When implementing implosion therapy, the therapist "floods" the client with information regarding situations that activate their anxiety. The role of the therapist is to describe anxiety-provoking situations in vivid detail and then they are guided by the client's response; the more the client's anxiety is provoked, the more advantageous the therapeutic endeavor is. Therapy is continued until the topic or situation no longer causes inappropriate anxiety (Townsend, 2014). The difference between implosion and flooding is the client is exposed to the fear-provoking stimuli either in real life or in imagination, whereas in implosion therapy these scenes are presented to the client verbally in an exaggerated and dramatic way. The descriptions of the situations are unrealistic, and the length of imagining anxiety-provoking scenes are up to two or more hours, although 40 to 60 minutes session are more common (Jena, 2008).

CERTIFICATIONS, TRAININGS, AND LICENSURE REQUIREMENTS

While there is no available literature that states certifications, training and licensure requirements specifically for implosion therapy. However, there are certification programs for prolonged exposure therapy. The Medical University of South Carolina offers an online, interactive, training program designed to teach mental health providers how to implement Prolonged Exposure therapy. The Center for Treatment and Study of Anxiety (CTSA) at Perelman School of Medicine University of Pennsylvania has a prolonged exposure certification program. The program can lead to a prolonged exposure therapist, prolonged exposure consultant, and prolonged exposure trainer. The prolonged exposure therapist program requires completion of the four-day intensive workshop in prolonged exposure therapy conducted by a certified prolonged exposure trainer. Completion of prolonged exposure consultation and recommendation of the certified prolonged consultation to certify the therapist.

For the prolonged exposure consultant certification, completion of certified prolonged exposure therapist requirements, completion of at least five full prolonged exposure cases, and completion of the five-day prolonged exposure consultant workshop conducted or certified by CTSA. Lastly, the requirements for the prolonged exposure trainer certification requires completion of the certified prolong exposure supervisor requirements, completion of at least 15 full prolonged exposure cases, observation of two intensive workshops in prolonged exposure therapy conducted by certified prolonged exposure trainers, and completion of the three-day prolonged exposure trainer's workshop conducted or certified by the CTSA.

SCOPE OF PRACTICE ISSUES

Before beginning implosive therapy with clients there are several steps that must be completed first. An informed consent should be completed by the client and medical documents must be received. Prior to treatment, clients are informed that the phobia persists because the frightening object is usually avoided. They are also informed about the more contact is maintained with the feared object for a long enough period, the anxiety diminishes, and they will become comfortable. During this process, the therapist maintains a low-key, matter of fact supportiveness, helpfulness, and nonjudgmental objectivity. Clients are informed beforehand about everything that will happen and there will be no surprises. Clients will not be forced to progress faster than they can tolerate; however, they would be encouraged to push themselves to the limit, while maintaining anxiety at the maximum tolerable level. The phobic object is brought and moved rapidly closer to the client until they either refuse to have brought closer, or on the verge of running away. During the process clients are asked to rate their intensity of anxiety on a scale from 0 to 100. The therapist implements modeling, where the therapist demonstrates holding and handling the phobic object ("Flooding and Implosive Therapy", 2016).

CAUTIONS WHEN CONSIDERING USING IMPLOSION THERAPY

There are several critiques that should be noted about implosive therapy. From a behavioral standpoint, the utilization of psychodynamic features into exposure-based therapy has been questioned. Research has shown that the therapy is just as effective without the psychodynamic component. Clients that engage in implosive therapy may find it difficult to endure implosion as compared to a more graduated approach. The research that existed on implosive therapy involved case studies and not clinical trials. The reviews on the effectiveness of implosion therapy have been mixed. Some studies showed that implosive therapy reduced fear while other studies showed that it had not been any more effective than control conditions or other interventions, like systematic desensitization. When treating phobias, implosion therapy is not a choice treatment, even though it is recognized as an integral component to contemporary exposure treatment (Milosevic, 2015). Many clinicians felt that their clients would be harmed by the anxiety that is generated during direct exposure.

The concerns of clinicians were valid because they have been trained to relieve anxiety, and provoking anxiety, even for a short time, appeared to be inconsistent with the treatment goal (Boudewyns & Shipley, 1983). It was reported by Morganstern (1973) that the flooding and implosion therapy, were no more effective than systematic desensitization; that some of the disadvantages were high relapse or increased variability in outcome at follow-up; that they "produced negative side-effects such as nightmares and resistance to continued treatment" (Rachman & Wilson, 1980, p. 138). When working with children, Francis and Beidel (1995) warned that flooding and implosion therapy can cause a deal of distress in children, mainly younger children. Therefore, it was imperative that children received an explanation and understood the reasoning behind the treatment (Laurent & Potter, 1998).

KIND OF THERAPIST AND CLIENT THAT DOES WELL WITH IMPLOSION THERAPY

Implosive therapy has been proving to be effective for several disorders such as panic disorder, specific and social phobia, obsessive-compulsive disorder, and posttraumatic stress disorder (PTSD). It was reported by Stampfl and Levis (1967) that implosive therapy also works well for individuals that struggle with affective disorders, depression, alcoholism, speech disorders, and schizophrenia (Russell & Sheperis, 2009).

SUMMARY

Implosive therapy was designed to extinguish anxiety by repeatedly exposing the client to conditioned anxiety-eliciting stimulus through imagery. Additionally, implosive therapy is imagined based therapy only (Sapp, 2009). Implosive therapy as the therapy introduced hypothesized feared cues into the scenario. The hypothesis developed by the therapist is rooted in psychodynamic formulation of the client's fear problem. The emotional response of the client is used by the therapist to determine if the hypothesized cues are relevant. Implosive therapy is an early variant of exposure therapy, it incorporates psychodynamic therapy and technique (Milosevic, 2015).

Dr. La Toya L Patterson is a native and current resident of Chicago, Illinois. Dr. Patterson attended Roosevelt University, where she received her BA in Psychology and MA in Clinical Professional Psychology. She has an MA in Forensic Psychology with a concentration in Law Enforcement from Argosy University. Dr. Patterson also received her PhD in Counselor Education and Supervision from Adler University. Dr. Patterson is a Licensed Clinical Professional Counselor (LCPC), and she is a National Certified Counselor (NCC). She has 15 years of experience working in the mental health/counseling field. Dr. Patterson has worked for various mental health organizations where she provided individual counseling to individuals that suffered from moderate to severe mental health conditions as well as substance abuse/dependency. She also worked for a local insurance company on the Ready Response Team, where she provided resources for individuals experiencing mental health crises. Dr. Patterson is currently an Assistant Professor at Chicago State University, where she teaches master-level students in the CMHC program, and she also has her own private practice in counseling.

The Essence of Healing LLC
essenceofhealingllc.com
847-643-1016

REFERENCES

Boudewyns, P. A. & Shipley, R. H. (1983). Flooding and Implosive Therapy: Direct therapeutic exposure in clinical practice. Plenum Press

Hackmann, A. (1998). Implosion and Imaginal Flooding. **Implosive Therapy - an overview | ScienceDirect Topics**

Laurent, J., & Potter, K. I. (1998). Anxiety-related difficulties. In T. S. Watson & F. M. Gresham (Eds.), *Handbook of child behavior therapy* (371-392). Springer Science+Business Media, LLC

Milosevic, I. (2015). Implosive Therapy. In I. Milosevic & R. E. McCabe (Eds.), *Phobias: The psychology of irrational fear* (203-205). ABC-CLIO, LLC

"PE Certification Program" (2023). Retrieved **PE Certification Program | Center for the Treatment and Study of Anxiety | Perelman School of Medicine at the University of Pennsylvania (upenn.edu)**

"Prolonged Exposure Emotional Processing Therapy" (2023). Retrieved **PE Web (musc.edu)**

Rachma, S. J. & Wilson, G. T. (1980). The effects of psychological therapy. Pergamon Press

Russell, D.R. & Sheperis, C. J. (2009). Implosive Therapy. In J. O. Johnson (Ed.), *The ACA encyclopedia of counseling* (278-279). American Counseling Association

Sapp, M. (2009). Psychodynamic, affective, and behavioral theories to psychotherapy. Charles C. Thomas

Townsend, M.C. (2014). Essential of psychiatric mental health nursing: Concepts of care in evidence-based practice. F.A. Davis Company

Imposter Phenomena/Imposter Syndrome

DR. SADÉ DUNN, ED. D, LCPC, LPC, NCC, BOARD APPROVED SUPERVISOR, RYT-200

DR. KEYONA HALL, ED.D, LCPC, LPC, NCC, CCTP, BOARD APPROVED SUPERVISOR

First discovered in 1978 by Pauline Rose Clance & Suzanne Imes, the imposter phenomenon, also referred to as imposter syndrome, is described as the self-doubt of intellect, skills, or accomplishments of those who are high-achieving individuals (Huecker et al., 2023). These individuals struggle to accept their achievements and compliments, and they struggle with their professional identity. Huecker et al., 2023, describe the cycle they sometimes experience due to Imposter Syndrome/Phenomena. This cycle includes overpreparation and procrastination. In the over-preparation portion of the cycle, they tend to feel they have to over-prepare for the task at hand, working harder than others for fear of failure; the procrastination portion includes them feeling like they will be exposed as a failure or fraud because they waited until the last minute to prepare for the assignment (Huecker et al., 2023).

Some other components of Imposter syndrome are perfectionism, super-heroism, atychiphobia or fear of failure, achievement phobia or fear of success, and denial of their capabilities (Huecker et al., 2023). This plagues them and causes a lot of emotional distress, including intellectual self-doubt, low self-esteem, feelings of inadequacy, anxiety, depression, burnout, and the development of a maladaptive personality. In professional arenas, they often compare themselves to their peers.

SCALES FOR EVALUATION

Several scales have been developed to help evaluate individuals for IP. Huecker et al. (2023) identified the following:

- The Clance Imposter Phenomenon Scale (The Clance Imposter Phenomenon Scale),
- Harvey Impostor Phenomenon Scale
- Young Imposter Scale
- Leary Imposter Scale (Leary Imposter Scale),
- Perceived Fraudulence Scale

Although no specific training or certification exists for Impostor Syndrome, many agencies and healthcare organizations incorporate Impostor Syndrome professional development training opportunities. Approved CE programs within the profession offer a few well-known continuing education courses. The PESI course on Impostor Syndrome is entitled "*Imposter Syndrome: Treating Anxiety, Depression, and Burnout in Clients Who Feel Like Frauds*" (Imposter Syndrome PESI training) The National Institute for the Clinical Application of Behavioral Medicine also provides a course on Impostor Syndrome, entitled *Working with Impostor Syndrome: Expert Strategies to Help Clients Struggling with Shame, Self-Doubt, and Feelings of 'Never Good Enough'* (Nicabm Imposture Syndrome Course).

TREATMENT RECOMMENDATIONS

Some treatment recommendations for imposter syndrome include counseling, cognitive behavioral therapy, gratitude exercises, and metacognition. (Huecker et. al., 2023). Counseling can provide support and guidance in addressing the root causes of imposter syndrome, such as childhood experiences or perfectionism. Cognitive behavioral therapy can help individuals identify and challenge negative thoughts and beliefs about competence and self-worth, which are common in imposter syndrome. Gratitude exercises can shift focus from feelings of inadequacy to recognizing accomplishments and strengths, fostering a more positive self-view. Metacognition, or thinking about one's thinking, can help individuals become aware of and challenge their self-doubting thoughts and develop more realistic self-assessments. Additionally, creating a positive environment focused on self-awareness helps individuals explore their strengths and weaknesses, recognize accomplishments, and develop a more compassionate and realistic self-view. (Clance & Imes, 1978).

SUPERVISION RECOMMENDATIONS

Supervisors should prioritize creating a safe and supportive learning environment where supervisees feel comfortable discussing their experiences with imposter syndrome. Education on the prevalence and impact of imposter syndrome, particularly among high-achieving individuals and specific populations, is crucial. Supervisors can help supervisees identify and challenge their imposter thoughts and model healthy coping strategies. Resources like articles, books, and continuing education opportunities can further enhance supervisees' understanding. Role-playing and case studies can help supervisors practice applying interventions and techniques for addressing imposter syndrome in clients. Finally, supervisors should encourage self-reflection and self-compassion, emphasizing recognizing and celebrating successes.

WHO STRUGGLES WITH THIS?

Originally, imposture phenomena/syndrome (IP) were discovered in high-achieving women (Clance & Imes, 1978). It is especially high in those who identify as BIPOC or minority populations (Abramson, 2021). Clance & Imes (1978) found that men struggle with IP at a much more intense rate and frequency than women do. Some have also found that IP is specifically among high-achieving medical and healthcare professionals (Huecker et al., 2023).

A seasoned professional or one specifically trained to work with high-achieving individuals would be best suited for this population. A newly licensed professional, under the supervision of an experienced individual specializing in high-achieving clients, may also be effective. Furthermore, it is essential for all professionals, regardless of their expertise level, to engage in continuing education focused on imposter syndrome to be well-prepared to treat those who experience it.

SUMMARY

IP was initially discovered and researched by Pauline Rose Clance & Suzanne Imes in 1978, after which Dr. Clance published a book in 1985 (Hawley, 2016). Imposter phenomena and imposter phenomena are often used interchangeably. This phenomenon was discovered initially in high-achieving women (Clance & Imes, 1978). Others have added to their research to include medical and healthcare professionals (Huecker et al., 2023) and those in the BIPOC or minority populations (Abramson, 2021). Several evaluation/assessment tools have been developed to help those who struggle with IP. Research is still being done on this fantastic phenomenon, so we can expect more articles, studies, and assessments/evaluations on Imposter Phenomena/Syndrome.

Dr. Sadé Dunn is the founder of Methods Therapy, LLC, and is recognized for her expertise and compassion in counseling and mental health. She holds the titles of Approved Supervisor and Licensed Professional Counselor across Washington, D.C., Maryland, and Virginia, contributing a wealth of knowledge to her practice.

An alumna of Governors State University and Bowie State University, Dr. Dunn is actively involved in professional organizations. She served on the Maryland Counselors for Social Justice board as a counselor representative from 2019 to 2022. She was an Emerging Leader with the Maryland Counseling Association during the 2020-2021 term, highlighting her commitment to advocacy and social change.

In addition to her academic and professional roles, Dr. Dunn is a Reiki Level II Practitioner and a registered yoga teacher (200-hour level). She is pursuing advanced yoga studies to obtain a 500-hour certification, reflecting her dedication to holistic wellness.

Her research interests include perinatal mental health, positive parenting, trauma-focused therapy utilizing Eye Movement Desensitization and Reprocessing (EMDR), and the identity development of mental health professionals. Dr. Dunn's work addresses the challenges faced during pregnancy and postpartum, explores strategies to enhance parent-child relationships, and investigates trauma recovery methods. She also examines the interplay of personal and professional identities among mental health professionals, aiming to inform strategies for professional growth and self-care.

Dr. Sadé Dunn exemplifies excellence and compassion and is committed to empowering individuals and communities on their wellness journeys.

Methods Therapy, LLC https://www.methodstherapy.com/

Dr. Keyona Evans Hall is a distinguished National Certified Counselor (NCC) and Licensed Clinical Professional Counselor (LCPC) in Maryland, known for her extensive contributions to mental health services and education. With over 16 years of professional experience, she has made significant strides in community mental health program administration. She is adept at providing direct and indirect services to children, adolescents, adults, and families.

Dr. Hall is an adjunct faculty member at two prestigious universities in Maryland, where she imparts her vast knowledge and experience to students pursuing counseling and mental health careers. She also owns a private practice in Maryland, Enlighten Therapuetic & Consulting Services, LLC, where she delivers expert care rooted in a compassionate and non-judgmental approach.

As an approved supervisor in Maryland and a Certified Clinical Trauma Professional, Dr. Hall specializes in addressing complex issues faced by those who have experienced trauma. Her clinical expertise extends to treating various diagnoses, including complicated traumas, depression, bipolar disorder, PTSD, anxiety, ADHD, and oppositional defiant disorder.

In addition to her clinical and educational roles, Dr. Hall earned her Counseling Education and Supervision doctorate. This qualification empowers her to provide high-level consultation and clinical supervision to emerging and established clinicians, bolstering their skills and confidence in the mental health field.

Dr. Hall's dual role as an educator and practitioner, alongside her dedication to mentorship, significantly enriches her impact on individual clients and the broader mental health community.

Enlighten Therapuetic & Consulting Services, LLC https://enlightentherapeutic.com/

REFERENCES

Abramson, A. (2021, June 1). How to overcome impostor phenomenon. *Monitor on Psychology, 52*(4). https://www.apa.org/monitor/2021/06/cover-impostor-phenomenon

Clance, P. R., & Imes, S. (1978). The imposter phenomenon in high achieving women: Dynamics and therapeutic intervention. *Psychotherapy: Theory, Research & Practice, 15*(3), 241-247. https://doi.org/10.1037/h0086006

Hawley, K. (2016, July 19). *Imposter syndrome: Feeling a fraud? It's not your fault!* Psychology Today. Retrieved August 18, 2024, from https://www.psychologytoday.com/us/blog/trust/201607/feeling-a-fraud-its-not-your-fault

Huecker MR, Shreffler J, McKeny PT, et al. Imposter Phenomenon. [Updated 2023 Jul 31]. In: StatPearls [Internet]. Treasure Island (FL): StatPearls Publishing; 2024 Jan-. Available from: https://www.ncbi.nlm.nih.gov/books/NBK585058/

Industrial-Organizational Psychology (I/O)

Morgan Ashworth, MSIOP, MSL, SHRM-SCP

Industrial-organizational psychology (I/O psychology) applies psychological theories to enterprise. The field started in the early 1900s but has gained increased popularity in the 21st century. According to the APA, it is "the scientific study of human behavior in organizations and the work place. The specialty focuses on deriving principles of individual, group and organizational behavior and applying this knowledge to the solution of problems at work" (APA Career). I/O psychologists (I/Os) use psychological principles to improve the workplace through employee initiatives. Using theories of human behavior in concert with statistical analyses, I/Os help organizations and organizational leaders select, train, support, and motivate employees through their focus on employee well-being.

More often than not, I/Os work in people operations for organizations, though it is possible to find oneself working in a broader scope of business such as sales, marketing, finance, etc. People operations is employee focused, and with employees running all parts of an organization, it is possible I/Os can find themselves practicing organizational development in general or in a specific sector.

CERTIFICATIONS, TRAININGS, AND LICENSURE REQUIREMENTS

There are no specific certification, training, or licensure requirements to become an I/O psychology practitioner in the U.S. Conversely, elsewhere in the world, practitioner experience is required in conjunction with degree requirements, which ultimately leads to licensure. To become an I/O psychologist in the U.S., and use the term as one's title, a license is required. Oftentimes, professionals will utilize the term I/O psychology practitioner in place of I/O psychologist, and simply attain a Master's over a Doctorate and license.

General Cost

Cost is dependent on the higher education program attended. At minimum, to achieve a 'terminal degree,' 6 years or the equivalent to 6 years of education is necessary. A bachelor's degree in any subject matter, on average, costs $26,027 per year for in-state public schools, $27,091 per year or for out-of-state students, or $55,840 per year for private school attendees (Hanson, 2023). An online master's degree in industrial-organizational (I/O) psychology can cost between $20,350 and $37,000 for a 2-year program, though in-person costs can reach upwards towards $68,000+ due to the average cost of private school master programs (Colton, n.d.; 2024 Harvard Extension School). In total, for a terminal Master's degree, the lowest cost one could incur is roughly $124,458 with a high of $291,360+. This does not take into account factors of other cost savings such as additional scholarships other than school provided ones, online undergraduate programs, express programs, pre-college credits, living at home, etc. In addition to the cost of tuition and living expenses, one will purchase school materials including textbooks, which equates to a cost of roughly $33 per class or $1,215 per year (Welding, 2023).

If one chooses to move onward towards a Doctoral program, most commonly a PsyD or PhD, the costs equal $30,000 to $50,000 for a 4-to-5-year program, so an additional total of up to $250,000 dis-including material and living expenses (Williams, 2024; 2023 AllPsychologySchools.com). Programs can take upwards towards 8 years to complete, though costs remain relatively the same since these are part-time programs. If one chooses to subsequently be licensed, an additional cost of $125 for the application fee and $750 in oral and written exams are adopted to become a board-certified I/O psychologist (Perry, 2024). The additional costs of over $250,000 with licensure are not required for success as an I/O psychology practitioner.

Additional, optional certification costs include anywhere from $200 to $2,000+ for recommended certifications and their training programs.

IDENTIFIED AS GOLD STANDARD, BEST PRACTICE, EMERGING PRACTICE, OR EBP

There are no identified gold standards, best practices, emerging practices, or EBPs for the industry of I/O psychology.

CERTIFICATION AVAILABLE/REQUIRED/RECOMMENDED

Supplementary forms of education exist in certification programs. Most secondary-education institutions offer certificates in a variety of subjects, from organizational development, to economics, marketing, finance, leadership, and others. To supplement a specific profession, a variety of certifications are available. For example, many I/Os find themselves involved in HR certifications through companies like Academy to Innovate HR (AIHR) or Society for Human Resources Management (SHRM), or HR Certification Institute (HRCI). There are, however, no requirements for certification. Depending on one's field, it is recommended to receive a certification in their specialty.

Certifications one may choose to acquire can further credit one's specialization in the I/O sphere. For example, if one focused on employee testing or statistics, they may look into becoming a certified psychometrist through the CSP (Certified Specialist in Psychometry) exam. Conversely, if one finds themselves in the HR or people operations fields, one may go after an HRCI or SHRM certification. The HR Certification Institute (HRCI) has a number of certifications to choose from with Associate, Professional, Senior, and Global levels, some of which are further specialized to cover the state of California or International. The Society for Human Resource Management (SHRM) has two main certifications, the SHRM-Certified Professional (SHRM-CP) and SHRM-Senior Certified Professional (SHRM-SCP). Both organizations have additional courses, which provide specialized certificates in different areas applicable to the I/O and HR industries.

Certifications certainly put candidates a step above their peers in the application process, and increases the likelihood for salary negotiation and promotion. I/Os can train and receive certificates in software programs common to their profession like becoming an IBM Certified Specialist on SPSS, Workday Certified, NetSuite Administrator Certified, or other specific HRIS program certifications. HRIP Certification from IHRIM is a general HRIS certification, as well as the SHRM and HRCI certifications.

Lastly, like the SHRM and HRCI certificates, one may choose to get a certificate to show an advanced understanding of a particular area within I/O. Linked-In, SHRM, HRCI, Academy to Innovate HR (AIHR), and a number of other organizations and universities have education programs available to receive such certificates. Those certificates may be one of the numberless topics as listed below. The list is not exhaustive of the learning certificate and credential opportunities available:

- Compensation & Benefits
- Training Employees
- Employment Law
- People Analytics
- Talent Management
- Diversity, Equity, & Inclusion
- HR Ethics
- Organizational Development
- Behavioral Interviewing
- People Management
- Total Rewards
- AI and HI Specialty
- Workplace Investigations
- Succession Planning
- Learning & Development
- HR Metrics
- Conflict Mediation
- Talent Acquisition
- Culture Development
- Coaching & Mentoring
- Organizational Theory
- Business Strategy
- Consumer Behavior
- Marketing Psychology

Degree Requirements

Higher education is necessary to practice I/O psychology. At minimum, a Bachelor's degree will be required to work most positions that fall under the realm of I/O psychology, and most will ask the major be I/O psychology or psychology. It is possible to study other majors such as business as well, but these do not always formally introduce students to psychological theories as is needed for a profession in I/O psychology. A Bachelor's degree alone, however, will diminish one's ability towards career growth. Significant experience and skill will be required for advancement. Instead, most professionals receive a Bachelor's in psychology followed by a Master's in I/O psychology.

A Master's is considered a terminal degree, though some professionals move on to receive a Doctoral degree of some sort. In order to become licensed as an I/O psychologist, one is most often required to have a Doctoral degree in the United States, though it is state specific. Oftentimes, professionals will utilize the term I/O psychology Practitioner in place of I/O psychologist, and simply attain a Master's over a Doctorate. The Master's degree should be in I/O psychology, though others practice I/O psychology with varying, related degrees. The choice between a Master's and Doctorate degree, then, becomes a personal one. One must look at their desired profession in I/O psychology to ensure their education matches the requirements for their profession. Almost always a Master's degree is as sufficient as a Doctoral degree. I have colleagues who state that they took the same exact course in a Master's and a Doctoral degree, if not very similar courses, so felt the addition of a Doctorate degree was not needed. Unless your profession specifically requires a Doctoral degree, it is advantageous to first begin with a Master's as experience is more highly valued in enterprise than education. One could aways return for a Doctorate later on, but it may not be necessary for success in one's vocation.

CAUTIONS OR LIMITATIONS

With a focus on applying psychological principles to the workplace, there are numerous ethical considerations in I/O Psychology, though none so prominent as to overshadow the rest. As in any field of psychology, the main ethical consideration is its mission to strive to benefit those with whom they work and take care to do no harm (APA Ethics). The Society of Industrial Organizational Psychology (SIOP) has adopted the APA Ethical Principles of Psychologists and Code of Conduct (SIOP Ethics). The 7 main ethical principles of psychology include informed consent, voluntary participation, disclosing risks, disclosing benefits, confidentiality, compensation, and contact information (APA Ethics).

Those practicing I/O psychology have an increased focus on business ethics as well. Depending on the resource, there are between 7 to 12 business ethical principles. The 12 that one may consider are honesty, fairness, leadership, integrity, compassion, respect, responsibility, loyalty, law-abiding, transparency, and environmental concerns (Twin, n.d.). There are numerous legal considerations as well, most prominent for those working in human resources due to state and federal labor laws.

The barriers one faces in practicing I/O psychology tends to be the lack of understanding those in the business world have of its practice and applicability. It is a less known subject so those practicing I/O psychology find themselves educating others regarding the field. Further, some say there is a gap between I/O psychology research and practice. This gap could be due to a lack of awareness of what the other side knows, a lack of confidence in the other side's knowledge, or a lack of implementation of ideas (Rynes, 2009). It is important the two be connected through research translation in order to bridge the gap. Finally, trends in the industry and in the business-scape can severely affect the way in which the field is depicted. Currently, I/O psychology professionals have an overemphasis on theory, a fixation on methodological minutiae, and an obsession with publication (Turner, 2017). This further creates a research-practice gap. The business-scape's orientation toward globalization and a remote workforce poses challenges for I/O psychologists, such as collaboration, communication, and building a sense of teamwork, due to a lack of connection between people. To solve these issues, I/O psychology professionals must ensure to retain the scientist-practitioner model to research and workplace integration.

SUMMARY

Industrial-organizational psychology has a vast range of applicability. It applies to any workplace and any type of professional. Current applications to I/O psychology include applying theories about leadership, motivation, retention, job satisfaction, consumer psychology, teamwork, remote work, burnout, generational differences, and more to the business-scape. With an ever-changing business landscape because of the evolving needs of a diverse set of individuals, I/O psychology is needed now more than ever. With a direct translation to human resources and people operations, and labor laws being disorderly across state and federal government, professionals well versed in law and the psychological principles behind people and change at work are at an advantage to solve workplace upset and ensure calm, content work environments.

WHAT KIND OF PERSON WOULD DO WELL IN MODEL/APPROACH

Dependent on one's path in the industry, different competencies are necessary. I/O psychologists can attain many titles, and can participate in a variety of industries. According to the Society of I/O Psychology (SIOP), there are four main paths an I/O can follow: 1) consulting, 2) government, 3) academia, and 4) industry. Too many believe consulting, specifically external consulting, is the only tract, meanwhile, industry is a prospering path to follow as so many titles exist in organizations that attract and allow I/Os to accomplish their purpose.

The consulting track involves internal and external consulting of organizational operations of all sorts. Consultants can be specific to one subject or cover a wide variety of topics in helping businesses. According to the SIOP, there are 5 job levels for an I/O psychology practitioner, among 2 paths. One path entails becoming a specialist and the other supervising staff within an organization. For external consultants, they could work as a team of one or internally at a consulting organization. For internal consultants, they work at non-consulting organizations in the people operations or management teams. Internal consultants may also work as a team of one or overseeing a department of employees.

The academia track enters one into the sphere of secondary education, where careers focus on educating others entering the field themselves and/or completing research. According to the SIOP, those entering the academia path have a 3-level career path that can ebb-and-flow depending on the interest of said professional. One can be a professor, a dean, or earn a higher position at a university. In order to attain tenure in organizations and receive a dean or similar position, like any academia professional, one must have a Doctoral degree. It is possible to become a professor with a Master's degree, but they are more often known as adjunct faculty members and find it difficult to advance.

The industry track enters one into the day-to-day business of an organization. One can act as an internal consultant, OD specialist, HR specialist, and other vocations within the industry path. According to the SIOP, those entering into the industry track have a 5-level career path. Similar to the consulting career ladder, there are two paths one can take. One entails becoming a specialist and team of one or few while the other involves supervising other staff and becoming an organizational manager. Further within the industry track, one may take on a specialty or choose to remain generalized in the field. From management consulting, to marketing, sales and consumer behavior, organizational development and/or strategy, learning, development and training, recruitment and talent acquisition, compensation and benefit analysis, employee testing, applied behavioral analysis, performance management, and others, I/Os have a number of opportunities available to them through industry.

The Government track is as it sounds, working in the government as an I/O psychology professional. Similar to the professions one can attain as an I/O psychologist, one would participate in the business of governmental operation. One difference than working in industry, however, is that research is more heavily required in the government path. Governmental positions are more likely, than consulting and industry, however, to require a doctoral degree.

HOW CAN MENTAL HEALTH PROFESSIONALS USE IT?

Mental health professionals will utilize I/O psychology if they enter the professional world as a business-person. They are less likely to use I/O psychology in treating patients clinically, though the knowledge that comes with theories of I/O psychology can be of help when discussing patients' workplace. There are many professionals who have since moved from clinical psychology to practicing I/O psychology. If a mental health professional wants to make beneficial change for people, but is not interested in the clinical route, then they can do so through enterprise working within the confines of business.

OVERALL PERSONAL AND PROFESSIONAL QUALITIES NEEDED

Becoming an I/O psychology professional will allow one to develop specific, deeper skills as they continue in a certain specialty, but for one to start they must be curious thus apt to learn. Separate from a willingness to research and teach themselves, they must have top-tier assessment and communication skills to ensure they have the capacity for research translation. Oftentimes, research is presented to business leaders in layman terms over scientific labels. Having the independent capability to problem solve and make good judgements is critical to ensure projects and suggestions are well-thought out prior to implementation. Those who will find the most success in the field are passionate and determined yet open to constructive criticism. The field is not for the weak-hearted as practitioners often find themselves negotiating between employees and employers and persuading groups to buy-in to recommended interventions and change. Further, with the existing difficulties in today's job market, committed individuals willing to explain their field and do the work will find themselves more quickly practicing in the field as well as advancing into their ideal job.

Morgan Ashworth is a dedicated industrial-organizational psychology professional with a strong passion for business and a profound understanding of human behavior in the workplace. She holds a B.A. in Psychology from the University of Vermont (UVM) and an M.S. in Psychology with a concentration in Industrial-Organizational Psychology from Southern New Hampshire University (SNHU). Although she has not pursued a doctorate, and therefore does not use the title "psychologist" as defined in the U.S., Morgan's expertise in her field is evident through her impactful work and leadership. While working in the field, Morgan attended Northeastern University for her MLS degree and pursued her SHRM-SCP certification.

Morgan began her career in human resources, focusing on a combination of administrative responsibilities and organizational development initiatives. Through her curiosity and drive, she quickly became adept at analyzing and improving organizational processes. She attributes much of her success to her willingness to immerse herself in every facet of an organization's operations, enabling her to design and implement tailored interventions that drive meaningful change.

Currently, Morgan serves as the Chief People Officer at Ashworth Awards, where she leads with a focus on enhancing employee engagement, organizational culture, and strategic development. She also hosts the podcast Organizational Sherlocks, where she shares her insights on applying organizational principles to real-world workplace challenges. Additionally, Morgan consults with small companies, offering tailored guidance on organizational structure, culture, and processes to help them thrive.

Morgan believes deeply in the importance of understanding the unique intricacies of each organization when designing and implementing change. Her advice to aspiring industrial-organizational psychology professionals is clear: "It is possible to make effective change as an external consultant, but one must ensure they are well-versed in the company's operations, financial capabilities, and other key factors. No matter the path you take, developing a deeper understanding of the enterprise and sector you work in is essential to ensure the success of any changes you suggest."

Morgan's career exemplifies the power of combining psychological expertise with business acumen, making her a dynamic force in her field.

Ashworth Awards www.ashworthawards.com

Organizational Sherlocks www.organizationalsherlocks.com

Linked-In: https://www.linkedin.com/company/organizational-sherlocks/

Streaming: https://open.spotify.com/show/1TaSJmsCjxuVjiCJmt5F41

https://www.linkedin.com/in/morgan-s-ashworth

REFERENCES

American Psychological Association. (n.d.). Industrial and Organizational Psychology provides workplace solutions. American Psychological Association. https://www.apa.org/education-career/guide/subfields/organizational#:~:text=Industrial%20and%20organizational%20(I%2FO)%20psychologists%20focus%20on%20the,communication%2C%20professional%20satisfaction%20and%20safety. > Cited as, APA Career

American Psychological Association. (n.d.). Industrial and Organizational Psychology provides workplace solutions. American Psychological Association. https://www.apa.org/ethics/code. >> Cited as, APA Ethics

Colton, A. (n.d.-a). *Online industrial-organizational psychology master's degree | usnews.com*. U.S. News & World Report, Education. https://www.usnews.com/education/online-education/industrial-organizational-psychology-masters-degree

Colton, A. (n.d.-b). *Ph.d. in industrial-organizational psychology online | usnews.com*. U.S. News & World Report, Education. https://www.usnews.com/education/online-education/industrial-organizational-psychology-doctorate-degree

Colton, A. (n.d.-c). *Ph.d. in industrial-organizational psychology online | usnews.com*. U.S. News & World Report, Education. https://www.usnews.com/education/online-education/industrial-organizational-psychology-doctorate-degree

Hanson, M. (2023, November 18). *Average cost of college [2023]: Yearly tuition + expenses*. Education Data Initiative. https://educationdata.org/average-cost-of-college#:~:text=The%20average%20cost%20of%20attendance,or%20%24223%2C360%20over%204%20years.

Industrial-Organizational Psychology Master's degree program. Harvard Extension School. (2024, April 15). https://extension.harvard.edu/academics/programs/industrial-organizational-psychology-graduate-program/

Perry, C. (2024, March 4). *How to become an industrial-organizational psychologist*. Forbes. https://www.forbes.com/advisor/education/psychology-and-counseling/become-an-industrial-organizational-psychologist/#:~:text=Industrial%2DOrganizational%20Psychologist%20Certification,the%20two%20exams%20total%20$750.

Rynes, Sara. (2009). The Research-Practice Gap in I/O Psychology and Related Fields: Challenges and Potential Solutions. The Oxford Handbook of Organizational Psychology. 1. 10.1093/oxfordhb/9780199928309.013.0013.

Society for Industrial and Organizational Psychology. (n.d.). https://www.siop.org/Events-Education/Continuing-Education. >> Cited as, SIOP

Society for Industrial and Organizational Psychology. (n.d.). https://www.siop.org/Career-Center/Professional-Ethics#apa >> Cited as, SIOP Ethics

Twin, A. (n.d.). *What is business ethics? definition, principles, and importance*. Investopedia. https://www.investopedia.com/terms/b/business-ethics.asp

Turner, M. (2017, April 1) *Has Industrial-Organizational Psychology Lost Its* Way?. SIOP.
https://www.siop.org/Research-Publications/Items-of-Interest/ArtMID/19366/ArticleID/1550/Has-Industrial-Organizational-Psychology-Lost-Its-Way#:~:text=world%20of%20work.-,1,Overemphasis%20on%20Theory

Welding, L. (2023, September 25). *Average cost of college textbooks: Full statistics: Bestcolleges.* BestColleges.com.
https://www.bestcolleges.com/research/average-cost-of-college-textbooks-statistics/#:~:text=Data%20Summary,per%20class%20on%20course%20materials.

Williams, Dr. K. (2024, May 14). *Doctorate in psychology (Ph.d. and psy.D.) - everything you need to know in 2024.* PsychologyJobs.com. https://psychologyjobs.com/psychology-degrees/doctorate/

A [complete] guide to earning a doctorate degree in psychology. AllPsychologySchools.com. (2023, November 10). https://www.allpsychologyschools.com/degrees/doctorate-in-psychology/

Infant Developmental Movement Education (IDME)

CARA ANGELA LIGUORI, MS, MHC-LP, IDME, RSME

An outgrowth of Bonnie Bainbridge-Cohen's BodyMind Centering® (BMC®), Infant Developmental Movement Education (IDME) is a somatic approach to supporting infant development and early bonding while empowering new parents and caregivers with an internalized sense of agency and self-trust.

IDMEs primary objective is to educate caregivers on how to support the emergence of their infants' developmental movement patterns. To do this, IDMEs focus on providing infants with early movement experiences that enhance their agility, coordination, and sense of autonomy. IDMEs also model for parents and caregivers how to avoid restrictive movement patterns that are often unconsciously imposed and can inhibit the unfolding of their babies' full potential (Bainbridge-Cohen, n.d.).

IDME focuses on babies' experiences of movement and touch. While it is widely accepted that neurological development influences movement, IDME uniquely highlights the reciprocal relationship between movement and neurological development. That is, a thorough and well-supported experience of movement in all spatial planes during infancy provides sensory nourishment for babies' developing brains (Bainbridge-Cohen, n.d.; Rupert, 2022; Faber, 2017). This emphasis on caregiver touch, handling, and co-regulation skills distinguishes IDME in the field of perinatal services. Rupert (2021) states, "there is a lack of research into the specific ways in which movement is being used to affect neurodevelopment and which specific types of movement most benefit neurodevelopment" (p. 2) in babies aged 0 - 3. With its primary focus on touch and movement, the IDME approach offers a valuable, but currently overlooked perspective on the importance of infant handling (personal communication, S. Murdock, April 26, 2024) that could add significant depth to this growing field of research which highlights maternal attentiveness mostly through language and facial mirroring (Kim, 2024; Beebe et al., 2018).

Further, because of IDMEs' in-depth knowledge regarding developmental movement and reflexes, IDME practitioners can skillfully emphasize *all that is going well* for infants and new families throughout the developmental process, even when milestones aren't met on a standard timeline. This aspect of the IDME work can provide a profoundly uplifting perspective, especially for families whose infants are experiencing developmental interruptions such as NICU hospitalizations or diagnoses requiring early intervention services.

The IDME paradigm is child-led and relationship-centered. The approach is non-pathologizing, strengths-based, trauma-informed, systems-informed, and culturally sensitive. IDME departs distinctly from instructional newborn care by engaging caregivers' genuine curiosity about what experiencing the world for the first time might be like for their babies, and, further, how deepening their own curiosity about babies' experiences, might shape the way they learn to relate and respond as parents. During sessions, information is imparted both experientially (i.e., through modeling and practice) and via psychoeducation. IDME does not rely on a one-size-fits-all protocol model to facilitate effective dyadic interactions. Instead, IDME offers an embodied practice that emphasizes the basics of relational intimacy (Bainbridge-Cohen, n.d.) and mindful observation to support the organic development of parental-infant bonding, caregiver skills, and confidence. IDME embraces that infants' internal maps of their perceptual experiences are carved into neural networks as a result of their bodies moving in space and exploring relationships (Ciaunica et al., 2021). Thus, beyond interactional techniques, IDME offers an embodied philosophy that reorients caregivers to *be with* their babies, to bear witness to their infant's growth (Barnaby & Matthews, n.d.), to be curious about the infant experience, and to understand that the cocreated patterns set in motion during early infancy set the stage for parenting style and attachment dynamics throughout a family's lifespan (Heller, 2019).

As a modality, IDME can be applied across settings. In-person and virtual sessions are common for families individually, in pods, or in small groups. Groups expand participants' peer networks which can be essential for combatting the sense of isolation faced by many new parents (U.S. Department of Health and Human Services, 2024). IDME sessions can take place during in-home visits that may initially resemble *listening visits,* an evidence-based non-directive counseling intervention for individuals with perinatal mood and anxiety disorders (PMADs) (McCabe et al., 2021). While sessions are typically framed as infant play or movement observation and support, the principles of IDME can be applied as parenting psychoeducation during the fourth trimester for individuals at high risk for or diagnosed with PMADs (personal communication, S. Murdock, December 12, 2024). IDME can also be introduced as experiential psychoeducation for prospective caregivers during or before pregnancy as preparation for the developmental process and role transition of becoming a parent.

CERTIFICATIONS, TRAININGS, AND LICENSURE REQUIREMENTS

Intended to provide in-depth training in the evaluation and facilitation of normal infant development, IDME certification begins with four core developmental modules: Senses & Perception, Basic Neurocellular Patterns, Primitive Reflexes, Righting Reactions, & Equilibrium Responses, and Ontogenetic Development, ~175 hours of in-person study. These courses are followed by two modules that address working with infants, an additional 160 hours of in-person study. The training modules range from 4 - 10 consecutive days. Throughout the completion of coursework, prospective IDMEs are expected to complete eight study sessions or small public presentations of IDME concepts, 20 infant observations, 12 interactive infant play sessions, and a total of 8 guidance, personal learning, and supervision sessions with certified IDME practitioners and instructors. Each of these requires a concise written report. An educational/promotional project and a video presentation of an infant observation are also required (Bainbridge-Cohen, n.d.).

Training modules are offered in movement studios. Organizations licensed by the School for BodyMind Centering® to provide IDME curriculum are currently located in New York, Spain, France, Germany, and Slovakia, while IDME prerequisite courses can be taken in 16 countries with English translation. Prerequisites can be pursued in any order and across multiple training facilities, while practical application coursework must be completed with an organization identified as the trainee's primary study location (Bainbridge-Cohen, n.d.). The time it takes to complete the IDME certification coursework and assignments varies by individual. The process is accredited by the International Somatic Movement Education and Therapy Association (ISMETA) with guidelines set by ISMETA's professional standards committee. Professional licensure is not required.

General Cost

At the time of publication, the core developmental modules cost $3,300 and IDME training modules I and II cost an additional $3,000, for a total cost of $6,300. Early bird registration discounts lower the cost to $5,670, with some scholarships available for students who intend to share IDME work with diverse and underserved communities. These amounts do not include the cost of sessions that are required for homework, for which fees vary by location. All learning materials are provided. The cost of travel and lodging must also be factored in to estimate the total cost of the IDME certification process, as all modules require in-person attendance.

IDENTIFIED AS AN EMERGING PRACTICE

IDME is an emerging practice. BodyMind Centering® theory and techniques, which provide the foundation for IDME, are also well represented in qualitative and theoretical research, largely in the field of dance and movement therapies as well as trauma therapies employing somatic interventions (Frank, 2021; Payne et al., 2016; Shafir, 2015).

Certification and Degree Requirements

There are currently no degree requirements for entry into the IDME certification program. Individuals who pursue this specialization include movement professionals (e.g. yoga instructors), bodyworkers (e.g. massage therapists, craniosacral practitioners, chiropractors), somatic educators, day-care professionals, and early-childhood educators, social workers, mental health professionals, doulas, parents, lactation counselors, caregivers, medical professionals including OT, PT, speech, and auditory specialists (Bainbridge-Cohen, n.d.). To date, there are no requirements for maintaining certification status as an IDME, however, certification is required to provide IDME services.

SCOPE OF PRACTICE ISSUES

The interventions offered by IDMEs are as minimal as possible, designed to allow professionals from diverse backgrounds to facilitate the work. With this in mind, the following scope of practice concerns may arise and ought to be considered by IDME practitioners.

CAUTIONS AND LIMITATIONS

Practicing IDMEs should abide by the scope of practice and ethical boundaries indicated by the primary profession within which they are practicing or providing services (e.g., LMSW, yoga teacher, doula). IDME practitioners are encouraged to acquire full coverage liability insurance and to work in spaces that are safe, clean, and baby-proofed. Many parents of newborns also prefer that practitioners coming into close contact with their infants are up to date on appropriate vaccines. Further, as touch is a large part of IDME work, practitioners should engage families in ongoing consent in regard to the practitioner's use of touch and baby handling.

Of note, families raising infants frequently interact with medical professionals to support their babies' health and development. IDMEs are advised to articulate their scope of expertise with families clearly and to provide psychoeducation on developmental movement processes in a fashion that does not contraindicate any advice families are receiving from medical professionals while providing access to the most up-to-date research. IDMEs often receive questions regarding lactation, infant sleep, lip tie, tongue tie, and other common infant care concerns. With this in mind, IDMEs should stay abreast of the latest research on infant development, care practices, and medical interventions while building networks of allied professionals to provide clients with appropriate resources, referrals, and support.

POPULATION SUITABILITY

New caregivers' resources and their dimensions of privilege and oppression will impact their capacity to participate in the traditional IDME model. While IDME embraces the neuroplasticity of infancy to enhance developmental outcomes for all kinds of babies during a critical developmental window, at the same time, the modality seizes the opportunity to assist parents in practicing healthy ways of relating during matrescence and patrescence, when they, too, are neurologically wired to learn new patterns (Kim et al., 2014). Well-resourced individuals and families with time to be curious about their babies' development are a natural fit for this work. However, individuals experiencing PMADs or personal life challenges (e.g., single parenting, pre-term birth, a baby with developmental delays, unemployment, or food, housing, or diaper insecurity) can also benefit greatly from IDME support before and after birthing a child. Practitioners working with under-resourced individuals must adapt IDME principles to meet the family's immediate needs (personal communication, A. Matthews, March 17, 2023). Their focus should be on ensuring safety, providing comfort, supporting bonding, and offering nervous system education. Virtual groups and responsive collaborations with social service organizations are avenues for further exploration such that the IDME approach can reach vulnerable and high-risk perinatal adults (personal communication, S. Murdock, December 12, 2024).

SYMPTOM BARRIERS

IDME can be supportive of the full range of human developmental experiences, not only in the support it offers infants but also through the relational support and skill building it provides parents and caregivers of babies with a broad spectrum of developmental outcomes. That said, IDME should not be considered a replacement for medical treatment and contraindications should be explored with any medical professionals involved in an infant's care.

WHAT KIND OF PERSON WOULD DO WELL WITH IDME?

Somatic-, experiential-, developmentally-oriented, attachment-based, and neuroscience-informed psychotherapists, practitioners with a family systems lens, dyadically trained counselors, and especially perinatal and reproductive mental health counselors, psychiatrists, social workers, and psychiatric nurse practitioners, who come into contact with individuals during the perinatal period will seamlessly incorporate IDME principles into their existing practices. Practitioners who enjoy experiential learning environments, who are willing to step outside of their clinical comfort zones, and who prefer to be responsive and improvisational in their approach to client interactions rather than providing routinized treatments, will find themselves well suited to IDME. Psychotherapists who would like to incorporate group work, movement, and more creativity into their practice, as well as the joy and delight of interacting with infants, will also do well in this model.

UPDATES, SUMMARY, AND REVIEW

As mentioned earlier, IDME emphasizes the co-creative relationship between movement and neurological development, especially focusing on the ways that early movement experiences nourish a baby's growing brain. Through its somatic principles and techniques, IDME guides caregivers and new parents, bringing special attention to the value of infant handling, observation, and co-regulation skills in shaping infants' early experiences and attachment styles. At its core, IDME offers a back-to-basics philosophy encouraging caregiving adults to be with babies in a mindful fashion that privileges the richness of embodied relational process over milestone-driven achievement schedules and consumer-driven learning products.

IDME has the potential to add significant value to the field of perinatal mental health services (personal communication, S. Murdock, January 22, 2024). By interweaving psychoeducation and experiential learning, IDME helps caregivers, including those at risk for PMADs, to build confidence in parenting skills, to deepen attunement with their babies, and to adopt a beginner's mind in regard to the developmental arc of their family lifespan. Accessible and adaptable, the IDME approach can be particularly beneficial for families with infants facing developmental challenges or caregivers experiencing perinatal mood and anxiety disorders (PMADs), as well as for families who are well and seeking community connection and support. In a recent pilot virtual IDME program called *Bonding with your Baby*, sponsored by the Postpartum Resource Center of New York and facilitated by a Mental Health Counselor and IDME, new parents at high risk for suicide and infanticide reported significant benefits from participation, many saying they felt improvements in confidence and mood after 1 - 2 group meetings (personal communication, S. Murdock, December 13, 2024). With all of this in mind, IDME shows great promise as a model for engaging, educating, empowering, and partnering with communities, as suggested by SAMHSA's (2024) Task Force on Maternal Mental Health, in service to improving the lives of new parents and caregivers while enhancing developmental outcomes for infants at the same time.

Cara Angela Liguori, MS, MHC-LP is a Mental Health Counselor in New York State, a Somatic Movement and Infant Developmental Movement Educator from the School for BodyMind Centering®, a certified Zero Balancing Bodymind Therapy practitioner, and a Natural Dreamwork practitioner. She is on the certification track for EMDR trauma therapy, and she specializes in reproductive mental health and dreams. Cara is a creative, person-centered counselor who is passionate about social justice and advocating for the needs of those who face systemic barriers to success, especially babies.
caraliguoriwellbeing.com
cara.liguori@gmail.com

REFERENCES

Bainbridge-Cohen, B. (n.d.). *Infant developmental movement education*. BodyMind Centering®: An embodied approach to movement, body, and consciousness. Retrieved December 28, 2024 from https://www.bodymindcentering.com/program/infant-developmental-movement-education/

Barnaby, S. & Matthews, A. (n.d.). *babies project*. Retrieved December 21, 2024 from https://babiesproject.org/

Beebe, B., Myers, M., Lee, S. H., Lange, A. Ewing, J., Rubinchik, N., Andrews, H. Austin, J. Hane, A., Margolis, A., Hofer, M., Ludwig, R., Welch, M. (2018). Family nurture intervention for preterm infants facilitates positive mother-infant face-to-face engagement at four months. *Developmental Psychology, 54*(11), 2016-2031. http://dx.doi.org/10.1037/dev0000557

Ciaunica, A., Safron, A., & Delafield-Butt, J. (2021). Back to square one: The bodily roots of conscious experiences in early life. *Neuroscience of Consciousness, 7*(2), 1 - 10.

Faber (2017). Dance and early childhood cognition: The isadora effect. *Arts Education Policy Review, 118*(3), 172 - 182.

Frank, R. (2021). The lived-body: A moving-feeling experience. *Gestalt Review, 25*(1), 11 - 30.

Heller, D. P. (2019). *The power of attachment: How to create deep and lasting relationships*. Sounds True Adult.

Kim, P., Rigo, P., Mayes, L. C., Feldman, R., Leckman, J. F., & Swain, J. E. (2014). Neural plasticity in fathers of human infants. *Social Neuroscience, 9*(5), 522 - 535.

Kim, S. (2024, July). A window into early brain development: Early parenting shapes the amygdala-prefrontal circuitry development [Editorial]. *Journal of the American Academy of Child & Adolescent Psychiatry, 63*(1), 17-19.

McCabe, J. E., Wickberg, B., Deberg, J., Chuffo Davila, R., & Segre, L. S. (2021). Listening visits for maternal depression: A meta-analysis. *Archives of Women's Mental Health, 24*(4), 595 - 603.

Payne, H., Warnecke, T., Karkou, V., & Westland, G. (2016). A comparative analysis of body psychotherapy and dance movement psychotherapy from a european perspective. *Body, Movement and Dance in Psychotherapy, 11*(2-3), 144 - 166.

Rupert, A. (2022). Dance/movement therapy for neurological development in ages 0–3: A critical review of the literature. *Social and Behavioral Sciences Commons.* **https://digitalcommons.lesley.edu/cgi/viewcontent.cgi?article=1640&context=expressive_t heses**

Shafir, T. B. (2015). Bridging the trauma-adult attachment connection through somatic movement. *Body, Movement and Dance in Psychotherapy, 10(4), 243 - 255.*

U.S. Department of Health and Human Services. (2024). *Parents under pressure: The U.S. surgeon general's advisory on the mental health and well-being of parents.* [Press Release].

Infant Mental Health Endorsement (IMH-E)

ISABELLA SAVAGE, BA

Infant Mental Health Endorsement® (IMH-E) was created in 1977 by the Michigan Association for Infant Mental Health (MI-AIMH) in order to "promote and support the optimal development of infants, young children, and families" ("Competency guidelines - infancy onward," 2017, p. 4). While IMH-E is not a license or certification, it is a widely accepted coalition under the Michigan Association for Infant Mental Health Alliance, which includes thirty states and two international countries ("I/ECMH endorsement," 2022).

Endorsement® provides a conceptual framework for professionals to best serve this population. Working under the practices of the Endorsement®/Alliance creates assurance in the mental health community, and in clients, that the clinician has specialization and in-depth knowledge of this population. The Alliance also allows clinicians to have a universal framework to utilize in order to better communicate, research, and serve infants and pregnant people.

Endorsement® is a nationally recognized title for people working with pregnant people and infants ages 0-3. There are four categories of IMH Endorsement® and a Reflective Supervisor role, and each has its own set of competency standards and levels of knowledge required to obtain Endorsement®.

It will be helpful to note for the images included in this chapter that there are two types of Endorsement®: IMH-E® and the ECMH-E® (early childhood mental health Endorsement® for those working with ages 3-6). Only the IMH-E® will be discussed in this section due to the large overlap between the two Endorsements.

ENDORSEMENT® REQUIREMENTS FOR IMH-E

Training

To further emphasize, Endorsement® is not a license, but it is acknowledged by the World Association for Infant Mental Health. Endorsement® is not required to serve infant populations. However, many psychologists have found the Endorsement® helpful in increasing their understanding of IMH and promoting specialized support (McCormick & Eidson, n.d.). Selection of Endorsement® category will correlate with different levels of knowledge required, experience, and skills obtained.

Within the four categories, there are five types of roles (Infant Mental Health Requirements, n.d.):

1. Infant Family Associate (IFA): this role works in promotion of positive interactions between parent and child (i.e., Early Childhood Educator, Court Appointed Special Advocate (CASA), Lactation Consultant, Early Head/Head Start Teacher, Program Administrator, Home Visitor, Pediatric Health Care Provider, Early Intervention provider).

2. Infant Family Specialist (IFS): this role works in prevention or early intervention (i.e., Early Intervention Provider, Infant/Toddler Coach, Home Visitor, Early Childhood Mental Health Consultant, Child Welfare Case Manager).

3. Infant Family Reflective Supervisor (IFRS): this role works in direct service within reflective supervision and prevention/intervention.

4. Infant Mental Health Specialist (IMHS): this role is for those who use direct clinical intervention such as infant/parent psychotherapy (i.e., Parent-Infant Psychotherapist, Parent-Child Psychotherapist, Early Childhood Mental Health Specialist, Private Practice Therapist).

5. Infant Mental Health Mentor (IMHM): this role is for those who work in macro or indirect mental health work (three types: mentor-clinical, mentor-policy, mentor-research/faculty).

Image 1. Scope of Practice. From Alliance for the Advancement of Infant Mental Health.

	Infant Family Associate	Infant Family Specialist	Infant Family Reflective Supervisor	IMH Specialist	IMH Mentor - Clinical, Research/Faculty, or Policy
Scope of Work	PROMOTION	PREVENTION/ EARLY INTERVENTION	PREVENTION/ EARLY INTERVENTION & PROVIDER OF RSC	CLINICAL INTERVENTION/ TREATMENT	MACRO
Education	Any academic degree[1]	No Degree	No Degree	Masters, Post-Graduate	Masters, Post-Graduate
Work Experience	Min. 2 yrs. of infant/early childhood related work experience or volunteer experience in an applicable role[2]	Min. 2 yrs. of prevention and/or early intervention services with 0-36 mo. olds & their caregivers/families; served a min. of 10 families	Min. 2 yrs. of prevention and/or early intervention services with 0-36 mo. olds & their caregivers/families; served a min. of 10 families **PLUS** provider of RSC for 1+ yr.	Min. 2 yrs. post-masters IMH practice working on behalf of caregiver-infant relationship	Min. 3 yrs. as an IMH practice leader Plus provider of RSC for 3+ yrs. (Clinical)
In-Service Training	Min. 30 hrs.	Min. 30 hrs.	Min. 48 hrs.	Min. 30 hrs.	Min. 33 hours (Policy & Research/Faculty) Min. 48 hours (Clinical)
References	3	3	3	3	3
Reflective Supervision with a Qualified Provider	Not required	Min. 24 hrs. received	Min. 24 hrs. received; 12 hours about the provision of RSC	Min 50 hrs. received	Min. 50 hrs. received; 25 hours about the provision of RSC (Clinical only)
Written Exam	No	No	No	Yes	Yes

1 Family Associate applicants need to meet the Education OR the Work requirement they do not need to meet both.

2 For Family Associate applicants, volunteer experience may meet the work criterion if it was a) supervised experience with women during pregnancy or with infants, toddlers, & families AND b) included specialized training. Examples include CASA, Doula, Child Life Specialist.

Image 2 will help you determine which Endorsement® level to choose.

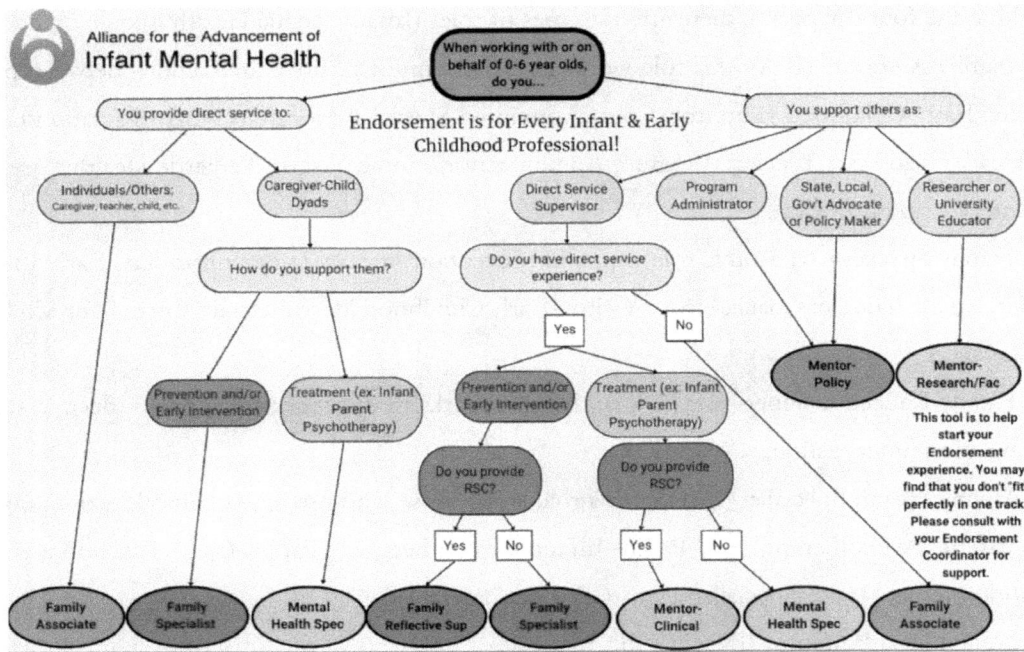

Image 2. Category Flow Chart. From Alliance for the Advancement of Infant Mental Health.

Requirements for application vary by Endorsement® category, as outlined in image three below.

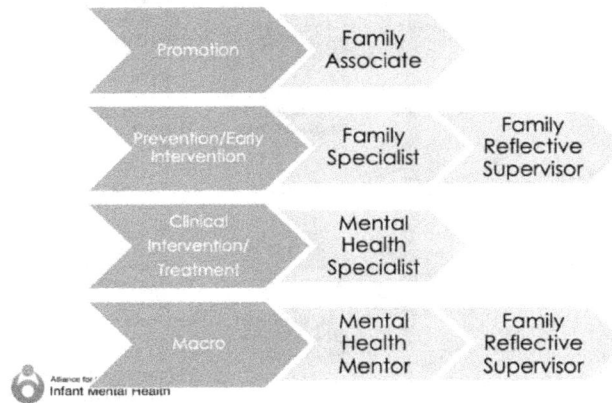

Image 3. Endorsement® Categories. From Alliance for the Advancement of Infant Mental Health.

General Cost

The associated costs of Endorsement® for the four different categories are listed in image 4 below. IMH-E includes IFA, IFS, IMHS, and IMHM. No prices were listed for Infant Family Reflective Supervisor (IFRS), so the cost likely correlates to the category related to the scope of practice (Infant Family Specialist or Infant Mental Health Mentor) based on image 1.

Image 4. Endorsement® Fees. From Alliance for the Advancement of Infant Mental Health.

Endorsement Fees

	IFA/ECFA (I)	IFS/ECFS (II)	IMHS/ECMHS (III)	IMHM/ECMHM (IV)
Membership in INfancy Onward	$50	$50	$50	$50
Application Fee	$15	$25	$25	$25
Processing Fee	$25	$50	$200	$300
Total Cost:	$90	$125	$275	$375

Caveats to Obtaining Endorsement®

It is important to know only one credential can be obtained at a time, and you must wait at least a year of after obtaining an Endorsement® before applying for another category ("I/ECMH endorsement," 2022). Once Endorsement® is obtained, it is required that you participate in 15 clock hours of training experiences that promote mental health per year (First3Years, 2022).

SCOPE OF PRACTICE

Supervision Required

Reflective Supervision/Consultation (RSC) is required for all categories of Endorsement®, except the Infant Family Associate (Infant Mental Health Requirements, n.d.). RSC is the continued understanding of all of the relationships in the therapeutic process, including clinician, client, and supervisor. A minimum of 12 hours of reflective supervision is required annually with a qualified provider for these four categories.

Ongoing Responsibilities

Once Endorsed®, you must maintain membership in an Infant Mental Health Association and receive fifteen hours of annual training on relationship-based education or the principals of IECMH with at least one hour dedicated to diversity, equity, and inclusion. Three of these hours must be about reflective supervision and consultation if you provide supervision.

SUMMARY

Review of Training

Endorsement® was created for those working with pregnant people, infants, very young children, and their families. If you work with these populations, want to gain more knowledge, and become part of a vast network of like-minded individuals, Endorsement® may be for you. The training encompasses eight domains of competency: theoretical foundations; law, regulation, and policy; direct service skills; working with others; communicating; systems expertise; thinking; and reflection (Infant Mental Health Requirements, n.d.). A general outline of the Endorsement® process is outlined below.

If you are interested in the Endorsement® title and its requirements, the steps for becoming Endorsed® are outlined below ("I/ECMH endorsement," 2022).

1. Contact your state's Endorsement® coordinator to learn more about category and requirements and receive guidance on the Endorsement® process.

2. Register as a member with your infant mental health state association.

3. Register on your state association's EASy portal.

4. Meet application requirements.

5. Gather documentation of competencies in education and training.

6. Submit application.

7. Exam (IMHS and IMHM only).

8. Become Endorsed® or deferred.

Isabella Savage is a 2nd-year Clinical Psychology Psy.D. student at Midwestern University's Glendale campus. She grew up in Austin, Texas, where she became interested in school psychology. She then went to the University of Virginia where she received her Bachelor of Arts in Cognitive Science and minored in Art History. While in university, she explored numerous areas of psychology, including school psychology, neuroscience, and IO psychology. She is now pursuing clinical psychology and has a wide range of interests. Her main interests include working with child and adolescent populations, immigrant and minority populations, and people experiencing trauma and anxiety-related disorders. She is also an active member of her state association and strives to be a future leader in the field with her extracurricular engagements. Outside the field, she spends her time volunteering at animal shelters, playing ultimate frisbee, and learning to use different art modalities.

(512) 574-0004

Isabella.savage@midwestern.edu

Isabella.s.savage@gmail.com

REFERENCES

Competency guidelines - infancy onward. INfancy Onward. (2017). Retrieved January 17, 2023, from https://www.infancyonward.org/wp-content/uploads/2022/07/IECMH-Competency-Guidelines-2022-Update.pdf

First3Years endorsement. First3Years. (2022, March 8). Retrieved March 5, 2023, from https://first3yearstx.org/endorsement/

How to license. allianceaimh. (n.d.). Retrieved February 27, 2023, from https://www.allianceaimh.org/endorsement-licensing

I/ECMH endorsement®. INfancy Onward. (2022, December 23). Retrieved January 17, 2023, from https://www.infancyonward.org/i-ecmh-endorsement/#:~:text=What%20is%20it%3F-,Infant%20Mental%20Health%20Endorsement%C2%AE%20(IMH%2DE%C2%AE)%20and,are%20so%20crucial%20to%20a

IMH endorsement® categories. INfancy Onward. (2022, July 19). Retrieved January 17, 2023, from https://www.infancyonward.org/i-ecmh-endorsement/imh-endorsement-categories-of-competency/

Infant Mental Health Requirements. allianceaimh. (n.d.). Retrieved March 5, 2023, from https://www.allianceaimh.org/endorsement-requirements-guidelines

McCormick, A., & Eidson, F. (n.d.). *Endorsement® is Good for Babies.* First 3 Years. Retrieved February 27, 2023, from https://first3yearstx.org/wp-content/uploads/2020/10/Endorsement-is-Good-for-Babies_FINAL_20200929.pdf

Infant-Family and Early Childhood Mental Health Specialists (IFECMHS)

Keran Flynn-Kroska, PhD, MS, LMFT-S, Certified PCIT Therapist, PCIT Within Agency Trainer, Certified ABC Therapist

Carol Messmore, PhD, LMFT

Natalie Richardson, PhD, LMFT

Infant Mental Health and Early Childhood Mental Health (I-ECMH)

Infant Mental Health (IMH) is a multidisciplinary scope of practice based on the work of Selma Fraiberg and Infant Parent Psychotherapy. Fraiberg's original work focused on the relationship patterns between very young children, age from birth to 3 years old, and their parents/caregivers. The concept of I-ECMH expanded the age range of the child, and covers clinical practice, research, policy, and advocacy work, all supporting the social and emotional competency of children aged from birth to 5 years (Zeanah & Zeanah, 2009). Different from Child-Parent Psychotherapy, I-ECMH practice focuses on the strengths of the parent/caregiver and the child to support the continued development and wellbeing of the relationship system. Zeanah and Zeanah (2009) maintain that very young children are "best understood, assessed, and treated in the context of their primary caregiving relationships" (p. 9).

Certifications, Trainings, and Degree and Licensure Requirements

The Michigan Infant Mental Health Association (MI-AIMH)/Alliance for the Advancement of Infant Mental Health (2022) report 33 U.S. state alliances offering endorsement credentials for IMH practice. The endorsement is offered through state level IMH alliances or associations and the credential includes multiple levels which make it accessible to paraprofessionals and to clinicians. The distinctions for each level are specific to competencies developed by the MI-AIMH in 2002 and the endorsement through the MI-AIMH is recognized by all 35 state alliances, making the endorsement portable across states. The MI-AIMH endorsement credential offers two categories, the infant family category for those working primarily children age birth to 3, and the early childhood category for those working primarily with children aged 3 – 6 years. The competencies for both categories are the same. Without the completed endorsement, the I-EC provider titles cannot be used professionally.

Training and Certification

The training to meet endorsement levels ranges from experience only, without an academic credential for three levels, and two clinical levels for those providers with a master's degree or post graduate clinical training. The scope of work and clients served determine the endorsement category and level, which also determines the training requirements.

The endorsement levels which require a master's degrees or post graduate training are the Infant Mental Health Specialist or Early Childhood Mental Health Specialist (I-ECMHS); and the Infant Mental Health Mentor or Early Childhood Mental Health Mentor (I-ECMHM). These two endorsement levels are for clinicians who provide mental health services to children and families (MI-AIMH, 2022). The clinical level of endorsement also requires the applicants to pass a national examination which is a combination of multiple-choice questions and clinical practice vignettes. Endorsement can only be awarded after successful completion of the examination.

The endorsement levels requiring work experience only are the Infant Family Associate or Early Childhood Family Associate (I-ECFA); the Infant Family Specialist or Early Childhood Family Specialist (I-ECFS); and the Infant Family Reflective Supervisor or Early Childhood Family Reflective Supervisor (I-ECFRS). These endorsement levels are for those providers who implement promotion, prevention, and early intervention services.

The required training for endorsement can be met through training programs offered by university degree programs, national workshops, training centers or agencies. The in-service didactic training requirement for the I-ECFA averages 40 hours, the I-ECFS averages 50 hours, and the I-ECFRS, I-ECMHS, and the I-ECMHM average 75 average hours. All levels require a minimum of 2 years working experience with very young children and their families. Each state Infant Mental Health association or alliance website lists the requirements specific to each level for the didactic training content, in-service training, work requirements, and reflective supervision for endorsement.

Cost

Endorsement requires membership in a state IMH alliance or association which averages $70-$100, and cost of the state endorsement varies by level. The cost of the I-ECFA, I-ECFS, and the I-ECFRS endorsement vary by state and average $100 - $150 for the initial endorsement plus a registration fee of $15 - $25. The cost of the clinical level endorsements I-ECMHS and I-ECMHM averages $300 - $400 for the initial endorsement plus a registration fee of $25.

Annual renewal of the endorsements includes maintaining membership in the IMH alliance or association ($70-$100), 15-30 hours of in-service training (varies by state) plus an average of 12 hours of reflective supervision (which is offered free of charge by some state IMH associations or alliances). There is not a renewal fee for the endorsement.

The endorsement in-service didactive training can be found at lower costs through state associations or alliances (averaging $50/3-hour workshop); the total cost of in-service training could run from $600 - $1250 depending upon the endorsement level and the reflective supervision is offered free of charge to association and alliance members. There are also full training programs inclusive of the required didactic courses plus reflective supervision offered through private and public organizations and academic institutions; the cost varies in the range of $2500 - $5500.

Degree Requirements

A degree is required only for the clinical practice levels, I-ECMHS and the I-ECMHM. A master's degree, post graduate training, or doctorate is required. Ideally the degree includes a focus on family-centered practice, family dynamics, assessment, interventions, and child development which can count towards the endorsement requirements. Clinical degrees such as counseling, social work, marriage and family therapy and psychology do have an easier process of endorsement as the content areas align and the degree holder is able to work professionally with the required age group (MI-IAMH, 2022).

Cautions and Contraindications

I-ECMH providers working with families of young children often find their clients involved with families at risk facing parental rights termination, issues of child custody and violent home situations. The service providers should be trained to assess issues of safety as often the provider works with the family in their home. It is also very possible that the family may disclose information, or the provider might see behaviors which require a report to the state child welfare abuse and neglect hotline. This can challenge the relationship with the clients, however as mandated reporters the provider has no other option. Working closely with families can create a strong relationship and service providers must be mindful of their professional boundaries, closing cases may be difficult for both the child client and the provider. The work of an Infant or Early Childhood service provider can be very rewarding, however can also be emotionally draining. Self-care and reflective supervision are a critical need for those working in this field.

Current Research and Model Evolution

As a multidisciplinary scope of practice, I-ECMH services are provided within evidenced-based programs such as ABC and CPP. A review of the research on I-EC services across states and provision levels completed by Silver et al. (2023) found that the outcomes of the programs studied provided positive changes for the child in at least one domain of social-emotional competency. There was also consistency across the research despite the differences in the providers (level of service) and provision environment (schools, homes, clinics). There is room for more service models to work towards evidenced-based outcomes as the field progresses. Also noted by Silver et al. (2023) is a need for research specific to service provision setting and provider level, learning "what works for whom" (p. 24).

CONCLUSION

Infant and Early Childhood mental health is a necessary service provision area. Between 10-16% of very young children in the United States are reported to have mental health issues, the number increases to 22% when poverty levels are factored in (Zero to Three, 2024). The expanding credentialing process has started a regulation of the quality and skills required for the multiple levels of service provision which supports the professional standing of the service provision. The training costs vary by level and for the clinical service levels can range from $600 - $5500. A master's or doctoral degree is required to begin the endorsement process for the mental health service providers and a clinical degree in counseling, marriage and family therapy, social work or psychology can streamline the process. for the training and the ability to work with children and families as part of the training process because direct service provision is required. Research on I-EC services has found positive outcomes across service levels and is an excellent choice for clinicians working with children and families experiencing relationship issues.

IS I-ECMH FOR YOU?

I-ECMH is best suited for providers who want to become specialists with very young children who are experiencing disruptive behavior and relationship issues. Services can be provided in various settings from homes, schools, agencies, and childcare centers. I-ECMH is relationship based and recognizes the unique culture and values of every family. Clinical professionals may be interested in the I-ECMH endorsement process which supports the quality of care and professional development of the service provider. There are multiple certifications and trainings that might be more attainable than endorsement, including Attachment bio-behavioral catchup, Circle of Security Parenting, Child-Parent Psychotherapy, Parent-Child Interaction Therapy, and Sand Tray Therapy. These have a specific focus and may take less time to achieve. Whether pursing endorsement or a certitication, clinicians interested in making a difference with families and young children experiencing challenges will find the work fulfilling.

Attachment Bio-Behavioral Catchup (ABC)

Attachment bio-behavioral catchup (ABC) is an evidence-based model specifically developed for at risk parent(s)/caregiver(s) and their infants and toddlers (Attachment Bio-behavioral Catchup, 2017). The model was developed by Dr. Mary Dozier and her lab at the University of Delaware to help parent(s) of infants and toddlers successfully increase secure attachment (Attachment Bio-behavioral Catchup, 2017b). The model is brief; just 10 one-hour sessions in the family's home. There is a wealth of research to support ABC and it is a gold standard evidence-based model (Attachment Bio-behavioral Catchup, 2017d). The main goal in ABC is to increase secure attachment and decrease parental/caregiver frightening and intrusive behaviors which then allows for improved parental ability to assist children in regulating their emotional states and decreasing stress-reactivity (Dozier et al., 2008). The theoretical foundations of ABC are attachment theory and developmental neurobioloendorsegy (Dozier & Bernard, 2017).

CERTIFICATIONS, TRAININGS, AND DEGREE AND LICENSURE REQUIREMENTS

All training and certification are managed by ABC (Attachment Bio-behavioral Catchup, 2017a). Certification is required for this model as it includes reviewing video footage and coding content with an ABC trainer/supervisor (Attachment Bio-behavioral Catchup, 2017a). The certification process can take between six months to 1 year as you must successfully complete the model with two families. Certification is available only through ABC (Attachment Bio-behavioral Catchup, 2017a).

Cost

The cost of training and certification is not available through the ABC website, yet you can contact them for the cost of the program (Attachment Bio-behavioral Catchup, 2017a). State DHHS grants are often available to agencies in which there is a "grantee" contract with the DHHS in which providers can access training for free if they choose to become certified in the model. As an example, the Minnesota Department of Human Services (DHS) offers grant opportunities for training in children's mental health to agencies within the state (Minnesota Department of Human Services, 2021).

Degree Requirements

Most often, a master's degree in marriage and family therapy, counseling, or social work, or a degree in psychology (PhD or PsyD) is required to be trained and certified in ABC. Post-degree providers working toward full licensure can be trained and certified, but if training is provided to grantee agencies through a state's Department of Human Services, training requirements may be limited to only independently licensed providers.

CAUTIONS AND CONTRAINDICATIONS

It is important to understand contraindications as the success of families is based in the fit of the model to the needs of the family, or what the needs are related to the expectations of courts and social services if child protection is involved. ABC is contraindicated if a parent is not the primary caregiver and spends little time with the child. ABC should then be utilized with the guardian instead as they are the consistent caregiver (Dozier & Bernard, 2017).

CURRENT RESEARCH AND MODEL EVOLUTION

ABC has a long history of research to support its effectiveness as an evidence-based model (Attachment Bio-behavioral Catchup, 2017d). Currently, research is ongoing to develop ABC model adaptations for newborns, children over the age of four, and children adopted internationally (Attachment Bio-behavioral Catchup, 2017c). Currently, use of ABC is being studied with high-risk birth parents, maternal opioid dependence, and strengthening relationships between foster and birth parents (Attachment Bio-Behavioral Catchup. (2017c).

SUMMARY

ABC is an evidence-based model with two decades of research proving its effectiveness with very young children experiencing inconsistent parenting and insecure attachment. ABC is a terrific model to use with parents in the child protection and foster parents. Training and certification take six-12 months on average, and costs can be variable (Attachment Bio-Behavioral Catchup. (2017a). A master's or doctoral degree is required as is independent licensure in a mental health field to qualify for training. Some contraindications are important to note for use of the model, yet ABC is an excellent choice for those families in which inconsistent parenting/caregiving and child insecure attachment are the key presenting issues.

Is ABC for You?

ABC would be best suited for those providers who want to become early childhood mental health specialists. As an evidence-based treatment, ABC can be attractive to providers who want to utilize home-based model that has been proven to be effective for children and families who are from diverse socio-economic, ethnic, and racial backgrounds (Attachment Bio-behavioral Catchup, 2017d). ABC is attractive to those providers who may be newer to the field, and who want to work effectively with at risk families with very young children who are in the child protection and foster care systems. As an evidence-based treatment, ABC is easy to utilize with training, and treatment is brief (10 home-based sessions), so those providers in community mental health (rural, urban, inner-city, suburban) can see progress quickly with changes over different contexts such as home, school, and community.

Circle of Security Parenting (COS-P)

Circles of Security (COS) is an intervention program designed to enhance the quality of parent-child relationships and promote secure attachment bonds. Developed by Glen Cooper, Kent Hoffman, and Bert Powell (The Circle of Security International [COSI], 2022), this approach is grounded in attachment theory, which emphasizes the importance of early relationships in shaping a child's emotional development and overall well-being.

Circles of Security includes a group-based protocol that includes both educational and therapeutic interventions (Marvin, Cooper, Hoffman, & Powell, 2002). Founding principles that underlie the COS intervention highlight the connection between early childhood attachment problems with psychopathology in later life and acknowledge the protective nature of secure attachment relationships, setting a strong foundation for social-emotional functioning (COSI, 2022). The co-originators of Circles of Security firmly believe that all caregivers want what is best for their children and that lasting change within attachment relationships comes from caregivers' developing specific relationship capacities rather than learning techniques to manage behavior (COSI, 2022).

The five primary goals of COS are to (a) establish a secure base with the participant group from which caregivers can explore their relationship with their child; (b) increase caregiver awareness and appropriate responsiveness by providing a "map" of children's attachment needs; (c) increase caregivers' understanding and recognition of the various cues children use to communicate their needs when their caregiver serves as a safe and secure base; (d) support reflective practices related to parent-child interactions to enhance empathy; and (e) increase caregiver reflection about the impact of their own childhood experiences and early development on their caregiving practices (Hoffman, Marvin, Cooper, & Powell, 2006).

Circles of Securities uses a standardized, video-based group model to deliver a weekly protocol to participants, introducing caregivers to children's core needs for exploration and attachment using visual graphics and giving language to their own defensive practices (referred to as "shark music" within the COS protocol; Hoffman et al., 2006) in order to promote positive parent-child interactions.

CERTIFICATIONS, TRAININGS, AND DEGREE AND LICENSURE REQUIREMENTS

Circles of Security International, Inc. (COSI) provides various in-person and online trainings that lead to endorsement as a Circles of Security Parenting (COSP) Facilitator, including a 4-day in-person facilitator training offered in numerous languages, a 1-week (approximately 35+ hour) immersive online training, a 2-week online training, inclusive of both synchronous and asynchronous sessions, as well as Norwegian-based trainings available either online/live streamed or in-person. COSP trainings are held in more than 20 countries, and the COSP program has been translated into many languages. Additional training is available for educators interested in applying COS to classroom settings as a COSP Classroom Facilitator. Additional information can be found online through COSI (https://www.circleofsecurityinternational.com/).

Cost

The general cost of training is $1000.00, respectively. The cost of international or non-English language trainings may vary. Additional training and CEUs are available through COSI for additional fees.

Degree Requirements

Circle of Security International, Inc. is accredited by the International Accreditors for Continuing Education and Training (IACET) and offers IACET CEUs for its various learning events and trainings. Successful completion of the Circles of Security Parenting (COSP) facilitator training (either virtually or in-person) is required to become a Registered COSP Facilitator. While the Circle of Security Parenting program can be conducted by anyone who has completed the COSP training, only clinicians with experience as psychotherapists are able to be trained in the Circle of Security-Intensive model (COSI, 2022).

CAUTIONS AND CONTRAINDICATIONS

Because the Circle of Security Parenting program can be conducted by anyone who has completed the COSP training, the scope of practice may vary based on the setting of services or the specific role/license of the facilitator. When working with caregivers or minor children, practitioners must be mindful of any state laws or professional ethical codes that may play a role when it comes to mandated reporting (e.g., signs/reports of child abuse or neglect). Trained facilitators will have access to COSP Materials through Circle of Security International, Inc. Practitioners should familiarize themselves with copyright laws and agreements with COSI related to the distribution or reprinting of materials once trained.

CURRENT RESEARCH AND MODEL EVOLUTION

Circles of Security is an evidence-based practice with empirical support for its positive impact on parent-child relationships for various populations, including but not limited to low-income families (Cassidy et al., 2017), mothers of children with Autism Spectrum Disorder (Kubo et al., 2021), mothers in residential substance abuse treatment (Horton & Murray, 2015), Japanese parent-child relationships (Kitagawa et al., 2021), foster families (Krishnamoorthy et al., 2020), and via telehealth during the COVID-19 pandemic (Cook et al., 2021).

The original Circle of Security Intensive model, although effective, was time-intensive and required advanced clinical training and supervision, which meant that providers without clinical training could not access the COS materials. Thus, in 2010, the co-originators developed and released the parent reflection program (i.e., COSP) that allowed facilitators to use video clips of parents and children that were captured with the specific goal of introducing attachment theory in an accessible manner (COSI, 2022). The COS-Intensive training program still exists and is available to clinical practitioners but is not required as a COSP facilitator.

SUMMARY

COS serves as a valuable tool for enhancing attachment relationships between caregivers and children. By offering caregivers insights into their child's emotional needs and behaviors, as well as practical strategies for nurturing secure attachments, the intervention aims to foster healthy development and resilient relationships. Through a structured approach that emphasizes the importance of both safety and exploration, caregivers are empowered to provide a secure base from which children can confidently explore the world.

IS CIRCLE OF SECURITY FOR YOU?

Circle of Security International, Inc. trains providers from various backgrounds and many different disciplines to help caregivers connect with the children in their lives using an attachment-based approach (COSI, 2022). Practitioners interested in working with at-risk families, parents, and young children to nurture strong attachment relationships using a group-based protocol may find this model most helpful in their work.

Child-Parent Psychotherapy (CPP)

Child-Parent Psychotherapy (CPP) is a relationship-based treatment model for young children aged from birth to 6 years old, and their parents who have experienced trauma. Developed by Alicia Lieberman, Ph.D. in collaboration with Patricia Van Horn J.D, Ph.D., and Chandra Ghosh Ippen, Ph.D. at the Child Trauma Research Project (CTRP). The evidenced based model is used extensively with children involved in the family court system and by clinicians working with children who have experience trauma such as violence in the home or community, separation from primary caregiver(s), stressful events such as national disasters (ChildParentPsychotherapy.com, 2022).

The treatment process is based is attachment based and works within the relationship of the child who has experienced trauma and the primary caregiver/parent. The treatment's goal is to support the young child in regulating emotions, resulting in age-appropriate and less aggressive behaviors. The point of intervention is the relationship between the child and the primary caregiver/parent and seeks to expand the awareness and understanding each has for the other (Lieberman et al., 2015). Young children learn through observation and interaction. Children who experience trauma at an early age will react in ways that they have observed and imitate what has been received. As a result, the child's behavior can be socially and age inappropriate and the child is unable to regulate emotional responses through any type of coping mechanism or self-soothing skills. The goal of treatment is to support the young child's social and emotional wellbeing through a strengthening of the parent-child relationship. CPP is used internationally by clinicians in community-based agencies and child welfare services.

The theoretical foundation for CPP is attachment theory (Lieberman et al., 2015), the quality of the relationship between the parent or caregiver is based on the sensitive and consistent responsiveness of the parent to the child (Ainsworth & Bowlby, 1991). Child developmental stages and family culture are also considered as part of the foundation of CPP (ChildParentPsychotherapy.com, 2022). Research has demonstrated that child and parent dyads treated with CPP have positive outcomes; reduced symptoms of behavioral distress in the child and increased empathy of the parent and increased interaction in dyad (ChildParentPsychotherapy.com, 2022a; Ippen et al., 2011).

CERTIFICATIONS, TRAININGS, AND DEGREE AND LICENSURE REQUIREMENTS

Master's and doctoral level clinicians (marriage and family therapists, clinical social workers, mental health counselors and psychologists) are eligible to participate in training. The initial training process includes didactic sessions, practice with families and reflective supervision over 18 months and must be conducted by an endorsed CPP trainer. Training opportunities are provided through Child Parent Psychotherapy (ChildParentPsychotherapy.com, 2022b).

General Cost

The initial training cost is approximately $2500 per individual which includes the didactic course plus the reflective supervision sessions. Training materials include the CPP manual, Don't hit my mommy: A manual for child-parent psychotherapy with children exposed to violence (Liberman et al., 2015) which is available through Zero to Three for $19 - $24. There are multiple other recommended and required texts to supplement the training which add additional costs and vary by the training instructor. There are opportunities for agencies in selected geographic areas to receive training for their providers at no cost through SAMSHA grant to increase the availability of CPP in rural areas (ChildParentPsychotherapy.com, 2022c).

Degree Requirements

A conferred clinical master's degree in marriage and family therapy, counseling, or social work, or a degree in psychology (PhD or PsyD) is required to be trained in CPP. A full clinical license is not required, but the trainee must work independently with clients (as defined by their state licensure board) during the CPP training process.

CAUTIONS AND CONTRAINDICATIONS

Clinicians providing CPP services might find themselves involved with legal disputes such as child custody disagreements, parental rights termination, and violent home situations. It is critical for the clinician to assess issues of safety when conducting home visits to not place oneself danger. It is also possible that the clinician will observe or hear information that requires a child abuse or neglect report to the state child welfare agency; as mandated reporters, clinicians have no leeway to not report despite beliefs in the client for change. Court systems and parents also often ask clinicians working with the children in these types of legal disputes to testify on what is best for the child. In these cases, the clinician must understand the boundaries of the work as a mental health clinician for the child and parent, and a forensic evaluation, and apply to any testimony. CPP work can be very fulfilling, however it can also be very emotionally draining, self-care and reflective supervision is essential for CPP providers.

CURRENT RESEARCH AND MODEL EVOLUTION

CPP has extensive research studies conducted across racially and ethnically diverse families presenting with issues of maternal depression, child maltreatment and domestic violence. The research results consistently showed decreased negative symptoms for the children and the parent/caregiver. CPP is being implements internationally with efficacy research happening outside of the United States in Israel and Sweden. The model also was adapted to address Perinatal maternal mental health issues and research is ongoing for development of the Perinatal CPP model (ChildParentPsychotherapy.com, 2022d). Maternal Mental Health is a rapidly expanding area of research and practice (Policy Center for Maternal Mental Health, 2023), the Perinatal CPP is a solid addition to support these efforts.

SUMMARY

CPP is an evidence-based model with outcome research demonstrating effectiveness with children age birth – 6 years old who have experienced trauma and/or stress and their parent/caregivers. The model works with diverse families and has been implements in the United States and Internationally. Training is the model is required and takes at least 18 months to complete. The training costs vary by instructor, with an average of $2500, and are offered virtually as well as in person on the ground. A clinical master's or doctoral degree is required for the training and the ability to work with children and families as part of the training process. CPP is an excellent choice for clinicians working with children displaying negative and/or not age-appropriate behaviors who have been exposed to violence, trauma, and stressful situations.

Is CPP for You?

CPP is best suited for providers who want to become specialists with very young children who have experienced trauma and/or stress. As an evidenced-based model, it has been proven effective with children aged birth to 6 years old, which supports work in grant-funded agencies or programs requiring evidence-based modalities. Clinicians who are interested in providing services to families involved with the foster care system or child protection systems would be interested in CPP training which can be provided in agency offices, playrooms, or home-visiting settings. CPP is relationship based and considers the culture of the family making it appropriate to implement in rural or urban settings and supports parents and other primary caregivers. CPP training is an excellent complement to the clinical programs as it provides more intense training on interventions with very young children and parents.

Parent-Child Interaction Therapy (PCIT)

Parent-child interaction therapy (PCIT) is an evidence-based treatment model for children ages 2 years-7 years and their parent(s)/caregiver(s). PCIT has been called the "bug in the ear" model as caregivers wear an earpiece to listen to coaching from the provider. The "bug in the ear" allows clinicians to prompt and reinforce caregivers in interacting with their children in specific ways (PCIT International, 2023c). The model was developed in the 1970s by Shiela Eyberg (PCIT International, 2023a). PCIT is a leading treatment for children who have experienced developmental trauma, although the treatment does not actually address trauma (Gurwitch & Warner-Metzger, 2022). PCIT has a long history of research with a variety of client populations, utilizing in-office, online, and hybrid models (PCIT International, 2023). PCIT is identified as a gold standard treatment model with decades of research to support its development and use.

The theoretical foundations of PCIT are social learning theory and attachment theory (PCIT International, 2023c). What makes this model so successful is the different ways in which caregivers can quickly see positive changes. Some of the ways that success is measured are in the assessment process utilizing the Eyberg Child Behavior Inventory (ECBI; Early Intervention Foundation, 2020) in which caregivers can visually see weekly decreases in negative behaviors, an increase in listening and minding by the child, and increased relationship satisfaction as parents become more masterful at playing with their children and increasing secure attachment (PCIT International, 2023c).

CERTIFICATIONS, TRAININGS, AND DEGREE AND LICENSURE REQUIREMENTS

All training and certification are managed by PCIT International (PCIT International, 2024) or approved training centers located in universities or agencies (PCIT, 2023; PCIT International, 2023). Certification is not necessary, yet training by a certified trainer is highly recommended. While PCIT is a manualized model, training is crucial to accurate assessment and utilization of the model. Certification is available only through PCIT International (PCIT International, 2023).

Cost

The cost of PCIT training can vary depending on whether training is accessed via PCIT International (2023) or through mental health grants available from the Department of Health and Human Services (DHHS) in your state. Trainings by PCIT global trainers, within agency trainers, and regional trainers differ in cost (PCIT International, 2023c). Training through PCIT International training modalities can cost $4,000 and up and non-PCIT International training can start at $3,000 (parentchildinteractiontherapy.com, 2021). State DHHS grants are often available to agencies in which there is a "grantee" contract with the DHHS in which providers can access training for free if they choose to become certified in the model. As an example, the Minnesota Department of Human Services (DHS) offers grant opportunities for training in children's mental health to agencies within the state (Minnesota Department of Human Services, 2021).

Degree Requirements

Most often, a master's degree in marriage and family therapy, counseling, or social work, or a degree in psychology (PhD or PsyD) is required to be trained and certified in PCIT. Often, post-degree providers working toward full licensure can be trained and certified, but if training is provided to grantee agencies through a state's Department of Human Services, training requirements may be limited to only independently licensed providers. Teacher-child interaction training (TCIT; Learn Ventures, LLC, n.d.) is utilized by teachers in the school system, so a teaching degree and certification is required as per the teacher's state licensure board. Child-adult relationship enhancement (CARE) can be utilized by police, first responders, non-clinical social workers, school staff, and others, and training is required (Gurwitch et al., 2016) but there is no certification process.

CAUTIONS AND CONTRAINDICATIONS

PCIT has been researched on different populations, and there are issues related to PCIT treatment and who is allowed to be involved in treatment that need to be understood. Wrap-around services are discouraged during active PCIT treatment as there can be conflicting information provided across providers, so if wrap around services is necessary PCIT must wait until the family is stabilized. Caregivers with a history of perpetrating child sexual abuse are never allowed in PCIT treatment. The rationale for this is that clinicians are training caregivers to increase secure attachment to children and to increase the child's compliance, so including those adults with predatory histories is never advisable. Other contraindications are parental mental health issues such as severe depression or personality disorders and active substance abuse which may impede treatment (Milestones Counseling and Consulting Services, 2023).

CURRENT RESEARCH AND MODEL EVOLUTION

PCIT is an evolving gold standard evidence-based model with a strong foundation of research utilized to identify current needs for therapeutic effectiveness (PCIT International, 2023a). A recent addition to the PCIT model is internet-based PCIT (I-PCIT) that was developed during the Covid pandemic to reach those families during social distancing when families could not access treatment in the office setting (PCIT International, 2023b). I-PCIT is still in use for those families in which office or home-based interventions are not accessible. PCIT has a strong decades-long research base strengthened by current research which increases the model's relevancy.

CONCLUSION

PCIT is an evidence-based model with decades of research proving its effectiveness with children experiencing behavioral challenges and families in child protection and foster care systems. Training in the model is required, yet certification is optional (although strongly encouraged). Costs for training vary greatly yet are available live or via self-study online or in-person (PCIT International, 2023; PCIT, 2021). A master's or doctoral degree is required as is independent licensure in a mental health field to qualify for training. Some contraindications are important to note for use of the model, yet PCIT is an excellent choice for those families in which inconsistent parents and child negative behaviors are the key presenting issues.

IS PCIT FOR YOU?

PCIT would be best suited for those providers who want to become specialists with young children and their parent(s)/caregiver(s). As a manualized model, it can be attractive to providers who want to utilize an evidence-based model that has been proven to be effective for children and families who are from diverse socio-economic, ethnic, and racial backgrounds (PCIT International, 2023c). PCIT is attractive to those providers who may be newer to the field, and who want to work effectively with at risk families who are in child protection and foster care systems. As a manualized treatment, PCIT is easy to utilize with training, and treatment can be brief (24-26 sessions), so those providers in community mental health (rural, urban, inner-city, suburban) can see progress quickly with changes over different contexts such as home, school, and community.

Sand Tray Therapy

Sand play therapy is a "hands-on" therapeutic approach, often used in conjunction with talk therapy, that utilizes creativity and tangible mediums to facilitate the psyches' natural capacity for healing. Most often incorporating a sand tray and a variety of miniature objects and figurines, practitioners support their clients in creating an external "world" within the sand tray using their imagination to facilitate the expression of thoughts, feelings, and experiences (Friedman & Mitchell, 2023). Developed by Swiss psychoanalyst Dora Kalff, sand play therapy is grounded in the theories of Carl Jung and emphasizes the symbolic nature of the unconscious mind. Participants are invited to create scenes and narratives in the sand, allowing unconscious material to emerge and be processed in a safe, contained, and nonverbal manner.

CERTIFICATIONS, TRAININGS, AND DEGREE AND LICENSURE REQUIREMENTS

A member society of the play International Society for Sandplay Therapy (ISST), Sandplay Therapists of America (STA) is a nonprofit organization established to train, support, and promote professional development in sandplay. STA offers a variety of certified sandtray training opportunities, as well as additional opportunities including sandplay intensives, regional workshops, and case consultation groups across the United States (US; STA, 2023). Distance learning, training, and consultation through Teaching Members are also available to those interested in sandplay therapy. Practitioners can also access international courses and training opportunities taught by teaching members outside the US and at conferences sponsored by ISST.

For certification as a Registered Sandplay Practitioner (RSP) and Certified Sandplay Therapist (CST), clinicians must complete a specific number of educational training hours on the following topic areas: (a) fundamentals/introduction to sandplay therapy; (b) clinical sandplay; (c) Jungian Theory; and (d) symbolism.

In addition to the pre-qualifications (later highlighted under "Degree Requirements") and educational requirements, those interested in becoming an RSP must develop and demonstrate a personal sandplay process (minimum of 40 hours with an STA/ISST certified member) and complete a minimum of 36 didactic and experiential sandplay education and training hours and 15 to 25 case consultation hours with an STA/ISST Teaching Member. The process of becoming a CST builds on the set of pre-qualifications and requirements for RSP, followed by additional education and training, personal development, and case consultation, including a minimum of 100 additional hours of personal sandplay process, 120 education and training hours, 120 case consultation hours, various written papers, and an advisory interview process (Sandplay Therapists of America Handbook, 2024).

For those interested in becoming an STA/ISST Certified Sandplay Therapist-Teacher (CST-T or Teaching Member) and supporting students through the training and certification processes, additional information can be found on the STA website and within the Sandplay Therapists of America Handbook (2024).

Cost

The overall cost of formal training in Sandtray therapy can be extensive and varies based on the training topic, format (intensive vs standard training), and location of the event, with an online fundamental course starting around $495. For certification, additional educational training and consultation hours are required.

Additional costs for certification would include annual STA membership and professional licensure fees, as well as the cost for sandtray materials, including a sandtray, sand, water toys, and a diverse collection of miniature figures – including nature objects, animals, people, spiritual figures, vehicles, structures, furniture, natural elements, equipment, building materials, etc. Further information about the composition of a sandplay collection can be found in "The Sandplay Collection" (Hegeman, 1992) and The Sandplay Categorical Checklist for Sandplay Analysis (Gruggs, 2005).

Degree Requirements

Pre-qualifications to become a Registered Sandplay Practitioner (RSP) or Certified Sandplay Therapist (CST) include (a) associate membership of STA, (b) a graduate degree in a helping profession (e.g., medicine, marriage and family therapy, school counseling, art therapy, psychology, social work, etc.) from a regionally accredited university, (c) an active mental health license, and (d) malpractice insurance (Sandplay Therapists of America Handbook, 2024).

CAUTIONS AND CONTRAINDICATIONS

When working with children or minors using Sandplay Therapy, practitioners should be aware of potential power imbalances within the therapeutic relationship. Additionally, sandplay therapists are expected to adhere to any local or state laws governing the jurisdiction in which they hold relevant licenses or practice, as well as all professional ethical codes if potential concerns for client safety ever arise. The STA also developed its own Standard for Professional Conduct intended to raise awareness of ethical issues that may arise during the course of sandplay practice and provide a set of organizational expectations for professional conduct for its members (STA Standards for Professional Conduct, 2024).

CURRENT RESEARCH AND MODEL EVOLUTION

A growing body of literature supports the efficacy and effectiveness of sandplay therapy in the treatment of children and adults with a wide variety of presenting challenges, supporting sandplay therapy as an evidenced-based approach (Razzi Freedle, 2022). Systemic reviews of the effectiveness of sandplay therapy support the use of this approach when treating a range of challenges in both children and adults, including anxiety, depression, traumatic stress, addiction, and personality disorders, and other psychosocial, emotional, somatic, and behavioral issues (Razzi Freedle, 2022; Roesler, 2019, Wen et al., 2019). Due to the non-verbal nature and use of imagery and play techniques with less emphasis on verbal communication or insight orientation, sandplay therapy has been found as an appropriate treatment approach for those impacted by traumatic stress, disabilities, or language impairments (Razzi Freedle, 2022; Roesler, 2019.

As a "cross-cultural, trauma-sensitive, multi-sensory therapeutic method," sandplay is practiced around the world with adults and children impacted by various mental health concerns (Razzi Freedle, 2022, pp. 129-130). Because it is not dependent on verbal language and the flexibility of use with individuals, families, or groups, sandplay therapy can be adapted and used in a multitude of settings (e.g., outpatient clinics, private practice, community-based settings, schools, hospitals, etc.) and used as a short-term or long-term intervention (Razzi Freedle, 2022). Additional empirical support can be found in the Journal of Sandplay Therapy.

SUMMARY

Sandplay is a creative form of therapy that provides a "free and protected space" for clients to express their internal symbolic worlds. While the name may suggest this intervention is most appropriate when working with children, sandplay therapy can be effective for both children and adults. Participants of sandplay (whether adults or children) work within the sand to create "worlds," which allow them to express their inner experiences and emotions and to enhance perspective into their challenges (STA, 2023).

IS SAND TRAY THERAPY FOR YOU?

The training, application, and certification journey to becoming an RSP and CST requires an immense amount of dedication of both time and financial commitment. Sandplay therapy would be most suitable for licensed mental health providers with experience in the field of family therapy or play therapy with an immense passion for advancing their clinical and educational skills with both children and adults to include an advanced play-oriented approach rooted in Jungian theory.

Dr. Flynn-Kroska is a licensed marriage and family therapist who has worked in rural mental health since 2008 as a therapist, supervisor, evidence-based trainer, and consultant. Dr. Flynn-Kroska is a certified therapist and certified trainer in parent-child interaction therapy (PCIT), is certified in attachment bio-behavioral catchup (ABC) for infants and their caregivers, is trained in eye movement desensitization and reprocessing (EMDR), internal family systems (IFS), accelerated resolution therapy (ART), clinical hypnosis, and Sand Tray therapy. She is an early childhood mental health specialist rostered with the state of Minnesota Department of Health and Human Services.

Dr. Flynn-Kroska has presented on rural mental health at the Minnesota Association of Marriage and Family Therapy conference and the St. Louis County Health and Human Services conference. She is a specialist in trauma and has worked primarily with legacy burdens, colonialization, and generational trauma with Indigenous populations. Dr. Flynn-Kroska has presented on legacy burdens and generational trauma for Bois Forte Tribal Behavioral Health.

Dr. Flynn-Kroska lives in an off-grid homestead in the wilderness of northeastern Minnesota with her husband, dog, and cat.

Capella University

School of Social and Behavioral Sciences

Marriage and Family Therapy MS Program, Advanced Studies in Human Behavior PhD Program

https://www.capella.edu

Keran.Flynn-Kroska@Capella.edu

Dr. Carol Messmore is an associate professor in the COAMFTE accredited Marriage and Family Therapy program at Capella University. She is a licensed marriage and family therapist, trainer, supervisor, and consultant with over 25 years of experience in academia and clinical practice. Dr. Messmore has experience working with children and families in school settings, community-based agencies, and private practice. Her master's degree and doctoral degree are in Marriage and Family Therapy, and she has a two-year post graduate training in Infant Mental Health through the Florida State University Harris Institute for Infant Mental Health. She has worked extensively with families involved with foster care services, child abuse and neglect. Dr. Messmore was also a member of the Palm Beach County Children's Services Council training faculty for TouchPoints and Infant Mental Health initiatives. Dr. Messmore has presented on topics related to infant mental health at Zero to Three national conferences, American Counseling Association national conference, the Solution-Focused Brief Therapy conferences, and the Florida Infant Mental Health Association conference. She has also published in the Zero to Three Journal, the Journal of Counseling and Human Development and has two recent book chapters focused on issues of early childhood. Currently, Dr. Messmore is a COAMFTE accreditation volunteer and serves on the board of a large community-based agency which provides services for families with young children. A resident of South Florida, she lives with her husband, three dogs and one cat.

Capella University

School of Social and Behavioral Sciences

Marriage and Family Therapy MS Program, Advanced Studies in Human Behavior PhD Program

https://www.capella.edu

Carol.Messmore@Capella.edu

Dr. Natalie Richardson is a Licensed Marriage & Family Therapy (LMFT) and the Assistant Academic Program Director of the COAMFTE-Accredited Marriage and Family Therapy MS program at Capella University. A doctoral alumna of East Carolina University with a background in Medical Family Therapy, Richardson has served in numerous clinical and research roles focused on moral injury, traumatic stress, adverse childhood experiences, the biopsychosocial-spiritual health of military personnel, and integrated behavioral health care. She has presented at various state and national conferences on her scholarly publications focused on moral injury and adverse childhood experiences. Dr. Richardson has received training in Parent-Child Interaction Training (PCIT), Trauma-Focused Cognitive Behavioral Therapy (TF-CFT), Filial Therapy, and Eye Movement Desensitization and Reprocessing (EMDR). As an educator and AAMFT-Approved Supervisor of therapists in training, Dr. Richardson finds passion and purpose in helping her students grow in their competence and confidence of providing compassionate systemic therapy while expanding their understanding of systems-thinking to include important aspects of oppression, diversity, equity, inclusion, and accessibility using trauma-informed and attachment-based lenses. Dr. Richardson resides in Oklahoma, and in her free time enjoys being a fur parent to her Bernedoodle (Sullivan), baking, and spending time with her amazing nieces and nephews.

Capella University

School of Social and Behavioral Sciences

Marriage and Family Therapy MS Program, Advanced Studies in Human Behavior PhD Program

https://www.capella.edu

Natalie.richardson@capella.edu

REFERENCES

Ainsworth, M. D. S., & Bowlby, J. (1991). An ethological approach to personality development. *The American Psychologist, 46*(4), 333-341. https://doi.org/10.1037/0003-066X.46.4.333

Attachment Bio-Behavioral Catchup. (2017). About ABC. Retrieved from https://www.abcintervention.org/aboutabc/

Attachment Bio-Behavioral Catchup. (2017a). Become a parent coach. Retrieved from https://www.abcintervention.org/becomeaparentcoach/

Attachment Bio-Behavioral Catchup. (2017b). Mary Dozier. Retrieved from https://www.abcintervention.org/mary-dozier/

Attachment Bio-Behavioral Catchup. (2017c). Research projects. Retrieved from https://www.abcintervention.org/abc-research-projects/

Attachment Bio-Behavioral Catchup. (2017d). Research supporting ABC. Retrieved from https://www.abcintervention.org/reasearch-supporting-abc/

Belanger, K., Gennis, H., Ottenbreit, N., & Racine, N. (2023). Enhancing attachment-based aspects of PCIT for young children with a history of maltreatment. *Frontiers in Psychology, 14*, 1229109-1229109. https://doi.org/10.3389/fpsyg.2023.1229109

Cassidy, J., Brett, B., Gross, J., Stern, J., Martin, D., Mohr, J., & Woodhouse, S. (2017). Circle of Security–Parenting: A randomized controlled trial in Head Start. *Development and Psychopathology, 29*(2), 651-673. https://doi.org/10.1017/S0954579417000244

Child-Parent Psychotherapy (2022). CPP developers. Retrieved from https://childparentpsychotherapy.com/about/cpp-developers/

Child-Parent Psychotherapy (2022a). CPP Research. Retrieved from https://childparentpsychotherapy.com/about/research/

Child-Parent Psychotherapy (2022b). CPP Training. Retrieved from https://childparentpsychotherapy.com/providers/training/

Child-Parent Psychotherapy (2022c). CPP Training events. Retrieved from https://childparentpsychotherapy.com/events/

Child-Parent Psychotherapy (2022d). CPP Research Summary. Retrieved from https://childparentpsychotherapy.com/wp-content/uploads/2018/05/CPP-Research-Summary_FINAL_051818.pdf

Cook, A., Bragg, J., & Reay, R. (2021). Pivot to Telehealth: Narrative Reflections on Circle of Security Parenting Groups during COVID-19. *Australian and New Zealand Journal of Family Therapy, 42*(1) 106-114. https://doi.org/10.1002/anzf.144

Dozier M, Bernard K. (2017). Attachment and Biobehavioral Catch-up: Addressing the needs of infants and toddlers exposed to inadequate or problematic caregiving. *Curr Opin Psychol.* Jun;15:111-117. doi: 10.1016/j.copsyc.2017.03.003. PMID: 28649582; PMCID: PMC5477793. Retrieved from https://www.ncbi.nlm.nih.gov/pmc/articles/PMC5477793/

Dozier, M., Peloso, E., Lewis, E., Laurenceau, J., & Levine, S. (2008). Effects of an attachment-based intervention on the cortisol production of infants and toddlers in foster care. *Development and Psychopathology, 20*(3), 845-859. https://doi.org/10.1017/S0954579408000400

Friedman, H., & Mitchell, R. R. (2023). What is sandplay therapy? Retrieved from https://www.sandplay.org/about-sandplay/what-is-sandplay/

Grubbs, G. (2005). *The sandplay categorical checklist for sandplay analysis.* Woodinville, WA: Rubedo Publications.

Gurwitch, R. H., Messer, E. P., Masse, J., Olafson, E., Boat, B. W., & Putnam, F. W. (2016). Child–Adult relationship enhancement (CARE): An evidence-informed program for children with a history of trauma and other behavioral challenges. *Child Abuse & Neglect, 53,* 138-145. https://doi.org/10.1016/j.chiabu.2015.10.016

Gurwitch, R.H. & Warner-Metzger C.M. (2022). Trauma-directed interaction (TDI): An adaptation to parent-child interaction therapy for families with a history of trauma. *International Journal of Environmental Research and Public Health.* 2022 May 17;19(10):6089. doi: 10.3390/ijerph19106089. PMID: 35627624; PMCID: PMC9140737.

Hegeman, G. (1991). The sandplay collection. *Journal of Sandplay Therapy, 1*(2), 101-106.

Hoffman, K. T., Marvin, R. S., Cooper, G., & Powell, B. (2006). Changing toddlers' and preschoolers' attachment classifications: the Circle of Security intervention. *Journal of Consulting and Clinical Psychology, 74*(6), 1017–1026. **https://doi.org/10.1037/0022-006X.74.6.1017**

Horton, E., & Murray, C. (2015). A quantitative exploratory evaluation of the circle of security- parenting program with mothers in residential substance-abuse treatment. *Infant Mental Health Journal, 36*(3), 320–336. **https://doi.org/10.1002/imhj.21514**

Ippen, C.G., Harris, W.W., Van Horn, P., & Lieberman, A.F. (2011). Traumatic and stressful events in early childhood: Can treatment help those at high risk? *Child Abuse & Neglect, 35,* 504-513.

Kitagawa, M., Iwamoto, S., Umemura, T., Kudo, S., Kazui, M., Matsuura, H., & Mesman, J. (2021) Attachment-based intervention improves Japanese parent-child relationship quality: A pilot study. *Current Psychology,* **https://doi.org/10.1007/s12144-020-01297-9**

Krishnamoorthy, G., Hessing, P., Middeldorp, C., & Branjerdporn, M. (2020). Effects of the 'Circle of Security' group parenting program (COS-P) with foster carers: An observational study. *Children and Youth Services Review,* (115). https://doi.org/10.1016/j.childyouth.2020.105082

Kubo, N., Kitagawa, M., Iwamoto, S. & Kishimoto, T. (2021). Effects of an attachment-based parent intervention on mothers of children with autism spectrum disorder: preliminary findings from a non-randomized controlled trial. *Child Adolescent Psychiatry Mental Health 15,* 37. https://doi.org/10.1186/s13034-021-00389-z

Learn Ventures, LLC. (n.d). About TCIT. Retrieved from http://www.tcit.org/home/about/

Lieberman, A.F., Ippen, C.G., &Van Horn, P. (2015). Don't hit my mommy: A manual for Child-Parent Psychotherapy with young witnesses of family violence (2nd ed.). Zero to Three.

Marvin, R., Cooper, G., Hoffman, K., & Powell, B. (2002). The Circle of Security project: attachment-based intervention with caregiver-pre-school child dyads. *Attachment & Human Development, 4*(1), 107–124. **https://doi.org/10.1080/14616730252982491**

Michigan Association of Infant Mental Health and the Alliance for the Advancement of Infant Mental Health. (2022). Endorsement Brochure. Retrieved from https://mi-aimh.org/wp-content/uploads/2022/10/Endorsement-Brochure-IECMH-2022-1.pdf

Milestones Counseling and Consulting Services. (2023). Parent-child interaction therapy. Retrieved from https://milestonesccs.com/pcit-therapy/#:~:text=In%20the%20case%20of%20PCIT,to%20participate%20effectively%20in%20therapy.

Minnesota Department of Human Services. (2021). Behavioral health division grants. Retrieved from https://mn.gov/dhs/partners-and-providers/grants-rfps/bh/

Nelson, M. M., & Bussing, R. (2022). Parent-child interaction therapy (PCIT): The evidence base and applications to new populations. *Journal of the American Academy of Child and Adolescent Psychiatry, 61*(10), S338-S338. https://doi.org/10.1016/j.jaac.2022.07.777

PCIT. (2021). Upcoming PCIT trainings. Retrieved from https://www.parentchildinteractiontherapy.com/upcoming-pcit-trainings

PCIT International. (2023). Description of training types. Retrieved from https://www.pcit.org/training-types.html

PCIT International. (2023a). PCIT research. Retrieved from https://www.pcit.org/pcit-research.html

PCIT International. (2023b). Resources for providing telehealth. Retrieved from https://www.pcit.org/resources-for-providing-pcit-via-telehealth.html

PCIT International. (2023c). What is PCIT for professionals? Retrieved from https://www.pcit.org/what-is-pcit-for-professionals.html

Razzi Freedle, L. (2022). Sandplay therapy: An evidenced-based treatment. *Journal of Sandplay Therapy, 31*(1), 129-136.

Roesley, C. (2019). Sandplay therapy: An overview of theory, applications, and evidence base. *The Arts in Psychotherapy, 64*, 84-94. https://doi.org/10.1016/j.aip.2019.04.001

Sandplay Therapists of America. (2023). Education and training overview. Retrieved from https://www.sandplay.org/education-training/education-training-overview/

Sandplay Therapists of America Handbook. (2024). Requirements and procedures for registered sandplay practitioners, certified sandplay therapists, and certified teaching members. Retrieved from https://www.sandplay.org/wp-content/uploads/STA-Handbook-2024.pdf

Sandplay Therapists of America. (2024). Sandplay Therapists of America Standards for Professional Conduct. Retrieved from https://www.sandplay.org/wp-content/uploads/STA-Standards-of-Professional-Conduct-2024.pdf

Silver, H. C., Davis Schoch, A. E., Loomis, A. M., Park, C. E., & Zinsser, K. M. (2023). Updating the evidence: A systematic review of a decade of Infant and Early Childhood Mental Health Consultation (IECMHC) research. *Infant Mental Health Journal, 44(1),* 5–26. https://doi-org.library.capella.edu/10.1002/imhj.22033

The Circle of Security International. (2022). COSP facilitator training: Train to become a registered COSP facilitator. Retrieved from **https://www.circleofsecurityinternational.com/cosp-facilitator-training/**

The Policy Center for Maternal Mental Health. (2023, May). 2023 Maternal Mental Health Roadmap. https://www.2020mom.org/2023-maternal-mental-health-roadmap

Wen, L., Li, Q., & Zhang, X. (2019). Sandplay therapy for mental disorders. *International Medicine and Health Guidance, 25*(2), 201-203.

Zeanah, C.H. & Zeanah, P.D. (2009). The scope of infant mental health. In C.H. Zeanah (Ed.), *The handbook of infant mental health (3rd ed.,* pp. 5-21). The Guilford Press.

Zero to Three. (2024). Infant and Early Childhood Mental Health. Retrieved from https://www.zerotothree.org/issue-areas/infant-and-early-childhood-mental-health/

Inference-Based Cognitive Behavioral Therapy (I-CBT)

BILL OWENBY, EDD, MC, FAAETS, DAAETS, DCMHS, LPC, LAAC, NCC, CCMHC, ACS, DIPLOMATE, FELLOW

Inference-Based Cognitive Behavioral Therapy (I-CBT) is a specialized form of cognitive-behavioral therapy designed specifically for individuals with Obsessive-Compulsive Disorder (OCD). Developed by Dr. Kieron O'Connor and colleagues, I-CBT offers an alternative to traditional exposure and response prevention (ERP) by addressing the reasoning errors and cognitive distortions that underpin obsessive-compulsive symptoms. Instead of focusing on reducing compulsions through behavioral exposure, I-CBT targets the faulty inferences that cause individuals to misinterpret intrusive thoughts as evidence of real danger or risk.

I-CBT shifts the therapeutic focus from behavior to cognition, helping clients recognize how hypothetical and imagined possibilities override their sensory reality. By resolving this "inferential confusion," clients can regain trust in their senses, break free from obsessional doubts, and reduce compulsive behaviors without the need for distressing exposure exercises.

THEORETICAL UNDERPINNINGS

I-CBT is grounded in the understanding that OCD is not driven by fear itself, but by a breakdown in reasoning that causes individuals to misinterpret ordinary, benign thoughts. Central to this process is **inferential confusion**, a cognitive distortion where imagined scenarios and hypothetical threats take precedence over actual evidence. Unlike traditional CBT, which emphasizes challenging catastrophic thinking or engaging in exposures, I-CBT identifies the following key mechanisms:

- **Doubt and Distrust of Sensory Information**: Clients with OCD frequently doubt their senses (e.g., "I might not have turned the stove off") and instead rely on imagined possibilities.

- **Over-Reliance on Imagination**: Hypothetical scenarios (e.g., "What if my hands are still dirty?") override real-world evidence, reinforcing obsessions and driving compulsions.

- **Faulty Reasoning**: Clients make inferences based on remote possibilities rather than actual probability.

    I-CBT works to dismantle these reasoning errors by encouraging clients to:

- Identify when inferential confusion occurs.

- Reconnect with sensory experiences and objective reality.

- Replace imagined catastrophic outcomes with accurate, reality-based information.

- By focusing on cognitive processes rather than behavioral responses, I-CBT provides clients with a structured method for overcoming obsessive-compulsive patterns.

Training in I-CBT is typically aimed at licensed mental health professionals, including psychologists, psychiatrists, counselors, and clinical social workers. As a growing therapeutic approach, I-CBT training programs are offered primarily through reputable institutions and workshops facilitated by the creators of the model or their affiliates.

Available Training Options:

1. **The OCD Clinic Montreal**: Founded by Dr. Kieron O'Connor, this clinic offers formal training for clinicians interested in I-CBT. Workshops and online modules provide comprehensive instruction on theoretical foundations, assessment strategies, and intervention techniques.

2. **CBI Center for Education**: Provides advanced workshops on I-CBT, including case conceptualization, treatment planning, and practical tools for implementation.

3. **International OCD Foundation (IOCDF)**: While primarily focused on ERP, the IOCDF hosts educational events and webinars featuring I-CBT as an alternative approach for OCD treatment.

   For more information, visit The OCD Clinic Montreal and IOCDF.

General Cost

The cost of I-CBT training varies depending on the provider and format:

- **Workshops and Webinars**: $200–$500 per course, with multi-day workshops costing $600–$1,000.
- **Self-Paced Online Courses**: $100–$600 for clinicians.

Current providers of I-CBT:

- https://icbt.online/ - The original program and founder's website.
  - $99 for the initial course: https://www.icbtonlinelearning.com/icbttraining
- https://www.ocdtrainingschool.com/
  - $175 for the comprehensive course:
    https://www.ocdtrainingschool.com/comprehensive-i-cbt-basic-training-home-study-resources-hub?gad_source=1&gclid=CjwKCAiApY-7BhBjEiwAQMrrEeZO5cb5b628RCBNi5U3Ra_INvBO2_tLS_PQOFDy8vjn0J2L5fGGIhoCA1QQAvD_BwE
- https://www.ocdtrainingschool.com/intro-to-inference-based-cbt
  - $35 for the intro to I-CBT, for those who are curious but don't want to spend more at this time.

These trainings are only the initial options. Various types such as on demand, live, workshops, and conferences will all entail additional or different costs, depending on convenience, location, and opportunity for you.

While training costs can vary, the investment ensures that professionals gain a thorough understanding of I-CBT principles and techniques to provide effective treatment for OCD.

I-CBT is considered an emerging evidence-based practice for the treatment of OCD. While ERP remains the most widely recognized gold-standard intervention for OCD, recent studies have demonstrated the efficacy of I-CBT as a viable and less distressing alternative. Research findings highlight the following benefits of I-CBT:

- Comparable symptom reduction to ERP without requiring direct exposure.

- Improved client adherence due to reduced discomfort and avoidance behaviors.

- Long-term cognitive changes that address the root causes of obsessional thinking.

Key Studies and Findings:

- O'Connor, K., Aardema, F., & Pélissier, M.-C. (2005). Beyond reasonable doubt: Reasoning processes in obsessive-compulsive disorder.

- Aardema, F., & O'Connor, K. (2012). Findings suggest that targeting inferential confusion significantly reduces OCD symptom severity.

While more large-scale clinical trials are needed, the growing body of evidence supports I-CBT as an effective and client-friendly intervention for OCD treatment.

Certification Available/Required/Recommended

Certification in I-CBT is not universally required, but it is recommended for clinicians seeking to offer this approach competently and ethically. Certification programs ensure that therapists are equipped with:

- The theoretical knowledge of I-CBT principles.

- Skills for identifying inferential confusion.

- Practical tools for intervention and relapse prevention.

Professionals interested in certification should prioritize training programs facilitated by recognized experts in I-CBT, such as Dr. Kieron O'Connor and his colleagues.

Degree Requirements

I-CBT is suitable for licensed mental health professionals with degrees in psychology, counseling, social work, or psychiatry. Practitioners must have foundational clinical training and licensure to provide psychotherapy and treat OCD.

CAUTIONS OR LIMITATIONS

While I-CBT is a promising approach, it may not be suitable for every client. Limitations include:

- Clients with severe OCD or treatment-resistant symptoms may require additional interventions or a combination of therapies (e.g., ERP or medication).

- The model requires clients to engage in cognitive reflection, which may be challenging for individuals with limited insight.

- I-CBT is still emerging, and while research is promising, it may not yet be widely available in all clinical settings.

Clinicians should assess client readiness and tailor treatment plans to ensure the most effective outcomes.

SCOPE OF PRACTICE ISSUES

I-CBT is designed for treating OCD and related obsessive-compulsive symptoms. Licensed clinicians must operate within their scope of practice, ensuring that I-CBT is implemented ethically and appropriately. Therapists should refer clients with severe or complex cases to specialists when necessary.

WHAT KIND OF PERSON WOULD DO WELL IN THIS MODEL?

Practitioners who excel in I-CBT are often:

- Analytical and detail-oriented, with strong cognitive restructuring skills.
- Empathetic and collaborative, creating a safe environment for clients to explore their reasoning processes.
- Trained in cognitive-behavioral techniques and comfortable addressing cognitive distortions.

If you would like further insight into your own level of training need and recommendations on which level of training is recommended for you, consider: https://iocdf.org/professionals/training-institute/self-assessment-test/

Clients who benefit most from I-CBT include individuals who:

- Prefer cognitive-based interventions over exposure-based methods.
- Are motivated to explore and challenge faulty reasoning patterns.
- Experience distress due to obsessional doubts but struggle with ERP adherence.

SUMMARY & REVIEW

Inference-Based Cognitive Behavioral Therapy (I-CBT) is a unique and effective approach for individuals with OCD, targeting the cognitive reasoning errors that drive obsessions and compulsions. By addressing inferential confusion, I-CBT empowers clients to reconnect with sensory reality, reduce obsessional thinking, and achieve long-term symptom relief. As an emerging evidence-based practice, I-CBT provides a less distressing alternative to traditional ERP, making it a valuable addition to OCD treatment options.

I hold two independent licenses in the states of Arizona and Ohio, supervisory status in Arizona, along with a substance abuse license in Arizona. I am board certified as a Diplomate and Clinical Mental Health Specialist, an Approved Clinical Supervisor, Nationally Certified Counselor, a Certified Clinical Mental Health Counselor, NeuroLinguistic Programming Practitioner, and a Clinical Trauma Specialist for Individuals and Family including EMDR Therapy and NET. I completed my training in Animal-Assisted Therapy and Pet Handlers certification in order to evaluate and incorporate the human-animal bond in therapy. I am the sole author and creator of the SxC Model of ESA Evaluation. My research interests surround post-traumatic growth, resiliency, strengths-based therapy, positive psychology, mindfulness, Animal-Assisted Therapy, Sandtray Therapy, Creative approaches in therapy, and martial arts in mental health. I have presented at local, state, regional, national, and international levels on various topics including personality traits, licensure reciprocity challenges, Sandtray and supervision, and Animal-Assisted Therapy within supervision. eonbllc@gmail.com

REFERENCES

Aardema, F., & O'Connor, K. (2012). The menace within: Obsessions and the self. *Journal of Cognitive Psychotherapy, 26*(3), 182–195. https://doi.org/10.1891/0889-8391.26.3.182

American Psychological Association. (2020). *Publication manual of the American Psychological Association* (7th ed.). Washington, DC: Author.

Neal, A., & Radomsky, A. S. (2015). Further developments and validations of the inference-based approach to treating obsessive-compulsive disorder. *Journal of Obsessive-Compulsive and Related Disorders, 6,* 33–41. https://doi.org/10.1016/j.jocrd.2015.05.003

O'Connor, K., & Aardema, F. (2012). The inference-based approach to obsessive-compulsive disorder: A comprehensive review. *Cognitive and Behavioral Practice, 19*(2), 221–233. https://doi.org/10.1016/j.cbpra.2011.03.002

O'Connor, K., Aardema, F., & Pélissier, M.-C. (2005). *Beyond reasonable doubt: Reasoning processes in obsessive-compulsive disorder and related disorders.* John Wiley & Sons.

Recommended Readings

O'Connor, K., & Aardema, F. (2012). *The inference-based approach to OCD: Theory and practice.* Routledge.
Radomsky, A. S., & Dugas, M. J. (2015). Cognitive approaches to OCD and anxiety disorders. *Clinical Psychology Review, 40,* 77–90.
Salkovskis, P. M. (1999). Understanding and treating obsessive-compulsive disorder. *Behaviour Research and Therapy, 37*(S1), S29–S52.

Inner Relationship Focusing

BILL OWENBY, EDD, MC, FAAETS, DAAETS, DCMHS, LPC, LAAC, NCC, CCMHC, ACS, DIPLOMATE, FELLOW

Inner Relationship Focusing (IRF) is a mindfulness-based therapeutic approach that emphasizes cultivating an empathetic and non-judgmental relationship with one's inner experiences. Developed by Ann Weiser Cornell and Barbara McGavin, IRF builds upon Eugene Gendlin's Focusing method, offering a structured framework for exploring emotions, sensations, and thoughts as they arise in the body.

The core principles of IRF include:

- **Inner Empathy:** Encouraging a compassionate and curious attitude toward inner experiences, fostering self-acceptance and healing.
- **Embodied Awareness:** Utilizing bodily sensations as entry points to explore deeper emotional and psychological layers.
- **Self-in-Process:** Viewing the self as dynamic and evolving, capable of transformation through mindful attention and understanding.

IRF is particularly effective for individuals seeking to address emotional blocks, enhance self-awareness, and navigate complex feelings or decisions.

CERTIFICATIONS, TRAININGS, AND LICENSURE REQUIREMENTS

Practitioners interested in IRF typically engage in specialized training programs that integrate theory and experiential practice. Key details include:

- **Education:** Training programs do not require prior licensure but often attract professionals in counseling, coaching, or related fields. Individuals with prior experience in mindfulness, somatic practices, or related therapeutic approaches may find the program particularly accessible.
- **Certification:** Certification in IRF is offered by accredited organizations such as The Focusing Institute and Focusing Resources. Certificates verify proficiency in IRF techniques and allow practitioners to integrate these methods into their existing practices.
- **Prerequisites:** While no formal prerequisites exist, familiarity with mindfulness, somatic approaches, or basic therapeutic concepts is recommended.
- **Continuing Education:** Advanced workshops, supervision, and mentoring are recommended for practitioners seeking to deepen their skills and maintain their certifications.

Training Programs

In-Person Programs
1. **Focusing Resources (USA):**
   o Offers comprehensive in-person and hybrid training programs in Inner Relationship Focusing.
   o Programs include experiential learning, mentorship, supervised practice, and peer collaboration.
   o Certification tracks are available for beginners and advanced practitioners.
   o Website: Focusing Resources

2. **The International Focusing Institute (Global):**
   - o Provides workshops, professional certification programs, and advanced training for individuals and mental health professionals.
   - o Offers immersive training experiences in both foundational and advanced Focusing techniques.
   - o Website: The Focusing Institute

Online Programs
1. **Inner Relationship Focusing Online (Focusing Resources):**
   - o Features beginner and advanced certification courses, delivered through live virtual sessions and self-paced modules.
   - o Includes practice groups, video demonstrations, and individualized feedback from trainers.
   - o Website: Focusing Resources Online
2. **Focusing Partnership Training:**
   - o Provides online modules designed to teach individuals how to facilitate the IRF process in partnership with clients or peers.
   - o Includes interactive assignments, peer feedback, and live Q&A sessions.
   - o Website: Focusing Partnership Training
3. **Advanced Certification Tracks:**
   - o Online options for deepening expertise in IRF include mentor-led supervision, case consultations, and advanced theory integration.

General Cost
The financial investment for training and practicing Inner Relationship Focusing includes:

- **Training Fees:** $1,000–5,000 for certification programs, depending on the level of training and format.
- **Workshops and Advanced Training:** $200–1,500 per session for specialized workshops or advanced certification tracks.
- **Practice Integration:** Minimal costs, requiring only a quiet and comfortable setting for sessions. Optional investments include additional resources such as books or video courses.

IDENTIFIED AS EMERGING PRACTICE

Inner Relationship Focusing is recognized as an emerging practice with growing anecdotal evidence supporting its effectiveness. Research into mindfulness and somatic therapies aligns closely with the principles of IRF, providing a foundation for its continued integration into therapeutic settings. While empirical validation is ongoing, testimonials and practitioner feedback highlight its transformative potential.

Certification Available/Required/Recommended
Certification is recommended for practitioners aiming to specialize in IRF or integrate its techniques into existing practices. Notable certifications include:

1. **Inner Relationship Focusing Certification (Focusing Resources):**
   - o A structured program covering foundational and advanced IRF techniques.
   - o Certification involves completing practice hours, submitting case studies, and receiving supervision from certified trainers.
2. **Certified Focusing Professional (The Focusing Institute):**
   - o A broader credential encompassing various Focusing modalities, including IRF.
   - o Requires a combination of theoretical study, practice hours, and mentorship.
3. **Advanced Practitioner Certification:**
   - o Offered by both Focusing Resources and The Focusing Institute who seek mastery in IRF.
   - o Includes specialized modules on trauma-informed applications and integration with other therapeutic modalities.

Degree Requirements

While a formal degree is not required, professionals with backgrounds in counseling, coaching, somatic therapies, or mindfulness practices may find IRF particularly complementary to their skill sets. IRF training is also accessible to individuals seeking personal development or career enhancement within adjacent fields.

CAUTIONS OR LIMITATIONS

While Inner Relationship Focusing is generally accessible and beneficial, considerations include:

- **Client Readiness:** Clients with severe trauma may require additional support or adaptations to safely engage with embodied exploration. Practitioners should assess readiness and ensure a supportive therapeutic environment.
- **Practitioner Expertise:** Effective facilitation requires skill in guiding clients through emotional intensity while maintaining a safe and non-judgmental space.
- **Limited Awareness:** As a niche modality, IRF may require practitioners to invest additional effort in educating clients and colleagues about its benefits and applications.

SCOPE OF PRACTICE ISSUES

Practitioners must operate within their licensure and training limits, ensuring that IRF is integrated ethically and appropriately into their professional scope. Supervision and collaboration with other professionals may enhance outcomes for complex cases.

WHAT KIND OF PERSON WOULD DO WELL IN THIS MODEL?

Inner Relationship Focusing is ideal for:

- Practitioners interested in mindfulness, somatic exploration, and self-compassion practices.
- Clients seeking a gentle and introspective approach to emotional healing.
- Individuals navigating complex decisions or seeking deeper self-awareness.

SUMMARY

Inner Relationship Focusing offers a compassionate and embodied approach to emotional exploration and healing. By fostering inner empathy and mindful attention, this modality empowers clients to navigate their inner world with greater clarity and acceptance. As interest in mindfulness and somatic therapies grows, IRF continues to provide a valuable pathway for personal and therapeutic transformation.

I hold two independent licenses in the states of Arizona and Ohio, supervisory status in Arizona, along with a substance abuse license in Arizona. I am board certified as a Diplomate and Clinical Mental Health Specialist, an Approved Clinical Supervisor, Nationally Certified Counselor, a Certified Clinical Mental Health Counselor, NeuroLinguistic Programming Practitioner, and a Clinical Trauma Specialist for Individuals and Family including EMDR Therapy and NET. I completed my training in Animal-Assisted Therapy and Pet Handlers certification in order to evaluate and incorporate the human-animal bond in therapy. I am the sole author and creator of the SxC Model of ESA Evaluation. My research interests surround post-traumatic growth, resiliency, strengths-based therapy, positive psychology, mindfulness, Animal-Assisted Therapy, Sandtray Therapy, Creative approaches in therapy, and martial arts in mental health. I have presented at local, state, regional, national, and international levels on various topics including personality traits, licensure reciprocity challenges, Sandtray and supervision, and Animal-Assisted Therapy within supervision. eonbllc@gmail.com

REFERENCES

Cornell, A. W. (1996). *The Power of Focusing: A Practical Guide to Emotional Self-Healing.* New Harbinger Publications.

Gendlin, E. T. (1981). *Focusing.* Bantam Books.

Recommended Online Resources

Focusing Resources
The International Focusing Institute
Inner Relationship Focusing Online

InSight Exercise and InSHAPE Program

ALYSON POMPEO-FARGNOLI, PH.D., LPC, SAC, NCC

SAMANTHA WICKETT, BS

Obesity is a perilous condition that is escalating in prevalence in the United States, with 41.9% of Americans falling into this category (CDC, 2021). Conditions associated with obesity and being overweight encompass, but are not restricted to, coronary heart disease, cancer, and a diminished quality of life. Notably, obesity has more severe repercussions on individuals with mental illnesses, such as depression, schizophrenia, and bipolar disorder, when compared to those without mental illnesses (Allison et al., 2009). According to the Third National Health and Nutrition Examination Survey (CDC, 2021), 60% of women and 29% of men with serious mental illness were found to be obese. This disparity becomes significant when contrasted with the general population, where obesity rates are 28.5% for women and 17.5% for men without mental illness. Several implications for this disparity arise, including the impact of medications used to treat mental illness. Antipsychotics and mood stabilizers have been linked to weight gain, posing a greater challenge to weight loss for individuals with serious mental illness (SMI) (Allison et al, 2009.). While some medications carry a lower risk of inducing weight gain, maintaining medication stability is paramount in the treatment of mental illness. Additionally, although weight loss surgeries such as gastric bypass and bariatric surgery can reduce BMI, they come with various risks. Furthermore, long-term data indicates that these surgeries are not effective for the majority of patients (Allison et al., 2009). Individuals with SMI face a multitude of risk factors that exacerbate the difficulties of behavior change and weight loss.

Long-term risk factors for obesity include adverse metabolic effects such as lipidemia, insulin resistance, elevated cholesterol and triglycerides, coronary heart disease, and stroke. Moreover, obesity and being overweight disproportionately affect individuals from lower socioeconomic status. Various barriers associated with low SES areas, including limited access to healthcare (due to factors such as location, cost, and availability), affordability of nutritious food, substance abuse, and tobacco/nicotine consumption, contribute to this disparity (Mendis, et al., 2011). A sedentary lifestyle is a major contributor to these comorbidities. Physical inactivity not only exacerbates mental health symptoms but also leads to weight gain (Muralidhara et al., 2018).

Lifestyle interventions have shown clinical significance in improving the health of individuals with serious mental illness and who are overweight. It has been shown that through long-term (at least 12 months) lifestyle intervention, it is possible to achieve a loss of body weight, a decrease in BMI, and a reduced fasting glucose level (Naslund et al., 2015a; Daumit et al., 2013; Green et al., 2015). Such lifestyle interventions have included an increase in exercise and having lifestyle change mentors. Such mentors have been trained in fitness and nutrition, as well as having knowledge and tools for working with individuals with mental illnesses (from mental health professionals specializing in motivation and behavior change). This idea of supporting individuals through a holistic lifestyle change approach can be found within Insight-Oriented therapy, the modality of Insight Personal Exercise, and via related programs such as InSHAPE.

INSIGHT-ORIENTED THERAPY: PAVING THE WAY FOR INSIGHT-PERSONAL EXERCISE

Insight-Oriented Therapy is utilized by therapists in order to help their clients recognize how their own personal experiences through life have contributed to their current personalities and behaviors (Cuncic, 2022). Much of what is covered through Insight-Oriented Therapy revolves around internal feelings that will attempt to be brought to light and confronted by both the client and therapist. Moreover, this approach can be very helpful for individuals struggling with a mental health disorder such as anxiety and depression. Stemming from Insight-Oriented Therapy, studies have shown that a person's exercising habits also relate to their personality. Insight Personal Exercise modality can be used by fitness instructors to determine if the client needs an increase in physical activity. Along with certain demographics such as gender and age, personality can have a large impact on an individual's fitness choices, and may allow fitness instructors to better help by placing the person in the proper setting, whether that be a group, personal training, or other options (Schneider, et al., 2009). Higher levels of exercise are also connected to better health and socialization. Insight Personal Exercise Modality has paved the way for InSHAPE, which is a program designed to assist people with mental health disorders to create a positive healthy fitness and nutrition journey.

THE InSHAPE PROGRAM

Individualized Self-Help Action Plan for Empowerment (InSHAPE) is an evidence-based fitness and nutrition program designed specifically for individuals diagnosed with serious mental health disorders (United Services, 2023). Its origins trace back to a small trial group in New Hampshire, initiated by Ken Jue, the director of Monadnock Family Services. Dr. Stephen Bartels of Dartmouth Centers for Health and Aging quickly recognized the program's potential and partnered with Jue, offering additional resources from Dartmouth. The driving force behind InSHAPE was the alarming premature mortality rate among patients in their 40s and 50s, largely attributed to unhealthy habits such as obesity and smoking (Dartmouth Medicine Magazine, 2011.)

The InSHAPE program is described as beneficial for anyone who is interested in making healthy lifestyle changes, has received clearance from a medical professional, has a mental health disorder diagnosis, and is motivated to improve their health. In addition, it is noted that there is an opportunity for children to even participate in this program (mhcgm.org, 2023). One of the unique and important aspects of the program is that it includes the support of a certified personal trainer/wellness coach (United Services, 2023). InSHAPE comprises several additional core components, including an initial health assessment, a tailored fitness and nutrition plan, weekly goal-setting meetings with mentors trained in the InSHAPE program, membership to gyms or fitness facilities, exercise classes, education in healthy eating skills, smoking cessation support, and motivational activities (Green, et al., 2015; United Services, 2023).

Clients who partake in the InSHAPE program often show significant improvements in their overall health. These improvements included reduced waist measurements, enhanced BMI, better dietary choices, and increased physical activity. The program's effectiveness has led to its recognition as the State and National Model for comprehensive wellness programs (Dartmouth Medical Magazine, 2011). InSHAPE stands as an impactful solution for addressing the health disparities faced by individuals with serious mental health disorders, ultimately empowering them to enhance their overall well-being (Lunardenie, et al., 2011).

RESEARCH SUPPORT FOR INSHAPE

In studying the impacts of the InSHAPE program, individuals who were overweight and dealing with serious mental illness (major depression, schizoaffective disorder, bipolar disorder, schizophrenia) received medical clearance from their healthcare provider to participate in the InSHAPE program. This lifestyle intervention was found to positively improve the fitness and weight loss of participants (Bartels, et al., 2013; Naslund, et. al., 2015a; Naslund, et al., 2015b). While research for the InSHAPE program has primarily focused on the adult population, and limited investigation has been conducted regarding the effectiveness of lifestyle intervention on children, InShape does offer consideration of program enrollment for minors. It has been described that Insight Personal Exercise's lifestyle intervention may serve as an effective treatment approach for young individuals grappling with negative mental health symptoms and overweight/obesity by enhancing their understanding of healthy nutrition, the positive impact of an active lifestyle, and additional support for behavior change (mhcgm.org, 2023).

LIFESTYLE COACHES/MENTAL HEALTH PROFESSIONALS

An important aspect of the InSHAPE lifestyle intervention is support of mental health professionals and fitness experts, often referred to as mentors or lifestyle coaches. Coaches are typically mental health professionals with an interest in physical health, and certified fitness instructors specializing in working with individuals with mental illness. In the InSHAPE trial, mentors undergo a minimum 3-day training period and participate in weekly phone calls with nutritionists and mental health professionals specializing in behavior change and motivation. Additionally, mentors typically conduct weekly group or individual sessions to address topics such as healthy eating habits, nutrition, and skill development (Bartels, et al., 2013).

While this framework has been developed based on clinical research, similar training for real-world counselors may prove effective. Research indicates that mental health counselors with intensive training in three areas—exercise, nutrition, and behavior change—are better equipped to assist clients in achieving healthier mental and physical states (mhcgm.org, 2023). Prior research has been conducted in both outpatient and inpatient care settings, as well as by mental health professionals employed by community organizations (Bartels, et al., 2013; Daumit, et al., 2015).

TRAINING AND CERTIFICATIONS

The founders of InSHAPE have designated the Mental Health Center of Greater Manchester as the international hub for the practice. However, with the success of InSHAPE, there is an opportunity for other facilities to adopt the model and expand its reach (mhcgm.org). Along with this is the opportunity for professionals to be trained in the model.

Counselors implementing this lifestyle intervention in practice with clients must maintain regular consultation with nutrition and fitness professionals. Nutritionists and dietitians can provide essential information on healthy eating that counselors may use to educate their clients. Emphasizing healthier food choices and nutritionally dense meals is integral to reducing body weight. Physical activity is another crucial component of weight loss and improved overall health. Counselors must also consult with fitness professionals to gain a fundamental understanding of physical activity principles (mhcgm.org, 2023; Muralidhara, et al., 2018).

The Mental Health Center of Greater Manchester offers educational opportunities for mental health professionals. Included in this are in person and virtual trainings in the InSHAPE wellness program. They consist of 6 weekly sessions of "Lifestyle Changes Class" for mental health professionals. These sessions are signed up for in blocks (one course sign up consists of 6 hourly virtual meetings) and at a cost of $180. The registration does not mention any prerequisites or required licensures to attend. To view the course schedule and book it, you may visit **www.mhcgm.org/training-and-education/upcoming-trainings/**

The Mental Health Center of Greater Manchester also provides continuing education, consultation, and health podcasts, and other educational resources around InSHAPE training as well as general mental health topics (mhcgm.org, 2023). For more information, please access the Mental Health Center of Greater Manchester's website at: **www.mhcgm.org** or contact them at 401 Cypress Street, Manchester, NH 03103 – Phone: (603) 668-4111.

Suggested Certification: Motivational Interviewing

Currently, there is no graduate-level program, certification, or licensure specifically tailored to this type of intervention. However, counselors interested in implementing Insight Personal Therapy must possess a foundational understanding of fitness, nutrition, and skills related to motivation and behavior change (mhcgm.org, 2023). Counselors can attain a Motivational Interviewing (MI) certificate through MINT. For novice trainers, MI training typically spans 3-4 days of in-person instruction or completion of an online asynchronous course to obtain their MI certificate. After completing the training, new trainers may apply to join the international Motivational Interviewing Network of Trainers (MINT) (MINT, 2021).

Additional Considerations

Lifestyle intervention aimed at promoting healthy living and alleviating negative mental health symptoms can prove effective for obese/overweight individuals with serious mental illness. Multiple resources are necessary in such a program. Mentors or coaches must possess relevant backgrounds and be available for skill acquisition/training in the lifestyle intervention, meet regularly with the clients, seek continuous professional development, and have the ability to design individualized or group-based plans. Counselors implementing this lifestyle intervention in practice with clients must remain competent and up-to-date on the interventions utilized, and seek continual professional development. Such counselors must also maintain regular consultation with nutrition and fitness professionals, and not provide advice or treatment outside of their scope of practice. Nutritionists and dietitians can provide essential information on healthy eating that counselors may use to educate their clients, but all information should come from a certified resource.

Furthermore, this lifestyle intervention requires financial investments in gym memberships, clinical treatment, and mentor training. Time is another valuable resource, as empirical data indicates that this intervention is most effective when implemented for at least 12 months. A weekly time commitment is also essential, including participant exercise time (with a goal of 150 minutes per week) and one hour of counseling (Bartels, 2013; Naslund, et al., 2015a; Naslund, et al., 2015b).

SUMMARY

Obesity is a pressing concern in the United States, affecting a significant portion of the population and leading to various health complications. Insight personal exercise is a lifestyle intervention that is proven to decrease body weight and increase physical movement and health. Through comprehensive, long-term approaches that include physical activity, nutrition education, and behavior change strategies, individuals with SMI can make meaningful progress toward weight loss and improved mental health. It is essential to acknowledge that these interventions require substantial resources, both in terms of trained mentors and financial investments. Moreover, sustaining these interventions over an extended period is crucial for achieving lasting benefits. Therefore, policymakers, healthcare providers, and mental health professionals must collaborate to make such interventions accessible and sustainable. The relationship between obesity and serious mental illness is a critical public health concern. By embracing evidence-based lifestyle interventions and addressing the associated challenges, we can work towards enhancing the well-being of individuals with SMI, reducing the burden of obesity-related comorbidities, and ultimately improving the overall health of this vulnerable population.

Dr. Alyson Pompeo-Fargnoli is a nationally certified counselor (NCC), licensed practicing counselor (LPC) in the state of New Jersey. Dr. Pompeo-Fargnoli also holds a Substance Abuse and Addictions Counseling Certification. She is an associate professor in Education counseling at Monmouth University, where she brings her 10 years of experience as a student affairs professional and 10 years of clinical counseling experience to the forefront of preparing her students for their careers. Additionally, Dr. Pompeo-Fargnoli has a wealth of over 25 publications ranging from the ethical obligation of counselor self-awareness and consultation, animal-assisted therapy, ecofeminist therapy, college admissions, and the effects of COVID-19 on mental health. She also regularly gives professional presentations at professional conferences, including a talk at the American Counseling Association (ACA) conference. Despite a busy professional life, Dr. Pompeo-Fargnoli still finds the time to enjoy life with her husband and two sons.

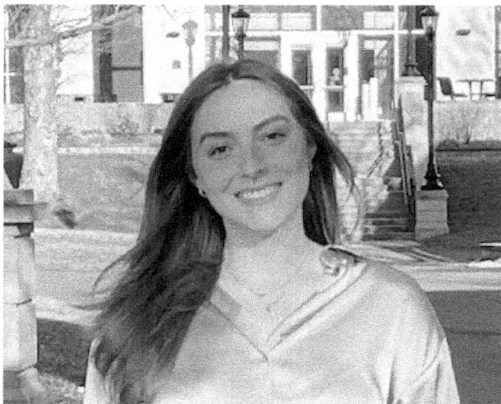

Samantha Wickett attended the University of Pittsburgh and obtained a BS in Psychology with a focus in Anthropology. She spent time in Pittsburgh working at a high-needs high school as an Americorps member where she found her love of school counseling. Currently she is a M.S. Ed. in School Counseling student at Monmouth University where she serves as an ambassador to the program, is a member of the Education Counseling Student Association (ECSA), and Chi Sigma Iota. Her anticipated graduation date is Dec. 2024. Samantha is a member of the American School Counseling Association (ASCA) and the Bergen County School Counseling Association (BCSCA). She currently resides in Bergen County, NJ where she spends time doing yoga and hanging out with friends, family and her cat, Slinky.

REFERENCES

Allison, D. B., Newcomer, J. W., Dunn, A. L., Blumenthal, J. A., Fabricatore, A. N., Daumit, G. L., Cope, M. B., Riley, W. T., Vreeland, B., Hibbeln, J. R., Alpert, J. E. (2009). Obesity among those with mental disorders: A National Institute of Mental Health meeting report *American Journal of Preventive Medicine* *36*(4) 341-350. https://doi.org/10.1016/j.amepre.2008.11.020

Bartels S.J., Pratt S.I., Aschbrenner K.A., Barre L.K., Jue K., Wolfe R.S., Xie H., McHugo G., Santos M., Williams G.E., Naslund J.A., Mueser K.T. Clinically significant improved fitness and weight loss among overweight persons with serious mental illness. *Psychiatric Services 64(8)*:729-36. doi: 10.1176/appi.ps.003622012. PMID: 23677386; PMCID: PMC5662189.

Centers for Disease Control and Prevention (2021). **National Health and Nutrition Examination Survey (NHANES). Surveillance Systems | Overweight & Obesity | CDC**

Cuncic, A. (2023). *What is Insight Oriented Therapy.* VeryWellMind.com

Daumit, G. L., Dickerson, F. B., Wang, N. Y, Dalcin, A., Jerome, G. J., Anderson, C. A. M., Young, D. R., Frick, K. D, Yu, A., Gennusa, J. V., Oefinger, M., Crum, R. M. (2013). A behavioral weight-loss intervention in persons with serious mental illness. *The New England Journal of Medicine* 368 1594-1602. .DOI: 10.1056/NEJMoa1214530

Green, C. A., Yarborough, B. J. H., Leo, M. C., Yarborough, M. T., Stumbo, S. P., Janoff, S.

L., Perrin, N. A., Nichols, G. A., Stevens, V. J. (2015). The STRIDE weight loss and lifestyle intervention for individuals taking antipsychotic medications: A randomized trial *American Journal of Psychiatry* https://doi.org/10.1176/appi.ajp.2014.14020173

Lunardenie, R (2011) In Shape: Local pilot becomes national model. *Dartmouth Medicine Magazine.* **https://dartmed.dartmouth.edu/winter11/html/vs_in_shape/**

Mendis, S., Puska, P., Norrving, B. (2011) 10 Obesity: A risk factor of CVDs. *Global Atlas on Cardiovascular Disease Prevention and Control,* 36-37. https://www.jstor.org/stable/resrep30133.14

The Mental Health Center of Greater Manchester (2023). *InShape: Self-help action plan for empowerment.* https://www.mhcgm.org/our-programs/adult-services/inshape/

Motivational Interviewing Network of Trainers (2021). *MINT excellence in motivational interviewing.* **https://motivationalinterviewing.org/training-expectations**

Muralidhara, A., Niv, N., Brown, C. H., Olmos-Ochoa, T. T., Fang, L. J., Cohen, A. N.,

Kreyenbuhl, J., Oberman, R. S., Goldberg, R. W., Young, A. S. (2018). Impact of online weight management with peer coaching on physical activity levels of adults with serious mental illness *Psychiatric Services* *69*(10) 1062-1068. https://doi.org/10.1176/appi.ps.201700391

Naslund, J. A., Aschbrenner, K. A., Scherer, E. A., Pratt, S. I., Wolfe, R. S., & Bartels, S. J. (2015a). Lifestyle intervention for people with severe obesity and serious mental illness *American Journal of Preventive Medicine 50*(2), 145-153. https://doi.org/10.1016/j.amepre.2015.07.012

Naslund, J.A., Aschbrenner, K. A., Pratt, S. I., Bartels, S. J. (2015b). Comparison of people with serious mental illness and general population samples enrolled in lifestyle interventions for weight loss. *Schizophrenia Research 169*(1-3) 486-488. **https://doi.org/10.1016/j.schres.2015.09.016**

Schneider, M. L., & Graham, D. J. (2009). Personality, physical fitness, and affective response to exercise among adolescents. *Medicine and Science in Sports and Exercise, 41*(4), 947–955. doi:10.1249/MSS.0b013e31818de009

United Services Incorporated (2023). *InShape*. **https://www.unitedservicesct.org/our-services/mental-health/mental-health-supportive-services/inshape/**

Insight-Oriented Therapy (IOT)

Yuji Su, BA

Insight-Oriented Therapy (IOT) is a kind of psychodynamic therapy. It helps people understand the deeper reasons behind their thoughts and actions. It helps people to find out how their behaviors are influenced by their past experiences (Messer & McWilliams, 2007). Clients can resolve their difficulties in a healthier way when they transfer this unconscious into their realization.

IOT is developed on Freud's idea about unconsciousness and how our experiences build our personalities (Messer & McWilliams, 2007). Over time, this kind of therapy has shifted its focus to more on the relationship between the therapist and the client and the emotional insights that happen during sessions.

A key idea in IOT is the difference between two types of insight. Intellectual insight means understanding problems on a thinking level without strong emotions involved. Emotional insight combines thoughts and feelings for deeper understanding (Messer & McWilliams, 2007). Emotional insight is seen as more effective for lasting change because it connects what clients realize with how they feel about it.

CERTIFICATIONS, TRAININGS, AND LICENSURE REQUIREMENTS

For certification, there isn't any specific one for Insight-Oriented Therapy (IOT). However, if you want to specialize in IOT, you can get training in psychodynamic therapy which most of the IOT rules are covered in (Messer & McWilliams, 2007). Mental health professionals like psychologists, counselors, social workers, and psychiatrists can use IOT after getting the necessary education and licenses in their fields.

Generally, there are two steps that need to be taken before being a therapist who specializes in IOT. First, you need a master's degree in related fields, such as psychology, counseling or social work. Second, you need to gain a license to practice counseling in your living area. This kind of license requires completing supervised clinical hours and passing an exam.

For formal training in IOT, you can enroll in programs in psychodynamic therapy offered by accredited institutions. These programs teach you about the history, theories, and techniques of IOT and often include supervised therapy sessions (Messer & McWilliams, 2007). Ongoing supervision is important because IOT involves complex skills. You need to understand unconscious processes and learn how to manage transference and countertransference.

General Cost

The cost of training in IOT varies widely. Since there's no standardized certification for IOT, expenses might include tuition fees for courses and workshops, ranging from a few hundred to several thousand dollars. Added costs might include books and materials, costing between $100 and $500.

If therapists need supervised clinical hours, paying for supervision can add to the cost. Supervision fees depend on the supervisor's experience and the region. Continuing education, like attending conferences or extra training, can also add to expenses but helps therapists stay updated.

Professionals should research different programs to understand financial commitment. Some institutions may offer scholarships or sliding scale fees.

IDENTIFIED AS EVIDENCE-BASED PRACTICE

Research shows that Insight-Oriented Therapy (IOT) can help people with various psychological issues. For example, in Nigeria, patients with substance use disorders took part in IOT. The therapy reduced symptoms like hallucinations and delusions. It also increased their motivation to recover and helped them develop healthier coping strategies (Adegbola et al., 2018). This suggests that IOT can be effective for treating substance use disorders, even in places where resources are limited.

In another study, couples experiencing marital distress took part in IOT. The couples showed significant improvements in their relationships and personal well-being, and these positive changes were kept over time (Snyder & Wills, 1989). This shows that IOT can be just as effective as other therapies in addressing marital problems.

For individuals dealing with anxiety and depression, IOT led to noticeable reductions in symptoms. What's more, these improvements continued long after the therapy had ended (Cross et al., 1982). This shows that IOT can bring about lasting positive changes in a person's mental health.

Furthermore, during IOT sessions, moments when clients had emotional insights were linked to physical changes like increased heart rate and skin conductance. This supports the idea that IOT facilitates meaningful emotional experiences that aid in healing (Reidbord & Redington, 1992).

While there are some critiques—for instance, the notion that insights may not always be factually correct but can still provide therapeutic benefits (Jopling, 2001)—the overall evidence supports IOT as an effective therapeutic approach.

Certification Availability, Requirements, and Recommendations

There isn't a special certification just for Insight-Oriented Therapy (IOT). Therapists who want to focus on IOT usually get extra training in psychodynamic therapy or psychoanalysis (Messer & McWilliams, 2007). Even though certification isn't needed, advanced training can help therapists improve their skills. In order to get better understanding on therapist's own feelings, some program may require therapist experience personal counseling therapy themselves. To keep getting better at practicing IOT, therapists need to continue learning. (Messer & McWilliams, 2007).

Degree Requirements

You need at least a master degree in related field in counseling or social worker before you can practice IOT, even to be a therapist. However, if you want to specialize in psychiatry, you may need a doctorate or a medical degree.

CAUTIONS OR LIMITATIONS

Though effective, Insight-Oriented Therapy (IOT) has important issues. Concerns include ensuring clients benefit from insights. Some find "placebo insights" valuable despite their inaccuracies (Jopling, 2001). The therapist's role in helping clients understand themselves and stay emotionally well raises ethical issues.

Managing powerful treatment emotions is another problem. Because IOT tackles deep issues and hidden reasons, clients may feel tremendous emotions. Researchers showed that emotional awareness increases heart rate (Reidbord & Redington, 1992). Therapeutic environments must be secure and helpful for clients to process these feelings.

Transference and countertransference skills are also needed by therapists. When clients project feelings about key persons onto the therapist, transference occurs. Therapist countertransference is emotional response to client. These dynamics must be managed for effective therapy (Messer & McWilliams, 2007).

Cultural considerations are important too. Studies have shown the effectiveness of IOT in diverse cultural settings, like in Nigeria for treating substance use disorders (Adegbola et al., 2018).

SCOPE OF PRACTICE ISSUES

When they wish to understand themselves and achieve permanent changes, some people choose Insight-Oriented Therapy (IOT). For complex emotions, unresolved previous experiences, relationship issues, anxiety, and depression, it is ideal. It may not work for quick fixes or those who are unwilling to investigate themselves. IOT needs patience and a willingness to explore hidden emotions (Messer & McWilliams, 2007). Other therapies may provide quick relief. Psychodynamic therapy training is required for IOT, which incorporates complicated procedures including unconscious material interpretation and transference management (Messer & McWilliams, 2007). Therapists may lose effectiveness and hurt clients without sufficient training.

IOT may not be suitable for clients with acute psychosis or severe cognitive impairments. Before undertaking insight-oriented work, these people may need immediate, structured interventions or medical care.

WHAT KIND OF PERSON WOULD DO WELL IN THIS MODEL?

Therapists who are patient, compassionate, and comfortable with deep emotional interactions can do insight-oriented therapy. They must listen and create trust with clients to reveal concealed ideas and feelings (Messer & McWilliams, 2007). Clients willing to examine themselves can benefit from IOT. Complex emotions or unresolved prior experiences may benefit from this therapy. Understanding why customers use drugs helped (Adegbola et al., 2018). IOT works for clients who want to understand themselves and explore their feelings (Messer & McWilliams, 2007).

SUMMARY

IOT helps clients comprehend their thoughts and behaviors by bringing unconscious motivations and prior experiences into awareness to assist healing (Messer & McWilliams, 2007). Research has proved its efficacy in diverse settings. The therapist-client interaction and emotional insights during sessions have become central to IOT (Messer & McWilliams, 2007).

Some research show that IOT helps people identify concerns and build healthy coping strategies. IOT has a profound impact on clients, as emotional understanding in treatment is linked to heart rate increases. Compared to other therapy, IOT improves outcomes similarly. While other critiques argue that insights need not be technically correct to be effective, they nevertheless stress client emotional relief.

Overall, Insight-Oriented Therapy is still successful in modern psychotherapy. Through deeper self-understanding and emotional insight, it helps clients make permanent transformation (Messer & McWilliams, 2007).

Yuji Su graduated from The Ohio State University with a Bachelor of Arts in Psychology. Currently, Yuji is pursuing a Master of Science in Clinical Mental Health Counseling at Marquette University, focusing on addiction counseling. Yuji's professional interests include helping international students adjust to new environments and supporting the Asian LGBTQ+ population in dealing with family trauma and mental health issues. After graduating, Yuji plans to pursue a doctoral degree and may work in a hospital setting in the meantime.

Email: ysu297367@gmail.com

REFERENCE

Adegbola, A., Akinnawo, O. E., & Kumuyi, O. D. (2018). Response of substance use patients to Insight-Oriented Therapy at Federal Neuropsychiatric Hospital Aro, Abeokuta. International Journal for Psychotherapy in Africa, 3(1), 95–106. Retrieved from https://www.journals.ezenwaohaetorc.org/index.php/IJPA/article/view/951

Cross, D. G., Sheehan, P. W., & Khan, J. A. (1982). Short- and long-term follow-up of clients receiving insight-oriented therapy and behavior therapy. Journal of Consulting and Clinical Psychology, 50(1), 103–112. https://doi.org/10.1037/0022-006X.50.1.103

Jopling, D. A. (2001). Placebo insight: The rationality of insight-oriented psychotherapy. Journal of Clinical Psychology, 57(1), 19–36. https://doi.org/10.1002/1097-4679(200101)57:1<19::AID-JCLP4>3.0.CO;2-Z

Messer, S. B., & McWilliams, N. (2007). Insight in psychodynamic therapy: Theory and assessment. In L. G. Castonguay & C. E. Hill (Eds.), Insight in psychotherapy (pp. 11–32). American Psychological Association. https://doi.org/10.1037/11532-001

Reidbord, S. P., & Redington, D. J. (1992). Psychophysiological processes during insight-oriented therapy: Further investigations into nonlinear psychodynamics. The Journal of Nervous and Mental Disease, 180(10), 649–657. https://doi.org/10.1097/00005053-199210000-00007

Snyder, D. K., & Wills, R. M. (1989). Behavioral versus insight-oriented marital therapy: Effects on individual and interspousal functioning. Journal of Consulting and Clinical Psychology, 57(1), 39–46. https://doi.org/10.1037/0022-006X.57.1.39

Instinctual Trauma Response® (ITR)

Linda Gantt, PhD, ATR-BC, ITR-Traumatologist

ITR Co-Founder

Mary Carlson, ITR-CTRT

The Instinctual Trauma Response® (ITR) is a comprehensive, structured approach rooted in neuroscience, to achieving full trauma recovery. It integrates elements of parts psychology, art, narrative, and somatic therapies. ITR is designed to address the deepest roots of trauma memory, including prenatal and preverbal trauma, without requiring the individual to relive past experiences. This method is versatile and suitable for individuals to do on their own, or for practitioners to do in both group and individual sessions, in hourly sessions or intensive formats, and with individuals as young as three.

ITR uses the same protocol for any trauma, making it both straightforward to learn and easy to apply. Its simplicity enables individuals to take more control of their own recovery process. With tools that can be used independently, a person is equipped not only to address their current challenges but also to manage future ones effectively.

Addressing Complex Trauma with Innovation and Care

When dealing with complex trauma, ITR's gentle, noninvasive approach stands out. Unlike other methods that may cause overwhelming "flooding" sensations, ITR employs simple, yet effective, drawing (Graphic Narrative®) and writing (Externalized Dialogue®). These directed and specific techniques help to externalize distressing memories by transferring them from the mind onto paper or into the ITR web app. They provide substantial relief and offer multiple benefits, including grounding, uncovering dissociated memories, and stimulating dynamic bilateral brain activity.

The ITR structured process involves organizing "fragmented" trauma memories into a coherent sequence—beginning, middle, and end—drawn out and following the universal Instinctual Trauma Response. This culminates in the creation of a Graphic Narrative®, which integrates nonverbal memories and bodily sensations, later reinforced through verbal description. The second technique, Externalized Dialogue®, facilitates a profound conversation between an individual's True Self and their dissociated parts. This written or recorded dialogue can be revisited and continued, offering a consistent and comforting approach to dealing with triggers or activated parts.

A Legacy of Pioneering Trauma Treatment

ITR represents a groundbreaking approach to trauma recovery, rooted in decades of clinical practice. Dr. Louis Tinnin, a psychiatrist and early adopter and staunch supporter of art therapy, recognized its potential in the 1980s while working at Prince George's Hospital in Maryland. Together with Dr. Linda Gantt, a world renown art therapist, they refined the ITR method over 40 years, addressing a wide range of traumas in both hospital and clinical settings. Their work has shown that ITR can deliver rapid and profound relief from traumatic stress, with effects that are both significant and enduring.

Dr. Tinnin also observed early in his career that trauma was frequently misdiagnosed as mental illness. He stated, "Trauma is so pervasive that any condition requiring professional help may be rooted in trauma. Process the trauma first and see what remains. No one should have to live with even minimal trauma symptoms. It's easy to treat, and it doesn't take years to do it."

For more information, including outcomes and testimonials, please visit HelpForTrauma.com.

Certifications, Trainings, and Licensure Requirements

The ITR Training Institute is the exclusive provider of Instinctual Trauma Response® training and certifications. A mental health clinician can become certified as an ITR Certified Trauma Specialists (ITR-CTS), while a paraprofessional can achieve certification as an ITR Certified Trauma Recovery Technician (ITR-CTRT). Both certifications require the completion of the Accelerated Traumatology Courses (ATC) 101, 102/103, participation in two case presentations during 10 peer group consultation calls, and a final private exit call to demonstrate competency and adherence to the ITR model. The certification process can be completed in less than 3 months.

Additionally, there is an advanced certification, ITR Certified Traumatologist (ITR-CT), for those who have completed all available ITR courses and have applied ITR in the field for over five years with diverse populations.

The ITR Training Institute is committed to making trauma recovery accessible to everyone. No specific educational background is required to learn the ITR protocol. We firmly believe that trauma survivors can access their own readiness to engage in ITR work. With the desire and discipline to learn, along with the ability to ground oneself, relief from trauma symptoms is within reach. Even those who only complete the ITR psychoeducation provided in ATC 101 will experience significant benefits. We recommend that individuals who are triggered by the ITR techniques or have a complex trauma history seek the professional guidance of an ITR Certified Trauma Specialist to ensure successful outcomes. There is a Professional Directory on HelpForTrauma.com.

The ITR Training Institute also focuses on training first responders, chaplains, educators, foster/adoptive parents, child advocacy workers, and coaches to be trauma-effective and parts-informed. The Accelerated Traumatology Course (ATC) 101 provides essential ITR psychoeducation, while the full ITR protocol is taught in ATC 102/103. Additional courses are available to address specific subjects and populations including first responders and children and adolescents.

The ITR Training Institute is an approved provider with the National Board of Certified Counselors (NBCC) and the West Virginia Board of Social Workers (WV BSW).

General Costs

At the ITR Training Institute, we are committed to supporting professionals in making their services accessible and affordable. We recognize the dedication of those in the helping professions and aim to empower as many individuals as possible through our training.

Our certification program is competitively priced, offering excellent value compared to most similar programs. Costs may vary slightly depending on the time of year, but typically, participants can achieve ITR certification within 3 to 6 months at an approximate cost of $2,000.

THE FUTURE OF TRAUMA RECOVERY

Trauma is finally being recognized as an injury, not a mental illness, and it is a global epidemic. ITR is poised to become the gold standard in trauma recovery treatment. It is a structured approach that facilitates memory reconsolidation, neutralizes triggers, and calms internal parts significantly reducing or eliminating traumatic stress symptoms quickly. Engaging in ITR equips individuals with lifelong tools to manage any future traumas and work with the parts of one's inner landscape for lasting inner peace.

The ITR Training Institute is dedicated to spreading the Instinctual Trauma Response® worldwide, utilizing technology and tools to help eliminate the suffering caused by traumatic stress symptoms. With ITR, full recovery is not only possible but can be achieved swiftly.

ITR Practitioners

ITR practitioners must adhere to their state laws and remain informed about changes in regulations. Clinicians (ITR Certified Trauma Specialists) have found collaboration with certified paraprofessionals (ITR Certified Trauma Recovery Technicians) to be highly beneficial in managing the high demand for trauma recovery services.

The ITR Training Institute advocates for "intensive" trauma work, which involves sessions longer than the standard 50-minute hour. Even a 90-minute session can create momentum that accelerates the recovery process. Once a person understands the ITR process, they can progress rapidly through their timeline and positively move forward with their lives. Trauma is treatable, and it doesn't require years to resolve.

For more information, including a webinar on setting up a private practice with a focus on achieving a healthy work/life balance, visit the homepage of HelpForTrauma.com.

CAUTIONS

Grounding oneself is an essential skill for anyone engaged in trauma recovery. We strongly recommend watching the *Grounding a Person* video available on the HelpForTrauma.com homepage. Individuals can assess their ability to ground themselves and determine whether they can undertake their ITR work without professional guidance. However, those with a complex trauma history or who experience strong emotional or physical responses during the protocol should seek professional guidance. An ITR Certified Trauma Specialist can be found via the Professional Directory on HelpForTrauma.com.

The ITR Training Institute has developed a web platform, BraveStoriesApp.com to assist practitioners and individuals in performing the ITR process.

WHO WOULD BENEFIT FROM ITR?

- Individuals who view trauma as an injury to recover from, not a mental illness to manage.
- Individuals who have tried other approaches with little success and are seeking something new and effective.
- Individuals looking for a simple, fast, holistic, and effective approach to complete trauma recovery.
- Individuals who recognize that coping mechanisms and medications or psychedelics are not sufficient for trauma recovery.
- Individuals eager to learn how to assist and guide others to fully recover from trauma symptoms.
- Individuals who believe in the power of encouragement, training, and self-leadership in their own recovery journey.
- Individuals who understand the need for accessible and effective trauma recovery methods worldwide.

HelpForTrauma.com

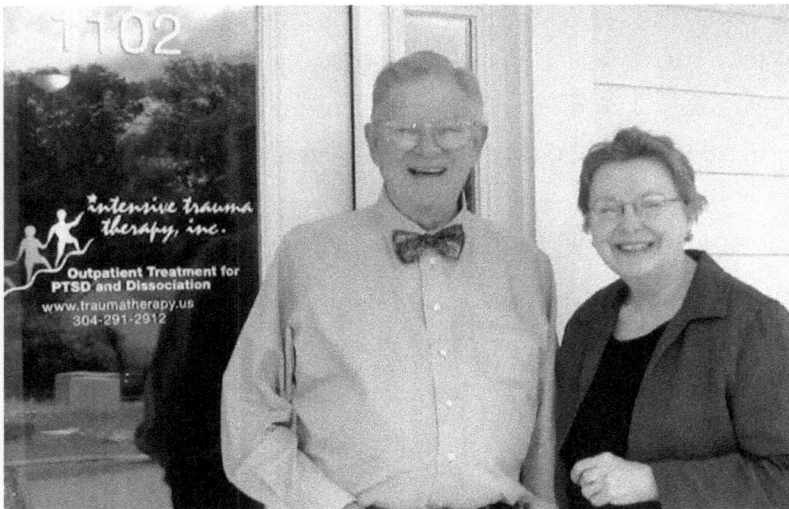

Dr. Linda Gantt has had a distinguished 45-year career in art therapy and trauma recovery. She is well known among art therapists having served as President of the American Art Therapy Association (AATA), editor of the first issue of the association's journal, and chair of the National Coalition of Art Therapies Associations. She has been awarded the Honorary Life Member citation, which is the highest accolade in AATA. Dr. Gantt has a master's degree in art therapy from the George Washington University and a doctorate in Interdisciplinary Studies from the University of Pittsburgh. She has taught in a number of graduate art therapy programs including the George Washington University, Vermont College, Notre Dame de Namur, and Florida State University.

Dr. Gantt developed Instinctual Trauma Response® (ITR) together with her late husband, psychiatrist Dr. Louis Tinnin. They held over 17 years of trauma conferences with West Virginia University. During those years they hosted many pioneers in the field and shared stages at other conferences with icons including Dr. Bessel van der Kolk who introduced Dr. Tinnin as "the greatest trauma mind of the 20th century."

Moreover, Dr. Gantt's Formal Elements Art Therapy Scale (FEATS), an assessment tool developed with Carmello Tabone, and is used nationally and internationally to make art therapy assessment more scientific. There is a paradigm shift toward greater use of art therapy in the mental health field and Dr. Gantt, with ITR and FEATS, is instrumental in that process.

Mary Carlson, co-owner of ITR Training Institute, is a filmmaker by trade. She is assisting Dr. Gantt in getting Instinctual Trauma Response® out to the world and making trauma recovery accessible to anyone who wants to learn through film and technology. She managed the virtual Intensive Trauma Recovery clinic with Dr. Gantt for 5 years. In January 2024, they closed the clinic to focus on training and promoting ITR practitioners.

Dr. Louis Tinnin and Dr. Linda Gantt in front of their last brick-and-mortar clinic in Morgantown, WV (picture above).

Mary Carlson, co-owner of ITR Training Institute, is a filmmaker by trade. She is assisting Dr. Gantt in getting Instinctual Trauma Response® out to the world and making trauma recovery accessible to anyone who wants to learn through film and technology. She managed the virtual Intensive Trauma Recovery clinic with Dr. Gantt for 5 years. In January 2024, they closed the clinic to focus on training and promoting ITR practitioners.

Institutional Psychotherapy (IP)

HANNAH L. BUTTON, B.A.

ABBEY SOWATZKE, B.S.

Institutional Psychotherapy (IP) is a humanistic group psychotherapy used in residential settings (Doan et al., 2017). It came about in the 1950's in Saint-Alban, France as an experimental therapeutic model run out of private psychiatric clinics, and was developed as an alternative to treatment based out of asylums (Robcis & Joice, 2017). The founders of this theory identified that people in need of psychiatric help faced alienation based not only on their mental illness, but also alienation inherent to the social structures of their communities (Doan et al., 2017). The asylum structure did little to alleviate this issue. Instead, they served to deprive clients of their sense of individuality, and treat them as if they were incapable of having any responsibilities (Lunov, 2019). Because of this, Institutional Psychotherapy is rooted in communitarian principles designed to address areas of isolation and deprivation, while also addressing mental health treatment at the institutional level. Care is provided to the entire community and not just the pathologized individuals living within it.

The intention of IP is to facilitate what is called a *therapeutic community*. The therapeutic community enables a greater degree of social connectedness, provides opportunities for patients to contribute to their community, and allows patients to feel as if they are in a home-like setting. This helps the patients feel they have a greater degree of freedom and comfort than they would in an asylum setting (Doan et al., 2017). This is where the theory deviates glaringly from the other treatment methods of its time, and even from many theories today: IP patients are given as much autonomy as possible. They are allowed to move about and leave as they wish, regulate their own time, take on jobs and roles in the community, and even participate in the greater organizational and leadership structures there through therapeutic clubs.

The clubs are a non-hierarchical, financially independent grouping of both patients and their caregivers, where they can mingle together and create change within the institution. They set up social and professional activities, publish a newsletter, host regular meetings, facilitate discussions of community concerns or requests, and provide other opportunities for patients to take on responsibilities. The ultimate purpose of the clubs and of IP in general is to put patients and caregivers on more equal footing, so that rather than patients feeling isolated, holed up, and stigmatized, they feel like capable and connected members of a community. It works to help clients experience the sense of belonging, responsibility, and importance that they were denied elsewhere.

CERTIFICATION AND TRAINING

With IP being born out of France, much of the training and resources related to IP are in French. When looking into how to become certified in IP, these authors found that there were one year training programs, mostly in France, at some institutions to allow people to become certified in IP. Unfortunately, when looking into these trainings, the authors could not find further information or found links that no longer worked. This feels appropriate as IP is more of a model for theoretical development and practice in psychiatric care over a modality that you gain certification in (Cano, 2006). IP presents itself as more of a psychiatric care reform movement over a practice or direction like other theoretical models. It is an essence or ideology of how to organize institutions to be the most supportive and therapeutic place possible (Lunov, 2019). For direct resources on training, visit this website and follow the links provided https://epg.pubpub.org/pub/03-institutional-therapy/release/1

SCOPE OF PRACTICE

While initially developed as a unique treatment for schizophrenia patients, IP is used to support clients facing a multitude of presenting issues. When designing a therapeutic community, IP practitioners intentionally mix clients from different pathologies and identities together, in order to further socialize these clients and destigmatize their experiences. However, because schizophrenia is usually considered a chronic condition, treatment in institutional psychotherapy is designed to be very time-intensive, which can be a deterrent for some clients as well as practitioners.

There is research establishing that institutional psychotherapy practices have a significant, positive impact on the patient's quality of life, social integration, and overall experience of their condition (Doan et al., 2017; Duprez, 2008). However, since little research on the theory is being conducted outside of France, information on the efficacy and scope of this theory is not widely accessible.

SUMMARY

In France during the 1950's, in the midst of asylums oppressing and abusing psychotic patients, and the anti-psychiatry movement pushing to abolish mental health institutions altogether, Institutional Psychotherapy began to develop a new way of approaching institution-based psychiatric care. Its founders examined the way existing mental institutions created an experience of alienation and they fought to overcome the harm widely accepted in asylums. At its core, IP is rooted in a profound respect for the client, and a belief that while psychotherapeutic treatment is necessary, promoting individuality and autonomy are equally important to the client's wellbeing.

As it stands, IP remains alive and well in France, and there is even information available on some training institutions in Greece and in Belgium, however many of those we found listed are no longer active today. Hopefully, both research and training in IP will become more widespread with time, allowing others throughout the world to learn and value the positive impacts that a collective, affirming, open institution has on a client's self-perception and wellness. In the meantime, for those who wish to seek out more information on the theory themselves, we would highly recommend researching how the theory came to be, the ideals and intentions behind its structures, and the perspective with which IP practitioners view their clients and their illnesses. Exploring and adopting the mindset of this theory could provide anyone within the helping professions, particularly those working in residential or inpatient care facilities, with a deepened understanding of and empathy for the clients they serve.

Hannah L. Button, B.A. is a student at Palo Alto University, pursuing their Masters in Clinical Mental Health Counseling with an emphasis in Marriage and Family Counseling. They completed their BA in communication, psychology, and a minor in sociocultural anthropology, which they use to develop an integrative perspective as a counselor. Hannah has over 15 years of experience working with nonprofits, fundraising for health care needs such as breast cancer research and treatment for children with HIV/AIDS, as well as environmental and social causes. They are currently working with seniors and at-risk youth, and have special interests in ADHD and autism, end-of-life care, and holistic or integrative therapeutic modalities. Recently, Hannah has been working as a research assistant, in admissions as a student interviewer, and assisting end-of-life doulas with clients pursuing medical aid in dying.

Abbey N. S. Sowatzke, B.S. is a student at Palo Alto University, working towards a Masters in Clinical Mental Health Counseling with an emphasis in Marriage and Family Counseling. She completed a BS in Psychology with an emphasis in Pre-Occupational Therapy. Abbey has previous experience working with a myriad of different populations in inpatient, residential, and outpatient treatment settings. Most recently, Abbey has worked as a group leader helping adolescents at high risk for suicide and self-harm learn coping skills through an integrative therapeutic approach focusing on DBT skills. She is currently working to provide counseling to underserved and at-risk clients aged 0-26 in a community mental health clinic. Abbey also works as a teaching assistant and research assistant with Palo Alto University. She hopes to integrate mind/body, play, and systemic therapy models into her future counseling work.

REFERENCES

Cano, N. (2006). Fondements éthiques de la psychothérapie institutionnelle. *L'Encéphale, 32*(2), 205–212. https://doi.org/10.1016/s0013-7006(06)76146-2

Doan, K., de Freitas, D., & Gargot, T. (2017). Institutional Psychotherapy. In EFPT Psychotherapy Guidebook (2nd ed.). https://doi.org/10.21428/fc0b32aa.19d22c72

Duprez, M. (2008). Réhabilitation psychosociale et psychothérapie institutionnelle. *L'information Psychiatrique, Volume 84*(10), 907–912. https://doi.org/10.1684/ipe.2008.0409

Lunov, V. (2019). *Institutional Psychotherapy in Terms of Maintaining the Subjectivity of an Individual.* https://doi.org/https://ssrn.com/abstract=3361332

Robcis, C., & Joice, K. (2017). Institutional Psychotherapy in France: An Interview with Camille Robcis. Retrieved from http://www7.bbk.ac.uk/hiddenpersuaders/blog/robcis-interview/.

Integral Breathe Therapy

BILL OWENBY, EdD, MC, FAAETS, DAAETS, DCMHS, LPC, LAAC, NCC, CCMHC, ACS, DIPLOMATE, FELLOW

Integral Breathe Therapy is a holistic therapeutic approach that utilizes conscious breathing techniques to address emotional, physical, and psychological imbalances. By accessing and altering breathing patterns, this modality aims to release stored trauma, promote relaxation, and enhance overall well-being. Rooted in practices such as breathwork, somatic psychology, and mindfulness, Integral Breathe Therapy integrates body, mind, and spirit for a transformative healing experience.

Key principles of Integral Breathe Therapy include:

- **Breath Awareness:** Focusing on the breath as a tool for accessing unconscious emotions and patterns.
- **Trauma Release:** Facilitating the release of stored emotional and physical trauma through deep, rhythmic breathing.
- **Holistic Integration:** Addressing the interconnectedness of emotional, mental, and physical health to promote balance and resilience.

This therapy is particularly effective for individuals dealing with anxiety, depression, trauma, and chronic stress, as well as those seeking spiritual growth and self-discovery.

CERTIFICATIONS, TRAININGS, AND LICENSURE REQUIREMENTS

Practitioners interested in Integral Breathe Therapy can undergo training through specialized programs. Key details include:

- **Education:** Programs often welcome individuals with backgrounds in counseling, coaching, or bodywork, though prior experience in breathwork is not always required.
- **Certification:** Certification programs are available through organizations such as the Integral Breath Therapy Institute.
- **Prerequisites:** Many programs require foundational knowledge of somatic or therapeutic practices.
- **Continuing Education:** Advanced workshops and retreats are encouraged for skill enhancement and staying updated on research.

TRAINING PROGRAMS

In-Person Programs

1. **Integral Breath Therapy Institute (USA):**
   o Offers in-depth training programs blending theoretical learning with experiential practice.
   o Includes supervised clinical work and personal breathwork sessions.
   o Website: Integral Breath Therapy Institute
2. **Transformational Breath Foundation (Global):**
   o Provides international training in breathwork techniques, including certifications for therapeutic practice.
   o Website: Transformational Breath

Online Programs

1. **Breathwork Alliance Online:**
   o Offers virtual courses on therapeutic breathwork techniques and integration.
   o Website: Breathwork Alliance
2. **Conscious Breathing Academy:**
   o Provides self-paced and live online training in breath-focused therapeutic practices.
   o Website: Conscious Breathing Academy

General Cost

The financial investment for training and practicing Integral Breathe Therapy includes:

- **Training Fees:** $2,000–8,000 for comprehensive certification programs.
- **Workshops and Retreats:** $500–3,000 for advanced training and personal development.
- **Practice Integration:** Minimal costs, typically requiring only a quiet space and basic equipment such as mats or cushions.

IDENTIFIED AS EMERGING PRACTICE

Integral Breathe Therapy is recognized as an emerging practice, with growing anecdotal and clinical evidence supporting its efficacy. Research into breathwork and somatic therapies aligns closely with its principles, providing a foundation for its integration into mental health and wellness fields.

Certification Available/Required/Recommended

Certification is recommended for practitioners integrating Integral Breathe Therapy into their practice. Notable certifications include:

1. **Certified Integral Breath Therapist (IBT):** Offered by the Integral Breath Therapy Institute.
2. **Transformational Breath Facilitator:** Focused on advanced breathwork techniques and applications.

Degree Requirements

While a formal degree is not required, professionals with backgrounds in counseling, psychotherapy, or bodywork may find this modality particularly complementary to their existing skill set.

CAUTIONS OR LIMITATIONS

While Integral Breathe Therapy is generally safe and effective, considerations include:

- **Physical Health:** Certain breathing techniques may not be suitable for individuals with specific health conditions, such as cardiovascular issues.
- **Emotional Intensity:** The release of stored trauma can be emotionally overwhelming for some clients, requiring careful facilitation and follow-up.
- **Practitioner Expertise:** Effective application requires thorough training and sensitivity to client needs.

SCOPE OF PRACTICE ISSUES

Practitioners must ensure that Integral Breathe Therapy is applied within their licensure and training scope. Collaboration with healthcare providers may be necessary for clients with complex medical or psychological conditions.

WHAT KIND OF PERSON WOULD DO WELL IN THIS MODEL?

Integral Breathe Therapy is ideal for:

- Practitioners interested in holistic and somatic approaches to healing.
- Clients seeking to address trauma, stress, or emotional imbalances through body-centered practices.
- Individuals exploring personal growth and self-awareness through mindfulness and breathwork.

SUMMARY

Integral Breathe Therapy offers a powerful and transformative approach to healing by harnessing the breath as a tool for emotional release and holistic integration. By addressing the mind-body connection, this therapy empowers clients to navigate their inner worlds with greater clarity and resilience. As interest in somatic and breath-centered modalities continues to grow, Integral Breathe Therapy provides a valuable framework for promoting health and well-being.

I hold two independent licenses in the states of Arizona and Ohio, supervisory status in Arizona, along with a substance abuse license in Arizona. I am board certified as a Diplomate and Clinical Mental Health Specialist, an Approved Clinical Supervisor, Nationally Certified Counselor, a Certified Clinical Mental Health Counselor, NeuroLinguistic Programming Practitioner, and a Clinical Trauma Specialist for Individuals and Family including EMDR Therapy and NET. I completed my training in Animal-Assisted Therapy and Pet Handlers certification in order to evaluate and incorporate the human-animal bond in therapy. I am the sole author and creator of the SxC Model of ESA Evaluation. My research interests surround post-traumatic growth, resiliency, strengths-based therapy, positive psychology, mindfulness, Animal-Assisted Therapy, Sandtray Therapy, Creative approaches in therapy, and martial arts in mental health. I have presented at local, state, regional, national, and international levels on various topics including personality traits, licensure reciprocity challenges, Sandtray and supervision, and Animal-Assisted Therapy within supervision. eonbllc@gmail.com

REFERENCES

Hendricks, G. (1995). Conscious Breathing: Breathwork for Health, Stress Release, and Personal Mastery. Bantam Books.

Rosenberg, J. L. (1990). Body, Self, and Soul: Sustaining Integration. Humanics Publishing Group.

Recommended Online Resources

Integral Breath Therapy Institute
Transformational Breath Foundation
Breathwork Alliance

Integrated Behavioral Health in Primary Care

VAIBHAVEE R. AGASKAR, PHD, LPC

Over the last few decades, there is a shift in the healthcare delivery system in the United States due to a variety of reasons, such as the passage of the Patient Protection and Affordable Care Act, push for the patient-centered medical homes, and the Triple Aim approach in healthcare. All these factors have started an innovative approach to healthcare delivery: integrated behavioral health services at primary care settings (Hunter et al., 2017). In this chapter, we will use the umbrella term 'behavioral health' which includes mental health, emotional health, substance use, life stressors and crises, and stress-related physical symptoms and health behavior (Agency for Healthcare Research and Quality, nd). First, I will elaborate on the integrated behavioral healthcare model and then I will distinguish between traditional specialty mental health and the integrated behavioral healthcare model to understand the nuances in the health delivery system. Lastly, I will shed light on the training and certificate programs in integrated behavioral health available for professional counselors.

INTEGRATED BEHAVIORAL HEALTH IN PRIMARY CARE SETTING

As per Robinson and Reiter (2007), up to 70% to 75% of primary care visits involve behavioral health elements which primary care physician needs to address in their office along with physical health concerns. Most physicians may not be able to manage behavioral health concerns in their offices due to patient volume, lack of time or resources, or training. Many patients do not have access to or lack medical coverage for behavioral health needs. Even if the referrals are made by physicians for the specialty mental health providers, many patients fail to make the appointment due to time constraints, lack of insurance for behavioral needs, stigma attached to seeking behavioral health care, or limited behavioral health providers in the patient's geographic area (Hunter et al., 2017). Thus, there is a movement toward multidisciplinary, comprehensive care for physical and behavioral health care in the primary care setting. It means primary care physicians and behavioral health providers will be available in primary care settings. Offering behavioral health services in the primary care setting will help reduce the stigma attached to mental illness and will also ensure that services can be offered in a very comfortable and familiar setting on the same day (Robinson & Reiter, 2007).

Integration of behavioral health services at primary care will facilitate accurate diagnosis, better treatment and dose management, shared resources, and trained professionals under one roof. All these integrated physical and behavioral health services need to be culturally sensitive; this cultural congruency in assessment, diagnosis, treatment, and prevention will help to close the gap in behavioral health disparities among ethnic minority clients (Hunter et al., 2017). There are many advantages to integrated care such as cost efficiency, outcomes, and patient and providers overall satisfaction of services (Sandoval et al., 2017). The mind/body connection has long been acknowledged and the role of mental well-being in physical illness outcomes and the importance of good physical health to mental health has also been proven (Shim & Rust, 2013). However, for many behavioral health providers (BHPs-psychologists, social workers, professional counselors, and family therapists), primary care providers (PCPs-family physicians, pediatrics, OBGYNs, etc.), and organizations, it is uncharted territory. Thus, the training and skills building of the providers and organizations will play a critical role in implementing integrated behavioral health at the primary care setting across the population. The goal of this chapter is to help the readers, especially future counselors, to give practical information about the integrated behavioral health at primary care approach.

Most of the time, collaborative care and integrated care are used interchangeably, however, collaborative care is not a specific model a concept that describes the accessibility and availability of behavioral services by using an interdisciplinary approach in the primary care setting (Hunter and Goodie, 2010). Models of collaborative care fall along a continuum of integration (Heath et al., 2013). At one end of this spectrum, collaboration occurs between PCPs and BHPs who work in separate facilities and deliver separate health care. This care model called coordinated care, involves minimal collaboration among providers who communicate as needed. When PCPs and BHPs interact more closely with each other and share the same location and resources, it is referred to as CO-LOCATED CARE. This model has been proven more effective in treating depression than standard primary care depression care (Katon, 2012). Some evidence-based models of co-located care are the Improving Mood-Promoting Access to Collaborative Treatment (IMPACT) model or the care management model (Katon et al., 2004 & Ell et al., 2010). Finally, INTEGRATED CARE exists on the other end of the continuum, where a prominent level of collaboration and communication occurs between PCPs and BHPs. In this model, the BHP is part of the PCP's team, collaborating as a consultant with the PCP to meet the population's needs. This model of integrated care, primary care behavioral health (PCBH), has been used widely by large healthcare systems such as Federally Qualified Health Centers, the Department of Defense, the Health Resources Services Administration (HRSA), and the Veterans Administration (Hunter et al., 2018). The PCBH model has also been successfully implemented in other settings such as university health centers and homeless Clinics (Reiter et al., 2018).

Integrated care is defined as "the care that results from a practice team of primary care and behavioral health clinicians working with patients and families, using a systematic and cost-effective approach to provide patient-centered care for a defined population. This care may address mental health and substance abuse conditions, health behaviors (including their contribution to chronic medical illnesses), life stressors and crises, stress-related physical symptoms, and ineffective patterns of health care utilization" (Peek & the National Integration Academy Council, 2013, p. 2). In a nutshell, integrated behavioral health at primary care is considered a 'one-stop shop' for physical and behavioral (mental health, emotional health, or substance use) needs.

ROLE OF BHPs IN THE PCBH MODEL

Most BHPs are trained in the traditional specialty mental health care model where usually the patient or client seeks services for anxiety, depression, or interpersonal issues for short-term duration (5 to 10 sessions) or long-term duration with one provider for 45-50 mins for individual psychotherapy. Traditionally, specialty mental health providers work in silos and hardly interact with primary care providers. In contrast, BHPs in the PCBH setting usually see a client for 15 to 30 mins compared to the traditional specialty mental health setting (Robinson & Reiter, 2007). Typically, primary care settings have a heavy caseload or many patients are sitting in the waiting room to be seen by the PCP, and thus 15 to 30 mins of meetings with BHPs and patients or consistent with the primary care workflow. Providers (PCPs or BHPs) are moving from one examination room to another other than patients moving from one setting to another. Usually, PCPs will do "warm hands-off" and introduce the role of BHPs in the treatment goals. BHP may use some universal screening such as depression or substance use inventory as a standard operating protocol integrated into their clinical pathways (Hunter et al., 2017). Then, BHPs will engage in the functional assessment to determine the treatment approach for the patient. BHPs and PCPs work together and exchange information on patients' progress or barriers to progress through the Electronic Medical Record system and in-person meetings like huddle room discussions (Hunter et al., 2017).

In PCBH setting will also have a care coordinator to support patients in their health journey. BHP may implement various evidence-based innervations appropriate to the primary care setting such as motivational interviewing, mindfulness excises, assertive communication, and behavioral self-analysis for the prevention and treatment of acute and chronic issues. BHPs may not have assigned caseloads and can see the patient multiple times till the patient has made considerable progress. BHPs can work with individuals, groups, couples, or families by offering evidence-based services for both the physical and behavioral needs of the patient (Getch & Lute, 2019). They might refer a patient for traditional specialty behavioral health services depending on the patient's diagnosis and need such as if the patient is not improving and need more intense care (Reiter et al., 2018). Providers in the PCBH, especially BHPs, need to be flexible and willing to work at a fast pace in the primary care setting. Robinson and Reiter (2016) came up with the acronym "GATHER" to accurately describe the role and responsibilities of the BHPs. In that acronym, "G" stands for a "Generalist approach"; "A" is "Accessibility"; "T" means "Team-based"; "H" is for "High productivity"; "E" emphasizes BHPs role as an "Educator"; and finally, "R" means "Routine". Please refer to Robinson and Reiter (2016) and Retier et al (2017) for a detailed description of the "GATHER". BHPs also need to be trained in population health management approaches (Hunter et al., 2018).

FUTURE OF INTEGRATED BEHAVIORAL HEALTH IN PRIMARY CARE SETTING

Organizations and providers may choose their collaborative care model and style of practice based on their population's needs and the resources available at each facility. The future of integrated health care also depends on financial sustainability, state and federal insurance or employed-purchased health care insurance, and reimbursement policies (National Council of Behavioral Health, 2013). The major challenges in implementing integrated health practice are workforce readiness, lack of reimbursement for the services, updated technology, and lack of uniformity in implementing integrated care. During the last few years, many community organizations all over the U.S. have received funding from SAMSHA (Substance Abuse and Mental Health Service Administration) and other private and state-level funding agencies to train the workforce and implement integrated behavioral health at the primary care setting (National Association of State Mental Health Program Directors [NASMHP], 2011.). Similarly, HRSA-BHWET (Health Resources and Services Administration-Behavioral Health Workforce Education and Training) has been given funding to universities to train the future workforce in integrated health care (NASMHP, 2011). Unfortunately, these funds were not available to members of the counseling profession. In 2013, the National Board of Certified Counselors (NBCC) advocacy work helped counseling programs become eligible for HRSA- BHWET grants that previously were restricted to social work and psychology programs. With the recent approval of the Mental Health Access Improvement Act, Mental Health Counselors will be eligible for Medicare Reimbursement along with psychologists and social workers (NBCC, 2023). This Medicare expansion will bring more opportunities for professional counselors in the integrated healthcare area, and it will also open some more training avenues for counselors. Thus, preparing the counseling workforce in integrated health care will be crucial in the coming few years.

CERTIFICATIONS, TRAINING, AND LICENSURE REQUIREMENTS FOR INTEGRATED BEHAVIORAL HEALTH IN PRIMARY CARE SETTING

Following is the list of where BHPs can get trained in Integrated Health Care at the Primary Care setting: Please note that author has not received any monetary or other benefits by compiling a list of training programs in Integrated behavioral health. There might be more certificate programs or training available in the integrated healthcare domain, but those programs are more geared towards psychologists or social workers or physicians and I have tried to compile a list of training programs for professional counselors. For all the following certificate programs, candidates need their masters in clinical mental health or a related field from an accredited university. Ideally, the candidate also needs a license or license eligibility in clinical mental health or related field.

- National Council for Mental Wellbeing's Centre of Excellence for Integrated Health Solutions, which is funded by the Substance Abuse and Mental Health Services Administration (SAMSHA) offers various training programs and resources on behavioral health integration. Most of the training programs and resources are free and available for professional counselors, however, these free training is not approved as Continuous Education Units (CEUs) by the NBCC: https://www.thenationalcouncil.org/program/center-of-excellence/

- The Center for Integrated Primary Care (CIPC), based at the University of Massachusetts Chan Medical School, offers various online or in-person courses, workshops, and webinars in Integrated Behavioral Health. CIPC also offers some free resources such as videos demonstrating motivational interviewing or warm handoffs. In addition, CIPC offers an online self-paced 22-module Certificate Course in Primary Care Behavioral Health four times each academic year. This course has been approved by the NBCC as an approved continuing education provider and counselors can earn up to 36 credits. Fees for this certificate course along with the continuous education are listed as $1600 on the website https://www.umassmed.edu/cipc/

- University of Washington's Advancing Integrated Mental Health Solutions (AIMS) Center offers online Collaborative Care training for Behavioral Health Case Managers at a very reasonable rate ($ 379 per individual user and a 20% discount as a group member). The course consists of nine hours of self-paced modules which the candidate must complete within three months of registration. AIMS is also offering CEUs for the various behavioral health providers including licensed mental health counselors, but NBCC is not listed as their approved provider https://aims.uw.edu/online-bhcm-modules

- Only a handful of universities or institutions have been offering a doctoral program in behavioral health. Arizona State University, Freed-Hardeman University, Grand Canyon University, and Walden University offer a doctorate program either in Behavioral Health with a Clinical concentration or a non-clinical (leadership) concentration where master's level clinicians can get trained in integrated care.

- https://www.gradschoolcenter.com/best-doctor-behavioral-health/

- Cummings Graduate Institute for Behavioral Health Studies offers a doctorate program in Behavioral Health and various certificate programs in Integrated Behavioral Healthcare.
- https://cgi.edu/academic-programs/
- Cherokee Health System, a Federally Qualified Health Center (FQHC), and Community Mental Health Center (CMHC) offer training in Integrated Care based on their leading best-practice program in the integration of behavioral health and primary care services.
- https://www.cherokeehealth.com/professional-training/integrated-care-training-academy

Some other universities and institutes such as Fairleigh Dickinson University, the University of Michigan's School of Social Work, and the University of Maryland's School of Medicine also offer training in Integrated Behavioral Health for social workers, psychologists, or physicians. The National Register of Health Service Psychologists (NRHSP) offers a web-based Integrated Healthcare training series (Corso, 2018). In 2012, the Council on Social Work Education (CSWE) and the National Association of Deans and Director of Schools of Social Work (NADDSSW) created a free curriculum and competencies for social work students in integrated healthcare settings (NADDSSW, nd). Then, American Psychology Association (2015) developed competencies for psychology practice in primary care. Recently, the American Mental Health Counselor Association (AMHCA, 2020) standards for Integrated Behavioral Health Counseling offered the most comprehensive and robust competencies for Clinical Mental Health Counselors.

Besides the above list, I will highly recommend the book Training to Deliver Integrated Care: Skills Aimed at the Future of Healthcare by Macchia and Kessler (2021). This book has two chapters devoted to Graduate Internship Training and overall workforce development, including continuing education for Integrated Behavioral Healthcare.

SUMMARY

Overall, there has been a movement towards integration of behavioral health in primary care in the last few years at the federal level as well as at some private healthcare delivery systems. Training the future behavioral health and primary care workforce to deliver integrated services will be important to achieve healthcare delivery goals. Hopefully, the future behavioral healthcare workforce, especially professional counselors will find this chapter useful to understand the basics of behavioral health integration at the primary care settings and resources for educational training and certification in this healthcare delivery model.

Dr. Vaibhavee Agaskar is an associate professor at New Jersey City University's Counselor Education Department. She enjoys teaching master's level course work such as research, assessments, and internship. She has served as the principal investigator and the director for a Behavioral Health Workforce Education and Training grants funded by the U.S. Health Resources and Services Administration to expand behavioral workforce in integrated health care at primary care settings. She also serves as a CACREP (Council for Accreditation of Counseling and Related Educational Programs) liaison and Team Site Member. She has published her research work on integrated health care training and outcome research. She has created an elective curriculum in integrated health care for graduate level counseling students. She has worked as a behavioral health therapist with children and adolescents at in- and out-patient facilities at the national and international levels for many years before entering the academic arena. She has been involved in outreach work and community engagement work along with her students. Currently, she is maintaining a small private practice. She lives in Jersey City with her two school-going boys and husband enjoys traveling and exploring novel places and food.

vagaskar@njcu.edu

REFERENCES

Agency for Healthcare Research and Quality. (n.d). Behavioral Health.
https://www.ahrq.gov/topics/behavioral-
health.html#:~:text=Behavioral%20health%20problems%2C%20which%20include,funding%20for
%20behavioral%20health%20research.

American Mental Health Counselor Association. (2020). *AMHCA standards for the practice of Clinical Mental Health Counseling*. https://www.amhca.org/events/publications/standards

American Psychological Association. (2015). *Education and training for psychology practice in primary care*. https://www.apa.org/ed/graduate/primary-care-psychology

Corso, K. A. (2018). Review of integrated healthcare training series. *Families, Systems & Health: The Journal of Collaborative Family Healthcare, 36*(4), 541–542. https://doi.org/10.1037/fsh0000383

Ell, K., Katon, W., Xie, B., Lee, P. J., Kapetanovic, S., Guterman, J., & Chou, C. P. (2010). Collaborative care management of major depression among low-income, predominantly Hispanic subjects with diabetes: A randomized controlled trial. *Diabetes Care, 33*(4), 706–713. http://www.ncbi.nlm.nih.gov/pubmed/20097780

Getch, S. E., & Lute, R. M. (2019). Advancing Integrated Healthcare: A Step by Step Guide for Primary Care Physicians and Behavioral Health Clinicians. *Missouri medicine, 116*(5), 384–388.

Heath, B., Wise, R. P., & Reynolds, K. (2013). A standard framework for levels of integrated healthcare. SAMHSA-HRSA Center for Integrated Health Solutions. https://www.pcpcc.org/sites/default/files/resources/SAMHSA-HRSA%202013%20Framework%20for%20Levels%20of%20Integrated%20Healthcare.pdf

Hunter, C.L., Dobmeyer, A.C. & Reiter, J.T. (2018). Integrating Behavioral Health Services into Primary Care: Spotlight on the Primary Care Behavioral Health (PCBH) Model of Service Delivery. *Journal of Clinical Psychology in Medical Settings,25*, 105–108. https://doi.org/10.1007/s10880-017-9534-7

Hunter, C. L., Funderburk, J. S., Polaha, J., Bauman, D., Goodie, J. L., & Hunter, C. M. (2017). Primary care behavioral health (PCBH) model research: Current state of Science and a call to action. *Journal of Clinical Psychology in Medical Settings, 25*, 127-156. https://doi.org/10.1007/s10880-017-9512-0.

Hunter, C. L., & Goodie, J. L. (2010). Operational and clinical components for integrated-collaborative behavioral healthcare in the patient-centered medical home. *Families, Systems, & Health, 28*, 308–321. doi:10.1037/a0021761

Hunter, C. L., Goodie, J. L., Oordt, M., & Dobmeyer, A. C. (2017). *Integrated behavioral health in primary care: Step-by-step guidance for assessment and intervention* (2nd ed.). Washington, DC: American Psychological Association.

Katon, W. J., Von Korff, M., Lin, E. H. B., Simon, G., Ludman, E., Russo, J., … Bush, T. (2004).

The Pathways Study: A randomized trial of collaborative care in patients with diabetes and depression. Archives of General Psychiatry, 61(10), 1042–1049. http://www.ncbi.nlm.nih.gov/pubmed/15466678

Macchi, C.R & Kessler, R. (Eds) (2021).Training to Deliver Integrated care: Skills Aimed at the Future of Healthcare. Springer. Switzerland.

National Association of State Mental Health Program Directors. (2011). *NASMHPD policy brief: Workforce and the public mental health system.* Retrieved from:
https://www.nasmhpd.org/sites/default/files/Workforce%20_Policy_Brief.pdf

National Board of Certified Counselors (2013). *NBCC government affairs update.* Retrieved from:
https://www.nbcc.org/Assets/Newsletter/Issues/Fall2013.pdf

National Board of Certified Counselors (2023). Medicare. https://nbcc.org/govtaffairs/medicare

National Council for Behavioral Health. (2013). *Integrating Behavioral and Primary Care for Children and Youth.*
https://www.integration.samhsa.gov/integrated-care
models/Integrated_Care_System_for_Children_final.pdf

National Association of Deans and Directors of Social Work. (n.d.). *Advanced social work practice behaviors to address behavioral health disparities.* Retrieved from http://www.cswe.org/getattachment/Centers-Initiatives/InstitutionalResearch/Social-Work-and-Integrated-Behavioral-Healthcare-P/Learning-Network-Resources/NADDBehavioralHealthDisparities-(1).pdf.aspx

Peek, C.J & the National Integration Academy Council. (2013). *Lexicon for behavioral health and primary care integration: Concepts and definitions developed by expert consensus, 13-IP001-EF.* Agency for Healthcare Research and Quality Publication. Rockville, MD. Retrieved from
http://integrationacademy.ahrq.gov/sites/default/files/Lexicon.pdf.

Reiter, J. T., Dobmeyer, A. C., & Hunter, C. L. (2018). The Primary Care Behavioral Health (PCBH) Model: An Overview and Operational Definition. *Journal of Clinical Psychology in Medical Settings, 25*(2), 109-126.
https://doi.org/10.1007/s10880-017-9531-x

Robinson, P. J., & Reiter, J. T. (2007). *Behavioral consultation and primary care: A guide to integrating services.* US: Springer Science; Business Media. http://dx.doi.org/10.1007/978-0-387-32973-4

Robinson, P. J., & Reiter, J. T. (2016). Behavioral consultation and primary care: A guide to integrating services (2nd ed.). Geneva: Springer.

Sandoval, B. E., Bell, J., Khatri, P., & Robinson, P. J. (2018). Toward a Unified Integration Approach: Uniting Diverse Primary Care Strategies Under the Primary Care Behavioral Health (PCBH) Model. *Journal of Clinical Psychology in Medical Settings, 25*(2), 187-196. https://doi.org/10.1007/s10880-017-9516-9

Shim, R., & Rust, G. (2013). Primary care, behavioral health, and public health: partners in reducing mental health stigma. *American journal of public health, 103*(5), 774–776.
https://doi.org/10.2105/AJPH.2013.301214

Integrated Energy Therapy (IET)

BILL OWENBY, EdD, MC, FAAETS, DAAETS, DCMHS, LPC, LAAC, NCC, CCMHC, ACS, DIPLOMATE, FELLOW

Integrated Energy Therapy (IET) is a healing modality that combines spiritual principles, energy work, and therapeutic techniques to clear energy blockages and promote emotional, physical, and spiritual well-being. Developed by Stevan J. Thayer, IET focuses on identifying and releasing suppressed emotions stored in the body, fostering harmony and self-empowerment.

OVERVIEW OF INTEGRATED ENERGY THERAPY

IET operates on the premise that unresolved emotional experiences can manifest as energy blockages within the body. By addressing these blockages, practitioners help individuals experience emotional release, self-awareness, and renewed vitality.

CORE PRINCIPLES OF IET

1. **Energy Anatomy**
   o Recognizes nine energy centers in the body where suppressed emotions are stored.
   o Uses a gentle, hands-on technique to clear blockages and restore energy flow.
2. **Empowerment**
   o Encourages individuals to reconnect with their authentic selves.
   o Emphasizes the client's role in their own healing journey.
3. **Angelic Support**
   o Integrates the belief in angelic energies that assist in the healing process.
   o Utilizes angelic guidance to promote peace and emotional clarity.

APPLICATIONS OF IET

Emotional Healing

- Clears suppressed feelings like guilt, fear, and resentment.
- Promotes emotional balance and self-compassion.

Stress and Anxiety Management

- Calms the nervous system and reduces emotional distress.
- Helps individuals feel grounded and centered.

Spiritual Growth

- Enhances connection to higher consciousness and spiritual guidance.
- Supports individuals on their spiritual journeys.

Physical Wellness

- Addresses the energetic roots of physical symptoms.
- Enhances overall vitality by clearing energetic stagnation.

Techniques in IET

1. **Energy Blockage Clearing**
   - Practitioners use a hands-on approach to identify and release energy blockages.
   - Focuses on specific areas of the body associated with emotional storage.
2. **Empowerment Imprints**
   - After clearing blockages, practitioners use positive affirmations to imprint empowering energy patterns.
   - Reinforces self-worth, courage, and love.
3. **Angel Card Readings**
   - Provides additional insight and guidance from angelic energies.
   - Complements the healing process by offering personalized messages.
4. **Integration Exercises**
   - Includes mindfulness, visualization, and journaling techniques.
   - Helps clients process and integrate the healing experience.

TRAINING AND CERTIFICATION IN IET

Educational Pathways

1. **Basic Level Training**
   - Introduction to IET principles and techniques.
   - Typically involves a one-day workshop.
2. **Intermediate Level Training**
   - Focuses on clearing deeper energy blockages.
   - Includes additional techniques for empowerment and self-healing.
3. **Advanced Level Training**
   - Teaches spiritual alignment and advanced energy techniques.
   - Covers professional application for certified practitioners.

Certification

1. **Requirements**
   - Completion of Basic, Intermediate, and Advanced training levels.
   - Submission of documented practice sessions.
   - Adherence to ethical guidelines set by the Center of Being, Inc.
2. **Time Commitment and Cost**
   - Basic training: 1 day, $200–$300.
   - Intermediate training: 1 day, $250–$350.
   - Advanced training: 1–2 days, $300–$500.
   - Full certification typically requires 3–6 months.
3. **Accrediting Organization**
   - The Center of Being, Inc., founded by Stevan J. Thayer, offers official IET training and certification programs.

BENEFITS AND LIMITATIONS

Benefits

- **Holistic Healing:** Addresses emotional, spiritual, and physical aspects of well-being.
- **Accessible Techniques:** Easy-to-learn methods suitable for practitioners and individuals.
- **Empowerment Focus:** Encourages clients to take an active role in their healing.

Limitations

- **Scientific Validation:** Limited empirical research on the efficacy of IET.
- **Spiritual Framework:** May not align with all clients' belief systems.
- **Scope of Practice:** Practitioners must clearly define IET as complementary rather than a substitute for medical or psychological treatment.

ETHICAL CONSIDERATIONS

1. **Informed Consent**
   - Clients should be informed about the spiritual components of IET.
   - Practitioners must ensure that clients understand the scope and limitations of IET.
2. **Cultural Sensitivity**
   - Techniques should respect clients' cultural and spiritual beliefs.
3. **Professional Boundaries**
   - Practitioners must clearly distinguish IET from clinical psychotherapy or medical treatment.

SUMMARY

Integrated Energy Therapy is a powerful modality that blends energy healing, spirituality, and therapeutic principles to support holistic well-being. With its focus on clearing emotional blockages and fostering empowerment, IET provides a pathway to greater self-awareness and emotional resilience. For practitioners and individuals seeking a transformative healing experience, IET offers accessible and effective tools for personal growth and renewal.

I hold two independent licenses in the states of Arizona and Ohio, supervisory status in Arizona, along with a substance abuse license in Arizona. I am board certified as a Diplomate and Clinical Mental Health Specialist, an Approved Clinical Supervisor, Nationally Certified Counselor, a Certified Clinical Mental Health Counselor, NeuroLinguistic Programming Practitioner, and a Clinical Trauma Specialist for Individuals and Family including EMDR Therapy and NET. I completed my training in Animal-Assisted Therapy and Pet Handlers certification in order to evaluate and incorporate the human-animal bond in therapy. I am the sole author and creator of the SxC Model of ESA Evaluation. My research interests surround post-traumatic growth, resiliency, strengths-based therapy, positive psychology, mindfulness, Animal-Assisted Therapy, Sandtray Therapy, Creative approaches in therapy, and martial arts in mental health. I have presented at local, state, regional, national, and international levels on various topics including personality traits, licensure reciprocity challenges, Sandtray and supervision, and Animal-Assisted Therapy within supervision. eonbllc@gmail.com

REFERENCES

Thayer, S. J. (1999). *The Healing Angels of the Energy Field.* Center of Being, Inc.

Eden, D. (2008). *Energy Medicine: Balancing Your Body's Energies for Optimal Health, Joy, and Vitality.* TarcherPerigee.

The Center of Being, Inc. (2024). Official Integrated Energy Therapy training guidelines. Retrieved from https://www.learniet.com

Recommended Resources

The Center of Being, Inc.: https://www.learniet.com
Energy Medicine Association: https://www.energymedicineassociation.com
International Association of Reiki Professionals: https://iarp.org

Integrative Cognitive-Affective Therapy (ICAT)

BILL OWENBY, EdD, MC, FAAETS, DAAETS, DCMHS, LPC, LAAC, NCC, CCMHC, ACS, DIPLOMATE, FELLOW

Integrative Cognitive-Affective Therapy (ICAT) is an innovative, evidence-based therapeutic approach that combines cognitive and emotional processes to address psychological challenges. Initially developed to treat eating disorders, ICAT has demonstrated versatility in addressing a broad range of mental health issues by fostering emotional awareness, improving cognitive flexibility, and enhancing self-regulation.

CORE PRINCIPLES OF ICAT

Cognitive-Affective Integration

- Recognizes the interplay between thoughts and emotions in shaping behavior.
- Promotes the identification and modification of maladaptive thought-emotion patterns.

Focus on Emotional Awareness

- Emphasizes understanding, accepting, and processing emotions as a pathway to change.
- Aims to reduce emotional avoidance and develop adaptive coping strategies.

Behavioral Activation and Problem Solving

- Encourages clients to engage in meaningful activities that align with their values.
- Teaches practical problem-solving skills to address life challenges.

Client-Centered Flexibility

- Adapts therapeutic strategies to meet the unique needs and goals of each individual.

APPLICATIONS OF ICAT

Eating Disorders

- Originally developed to treat conditions like bulimia nervosa and binge eating disorder.
- Targets cognitive distortions about body image, emotional triggers for eating, and dysfunctional eating behaviors.

Mood Disorders

- Addresses emotional dysregulation and negative thought patterns in depression and anxiety.

- Supports clients in building resilience and emotional stability.

Trauma and PTSD

- Helps clients process trauma-related emotions while reframing maladaptive cognitive beliefs.
- Provides tools for managing intrusive thoughts and emotional flashbacks.

General Mental Health

- Enhances emotional intelligence and self-awareness in clients across diverse populations.

Key Techniques in ICAT

Emotional Awareness Training

- Guides clients in identifying, naming, and validating their emotions.
- Uses mindfulness and reflective exercises to foster emotional connection.

Cognitive Restructuring

- Challenges and modifies unhelpful thought patterns that perpetuate emotional distress.
- Encourages the development of balanced, realistic perspectives.

Behavioral Activation

- Encourages clients to engage in activities that provide a sense of purpose and satisfaction.
- Focuses on breaking cycles of avoidance and inactivity.

Relapse Prevention Planning

- Teaches clients to identify potential triggers and develop strategies to maintain progress.
- Promotes long-term recovery through self-monitoring and adaptive problem-solving.

TRAINING AND CERTIFICATION IN ICAT

Educational Requirements

- Typically requires a background in psychology, counseling, or social work.
- A master's or doctoral degree in a mental health-related field is often preferred.

Training Programs

- Offered through specialized workshops, online courses, and accredited institutions.
- Training includes didactic instruction, case studies, and supervised practice.

Certification Process

1. **Introductory Training**
   - Covers ICAT principles, applications, and foundational techniques.
   - Costs range from $500 to $1,500 for a 2–3-day workshop.
2. **Advanced Training**

- Includes in-depth exploration of ICAT for specific disorders, such as eating disorders or trauma.
- Typically involves several months of study and practice, costing $2,000 to $5,000.
3. **Supervised Practice**
   - Practitioners complete a set number of supervised ICAT sessions to demonstrate competency.
4. **Continuing Education**
   - Ongoing professional development ensures practitioners stay updated on research and best practices.

Recommended Training Providers

- **Academy for Eating Disorders (AED)**
- **International Society for Emotion-Focused Therapy (ISEFT)**

BENEFITS OF ICAT

For Clients

- **Improved Emotional Regulation**: Empowers clients to manage emotions constructively.
- **Cognitive Flexibility**: Reduces rigid, negative thought patterns.
- **Enhanced Resilience**: Builds coping strategies for long-term mental health.

For Therapists

- **Holistic Framework**: Integrates cognitive and emotional strategies for a comprehensive approach.
- **Versatile Application**: Suitable for diverse client populations and presenting issues.
- **Professional Growth**: Expands therapeutic skillsets through advanced training and techniques.

For Communities

- **Better Outcomes**: Promotes recovery and resilience, reducing the burden on healthcare systems.
- **Increased Awareness**: Encourages understanding of the link between cognition, emotion, and behavior.

ETHICAL AND PRACTICAL CONSIDERATIONS

Cultural Sensitivity

- Tailors interventions to align with clients' cultural values and emotional expressions.

Client Readiness

- Assesses clients' willingness to engage with emotional exploration and cognitive restructuring.

Informed Consent

- Ensures clients understand the purpose and methods of ICAT, including potential emotional challenges.

Professional Boundaries

- Maintains clear boundaries to ensure therapeutic integrity and effectiveness.

CHALLENGES IN IMPLEMENTING ICAT

Emotional Resistance

- Clients may initially resist exploring difficult emotions, requiring patience and support.

Resource Limitations

- Access to ICAT-trained professionals may be limited in some areas.

Training Barriers

- Certification programs may be costly or geographically inaccessible for some practitioners.

SUMMARY

Integrative Cognitive-Affective Therapy (ICAT) represents a powerful approach to addressing the interplay between thoughts and emotions in mental health treatment. By fostering emotional awareness, cognitive flexibility, and behavioral activation, ICAT equips clients with tools for lasting change and resilience. For therapists, mastering ICAT provides a versatile framework for addressing diverse client needs and enhancing therapeutic outcomes.

I hold two independent licenses in the states of Arizona and Ohio, supervisory status in Arizona, along with a substance abuse license in Arizona. I am board certified as a Diplomate and Clinical Mental Health Specialist, an Approved Clinical Supervisor, Nationally Certified Counselor, a Certified Clinical Mental Health Counselor, NeuroLinguistic Programming Practitioner, and a Clinical Trauma Specialist for Individuals and Family including EMDR Therapy and NET. I completed my training in Animal-Assisted Therapy and Pet Handlers certification in order to evaluate and incorporate the human-animal bond in therapy. I am the sole author and creator of the SxC Model of ESA Evaluation. My research interests surround post-traumatic growth, resiliency, strengths-based therapy, positive psychology, mindfulness, Animal-Assisted Therapy, Sandtray Therapy, Creative approaches in therapy, and martial arts in mental health. I have presented at local, state, regional, national, and international levels on various topics including personality traits, licensure reciprocity challenges, Sandtray and supervision, and Animal-Assisted Therapy within supervision. eonbllc@gmail.com

REFERENCES

Wonderlich, S. A., et al. (2014). "Integrative Cognitive-Affective Therapy: A New Approach for Eating Disorders." *Clinical Psychology Review.*

Fairburn, C. G. (2008). *Cognitive Behavior Therapy and Eating Disorders.* Guilford Press.

Linehan, M. M. (2015). *DBT Skills Training Manual.* Guilford Press.

Recommended Resources

- **Academy for Eating Disorders (AED):** www.aedweb.org
- **International Society for Emotion-Focused Therapy (ISEFT):** www.iseft.org
- **ICAT Practitioner Training Programs:** Search online for accredited workshops and courses.

Integrative Medicine and Nutrition Certification

The Brainbow Blueprint® Methodology

DR. LESLIE KORN, PHD, MPH, LMHC, FNTP

CREATOR OF BRAINBOW BLUEPRINT

Mainstream modern health care is segmented and fragmentary, focusing on individual diseases rather than the whole person. Dr. Leslie Korn developed the methodology known as the Brainbow Blueprint® over 45 years of research and practice in integrative mental health care, to bridge the gaps in the field and provide a flexible roadmap to not only symptom resolution but the deeper integration that mental health clients seek.

The Brainbow Blueprint combines the fields of psychotherapy, somatics, nutrition, biology, herbal medicine, and spirituality to address the needs of the whole person. Dr. Korn pioneered its use and applies it successfully in her own private practice to treat complex trauma, PTSD, depression, anxiety, addiction, chronic pain, OCD, ADHD, insomnia, and autoimmune and digestive disorders.

As one of the developers of integrative mental health care, Dr. Korn also trains other clinicians in incorporating the Brainbow Blueprint into their existing practice to provide more personalized and effective solutions for clients. Her website (www.drlesliekorn.com) lists all her current course, certification, and supervision offerings; summaries of her books and various other publications; and a blog and glossary of terms in integrative medicine and nutrition.

CERTIFICATIONS, TRAININGS, AND LICENSURE REQUIREMENTS FOR THE BRAINBOW BLUEPRINT®

The Brainbow Blueprint developed by Dr. Korn is interdisciplinary and holistic by design, and those interested in studying it comes from a wide range of professional backgrounds. The certification trainings Dr. Korn teaches have been designed for helping professionals in the broadest sense, including: counselors, psychologists, case managers, psychotherapists, social workers, marriage & family therapists, addiction counselors, psychiatrists, physicians' assistants, occupational therapists, occupational therapists' assistants, nurses, massage therapists, nurses, nurse practitioners, physical therapists, nutritionists and registered dietitians, program administrators, and other professionals.

Many of Dr. Korn's courses are also accessible to non-professionals with interest in their own health and well-being.

The three certifications Dr. Korn offers as of 2023 are described below. A range of short, introductory, and lower-cost courses are also available at drlesliekorn.com.

PTSD, Complex Trauma, and Traumatic Brain Injury

The general cost of this 30-hour CE and certification training is $1279, with discounts offered throughout the year.

This certification training provides participants an integrative approach to the mind-body treatment of PTSD and complex trauma. It examines biology down to the level of the cell, as well as considerations of cultural, ethnic, and genomic dimensions unique to each client, enabling participants to tailor their interventions precisely client by client.

The 30-hour training also features an invitation to join Dr. Korn's Live Advanced Applications program (coaching and case consultation), an exclusive listing in her referral network, numerous practical videos and handouts to use with your clients, nutritional recipes for your clients, clear assessment demonstrations, and multiple case reviews.

Those who complete the program successfully can earn 30 CE Credits in Mental Health, Nursing, or Nutrition, and qualify to immediately become Certified in Integrative Medicine and Nutrition for Trauma Treatment (CIMNTT) through the Leslie Korn Institute for Integrative Medicine.

With 107 learning objectives addressed throughout the course, this certification training is arguably the most comprehensive, integrative trauma recovery program available today.

Mental Health Integrative Medicine Provider Certification

The general cost of this certification training is $749, with discounts offered throughout the year.

This 20-hour training is designed to breathe new life into providers' clinical treatment plans for clients looking for holistic approaches to health and healing. Because this certification course is interactive online, participants in the training can interact with a community of peers and mentors who are equally focused on helping clients succeed.

The 26 learning objectives in the training include: evidence-based protocols for nutritional and herbal approaches for seven DSM-5™ categories, the assessment of drug-nutrient-herb interactions, a simple psycho-educational method to assess food and mood interactions, and methods for analyzing the differences between mental illness versus nutritional and hormonal imbalances.

Upon successful completion of the training, participants can earn 20-24 CE credits in Mental Health, Nursing, or Nutrition, and they also qualify to immediately become a Certified Mental Health Integrative Medicine Provider (CMHIMP) through the Leslie Korn Institute for Integrative Medicine.

Diabetes Type 2, Cognitive Decline, and Alzheimer's Certification

The general cost of this certification training is $999, with discounts offered throughout the year.

This 30-hour training provides state-of-the-art methods to prevent type 2 diabetes and Alzheimer's and to treat the whole person, with evidenced-based methods that are designed to integrate seamlessly and safely into the provider's existing practice. The course delves deeply into the biology and psychology of both diseases, as well as the role of circadian rhythms and hormones, digestion and diet, culinary, spice, and herbal medicine, assessment and evaluation, ethics and scope of practice, and other topics.

Upon completion of this training, participants qualify to immediately become an Integrative Medicine and Nutrition for Diabetes and Alzheimer's Provider (IMNDAC) through the Leslie Korn Institute for Integrative Medicine.

Participants can also earn 25 CE credits in Mental Health, Nursing, or Nutrition through the completion of this certification.

Degree Requirements

Anyone may take the certifications; however, professional practice of nutrition is limited depending upon the state in which one practices. States define the scope of practice of nutritional therapies. Most states allow total or some limited inclusion of nutrition into clinical practice. For example, herbal medicine can be practiced by anyone in the United States. Each course contains a module on ethics and scope, including the roles of psychoeducation and collaboration with other professionals. Over 35,000 mental and physical health professionals have attended at least one certification.

Advanced Study

Following completion of one certification, licensed clinicians may attend live, advanced case consultation CE groups with Dr. Korn.

Ongoing study is required or recommended to maintain certification credentials; one must obtain 12 hours of study in a related field every 2 years.

Certification Fee: The first year certification is free. Following the first year, a fee of $49.00 is assessed every 2 years.

SUMMARY

Any clinician interested in holistic or integrative methods, either as a primary lens or to complement their existing practice model, will benefit from these trainings. Clients today are experimenting with self-care, reading Dr. Google, and taking advice from friends and family which may or may not be helpful for them specifically. These trainings explore the bioindividual needs of clients that can be integrated seamlessly into any practice model with an emphasis on developing the "self-care muscle." In addition, clinicians often use the knowledge gained in these trainings for their own self-care and burn-out prevention, in order to thrive and stay healthy in their clinical practice.

Dr. Leslie Korn began her training in the jungle of Mexico more than 45 years ago and completed her training in the jungle of Harvard Medical School. She is an Integrative Medicine clinician, scientist, educator, and author of 10 books who specializes in the intersection of trauma, cognition, and chronic physical illness. Dr. Korn is a licensed psychotherapist, certified in Functional Nutrition, board-certified in both Polarity therapy and Bodywork and Massage therapy, and is a national board-approved clinical supervisor. In her private practice, she works with clients to improve mental health and reduce or eliminate medications using natural medicines. She also mentors clinicians who want to enter the field and provides supervision for clinicians. She has been in clinical practice for more than 40 years and as a public health activist works in the fields of health disparities and food insecurity. She is Research Director at the Center for World Indigenous Studies.

www.DrLeslieKorn.com

drleslie@protonmail.com

REFERENCES

Korn, L. (2013, 2023). Rhythms of Recovery: Integrative medicine for PTSD and Complex Trauma. Routledge, NY.

Korn, L. (2023) The BrainBow Blueprint. PESI Publishing,WI

Korn, L. 2019 Natural Woman: herbal remedies for radiant health at every ages and stage of Life

Korn, L. (2016) Nutrition Essentials for Mental Health, Norton, NY.

Krystal, J. H., Davis, L. L., Neylan, T. C., A Raskind, M., Schnurr, P. P., Stein, M. B.,

Vessicchio, J., Shiner, B., Gleason, T. C., & Huang, G. D. (2017). It is time to address the crisis in the pharmacotherapy of posttraumatic stress disorder: A consensus statement of the PTSD psychopharmacology working group. Biological Psychiatry, 82(7), e51–e59. https://doi.org/10.1016/j.biopsych.2017.03.007

Integrative Milieu Therapy (IMT)

Bill Owenby, EdD, MC, FAAETS, DAAETS, DCMHS, LPC, LAAC, NCC, CCMHC, ACS, Diplomate, Fellow

Integrative Milieu Therapy (IMT) is a holistic, environment-based therapeutic approach that emphasizes the role of the therapeutic milieu—or structured environment—in supporting client healing and well-being. This model integrates components from psychotherapy, social work, and behavioral interventions while creating a safe and supportive environment that fosters personal growth. IMT is often applied in residential, inpatient, and school-based settings where clients can benefit from consistent, structured support. It has proven particularly effective for individuals dealing with trauma, severe emotional dysregulation, substance abuse, and complex behavioral challenges.

Milieu therapy, at its core, focuses on creating an atmosphere of trust, safety, and engagement. Integrative Milieu Therapy expands on this foundation by incorporating evidence-based therapies such as cognitive-behavioral therapy (CBT), group therapy, mindfulness, trauma-informed care, expressive therapies, and family systems interventions to meet the individual needs of clients. IMT emphasizes community dynamics and interpersonal relationships as critical components of healing, allowing clients to learn, practice, and generalize healthier behaviors and emotional regulation strategies in a real-world setting. These principles encourage clients to actively engage in their own healing process while contributing to the growth and development of the therapeutic community.

IMT is a client-centered, flexible model that can be adapted for use across diverse populations, including children, adolescents, adults, and families. The model's emphasis on structure, relationships, and evidence-based practices allows it to provide an immersive and transformative experience for individuals struggling to thrive in traditional outpatient therapy settings.

THEORETICAL UNDERPINNINGS

Integrative Milieu Therapy combines principles from several theoretical frameworks to create a comprehensive and client-centered approach:

1. **Systems Theory**: IMT operates on the idea that individuals are part of larger systems—including families, peer groups, and therapeutic communities—that influence behavior and emotional well-being. By improving these relational systems, clients experience broader, sustainable change.

2. **Behavioral Theory**: The structured environment of IMT provides consistent reinforcement for positive behaviors while addressing maladaptive patterns. Through behavior modification and positive reinforcement, clients learn healthier coping mechanisms and interpersonal skills.

3. **Trauma-Informed Care**: IMT recognizes the pervasive impact of trauma and focuses on creating a safe, predictable environment that supports emotional healing. The model emphasizes safety, choice, collaboration, trustworthiness, and empowerment.

4. **Humanistic and Psychodynamic Models**: IMT emphasizes empathy, self-awareness, and the exploration of past experiences as key components of personal growth. By fostering emotional exploration and self-reflection, IMT encourages clients to process unresolved issues.

5. **CBT and Skills-Based Interventions**: Cognitive and behavioral strategies are integrated into the therapeutic milieu to teach emotional regulation, coping skills, and interpersonal effectiveness. Skills-based interventions, such as DBT (Dialectical Behavior Therapy), mindfulness practices, and social skills training, are frequently utilized.

6. **Expressive Therapies**: IMT often incorporates art therapy, music therapy, and movement-based interventions to provide creative outlets for emotional expression, particularly for individuals who struggle with verbal communication.

By blending these frameworks, IMT offers a dynamic approach to addressing a range of psychological, emotional, and behavioral concerns, particularly for individuals requiring structured, long-term care.

CERTIFICATIONS, TRAININGS, AND LICENSURE REQUIREMENTS

While there is no universal certification specifically for Integrative Milieu Therapy, training and licensure requirements vary depending on the professional setting and role:

- **Licensed Mental Health Professionals**: Therapists (e.g., LCSWs, LPCs, LMFTs, and clinical psychologists) working in IMT settings must hold appropriate licensure to provide individual, group, and family therapy services.

- **Milieu Coordinators and Behavioral Specialists**: Professionals overseeing the therapeutic environment often complete specialized training in behavioral interventions, trauma-informed care, systems theory, and milieu management.

- **Expressive Therapy Certifications**: Practitioners incorporating art, music, or movement-based therapies within IMT may pursue certifications in these specialties.

- **Professional Development Workshops**: Training programs focusing on trauma, behavioral management, skills-based therapies, and integrative approaches provide continuing education for IMT practitioners.

Organizations such as the National Association of Therapeutic Schools and Programs (NATSAP), the Association for Child and Adolescent Mental Health (ACAMH), and the Trauma-Informed Care Network offer workshops and resources to enhance professional competence in milieu-based interventions.

Further information can be found on https://www.oliveleaftherapy.com/blog/treatment-method-milieu-therapy for what, how, and why to implement it. Overall, Milieu therapy is a generalized, intentional approach rather than an individualized treatment to be learned through a certification process or training program.

General Cost

Costs associated with Milieu Therapy are difficult to ascertain due to no formal trainings, certifications, or credentialing; Milieu Therapy is more of an approach and philosophy rather than a training technique. Costs for implementing IMT in clinical, school-based, or residential settings may also include staff training expenses, therapeutic program materials, and facility upgrades.

IDENTIFIED AS BEST PRACTICE

Integrative Milieu Therapy is considered a best practice in residential, inpatient, and therapeutic school settings. While not a standalone evidence-based treatment, IMT integrates numerous evidence-based practices (e.g., CBT, trauma-informed care, DBT) within a structured, supportive environment to produce positive client outcomes.

Research highlights the effectiveness of milieu-based interventions for clients experiencing:

- Severe emotional and behavioral dysregulation
- Trauma and attachment disorders
- Substance use disorders
- Anxiety, depression, and other mental health conditions

Studies also show that therapeutic milieu settings foster interpersonal growth, social connectedness, and skill generalization, leading to improved long-term outcomes for individuals with complex treatment needs.

CAUTIONS OR LIMITATIONS

While IMT is effective in structured environments, it may present challenges, including:

1. **Cost and Accessibility**: Residential and inpatient programs can be costly, limiting access for some clients.
2. **Dependence on the Environment**: Clients may struggle to generalize skills learned in IMT settings to less structured environments. Transition planning is critical.
3. **Staff Training and Consistency**: Successful implementation of IMT requires well-trained, consistent staff capable of creating and maintaining a therapeutic milieu.
4. **Emotional Intensity**: Clients and staff alike may face emotional challenges in immersive therapeutic settings. Regular supervision and self-care are essential.

To address these challenges, programs must emphasize family involvement, transition planning, and relapse prevention to support long-term client success.

SCOPE OF PRACTICE ISSUES

IMT practitioners must operate within their professional licensure and training, collaborating with multidisciplinary teams to meet client needs. Practitioners should:

- Refer clients to specialized providers for psychiatric care, substance use treatment, or advanced trauma interventions when appropriate.
- Avoid scope drift by ensuring adherence to evidence-based practices.

WHAT KIND OF PERSON WOULD DO WELL IN THIS MODEL?

IMT is well-suited for practitioners who:

- Are skilled in creating structured, supportive, and collaborative environments.
- Excel at integrating evidence-based practices into a comprehensive treatment framework.
- Possess strong communication, empathy, and interpersonal skills.
- Are flexible, patient, and adaptable to clients' unique needs.

Clients who benefit most from IMT include individuals who:

- Require immersive, intensive care for emotional, behavioral, or trauma-related issues.
- Thrive in predictable environments that promote learning and growth.
- Benefit from community-based and experiential therapeutic interventions.

SUMMARY

Integrative Milieu Therapy (IMT) is a holistic, environment-based approach that blends evidence-based practices with structured, immersive care to promote healing, emotional regulation, and behavioral change. By combining principles from systems theory, trauma-informed care, expressive therapies, and CBT-based interventions, IMT creates a dynamic therapeutic milieu that supports clients with complex needs. Its effectiveness in residential, inpatient, and school-based settings highlights its value as a best practice for individuals requiring consistent, intensive therapeutic support.

I hold two independent licenses in the states of Arizona and Ohio, supervisory status in Arizona, along with a substance abuse license in Arizona. I am board certified as a Diplomate and Clinical Mental Health Specialist, an Approved Clinical Supervisor, Nationally Certified Counselor, a Certified Clinical Mental Health Counselor, NeuroLinguistic Programming Practitioner, and a Clinical Trauma Specialist for Individuals and Family including EMDR Therapy and NET. I completed my training in Animal-Assisted Therapy and Pet Handlers certification in order to evaluate and incorporate the human-animal bond in therapy. I am the sole author and creator of the SxC Model of ESA Evaluation. My research interests surround post-traumatic growth, resiliency, strengths-based therapy, positive psychology, mindfulness, Animal-Assisted Therapy, Sandtray Therapy, Creative approaches in therapy, and martial arts in mental health. I have presented at local, state, regional, national, and international levels on various topics including personality traits, licensure reciprocity challenges, Sandtray and supervision, and Animal-Assisted Therapy within supervision. eonbllc@gmail.com

REFERENCES

Burns, B. J., & Hoagwood, K. (2002). Community treatment for youth: Evidence-based interventions for severe emotional and behavioral disorders. *Oxford University Press.*

Jones, M. (1968). *Social psychiatry in practice: The idea of the therapeutic community.* Penguin Books.
T
rieschman, A. E., Whittaker, J. K., & Brendtro, L. K. (1969). *The other 23 hours: Child-care work with emotionally disturbed children in a therapeutic milieu.* Aldine Publishing Company.

Recommended Readings

Bettelheim, B. (1950). *Love is not enough: The treatment of emotionally disturbed children.* Free Press.

Maier, H. W. (1987). *Developmental group care of children and youth: Concepts and practice.* Haworth Press.

Whittaker, J. K., Del Valle, J. F., & Holmes, L. (2015). *Therapeutic residential care for children and youth: Developing evidence-based international practice.* Jessica Kingsley Publishers.

Integrative Therapy

JoAnna Marquis, M.A., APCC, LMFT

Integrative Therapy is a holistic approach to psychotherapy that casts a large net to include the affective, cognitive, behavioral, spiritual, social, and physiological systems into the conceptualization of the individual's psychological state. The interplay of these fluid dimensions are utilized to understand the needs, sensitivities, crises, and opportunities for new learning unique to the client. The approach takes into account any and all psychological theories including psychodynamic, behaviorist, cognitive, Gestalt, somatic/body-based, object relations, and transactional analysis into a dynamic systems understanding (O'Brien & Houston, 2014). This multi-modal approach encourages the clinician to take a critical and evaluative stance to investigate the individual's deepest values, emotions, inter- and intrapersonal relationships, along with their relationships with the physical and spiritual world. Expanding factors outside of pure symptomology encourages an exploration of the "root" of psychological distress rather than a narrow focus on diagnosis of a specific psychopathology and reduction of symptoms.

Because Integrative Therapy considers multiple domains, unlimited frameworks and interventions can be pulled from to address different issues. Sometimes confused for Eclectic Therapy, Integrative Therapy differs in that it expands the idea of what therapy can be and entails, rather than just pulling interventions from different theories (Cherry, 2021). Integrative Therapy utilizes 'theoretical integration' where one approach is used to bring together different models in conversation with one another, rather than 'technical eclecticism' where the therapist chooses techniques from different schools of thought (American Psychological Association). The freedom to pull from multiple modalities and interventions, while also integrating other sociological realms, allows Integrative Therapy to be useful in many arenas outside of traditional private practice psychotherapy. Integrative Therapy is well suited for the treatment of behavioral health concerns in community mental health organizations, crisis stabilization centers, and school-based counseling programs. It is also particularly useful in medical institutions such as hospitals as a way to address mental health with concurrent physical ailments/diagnosis to improve coping and treatment outcomes.

EXAMPLES OF INTEGRATIVE THERAPY IN CLINICAL SETTINGS

In a hospital setting, an Integrative Therapy approach may look like reviewing a patient's medical record and consulting with medical staff to take into account the physical and cognitive effects of the medical malady and accompanying psychological stress. Inquiring about and incorporating the patients religious or spiritual practices and offering relevant interventions like shared prayer or guided meditation can bring a sense of peace or comfort. Information regarding a patient's wider support network and living environment can be gleaned from direct conversation or consultation with the case worker or medical social worker to allow for planning of continued care and support post hospital admission. A Feminist Theory systems based approach could bring awareness to social structures and historical precedents contributing to distrust in the medical system or institutional bodies. Finally, an exploration of the patient's cultural background can help guide appropriate theoretical approaches and interventions. For example, some clients may be very comfortable getting deep with existential conversations, while others will respond better to CBT interventions directed at addressing pain or anxiety, and some others may appreciate expressive art therapy exercises aimed at articulating emotion where words fail or outward expression of emotion are discouraged.

A therapist utilizing an Integrative approach will need to be committed to the pursuit of knowledge in the field of psychotherapy and its associated fields like sociology and public health. Dialogue with colleagues of diverse orientations and interdisciplinary fields like medical practitioners, community ambassadors, and social workers is necessary to aid in the holistic understanding of the individual to best serve their needs and coordinate appropriate care. By consulting and collaborating with other professionals involved in the clients care, Integrative Therapy facilitates the understanding of the wholeness that is the person's being, psychological state, and functioning in the intrapsychic, interpersonal, physical, and sociopolitical space.

CERTIFICATIONS, TRAININGS, AND LICENSURE REQUIREMENTS

General Cost

- Varies based on certification or extra training in modalities/behavioral health

Training required/recommended

- Recommended: knowledge of multiple modalities from traditional theories (humanistic/psychodynamic/cognitive) as well as *other* theoretical lenses (expressive arts therapy, transpersonal therapy, etc)

- Behavioral Health/ Physiological influence on psychological states

- Personality theory

- Somatic modalities

Trainings offered if no certification available

- There are many supplemental online training options through organizations like:
  - www.integrativetherapy.com
  - www.integrativecounseling.us
  - www.citintegral.com

- Some colleges offer Integrative/Holistic Psychology bachelors or post-baccalaureate certifications:
  - National University (online)
  - Drexel University (online)
  - Bastyr University (Washington)
  - Lesley University (Massacheusets)
  - Cambridge College (Massacheusets)
- Graduate level offerings:
  - Pacifica Graduate Institute (California)
    - PhD in Depth Psychology/Integrative Therapy
  - International University of Professional Studies (online)
    - PhD & MA of Holistic Psychology
  - The Center for Integrative Psychology (California)
    - PsyD Clinical Psychology with Integrative Psychology Emphasis
- Post grad traineeship/internship programs:
  - California Pacific Medical Center (CPMC) Integrative Therapy Traineeship

Degree Requirements (if any/applicable)

- At least a graduate degree in the expected field and licensed to practice within one's state

SCOPE OF PRACTICE ISSUES

Training required or recommended

- Recommended: knowledge of multiple modalities from traditional theories (humanistic/psychodynamic/cognitive) as well as *other* theoretical lenses (expressive arts therapy, transpersonal therapy, etc)
- Behavioral Health/ physiological influence on psychological states
- Personality theory
- Somatic modalities

Supervision required or recommended

- If no background in Behavioral Health/medicine then supervision in this area will be of use depending on nature of site

Ongoing CEU required or recommended

- No

Ongoing annual fees required or only if joining the membership, association, etc

- No

SUMMARY

Integrative Therapy is an approach well suited for many modalities, populations, and sites because it gathers a holistic understanding of the client and considers a wide variety of factors that could be influencing their mental health. Postgraduate certifications as well as specialized training and degree programs are available to educate and train the clinician in the multi-faceted discipline. Practitioners must be licensed to provide psychotherapy in the state they are practicing in, but the macro, mezzo, and micro view of the cognitive, emotional, physical, and spiritual understanding is a lens that can be utilized whether providing psychotherapy or any other form of social service.

JoAnna Marquis is an Associate Marriage and Family Therapist and Associate Professional Clinical Counselor currently based in San Francisco, California. She completed her practicum at California Pacific Medical Center's Integrative Therapy Program designed and curated by Dr. Craig Garfinkel, PhD. Her passion lies in community mental health working with serious mental illness and co-occurring substance use disorders. JoAnna also maintains a small private practice caseload virtually for adult and teen clients in California.

Licensed Marriage and Family Therapist # 153515
Associate Professional Clinical Counselor # 12013
joannavtherapy@gmail.com

REFERENCES

American Psychological Association. (n.d.). *Theoretical Integration*. American Psychological Association. Retrieved January 31, 2023, from https://dictionary.apa.org/theoretical-integration

American Psychological Association. (n.d.). *Technical eclecticism*. American Psychological Association. Retrieved January 31, 2023, from https://dictionary.apa.org/technical-eclecticism

Cherry, K. (2021, October 2). *How integrative therapy works*. Verywell Mind. Retrieved January 31, 2023, from https://www.verywellmind.com/integrative-therapy-definition-types-techniques-and-efficacy-5201904

O'Brien, M., & Houston, G. (2014). *Integrative therapy: A practitioner's guide*. Sage.

Intellectual/Developmental Disabilities
Systemic, Therapeutic, Assessment, Resources, and☐Treatment (START)

MONICA JOHNSON, M.A., CERTIFICATE IN SCHOOL PSYCHOLOGY, LPC-S, LSSP

HISTORY AND NEED

Individuals with intellectual and developmental disabilities (IDD) often experience mental distress at much higher rates, almost five times more often, than adults without disabilities (Schwartzman, Kujawa, Neul, 2023). Despite this high prevalence, there is limited understanding of the most effective methods for addressing the needs of individuals with IDD who also have mental health challenges. People with IDD may encounter various psychiatric disorders. Still, unlike the general population, their psychiatric symptoms are frequently attributed to their disability (Huff, 2021) rather than recognized as signs of mental illness, a phenomenon known as "diagnostic overshadowing." This diagnostic overshadowing leads to detrimental effects. A recent study examining suicide rates in Utah discovered that individuals with autism spectrum disorder (ASD) were more likely to die by suicide from 2013 to 2017 compared to those without an ASD diagnosis (Kirby, Bakian, Zhang, Bilder, Keeshin, Coon, 2019). Additional studies underscore the scarcity of mental health services for the need and availability Camm-Crosbie (2019) found in an online survey of 200 adults living with autism, nine out of ten of the participants reported they had a mental health diagnosis, most often anxiety or depression. Camm-Crosbie flatly titled the study "People Like Me Don't Get Support."

Intellectual and developmental disabilities, or IDDs, are differences present at birth that uniquely affect an individual's physical, intellectual, and emotional development (NICHD, 2021). These conditions often impact multiple body parts or systems. Intellectual disability typically begins before age 18 and involves differences in intellectual functioning and adaptive behavior. The term "developmental disabilities" encompasses a broader category of lifelong challenges, including intellectual, physical, or both. "IDD" is commonly used to describe situations involving intellectual disability and other disabilities. As individuals with IDD live longer, they encounter various mental health challenges which exceed the available mental health professionals available. This group has needed quality mental health care for years. While awareness and resources to help the mental health and well-being of this population have improved in recent years, there are not many counselors, therapists, and psychologists available with experience providing care for individuals with IDD (NICHD, 2021). Mental health professionals can address the access gap by consulting with trained colleagues. Generally, practitioners can adapt their approach to the client's cognitive level and other characteristics when working with individuals with IDD-MH. They should work hard and not primarily just interact with a family member or caregiver; this can damage rapport and erode trust (Huff, 2021). While these adaptations can be beneficial, refining a skill set and strategies would be most effective.

Providing a clear base of foundational knowledge interventions to avoid the blind leading the blind is where the START model shines. Recognizing the growing need and trying to fill this access gap, Dr. Joan Beasley, Research Professor at the University of New Hampshire, conducted decades-long research on the mental health areas of IDD. Beasley, Kroll, and Sovern (1992) published papers outlining protocols that would later develop into the Systemic, Therapeutic, Assessment, Resources, and Treatment (START)/Sovner Center Model. Dr. Joan Beasley and her colleagues established The National Center for START Services (NCSS) in 2011 at the University of New Hampshire's Institute on Disability. Today, the START model is an evidence-based intervention focused on building capacity within systems, including training mental health professionals to support individuals with intellectual developmental disabilities and mental health (IDD-MH).

INTRODUCTION TO START

The START model includes center-based services and therapeutic supports. Determined not to view individuals from a purely medical model, which can often focus on fixing the problem or addressing weaknesses, the therapeutic supports at START take a strengths-based or positive psychology approach, improving life satisfaction, building individuals' strengths, and highlighting their well-being (Seligman & Csikszentmihalyi, 2000). START's therapeutic approach incorporates these essential elements based on positive psychology: promoting positive experiences, identifying individual strengths, and recognizing intact abilities and ambitions (National Center for Start Services Institute on Disability University of New Hampshire, 2022). Therapeutic supports offered by START include planned and emergency center-based support and community-based therapeutic coaching. These supports aim to provide an alternative to mental health in-patient admission, offer assessment and assistance to individuals in distress, help those discharged from a mental health in-patient facility, and provide ongoing support to individuals who live with family, unable to access or benefit from traditional respite programs. START services promote person-centered approaches and training to individuals, families, and caregivers (National Center for Start Services Institute on Disability University of New Hampshire, 2022).

CERTIFICATIONS, TRAININGS, AND LICENSURE REQUIREMENTS FOR START

The National Center for START Services Training Department develops, coordinates, and delivers evidence-based and culturally responsive training and professional development on issues related to IDD-MH, independent living, and community engagement beyond traditional training programs. The organization's goal is to prepare leaders in the field of IDD-MH. These didactic learning opportunities include the perspective and lived experience of individuals of IDD-MH (National Center for Start Services Institute on Disability University of New Hampshire, 2022). To be more accessible, the organization goes beyond training and offers technical assistance, clinical knowledge, and consultation services.

Professional Development Series

The National Center for START Services Training Department developed the IDD-MH Professional Development Series, introductory-level courses to address specific roles in the human services system. The courses cover foundational concepts and an evidence-based approach to treating and supporting individuals with IDD and mental health needs for mobile crisis responders, direct support professionals, and care coordinators.

Direct Support Professionals Course

The NCSS recommends the course for direct support professionals, functional support specialists, residential/ home care providers and staff, day habilitation, and residential supervisors. It costs $149 and delves into therapeutic interventions such as utilizing trauma-informed care, positive identity formation, emotion regulation, and creative expression.

Care Coordinators & Case Managers Course

The Care Coordinators & Case Managers course would be most interesting to practitioners working as case managers, supervisors, program managers, or intake/intervention specialists. This training focuses on providing strengths-based, trauma-informed, culturally competent service coordination to individuals with IDD and mental health needs. The registration fee is $299 per person. Participants will receive University of New Hampshire Continuing Education Units and a Certificate of Completion for IDD-MH Training for Care Coordinators & Case Managers. Participants walk away knowing how to include the individual receiving care and their family in service delivery planning, practical strategies for improving systemic engagement and identifying common mental health presentations in individuals with IDD.

Mobile Crisis Responder Course

The NCSS recommends the Mobile Crisis Responders course for mental health and IDD case managers/service coordinators, emergency services clinicians, mobile crisis responders, clinicians, and supervisors. The training teaches participants best practices in emergency management, crisis assessment, and response. The registration fee is $149 per person. At the end of the course, participants can recognize the presentation of common mental health conditions in individuals with IDD, identify the most frequently diagnosed mental health conditions in the IDD population, and differentiate between a person's presentation and their diagnostic understanding.

Recently, START Services released an online asynchronous $49 course on suicide screening for people with autism spectrum disorder (ASD) or IDD. The training facilitates improved support and assistance to individuals with IDD-MH through equipping 988 National Suicide Lifeline Counselors. Participants leave the course able to identify appropriate suicide screening tools for individuals with ASD and IDD, effectively engage with this population, and recognize the signs and symptoms of suicidality amongst individuals with ASD-IDD.

START Coordinator Certification

The START Coordinator Certification is designed to equip professionals with the necessary skills and knowledge to support individuals with intellectual and developmental disabilities effectively (IDD) and mental health (MH) needs. To pursue this certification, candidates must engage in a structured training program that includes both didactic learning and practical application of the START model principles. This training emphasizes evidence-based practices, cultural competency, and a person-centered approach to care. While supervision is required during the certification process, ensuring that coordinators apply their knowledge effectively within their practice settings is essential. The certification renewal process occurs every two years, promoting ongoing learning and adherence to the START model's evolving standards.

SCOPE OF PRACTICE ISSUES

When working within the START framework, professionals should be aware of the scope of practice issues that may arise. Practitioners are encouraged to pursue additional training and professional development to enhance their competencies in this specialized area. While certification is not mandatory for all practitioners working with individuals with IDD and MH needs, those seeking to become START Coordinators must adhere to specific training and supervision requirements. Ongoing continuing education units (CEUs) are recommended to maintain and expand knowledge in the field, although they are not strictly required. Certification is straightforward, without the burden of annual fees or complex membership requirements. This accessibility allows practitioners to focus on their professional growth and the needs of the populations they serve.

The NCSS recommends that practitioners pursue training and professional development; supervision is only required if pursuing the START Coordinator Certification. Ongoing CEUs are a recommendation, though not required. There are no annual fees or association memberships to track and fret over. The process is simple; it is neither time-intensive nor a money grab. The National Center for START Services Institute on Disability at the University of New Hampshire genuinely seems interested in helping a group of marginalized individuals we've neglected for far too long.

SUMMARY

While there is no universally accepted gold standard for the mental health treatment of individuals with intellectual and developmental disabilities (IDD), the START model effectively integrates evidence-based practices such as person-centered care, positive psychology, and self-determination. This model encourages counselors to engage in collegial consultation, fostering the expansion of their knowledge and skills related to IDD.

Importantly, certification to treat mental health concerns in individuals with IDD is not mandatory, nor is a specific degree required. For many clinicians, developing competency in this area may represent a significant shift in their practice. As Neitzke, an assistant professor in the Department of Psychology at the University of Nebraska Medical Center, aptly noted, "You might have to make a few adaptations, but you have the skill set, you know the content, you know the strategies to utilize. Then it's more of refining the art of the therapy" (Huff, 2021). The START model serves as an excellent framework for practitioners seeking structured protocols and guidance on evidence-based interventions tailored to the needs of individuals with IDD. It offers a comprehensive approach to addressing their mental health needs, with a well-structured training process that equips participants with both theoretical knowledge and practical skills essential for effective intervention.

Other practitioners' experience with the certification process has been overwhelmingly positive, underscoring the National Center for START Services' commitment to cultivating skilled professionals who serve this marginalized population. Individuals who thrive within the START model typically possess a solid foundation in mental health practices, a genuine passion for supporting individuals with disabilities, and a commitment to ongoing learning. This approach is particularly well-suited for mental health professionals, educators, and caregivers eager to adapt their practices to meet the unique needs of individuals facing IDD and mental health challenges. By embracing the principles of the START model, practitioners can significantly enhance the quality of care and support provided to this vulnerable group.

Monica Johnson, MA, LPC-S, LSSP, is a mental health professional specializing in trauma and crisis counseling and related services in educational settings. She has been instrumental in crisis assessment teams, focusing on multiculturalism and inclusivity. Formerly a special education counselor in K-12 settings, Monica serves as an Education Specialist in Transition and Mental Health for Students with Disabilities, supporting students with disabilities in their educational journey. She researches school-wide positive behavior interventions and supports (PBIS) and is dedicated to enhancing student and educator mental health and wellness in public schools. Monica advocates for student and educator wellness in the mental health community.

mdj0091@sbcglobal.net

REFERENCES

Beasley, J., Kalb, L.G., & Klein A. (2018). Improving mental health outcomes for individuals with intellectual disability through the Iowa START (I-START) program. *Journal of Mental Health Research in Intellectual Disabilities*, 11(4), 287-300. https://doi.org/10.1080/19315864.2018.1504362

Beasley, J., Kroll, J., & Sovner, R. (1992). Community-based crisis mental health services for persons with developmental disabilities: The START model. *The Habilitative Mental Healthcare Newsletter*, 11(9), 55-58.

Camm-Crosbie, L., Bradley, L., Shaw, R., Baron-Cohen, S., & Cassidy, S. (2018). "People like me don't get support": Autistic adults' experiences of support and treatment for mental health difficulties, self-injury and suicidality. *Autism*, 23(6), 1431–1441. https://doi.org/10.1177/1362361318816053

Helker, W., & Morrison Bennet, M. (2019). *Child-Parent Relationship Therapy (CPRT)* (2nd ed.). Routledge.

Huff, C. (2021, November 1). Working with adults with developmental disabilities. *Monitor on Psychology*, 52(8). https://www.apa.org/monitor/2021/11/feature-developmental-disabilities

Kirby, A. V., Bakian, A. V., Zhang, Y., Bilder, D. A., Keeshin, B. R., & Coon, H. (2019). A 20-year study of suicide death in a statewide autism population. *Autism Research*, 12(4), 658–666. https://doi.org/10.1002/aur.2076

National Center for Start Services Institute on Disability University of New Hampshire. (2022, September 21). *START Model*. National Center for START Services. https://centerforstartservices.org/START-Model

National Institute of Child Health and Human Development. (2021, November 9). *About Intellectual and Developmental Disabilities (IDDs)*. Https://Www.nichd.nih.gov/. https://www.nichd.nih.gov/health/topics/idds/conditioninfo

Schwartzman, J., Rodrigues, V., Kujawa, A., & Neul, J. (2023, March 30). *Mental Health in Individuals with Intellectual and Developmental Disabilities*. Vanderbilt Kennedy Center Conversation Series on Research in Intellectual and Developmental Disabilities. https://vimeo.com/813653291

Seligman, M. E. P., & Csikszentmihalyi, M. (2000). Positive psychology: An introduction. *American Psychologist*, 55(1), 5–14. https://doi.org/10.1037/0003-066X.55.1.5

Senior, K. (2009-04-01). "Greater needs, limited access". *Bulletin of the World Health Organization*. 87 (4): 252–253. doi:10.2471/blt.09.030409. ISSN 0042-9686. PMC 2672575. PMID 19551229.

Intensive Short-Term Dynamic Psychotherapy (ISTDP)

Johannes Kieding, LCSW

ISTDP was developed by Dr. Habib Davanloo, an Iranian born psychiatrist originally trained in psychoanalysis who spent most of his psychiatric and teaching career operating out of McGill university. Dr. Davanloo became interested in finding a more effective and expedient way of helping psychotherapy patients. Dr. Davanloo referred to what he called the "Central Dynamic Sequence" as the foundation of the model. The Central Dynamic Sequence, a series of therapeutic phases, is navigated with an interactive diagnostic roadmap to the patient's psychological conflicts and to the patient's unconscious. The model entails an organized body of knowledge that not only captures a set of interventions, but also a way of assessing the patient's responses to those interventions which then informs the clinician's next intervention and ensures that the therapist is not working above or below the patient's capacities.

Ultimately the aim is not just symptom relief, but character change. This is accomplished by helping the patient become acquainted with his or her repertoire of psychological defense mechanisms, helping the patient see how these defenses perpetuate their presenting problems and symptomatology, and then encouraging the patient to relinquish their maladaptive defenses in favor of facing the underlying thoughts, longings, and emotions that have been repressed or disavowed from conscious awareness. Depending on the patient's psychological make-up, this can take different forms. What remains constant is a very careful attention to the patient's response to the therapist's intervention, as this response will inform the therapist's next intervention.

Central to Dr. Davanloo's development of ISTDP was reviewing video recordings of therapy sessions he conducted with his patients. Dr. Davanloo's protocol for successful therapy was no return of presenting symptoms in 5 years, with intervals for 6 months, 1 year, and 5-year follow-ups — those follow-up meetings with patients were video recorded as well (Marvin Skorman, Personal communication, 2019).

Richard Meyer, MD., a long-time student of Dr. Davanloo, articulated a thumbnail description of the method in this way:

"Davanloo created a technique that was based on psychoanalytic principals but approached the core problems in a new way that was clearly articulated. In his technique the therapist is not passive. The therapist puts active pressure on the patient's defenses so that they can disappear resulting in the quick emergence of unconscious processes that can then be resolved" (personal communication, 2018).

DISORDERS TREATED BY ISTDP

ISTDP has been found to be effective for a wide range of psychological disturbances. For an overview of the available evidence and outcome data, I refer you to the following website: https://medicine.dal.ca/departments/department-sites/psychiatry/research/emotions-health/research/publications.html

CERTIFICATIONS, TRAININGS, AND CONSIDERATIONS

Unfortunately, Dr. Davanloo never codified a formal certification program in ISTDP. The training program that does lead to formal certification through an organization called the "IEDTA" does not bear Dr. Davanloo's stamp of approval. Marvin Skorman, LMHC, my former teacher and supervisor and a close student of Dr. Davanloo in the late 1980s had this to say when I asked him about the issue of credentialing:

"I decided to carry on Davanloo's tradition of looking at each supervisee and what they can actually accomplish with their clients rather than establishing a more formalized tiered certification process. I find that much more meaningful. That doesn't mean the more formal tiered process is wrong. It just is not my style and does not have much meaning to me, but others may be fine with it and that is okay too" (personal communication, 2021).

My training background consisted of weekly audio-visual supervision with Marvin Skorman from 2013 through the end of 2021, when Mr. Skorman retired. The total number of hours of supervision must have approached around 800-hours. I also attended two training events led by Dr. Davanloo in 2012 and 2013. When Mr. Skorman deemed me ready to teach and supervise in 2017, I began to do so. Because of my own experience, I am biased towards the idea that the best way to train in ISTDP is to have weekly audio-visual supervision with an accomplished supervisor who either was trained directly by Davanloo or who was trained by someone who was trained directly by Davanloo. Others prefer to go through the training that the IEDTA offers which leads to IEDTA certification after 3-years, but again, this certification does not bear Dr. Davanloo's stamp of authority or approval. For more information about the IEDTA and their certification programs, visit this website: https://iedta.net/iedta/certification/

Out of respect for Dr. Davanloo, I prefer to refer to what I do as 'ISTDP-informed' rather than ISTDP, as it is well known that Dr. Davanloo experienced displeasure that clinicians who had not been sanctioned by him to teach referred to what they did as ISTDP.

I maintain a small private practice in Tucson, Arizona. I provide ISTDP-informed psychotherapy, trainings, and consultations to clinicians all over the world. I intermittently serve as an adjunct faculty member at the Rochester Institute of Technology where I train and supervise their clinicians in ISTDP-informed psychotherapy, and I also intermittently supervise graduate level social work students at Arizona State University.

www.johanneskieding.com

Internal Family Systems (IFS)

RASHUNDA MILLER REED, PhD, LPC, LMFT, NCC
LEVEL 2 TRAINED THERAPIST

Internal Family Systems, also known as IFS, was founded and developed by Richard C. Swartz, PhD. The goal of IFS therapy is to acknowledge parts, help them heal, and eventually help people heal. IFS is a non-pathologizing approach, therefore, what might be a diagnosis in traditional mental health approaches are also approached from a parts perspective (i.e., narcissism, dissociative identity disorder, and depression). In fact, the founder of IFS, Dr. Swartz began his work with clients struggling with eating disorders (1987). He paid attention to how clients spoke about what was happening…as if parts would lash out. Imagine feeling more confidence, ease, clarity, and connected with clients instead of exhausted or overwhelmed. In the deepest sense, IFS is an approach where the clients really get to be experts of their lives. The model works with both intuition and intentionality in ways that allow for deeper awareness, exploration, appreciation, and integration.

The premise behind IFS is that we all have parts that are characterized as managers, firefighters, and exiles who make up our inner system. These parts, in their own ways really try to protect and help. Manager parts keep things running smoothly and try to circumvent possible distress. For example, they plan and make lists. Firefighter parts come in for emergencies or situations that are beyond managers expertise, awareness, or control. They attempt to quickly address distress, however, haphazardly can provide more of mess. Examples of firefighter parts include anger, addictions, and impulsivity. Exiles are parts that have been hidden or locked away because of the real or anticipated harm the system might experience. They can be young parts who have experienced deep trauma or carry other burdens. Again, the goal is to create a system where all parts are acknowledged, healed, and integrated into the system is ways that work for clients. Clients learn how parts show up in their bodies and how to allow SELF to respond instead of parts. More about the model can be found from the IFS Training Manual (Anderson and colleagues, 2017).

CERTIFICATIONS, TRAININGS, AND LICENSURE REQUIREMENTS

Official Internal Family Systems training, in entirety consists of 3 levels. Within each level, participants can choose specialties. Each level is typically offered North American and International Trainings. Enrolling in training is highly competitive. In some instances, participation is prioritized. It is common for potential attendees to get waitlisted or wait months prior be being accepted into a training course.

Level 1, which is 72-80 hours is the basic course with provides that foundation for Internal family systems. At this level, participants learn about parts, how these parts show up, the 6 F's which include helping parts unblend and unburden withing the system, 6 F's. Parts consist of Managers, Firefighters, and Self-like parts. Parts have agendas that are often less helpful than they intend. For example, a manager part that likes to plan everything. For some manager parts keep them focused and on track. That behavior probably works some time. Over time or for other situations the planning part might be too rigid to develop a connection and more spontaneity is needed. The goal of IFS is to help parts heal and develop a system of SELF- Leadership. The core SELF is characterized by the 8 C's: clarity, compassion, courage, confidence, curiosity, creativity, calmness, and connectedness.

Level 2 has a variety of topics that clinicians can choose. Past options have included a deepening and expanding (continuation of level one), shame, depression, couples work,

Level 3 is taught by a variety of Lead trainers, yet the curriculum is the same. The focus of level 3 is helping therapists to become more self-led and determine their niche within Internal Family Systems.

Two certifications are offered, one for IFS Therapists who are licensed in a mental health field (counseling, social work, psychology) and one for IFS Practitioners who are in other recognized helping professionals such as nurses, pastors, and so forth. Those interested in certification should visit the IFS Institute website for the most updated information. In the past, certification has consisted of the following:

- Completion of Level 1 comprehensive course
- One year since completion of Level 1 and 200 hours of IFS practice
- 30 hours of IFS trainings/consultations by approved IFS providers
- Review of IFS session by an approved reviewer
- Certification fees

To maintain certification an initial the following is required. Visit the IFS Institute website at https://ifs-institute.com/trainings/ifs-certification/ifs-certification-policy for further information.

General Cost

The cost for IFS training varies greatly. Anyone interested in IFS training should refer to training brochures for specific details. First, clinicians must choose if they want comprehensive training or an introduction. Next, trainings can be taken in the US and abroad. There are also online, hybrid, and in-person options to consider. Trainings provided through the IFS Institute have accompanying online brochures that specify details and fees for particular trainings. For example, retreat style or international trainings have additional costs for the training and other travel-related fees for attendees. Attendees are responsible for making their own travel arrangement. There is a non-refundable application fee, usually around $15 and trainers decide book(s) and other required materials for courses. Many of the resources can be purchased directly from IFS institute or popular vendors. Scholarships are available on a limited basis for qualifying attendees. Continuing education credits for trainings range from 1 CE to 80 CEs. Clinicians are responsible for checking if CEs are appropriate for their licensing boards. Level 1, the comprehensive course, is highly recommended to have a thorough understanding and immersion in the IFS model. In addition, training is provided by other IFS professionals.

GETTING STARTED

The initial investment for IFS varies. Clinicians can obtain training locally and through online platforms that range from zero dollars to $3000 for retreat style learnings. Training might range from 1 CE to 80 CEs.

- Level 1. Clinicians who desire comprehensive online learning experience for Level 1 can easily invest $2000 to $3500 for Level 1 training through the IFS Institute and affiliated organizations. Through the IFS instituted there has typically been a non-refundable application fee and deposit, ranging from $215 to $315. Again, potential attendees should see the accompanying brochures for the exact fees.

- Level 2. Clinicians who desire the full online learning experience for Level 1 can easily invest $2800 or more for a Level 2 training through the IFS Institute and affiliated organizations. Level 1 must be completed in months prior to registering for Level 2.

- Level 3. Clinicians who desire the full online learning experience for Level 3 can easily invest $2500 or more for Level 3 training through the IFS Institute and affiliated organizations. Level 1 must be completed in months prior to registering for Level 3.

Certification

Please visit the IFS Instituted website for updated information on certification fees. Currently, the investment for certification consists of an application fee of $50, certification fee of $150, and reviewer fee for DVD or live session of $150. On average those interested can expect to invest $3,350 for the path to certification.

Recertification

Training costs vary from zero dollars to thousands of dollars. In addition, a biannual recertification fee for video reviews typically applies.

Authors Training Investment

Prices can vary for training. As a participant, I took the level one training through Central Connecticut State University (CCSU) online for $3450 including a $200 non-refundable deposit. For Level 2, I enrolled in Intimacy from the Inside Out® IFIO basic training which is an IFS inspired model for couples developed by Toni Herbine-Blank. Fees were $2850 including a $300 non-refundable deposit. IFS therapy, which is also recommended, totaled about $3500 for one year.

Organizational Costs

Organizations may contact the IFS institute directly to set up trainings and costs.

IDENTIFIED AS AN EVIDENCED-BASED PRACTICE

According to the website, IFS was indicated by SAMHSA as an evidenced based practice for (2014, Foundation for Self-Leadership; See Shadick et al., 2013). Unfortunately, I could not confirm through the SAMHSA. In addition, the National Registry of Evidenced-Based Practices and Programs (NREPP) database was inaccessible at the time this chapter was written. Jenn Matheson, PhD, LMFT, Foundation's Senior Coordinator for Research is listed on the website as the contact for more information (Research@FoundationIFS.org).

Training Required/Recommended

At the least IFS-Level one basic training is recommended, which provides about 70 hours of training over months or weeks. The advantages of the comprehensive training offered through IFS are the immersion components and practice groups. Learners can immerse themselves in the IFS approach, see several full demonstrations, and get questions answered quickly. Because training occurs over time (week or months, there is also time to sit with questions that might come up and reach out to trainers) as opposed to one day trainings. Internal Family Systems might be particularly attractive to clinicians who embrace creativity, meditation, evidence -based approaches, yet also want a model that is intentional and intuitive. A huge benefit of the comprehensive training it that attendees have direct contact with lead trainers and program assistants who can assist in developing their own SELF energy as well as skills related to the model. As a systems-trained therapist, I believe clinicians without systems training might have more of a learning curve with some of the concepts within IFS model. All concepts are fully explained, and the training courses are open to those without systems training.

Trainings Offered if no Certification Available

Training, including webinars and videos are offered through the IFS Institute and other organizations for those not wanting a comprehensive course or IFS certification.

Certification Available/Required/Recommended?

Certification is recommended for clinicians wanting to advance in IFS practice, research, and supervision. There are several opportunities for leadership related to IFS, such as becoming a program assistant, consultant, assistant trainer, and lead trainer. This information is provided on the IFS Institute website.

Degree Requirements

IFS is open to various licensed mental health professionals (counselors, social workers, psychiatrists, psychologists, addiction counselors) and other helping professionals such as nurses, holistic practitioners, and clergy.

ANY CAUTIONS OR LIMITATIONS PROFESSIONALS AND STUDENTS SHOULD KNOW ABOUT?

IFS is a healing approach intended to improve mental health. Those wanting to use IFS would need to ensure that it falls within their clinical scope. Graduate students are eligible for training. Currently, only licensed professionals are eligible for certification as an IFS therapist. Furthermore, only those certified can used the designated title of IFS therapist. The IFS institute provides a voluntary directory of providers and their training level for IFS. In briefly reviewing the directory, many clinicians were licensed as counselors, marriage and family therapists, and social workers.

SCOPE OF PRACTICE ISSUES

Tenets of IFS can be immediately incorporated. IFS is a non-pathologizing approach. Therefore, clinicians who are required to diagnose will need to determine how to best do that while incorporating the IFS model. Professionals should always practice withing the scope of licenses (title and practice) as indicated in state laws.

Recommended Websites

Full Comprehensive trainings: https://ifs-institute.com/trainings

Podcasts: https://internalfamilysystems.pt/ifs-talks

Online courses/Learning Circles: https://courses.ifs-institute.com/

Books/Videos: https://ifs-institute.com/store

Supervision Required or Recommended

IFS consultation (group or individual) is highly recommended to help clinicians continue to develop their own SELF energy as well as address practice issues from an IFS perspective. Obtaining at least 10 hours of consultation (group or individual) is required for certification.

Ongoing CEs Required or Recommended

Ongoing CEs are recommended for anyone practicing IFS. Like any model, it is evolving as it is more widely accepted and applied. Ongoing CEs are required for certified IFS therapists and Practitioners. They must obtain 20 CEs each year through the IFS Institute or other approved organizations. Failure to certify within a year of recertification date requires 30 hours of CE.

Ongoing Annual Fees

Ongoing fees are only required for those who want to become certified. To date, there are several regional and social media IFS groups that do not currently require membership fees.

WHAT KIND OF PERSON WOULD DO WELL IN IFS OR WHERE YOUR APPROACH IS BEST CONDUCTED?

IFS can be integrated with a variety of populations, practice settings, modalities, and theoretical approaches. Those who have willingness to open their heart to a more inclusive approach are likely to find IFS a good fit. IFS pulls from tenets of systems theory. Clinicians may be drawn to IFS who have and appreciation for works of Carl Jung, Virginia Satir, Murray Bowen, Carl Whitaker, and other approaches that promote self-actualization and self-mastery. IFS is a validating approach.

SUMMARY

The trainings provided through or in connection with the IFS institute are worth the experience. Clinicians can choose to use the mode in part or in entirety. Furthermore, the training also provides an opportunity for personal growth and to build community with other attendees. I noticed some limitations when using the model with clients who have parts that are literal, struggle with embracing ambiguity. It could be that additional training is required. The idea of going in can be illusive. The IFS model provides an approach for those who struggle to go in called direct access. Instead of clients going in, with permission client have parts embody them. IFS organizers seem to recognize the importance of cultural humility and diversity, and recruiting more diverse trainers is in progress. There are international trainers and training which meets some demands for geographical, ethnic, and language diversity. The model itself adequately addresses those dimensions. In the past, IFS has partnered with organizations such as Black Therapist Rock to provide IFS trainings to clinicians of color (Foundation for Self-Leadership, 2022).

Rashunda's desire is to help build relationships where people learn to be with themselves and others. She offers a warm, yet down-to-earth approach for strengthening relationships. Her approach, informed by systems thinking starts with being present. This can be uncomfortable initially as many people are not accustomed to being seen and heard with such intention. She is trained in Internal Family Systems (IFS) Level 1, IFS Level 2 Intimacy from the Inside Out (IFIO), and Discernment Counseling (which is not really counseling). When not counseling, she enjoys teaching and supervising future counselors and talking about relationships, integrated care, and ethics. Going to museums, celebrating successes, wearing cowboy boots, watching mystery movies, and road trips with her family are a few of her favorite things. Rashunda is the founder of Relationships Matter LLC, a practice dedicated to healing parts related to partnering, parenting, and professionalism.

Visit www.rashundareed.com for more information.

References

Anderson, F. G., Sweezy, M. & Swartz, R. C. (2017). *Internal family systems skills training manual: Trauma-informed treatment for anxiety, depression, ptsd, and substance abuse.* Pesi Publishing & Media

Foundation for Self-Leadership. (2022). Black therapists Rock and IFS – A growing partnership. Foundation News. Retrieved from https://ifs-institute.com/news-events/news/black-therapists-rock-and-ifs-growing-partnership

Foundation for Self Leadership (2014). IFS, and evidenced-based practice. Foundation News. Retrieved from https://foundationifs.org/news-articles/79-ifs-an-evidence-based-practice#:~:text=Interventions%20listed%20in%20NREPP%2C%20now%20including%20IFS%2C%20have,IFS%20on%20NREPP%20was%20submitted%20in%20April%202014.

Shadick, N. A., Sowell, N. F., Frits, M. L., Hoffman, S. M. Hartz, S. A., Booth, F. D., Sweezy, M., Rogers, P. R., Dubin, R. L., Atkinson, J. C., Friedman, A. L., Augusto, F., Iannaccone, C. K., Fossel, A. H., Quinn, G., Cui, J., Losina, E., and Schwartz, R. C. (2013). A randomized controlled trial of an internal family systems-based psychotherapeutic intervention on outcomes in rheumatoid arthritis: a proof-of-concept study. *Journal of Rheumatology*, *40*(11), 1831-1841. doi: 10.3899/jrheum.121465

Swartz, R. (1987). Our multiple selves: Apply systems thinking to the inner family. *The Family Therapy Networker*, 21-31. Retrieved from https://foundationifs.org/images/Schwartz_1987_Our_Multiple_Selves.pdf

Interpersonal Neurobiology (IPNB)

CHRISTINA VILLARREAL-DAVIS, PHD, LPC-S, NCC, RPT-S™

"People will forget what you said, people will forget what you did, but people will never forget how you made them feel."

-Maya Angelou

This brief chapter attempts to describe and provide an overview of Interpersonal Neurobiology (IPNB) from a clinical counseling perspective. In this overview, the five foundations of IPNB will be explored along with the twelve integrative principles, the intersection of IPNB and social injustices, and IPNB best practices. The second half of this chapter describes the current training and certificate programs in IPNB.

IPNB OVERVIEW

IPNB was developed and coined by Daniel Siegel, a child and adolescent psychiatrist, in the early 1990s in an attempt to highlight common beliefs across varying scientific disciplines (Sigel, 1999, 2012, 2020). Siegel (1999) theorized that the mind was developed and shaped by one's interpersonal relationships and emphasized that interpersonal experiences play "a special organizing role in determining the development of brain structure early in life and the ongoing emergence of brain functioning throughout the lifespan" (p. 21). Siegel (2021) also emphasizes that IPNB's clinical application is not necessarily a standalone theoretical approach in counseling or any other mental health field, but rather it is a "consilient framework for understanding reality that can *inform* therapy…" (p. 2) along with other supportive fields (e.g., education, parenting, systems of government, and so forth). According to Siegel (2012), IPNB is:

> a consilient field that embraces all branches of science as it seeks the common, universal findings across independent ways of knowing in order to expand our understanding of the mind and well-being…this field explores the ways in which relationships and the brain interact to shape our mental lives. IPNB is meant to convey the embracing of everything in life from society (interpersonal) to synapses (neurobiology). (p. A1-42)

From a mental health counseling/clinical perspective, this author would define IPNB as an integrative and relational approach in being with and connecting with others that considers the brain, body, and mind connection in the healing and therapeutic process of mental health counseling.

Five Foundations of IPNB

Within the various mental health fields (e.g., psychotherapy/counseling, psychology, psychiatry, nursing, and social work), there is no common ground that joins the field of science and the treatment of mental health concerns and suffering (Siegel, 2021). As such, Siegel (1999) developed IPNB to present the case for a more collaborative approach (e.g., the consilient framework) to better inform counseling and other ways of being within relationships. As such, IPNB offers "a definition of the mind and what a healthy mind might be considered to be—and then shows how to cultivate well-being and human flourishing beyond just reducing mental suffering" (Siegel, 2021, p. 2). To further explore IPNB, Siegel's (2021) outlines five foundational principles that guide IPNB:

1. The need to link the empirical research from the consilient fields to psychotherapy practice to better understand mental health,

2. Relationships are significant and can positively or negatively impact mental health,

3. Relational experiences are directly related to what occurs inside our bodies (the "inter" and "inner"/"personal" focus of IPNB),

4. Neuroscience and neurobiology are foundational in the development of the mind and mental health (e.g., "neuro" refers to the whole nervous system throughout our bodies), and

5. IPNB is a framework for comprehending the mind, brain, and body connection that "may provide initial common ground but then offer very different strategies of cultivating health" (p. 3).

Twelve Integrative Principles

In building upon the five foundational principles as well as discoveries from various fields of science, IPNB has found some common ground in 12 integrative principles, which will be explored next. The first principle is the "Mind is broader than the brain and bigger than the body" (Siegel, 2021, p. 4). Oftentimes the mind and brain are used interchangeably; however, there is a distinct difference between the two. Siegel (2012) describes the mind as "our inner subjective experience and the process of being conscious or aware" (p. 1-1), whereas the brain is the actual cluster of cells that are incased in the skull.

The mind also regulates the flow of energy and information throughout the brain and body as well as within and between relationships, which leads to the second and third integrative principles. The second principle states, "Energy and information flow is fundamental to mind" (Siegel, 2021, p. 4). In other words, the mind's main job centers on the movement of energy and information throughout the entire body. The third principle states, "Energy and information flow occurs within an individual, and between the individual and the world of other people and the planet—the world of nature" (Siegel, 2021, p. 5), which identifies the relational aspects of the mind with others and the world.

Further expanding on the mind, Siegel (2021) identifies the fourth principle, "'mind' involves at least four facets: subjective experience, consciousness, information processing, and self-organizing" (p. 5). Siegel (2021) emphasizes these four facets as emergent properties that are a part of a complex, yet fascinating, system. These emergent properties become trailblazers for the flow of energy and information, which is both an embodied and relational experience. This notion leads to the fifth principle, "One facet of mind can be defined this way: An emergent, self-organizing, embodied, and relational process that regulates the flow of energy and information" (Siegel, 2021, p. 6). In a quest for equilibrium, the emergent properties of the mind, this very complex system, is trying to figure out a way to balance itself through self-organization, which is felt within (e.g., embodied) and between (e.g., relationally).

In this quest for equilibrium, Siegel (2021) calls attention to the healthy mind, which seeks to "cultivate integration, within and between" (p. 6), the sixth principle of IPNB. Integration is the "linkage of differentiated parts of a system" (Siegle, 2012, p. 16-1), which refers to the various, but distinct, parts of the mind that are part of this complex system of the mind. However, in circumstances of an unhealthy mind, impaired integration emerges, the seventh principle of IPNB. Siegel (2021) provides an acronym connected to the analogy of a smooth flowing river where healthy integration exists. This FACES flowing river is "**F**lexible, **A**daptive, **C**oherent (resilient over time), **E**nergized, and **S**table (reliable, not ridged)" (p. 6). Within and between healthy relationships, such as a secure attachment between parent and child, FACES is experienced, both embodied and relationally, leading to optimal self-organization and linkage of the complex system, cultivating healthy integration. However, within and between unhealthy relationship, such as an insecure attachment between a parent and child, FACES is not experienced (or not consistent and reliable as evident in anxious-ambivalent or avoidant attachment styles), both embodied and relationally, leading to deprived self-organization, inadequate linkage, and impaired integration.

On a positive note, impaired integration is not the end of one's story. There is hope and healing that can be found when one experiences compassionate, caring, and respectful relationships. This leads to Siegel's (2021) eighth and ninth principles, respectively: "Relational and neural integration are mutually reinforcing" (p. 7) and "Where attention goes, neural firing flows, and neural connection grows" (p. 7). One of the most well-known neurobiological concepts often discussed in the mental health field is *neuroplasticity*, meaning neurons that fire together, wire together. Siegel (2012) defines neuroplasticity as "the ability of the brain to change its structure in response to experience" (p. 8-1). For example, the pure experience of a counseling relationship where safety, compassion, kindness, and presences are felt (e.g., felt embodied experiences) over time, provides the foundation and cultivation of the rewiring of healthier, adaptive, and integrative neural networks.

The tenth principle centers on the roles of the mind. According to Siegel (2021), "Mind in its regulatory role both monitors and modifies energy and information flow, and these are learnable mindsight skills" (p. 8). Furthermore, Siegel points out that monitoring, in order to stabilize or modify, involves these three key aspects of the mind: openness, objectivity, and observation.

The eleventh principle defines the term *mindsight*. According to Siegel (2021), mindsight refers to "the capacity to have insight into one's own inner state of energy flow, to sense that in others as empathy, and to modify that flow within and between toward integration" (p. 8). Cultivating a healthy mind is accomplished through the development of the twelfth and final principle, the "nine domains of integration" (p. 9). These nine domains include the following: integration of consciousness (the experience of awareness of self and others), vertical integration (subcortical energy flow throughout the brain and body), bilateral integration (flow of energy and information in both hemispheres of the brain), memory integration (understand and processing explicit and implicit memory), narrative integration (the storyline of our memories and lived experiences), state integration (referring to the brain and body connection, the embodied brain, sensed throughout the body and often in one's gut and heart), interpersonal integration (reaching healthy attachment and differentiated self), temporal integration (the longing for immortality while facing the reality of mortality), and identity integration (self as well as self in relationships) (Siegel, 2021, p. 9-12).

Intersection of IPNB and Social Injustices

The very nature of IPNB, which respects and values differences while honoring one's subjective experiences, provides the foundation of unconditional and nonjudgmental acceptance, kindness, and love. IPBN is the essence of acceptance, equality, equity, and inclusion to help promote social justice and overcome social inequities and disparities. Where belonging and acceptance of differences does not exist, chaos and rigidity exist, and when a group of people suffer in this manner, society ultimately suffers in this chaos and rigidity of impaired integration. However, through IPNB and its importance on integration being at the heart of health, the goal is "keeping hope alive as a steward of justice emerges out of differentiating our histories from one another and then cultivating the compassionate connection that honors those difference, without losing track of them" (Siegle, 2021, p. 15). In quintessence, hope can be accomplished through helpful and supportive methods such as advocacy, healing and restoring relationships (e.g., race relations), and providing safe spaces that decrease and/or eliminate biases and hate.

As with any theory or model/approach in counseling, or in this case the IPNB framework that informs counseling, the educational experience and supervised application of the theory/model/framework are essential in fostering the proper implementation and efficacy of IPNB. A review of the literature did not reveal scope of practice issues or IPNB best practices; however, the American Counseling Association (ACA) addresses scope of practice issues in their *2014 ACA Code of Ethics* (2014). Concerning boundaries of competence, ACA's code C.2.a. maintains that "Counselors practice only within the boundaries of their competence, based on their education, training, supervised experience, state and national professional credentials, and appropriate professional experience" (ACA, 2014, p. 8). Concerning new specialty areas of practice, ACA's code C.2.b. asserts that "Counselors practice in specialty areas new to them only after appropriate education, training, and supervised experience. While developing skills in new specialty areas, counselors take steps to ensure the competence of their work and protect others from possible harm" (p. 8). Concerning the monitor of effectiveness, ACA's code C.2.d. affirms that "Counselors continually monitor their effectiveness as professionals and take steps to improve when necessary. Counselors take reasonable steps to seek peer supervision to evaluate their efficacy as counselors" (p. 8). Lastly, counselors are ethically obligated to seek consultation as needed regarding professional practice (see ACA code C.2.e.) as well as recognize the need for continued education to maintain competence (see ACA code C.2.f.). Applying these ethical codes, along with the heart of IPNB, which values the felt sense of safety in counseling and neural healing through integration, the IPNB counselor-in-training will due their due diligence to obtain the continued education and supervised experience that honors the foundational beliefs and principles of IPNB. The next section offers three certification programs that provide a great starting point for best practices.

TRAINING AND CERTIFICATION

Currently, at the time of this writing, there is not a credential or licensure in IPBN. However, there are a few institutions that offer a certificate in IPNB including the Mindsight Institute, Portland Community College, and Southwestern College.

Mindsight Institute

Dr. Siegel offers a comprehensive IPNB course titled "The Mindsight Approach to Well-Being: A Comprehensive Course in Interpersonal Neurobiology" through his educational organization, the Mindsight Institute (Mindsight Institute, 2024). The course offers 36 CE credits, 36 prerecorded hours of content training, 9 hours of live Q & A discussions with Dr. Siegel (archival access to the Live Q & As), online learning community, online study groups, and lifetime access to the course content. The training is offered in the following segments:

- Segment 1: Mind, Brain, and Relationships in the Cultivation of Well-Being,
- Segment 2: Attachments and How Close Relationships Shape Who We Are,
- Segment 3: The 1st Domain of Integration: Consciousness and Dr. Siegel's Reflective Practice, "The Wheel of Awareness,"

- Segment 4: The 2nd, 3rd, and 4th Domains of Integration: Linking the Two Sides of the Brain, the Embodied Brain, and Memory,

- Segment 5: The 5th and 6th Domains of Integration: Making Sense of Life through our Narratives and States of Mind, and

- Segment 6: The 7th, 8th, and 9th Domains of Integration: Interpersonal Relationships, Dimensions of Time, and Facets of Identity.

The total cost for the training is $890.00 with the choice of a 6-month option that is paid in $89.00 monthly installments over 10 months or a 6-week option that is paid in $89.00 weekly installments over 10 weeks. The 6-month option offers monthly live Q & As over 6 months in January through July, whereas the 6-week option offers weekly live Q & As over 6 weeks in February through March. Participants also have the option of purchasing just the course for $690.00 (10 weekly installments of $69.00), which includes 36 CE credits, 36 hours of course video, and lifetime access to the course content. All three options offer a savings of $40.00 (course only option) or $41.00 (Live Q & A options) if paid in full at the time of purchase. For more information, visit the Mindsight Institute's comprehensive IPNB course website at

https://mindsightinstitute.com/product/the-mindsight-approach-to-well-being-a-comprehensive-course-in-interpersonal-neurobiology/.

Portland Community College (PCC)

The CLIMB Center at PCC offers a 7-month certificate program entitled *Foundation of Interpersonal Neurobiology (IPNB) Certificate*. This program "explores the theory and practical working models that inform human development, attachment and trauma, and functions as a product of the relationship between the body, mind, and relationships" (PCC, 2024, para. 1). This certificate program offers 125 hours of CE over 2 terms through online weekly synchronous classes, online weekly asynchronous readings and assignments, and an in-person immersion weekend (4 days of embodied practicum). While strongly encouraged to attend the live weekly, zoom-based class sessions in order to explore and cultivate the concepts of IPNB with one's fellow classmates, students unable to attend the live sessions can view the class recording later. Course topics include the following: Introduction to IPNB (20 CE hours), IPNB Navigation and Integration (8 CE hours), Science of IPNB (25 CE hours), A Mind for Learning Seminar (3 CE hours), IPNB of Attachment and Trauma (18 CE hours), Bridging Relational Neuroscience Across Difference (20 CE hours), Embodied Systems and Mindful Resilience (12 CE hours), Leadership Seminar (3 CE hours), and IPNB of Connection and Community (16 CE hours). Ethics from an IPNB Perspective (6 CE hours) is woven throughout the certificate program. Tuition for this program totals $2,499.00 plus a $45.00 application fee and tuition can be paid at registration or through a 6-month payment plan. For more information, visit PCC's IPNB certificate program website at https://www.pcc.edu/climb/health/mental/ipnb/. This author completed this certificate program during Fall 2021 – Spring 2022. According to this author, the most enjoyable and fascinating part of this certificate program occurred during the immersion experience she had the opportunity to dissect an animal brain and explore its various structures.

Southwestern College

The New Earth Institute of Southwestern College (2024) offers a 6-course certificate program entitled *Applied Interpersonal Neurobiology Certificate*. Each course is typically offered on a weekend and on camps at Southwestern College located in Santa Fe, New Mexico. According to the New Earth Institute of Southwestern College, the program courses are "crafted to provide the most current theory and practices from relational neuroscience and a toolbox of practical, experiential skills grounded in IPNB for working with people of diverse backgrounds in individual and group settings" (para. 4). Furthermore, "through personal exploration and experiential practice, participants can enrich their capacity for bringing mindful, attuned, embodied connection to their relationships, their work and their lives" (para. 4). The 6-course certificate program offers 96 CE hours (16 CE hours for each course) through the completion of any 6 of the following 7 courses:

- The Neurobiological Foundations of Therapeutic Practice: Integrating Brain, Body and Heart Intelligence

- Neurobiological Roots and Applications of Psychodrama and Action Methods

- Mindfulness-Based Emotional Processing (MBEP): Minding the Body, Embodying the Mind

- The Psychedelic Experience: Promises and Perils

- Moving Toward Wholeness: The Intrinsic Wisdom of Body/Mind/ Spirit through Holotropic Breathwork

- A New Perspective on the Essentials and Practice of Group Work

- Earth Body/Earth Mind

- Other courses may be offered and are listed in their quarterly schedules.

Tuition for this program is $375.00 per course for a total of $2,250.00 for the certificate. It is important to note that current graduate students taking the course to meet a graduate degree program must pay the current graduate tuition rate. Students or community members must complete all classes required for the certificate within six years of taking the first class. For more information, visit The New Earth Institute of Southwestern College certificate program website at https://www.swc.edu/applying-to-certificate-specialty-programs/applied-interpersonal-neurobiology/#.VPJ0uP05CM8.

SUMMARY

IPNB is more than a set of five foundational beliefs and twelve integrative principles. It is a *way of being* that provides a felt sense of safety and safe embodiment that provides hope and healing through relational healing. According to Bonnie Badenoch (2021), "Interpersonal neurobiology is more than a theory drawn from the discoveries of relational neuroscience. It is an invitation to make direct contact with the heart of our genetic human inheritance" (p. 116). Humans are genetically encoded to need and want healthy connection with others. Our complex system is continuously on a quest for connection, seeking the most nurturing connection and attachment it can fathom (Siegel, 2020). Therefore, the ultimate goal of the IPNB counselor is to become a therapeutic presence in the counseling room in order to provide neurobiological hope and healing for the clients that enter such room.

Christina Villarreal-Davis, PhD, LPC-S, NCC, RPT-S™ is an Associate Professor at Liberty University and the Clinical Director of Wellspring of Life Counseling & Play Therapy Center, PLLC in San Antonio, TX. She received her master's degree in Community Counseling from St. Mary's University in 2002 and her Doctorate in Counselor Education and Supervision (CES) from Regent University in 2007. She has over 20 years of experience in working with children, adolescents, adults, families, and couples with various emotional and mental health concerns by incorporating an interpersonal neurobiology (IPNB) framework and utilizing Child-Centered Play Therapy (CCPT), Child-Parent Relationship Therapy (CPRT), and Person-Centered Therapy. Her research and writing interests include CCPT, CPRT, multiculturalism and cultural humility, IPNB, sandtray therapy, and utilizing creativity in counseling and CES. She has presented on these topics locally, as well as at state, national, and international conferences. Dr. Villarreal-Davis is a member of several organizations, including the Association for Play Therapy (APT), Texas Association for Play Therapy (TxAPT), American Counseling Association, Texas Counseling Association, and the American Association for Christian Counselors. She has served as a member and chair of the Leadership Academy at APT as well as Treasurer and a 3-year Presidential term at TxAPT. She has also authored or co-authored several articles in peer-reviewed journals and magazines as well as 11 book chapters on these topics. In her free time, Dr. Villarreal-Davis enjoys spending time with her family, playing sports, working out at Orange Theory Fitness, traveling, reading, and learning!

REFERENCES

American Counseling Association. (2014). *2014 ACA code of ethics.*
https://www.counseling.org/docs/default-source/default-document-library/ethics/2014-aca-code-of-ethics.pdf?sfvrsn=55ab73d0_1

Badenoch, B. (2021). Becoming a therapeutic presence in the counseling room and the world. In

D. J. Siegel, A. N. Schore, & L. Cozolino (Eds.), *Interpersonal neurobiology and clinical practice* (pp. 113-133). W. W. Norton & Company, Inc.

Mindsight Institute. (2024). Dr. Dan Siegel's comprehensive interpersonal neurobiology (IPNB) course. Mind Your Brain, Inc. https://mindsightinstitute.com/product/the-mindsight-approach-to-well-being-a-comprehensive-course-in-interpersonal-neurobiology/

Portland Community College. (2024). Foundations of interpersonal neurobiology (IPNB) certificate. Author. https://www.pcc.edu/climb/health/mental/ipnb/

Siegel, D. J. (1999). *The developing mind: How relationships and the brain interact to shape who we are.* Guilford.

Siegel, D. J. (2012). *Pocket guide to interpersonal neurobiology: An integrative handbook of the mind.* W. W. Norton & Company, Inc.

Siegel, D. J. (2020). *The developing mind: How relationships and the brain interact to shape who we are* (3rd ed.). Guilford.

Siegel, D. J. (2021). Interpersonal neurobiology from the inside out: A brief overview of a consilient approach to personal, public, and planetary flourishing. In D. J. Siegel, A. N.

Schore, & L. Cozolino (Eds.), *Interpersonal neurobiology and clinical practice* (pp. 1-26). W. W. Norton & Company, Inc.

The New Earth Institute of Southwestern College. (2024). *Applied interpersonal neurobiology certificate.* Southwestern College Santa Fe, NM. https://www.swc.edu/applying-to-certificate-specialty-programs/applied-interpersonal-neurobiology/#.VPJ0uP05CM8

Interpersonal Psychoanalysis Therapy

RACHEL BREJCHA, PHD, LPC, QS, NCC

Interpersonal Psychoanalysis therapy was developed by an American Psychiatrist, Harry Stack Sullivan. Sullivan's theory focuses on the impact of the client's interpersonal relationships in childhood with primary caregivers on the development of personality and mental health concerns. Sullivan (1968) coined the term "interpersonal anxiety" to help conceptualize and understand how people develop and maintain interpersonal relationships. Sullivan argued that anxiety was the central motivation for human behavior (Teyber, 2006). Interpersonal anxiety develops through the rejection and disapproval of primary caregivers. Through interpersonal anxiety, Sullivan (1968) theorized that one's personality develops through interpersonal strategies to help reduce anxiety, and rejection from primary caregivers and to create a sense of self-worth (Sullivan, 1968; Sullivan, 1970; Teyber, 1997). For example, a child that was ridiculed by their mother for expressing emotion may have difficulty being emotionally available for a partner in adulthood due to the shame internalized by their primary caregiver.

In Interpersonal Psychoanalysis, the main goal of treatment is to identify relational themes and to provide analytic neutrality so the client(s) can have a corrective emotional experience. A corrective emotional experience is defined as empowering the client to feel safe and validated enough to express their authentic self in session with the counselor in hopes of applying their desired behavioral, psychological, and cognitive self with the counselor (and others; Teyber, 2006). The counselor will be accepting instead of re-enacting harmful relational patterns and schemas from the client's past with primary caregivers; hence, the corrective emotional experience.

The therapeutic relationship is the main vehicle of change, and the counselor must enter the subjective reality of the client's world within each counseling session and therefore, is part of the therapeutic process. The counselor is an active part of therapeutic change and contributes to the client's healing from interpersonal traumas. In conclusion, Interpersonal Psychoanalysis focuses on improving the quality and range of interpersonal relationships in the client's life in hopes of reducing psychological distress and mental health concerns associated with interpersonal anxiety.

EXPERIENCE- CERTIFICATE OF COMPLETION

Online Intensive Psychoanalytic Psychotherapy Program (Online IPPP)

This program is offered through the William Alanson White Institute of Psychiatry, Psychoanalysis & Psychology in New York, NY. The curriculum for the online IPPP includes 28-weeks of four modules over seven weeks each focused on the interpersonal psychoanalytic perspective. All coursework is completed via Zoom and the program tuition is $3,000 and nonrefundable. The application requires a $75 fee, professional liability insurance and to have current psychotherapy clients for class discussions and seminars.

All applicants must be licensed in a mental health field including one of the following: psychiatrists, psychologists, social workers, nurse practitioners, family therapists, couple's therapists, clinical professional counselors, and art therapists. In addition, professionals whose licensed scope is within the practice of psychotherapy may also apply. A certificate of completion of coursework is awarded at the end of the program and allows psychotherapists to apply for the Contemporary Clinical Workshop.

Link to the application: The Online IPPP Application Form 2024 (wufoo.com)

SUMMARY

Experience in Interpersonal Psychoanalysis Therapy is best suited for a mental health professional who works primarily in the here and now while incorporating the impact of childhood interpersonal relationships with primary caregivers on current interpersonal relationship dynamics. This type of therapy utilizes the therapeutic working alliance as the main vehicle of change. Interpersonal Psychoanalysis can be effective when working with clients with interpersonal trauma histories, grief and loss, anxiety and depression, self-esteem and identity concerns, relationship concerns, and more.

The Interpersonal Psychoanalysis program strongly suggests that you seek personal counseling as you navigate the curriculum to continue to be self-aware and to work on healing your own interpersonal concerns. Interested mental health professionals must be ready to dive deeper into their own narratives while providing space for clients to do the same work and emotionally heal from interpersonal dynamics and concerns that contribute to the development of mental health concerns.

Rachel Brejcha, PhD, LPC, NCC is an Assistant Professor and Fieldwork Coordinator of the Clinical Mental Health Counseling Program at Catawba College. Dr. Brejcha is a Licensed Professional Counselor (LPC) in Michigan and South Carolina, as well as a National Certified Counselor (NCC). She is also a Qualified Supervisor (QS) and provides supervision to mental health clinicians with provisional licenses. Dr. Brejcha specializes in college student development, teaching, and clinical supervision. Dr. Brejcha has clinical experience working with college students, medical students, and within perinatal mental health. Her research interests include the theory of clinical supervision, the therapeutic working alliance, and bridging the gap between research and clinical practice. Dr. Brejcha earned her BS at DePaul University, her MS at the University of North Carolina-Greensboro, and her Ph.D. at Oakland University. In her free time, Dr. Brejcha enjoys spending time with her family, trying new coffee shops, and traveling.

REFERENCES

Robertson, M. (2008). Interpersonal psychotherapy: an overview. *Psychotherapy in Australia, 14*(3), 54.

Sullivan, H. (1968). *The interpersonal theory of psychiatry*. New York: Norton.

Sullivan, H. S. (1970). *The psychiatric interview*. New York: Norton.

Teyber, E. (2006). *Interpersonal process in therapy: An integrative model* (5th ed.). Belmont: Thomson Brooks/Cole.

Training and Education. William Alanson White Institute. Retrieved April 13th, 2023, from <u>Training & Education – William Alanson White Institute (wawhite.org)</u>

Interpersonal Psychotherapy (IPT)

LAUREN FLYNN, PH.D., NCC

Interpersonal Process Therapy, which has been referred to as Interpersonal Process Therapy or simply (IPT) is a type of therapy that focuses on a client's relationships and interactions with others as a way to understand and treat their clinical concerns. IPT is based on the idea that emotional and behavioral problems often stem from difficulties in relationships and interactions with others, and that addressing these difficulties can alleviate psychological distress and promote emotional well-being. This approach is centered around exploring the connections between a client's clinical concerns and their interpersonal relationships. Thus, examining how interpersonal conflict and experiences contribute to emotional and behavioral symptoms. IPT is a brief goal-oriented and structured approach with treatment typically spanning 12-16 sessions. This approach was originally developed in the 1970s by Dr. Gerald Klerman and Dr. Myrna Weissman as a treatment for depression, however it has been shown to be effective in international research trials across a variety of mental health diagnoses including anxiety, bipolar disorder, eating disorders, and phobias. When it was first developed, IPT was created as a research intervention, and until recently all practitioners of IPT were researchers. The success of IPT in research studies led to growing interest in IPT among clinicians, and subsequently the global use of IPT in clinical practice. Some principles and techniques core to IPT include personal inventory, or the evaluation of current relationships, capacity for intimacy, and relationship patterns, exploration of interpersonal signals or self-expression, assessment of ability to assert needs and wishes within interpersonal encounters and taking appropriate social risks.

CERTIFICATIONS, TRAININGS, AND LICENSURE REQUIREMENTS FOR IPT

As IPT began as a research intervention, the training requirements for becoming an IPT researcher have predated IPT clinical training requirements. The standards for clinical training for non-researchers are still being defined. Though no single body has been recognized as the gold standard of IPT training, there are several organizations that offer trainings and certifications to IPT clinicians. Multiple online training platforms offer brief introductory trainings to IPT, but International Society of Interpersonal Psychotherapy (ISIPT) and Interpersonal Psychotherapy Institute (IPT) are the primary organizations for IPT training, each offering numerous IPT certifications. Though the International Society for Interpersonal Psychotherapy is identified as the international umbrella organization for IPT, it allows countries to develop their own credentialing processes for IPT and Interpersonal Psychotherapy Institute was formed to offer courses in the US and over 30 other countries. The requirements for each certification type within both organizations are outlined below.

International Society of Interpersonal Psychotherapy (ISIPT) Certifications

<u>Therapist Certification</u>

Requirements:

- Completion of terminal degree in field including but not limited to Counseling, Social Work, Marriage and Family Therapy, Psychiatric Nursing, and Clinical Psychology or hold a clinical license in one's designated field.

- Minimum of 150 hours of supervised training in designated field and be license-eligible within two years.

- Minimum of 16 hours of introductory IPT training workshop or equivalent of IPT coursework by an ISIPT endorsed trainer. Documentation of activity completion must be provided.

- Completion of at least three supervised cases representing early, middle and late sessions, each by ISIPT endorsed supervisor

- Completion of online application

Maintenance of Certification:

- All providers must recertify every five years.

- Therapists are required to submit documentation of participation in 40 continuing educations hours of IPT training over the past five

- Therapists must have maintained their membership in ISIPT over the previous five years.

- Therapists must have maintained their professional license or credentials

Cost = Therapist Certification fee is $250.00 USD.

<u>Trainer Certification</u>

Requirements:

- Active ISIPT membership
- Completion of terminal degree in field including but not limited to Counseling, Social Work, Marriage and Family Therapy, Psychiatric Nursing, and Clinical Psychology.
- Certified as an IPT therapist
- Received supervision on the treatment of 2 additional IPT cases for a total of 5 supervised cases for themselves.
- Continued use of IPT treatment approach with cases for a minimum of a year after therapist certification.
- Completion of a specific trainer's training.
- Led or co-led a minimum of 100 hours of IPT teaching in clinical IPT training workshops or IPT academic course, or IPT research study.

Maintenance of Certification:

- Trainers must recertify every five years.
- Trainers are required to submit documentation of three trainings or a minimum of eight hours of training workshops over the last five years
- Trainers must have maintained their membership in ISIPT over the previous five years.
- Trainers must have maintained their professional license or credentials.

Cost= Trainer certification fee is $300.00 USD. If applying for Supervisor and Trainer certification concurrently the fee is $450.00 USD

Supervisor Certification

Requirements:

- Active ISIPT membership
- Must currently use IPT in clinical, academic or research practices.
- Already certified as an IPT therapist
- Must have an identifiable track record of providing IPT supervision which includes a minimum of supervising four different clinicians.
- Completion of specific supervisor's training, mentoring, academic course, self-study, or training through a research project that covered the core competencies and adherence elements of IPT supervision where available.

Maintenance of Certification:

- Supervisors must recertify every five years.
- Supervisors are required to submit documentation of 40 hours of supervision of at least three supervisees over the last five years or a minimum of eight hours of supervisor trainings, or a minimum of eight hours of training workshops, consultations, webinars, etc. that have helped maintain supervising skills, knowledge and experience since initial certification.
- Supervisors must have maintained membership in ISIPT over the previous five years.
- Supervisors must have maintained professional license or credentials.

Cost = Supervisor certification fee is $300.00 USD. If applying for Supervisor and Trainer certification concurrently the fee is $450.00 USD.

Interpersonal Psychotherapy Institute (IPT) Trainings & Certifications

IPT Clinical Training Level A

This Level A clinical training is an introductory course for individuals with professional clinical training in mental health at the graduate or professional level. This course is a prerequisite for all IPT certifications. Prior to the training, participants are asked to be familiar with the IPT textbook. The course, either live on-line or in person, is 16 hours and involves didactic instruction in IPT along with video review and discussion, small group interactions, and practice of IPT skills and techniques.

Cost = Price of Level A training not listed on the Interpersonal Psychotherapy Institute (IPT) organization website.

IPT Community-Based Therapist Certification Level B

After completing Level A training, individuals are eligible to begin the Community-Based Therapist Certification Level B training program. This program is multifaceted and is designed to be completed within 6-8 months. The requirements for this certification are outlined below:

Requirements:

- Completion of an IPT Institute accredited Level A IPT Course within the last three years.
- Licensure or student status sufficient to conduct clinical work with patients.
- Completion of at least 10 consultation hours. These hours may include either individual consultation or small-group consultation as is typical for the Community-Based Training programs. Consultation must be provided by an IPT Institute accredited consultant.
- Completion of two IPT Portfolios (one portfolio for two different clients). Each portfolio must obtain a passing grade as rated by an IPT Institute accredited Consultant. Each portfolio must include Case Report of the IPT treatment provided, Interpersonal Inventory, Interpersonal Formulation, Interpersonal Summary, Self-Evaluation Rating, Patient Outcome Measures, and an audio or videotape of one session of the IPT treatment. The two portfolios should capture different time points in the treatment process.
- Completion of an IPT Booster or Advanced Course of at least 8 hours.

Cost= Prices for the required training, consultation hours, and IPT booster or Advanced Course not listed on the Interpersonal Psychotherapy Institute (IPT) organization website.

IPT Certified Therapist Level C

For those who complete the Level B training program and wish to continue to become IPT Certified Therapists, they must receive a nomination for Level C Training by IPT Institute Consultant. Following nomination, individuals must complete two more individually supervised cases and satisfactory portfolios, with the same portfolio requirements as outlined in Level B requirements.

Cost= Prices for the case supervision are not listed on the Interpersonal Psychotherapy Institute (IPT) organization website.

IPT Certified Supervisor Level D

This certification is limited to individuals with professional licensure. In order to become an IPT Certified Supervisor Level D, one must complete Level C training and be nominated for Level D training by an IPT Institute Consultant.

Requirements:

- Completion of an IPT Institute accredited Level D IPT Course. The course must include 8-16 hours of instruction.

- Adequate reliability in using the IPT Quality and Adherence Rating Scale.

- Completion of two group consultations (10 or more hours each) as a co-consultant with an IPT Institute Certified Consultant.
  - Reviews of the written portfolio feedback provided by the consultant in training must be at least a high proficiency grade rated by an IPT Institute Certified Consultant.
  - Reviews of the consultant in training provided by the Certified Senior Co-Consultant must be at least a high proficiency grade.

- Nomination by that Certified IPT Consultant for continuation to lead a consultation group as a solo consultant.

- Displayed ongoing commitment to training in IPT including maintaining clinical practice in IPT, participating in IPT consultants' mentoring groups and yearly training in IPT updates, and maintaining an average of 3.5 or greater on reviews by supervisees.

Cost= Prices for the Level D course and consultation hours are not listed on the Interpersonal Psychotherapy Institute (IPT) organization website.

IPT Certified Instructor Level E

IPT Certified Instructor Level E is reserved for very experienced IPT clinicians and requires extensive coursework, co-teaching, and teaching at a satisfactory level. To begin this certification process, an individual must be nominated by their supervisor and trainer. The Level E requirements are outlined below:

Requirements:

- Completion of an IPT Institute accredited Level E IPT Course. The course must include 14-16 hours of instruction.

- Co-teaching at least two IPT training courses (16 hours or more) with an IPT Certified Instructor.
  - Written teaching reviews provided by course participants must be at least a high proficiency grade.
  - Reviews of the instructor in training provided by the Certified Senior Co-Instructor must be at least a high proficiency grade.

- Co-instruction must be done with consecutive courses rather than concurrent courses.

- Nomination by that Certified IPT Instructor for continuation to teach an IPT Course as a solo instructor.

- Teaching at least one IPT course (14 or more hours each) as a solo instructor. Ratings for each course must be a high proficiency grade as rated by an IPT Institute accredited Instructor and an average of 4.0 as rated by the course participants.

- Demonstrate ongoing commitment to training in IPT including as outlined in Level D requirements.

Cost= Prices for the Level E course and consultation hours are not listed on the Interpersonal Psychotherapy Institute (IPT) organization website.

SCOPE OF PRACTICE ISSUES

The training requirements and certification titles differ substantially according to each training track and certifying organization. To progress further in IPT trainings and certifications, the requirements can be extensive and potentially costly, though there is a lack of clarity regarding fees for Interpersonal Psychotherapy Institute trainings. Similarly, International Society of Interpersonal Psychotherapy outlines clear requirements for certification management while Interpersonal Psychotherapy Institute's demonstration of ongoing commitment requirements are vaguer. Though as the international IPT umbrella organization, the International Society of Interpersonal Psychotherapy defers to individual countries to set their own credentialing processes for IPT, this organization seems to offer the most transparent training routes to certification. It is important to note that IPT is an add on therapy to existing approaches and is not a standalone theoretical framework. Thus, clinicians must have a strong theoretical background prior to adding IPT to their repertoire. Though research studies have not identified a population or clinical concern in which IPT is not effective, due to its relational focus, IPT may be particularly well suited for clients of collectivist cultures and its use may be more challenging with clients of individualistic cultures.

SUMMARY

IPT, originally developed by Dr. Gerald Klerman and Dr. Myrna Weissman as a research intervention targeting depression, is a brief evidence-based clinical approach for the treatment of a variety of mental health concerns. IPT proposes that clinical concerns often stem from difficulties in relationships, and thus centers the client's interpersonal relationships as the mechanism for healing. Though there is not an identified gold standard for clinical training in IPT, there are several organizations that offer IPT trainings and certifications for therapists, supervisors, trainers, and instructors. Though IPT is a fairly simple treatment approach for already experienced clinicians to add to their practice, the training and credentialing processes may be time consuming. Still, the dues may be well worth the outcome as IPT is a valuable evidence-based treatment and its relational focus allows clinicians to build on and pull from the client's social resources and help them feel more connected with those around them throughout the healing process. Clinicians with relational perspectives such as Relational Cultural Theory (RCT) or Family Systems Theory may be particularly interested in using IPT in their clinical practice.

Lauren Flynn, Ph.D., NCC, is a mental health counselor and adjunct professor in San Diego, California. She earned her doctorate in Counselor Education and Practice from Georgia State University. Dr. Flynn specializes in the treatment of trauma and addiction, and her research and teaching interests lie in the intersection of trauma and addiction. She can be reached by email at Lflynn@sandiego.edu

REFERENCES

Bäck, M. (n.d.). International Society of Interpersonal Psychotherapy - ISIPT. https://interpersonalpsychotherapy.org/

Markowitz, J. C., & Weissman, M. M. (2004). Interpersonal psychotherapy: principles and applications. PubMed. https://pubmed.ncbi.nlm.nih.gov/16633477

Perishable. (n.d.). IPT Institute. Copyright Interpersonal Psychotherapy Institute - All Rights Reserved. https://iptinstitute.com/

Interpersonal and Social Rhythm Therapy (IPSRT)

BILL OWENBY, EDD, MC, FAAETS, DAAETS, DCMHS, LPC, LAAC, NCC, CCMHC, ACS, DIPLOMATE, FELLOW

DEFINITION AND OVERVIEW

Interpersonal and Social Rhythm Therapy (IPSRT) is an evidence-based psychotherapy initially developed for the treatment of bipolar disorder. It combines principles from interpersonal psychotherapy (IPT) and social rhythm therapy, aiming to stabilize daily routines and interpersonal relationships to help manage mood fluctuations. IPSRT is rooted in the idea that disruptions in biological and social rhythms can trigger mood episodes, particularly among individuals with mood disorders.

HISTORICAL BACKGROUND

IPSRT was developed by Ellen Frank, Ph.D., and her colleagues at the University of Pittsburgh. Their research into the connection between circadian rhythms and mood regulation in individuals with bipolar disorder led to the creation of this therapeutic model. It was first introduced formally in the early 2000s following successful clinical trials demonstrating its effectiveness in prolonging periods of wellness and reducing the recurrence of mood episodes (Frank et al., 2005).

CORE COMPONENTS OF IPSRT

IPSRT integrates two key domains:
1. **Interpersonal Therapy (IPT):** Focuses on resolving interpersonal conflicts, role transitions, grief, and interpersonal deficits that may contribute to mood instability.
2. **Social Rhythm Therapy:** Encourages regular daily routines (sleep, meals, socialization, physical activity) to enhance circadian stability and reduce biological stressors.

APPLICATIONS IN MENTAL HEALTH PRACTICE

IPSRT is especially effective in treating:

- Bipolar I and II Disorder
- Cyclothymic disorder
- Recurrent major depressive disorder with circadian instability
- Clients with mood disorders affected by life transitions, grief, or disrupted social rhythms

Techniques Used

- Daily mood and activity charting using a Social Rhythm Metric (SRM)
- Psychoeducation about circadian biology and bipolar disorder
- Identification and resolution of interpersonal issues
- Goal-setting and behavioral activation to establish stability

TRAINING AND CERTIFICATION REQUIREMENTS

While there is no universal governing body for IPSRT certification, structured training programs are available through research institutions and individual trainers:

1. **University of Pittsburgh's Western Psychiatric Institute and Clinic:** The birthplace of IPSRT, offers periodic professional development workshops and clinical supervision.
2. **IPSRT.com:** Offers virtual training options from clinicians closely associated with the model's originators.
3. **Training Components Include:**
   o Didactic sessions on the theoretical foundation of IPSRT
   o Practice with the Social Rhythm Metric
   o Case consultation and supervision
   o Role-play exercises and review of clinical application

General Cost and Time Commitment
- Online introductory trainings range from $250 to $500
- Advanced courses or supervised practicums may cost up to $1,200
- Time commitment ranges from 8 to 40 hours depending on level of training

SCOPE OF PRACTICE

IPSRT is a specialized therapeutic approach typically implemented by licensed mental health professionals with advanced training in psychotherapy. These include:

- Licensed Professional Counselors (LPCs)
- Psychologists
- Social Workers (LCSWs)
- Marriage and Family Therapists (LMFTs)
- Psychiatrists and Psychiatric Nurse Practitioners
  While IPSRT techniques (like routine tracking) can be taught in paraprofessional contexts, full implementation is best reserved for licensed providers due to its clinical complexity and focus on mood disorders.

IDEAL CLIENTS

- Individuals with bipolar disorder seeking structure and rhythm
- Clients experiencing mood swings exacerbated by chaotic schedules
- Those undergoing grief or interpersonal changes impacting emotional regulation

IDEAL PROFESSIONALS

- Mental health clinicians with a background in mood disorder treatment
- Providers with training in CBT, IPT, or DBT who want to expand their scope
- Therapists interested in chronotherapy or circadian-focused mental health interventions

CAUTIONS AND LIMITATIONS

- IPSRT requires client motivation and consistency; it may not be appropriate for individuals with severe cognitive impairment or non-adherence challenges
- Limited access to formal training and supervision may hinder consistent implementation
- Requires time-intensive data tracking, which may not appeal to all clients

SUMMARY

IPSRT represents a unique blend of interpersonal psychotherapy and behavioral rhythm regulation that has proven effective, particularly in managing bipolar disorder. Its focus on lifestyle regularity and relational health makes it a versatile and powerful intervention for mood stabilization. As access to structured training expands, IPSRT stands to become an increasingly valuable modality in the clinician's toolkit for mood disorder treatment.

I hold two independent licenses in the states of Arizona and Ohio, supervisory status in Arizona, along with a substance abuse license in Arizona. I am board certified as a Diplomate and Clinical Mental Health Specialist, an Approved Clinical Supervisor, Nationally Certified Counselor, a Certified Clinical Mental Health Counselor, NeuroLinguistic Programming Practitioner, and a Clinical Trauma Specialist for Individuals and Family including EMDR Therapy and NET. I completed my training in Animal-Assisted Therapy and Pet Handlers certification in order to evaluate and incorporate the human-animal bond in therapy. I am the sole author and creator of the SxC Model of ESA Evaluation. My research interests surround post-traumatic growth, resiliency, strengths-based therapy, positive psychology, mindfulness, Animal-Assisted Therapy, Sandtray Therapy, Creative approaches in therapy, and martial arts in mental health. I have presented at local, state, regional, national, and international levels on various topics including personality traits, licensure reciprocity challenges, Sandtray and supervision, and Animal-Assisted Therapy within supervision. eonbllc@gmail.com

REFERENCES

Frank, E., Swartz, H. A., & Kupfer, D. J. (2005). Interpersonal and social rhythm therapy: Managing the chaos of bipolar disorder. *Biological Psychiatry*, 48(6), 593-604.

University of Pittsburgh School of Medicine. (n.d.). Interpersonal and Social Rhythm Therapy (IPSRT). Retrieved from https://www.psychiatry.pitt.edu/

IPSRT.com. (n.d.). IPSRT Training Resources. Retrieved from https://ipsrt.com

American Psychiatric Association. (2013). *Diagnostic and Statistical Manual of Mental Disorders (5th ed.)*. Arlington, VA: American Psychiatric Publishing.

Intimacy from the Inside Out

BILL OWENBY, EdD, MC, FAAETS, DAAETS, DCMHS, LPC, LAAC, NCC, CCMHC, ACS, DIPLOMATE, FELLOW

Intimacy from the Inside Out (IFIO) is a specialized therapeutic approach rooted in Internal Family Systems (IFS) therapy. This method focuses on enhancing intimacy and connection within relationships by addressing individuals' internal dynamics and fostering understanding and compassion between partners. Developed by Toni Herbine-Blank, IFIO emphasizes the importance of self-awareness, communication, and vulnerability as pathways to relational growth.

OVERVIEW OF INTIMACY FROM THE INSIDE OUT

IFIO integrates principles of IFS with relational therapy techniques to help individuals and couples navigate the complexities of their emotional lives and relationships. This approach recognizes that inner conflicts and protective parts often drive interpersonal difficulties, and it seeks to foster healing and connection both within individuals and between partners.

CORE PRINCIPLES OF IFIO

1. **Internal Family Systems Framework**
   - Recognizes the influence of different internal parts, such as protectors and exiles, on relational dynamics.
   - Encourages individuals to develop self-leadership and compassion for their internal systems.
2. **Relational Focus**
   - Highlights the interplay between individual internal processes and relational interactions.
   - Helps partners understand and respond to each other's vulnerabilities.
3. **Compassionate Communication**
   - Builds skills for empathetic listening and authentic expression.
   - Reduces blame and defensiveness in relationships.
4. **Fostering Vulnerability**
   - Encourages individuals to access and share their core emotions and needs.
   - Strengthens emotional bonds through mutual understanding.

APPLICATIONS OF IFIO

Couples Therapy
- **Conflict Resolution**: Identifies and addresses patterns of reactivity and blame in relationships.
- **Rebuilding Trust**: Provides a safe framework for partners to explore and heal breaches of trust.
- **Enhancing Emotional Intimacy**: Promotes deeper understanding and connection between partners.

Individual Therapy
- **Self-Understanding**: Helps individuals recognize how their internal dynamics influence their relationships.
- **Healing Past Wounds**: Addresses unresolved trauma and emotional pain that impact relational patterns.
- **Building Relational Skills**: Teaches practical tools for improving communication and connection.

Group Therapy
- **Peer Support**: Offers a shared space for individuals and couples to explore relational challenges.
- **Skill Development**: Provides opportunities to practice communication and vulnerability in a supportive environment.
- **Fostering Connection**: Encourages empathy and understanding among group members.

TRAINING AND CERTIFICATION IN IFIO

Educational Pathways

1. **Foundational Workshops**
   - Introductory training covering the principles of IFS and its application to relationships.
   - Typically 2–3 days in duration, designed for therapists new to IFS or relational work.
2. **Core Training Program**
   - In-depth training in IFIO techniques, including experiential practice and case consultations.
   - Delivered over multiple weekends or an intensive week-long format.
3. **Advanced Training**
   - Focuses on complex cases, advanced techniques, and refining therapeutic skills.
   - Includes supervised practice and peer consultation.

Certification Requirements

1. **Prerequisites**
   - Must complete IFS Level 1 training or demonstrate equivalent experience with IFS principles.
   - Background in psychotherapy, counseling, or a related field is required.
2. **Core Components**
   - Completion of foundational and advanced IFIO training modules.
   - Submission of recorded therapy sessions for evaluation.
   - Participation in ongoing supervision and peer consultation groups.
3. **Time and Cost**
   - Foundational workshops: $500–$800.
   - Core training: $3,000–$5,000, typically spanning 6–12 months.
   - Advanced training: $2,000–$4,000.
4. **Accrediting Organization**
   - Training is overseen by the IFIO Training Institute, founded by Toni Herbine-Blank.

BENEFITS AND LIMITATIONS

Benefits

- **Depth of Insight**: Combines internal and relational exploration for comprehensive growth.
- **Practical Tools**: Provides actionable strategies for improving communication and connection.
- **Trauma-Informed**: Addresses the impact of past experiences on current relational dynamics.

Limitations

- **Intensive Training Requirements**: Certification requires significant time and financial investment.
- **Limited Accessibility**: Training programs may not be available in all regions.
- **Emotional Intensity**: The vulnerability required in therapy can be challenging for some clients.

ETHICAL CONSIDERATIONS

1. **Informed Consent**
   o Clients should understand the emotional depth and vulnerability involved in IFIO therapy.
2. **Cultural Sensitivity**
   o Interventions must be adapted to respect clients' cultural and relational norms.
3. **Scope of Practice**
   o Therapists must ensure they have the requisite training and supervision to provide IFIO.

SUMMARY

Intimacy from the Inside Out is a transformative approach to relational therapy that integrates Internal Family Systems principles with relational techniques. By addressing internal conflicts and fostering vulnerability, IFIO helps individuals and couples build deeper connections and healthier relationships. For therapists, mastering IFIO offers an opportunity to support clients in navigating the complexities of intimacy with compassion and expertise.

I hold two independent licenses in the states of Arizona and Ohio, supervisory status in Arizona, along with a substance abuse license in Arizona. I am board certified as a Diplomate and Clinical Mental Health Specialist, an Approved Clinical Supervisor, Nationally Certified Counselor, a Certified Clinical Mental Health Counselor, NeuroLinguistic Programming Practitioner, and a Clinical Trauma Specialist for Individuals and Family including EMDR Therapy and NET. I completed my training in Animal-Assisted Therapy and Pet Handlers certification in order to evaluate and incorporate the human-animal bond in therapy. I am the sole author and creator of the SxC Model of ESA Evaluation. My research interests surround post-traumatic growth, resiliency, strengths-based therapy, positive psychology, mindfulness, Animal-Assisted Therapy, Sandtray Therapy, Creative approaches in therapy, and martial arts in mental health. I have presented at local, state, regional, national, and international levels on various topics including personality traits, licensure reciprocity challenges, Sandtray and supervision, and Animal-Assisted Therapy within supervision. eonbllc@gmail.com

REFERENCES

Herbine-Blank, T. (2018). Intimacy from the Inside Out: Courage and Compassion in Couple Therapy. IFS Institute.

Schwartz, R. (2013). Internal Family Systems Therapy. Guilford Press.

IFIO Training Institute. (2024). Training and certification guidelines for IFIO therapists. Retrieved from https://www.intimacyfromtheinsideout.com

Recommended Resources

IFIO Training Institute: https://www.intimacyfromtheinsideout.com
Internal Family Systems Institute: https://ifs-institute.com
Couples Therapy Network: https://www.couplestherapynetwork.com

Intra/Interpersonal Identity

Sedaria Williams, NBCC

There is an intricate tapestry of the human form that has a central theme to our being. We want to focus on understanding and integrating who we are within ourselves and with others. This focus allows a sense of self while also improving our relationships from an internal and external perspective. Intra/Interpersonal Identity is deeply rooted in therapy and counseling due to its self-awareness and relational dynamics approach. One must understand the internal self, consisting of our thoughts, emotions, and beliefs while navigating complex relationships with others. Focusing on the intrapersonal involves developing self-determination, establishing self-control, participating in mutual support groups, feeling the need to be accepted, and returning to a meaningful social role (Davidson et al., 2005). We want to feel connected and essential and that we matter, but this can only happen with an interpersonal perspective. It allows a focus on our identity and how those around us help to shape it.

Let us imagine a young woman who has struggled with feelings of inadequacy and a constant need for validation from those around her. Through therapy, she embarks on a self-healing, self-discovery journey that seeks to recognize and challenge negative self-issues and uncover the root cause of her insecurities. She does so by gaining a deeper understanding of self and seeks to understand interpersonal relationships. It includes identifying patterns of behavior such as dependency and how to create healthier boundaries, creating more genuine connections with her circle. How does she do this? Having a dual focus on intrapersonal and interpersonal identity enhances her ability to form meaningful and fulfilling relationships with herself and those around her. Therefore, exploring both interpersonal and intrapersonal will emphasize self-awareness and self-acceptance, which channels the ability to address conflicts between oneself and others.

INTRO TO INTRAPERSONAL IDENTITY THERAPY

Intrapersonal identity therapy is focused on helping persons understand and integrate their emotions, thoughts, and feelings, creating a cohesive sense of being and self. A person's introspective view is based on their sense of who they are and how they view themselves internally. What we often think of ourselves plays out in real-time. For example, Erickson (1968) postulated that identity formation is a dynamic life-long process that creates a sense of contribution towards self-based on constructing our identity. For example, a person may view their self-talk and decision-making as internal dialogues that affect their self-projection. Intrapersonal allows for more goal-oriented work that helps to create a compassionate and healthier focus within oneself. Identities serve as responses to the inquiry, "Who am I?" (Ashforth, Harrison, & Corley, 2008), and are constructed through the lens of roles and interpersonal relationships (Ashforth & Schinoff, 2016; Sluss & Ashforth, 2007). Thus, we seek to answer the question by forging our personal concepts of self and the roles we play while being influenced by our titles, ultimately leading to how others view us.

INTRO TO INTERPERSONAL IDENTITY THERAPY

Interpersonal identity therapy involves understanding and improving a person's relationships with others and how these relationships impact their sense of well-being. Individuals often define themselves through relationships and social interactions that shape their perception and role in others' lives. The simple way to see interpersonal identity is how people see and define themselves through their closest relationships and social circles. For example, a person with a strong identity or a dedicated employee and friend may have a sense of who they are based on these relationships and how others perceive them. Using interpersonal identity, we may understand the influences that affect a person's behavior and self-esteem. As we continue to work on ourselves, we can align with personal values and goals that are not tied to someone else's opinion of us.

HOW INTRA AND INTERPERSONAL IDENTITY THERAPY IS DIFFERENT THAN INTERPERSONAL PROCESS THERAPY

Intrapersonal identity therapy and interpersonal identity therapy are recognized as therapeutic approaches. The focus of their therapy is different from that of their counterparts, interpersonal process therapy (IPT). Lipsitz & Markowitz (2013) conceptualize interpersonal problems as central interpersonal problems, current crises or predicaments that disrupt social support. Improved relationships may increase one's mood, resulting in improved mental health. There is a direct change to address patterns and improve social functions that oftentimes lead to overall distress. Intra and Interpersonal Identity Therapy focuses on exploring and understanding one's identity, internally (intra) and about others (interpersonal). Intra and inter's primary focus is resolving conflicts that hinder awareness and affect one's identity (religious, ethnic, social, etc.). Each therapy offers valuable insights into personal growth. However, each one caters to different therapeutic goals.

CERTIFICATIONS, TRAINING, AND LICENSURE REQUIREMENTS FOR INTRA/INTER-IDENTITY THERAPY

Many clinical mental health clinicians can work with intrapersonal and interpersonal identity therapy. Standard training and licensure requirements for becoming a therapist and counselor include obtaining certifications such as the National Certified Counselor (NCC), which necessitates a master's degree. Additionally, state-specific certifications and licensure, such as the Licensed Marriage and Family Therapist (LMFT), are required and vary by state. Furthermore, the International Society of Interpersonal Therapy (IPST) offers certification to gain specialized hours and experience in using interpersonal identity therapy. The International Society of Interpersonal Psychotherapy (ISIPT) asks for several things to be met to maintain membership within working within interpersonal therapy. To get certified, candidates must have a terminal degree in a relevant field like Clinical Counseling, Marriage and Family Therapy, Psychiatric Nursing, or Clinical Psychology. They can also hold a clinical license appropriate for their field and region.

In addition, they need at least 150 hours of supervised training in therapy provision and must be license-eligible within two years. They must also complete at least 16 hours of introductory IPT training workshops or equivalent coursework by an ISIPT-endorsed trainer. Plus, candidates must document the completion of at least three supervised cases, covering early, middle, and late sessions, each supervised by an ISIPT-endorsed supervisor.

SCOPE OF PRACTICE ISSUES

Therapists and counselors working with interpersonal and intrapersonal identities should adhere to a holistic and comprehensive approach. However, a boundary exists based on the circumstances and the client's needs. Intra and interpersonal identity therapy may not work with clients experiencing severe mental health disorders such as schizophrenia or bipolar disorder. There may be a disconnect in understanding the introspective nature of identity therapy, where one needs structure and focused-driven interventions. Clients experiencing acute crisis need stabilization and immediate needs that either of these modalities can provide at the time. One would refer to interpersonal process therapy when a client has social interactions with many difficulties in those relationships. Let us imagine a client with unresolved interpersonal conflicts or role transitions; IPT can create a structured approach to these issues that intra and interpersonal identity cannot.

CAUTIONS OR LIMITATIONS OF THIS MODALITY

Any modality has limitations and boundaries, including intrapersonal and interpersonal identity. A level of introspection and self-awareness must exist, which may be problematic for someone who is not yet willing to engage in deep reflection or self-reflection. This modality style is less structured and, at times, has more in-depth approaches than most. In therapy, we explore many emotions and memories that may evoke strong emotions. Clients should be able to prepare for the intensity it brings, and sometimes unresolved trauma needs additional support that intra and interpersonal identity may not provide.

Time consumption is another limitation, which shows that the more unresolved trauma, the more time is needed. Therefore, a person must have an integrated sense of self and understand the ability to find solutions that may take time and space.

There is always a cultural, social, and contextual component to identity issues. To be effective in guiding diverse clients in their healing journeys, therapists must have cultural competence. Consequently, clients must be active, engaged, and committed to the therapeutic process.

SUMMARY

We delve into the intricate tapestry of human identity, focusing on intrapersonal and interpersonal dimensions. It highlights the significance of understanding and integrating one's emotions, thoughts, and beliefs to create a cohesive sense of self. Intrapersonal identity therapy seeks to center an individual's internal experiences, which assists with a sense of acceptance of self, leading to a more fulfilling social role. Internal identity focuses on the impact of relationships on oneself. By utilizing both modalities, we can foster a sense of self-awareness self-acceptance, and address conflicts in relationships that improve our overall well-being.

Sedaria Williams is a doctoral candidate at the University of Memphis in Counselor Education and Supervision. Sedaria earned her bachelor's degree in psychology from Christian Brothers University, master's degree in Sports Administration from Belhaven University, and a master's degree in Clinical Mental Health Counseling from the University of Memphis.

slwrght3@memphis.edu

REFERENCES

Ashforth, B. E., Harrison, S. H., & Corley, K. G. (2008). Identification in organizations: An examination of four fundamental questions. *Journal of Management*, 34: 325–374

Ashforth, B. E., & Schinoff, B. S. (2016). Identity under construction: How employees come to define themselves in organizations. *Annual Review of Organizational Psychology and Organizational Behavior*, 3: 111–137.

Davidson, L., Borg, M., Marin, I., Topor, A., Mezzina, R., & Sells, D. (2005). Process of recovery in serious mental illness: Findings from a multinational study. American Journal of Psychiatric Rehabilitation, 8, 177-201.

Lipsitz JD, Markowitz JC. Mechanisms of change in interpersonal therapy (IPT). Clin Psychol Rev. 2013 Dec;33(8):1134-47. doi: 10.1016/j.cpr.2013.09.002. Epub 2013 Sep 25. PMID: 24100081; PMCID: PMC4109031.

Sluss, D. M., & Ashforth, B. E. (2007). Relational identity and identification: Defining ourselves through work relationships. *Academy of Management Review*, 32: 9–32.

Intuitive Eating

MONIQUE RAHMAN, PHD, LPC, RPT, NCC

Intuitive Eating, conceptualized by dieticians Evelyn Tribole and Elyse Resch in 1995, offers a weight-neutral, evidence-based approach to nutrition and well-being (Tribole, 2017). It emphasizes the innate ability of individuals to regulate their eating habits by listening to and responding to the body's cues to meet physical and psychological needs. This chapter explores the theoretical underpinnings, certification requirements, limitations, and considerations for practice surrounding the Intuitive Eating model.

CERTIFICATION REQUIREMENT AND COST

The Original Intuitive Eating Pros® offer two certification types (Original Intuitive Eating Pros ®, 2020): Certified Intuitive Eating Counselor and Certified Intuitive Eating Lay Facilitator. Counselors are required to have at least a Bachelor's degree in one of the accepted allied health professions, including certified personal trainers, dentists, counselors, midwives, nurses, pharmacists, physicians, registered dietitian nutritionists, and yoga therapists. The founders have provided an application to verify if a career qualifies for certification.

On the other hand, Lay Facilitator certification is tailored for individuals interested in educating the community on Intuitive Eating but who are not health professionals. Examples of potential candidates include support group leaders, clergy, addiction or peer counselors with less than a Bachelor's degree, or some coaches.

As of 2020, both certification types require completion of the following requirements, which typically take at least nine weeks to complete:

Helm Publishing's Self-Study Intuitive Eating Course offers versions specific to either certification option, costing $445 and providing 46 continuing education hours.

Evelyn Tribole's Intuitive Eating PRO Webinar, conducted through live Zoom meetings over six weeks, costs $525 (discounted to $450 with early registration).

Three 45-minute supervision or coaching sessions with either Resch or Tribole themselves, costing $200 each for a total of $600. Tribole also offers 90-minute group sessions for a discounted total of $395 for three sessions.

The total cost to complete either certification route ranges between $1290-1570, depending on the options chosen. Upon certification completion, Counselors and Lay Facilitators gain membership in a closed Facebook Group for Certified Intuitive Eating Counselors, inclusion in a directory on the IntuitiveEating.org website, and licensed use of the "Trained & Certified by the Original Intuitive Eating Pros" logo.

To maintain certification, Counselors and Lay Facilitators must complete three supervision hours every five years.

LIMITATIONS AND CONSIDERATIONS FOR PRACTICE

Intuitive Eating stands in direct contrast to traditional dieting approaches and is not intended for weight loss. Research has consistently shown the ineffectiveness of diets, which often result in weight gain, increased body dissatisfaction, and perpetuation of weight stigma (Rothblum, 2018; O'Hara & Taylor, 2018). Despite this, misconceptions about Intuitive Eating persist, with some individuals mistakenly believing that it promotes unhealthy food choices or higher body weights (Avalos & Tylka, 2006). However, research consistently demonstrates that Intuitive Eating is associated with higher body satisfaction, self-esteem, and lower body mass indexes (Faw et al., 2021; Markey et al., 2022).

In clinical practice, mental health practitioners implementing Intuitive Eating must navigate various considerations. It plays a pivotal role in eating disorder treatment and recovery, shielding against and mediating the risk of developing eating disorders (Linardon, 2021) and aiding in eating disorder recovery (Koller et al., 2019). Practitioners should be adept at recognizing signs of disordered eating and engaging in conversations about unhealthy relationships with food and related trauma (DeVille, Erchull & Mailloux, 2021). Individuals with eating disorders face significant health risks, including one of the highest mortality rates among mental illnesses (Van Hoeken & Koek, 2020).

Because of the severity of eating disorders, mental health practitioners are encouraged to work in a treatment team and consult with registered dieticians and physicians who specialize in disordered eating (Novack, 2021; Yang et al., 2023). Collaboration within a multidisciplinary team is essential for providing comprehensive care and addressing the complex needs of individuals with eating disorders. Clients who focus on weight loss, diets, and BMI may inadvertently work against treatment goals, highlighting the importance of a non-diet approach like Intuitive Eating (Vlahoyiannis & Nifli, 2020). In actuality, restrained eating or rigid dieting has been associated with excess weight and unsuccessful food avoidance strategies, such as cutting down or eliminating carbohydrates or processed foods (Vlahoyiannis & Nifli, 2020).

Working in a treatment team and consulting with registered dieticians and physicians who specialize in disordered eating are crucial elements of effective practice (Novack, 2021; Yang et al., 2023). Collaboration within a multidisciplinary team is vital for providing comprehensive care and addressing the complex needs of individuals with eating disorders. Practitioners should also be mindful of potential barriers to adopting Intuitive Eating practices, such as socioeconomic factors, food insecurity, and parental feeding practices influencing children's eating habits (Burnette et al., 2023).

Practitioners must address potential challenges, including misconceptions about Intuitive Eating and resistance from clients accustomed to dieting. Despite these challenges, the holistic approach of Intuitive Eating empowers clients to develop a healthy and sustainable relationship with food and their bodies, promoting overall well-being and psychological health (Avalos & Tylka, 2006; Faw et al., 2021; Markey et al., 2022).

SUMMARY

Intuitive Eating offers a holistic approach to health and wellness, emphasizing mindfulness, body acceptance, and internal regulation of eating behaviors. Mental health practitioners who prioritize a client-centered, non-diet approach to nutrition and well-being will find Intuitive Eating to be a valuable framework in their practice. By fostering a supportive and inclusive environment, practitioners can empower clients to develop a healthy and sustainable relationship with food and their bodies.

This discussion highlights the importance of understanding the theoretical foundations, certification requirements, limitations, and considerations for practice associated with the Intuitive Eating model. By integrating these insights into clinical practice, mental health practitioners can effectively support clients in their journey towards improved overall health and well-being.

Monique is a graduate of Texas A&M University Honors Psychology Bachelor of Arts program with a minor in Neuroscience, the University of Houston – Victoria's Clinical Mental Health Counseling Master of Education, and St. Mary's University's Counselor Education and Supervision Doctorate of Philosophy program with a concentration in play therapy. Monique has had experience on a university helpline, at psychiatric hospitals (both inpatient and outpatient), community agencies and clinics, as well as private practices. Though the majority of Monique's experience has been with clients who are in crisis (suicidal, homicidal, psychotic), she also enjoys helping people deal with more common life stressors and becoming a happier version of themselves. Believing in a holistic view, she believes it is important to address all areas of wellness, and especially is interested in the wellness of counselors. As she believes people need to start conversations about emotional health from a young age, she is also a Registered Play Therapist.

REFERENCES

Avalos, L. C., & Tylka, T. L. (2006). Exploring a model of intuitive eating with college women. Journal of Counseling Psychology, 53, 486–497. https://doi.org/10.1037/0022-0167.53.4.486B

Burnette, C. B., Hazzard, V. M., Linardon, J., Rodgers, R. F., Loth, K. A., & Neumark-Sztainer, D. (2023). How parental feeding practices relate to young people's intuitive eating: Cross-sectional and longitudinal associations by gender and weight concern. Journal of Adolescent Health, 73(6), 1145–1152. https://doi-org.ruby.uhv.edu/10.1016/j.jadohealth.2023.07.018

Carbonneau, E., Carbonneau, N., Lamarche, B., Provencher, V., Bégin, C., Bradette-Laplante, M., Laramée, C., & Lemieux, S. (2016). Validation of a French-Canadian adaptation of the Intuitive Eating Scale-2 for the adult population. Appetite, 105, 37–45. https://doi-

DeVille, D. C., Erchull, M. J., & Mailloux, J. R. (2021). Intuitive eating mediates the relationship between interoceptive accuracy and eating disorder risk. Eating Behaviors, 41. https://doiorg.ruby.uhv.edu/10.1016/j.eatbeh.2021.101495org.ruby.uhv.edu/10.1016/j.appet.2016.05.01

Faw, M., Davidson, K., Hogan, L., & Thomas, K. (2021). Corumination, diet culture, intuitive eating, and body dissatisfaction among young adult women. Pers Relationship, 28, 406–426. https://doi.org/10.1111/pere.12364

Koller, K. A., Thompson, K. A., Miller, A. J., Walsh, E. C., & Bardone, C. A. M. (2020). Body appreciation and intuitive eating in eating disorder recovery. International Journal of Eating Disorders, 53(8), 1261–1269. https://doi-org.ruby.uhv.edu/10.1002/eat.23238

Linardon, J. (2021). Positive body image, intuitive eating, and self-compassion protect against the onset of the core symptoms of eating disorders: A prospective study. International Journal of Eating Disorders, 54(11), 1967–1977. https://doi-org.ruby.uhv.edu/10.1002/eat.23623

Markey, C. H., Strodl, E., Aimé, A., McCabe, M., Rodgers, R., Sicilia, A., Coco, G. L., Dion, J., Mellor, D., Pietrabissa, G., Gullo, S., Granero, G. A., Probst, M., Maïano, C., Bégin, C., Alcaraz, I. M., Blackburn, M., Caltabiano, M. L., Manzoni, G. M., & Castelnuovo, G. (2023). A survey of eating styles in eight countries: Examining restrained, emotional, intuitive eating and their correlates. British Journal of Health Psychology, 28(1), 136–155. https://doi-org.ruby.uhv.edu/10.1111/bjhp.12616

Novack, D. (2021). "It Takes a Village": Concurrent Eating Disorder Treatment and the Multiperson Field. Psychoanalytic Dialogues, 31(2), 181–196. https://doi-org.ruby.uhv.edu/10.1080/10481885.2021.1884081

Original Intuitive Eating Pros®. (2020). Certified Intuitive Eating Counselor (CIEC) Requirements [PDF]. Retrieved from https://www.intuitiveeating.org/wp-content/uploads/CIEC-Requirements-7-2020.pdf

Swami, V., Maïano, C., Todd, J., Ghisi, M., Cardi, V., Bottesi, G., & Cerea, S. (2021). Dimensionality and psychometric properties of an Italian translation of the Intuitive Eating Scale-2 (IES-2): An assessment using a bifactor exploratory structural equation modelling framework. Appetite, 166. https://doi-org.ruby.uhv.edu/10.1016/j.appet.2021.105588

Tribole, E. & Resch, E. (2012). Intuitive Eating (3rd ed). St. Martin's Press, NY: NY.

Tylka, T. L. (2006). Development and psychometric evaluation of a measure of intuitive eating. Journal of Counseling Psychology, 53(2), 226-240.

Tylka, T. L. (2013). A psychometric evaluation of the Intuitive Eating Scale with college men. Journal of Counseling Psychology, 60(1), 137-153.

van Hoeken, D., Hoek, H.W. (2020). Review of the burden of eating disorders: mortality, disability, costs, quality of life, and family burden. Curr Opin Psychiatry, 33(6), 521-527. doi: 10.1097/YCO.0000000000000641. PMID: 32796186; PMCID: PMC7575017.

Vlahoyiannis, A., & Nifli, A. (2020). Dietary restraint is associated with adiposity and repeated attempts of food avoidance since early adolescence. Physiology and Behavior, 218, 112826. https://doi.org/10.1016/j.physbeh.2020.112826W

Vintilă, M., Todd, J., Goian, C., Tudorel, O., Barbat, C. A., & Swami, V. (2020). The Romanian version of the Intuitive Eating Scale-2: Assessment of its psychometric properties and gender invariance in Romanian adults. Body Image, 35, 225–236. https://doi-org.ruby.uhv.edu/10.1016/j.bodyim.2020.09.009

Yang, Y., Conti, J., McMaster, C. M., Piya, M. K., & Hay, P. (2023). "I Need Someone to Help Me Build Up My Strength": A Meta-Synthesis of Lived Experience Perspectives on the Role and Value of a Dietitian in Eating Disorder Treatment. Behavioral Sciences, 13(11), 944. https://doi-org.ruby.uhv.edu/10.3390/bs13110944

Juris Doctor/Attorney and Mental Health Degree

BILL OWENBY, EdD, MC, FAAETS, DAAETS, DCMHS, LPC, LAAC, NCC, CCMHC, ACS, DIPLOMATE,

FELLOW

The integration of a Juris Doctor (JD) degree with a mental health degree, such as counseling, psychology, or social work, offers unique opportunities for professionals seeking to address the intersection of law and mental health. This combination allows practitioners to navigate complex legal and psychological issues, advocate for systemic change, and provide specialized services to diverse populations.

ADVANTAGES OF HOLDING BOTH DEGREES

1. **Expanded Career Opportunities:**
   o Legal expertise combined with mental health knowledge enables professionals to work in forensic psychology, family law, or policy advocacy.
   o Professionals can serve as expert witnesses, mediators, or consultants on cases involving mental health issues.
2. **Enhanced Client Advocacy:**
   o Understanding both fields allows for holistic support of clients navigating legal systems, such as custody battles, criminal cases, or disability claims.
   o Lawyers with mental health training can better address emotional and psychological dimensions of legal disputes.
3. **Policy and Systemic Change:**
   o Dual-degree holders are well-positioned to influence legislation, develop mental health policies, and advocate for marginalized communities.
4. **Specialized Private Practice:**
   o Professionals can offer niche services, such as therapeutic mediation or legal-psychological consultation.

CHALLENGES AND LIMITATIONS

1. **Time and Financial Investment:**
   o Completing both degrees is a significant commitment, often requiring six to eight years of study and substantial tuition costs, with JD programs averaging $80,000 to $200,000 and mental health degrees adding $30,000 to $100,000.
2. **Licensure and Certification Requirements:**
   o Professionals must meet licensure standards for both fields, which can be complex and time-consuming.
   o Maintaining continuing education credits for both professions may be challenging.
3. **Potential Role Conflicts:**
   o Ethical dilemmas may arise when balancing the roles of therapist and legal advocate.
   o Professionals must clearly define their scope of practice to avoid dual relationship issues.
4. **Burnout Risk:**
   o The emotional demands of navigating both legal and mental health challenges may increase

the risk of burnout.

TRANSITIONING BETWEEN FIELDS

Moving from Law to Mental Health:

1. **Education Requirements:**
   o Complete a Master's or Doctoral degree in counseling, psychology, or social work.
   o Some programs offer accelerated tracks for individuals with prior advanced degrees.
2. **Licensure:**
   o Pass state licensing exams, such as the LPC, LMFT, or LCSW, depending on the chosen mental health field.
3. **Practical Experience:**
   o Fulfill internship or supervised practice requirements, typically ranging from 2,000 to 4,000 hours.

Moving from Mental Health to Law:

1. **Education Requirements:**
   o Complete a Juris Doctor degree, typically a three-year program.
   o Consider programs that offer specialization in mental health law or family law.
2. **Bar Exam:**
   o Pass the bar exam in the state where you plan to practice.
3. **Specialized Practice Areas:**
   o Focus on areas such as disability law, criminal justice reform, or child advocacy.

Combined or Sequential Programs

Some universities offer joint JD and mental health degree programs, allowing students to complete both degrees in a reduced timeframe. Examples include:

1. **JD/PhD in Psychology:**
   o Combines legal training with advanced psychological research and practice.
2. **JD/MSW (Master of Social Work):**
   o Prepares graduates for roles in social justice, policy advocacy, and therapeutic practice.
3. **JD/MA in Counseling:**
   o Focuses on integrating legal and mental health expertise for mediation and client support roles.

ETHICAL CONSIDERATIONS

1. **Dual Roles:**
   o Professionals must avoid conflicts of interest, particularly when serving as both a legal advisor and mental health provider for the same client.
2. **Confidentiality:**
   o Navigating differing confidentiality standards between legal and therapeutic settings requires careful attention to ethical guidelines.
3. **Informed Consent:**
   o Clients must fully understand the professional's roles and limitations.

1. **Financial Investment:**
   o JD programs cost $80,000–$200,000; mental health degrees range $30,000–$100,000.
   o Scholarships, fellowships, and loan forgiveness programs can offset costs for dual-degree students.
2. **Earning Potential:**
   o Dual-degree holders often earn higher salaries due to specialized expertise, with forensic psychologists earning $80,000–$120,000 annually and mental health attorneys earning $100,000–$200,000, depending on experience and location.
3. **Career Flexibility:**
   o The ability to switch between legal and mental health roles provides long-term career resilience and adaptability.

Case Examples

1. **Therapeutic Mediation:**
   o A JD-LPC professional mediates high-conflict custody cases, integrating therapeutic techniques to reduce tension and facilitate agreements.
2. **Forensic Consultation:**
   o A psychologist-attorney provides expert testimony in criminal cases involving mental health evaluations.
3. **Policy Advocacy:**
   o A dual-degree holder drafts legislation to improve access to mental health services in underserved communities.

SUMMARY

Combining a Juris Doctor and a mental health degree offers unparalleled opportunities to bridge the fields of law and psychology. While this path requires significant dedication and comes with challenges, the ability to advocate, legislate, and provide comprehensive client care makes it a rewarding choice for professionals committed to systemic change and interdisciplinary practice.

I hold two independent licenses in the states of Arizona and Ohio, supervisory status in Arizona, along with a substance abuse license in Arizona. I am board certified as a Diplomate and Clinical Mental Health Specialist, an Approved Clinical Supervisor, Nationally Certified Counselor, a Certified Clinical Mental Health Counselor, NeuroLinguistic Programming Practitioner, and a Clinical Trauma Specialist for Individuals and Family including EMDR Therapy and NET. I completed my training in Animal-Assisted Therapy and Pet Handlers certification in order to evaluate and incorporate the human-animal bond in therapy. I am the sole author and creator of the SxC Model of ESA Evaluation. My research interests surround post-traumatic growth, resiliency, strengths-based therapy, positive psychology, mindfulness, Animal-Assisted Therapy, Sandtray Therapy, Creative approaches in therapy, and martial arts in mental health. I have presented at local, state, regional, national, and international levels on various topics including personality traits, licensure reciprocity challenges, Sandtray and supervision, and Animal-Assisted Therapy within supervision. eonbllc@gmail.com

REFERENCES

American Bar Association. (2020). Careers in mental health law. *ABA Journal.*

Zur, O. (2015). Dual relationships and boundaries in psychotherapy. *Zur Institute.*

Recommended Online Resources

American Psychological Association
National Association of Social Workers
American Bar Association

Ketamine/Psychedelic-Assisted Psychotherapy (KAP/PAP)

KATE KINCAID, MC, LPC, CMHC

When I became a therapist, I was so excited to use the tools I learned in graduate school to help people. In internship and in my early therapist positions, I was humbled by how slow the work can be. I quickly saw that healing is a lifestyle and a lifelong commitment. I, like most therapists, had to grapple with my clients' frustration and seek quicker relief. I wanted to find tools to help alleviate suffering as quickly and efficiently as possible while also still honoring that lasting change often requires patience and many slow, incremental changes in one's life.

Psychedelics played a role in my own healing journey long before I even knew that they could be used in a clinical setting. For me they were spiritual tools, and my Western training didn't exactly encourage integrating spirituality into the physical or psychological. In 2015, I heard about the Zendo project and all the important work that MAPS is doing and that was the first time I could see a possibility for using these medicines in my clinical work. I decided to be more intentional about my own personal and professional training with regards to psychedelic medicines for psychospiritual growth. The field is moving quickly so now it seems that more of these tools will be available for use sooner than later but a couple years ago I heard about ketamine and how it was legal and available for use now. In January 2021, I enrolled in an experiential training and immediately saw how ketamine could be used as a tool for clients to work with trauma, PTSD, depression, anxiety, and OCD. After that training and because of my enthusiasm, more of my colleagues at my practice sought training in ketamine assisted psychotherapy (KAP) and we worked diligently to open our own practice in October 2021. And to no surprise, we've seen incredible results with our treatment resistant clients, many of whom we've been working with for years in talk therapy. Ketamine has been a springboard to the faster and more robust results I dreamed about in graduate school.

TREATMENT RESISTANT DEPRESSION (TRD) AND POST TRAUMATIC STRESS DISORDER (PTSD)

In my clinical work, I provide preparation and integration services for people exploring all different psychedelics. Part of my prep work is slowing people down and helping examine any beliefs about the medicine being a cure all. The psychedelic worldview is a lifestyle change, not a one-time event or destination to reach. Currently, ketamine is the only legal psychedelic available outside of clinical trials at this time. That said, it's not a consolation prize while we wait for other medicines to become available (like MDMA or psilocybin); ketamine is proving to be a very powerful treatment for treatment resistant depression and PTSD.

TRD

Treatment Resistant Depression (TRD) is a form of Major Depressive Disorder that is persistent despite traditional antidepressant treatment. While TRD is still being debated over exact criteria for diagnosis, some researchers define it as a case of depression that doesn't respond to one or two different antidepressants from different classes. According to the Food and Drug Administration, an individual has TRD if they've had two or more adequate trials of antidepressants over a period of two years, but treatment has failed to alleviate the symptoms or put their depression into remission. The annual prevalence of TRD is estimated to be at 30.9% among adults with medication treated MDD, equating to about 2.8 million adults or 1.1% of the US adult population (Zhdanava et al., 2021).

While TRD often predicts poor response to standard antidepressant medications, there may be a better response to other forms of treatment, such as electroconvulsive therapy (ECT), medications like ketamine or esketamine, botox, or Transcranial Magnetic Stimulation. The best treatment is often a combination of medicine and therapy, but this can vary on a case-by-case basis.

PTSD

Posttraumatic stress disorder (PTSD) is a complex somatic, cognitive, affective, and behavioral reaction to psychological trauma. PTSD develops in some people who have experienced a shocking, scary, or dangerous event. PTSD is characterized by intrusive thoughts, nightmares and flashbacks of past traumatic events, avoidance of reminders of trauma, hypervigilance, and sleep disturbance, all of which lead to considerable social, occupational, and interpersonal dysfunction. The lifetime prevalence of PTSD ranges from 6.1 to 9.2 percent in national samples of the general adult population in the United States and Canada, with one-year prevalence rates of 3.5 to 4.7 percent (Sareen, 2022).

INTRODUCTION TO TREATMENT

Ketamine Assisted Psychotherapy is a relatively new modality. Most of the current research is based on IV ketamine being administered to chronic pain patients and providers started noticing a reduction in depressive symptoms. The ketamine alone has neurogenic effects which stimulates new neuronal pathways which can be helpful for combatting mental health concerns. There are very few studies to date evaluating KAP or in other words evaluating the efficacy of ketamine used concurrently with therapy.

Ketamine is a relatively safe medicine that has been used in anesthesia since the 1960s. However, there are some indications and contraindications for ketamine assisted psychotherapy. In low doses, it is useful as an analgesic (pain-relief) and anxiolytic (anxiety-reduction). More recently, its off-label use has been shown to improve a variety of mental health concerns such as depression, anxiety, and PTSD. It is available only by prescription and it is now widely considered a potent psychedelic. It is the only psychedelic legal for clinical use that is available outside of clinical trials. In a safe "set and setting", ketamine can contribute to profound psychological and spiritual insights. As with all other psychedelics, ketamine is not a magic pill and the most benefit is seen when used in conjunction with therapy and other lifestyle changes. The current indications described above are treatment resistant depression, PTSD and people are starting to recommend it for anxiety, OCD, and postpartum mood disorders. It is not recommended for people with thought disorders, unmanaged bipolar disorder as well as several other medical diagnoses such as uncontrolled high blood pressure, history of vascular issues such as stroke and anyone with kidney or liver function impairment.

There are different routes to administering ketamine but the most common are intravenously (IV), intramuscularly (IM) or sublingually (SL). The different routes have different bioavailability and subjective effects. When clients receive IV ketamine, it is slowly infused and typically the dose is meant to avoid a psychedelic effect. The infusion can be turned off and the effects dissipate quickly. This route is ideal for people with more complex health concerns as there is an increase in monitoring and the medication can be stopped quickly as well as rescue meds administered.

IM has a similar bioavailability and it is administered with a shot into the muscle. Once the dose is administered, the client is along for the ride until their body has metabolized the medicine. The effects wear off after about 45-90 minutes and clients report feeling quite clear-headed afterwards. Sublingual is done with a rapidly dissolving lozenge held under the tongue and either ingested or expectorated (i.e., spit out). This route takes the longest to take effect and lasts the longest. Subjectively, clients report this route is the most somatic, meaning they are aware of their body during the session. There is less bioavailability but that is mediated by the prescribing provider prescribing a higher dose, knowing much of it won't be absorbed.

PSYCHEDELICS AS AN ALTERNATIVE TREATMENT

A 2020 review reported on 24 prior studies on psychedelic drugs to treat anxiety symptoms. It said 65% of studies reported a reduction in anxiety with psychedelics (Weston et al, 2020). A 2021 study asked 164 people who reported experiencing a psychedelic experience to discuss their mental health symptoms. Participants reported significant reductions in depression, anxiety, and stress following the psychedelic experience. An analysis revealed that participants also had greater compassion and less frequent rumination (Fauvel et al 2021).

Chronic stress and depression are likely associated with increased glutamatergic neurotransmission and changes in neuronal plasticity, including dendritic remodeling and atrophy (Sanacora, Treccani, & Popoli, 2012). While these changes may be adaptive, they contribute to maintaining a variety of mental health conditions. Recent data shows that ketamine activates estrogen receptors so this suggests that ketamine may work with estrogen to increase glutamate levels (Abeallah, 2018). Glutamate is a neurotransmitter that may be central to understanding major depression. Glutamate deficits in certain regions of the brain have been strongly linked to depression (Murrough, 2017). Ketamine has been shown to activate glutamate transmission in the brain and explains its anti-depressant effects (Abeallah, 2018).

I know for me, doing my own ketamine assisted psychotherapy (KAP) changed my life and helped me heal from some postpartum induced anxiety and OCD. My first KAP session I recall the feeling (and the imagery) of my neurons being stretched and pulled like taffy. It felt like yoga asana for my brain, and I literally felt more spacious afterwards. I went into the first session with the intention to get to know some of my ruminative thought patterns and hopefully understand why I had a hard time letting them go. But instead, it felt like I had just forgotten what it was that I was obsessing about; they were just gone, and I didn't even want to try to look for them to understand them.

CERTIFICATIONS, TRAININGS, AND LICENSURE REQUIREMENTS FOR KAP

Psychedelic assisted therapy is a burgeoning field, and more and more certifications and training programs are popping up seemingly every day. A few master level therapy training programs are partnering with MAPS (Multidisciplinary Association of Psychedelic Studies) to bring trainings to their programs. The most well-known certificate programs are through the California Institute of Integral Studies (CIIS) and the Integrative Psychiatry Institute (IPI). Graduates of the CIIS program also leave with the coveted MAPS certification in MDMA assisted therapy. Clinicians can also do the MAPS training independently. It is rumored that if you want to work with MDMA when it becomes available, you will have to do the MAPS training specifically, but the truth is no one knows yet since the medicine is not on the market yet for clinical use.

Some have described what is happening with psychedelic assisted therapies as a "gold rush" so there are new trainings popping up every day and many are not legitimate. It's important to take training by people who have been working in the field for a long time and who are vetted and esteemed by other colleagues. Supervision is highly recommended even after you've completed your training. Working with non-ordinary states is exciting and dynamic work but a lot can come up that you haven't been used to working with in traditional clinical work. Fortunately, because it's such a burgeoning field, there's no shortage of trainings and webinars and continuing education series. The ketamine research institute KRIYA institute has a list of ketamine specific trainings they recommend with confidence. Polaris Insight is another popular training for ketamine specifically because they offer bite sized modules.

Ketamine is a unique tool and while it may be legal to prescribe when certain clinical criteria are met, it is also an unusual and experiential medicine and can induce psychedelic states. Hopefully working with psychedelics will be incorporated into training at the graduate level for all mental health professionals but in the meantime, anyone wanting to work with these tools should do their due diligence and get training on their own. Many of the current trainings are kind of like psychedelic 101s and are made for both therapists and prescribers alike. Our training arm of Tucson Counseling Associates is called Soma Psychedelics and we plan to offer our own modules which are heavily focused on the psychotherapeutic portion of working with Ketamine Assisted Psychotherapy (KAP). We are passionate about providing these ongoing trainings and support for clinicians in working with this powerful and transformative modality.

Kate Kincaid is a licensed professional counselor in Tucson, AZ. She runs a group private practice that specializes in working with LGBTQIA+ clients, people in ethically non-monogamous relationships and people seeking psychedelic integration therapy and Ketamine Assisted Psychotherapy. She has long been interested in non-ordinary states of consciousness and believes in the healing wisdom of plant medicines. She is a graduate of the CIIS Center for Psychedelic Studies and Research and her practice has applied to establish eligibility with MAPS PBC to offer MDMA-Assisted Psychotherapy if it becomes an approved treatment. She is also the co-creator of Southwest Love Fest, a conference on relationships, identity, and community. Kate's therapeutic style is informed by feminism and social justice, seeking to help collectively dismantle systems of violence and oppression. She believes that many issues clients come to therapy with are rooted in a logical response to an oppressive system that is then pathologized and stigmatized. She has an eclectic and intuitive approach that is influenced by attachment theory, humanistic psychology, somatics, and neuroscience.

Website: www.tucsoncounselingassociates.com

Email: kjkincai@gmail.com

Instagram @okatekincaid or @tucsoncounselingassociates

REFERENCES

Abeallah et al. The effects of ketamine on prefrontal glutamate neurotransmission in healthy and depressed subjects. Neuropsychopharmacology 2018. 43, 2154-2169

Becker, J. (2014). Regarding the transpersonal nature of ketamine therapy: An approach to the work. International Journal of Transpersonal Studies, 33(2), 151–159.. International Journal of Transpersonal Studies, 33 (2). http://dx.doi.org/10.24972/ijts.2014.33.2.151

Fauvel, B., Strika-Bruneau, L., & Piolino, P. (2021). Changes in self-rumination and self-compassion mediate the effect of psychedelic experiences on decreases in depression, anxiety, and stress. *Psychology of Consciousness: Theory, Research, and Practice*. Advance online publication. https://doi.org/10.1037/cns0000283

Murrough J.W. Targeting glutamate signaling in depression: progress and prospects. Nat Rev Drug Discov. 2017;17:472-86

Sanacora G, Treccani G, Popoli M. Towards a glutamate hypothesis of depression: an emerging frontier of neuropsychopharmacology for mood disorders. Neuropharmacology. 2012 Jan;62(1):63-77. doi: 10.1016/j.neuropharm.2011.07.036. Epub 2011 Aug 3. PMID: 21827775; PMCID: PMC3205453.

Sareen, J.S. (2022). Posttraumatic stress disorder in adults: Epidemiology, pathophysiology, clinical manifestations, course, assessment, and diagnosis. https://www.uptodate.com/contents/posttraumatic-stress-disorder-in-adults-epidemiology-pathophysiology-clinical-manifestations-course-assessment-and-diagnosis/print

Weston, N.M., Gibbs, D., Bird, C.I.V., Aster, D., Jelen, L.A. Knight, G. Goldsmith, D., Young, A.H., Rucker, J.J. Historic psychedelic drug trials and the treatment of anxiety disorders. First published: 05 July 2020 https://doi.org/10.1002/da.23065

Zhdanava M, Pilon D, Ghelerter I, Chow W, Joshi K, Lefebvre P, Sheehan JJ. The Prevalence and National Burden of Treatment-Resistant Depression and Major Depressive Disorder in the United States. J Clin Psychiatry. 2021 Mar 16;82(2):20m13699. doi: 10.4088/JCP.20m13699. PMID: 33989464.

Websites:
- CIIS: https://www.ciis.edu/research-centers/center-for-psychedelic-therapies-and-research?gclid=Cj0KCQiA99ybBhD9ARIsALvZavXrjGLF9qqyKlIOdQHqOsVHRiX5a6FZPHl_xFY2aI8-peS4_LoB9yEaAoJrEALw_wcB
- IPI: https://psychiatryinstitute.com/fellowship-program-g2020/?npclid=Cj0KCQiA99ybBhD9ARIsALvZavXUfAvB5ygrr7ypQj4LqmLHz0UeZ3g146evLpeiUYgaFdLUMD6iE8AaAsQ_EALw_wcB&utm_source=google&utm_medium=cpc&utm_term=ipi%20psychiatry&utm_campaign=Brand&gclid=Cj0KCQiA99ybBhD9ARIsALvZavXUfAvB5ygrr7ypQj4LqmLHz0UeZ3g146evLpeiUYgaFdLUMD6iE8AaAsQ_EALw_wcB
- KRIYA: https://www.kriyainstitute.com/
- MAPS: https://maps.org/
- Polaris Insight: https://www.polarisinsight.com/
- Tucson Counseling Associates/Soma Psychedelics: https://www.tucsoncounselingassociates.com/

Kleinian Therapy

ADAM DREGELY, M.A.ED.

Developed by Melanie Klein, Kleinian Therapy is a Neo-Freudian psychoanalytic intervention used with children and adults (Baker & Carlson, 2017). Klein's technique was described, by Klein herself, as based on the work of Freud with emphasis being placed on the role of transference and defenses. Kleinian techniques emphasize the role of the patient's anxieties as a starting point for understanding the unconscious through interpretation (Bott et al., 2011). Klein's work began in the early 1900's, in Vienna, where she sought to engage in the analysis of children (Bott et al., 2011). While both Sigmund and Anna Freud believed that analysis could not be successfully conducted with children, Klein persisted (Crann, 2010). Following her move to London, Klein began working with children and was invited to speak at the British Analytic Society regarding her advancements. While Klein's initial work focused on children it did grow to include adults over time; with much of the Kleinian technique being developed through work with clients experiencing psychosis and personality disorders (Bott et al., 2011).

CERTIFICATIONS, TRAININGS, AND LICENSURE REQUIREMENTS

While no certification in Kleinian therapy is provided, The Melanie Klein Trust (2023) provides links to additional training opportunities on topics salient to the work of Melanie Klein and Kleinian therapy. Recordings of previous events are available and include an "Authors in Conversation" series which explores the published works of psychoanalytic authors including Melanie Klein (The Melanie Klein Trust, 2023). While these conversations are available for purchase, no rigorous training on Kleinian Therapy is provided with this particular organization.

The Melanie Klein Trust (2023) does provide access to papers, video and audio files, as well as conference reports, and reading lists on subjects relating to both Klein and her work. For certifications, training, and licensure requirements, it is advantageous to reference Klein's influence on Object Relations Theory as such options exist in that realm.

SCOPE OF PRACTICE ISSUES

Kleinian Therapy requires scope of practice sufficient to practice psychoanalytic therapy. While the Melanie Klein Trust (2023) can provide orienting information the resources provided are insufficient to meet modern practice standards of practice as well as scope of training. Psychoanalytic services should be rendered by a clinician who has received appropriate training in psychoanalytic principles and has received supervision by a licensed psychoanalytic practitioner.

SUMMARY

Kleinian Therapy training should be obtained through psychoanalytic or Object Relations (see other chapter by this author) Therapy programs. While the Melanie Klein Trust can provide additional opportunities for learning for clinicians who are sufficiently oriented to psychoanalytic services, this organization does not provide professional preparation, certification, or credentialing opportunities.

Adam Dregely is a Clinical Psychology Doctoral Candidate at California Southern University. He completed his pre-doctoral internship in K-12 education under the supervision of an Object Relations practitioner. Adam currently works at Ottawa University teaching trauma counseling, ethics, and psychodiagnostic courses for graduate students.

REFERENCES

(2023). *The Melanie Klein Trust*. Melanie Klein Trust. Retrieved June 1, 2023, from https://melanie-klein-trust.org.uk

Baker, E. K. C., & Carlson, J. (2017). Kleinian Theory: A Neo-Adlerian Approach? *Journal of Individual Psychology*, *73*(2), 156–170. https://doi.org/10.1353/jip.2017.0013

Bott, S. E., Milton, J., Garvey, P., Couve, C., & Steiner, D. (2011). *The new dictionary of kleinian thought*. Taylor & Francis Group.

Crann, S. (2010). Profile of Melanie Klein. In A. Rutherford (Ed.), *Psychology's Feminist Voices Digital Archive*. Retrieved from https://feministvoices.com/profiles/melanie-klein

Knitting Therapy

BILL OWENBY, EdD, MC, FAAETS, DAAETS, DCMHS, LPC, LAAC, NCC, CCMHC, ACS, DIPLOMATE, FELLOW

KATHERINE CAMPBELL, MAED, LPC, LAAC, NCC

Knitting Therapy, or therapeutic knitting therapy, leverages the therapeutic benefits of knitting to support mental health and well-being. By engaging in this mindful, repetitive activity, clients can experience stress relief, emotional regulation, and a sense of accomplishment. Knitting Therapy is a creative, hands-on approach that has gained popularity as a supplementary tool in therapeutic settings.

FOUNDATIONAL PRINCIPLES OF KNITTING THERAPY

1. **Mindfulness and Relaxation**
   o Encourages clients to focus on the present moment through repetitive hand movements and patterns.
2. **Creativity and Expression**
   o Offers a platform for self-expression through the creation of unique knitted items.
3. **Embodied Engagement**
   o Integrates hand-eye coordination, tactile sensation, and focused attention to promote holistic well-being.
4. **Social Connection**
   o Provides opportunities for group interaction and shared experiences, fostering a sense of community.

APPLICATIONS OF KNITTING THERAPY

Knitting Therapy has been applied to address a variety of mental health concerns and developmental needs:

- **Anxiety and Depression**
  o Reduces stress and promotes relaxation through rhythmic movements.
- **Trauma Recovery**
  o Provides a grounding activity to help clients manage intrusive thoughts and emotions.
- **Chronic Pain Management**
  o Distracts from physical discomfort and enhances the release of endorphins.
- **Addiction Recovery**
  o Offers a constructive and creative outlet to support sobriety.
- **Group Therapy**
  o Encourages social interaction and collaboration in a supportive environment.

1. **Stress Reduction**
   o Repetitive motions calm the nervous system, lowering cortisol levels.
2. **Improved Focus**
   o Encourages sustained attention and mindfulness, reducing rumination.
3. **Enhanced Self-Esteem**
   o Completing a knitted project provides a sense of accomplishment.
4. **Motor Skill Development**
   o Improves fine motor coordination and dexterity.
5. **Social Support**
   o Group sessions foster relationships and reduce feelings of isolation.

Therapeutic Techniques in Knitting Therapy

1. **Mindful Knitting**
   o Clients are guided to focus on each stitch and their breathing, integrating mindfulness into the practice.
2. **Knitting Projects with Symbolism**
   o Therapists assign symbolic meaning to projects, such as knitting a scarf to represent personal growth.
3. **Progressive Projects**
   o Projects are scaled to match clients' skill levels, gradually increasing in complexity as confidence grows.
4. **Group Knitting Circles**
   o Facilitates a shared therapeutic experience that fosters community and mutual support.

TRAINING AND CERTIFICATION IN KNITTING THERAPY

Educational Pathways

- Training is open to therapists, educators, and recreational specialists. While a mental health background is not always required, having experience in counseling or expressive therapies is beneficial.

Training Structure

- **Introduction to Knitting Therapy**:
  o Workshops lasting 1–2 days, covering basic principles and practical techniques.
- **Advanced Training**:
  o In-depth courses on integrating knitting into therapeutic practice, including case studies and supervision.
- **Cost**:
  o Workshops typically range from $100 to $500, while advanced training programs may cost $1,000 to $3,000.

Certifications

- **Certified Knitting Therapy Practitioner (CKTP)**:
  o Offered by select organizations specializing in expressive and creative arts therapies.
- Certification requires foundational training, supervised practice, and submission of case studies.

- Opportunities include online courses, knitting retreats, and conferences focused on creative arts in therapy.

CHALLENGES AND LIMITATIONS

1. **Client Accessibility**
   - Physical or cognitive impairments may limit clients' ability to engage in knitting.
2. **Skill Acquisition**
   - Clients may require time and patience to develop knitting skills.
3. **Therapeutic Fit**
   - Not all clients may resonate with or benefit from this creative modality.
4. **Material Costs**
   - Yarn, needles, and other supplies can be a financial consideration.

SUMMARY

Knitting Therapy is a versatile and accessible modality that supports mental health and emotional well-being. By combining creativity with mindfulness, it empowers clients to engage in a calming and productive activity. For therapists, integrating Knitting Therapy offers a unique way to promote relaxation, self-expression, and connection in therapeutic settings.

I hold two independent licenses in the states of Arizona and Ohio, supervisory status in Arizona, along with a substance abuse license in Arizona. I am board certified as a Diplomate and Clinical Mental Health Specialist, an Approved Clinical Supervisor, Nationally Certified Counselor, a Certified Clinical Mental Health Counselor, NeuroLinguistic Programming Practitioner, and a Clinical Trauma Specialist for Individuals and Family including EMDR Therapy and NET. I completed my training in Animal-Assisted Therapy and Pet Handlers certification in order to evaluate and incorporate the human-animal bond in therapy. I am the sole author and creator of the SxC Model of ESA Evaluation. My research interests surround post-traumatic growth, resiliency, strengths-based therapy, positive psychology, mindfulness, Animal-Assisted Therapy, Sandtray Therapy, Creative approaches in therapy, and martial arts in mental health. I have presented at local, state, regional, national, and international levels on various topics including personality traits, licensure reciprocity challenges, Sandtray and supervision, and Animal-Assisted Therapy within supervision. eonbllc@gmail.com

Katherine is a local nonprofit integrative community health agency where she provides therapy. Katherine received her Masters in Arts in Education from the University of Akron. She is a published author, an award recipient, and has presented on the use of Therapy Animals in Supervision. She is trained as an LPC and LAAC, a trauma specialist, and a Nationally Certified Counselor. She was awarded the Tucson Hispanic Chamber of Commerce's 40 Under 40 in 2021, which means she got it before Bill, as well as beat out Bill in 2021, and yes, they joke about that all the time. Katherine lives with her spouse/co-captain/PIC/co-editor and their 2 cats Waffle and Pancake outside of Tucson, AZ.

REFERENCES

Riley, J. (2008). The Benefits of Creative Therapy in Mental Health Practice. Creative Arts Therapy Press.

Corkhill, B., Hemmings, J., Maddock, A., & Riley, J. (2014). Knitting and Well-Being: An Overview of the Evidence. Journal of Occupational Therapy.

Harvard Health. (2020). The Mindfulness Benefits of Knitting.

Recommended Resources

- **American Art Therapy Association (AATA):** www.arttherapy.org
- **Books on Knitting and Mental Health:** Available from online retailers and therapy resource platforms.
- **Local Knitting Therapy Workshops and Groups:** Search for offerings in your area for hands-on training.

Lacanian Psychoanalysis

DANIEL BARKER, M.A. IN PHILOSOPHY, M.A. CANDIDATE FOR COUNSELOR EDUCATION

Jacques Lacan's career spans from the 1930s to the 1980s. In the '50s and '60s he would become a major force in French psychoanalysis and French intellectual movements, partially due to his popular yearly seminars and partially due to the bombastic way he expressed theoretical disagreements. Some of his practicing methods were the subject of scrutiny by the International Psychoanalytic Association [IPA] which eventually made the French Society for Psychoanalysis' [SFP] membership conditional on Lacan's being stricken from the list of training analysts. He would go on to form the Freudian School of Paris [EFP] causing a significant split in the French analytic world.

Today his techniques and teaching inform therapists practicing primarily in France, Argentina, Italy, and Spain. His work was introduced into the United States primarily through French and Comparative Literature departments and has become associated more with an academic, political analysis of ideology than clinical practice. However, Lacanianism seems to be enjoying a resurgence of therapist interest in the English-speaking world and these therapists are often keen on using this framework to explore questions of how social, economic, and political dimensions function in the symptoms and desires that clients present.

THEORETICAL OVERVIEW

Ego Psychology and the Imaginary Register

Lacanian practitioners could take their points of departure from any given period of Lacan's prolific training and teaching, given in France by way of seminars from the 1950s to the 1980s. Because of this, there is no centralized school or methodology but rather several schools and individual analysts who have taken inspiration from specific ideas and/or periods. Lacan's earliest work focused on deriding the Anglo and American drift towards ego psychology embodied in the popular work of Anna Freud and Heinz Hartmann. Heinz Hartmann reframed psychoanalytic theory from a Freudian analysis of conflictual internal agencies to an evolutionary theory of man's adaptation to his social environment. Humankind is assumed to have intrinsic, natural instincts that predetermine and guide their activity, aims, and desires and mediate their interactions with their world (Black & Mitchell, 1995, pp. 34-38). This harmonious vision, accomplished as easily and automatically as a bird's "programmed" migration, is a far cry from Freud's own late-period nihilistic lamentations in the final pages of Civilization and its Discontents (1930/1961) where he expresses skepticism about the modern world's conviction that a progressive humanitarian ideal will necessarily shape our future.

Lacan advocated a "return to Freud" and ridiculed the contemporary trend of making ego strengthening and social adaptation the goal of analysis, to be carried out by client identification with the analyst's ego. Not only did this methodology imply closing analyst's ears to the specificity of what clients and their desires had to say, to the difference spoken through their suffering and symptoms, but Lacan believed that it also had the dangerous effect of potentially triggering a paranoid reaction on the part of the patient. The fragile sense of self that we associate with narcissistic personality disorder and paranoia was something Lacan felt wasn't just a rare disorder but was inherent in the way every ego develops and therefore a universal latent possibility.

At this point, Lacan introduced a distinction in what he would refer to as registers of the therapeutic situation, or analytical scene. The back and forth between the client and therapist could be described at different levels: the imaginary, symbolic, and real. These key terms, once introduced, would remain anchor points for Lacan's theoretical development, even if their characterizations might change over the course of his teaching. Lacan described the action of ego psychology as taking place on the imaginary level, the level of ego-to-ego interaction. This level of relation had a distinctly aggressive potential since Lacan described the ego as having a fundamentally paranoid and fragile structure. This level is associated with rigidly black-and-white, either-or thinking, where the stability and health of one subject's ego depends on the conquest of the others. Thus, ego-strengthening would always entail increasing the risk of triggering the fault or schism internal to every ego's structure (Lacan, 2007).

Lacan's alternative, the return to Freud, would be elaborated over the course of the '50s as an entreaty to analysts to begin, once again, to listen carefully to their client's speech. Here Lacan advocated that analysts break away from the imaginary register and pay more attention to the symbolic register, to what manifests in the therapeutic relationship as classical Freudian slips in speech (Lacan, 1966/2006, pp. 206-211). Lacan found that analysts were all too keen to stamp their own preconceptions onto what clients said, to dominate them by reducing their experience to what they already felt they understood. Instead, Lacan encouraged his trainees to postpone understanding (Fink, 2007, Chapter 1). Imaginary speech, or what he called 'empty speech', could be characterized as a transmission of bits of knowledge that are already readily understood. On the counselor's part, they may listen with ears full of stereotypes or overly-simplifying diagnostic categories that can be used to make the client too quickly comprehended. The client themselves, especially if they've been to counseling before, may have a fairly well-narrated story about themselves and their issues. But if the client already has a good story established, what does the counselor really bring to the table in repeating it? Lacan trained analysts to listen instead for the contours of what was carefully not being said, for what was being left out, for slips, parapraxes, etc... If the fragile, paranoid ego speaks about him or herself in easily understandable blocks of information, then what Lacan called the subject of the unconscious spoke its truth by misfirings, or errors in this first exchange. Analysts direct client attention to these slips and attempt to uncover the repressed truth that motivates them instead of shoring them up.

What is the nature of this unconscious speech conceived as symbolic? Lacan's answer to this takes its bearings in the 20th century's intellectual fascination with language, in what is often referred to as the linguistic turn. We could start by saying that the unconscious has its own rules and organized structure. Instead of conceiving of an unconscious id as a bundle of chaotic, biological instincts, Lacan sought to interpret it according to structural linguistics, giving rise to his well-known saying, "The unconscious is structured like a language." Preempting the next generation of philosophers like Derrida and Foucault, emphasis is given to the material word, the signifier, over the meaning this word conveys, the signified. This runs parallel to an emphasis on the effects of social structure in the unconscious subject as opposed to the conscious intentions of an egoic individual. In light of this privileging of the word over its meaning, devices like puns are the mechanisms for displaced and repressed thoughts. A whole systemic science of the unconscious might be written on the basis of this linguistic organization. These principles of the unconscious' organization were outlined by overlaying Roman Jakobson's linguistic analysis of metaphor and metonymy onto the classical Freudian primary processes, condensation and displacement. These mechanisms of linguistic functioning would partially guide identity formation and shape symptoms.

Lacan further distanced his clinical focus on client speech from the paranoid mastery of ego psychology by clarifying that desire was always first desire of the Other (Lacan, 1973/1998, p. 235). This repeated Freud's own contention that psychoanalysis continued the Copernican scientific tradition's decentering of mankind's hubris. If Freud posited that unconscious drives dethroned the ego from its pretensions to self-mastery, Lacan deepened the narcissistic wound by proposing that even the most intimate desires at the center of man's unconscious were not his own but were instead inscribed in him by the effects of a structure also deemed responsible for the total social symbolic order. This befuddles the distinction between the individual and society, a distinction that is indispensable for almost any intellectual discussion taking place in the modern era about nearly any of its big ideas, even and especially the concept of freedom.

A keen reader will have noticed a disagreement between the Lacanian analyst's attempt to listen carefully for a client's unique difference and the structuralist determinism outlined above. Where does human difference come from if even our secret, hidden desires are given in advance by social-symbolic paternalistic laws? And what use would freedom of expression be if real freedom were prohibited by an homogenization so complete it manifested at the level of desire? Shouldn't desire instead enable freedom? This would be a good place to introduce a third feature of Lacan's symbolic, its incompletion. This incompleteness of the symbolic is the third of Lacan's registers, the real. The incompletion or undecidability of the abstract structural order determining us manifests itself as desire. Against object relations schools, Lacan would offer a theory of desire as a theory of lack or subjective destitution rather than a theory of desire as having a corresponding positive object (Lacan, 1994/2020). Lacan emphasized how each love object, once obtained, frustrates and disappoints the desiring subject since what we aim at ultimately with our desire is the recovery of some more primary loss. So, the symbolic order is indeed determinative but ultimately not in the sense that it prescribes, in advance, a specific love object for us to desire but that it makes each object ultimately dissatisfying. Lacan emphasizes that it isn't the analyst's job to help the client successfully find a "normal" love object and thereby adapt and conform to social norms, a goal often achieved in therapy by scaffolding or modeling with the analyst's own ego. "The goal is not, as people believe, to adapt to a more or less well-defined or well-organized reality, but to get one's own reality-that is, one's own desire- recognized… to symbolize it" (Lacan, 2005/2013, p. 37). Part of bringing the client to a place where they're able to hear and interpret their own desire entails realizing the illusory nature of the client's fantasy that their own completeness will result with the conquest of this love object (Lacan, 1966/2006, pp. 80-81). To summarize, the constitutive role of loss in structuring unconscious desire implies that the deterministic system of the unconscious is open-ended at this key point. It is the analyst's job to lead the client to familiarity, within the context of their own life history and situation, with their own desire.

It's at this juncture that freedom and desire meet, leading Lacan to later write about psychoanalysis as a creative ethics of desire. Lacan elaborates that if the symbolic order ultimately doesn't determine an essential, natural object (for example, a man for a woman and a woman for a man) but leaves it undetermined, this indetermination is perfectly expressed in the anxiety-inducing message that it does code us with: "What do you want?" (Lacan, 1966/2006, p. 690). If some analysts had a tendency to interpret the contents of the unconscious through the lens of positivistic biology, as an instinctual tendency towards a natural object, Lacan instead found a question there rather than a positive answer. Here counselors who may be more familiar with existentialist counseling modalities will notice how Lacan's conception of the symbolic merges with the same popular philosophy of his time and place. Indeed, being determined to ask the question, "What do I want" or, "What is wanted of me" sounds quite a bit like Sartre's description of the human condition as being 'condemned to freedom'. Yet, however much Lacan owes to Sartre and existentialism, we should be careful to observe that he distances himself from Sartre's own reduction of intersubjective relations to relations of mastery (Lacan, 1966/2006, p. 80) and relegates that dynamic to the imaginary register. The introduction of the unconscious and the question of our desire as unconscious allows us to gain some freedom from always being implicated in social power relations aimed at marginalization, colonization, mastery, or sadistic capture of our neighbor.

Counselors and counseling students may find something of value in this way of thinking insofar as they find themselves conflicted about the role social norms play within the discipline. On one hand, we are asked to utilize the DSM whose diagnostic categories must make constant reference to hypothetical social norms. In diagnosed clients, deviance from these norms and the consequent social limitations are encoded as qualifying diagnostic criteria, a part of the definition of what it means to be mentally ill. On the other hand, we may have the experience that our client's unique suffering attests to an ethical-political injustice enabled by these norms and that their speech calls out for a different experience and order, and that they desire to be something other than the options the current social order offers. This conflict is salient to our specific challenges as counselors today in the 2020s, where we find transgender children and adults at the center of American political culture wars, domestic terror threats, and on the table at many a state legislature. Lacan's reinterpretation of classical Freudian thought gives a framework to think both the non-essential character of social norms as well as the nevertheless determining effect they have on us.

TRAINING

Practical Concerns

Those practicing psychoanalysis with a Lacanian lens are subject to all the other requirements of normal psychoanalytic training. In America, psychoanalytic institutes admit those with a license to practice in the helping fields. Training to become a psychoanalyst involves coursework but also requires that the candidate undergo their own rigorous training analysis with a psychoanalyst. Training analysts are also required to have a series of supervised analyses of a determinate length and frequency. Most programs also offer a truncated training in psychoanalytic psychotherapy, typically two years of coursework, and most also offer academic training for those outside the helping disciplines. These range in cost from institute to institute. A quick sampling of organizations showed around $3200 per semester at the Washington-Baltimore Center for Psychoanalysis or around $2000 for a semester of study at the Psychoanalytic Center of the Carolinas. 'The Lacanian Compass' appears to be the closest thing to an "authorized" school with Lacanian emphasis since it is linked to the New Lacanian School and the World Association of Psychoanalysis, both of which are associated with Jacques Alain-Miller, Lacan's son-in-law and authorized editor of his seminars. Lacanian Compass courses had $350 registration fees in 2024. Interested candidates for study should keep in mind that the financial demands of such programs also entail payment for supervision of required supervised analyses as well as one's own training analysis. Those pursuing attainment of full analyst status may find themselves in training past five years.

The EFP, Lacan's school, implemented a controversial procedure referred to as "the pass" for those who sought to accede to the rank of analyst of the school. On the one hand this procedure unburdened the training analysis from the pressure of being a requirement for acceding to analyst status. On the other hand, it removed the hierarchical structure this requirement gave to the school by disempowering training analysts of their gatekeeping function with regard to evaluating training analyses. Candidates to the pass were not nominated by higher-ranking members but could only be nominated by themselves. The jury hearing the candidate's testimony about their analysis was comprised not just of analysts of the school but also of three randomly chosen, simple members. Even these three higher-ranking analysts of the school were chosen at random. The director of the school, Lacan, was the seventh member of the jury. To make things even more complicated, the simple members, known as passeurs would hear from the candidate about his analysis and what warranted its ending. They would then give testimony before the jury and the jury of analysts would vote on this candidate's accession.

Tracy McNulty (2022) writes about her experience of the Lacanian procedure as a passeur in terms of the transmissibility of unconscious knowledge and desire. The validation of the candidate's analysis isn't the logical completion or tidiness of its trajectory but rather its ability to transmit unconscious contents incapable of being straightforwardly framed by language. In McNulty's article, these unconscious elements are registered instead in the form of bodily symptoms and bodily behavior contracted by the passeurs, in her case, headache, disorientation, social discomfort, and a blood sugar spike. Her descriptions of this experience reinforce the importance in Lacan of formalizing elements that elude symbolic, articulable experience.

The scope of practice for Lacanian psychoanalysis is hard to determine since 'Lacanianism' itself has always been amorphous. It has always ambivalently wavered between the dogmatic, captivated worship of a Godhead at one pole, and on the other, the disorganizations resulting from Lacan's institutional self-destructiveness, intentionally obfuscating writing, and an emphasis on the analytic importance of not understanding. Decades later, whatever may be called 'Lacanianism' involves a plurality of official and non-official organizations as well as individual, analytic-minded writers and thinkers who cite Lacan's teachings as their inspiration. The infamous seminars themselves bear witness against an orthodoxy insofar as his cryptic aphoristic formulations about different core concepts tended to change and shift over time, so much so that certain key concepts take on opposite formulations at different periods. This is rendered more difficult for readers to follow in that, unlike Freud for example, Lacan showed no inclination to draw attention to the experimental lability of his concepts but instead preferred to maintain the fascinating mystique of an internally coherent and consistent theoretical edifice whose watchword was always just out of reach. Despite his loud protests against Hegelianism, against a systemic thinking that attempts to comprehend all domains of knowledge, it's hard to credibly deny a tendency in Lacan's work towards an applicability to all sciences and similarly a claim for the clinical utility of his concepts to all clients. Against Freud, Lacan would try early on to extend the concept of transference past neurosis to psychotic clients, expanding the scope of practice to its once-excluded other. His work here is continued by many contemporary Lacanians and the '388' in Quebec, a psychoanalytic treatment center for young adult psychotics, is associated with GIFRIC [Group Interdisciplinaire Freudien de Recherche et d'Intervention Cliniques et Culturelles], a Lacanian group. Even contemporary symptom syndromes like 'depression' that were publicly criticized by Lacan are now subjects of anthologies by numerous practitioners who have found his thought useful for formulating case conceptualization and orienting treatment (Hook & Vanheule, 2023).

That being said, the same precautions that might apply to psychoanalysis in general will apply to Lacanian-oriented analysis. Counseling clients who present with significantly advanced eating disorders or substance use disorders will need to address these habits first or concurrently in order to find themselves capable of engaging in the introspective work demanded by the modality. Similarly, those dealing with significant emotional dysregulation may benefit from some practical skills work before this type of therapy.

With psychodynamic psychotherapy and psychoanalytic psychotherapy both prescribing multiple sessions per week, many clients will understandably find it challenging to find time in their schedules. While the notion that these modes of therapy cost more per session than the so-called evidence-based therapies isn't altogether accurate, it is true that they emphasize a more prolonged treatment since their therapy goals entail a more fundamental shift in personality organization and an overall increased self-understanding rather than the temporary amelioration of specific symptoms frequently decontextualized from their causal factors. In any case, the pursuit of any psychoanalytic or psychodynamic therapy is a significant commitment of client time and money and may not fit into the busy lives and schedules demanded of us by our contemporary conditions.

VALUE AND RELEVANCE TO COUNSELORS

Counselors interested in a theoretical framework that emphasizes economic, political, and social factors may find Lacanian theory and approach to be a fruitful option. Lacanian theory reimagines client suffering, desire, and symptom formation through this lens. Equally as important, counselors who find these factors to be determinative but who additionally find relativistic postmodern approaches to be lacking may find this direction even more appealing since it's equally opposed to biological and social reductivism. A third option, the psychoanalytic domain of the sexual first opened by Freud, is reinterpreted not as the successful determination of both nature and nurture but as the fateful effect of their overlapping misfire.

Socialization of Disorders

Lacan is often credited with introducing social dynamics into the understanding of symptoms or disorders. This component is so prominent that many Lacanian practitioners will often refer, for example, to 'paranoid structure' rather than describing someone as 'having paranoia'. One doesn't refer to a disease contracted by an individual but to a specific relationship of a unique individual to a contingent, ever-changing social reality. Psychotic, neurotic, or perverse structures are possibilities of existing comprised of one's specific mode of relating to social and cultural norms, economic systems, ideological frameworks, and gender relations.

As identity politics have come into vogue in broader swathes of American public discourse, increasingly more counselors may feel motivated to take a closer look at theoretical frameworks that require consideration of the above-listed factors when formulating cases. Clients increasingly expect therapists who consider that social factors are key to understanding them. With Lacan, therapists may find resources not just for thinking through ways that clients are formed by social factors but also for the important and unique ways that they exceed these determinations and limitations. Along these same lines, marginalized clients may benefit from a counseling style that considers the aim and goal of therapy to be the creation of new social-symbolic possibilities that speak to their own desires rather than adaptation to an ill-functioning society.

CRITIQUING EMPATHY AND UNDERSTANDING

Bruce Fink's Fundamentals of Psychoanalytic Technique (2007) does a good job of using Lacanian theory to demonstrate how many seemingly innocuous fundamentals taught by counseling programs can become detrimental to the client-counselor relationship. An overemphasis on empathy in early training, for example, could lead young therapists to an approach that feels rather invasive to a client if they perceive that the therapist hasn't taken adequate time to really listen and get to know the specificity of their experience. Excessively empathetic approaches may emphasize the importance of making the client feel heard and validated over actually hearing the client. For example, many may automatically nod their heads before they've had the time to comprehend the meaning or import of a bit of client communication. Not only can this limit, in advance, what we're receptive to hearing but it may also contribute to a sense of distrust for some clients when applied indiscriminately.

Along with this, many counselors may rush in to understand the client whereas Lacanian practice emphasizes suspending conclusions and postponing understanding. This may be done either to quell one's own anxiety in early moments of the relationship or perhaps out of an equally-anxious concern for establishing early rapport. This may feel invasive, invalidating, or disingenuous to some clients. Fink mentions that many clients already have a self-narrative, even if it's only implicit, that commits them to the symptoms, interpersonal styles, and repeated unpleasant experiences that bring them to therapy. The counselor's job isn't simply to understand and empathize with this tidy self-narrative but to find the cracks or inconsistencies in it that might be footholds toward change.

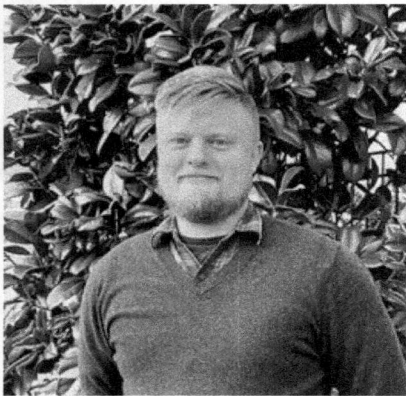

Mr. Barker is currently working towards his Master's Degree in Counselor Education at Adams State University and practicing under supervision in Raleigh, NC at The Center for Psychological & Family Services. Prior to his training as a therapist, he completed an M.A. in Philosophy at Miami University of Ohio and a B.A. in English Literature at Georgia Southern University, both of which enrich his understanding of the human experience. His areas of interest include grief, obsessive-compulsive disorder, and anxiety.

References

Black, M., & Mitchell, S. (1995). Freud and Beyond: a History of Modern Psychoanalytic Thought. BasicBooks.

Fink, B. (2007). Fundamentals of Psychoanalytic Technique. W. W. Norton & Company.

Freud, S. (1961). Civilization and its Discontents (J. Strachey, Ed. & Trans.). W. W. Norton & Company. (Original work published 1930)

Hook, D., & Vanheule, S. (Eds.). (2023). Lacan on depression and melancholia. Routledge.

Lacan, J. (1981). The Four Fundamental Concepts of Psychoanalysis (A. Sheridan, Trans.). W. W. Norton & Company. (Original work published 1973)

Lacan, J. (2020). The Object Relation (A. Price, Trans.). W. W. Norton & Company. (Original work published 1994)

Lacan, J. (2006). Ecrits: the First Complete Edition in English (B. Fink, Trans.). W. W. Norton & Company. (Original work published 1966)

Lacan, J. (2013). On the Names-of-the-Father (B. Fink, Trans.). Polity Press. (Original work published 2005)

McNulty, T. (2022). Untreatable: the Freudian Act and its Legacy. Crisis and Critique, 6(1), 227-251.

Mitchell, J. (1975). Psychoanalysis and Feminism: Freud, Reich, Laing and Women. Vintage Books.

Roudinesco, E. (1997). Jacques Lacan: Outline of a Life, History of a System of Thought (B. Bray, Trans.). Columbia University Press. (Original work published 1994)

Roudinesco, E. (1986). Jacques Lacan & Co.: a History of Psychoanalysis in France, 1925-1985 (J. Mehlman, Trans.). The University of Chicago Press. (Original work published 1990)

Laplanche Therapy

Elise Johns, PhD, LPCS, NCC, CCTP

Lauren Clark, PhD, LPC, NCC

Jean Laplanche's theory was developed after his years of training in Psychoanalysis. Laplanche's innovative views diverged from the original psychoanalytic concepts outlined by Freud. Whereas Freud abandoned his theory of seduction, Laplanche proposed a reexamination and extension of this original concept in his *general theory of seduction* (Fletcher, 2000). The goal of Laplanche's *general theory of seduction* was to explain the origin of the unconscious (Foiles, 2019). In the adult-child dynamic, the child is unable to interpret the sexual messages that are unconsciously sent from adult to child (Ahbel-Rappe, 2011). According to Laplanche, the unconscious should not be viewed as consistently pathological and the interaction between adult and child is characteristic of normal development (Ahbel-Rappe, 2011; Foiles, 2019). While the child is unable to fully grasp the adult's communication, the theory examines the way human sexuality is established (Ahbel-Rappe, 2011; Foiles, 2019).

CERTIFICATIONS, TRAININGS, AND LICENSURE REQUIREMENTS FOR LAPLANCHE THERAPY

General Cost

No certifications are available. General cost per training varies, however, has an average of $300-375 per training (https://internationalpsychoanalysis.net, https://www.laplancheinthestates, https://www.trontopsychoanalysis.com).

Identified as gold standard, best practice, or EBP

Jean Laplanche's theory is not associated with best practice, or evidence-based practice (EBP) designation in the same way that some therapeutic modalities are. Laplanche, as most psychoanalytic theory, is individual-specific and subjective in approach. It is important to note that psychoanalysis, including Laplanche's theories, is often considered a complex and evolving field with diverse perspectives and interpretations (Laplanche, 1997; Mitchell, & Black, 2014). To gain a thorough understanding of Laplanche's theory, it is recommended to engage in psychoanalytic training that encompasses his work.

Training required/recommended?

No current certifications exist on solely the work of Laplanche. Few sporadic trainings and continuing education courses exist on the topic. Thus, training is recommended, not required. In order to practice in the field of psychoanalysis, of which Laplanche is a theorist, training is required as with all mental health professions (McWilliams, 2011).

Trainings offered if no certification available?

Various trainings in Laplanche's theory are available (e.g., trainings to teach the theory and application). Most trainings require multiple sessions (e.g., 2 to 9 sessions). It is possible to complete trainings in psychoanalysis that provide a foundation for further education in Laplanche specific psychoanalytic theory. The American Psychoanalytic Society (APsA) host a variety of trainings, continuing education, and/or conferences on psychoanalysis with information available on their website (https://www.apsa.org). In the past, International Psychoanalysis has hosted Laplanche specific in-person trainings. It is possible to reach out to the organization to request information on past trainings or possible future trainings (https://internationalpsychoanalysis.net). In October of 2021, a virtual "Laplanche in the States Conference" was hosted. Information and related podcasts and book suggestions are still available on the website (https://www.laplancheinthestates). The Toronto Analytic Society offers a course "Entering Laplanche Through the Clinic: An Introductory Perspective" (https://www.trontopsychoanalysis.com).

Certification Available, Required or Recommended?

Certifications can be obtained in psychoanalysis. In order to practice psychoanalysis, one must follow appropriate ethical and professional standards set out by the profession (McWilliams, 2011). Certification is not required for Laplanche informed practice. To practice as a psychoanalyst, one must have appropriate educational credentials (McWilliams, 2011).

Degree Requirements

No specific degree requirements. However, as a theory prominent in psychoanalysis, common degrees include a graduate level degree in counseling and psychology.

ANY CAUTIONS OR LIMITATIONS PROFESSIONALS AND STUDENTS SHOULD KNOW ABOUT?

If intending to work with clients, a license in counseling or psychology is required to which the theory can be applied. If not intending to work with clients, the theory can be applied to scholarly discussions and research interests pertinent to the professional.

SCOPE OF PRACTICE ISSUES

When practicing psychoanalysis or applying any more specific theoretical framework to include Laplanche, it is important to adhere to guidelines of ethical and professional organizations. Making sure individuals receive appropriate training, taking a collaborative approach by seeking supervision and consultation, as well as considering other relevant theories and limitations of the theoretical framework one is applying are all important elements to consider when working within scope of practice (Gabbard, 2008).

Supervision Required or Recommended

As there is no certification or degree specific to Laplanche; no specific supervision is required. In order to become a psychoanalyst, graduate education, personal analysis, clinical experience, and supervision are required (McWilliams, 2011). When practicing in the field of mental health, particularly when acquiring new information, supervision is always recommended and in many instances, it is required; particularly when pursuing licensure (Watkins, Milne, 2017).

Ongoing CEU Required or Recommended

No ongoing fees associated with Laplanche continuing education.

Ongoing Annual Fees

There is no society or membership associated with Laplanche. One can become a member of numerous psychoanalytic societies; all include a variety of annual fees.

SUMMARY

Jean Laplanche, 1924-2012, was a French psychoanalyst, theorist, and philosopher whose seminal works include co-authoring the influential book, "The Language of Psychoanalysis" exploring the language and foundational concepts of psychoanalysis. Laplanche emphasized the early childhood experience and its influence on the subconscious with specific focus on the impact of sexual and erotic experiences during infancy and the formation of subconscious desire. The work of Laplanche also addressed the complex human sexuality and the role of language in psychoanalysis. (Laplanche, 1997; Laplanche & Pontalis, 1973). There are no certifications, fees, membership, or supervision requirements associated with Laplanche theoretical orientation and application. However, Laplanche is a psychoanalytic theory. To professionally practice as a psychoanalyst, one must pursue the appropriate degrees, uphold a professional standard, seek supervision and personal analysis, and pay all associated professional memberships and fees (McWilliams, 2011; https://www.apsca.org)

Dr. Johns has been in the field of mental health for 15 years. As a therapist in private practice she works primarily with grief and trauma. Dr. Johns has worked in the field of mental health in various capacities since her graduation from Troy University in 2009. Since 2009, Dr. Johns has worked with veterans, hospice, and in community mental health. She is a member of ACA, SACES and a current board member on the Louisiana State Board of Licensed Professional Counselors. Dr. Johns' professional presentations include topics on mindfulness, aging, and ethics in counseling.

elisejohns@gmail.com

Dr. Clark has been in the field of mental health for seven years and has worked with children, adolescent, and adult clients who are dealing with a wide variety of presenting problems. Dr. Clark obtained her Master's degree from Monmouth University in 2016 and her Doctoral degree from the University of New Orleans in 2022. She is a member of various national and state-level professional organizations, including ACA, ACES, LCA, and NJCA. Dr. Clark's professional presentations include topics on school violence prevention, counselor resilience, and

REFERENCES

Ahbel-Rappe, K. (2011). The seduction theory in the twenty-first century: Trauma, fantasy and reality [Review of the book *The seduction theory in the twenty-first century: Trauma, fantasy and reality*, by M. Good]. *APA Divisions,* https://www.apadivisions.org/division39/publications /reviews/seduction

Entering Laplanche Through the Clinic: An Introductory Perspective. (2023). Toronto Analytic Society. ((https://www.trontopsychoanalysis.com).

Fletcher, J. (2000). Gender, sexuality, and the theory of seduction. *Women: A Cultural Review, 11*(1/2), 95-108.

Foiles, J. (2019). Where does the unconscious come from? Examining Lapanche's theory of how the unconscious is formed. *Psychology Today.* https://www.psychologytoday.com/us/blog/the-thing-feathers/201908/where-does-the-unconscious-come

Gabbard, G.O. (2008). The Scope of Psychoanalytic Practice. Journal of the American Psychoanalytic Association 56 (1), 39-56

Laplanche, J. (1997). The Unfinished Copernican Revolution: An Attempt to Construct a Freudianism. International Journal of Psychoanalysis, 7(3), 357-366.

Laplanche in the States Conference. (2021). Laplanche in the States. https://:www.laplancheinthesatates.com

Laplanche, J., & Pontalis, J.B. (1973). The Language of Psycho-Analysis. W.W. Norton & Company.

Membership eligibility. (2023) American Psychoanalytic Association. https://www.apsa.org

Mitchell, S.A., & Black M.J. (2014). Freud and Beyond; A History of Modern Psychoanalytic Thought. Basic Books.

McWilliams, N. (2011) The challenges of contemporary psychoanalytic education. Psychoanalytic Psychology, 28 (3) , 385-403.

Watkins, C.E. Jr., & Milne, D. (2017). Supervision in psychotherapy: An integrative developmental approach. Psychotherapy, 54 (1), 7-15.

Laughter Yoga Leader Certificate (CLYL)

AUDREY S. AUTREY, MA, LPC, NCC, CLYL, CCTP, CHT

Laughter Yoga has a relatively short history, beginning in 1995 with the first laughter club being started by Dr. Madan Kataria, a medical doctor from Mumbai India, with just five people in a public park. He knew the medical benefits of laughter and they began just by telling each other jokes and funny stories, but soon ran out of them as we all have a limited repertoire of jokes. Dr. Kataria's wife, Madhuri Kataria, was a traditional yoga teacher, and the two of them together recognized the similarities in breathing during laughter as well as in yoga, and the fact that the body does not differentiate between acted and genuine laughter. They explained this to their small group and asked them to try to act out laughter with him for one minute, and despite the skepticism and doubt, they agreed to try and the results were surprising! For some, the acted laughter quickly turned into genuine laughter, which was contagious, and soon the group was laughing like never before and the laughter kept going for almost ten minutes!

Dr. Kataria reminds us that we don't need a sense of humor to laugh and that we can train ourselves to laugh for no reason at all. His techniques are effective even for people who seem to have lost their laughter or have absolutely no sense of humor. All that is needed is an openness and willingness to show up because laughter is so contagious. Once released, natural laughter is hard to stop. He talked about the link between body and mind and the theory of "Motion Creates Emotion". Laughter Yoga uses this mind/body link through voluntary movements such as repetitive clapping, chanting and specific body movements combined with laughter and breathing exercises.

Dr. William F. Fry (1924-2014), a professor of psychology at Stanford, was one of the first scientists to suggest in 1964 that laughter was a reasonable field to study and was the first to apply for public funding. However, this was during the Vietnam War, and all research projects were put on hold due to budgetary constraints. He pursued his interest informally and became the first self-proclaimed "Gelotologist", an expert in the science of laughter from the Greek root gelos, to laugh.

Norman Cousins (1915-1990) also raised a lot of public awareness about the healing power of laughter and positive emotions following a miraculous "laughter recovery" in 1964 from a fatal illness, ankylosing spondylitis (a rare form of degenerative arthritis). He claimed that 10 minutes of belly laughter would give him two hours of pain-free sleep, where previously even morphine could not help him. His story baffled the scientific community and inspired research. His 1979 book Anatomy of an Illness is a classic.

The American Association for Therapeutic Humor (www.aath.org) was founded in 1987 and the formation of the International Society for Humor Studies (www.humorstudies.org) based in Europe followed in 1988. These organizations bring together hundreds of professionals interested in integrating humor into a variety of therapeutic modalities and have published hundreds of articles on the health benefits of laughter.

My training is through the Dr. Kataria School of Laughter Yoga (www.laughteryoga.org) and was quite serendipitous in crossing my path. My partner had just recently died, and I was not doing well. I saw an ad in our local newspaper about a laughter yoga conference being held one weekend in our city, which seemed intriguing, but I let it pass. However, my curiosity was piqued, and I kept thinking how I wish I had gone to see what it was about. I soon saw an ad for a laughter yoga club and decided to go but when I got there, it was just the leader and myself. Despite that, we had a blast and within a few weeks that group grew rapidly and was truly my only bright spot through that difficult time.

CERTIFICATIONS, TRAININGS, LICENSURE REQUIREMENTS FOR LAUGHTER YOGA

As this is a relatively new training, it isn't very strenuously regulated. The training included two days of group training about the history and benefits of laughter yoga and lots of practice engaging in laughter, which was very fun! The cost was around $300 for the initial training. There is no ongoing CEU requirements or certification renewals. There are now trainings via Zoom via Dr. Kataria's school (www.laughteryoga.org).

A quick Google search showed several "diplomas" and certifications through many different places. The AATH has its own certificate program with different requirements than Laughter Yoga. So, my suggestion is to decide which of these programs best fits your own philosophy and keep bringing laughter into your life and into the lives of your clients because the benefits are real!

SCOPES OF PRACTICE ISSUES

There are no formal Code of Ethics for Laughter Yoga, but Dr. Kataria's founding ideas were to bring laughter to as many people as possible, and it was suggested in my training that we keep the laughter clubs free of charge to encourage more equality of opportunity to attend these clubs. I found that especially helpful advice as I was running my initial laughter clubs/groups out of a clinic for those without insurance and people were so thankful they could finally participate in a program without worrying about cost.

As for any licensed professional, one should continue to practice within their specific Code of Ethics, applying it to the practice of laughter yoga. I have found a few times that my counseling skills came in handy as a couple of individuals going through a difficult time were able to access emotions they had covered up until beginning to laugh for the first time in quite a while and ended up doing some individual therapy at those times. It has been rare that those issues have come up, but it is something to be aware of.

OVERALL RECOMMENDATIONS AND IMPRESSIONS OF MODALITY TRAINING

I personally have found Laughter Yoga to be a fun addition to my professional identity. Perhaps it is because of my own biases and interests, but of the possibilities for certification in laughter/humor, etc. Dr. Kataria's training has felt more genuine and comfortable for me. In such a difficult world we live in, the reminder to laugh is essential, and having the "excuse" of going to Laughter Yoga is a fun way to give yourself that permission to laugh more genuinely. As I mentioned above, my own personal reason for going to laughter yoga training was a life saver. Nothing else would have pulled me out of my grief and depression. I like that his training incorporates education about the physiology and psychology of laughter and really explains why and how it works. He incorporates all the benefits of laughter and even shows how it can be used in many different locations, such as in schools, in businesses, and in hospitals. I have personally made use of it in the hospital setting when things are really stressful. I will start with myself, watching Dr. Kataria's YouTube video of him laughing by himself (https://youtu.be/QvAkyoA7I4U) which always lightens my mood and helps me face whatever challenges come my way.

I think finding live trainings are always much more fun than online trainings for this modality. Part of the reason is how contagious laughter is and I've been involved in some laughter clubs online and don't always get the same effect as in person groups. The pandemic made online a necessity, but it is definitely much more fun in person!

Laughter Yoga is a fun addition to traditional therapy and can help people of all ages.

I am a master's level trained mental health counselor, licensed in the state of Arizona, holding a National Certification through the National Board of Certified Counselors, as well as a Certified Clinical Trauma Professional certification through PESI/Evergreen certifications, and a Certified Hypnotherapist through the International Board of Hypnotherapy. I did not set out to become a therapist, but it found me and then through the clients that ended up coming to me, I furthered my training with the additional certifications that would help me help my clients. The laughter yoga certification is a really nice ice breaker because it is such a unique training and people tend to want to know more. Having worked in hospital settings with severely medically ill and mentally ill patients, the addition of laughter yoga has been a nice change from the "serious" business of medicine and psychiatry. It reminds both counselor and clients that reconnecting to "childlike play" and "childlike curiosity" can be healing in itself! My hope is that Laughter Yoga will become a regular addition to many inpatient psychiatric facilities and will be used with staff in many different work situations to help reduce the stress that people feel in the workplace.

I co-founded a nonprofit organization working with epilepsy in New Mexico, Epilepsy Support and Education Services (https://epilepsysupportnm.org). Although I am no longer involved in the day-to-day functioning of that organization, it is the accomplishment I am most proud of because it was the first nonprofit organization for epilepsy in the state of New Mexico.

I am currently a psychiatric assessor in a local hospital emergency room, and work part time with a local counseling agency in Tucson, AZ.

REFERENCES

Kataria, M., 2010. Certified Laughter Yoga Leader Training Manual.

Lego® Therapy

Bill Owenby, EdD, MC, FAAETS, DAAETS, DCMHS, LPC, LAAC, NCC, CCMHC, ACS, Diplomate, Fellow

Katherine Campbell, MAED, LPC, LAAC, NCC

Lego® Therapy is an innovative, play-based therapeutic approach that uses Lego bricks and collaborative building activities to support social skills, communication, and emotional development. Originally developed by Dr. Daniel B. LeGoff, a clinical neuropsychologist, Lego Therapy has gained recognition for its effectiveness in helping individuals, particularly children with autism spectrum disorder (ASD) and other developmental challenges, to build meaningful connections and enhance interpersonal skills.

CORE PRINCIPLES OF LEGO THERAPY

Collaborative Play

Participants work together to build Lego creations, fostering teamwork and communication. Roles such as "Builder," "Engineer," and "Supplier" encourage turn-taking and collaboration.

Social Skills Development

The method emphasizes verbal and non-verbal communication, active listening, and conflict resolution. It promotes sharing, compromise, and group problem-solving.

Structured yet Flexible Approach

Therapists create structured activities but allow creativity and self-expression within the process. Lego Therapy is tailored to meet the unique needs and goals of each participant.

APPLICATIONS IN MENTAL HEALTH AND EDUCATION

Autism Spectrum Disorder (ASD)

Lego Therapy addresses social skills deficits by providing a structured environment for interaction. It builds confidence and reduces social anxiety.

ADHD and Behavioral Challenges

The approach encourages focus, impulse control, and positive peer interactions. It reinforces the importance of following rules and completing tasks.

Emotional Regulation

Lego Therapy provides a safe space for participants to express emotions through creative play. It teaches coping strategies and frustration tolerance.

General Child and Adolescent Therapy

This therapy enhances fine motor skills, cognitive development, and imaginative play. It also facilitates parent-child bonding and family therapy dynamics.

BENEFITS OF LEGO THERAPY

Enhanced Social Interaction

Participants learn to navigate social settings and develop meaningful relationships. Lego Therapy builds empathy and perspective-taking skills.

Fun and Engagement

The use of universally loved Lego bricks makes therapy enjoyable and motivating, increasing participation and retention in therapy sessions.

Accessible and Inclusive

Lego Therapy is suitable for a wide range of developmental levels and ages. It can be adapted for individual, group, or family therapy.

Promotes Creativity and Problem-Solving

Participants gain a sense of accomplishment through completing projects. The approach encourages innovative thinking and resilience.

TRAINING AND CERTIFICATION FOR LEGO THERAPY

Educational and Professional Background

Lego Therapy training is typically geared toward therapists, educators, and support staff working with children and adolescents. A background in psychology, social work, or special education is recommended.

Certification Programs

Certification is available through specialized organizations offering Lego Therapy training workshops. Programs cover core principles, practical applications, and strategies for integration into practice. Workshops typically range from $150 to $500, with more comprehensive certifications costing $1,000–$2,000.

Continuing Education

Many courses offer CE credits for mental health professionals. Topics include advanced techniques, adaptations for specific populations, and research updates.

Notable Training Providers

- The LEGO Foundation Initiatives
- Social Skills Training Institute (SSTI)
- Play-Based Therapy Programs

CHALLENGES AND LIMITATIONS

Limited Awareness and Resources

Lego Therapy is not widely known or accessible in all areas, requiring additional training and investment.

Potential for Overstimulation

The colorful and tactile nature of Lego Therapy can overwhelm some participants with sensory sensitivities.

Balancing Fun and Therapeutic Goals

Therapists must ensure that activities remain purposeful and aligned with therapeutic objectives.

Group Dynamics

Managing group interactions and resolving conflicts can be challenging, especially with diverse developmental levels.

IMPLEMENTATION IN PRACTICE

Starting a Lego Therapy Program

To begin, identify client needs and set measurable goals. Obtain Lego kits and designate a therapy space conducive to collaborative play.

Session Structure

Sessions typically last 30–60 minutes and include:

- Warm-up activities
- Collaborative building tasks
- Reflection and feedback

Integration with Other Therapies

Lego Therapy combines well with cognitive-behavioral therapy (CBT), occupational therapy, and social skills training.

FUTURE DIRECTIONS AND RESEARCH

Expanding Access

Efforts are underway to increase awareness and availability of training programs worldwide.

Evidence-Based Practice

Continued research is needed to validate the efficacy of Lego Therapy for diverse populations.

Technology Integration

Exploring the use of digital Lego tools and virtual therapy platforms can broaden accessibility.

SUMMARY

Lego Therapy offers a creative and engaging way to support social, emotional, and developmental growth. Its versatility, accessibility, and evidence-based foundation make it a valuable tool for mental health professionals, educators, and families. By integrating play with therapeutic practice, Lego Therapy helps individuals build connections—brick by brick.

I hold two independent licenses in the states of Arizona and Ohio, supervisory status in Arizona, along with a substance abuse license in Arizona. I am board certified as a Diplomate and Clinical Mental Health Specialist, an Approved Clinical Supervisor, Nationally Certified Counselor, a Certified Clinical Mental Health Counselor, NeuroLinguistic Programming Practitioner, and a Clinical Trauma Specialist for Individuals and Family including EMDR Therapy and NET. I completed my training in Animal-Assisted Therapy and Pet Handlers certification in order to evaluate and incorporate the human-animal bond in therapy. I am the sole author and creator of the SxC Model of ESA Evaluation. My research interests surround post-traumatic growth, resiliency, strengths-based therapy, positive psychology, mindfulness, Animal-Assisted Therapy, Sandtray Therapy, Creative approaches in therapy, and martial arts in mental health. I have presented at local, state, regional, national, and international levels on various topics including personality traits, licensure reciprocity challenges, Sandtray and supervision, and Animal-Assisted Therapy within supervision.

eonbllc@gmail.com

Katherine is a local nonprofit integrative community health agency where she provides therapy. Katherine received her Masters in Arts in Education from the University of Akron. She is a published author, an award recipient, and has presented on the use of Therapy Animals in Supervision. She is trained as an LPC and LAAC, a trauma specialist, and a Nationally Certified Counselor. She was awarded the Tucson Hispanic Chamber of Commerce's 40 Under 40 in 2021, which means she got it before Bill, as well as beat out Bill in 2021, and yes, they joke about that all the time. Katherine lives with her spouse/co-captain/PIC/co-editor and their 2 cats Waffle and Pancake outside of Tucson, AZ.

REFERENCES

LeGoff, D. B., et al. (2004). Social competence in children with autism: Using Lego therapy as a therapeutic intervention. JOURNAL OF AUTISM AND DEVELOPMENTAL DISORDERS.

Owens, G., & Granader, Y. (2008). The effectiveness of Lego-based therapy in children with social difficulties. AUTISM RESEARCH.

Peeters, T., & Gillberg, C. (2010). AUTISM AND PLAY. Routledge.

Recommended Resources

Brick by Brick: How to Use LEGO® in Therapy: **www.legotherapy.com**
Autism Research Centre: **www.autismresearchcentre.com**
The LEGO Foundation: **www.legofoundation.com**

Let me know if further changes are needed!

Liberation Therapy

FRANK GORRITZ FITZSIMONS, PHD, LPC, NCC

During this chapter, you will each gain an understanding of what Liberation Therapy consists of in a counseling context, as well as ways to apply the theory in counseling practice. Liberation Theory was originally founded by Ignacio Martín-Baró in 1986. However, it is important to note that Liberation Theory has global roots around the world, in places including, but not limited to Cuba (SÁNCHEZ & WIESENFELD, 1991), South Africa (Seedat, 1997; 2014; Seedat et al., 2001), the Philippines (Enriquez, 1994; Pe-Pua & Protacio-Marcelino, 2000), and New Zealand (O'Connor et al., 2011; Robertson & Masters-Awatere, 2008). Liberation Theory originally served as a counter-perspective to the lived experience of privileged individuals who were able to access counseling at their leisure, and instead focused on the lived experiences of minoritized communities who were exposed to structural violence and political oppression (Comas DÍAZ & Torres Rivera, 2020). Through various theoretical tenets, Liberation Therapy alters the focus from pathologizing a client towards instead connecting with the minoritized lived experiences of clients, especially as they are impacted by oppression based on various cultural identities and intersections such as race, gender, sexuality, etc.

THEORETICAL TENETS

- Reorientation of Psychology – This tenet asks counselors to prioritize the lived experiences of those who are exposed to oppression, discrimination, and poverty, rather than contribute to it through the psychological gaze of pathology that is commonly taught in Western Psychology (Comas DÍAZ & Torres Rivera, 2020; Martín-Baró, 1998; Summers & Nelson, 2023). In other words, this tenet emphasizes the idea that both the psychological and personal perspectives of oppressed communities are political and must be treated as such in the context of counseling.

- Recovering Historical Memory – This theoretical tenet focuses on how the history of the oppressed had been taken and reproduced through the lens of the colonizer, which plays a present role in oppressive tenets of counseling and psychology (Adams et al., 2015; Afuape, 2011; Akken & Taracena, 2007; Enriquez, 1994). An example of this tenet is currently and historically present through the anti-CRT legislation present in Florida, which consequently replaced Black/African American histories of slavery to state that Black and African slaves benefitted from slavery (Breen, 2023). Through providing space for clients to engage in collaborative story-telling, reclaiming one's cultural history and counter-narrative, as well as catharsis, healing elements are produced for clients during the therapeutic process (Chavez et al., 2016).

- Deideologizing Everyday Experience – This theoretical tenet encourages counselors to analyze dominant forms of discourse that distort the lived experiences of minoritized communities (Tate et al., 2013). Specifically, counselors must get to know the everyday experiences of their clients, to deconstruct dominant messages that distort minoritized lives, so that minoritized clients can begin to heal from their oppressive experiences in therapeutic spaces where counselors will fully listen to their lived experience (DOMÍNGUEZ ET AL., 2020).

- Virtues of the People – This tenet focuses on utilizing the strengths present within minoritized communities, to help minoritized clients create and recognize their own personal tools that can help them survive and thrive through oppressive obstacles. An example of theoretical models that explore the various strengths and virtues of minoritized communities includes the Community Cultural Wealth Model (Yosso, 2005). This model allows minoritized communities to explore various forms of capital that provide people with strengths and inspiration during times of adversity including aspirational capital (e.g., aspects of culture that help people maintain their hopes and dreams during times of adversity), familial capital (e.g., cultural knowledge and support provided through family), social capital (e.g., networks within one's community that can provide resources and support), navigational capital (e.g., skills of maneuvering through institutions with socially dominant values), resistant capital (e.g., knowledge and skills developed through challenging oppression), and linguistic capital (e.g., intellectual and social skills attained through communication in more than one language) (Yosso, 2005).

- Denaturalization – Through continuously questioning whose lived experiences are placed in the forefront and whose lived experiences are placed on the social margins, erroneous assumptions about minoritized communities can be explored and questioned within a counselor's perspective. To engage in Liberation Therapy successfully, denaturalization must be an ongoing work for the counselor, so that they can intercept any biases that could harmfully impact minoritized clients (Summers & Nelson, 2023).

- Problematization – This tenet focuses on shifting the counselor's lens to understanding the problems clients face from their perspectives, and not that of the practitioner's professional experience that is drawn from socially dominant systems of oppression (Summers & Nelson, 2023). Through discussion, questioning, and critical reflection, counselors can begin to problematize the ways they have learned about the lived experiences of minoritized people without their voices, and allows clients to explore the ways their lives should be compared to experiences of oppression one can experience (Rivera, 2020; Summers & Nelson, 2023; Tate et al., 2013).

- Conscientization – This theoretical tenet mainly focuses on building critical consciousness between both the counselor and client(s). Through immersing oneself through various tenets of Liberation Theory (among both the counselor and client), powerful insights can emerge that shape a client's empowerment from oppression in their lives. For example, through continuous immersion in problematization and exploring the virtues of the people, the counselor and client(s) can develop powerful insights that empower clients to continue moving through oppression with the power of voice, cultural wealth, and resilience.

- Transformation of the Social Scientist – This theoretical tenet highlights how through continuous immersion in a client's life, that both counselors and clients are forever changed by their genuine cultural immersion, curiosity, and critical consciousness building (DOMÍNGUEZ ET AL., 2020). This transformation is not only powerful for the counselor, but is also powerful for how counselors navigate their interactions with minoritized community members in the field, given that liberation-based transformation strengthens one's advocacy in counseling work.

- Power Dynamics – Counselors must continue to be mindful of the social dynamics that exist between a counselor and their clients to ensure the development of equitable counseling relationships, as well as maximize the effectiveness of culturally responsive therapy. Furthermore, disrupting power dynamics provides more space for clients' traditional customs and community networks to feel more included during the therapy process at the request of the client (Comas DÍAZ & Torres Rivera, 2020).

- Praxis – This final tenet illustrates the importance of social justice action during and post therapy with minoritized clients. To further contribute to the healing of minoritized clients, counselors must step forward and engage in social justice movements, to disrupt forms of oppression that harmfully impact the mental health, wellness, and lives of minoritized people.

Certifications, Trainings, and Licensure Requirements

While certifications are not mandated for counselors to provide effective therapy for minoritized communities, counselors must continuously apply the theoretical tenets of Liberation Therapy to successfully engage in its purposes and practice. Specifically, counselors must put into effect the tenets of "Reorientation of Psychology, Deideologizing Everyday Experience, Denaturalization, Problematization, Power Dynamics, and Praxis" on an ongoing basis to develop further competence in Liberation Therapy. However, counselors must keep in mind that all of the theoretical tenets are essential to apply if counselors are to apply authentic social justice-based therapies with minoritized clients in counseling work.

Degree Requirements

- Master's Degree Related to Counseling (Minimum Degree Needed to Become Licensed as a Counselor Per State)

ANY CAUTIONS OR LIMITATIONS PROFESSIONALS AND STUDENTS SHOULD KNOW ABOUT?

One does not necessarily need to have an independent counseling license to utilize Liberation Therapy in their work with minoritized communities. However, when working with minoritized communities and using Liberation Therapy, it is important to receive supervision from counselors who specialize in Liberation Therapy and have extensive experience in its use with minoritized clients, particularly when counselors may be novice. Ongoing self-awareness work is absolutely vital to becoming trained in Liberation Therapy. Specifically, all counselors must engage in ongoing training and self-reflection in regards to the perception of minoritized communities across the spectrum of gender, sex, sexuality, affectional orientation, race, ethnicity, religiosity, spirituality, ability, socioeconomic status, height, weight, as well as various minoritized identities that can represent salient aspects of one's identity.

Also, it is very important that counselors who wish to provide Liberation Therapy take the time to learn about their own cultural roots as they begin to immerse in others' cultures. Specifically, counselors can find it difficult to immerse themselves in another's culture when they struggle with being self-aware of their own cultural beliefs, assumptions, and values (Summers & Nelson, 2023). This need for awareness directly impacts how one can apply Liberation Therapy, given that the idea of liberation itself can carry different meanings across diverse cultural groups and social identities, especially for those impacted by systemic oppression.

It is also important to note that Liberation Therapy is a widely recognized theoretical orientation in the professional field of counseling, especially as social justice continues to be recognized as a driving force for effective counseling practice (Ratts, 2009). Given its sociocultural roots around the world, it is vital that Liberation Therapy is recognized and taught as a mainstream form of therapy that all counselors can be trained in, as part of promoting culturally affirming counseling across various social identities, as well as part of disrupting systemic harm that the counseling field traditionally stems from.

Supervision Required

Not required/Yet recommended.

Ongoing CEUs Centered on Liberation Therapy are Recommended for Effective Practice!

SUMMARY

All counselors must be aware of, as well as remain dedicated to the original values that shaped the counseling field. Specifically, counselors used to be known as social welfare reformers, which is now known today as social justice (Aubrey, 1977; Goodyear, 1984). To best accomplish this goal, counselors must continue to look back through the histories and herstories of minoritized communities, whose voices were rooted in the philosophy of liberation and social justice. As counselors come to understand Liberation Therapy, as well as its benefits, counselors can begin to fulfill their role as counselors as they engage in the fifth force of counseling effectiveness: social justice (Ratts, 2009).

Liberation Therapy is widely applicable across many theoretical orientations, including those of but not limited to humanistic therapies, feminist therapy, narrative therapy, and postmodern theories. Furthermore, Liberation Therapy is transformative for both counselors and clients as social justice takes a central role in the conceptualization of clients. The counselor's transformation is also highly necessary to apply this therapy effectively, given that to liberate someone else, psychologists and counselors must be liberated themselves (Comas DÍAZ & Torres Rivera, 2020). The nine theoretical tenets associated with Liberation Therapy are also flexible in use and serve similar purposes to help clients attain a sense of spiritual and psychological freedom from oppression (Comas DÍAZ & Torres Rivera, 2020). Overall, Liberation Therapy is a wholesome therapeutic approach and counseling theory that integrates social justice principles into the healing effects of therapy as it utilizes these principles to promote minoritized voices in counseling relationships.

However, it is important to note that Liberation Therapy is not an accent to traditional counseling therapies, and stands on its own as a valid counseling theory. Liberation Therapy has its own philosophical foundation that facilitates social change, action, and engagement with minoritized communities, understanding that the primary ills that impact human beings are related to oppressive political systems and structural violence (Comas DÍAZ & Torres Rivera, 2020). Therefore, this therapy is not to be used lightly by curious counselors and should be given the same consideration of importance given to traditionally recognized counseling theories.

As systemic oppression continues to be recognized as a significant hardship for diverse communities, social justice informed therapies, such as Liberation Therapy, will become the forefront of modern counseling approaches that support people during such unique and complex struggles. Furthermore, Liberation Therapy transforms the counseling field, and liberates the current counseling field, to encourage counselors to take social justice action outside of the therapy room if true social justice change is to occur. One of the most valuable lessons that Liberation Therapy teaches us all, is that all voices are essential to the liberation process, which is something we should be consistently uplifting to give life new ideas, new possibilities, and new futures.

Dr. Frank Gorritz FitzSimons received his Ph.D in Counselor Education and Supervision at the University of Georgia, with a cognate focus in Expressive Arts in Counseling, Diversity, Equity, and Inclusion, and Qualitative Research. Dr. Gorritz FitzSimons is a member of the American Counseling Association (ACA), International Association of Addictions and Offender Counselors (IAAOC), Counselors for Social Justice (CSJ), Association for Counselor Education and Supervision (ACES), and the Florida Counseling Association (FCA). He has presented nationally on topics including providing affirmative counseling care to queer and transgender communities of color, providing multicultural supervision, utilizing diverse approaches to counseling work, as well as addressing and disrupting white supremacy in counselor education. As an assistant professor at Florida Gulf Coast University, Dr. Gorritz FitzSimons utilizes his passions for social justice to empower students through andragogy as they develop their counseling and advocacy leadership skills.

fgorritz@fgcu.edu

239-590-7772

REFERENCES

Adams, G., Dobles, I., Gómez, L. H., Kurtis, T., & Molina, L. E. (2015). Decolonizing psychological science: Introduction to the special thematic section. *Journal of Social and Political Psychology*, *3*, 213-238. **https://dx.doi.org/10.5964/jspp.v3i1.564**

Afuape, T. (2011). *Power, resistance and liberation in therapy with survivors of trauma*. Routledge.

Akken, R. V. & Taracena, L. P. (2007). *La visión Indigena de la conquista* [The Indigenous vision of the conquest]. Serviprensa.

Aubrey, R. F. (1977). Historical development of guidance and counseling and implications for the future. *Personnel & Guidance Journal*, *55*(6), 288-295. **https://doi.org/10.1002/j.2164-4918.1977.tb04991.x**

Chavez, T. A., Torres Fernandez, I., Hipolito-Delgado, C. P., & Torres Rivera, E. (2016). Unifying liberation psychology and humanistic values to promote social justice in counseling. *The Journal of Humanistic Counseling*, *55*, 166-182.

Comas DÍAZ, L. & Torres Rivera, E. (2020). *Liberation psychology: Theory, method, practice, and social justice*. American Psychological Association.

DOMÍNGUEZ, D. G., HERNANDEZ-ARRIAGA, B., & PAUL, K. S. (2020). CRUZANDO FRONTERAS: LIBERATION PSYCHOLOGY IN A COUNSELING PSYCHOLOGY IMMERSION COURSE. JOURNAL OF LATINX PSYCHOLOGY, 8(3), 250-264. HTTPS://DOI.ORG/10.1037/LAT0000148

Enriquez, V. (1994). *From colonial to liberation psychology: The Philippine experience*. De La Salle Univeristy Press. Retrieved from **http://eaststemcell.com/files/storage.cloud.php?id=OTcxNTQyNTg4Nw==**

Goodyear, R. K. (1984). On our journal's evolution: Historical developments, transitions, and future directions [Editorial]. *Journal of Counseling & Development*, *63*(1), 3-9. https://doi.org/10.1002/j.1556-

Martín-Baró, I. (1998). Psicología de la liberación [Liberation psychology]. Editorial Trotta.

O'Connor, S., Tilyard, B. A., & Milfont, T. L. (2011). Liberation psychology: From Latin America to Aoteroa/New Zealand. *Journal of New Zealand Studies*, *11*, 151-170.

Pe-Pua, R. & Protacio-Marcelino, E. (2000). Sikolohiyang Pilipino (Filipino psychology): A legacy of Virgilio G. Enriquez. *Asian Journal of Social Psychology*, *3*, 49-71. **https://dx.doi.org/10.1111/1467-839X.00054**

Ratts, M. J. (2009). Social justice counseling: Toward the development of a fifth force among counseling paradigms. *The Journal of Humanistic Counseling, Education, and Development*, *48*(2), 160-172. **https://doi.org/10.1002/j.2161-1939.2009.tb00076.x**

Rivera, E. T. (2020). Concepts of liberation psychology. In L. Comas- DÍAZ & T. RIVERA (EDS.), LIBERATION PSYCHOLOGY: THEORY, METHOD, PRACTICE, AND SOCIAL JUSTICE (PP. 41-51). AMERICAN PSYCHOLOGICAL ASSOCIATION. https://doi.org/10.1037/0000198-000

Robertson, N. & Masters-Awatere, B. (2008). Community psychology in Aotearoa/New Zealand. In S. Reich, M. Reimer, I. Prilleltensky, & M. Montero (Eds.), *International community psychology: History and theories* (pp. 140-163). Springer Science + Media.

SÁNCHEZ, E. & WIESENFELD, E. (1991). COMMUNITY SOCIAL PSYCHOLOGY IN LATIN AMERICA [SPECIAL ISSUE]. APPLIED PSYCHOLOGY, 40(2).

Seedat, M. (1997). The quest for liberatory psychology. *South African Journal of Psychology, 27*, 261-270. **https://dx.doi.org/10.1177/008124639702700410**

Seedat, M. (2014). *Liberation psychology: 25 years on. Imagining Ignacio Martín-Baró and Steve Bantu Biko in conversation.* Retrieved from **http://libpsy.org/2014/11/16/liberation-psychology-25-years-on-imagining-ignacio-martin-baro-and-steve-bantu-biko-in-conversation/**

Seedat, M., Duncan, N., & Lazarus, S. (2001). *Community psychology: Theory, method and practice, South African and other perspectives.* Oxford University Press.

Summers, L. M. & Nelson, L. (2023). *Multicultural counseling: Responding with cultural humility, empathy, and advocacy.* Springer Publishing.

Tate, K. A., Torres Rivera, E., Brown, E., & Skaistis, L. (2013). Foundations for liberation: Social justice, liberation psychology, and counseling. *Revista Interamericana De Psicología/Interamerican Journal of Psychology, 47*, 373-382.

Yosso, T. J. (2005). Whose culture has capital? A critical race theory discussion of community cultural wealth. *Race Ethnicity and Education, 8*(1), 69-91. https://doi.org/ 10.1080/1361332052000341006

Life Coach

LORRIE-ANNE MONTE, PhD, MPH, CHES, NCC, LPC, PCS, BC-TMH

REAL BALANCE GLOBAL WELLNESS SERVICES CERTIFIED WELLNESS & HEALTH COACH

INTEGRATIVE NUTRITION HEALTH COACH

ROBBINS-MADANES TRAINED COACH

Our beliefs about what we are and what we can be, precisely determine what we will be.
-Tony Robbins

There are many definitions of life coaching but here is my personal favorite:

> Life coaching is a powerful human relationship in which trained coaches help people design their future rather than get over their past. Through a typically long-term relationship, coaches aid clients in creating visions and goals for all aspects of their lives and multiple strategies to support the achievement of those goals. Coaches recognize their clients' brilliance and their personal power to discover their own solutions when provided with support, accountability, and unconditional positive regard (Williams & Davis, 2007, p. xiii).

The growth of life coaching and many other types of coaching has been exponential since the 1990s (Grant & Cavanagh, 2018; Williams & Davis, 2007). Many therapists have chosen to pursue life coaching training and have added it to their repertoire of professional offerings, while others have transitioned completely into the coaching profession. It is important to note that coaching is not therapy. Coaching does not treat mental illness, it does not try to fix people, and it does not focus on the past. Coaching is about helping clients to use their own strengths and values to create personal goals that will help them to realize their own preferred future. Although there are many similarities between counseling and coach training, there are some coach competencies which are not taught in counseling programs. That is why it is important for counselors to obtain high quality coach training if they want to offer coaching services (Labardee et al., 2012; Williams & Davis, 2007).

OPTIONS FOR COACHING TRAINING & CERTIFICATION

If you are interested in becoming a life coach, there are many programs to choose from. You can complete a program and obtain a certificate of completion if you just want to increase your skills. Or you can become certified depending on the options provided by the coach training program. Every life coach training program is different with regards to modality of learning (in-person or online), hours required, cost, examinations, practical skills assessments, continuing education requirements, and annual fees.

It is extremely important to thoroughly research any life coach training programs that you are interested in to ensure that you are choosing a reputable program. Also, before you choose one and go for it, you should think carefully about your long-term goals. Many people who are truly dedicated to the coaching profession want to take their skills to the highest level possible, which means obtaining advanced coaching certifications. If that is of interest to you, you will need to understand the organizations that offer advanced credentials so that you can choose a coach training program that meets their standards.

With over 50,000 members, the International Coach Federation (ICF) is the largest coaching organization worldwide (ICF, 2022a). The ICF only accredits coach training programs that meet their specific requirements, and they offer three coaching credentials: Associate Certified Coach (ACC), Professional Certified Coach (PCC), and Master Certified Coach (MCC). Each credential has its own requirements regarding the number of coaching education and client coaching hours required along with examination and evaluation requirements. A list of ICF approved coach training programs can be found on their website (ICF, 2022b).

Another option for certification is the Center for Credentialing & Education (CCE), which is an affiliate of the National Board for Certified Counselors. The CCE offers various certifications for counselors, including the Board-Certified Coach (BCC) credential. It has multiple requirements for certification, such as educational experience, examination requirements, coach training, and coaching client hours completed. A list of CCE approved coach training programs can be found on their website (CCE, 2022). Other organizations that offer advanced certification include the International Association of Coaching and the European Mentoring and Coaching Council (EMCC) to name a few.

SUMMARY

Life Coaching is positive and exciting. It is about human potential, self-actualization, and helping others to become the best version of themselves. Ultimately, it is about thriving and flourishing as a human being. If the idea of helping others in this way resonates with you, then you might want to become a life coach.

When I first heard of the coaching profession, I was completely enamored. It spoke to my heart, mind, and soul. I already earned a Master of Science degree in Counseling with School Counselor Certification, and I was employed full-time as a high school counselor. I knew that the skills I would learn in coaching would help me to be a better school counselor. After extensive research, I started my coach training program journey. My first three coach training programs were focused on health and wellness coaching. You can read more about my experiences with health and wellness coaching training programs in the Health & Wellness Coach chapter in this book. Most recently, I completed the Robbins-Madanes Life Coach Training, Core 100 Training program. I chose this program because their life coach training program was a collaboration between Tony Robbins and Chloe Madanes. Tony Robbins is a legend in the coaching industry and Chloe Madanes is a legend in the field of family therapy. I loved the idea of the merger between the two and relished learning about life coaching from their perspective. The program did not disappoint. It provided me with 100 hours of fascinating life coach training.

Dr. Lorrie-Anne Monte is an Assistant Professor and the Fieldwork Coordinator in Counselor Education at Western Connecticut State University. Prior to that she was a high school counselor for over 18 years. She has a Bachelor of Science in Human Development and Family Relations from the University of Connecticut (UCONN). She also has a Master of Science in Counseling and a Master of Public Health from Southern Connecticut State University. She completed her 092 Educational Leadership coursework at Sacred Heart University. She also has a PhD in Educational Psychology: Counselor Education and Counseling Psychology from UCONN. Lorrie-Anne loves to learn, and constant personal and professional development is the air that she breathes. She is a Certified Health Education Specialist, a Real Balance Global Wellness Services Certified Wellness & Health Coach, an Integrative Nutrition Health Coach, a Robbins-Madanes Trained Coach, a National Certified Counselor, a Licensed Professional Counselor, a Pastoral Care Specialist, and a Board Certified-TeleMental Health Provider. Lorrie-Anne also strongly believes in being of service to others.

Western Connecticut State University
montel@wcsu.edu

REFERENCES

Center for Credentialing & Education. (2022). *BCC board certified coach (bcc)*. https://www.cce-global.org/credentialing/bcc

Grant, A. M., & Cavanagh, M. J. (2018). Life coaching. In E. Cox, T. Bachkirova, & D. Clutterbuck, (Eds.), *The complete handbook of coaching* (3rd ed.) (pp. 327-344). Sage.

International Coaching Federation. (2022a, January 24). *International coaching federation surpasses 50,000 ICF members worldwide*. https://www.prnewswire.com/news-releases/international-coaching-federation-surpasses-50-000-icf-members-worldwide-301465699.html

International Coaching Federation. (2022b). *What is an ICF credential*. https://coachingfederation.org/credentials-and-standards

Labardee, L., Williams, P., & Hodges, S. (2012, November 1). *Counselors who coach*. Counseling Today. https://ct.counseling.org/2012/11/counselors-who-coach/

Williams, P., & Davis, D. C. (2007). *Therapist as life coach*. W.W. Norton and Company.

Lifeline Technique Training Program

BILL OWENBY, EDD, MC, FAAETS, DAAETS, DCMHS, LPC, LAAC, NCC, CCMHC, ACS, DIPLOMATE, FELLOW

The Lifeline Technique is an integrative healing modality designed to address physical, emotional, and spiritual imbalances by activating the body's natural ability to heal itself. Developed by Dr. Darren Weissman, this technique blends elements of ancient healing traditions with modern neuroscience and energy medicine to create a holistic approach to well-being. The Lifeline Technique empowers practitioners and clients to transform negative emotions, limiting beliefs, and unresolved trauma into a state of balance, harmony, and vitality.

OVERVIEW OF THE LIFELINE TECHNIQUE

At its core, the Lifeline Technique is built upon the philosophy that symptoms and stress are the body's way of expressing subconscious imbalances. By accessing and harmonizing these imbalances, individuals can achieve lasting healing and transformation. The technique involves a specific flowchart of questions, gestures, and affirmations, guiding practitioners through a process of identifying and shifting energy blockages.

CORE PRINCIPLES OF THE LIFELINE TECHNIQUE

1. **Infinite Love and Gratitude**
   - A foundational mantra and gesture used to connect with the subconscious mind and promote healing.
   - Cultivates a mindset of acceptance, forgiveness, and empowerment.
2. **The Subconscious Mind**
   - Recognizes the subconscious as the storehouse of unresolved emotions and limiting beliefs.
   - Emphasizes the importance of addressing subconscious patterns to create sustainable change.
3. **The Five Basics for Optimal Health**
   - Focuses on physical, emotional, nutritional, environmental, and spiritual well-being as interconnected aspects of health.
4. **Holistic Integration**
   - Combines elements of Chinese medicine, Ayurvedic principles, neuro-linguistic programming (NLP), and quantum physics to create a multidimensional approach.

APPLICATIONS OF THE LIFELINE TECHNIQUE

Physical Health

- Addresses chronic pain, autoimmune conditions, and other physical symptoms as expressions of unresolved emotional energy.
- Supports the body's innate healing capacity through energy alignment.

Emotional Well-Being

- Identifies and releases suppressed emotions such as fear, anger, and sadness.
- Cultivates emotional resilience and self-empowerment.

Trauma Recovery

- Facilitates the release of trauma stored in the subconscious mind.
- Helps individuals regain a sense of safety and stability.

Personal Growth

- Encourages self-awareness and alignment with personal values and goals.
- Promotes a sense of purpose and fulfillment.

TRAINING AND CERTIFICATION IN LIFELINE TECHNIQUE

Educational Pathways

1. **Foundational Training**
   o The Lifeline Ignite program introduces the basic concepts and tools of the Lifeline Technique.
   o Typically delivered as a weekend workshop or online course.
2. **Advanced Training**
   o In-depth programs explore the full Lifeline Flowchart, advanced applications, and practitioner skills.
   o Includes hands-on practice, peer collaboration, and case study reviews.
3. **Mastery Certification**
   o Designed for professionals seeking to integrate the Lifeline Technique into their practice.
   o Focuses on advanced energy work, intuitive development, and client-centered techniques.

Certification Requirements

1. **Prerequisites**
   o No prior experience in energy work is required for foundational training.
   o Advanced training requires completion of foundational courses.
2. **Core Components**
   o Completion of all training modules.
   o Submission of case studies demonstrating proficiency in the Lifeline Technique.
   o Participation in mentorship and peer consultation groups.
3. **Time and Cost**
   o Foundational training: $300–$600 (2–3 days).
   o Advanced training: $2,000–$3,500 (3–6 months).
   o Mastery certification: $4,000–$6,000 (6–12 months).
4. **Accrediting Organization**
   o Training is overseen by The Lifeline Center, founded by Dr. Darren Weissman.

BENEFITS AND LIMITATIONS

Benefits

- **Holistic Healing**: Addresses multiple dimensions of health and well-being.
- **Empowerment**: Teaches clients and practitioners to harness the power of their subconscious mind.
- **Versatility**: Can be integrated into various professional practices, including psychotherapy, coaching, and holistic health.

Limitations

- **Accessibility**: Training programs may not be available in all regions.
- **Skepticism**: The integration of energy medicine and quantum physics may face criticism from traditional medical and scientific communities.
- **Time Commitment**: Certification requires significant investment in time and financial resources.

ETHICAL CONSIDERATIONS

1. **Informed Consent**
   - Practitioners must ensure clients understand the nature and scope of the Lifeline Technique.
2. **Scope of Practice**
   - Professionals should practice within their licensure and expertise, particularly when integrating energy work with clinical interventions.
3. **Cultural Sensitivity**
   - Techniques must be adapted to respect clients' cultural and spiritual beliefs.

SUMMARY

The Lifeline Technique offers a transformative approach to healing by harmonizing the mind, body, and spirit. Its integration of ancient wisdom and modern science provides a powerful framework for addressing physical symptoms, emotional challenges, and personal growth. With comprehensive training and adherence to ethical practices, professionals can use the Lifeline Technique to empower clients on their journey to wellness.

I hold two independent licenses in the states of Arizona and Ohio, supervisory status in Arizona, along with a substance abuse license in Arizona. I am board certified as a Diplomate and Clinical Mental Health Specialist, an Approved Clinical Supervisor, Nationally Certified Counselor, a Certified Clinical Mental Health Counselor, NeuroLinguistic Programming Practitioner, and a Clinical Trauma Specialist for Individuals and Family including EMDR Therapy and NET. I completed my training in Animal-Assisted Therapy and Pet Handlers certification in order to evaluate and incorporate the human-animal bond in therapy. I am the sole author and creator of the SxC Model of ESA Evaluation. My research interests surround post-traumatic growth, resiliency, strengths-based therapy, positive psychology, mindfulness, Animal-Assisted Therapy, Sandtray Therapy, Creative approaches in therapy, and martial arts in mental health. I have presented at local, state, regional, national, and international levels on various topics including personality traits, licensure reciprocity challenges, Sandtray and supervision, and Animal-Assisted Therapy within supervision.

eonbllc@gmail.com

REFERENCES

Weissman, D. (2013). The Power of Infinite Love & Gratitude: An Evolutionary Journey to Awakening Your Spirit. Hay House.

The Lifeline Center. (2024). Training and certification guidelines for the Lifeline Technique. Retrieved from https://www.thelifelinecenter.com

Lipton, B. H. (2005). The Biology of Belief: Unleashing the Power of Consciousness, Matter, and Miracles. Hay House.

Recommended Resources
The Lifeline Center: https://www.thelifelinecenter.com
Hay House Publishing: https://www.hayhouse.com
Infinite Love & Gratitude Community: https://www.infiniteloveandgratitude.com

Light Therapy

BILL OWENBY, EdD, MC, FAAETS, DAAETS, DCMHS, LPC, LAAC, NCC, CCMHC, ACS, DIPLOMATE, FELLOW

Light therapy, also known as phototherapy, is a non-invasive treatment that uses specific wavelengths of light to address various mental health, dermatological, and sleep-related conditions. This therapeutic approach has gained widespread recognition for its effectiveness in treating Seasonal Affective Disorder (SAD), depression, circadian rhythm disorders, and certain skin conditions like psoriasis.

CORE PRINCIPLES OF LIGHT THERAPY

1. **Wavelength-Specific Effects:**
   o Blue and white light are commonly used to regulate circadian rhythms and improve mood.
   o Red and near-infrared light are used for skin regeneration and wound healing.
2. **Timing and Duration:**
   o Treatments are typically conducted in the morning for 20-30 minutes to mimic natural daylight exposure.
3. **Intensity:**
   o Therapeutic light boxes provide an intensity of 10,000 lux, which is significantly brighter than standard indoor lighting.

APPLICATIONS IN MENTAL HEALTH AND WELLNESS

1. **Seasonal Affective Disorder (SAD):**
   o Light therapy is the first-line treatment for SAD, helping to alleviate depressive symptoms during fall and winter months.
2. **Depression:**
   o Studies show light therapy can augment antidepressant medications and benefit non-seasonal depression.
3. **Sleep Disorders:**
   o Effective in regulating sleep-wake cycles for individuals with insomnia, delayed sleep phase syndrome, or jet lag.
4. **Cognitive Function:**
   o Preliminary research indicates benefits for cognitive performance and mood stabilization in older adults.

NATURAL LIGHT VS. SIMULATED LIGHT

1. **Natural Light:**
   o Sunlight is the most accessible and powerful form of light therapy, containing the full spectrum of light essential for regulating circadian rhythms.
   o Benefits include:
      ▪ Stimulating vitamin D production.
      ▪ Regulating melatonin levels for better sleep.
      ▪ Enhancing mood and energy naturally.

- o Limitations:
  - Seasonal changes reduce sunlight availability.
  - Weather conditions or geographic location may limit access.
  - Overexposure to UV rays can pose risks of skin damage.
2. **Simulated Light:**
  - o Therapeutic light boxes replicate the effects of natural light without harmful UV rays.
  - o Advantages include:
    - Controlled exposure tailored to individual needs.
    - Usable during all seasons and weather conditions.
    - Portable and convenient for home or office use.
  - o Limitations:
    - May lack the full spectrum benefits of natural sunlight.
    - Requires proper calibration to ensure safety and efficacy.

CERTIFICATIONS, TRAINING, AND LICENSURE

1. **Education and Certification:**
   - o While no formal licensure is required for administering light therapy, several training programs and certifications are available.
2. **Training Programs:**
   - o **National Alliance on Mental Illness (NAMI):** Offers workshops on integrating light therapy for SAD and depression.
   - o **American Association of Sleep Technologists (AAST):** Provides training on light therapy applications for sleep disorders.
   - o **Photonic Therapy Institute:** Offers certifications for becoming a Certified Light Therapist (CLT), focusing on comprehensive phototherapy techniques. (Website)
   - o **Advanced Therapy Institute of Touch:** Provides a detailed Light Therapy Certification program that combines practical application with theoretical understanding. (Website)
   - o **PESI Certificate Course:** Offers a focused Red Light Therapy course tailored for mental health professionals, emphasizing safety and efficacy. (Website)
3. **Continuing Education:**
   - o Healthcare professionals can earn CE credits through these programs or courses offered by organizations like the American Psychological Association (APA).
4. **Device Safety Certification:**
   - o Ensure light therapy devices meet FDA guidelines for safety and efficacy.

COSTS OF TRAINING AND DEVICES

1. **Training Costs:**
   - o Workshops and courses range from $200 to $1,500, depending on format and duration. Advanced certifications, such as those from the Photonic Therapy Institute or PESI, may cost up to $2,500.
2. **Device Costs:**
   - o Therapeutic light boxes for personal use cost between $100 and $300, while clinical-grade devices can range from $500 to $2,000.

IDENTIFIED AS EVIDENCE-BASED PRACTICE

Light therapy is widely regarded as an evidence-based treatment for SAD and other circadian rhythm disorders. Research supports its efficacy, particularly when combined with traditional therapies like Cognitive Behavioral Therapy (CBT).

ETHICAL CONSIDERATIONS

1. **Contraindications:**
   o Not recommended for individuals with certain eye conditions or light sensitivity.
2. **Informed Consent:**
   o Clients should be informed about potential side effects, such as eye strain or headaches.
3. **Supervised Use:**
   o Sessions should be monitored to ensure proper device usage and exposure.

SCOPE OF PRACTICE

Light therapy should be integrated by licensed professionals as part of a comprehensive treatment plan. Collaboration with other healthcare providers, such as ophthalmologists or dermatologists, may enhance treatment outcomes.

WHAT KIND OF PERSON WOULD BENEFIT?

1. **Practitioners:**
   o Mental health professionals seeking non-pharmacological options for mood and sleep disorders.
   o Wellness coaches interested in holistic approaches to mental and physical health.
2. **Clients:**
   o Individuals with seasonal or chronic depression.
   o Those experiencing circadian rhythm disruptions.
   o Clients seeking adjunctive treatments for mood stabilization.

SUMMARY

Light therapy is a versatile and evidence-based treatment that addresses a range of mental health and physical conditions. By leveraging both natural and simulated light, it provides adaptable options for enhancing mood, sleep, and overall wellness. With accessible training programs and evolving research, practitioners can confidently integrate this modality into their practices. As interest in light therapy continues to grow, its potential to transform mental wellness and quality of life remains unparalleled.

I hold two independent licenses in the states of Arizona and Ohio, supervisory status in Arizona, along with a substance abuse license in Arizona. I am board certified as a Diplomate and Clinical Mental Health Specialist, an Approved Clinical Supervisor, Nationally Certified Counselor, a Certified Clinical Mental Health Counselor, NeuroLinguistic Programming Practitioner, and a Clinical Trauma Specialist for Individuals and Family including EMDR Therapy and NET. I completed my training in Animal-Assisted Therapy and Pet Handlers certification in order to evaluate and incorporate the human-animal bond in therapy. I am the sole author and creator of the SxC Model of ESA Evaluation. My research interests surround post-traumatic growth, resiliency, strengths-based therapy, positive psychology, mindfulness, Animal-Assisted Therapy, Sandtray Therapy, Creative approaches in therapy, and martial arts in mental health. I have presented at local, state, regional, national, and international levels on various topics including personality traits, licensure reciprocity challenges, Sandtray and supervision, and Animal-Assisted Therapy within supervision. eonbllc@gmail.com

REFERENCES

Golden, R. N., Gaynes, B. N., Ekstrom, R. D., et al. (2005). The efficacy of light therapy in the treatment of mood disorders: A review and meta-analysis. *American Journal of Psychiatry*.

Terman, M., & Terman, J. S. (2005). Light therapy for seasonal and nonseasonal depression: Efficacy, protocol, safety, and side effects. *CNS Spectrums*.

Recommended Online Resources

National Alliance on Mental Illness
American Association of Sleep Technologists
American Psychological Association
Photonic Therapy Institute
Advanced Therapy Institute of Touch
PESI Red Light Therapy Certificate

Logic-Based/Philosophical Therapy (LBPT)

ARIELLE JORDAN, PHD, MS, LCPC, NCC

Logic-Based/Philosophical Therapy (LBPT) is a therapeutic approach that focuses on helping individuals identify, evaluate, and modify their beliefs and thought processes. This treatment model is grounded in the principles of philosophy and logic and aims to promote rational thinking, emotional regulation, and improved decision-making.

The development of LBPT can be attributed to philosopher and psychotherapist Dr. Elliot D. Cohen, who founded the Institute of Critical Thinking and the National Philosophical Counseling Association (now the American Philosophical Practitioners Association) in the 1980s. Dr. Cohen's background in philosophy and psychology, along with his extensive research and publications, have contributed significantly to the establishment and popularization of LBPT.

The emergence of LBPT coincided with a growing interest in alternative forms of therapy and a cultural shift towards greater self-awareness and introspection. LBPT's underlying philosophy is rooted in the belief that many emotional and mental issues stem from irrational or faulty thinking patterns. By applying philosophical concepts and techniques, clients can identify, analyze, and modify these patterns to achieve greater clarity and insight.

Individuals may seek out LBPT for a variety of reasons, such as a desire to better understand their thought processes, beliefs, and values, or to address specific emotional or mental challenges. By fostering rational thinking and self-reflection, LBPT empowers clients to develop healthier perspectives and make more informed decisions in their lives.

The core principles of LBPT include:

- Identifying and analyzing irrational beliefs
- Developing logical reasoning skills
- Encouraging self-reflection and introspection
- Promoting ethical decision-making

Given the unique nature of this therapy, it is essential to discuss the certification, training, and licensure requirements for practitioners of LBPT.

CERTIFICATION AND TRAINING REQUIREMENTS

Several certification and training programs are available for those interested in pursuing LBPT. Some of the most notable programs include:

- The American Philosophical Practitioners Association (APPA) Certification Program Home - APPA

- The Logic-Based Therapy Institute's Certification Program PRIMARY & ADVANCED TRAINING PROGRAMS | Logic-Based Therapy.

Each program has its own set of requirements, such as completing specific courses, attending workshops, and demonstrating competency in the practice of LBPT. Prospective practitioners must research and compare these programs to determine which best aligns with their professional goals and needs.

LICENSURE REQUIREMENTS

Licensure requirements for practicing LBPT vary depending on the jurisdiction and the practitioner's background. In some cases, a license in a related mental health field (e.g., psychology, counseling, or social work) may be sufficient for practicing LBPT. However, it is essential to consult local regulations and guidelines to determine the specific licensure requirements for your area.

The process of obtaining a license typically involves:

- Completing the necessary education and training

- Passing a licensing examination

- Meeting any additional requirements, such as supervised practice or continuing education

SCOPE OF PRACTICE ISSUES

Practitioners of LBPT must be aware of the limitations and boundaries of their practice. Some considerations include:

- Ensuring that the therapy is appropriate for the client's presenting issues

- Recognizing when a referral to a different professional or treatment modality may be necessary

- Adhering to ethical guidelines and professional standards

Examples of situations that may pose scope of practice issues include:

- Clients presenting with severe mental health disorders that require specialized intervention

- Clients who may benefit from a different therapeutic approach that is outside the practitioner's expertise

- Ethical dilemmas, such as conflicts of interest or dual relationships

SUMMARY

In conclusion, Logic-Based/Philosophical Therapy is a unique treatment model that focuses on helping individuals develop rational thinking and emotional regulation skills. Practitioners must know the certification, training, and licensure requirements and the scope of practice issues associated with this therapy.

Advantages of LBPT include:

- A focus on rational thinking and self-reflection
- A strong philosophical foundation
- Applicability to a wide range of issues

Disadvantages may include:

- Limited research on its effectiveness compared to other therapies
- Potential challenges in navigating the scope of practice issues

We encourage readers to explore this therapy further and consider the resources provided by organizations such as the APPA and the Logic-Based Therapy Institute for additional information and training opportunities.

Dr. Arielle Jordan is an Army veteran, licensed clinical professional counselor (LCPC) in Maryland, nationally certified counselor, and EMDR consultant. She is the founder of Mindset Quality, a telehealth private practice providing trauma-informed counseling, consultation, and EMDR-based services. Her work focuses on trauma, PTSD, grief, complex stress, and racialized trauma, with an emphasis on culturally responsive and evidence-based care.

Dr. Jordan holds a Bachelor of Science in Psychology and a Master of Science in Clinical Mental Health Counseling, and she has completed her PhD in Counselor Education and Supervision. As an EMDR consultant and IFS-informed clinician, she brings a relational, neuroscience-informed, and systems-aware lens to both clinical practice and professional education.

In addition to her clinical work, Dr. Jordan is an international speaker, author, and educator passionate about clinician development, ethical practice, and expanding access to high-quality mental health care. She is especially committed to serving veterans, service-connected communities, and individuals impacted by systemic and racial stress while building meaningful, resilient lives.

Website: https://bio.ariellenjordan.com

REFERENCES

Cohen, E. D. (2003). What is Logic-Based Therapy? Retrieved from https://www.appa.edu/what_is_lbt.htm

Marinoff, L. (1999). Plato, Not Prozac!: Applying Eternal Wisdom to Everyday Problems. HarperCollins.

https://appa.edu/

https://www.philosophicalpractice.net/primary-advanced-training-programs

Logotherapy/Existential Analysis (LTEA)

CYNTHIA WIMBERLY, PHD

Finding Health in Meaning and Purpose

BACKGROUND

Logotherapy, founded by Viktor Frankl MD, PhD in the 1930's, is grounded in the premise that meaning is the primary motivation. Dr. Frankl, born in Vienna in 1905, became interested in the new study developed by Sigmund Freud, psychology. As a student of both Freud and Adler's work during the years between World War I and World War II, he came to the realization that there was a key dynamic missing in both the theory of psychoanalysis and individual psychology. Observing the lives of both his patients and those he interacted with, he began to recognize the fundamental role of discovering meaning in life.

Writing his first draft of what would become known as the theory of Logotherapy before his imprisonment in the concentration camps of WWII, Frankl often stated he "tested" his theory in Theresienstadt, Auschwitz, Dachau, and Turkheim. Returning to Vienna after his release from the camps, he began to again put his theory into writing. Using secretly kept records of his observations in the camps, he published a book in German entitled *Arztliche Seelsorge,* where he presented his new theory, Logotherapy. This book was translated into English in 1959, and in a revised and enlarged edition appeared as *The Doctor and the Soul: An Introduction to Logotherapy* in 1963.

However, for many, *Man's Search for Meaning,* written in 1946 where he described his experiences in the concentration camps, was their introduction to Logotherapy. By the time of Dr. Frankl's death, *Man's Search for Meaning* had been translated into 24 languages and reprinted 73 times and had long been used as a standard text in high school and university courses in psychology, philosophy, and theology.

When Viktor Frankl died in 1997, he had received 29 honorary doctorates from universities in all parts of the world, wrote over 30 books and became the first non-American to be awarded the American Psychiatric Association's prestigious Oskar Pfister Prize, served as a visiting professor at Harvard, Stanford and other universities in Pittsburgh, San Diego and Dallas, and lectured at 209 universities on five continents.

THEORY

The theory of Logotherapy is based on several key assumptions:

1. Humans are three-dimensional beings consisting of a body (soma), mind, (psyche), and spirit (noös).
2. Spirit or noös, however, refers to the uniquely human essence; not connected to a religious definition.
3. Each human is unique and irreplaceable as is each moment. Neither can be duplicated.
4. Because each person is unique and each situation is unique, the meaning potential in that moment is only available to that one individual at that one time.
5. Life itself has a demand quality to which each person is challenged to respond meaningfully. We each have unique life tasks to perform: we are here on purpose. Because we are unique, the meaning in each situation is unique to us, in that moment.
6. An individual has the free will to make a choice. Each is "response-able" in how we act.

These assumptions center on three basic tenets or principles:

1) Freedom of will

This freedom resides in the noetic (spiritual) dimension unique to humanity. It is the space where an individual has the ability to take a stand against challenges in the dimensions of the psyche and/or the soma (body). Each human has the opportunity to take a stand against internal (psychological) and external (biological and social) conditions. Freedom of will allows a human to act not simply react.

2) Will to Meaning

This desire to live a life with meaning is the primary motivation to live with purpose. It allows individuals to pursue life's meaning. (Meaning is not created by the individual but rather life offers us the ability to discover the meaning of the moment.) It is an individual journey unique to the person, the time, and the situation.

3) Meaning in Life

There is always meaning available; it is an objective reality. Each person is challenged to respond to the situation based on individual meaning potentials in a responsible manner. This response can be based in context of creativity or accomplishment (doing), experiential (experiencing, loving) or attitudinal (adapting attitude toward an unchangeable fate).

Frankl taught that each of us would deal with the tragic triad consisting of suffering, guilt and death. In each of these, he saw the opportunity to discover meaning; to respond by improving oneself. Specifically, LTEA is used to combat those dealing with an existential vacuum; a loss of meaning or reason for existence, brought about by the tragic triad, fate, or an issue beyond self-regulation (i.e. addiction, depression, anxiety, posttraumatic stress, etc.) However, as an adjunct LTEA can be useful in providing a complete treatment plan by addressing the noetic dimension.

The American Medical Society, the American Psychiatric Association and the American Psychological Association have officially recognized Dr. Frankl's Logotherapy as one of the scientifically based schools of psychotherapy.

INSTITUTE

The beginnings of the Viktor Frankl Institute of Logotherapy can be traced back to 1965 when Dr. Viktor Frankl gave a presentation at the Unitarian Church of Berkley in California. In the audience was an interested attendee by the name of Joseph Fabry. Fabry, like Frankl was a Jew who was forced out of his home during the Nazi invasion of Austria. Fabry intrigued by Frankl's comments, soon began to hold meetings in his home to share and study the concepts found in Logotherapy.

On February 14, 1978, the Institute of Logotherapy was incorporated. Soon afterwards, Vera Lieban Kalmar, PhD began organizing the first curricula for teaching the concepts of Logotherapy. In 1984, the *International Forum for Logotherapy* was copyrighted. In 1989 during the presidency of Bianca Hirsh, PhD, Viktor Frankl gave permission for the use of his name in the title of the institute.

Currently, information about the Institute can be found on the website **https://www.viktorfranklinstitute.org** In addition to the education courses, Logochats are held every other month, free to all registered participants on different topics of interest. World Congresses are held biannually with the last Congress held virtually in October 2023. The *International Forum for Logotherapy* is published twice a year and can be obtained online through the website. Additional information on workshops and topics of interest can also be found online. Interested individuals are encouraged to contact the Institute through **info@viktorfranklinstitue.org**

EDUCATION: COURSES LEADING TO CERTIFICATION

The VFIL offers education opportunities that provide continuing education credits. The Institute is approved by the American Psychological Association (APA) as a provider of Continuing Education units (CE) for psychologists. Many state licensing boards, and professional organizations accept CE units that are granted by the American Psychological Association.

Logotherapy Introductory Course

This course consists of 15 hours of on-site group instruction or 5 individual tutorial sessions with the instructor to discuss lesson. Cost: $450 (US)

Course: *Foundations of Logotherapy*

Prerequisite: none

Description: The Introductory course serves as a foundation in Logotherapy and familiarizes participants with Frankl's existential approach to the fundamental motivating factor in human existence, the search for meaning. As an introduction, the basic concepts, postulates, teachings, and philosophy that comprise the Third School of Viennese Psychiatry are covered. The Will to Meaning is contrasted with the Will to Pleasure and the Will to Power. Humans as conceptualized in three dimensions and the dynamic power of the human spirit are explored. Three ways to find meaning are presented and examples given. Socratic dialogue is practiced. Contemporary uses of Frankl's work are discussed. Students will develop a personal statement of meaning and discuss case studies. The course ends with a summary, review, and evaluation.

Required readings include *Man's Search for Meaning* by Viktor E. Frankl and additional readings as supplied by the instructor.

Logotherapy Intermediate Courses

The two intermediate courses focus on areas of Logotherapeutic application.

Each course is 30 hours of on-site instruction or 10 individual tutorial sessions with the instructor to discuss lesson. Cost per course: $600 (US)

Course: *Logotherapy: Attitudinal Change*

Prerequisite: Completion of the course Foundation of Logotherapy Description: Building upon information from the Foundations of Logotherapy course, this course develops the concept of attitudinal change and its importance in the utilization of Frankl's Logotherapy in understanding meaning. Key techniques and methods are explored. In addition, the concepts of Frankl's phenomenological theory, existential vacuum, and the components of the tragic triad are explored. The role of experiential activities in the development of attitudinal change in all areas of the meaning triangle (creative, experiential, and attitudinal) are explored. Case studies utilizing key concepts are provided. The course concludes with a summary, review, and evaluation.

Required readings include *Will to Meaning* by Viktor Frankl, *The Pursuit of Meaning* by Joseph Fabry and additional readings as supplied by the instructor.

Course: *Logotherapy: Meaning-Centered Interventions*

Prerequisite: Completion of the courses Foundations of Logotherapy and Attitudinal Change

Description: Following a natural progression of thought and practice from attitudinal change to Meaning-Centered Interventions, this course involves a study of the affirmative, future oriented, holistic approach of Logotherapy that seeks to reverse the trend of meaninglessness, depersonalization, and nihilism. The course focuses on helping to facilitate an awareness of dignity and uniqueness within the individual as a source of strength and well-being for making choices and taking responsibility for one's actions. In addition, Logotherapy's three-dimensional concept of the human being (somatic, psychic, *noetic*) as a significant resource for mental health is explored. Logotherapy's place in the discipline of psychotherapy, as well as when it is appropriate for it be used as an adjunct theory, is identified. Key topics include Logotherapy's use in crisis intervention and prevention, in addictions, in depression, and in exploring ethical concepts. As in the previous course, the role of experiential activities in the development of all areas of the meaning triangle are explored. Case studies utilizing key concepts are provided. The course concludes with a summary, review, and evaluation.

Required readings include The Doctor and the Soul (Part I) by Viktor Frankl, Viktor Frankl's Logotherapy by Ann V. Graber, and additional readings as supplied by the instructor.

Course: *Logotherapy Advanced Course*

Each course is 30 hours of on-site instruction or 10 individual tutorial sessions with the instructor to discuss the lesson. Cost per course: $600 (US)

Students will register for one (1) advanced course. In order to register for Logotherapy for Clinical Practice, a student is encouraged to hold a valid mental health license or to meet requirements in their country to practice.

Course: *Logotherapy for Clinical Practice*

Prerequisites: Completion of Introduction to Logotherapy and the two Intermediate courses in Logotherapy

Description: This is a practically oriented course for licensed professionals that provides a contemporary focus on logotherapy for behavioral health disorders. The course includes theoretical underpinnings, clinical applications, and clinical research. Broad concepts in ethics and culture are included. The learner is guided in navigating the dialectical paradoxes of holism and pluralism, objectivity and subjectivity, absurdity/facticity and meaning, and Frankl's dimensional ontology, in the unique phenomenologies of client life and existential distress. Emphasis will be on competency in case study analysis of creatively applying self-distancing and self-transcendence to support client's meaning-discovery. An emphasis on case demonstrations/illustrations is incorporated into the format of the course. The course concludes with a summary, review, and evaluation.

Required readings include *The Doctor and the Soul* (Part II) by Viktor Frankl, *On the Theory and Therapy of Mental Disorders* by Viktor Frankl, and additional readings as supplied by the instructor.

Course: *Contemporary Application of Logo-Philosophy: Logotherapy in Non-Clinical Settings*

Prerequisites: Completion of Introduction to Logotherapy and the two Intermediate courses in Logotherapy

Description: This course is designed for those who are interested in the application of logotherapy and logo philosophy in spaces outside of direct health care settings, including but not limited to coaching, education, business, consulting, and organizational life. The course is focused on the philosophy and posture of Logotherapeutic approaches, and applications in various aspects of life. Ample attention is given to ethical considerations. The course frames logo-philosophy application through the lens of maieutic presence, with attention to the importance of stillness, the awakening of conscience for its noetic discernment, techniques for values-discourse, and a variety of tools and interview-approaches to draw forth self-transcendence and self-distancing towards meaning-discovery in all areas of life and vocations.

Academic Associate Credential

The "Academic Associate" credential is available upon completion of four courses in Logotherapy: Introductory Course, two Intermediate Courses, and one Advanced Course. Application must be made to the Viktor Frankl Institute of Logotherapy.

Diplomate Credential

Qualified adult learners wishing to pursue the "Diplomate" credential will engage in supervised study after earning the Academic Associate credential. Students in both Diplomate tracks will submit a written paper presenting the student's areas of expertise. The individual topic will be determined in consultation with the supervising diplomate. Cost: $1500 (US)

DIPLOMATE FOR CLINICAL PRACTICE

PREREQUISITES: License to practice (at a minimum of the master's degree level) in one of the human services fields. Official transcripts, copies of state licenses, and Associate in Logotherapy credential must be on file in the Institute office.

Requirements:

- Practicum: Fifty (50) hours of individual and group counseling in which the concepts of logotherapy are integrated. (An approved Institute clinical faculty member of the candidate's choice will supervise.)

- Supervision: Twenty-five (25) hours (For every 2 hours of practicum experience, one hour of supervision shall be required). Through analysis of case studies presented by the candidate, proficiency must be demonstrated in the following areas: evaluation and diagnosis, appropriate intervention, and therapeutic techniques in which the concepts of Logotherapy are integrated, record keeping, consultation protocol with related professionals, and knowledge of ethical responsibilities.

- Research Paper: A written paper will be presented in APA format to the Institute focused on one area of the student's interests. This will be determined in consultation with the supervising diplomate.

DIPLOMATE IN LOGO-PHILOSOPHY

PREREQUISITES: Education at, or equivalent to, a minimum of the master's degree level OR appropriate life experiences as approved by the Institute. Applicable to those whose primary responsibilities do not include the clinical application of Logotherapy or for those interested in doing a research or other non-practicum project. Associate in Logotherapy credential must be on file.

Requirements:

Research Paper: A written research project in the work of Viktor E. Frankl, MD, PhD, as seen in Logotherapy presented in APA format. The supervising Diplomate (an approved Institute faculty member of the candidate's choice) will serve in a tutorial capacity during this advanced independent study to guide and encourage the Diplomate candidate to the successful completion of the stated goal. The Diplomate project will reflect the candidate's area of expertise and will be relevant to the chosen area of application.

Applicants for the Diplomate Clinician and Diplomate in Logo-Philosophy credential must be members of the Viktor Frankl Institute of Logotherapy and must MAINTAIN membership in the Institute in order to retain the validity of the Diplomate credential.

The Viktor Frankl Institute of Logotherapy maintains responsibility for the program and its content.

RESEARCH SUPPORTING LOGOTHERAPY

Dr. Frank encouraged both experimental and empirical validation of Logotherapy. Individuals who are interested in specific research are encouraged to review the work of James Crumbaugh, Robert Hutzell, Paul Wong, Alexander Batthayany, Stefan Schulenberg, and numerous dissertations, research studies, and case studies on Logotherapy in general or specific techniques or applications.

SUMMARY

Viktor Frankl's Logotherapy is both a life philosophy and a treatment modality. As a philosophy, it focuses on the meaning of human existence and on man's search for such meaning. As a therapy, it focuses on finding health through finding meaning. Although developed in the 1930's, the concepts in Logotherapy are as vital today as they were then.

The courses at the VFIL are open to anyone interested in learning new ways of finding meaning in the day to day, moment to moment existence called life. Viktor Frankl's life serves as a reminder to all, no matter how difficult the path may be, choosing to give up, before it has had the chance to fly, only holds the human spirit back. We welcome not only mental health professionals looking for methods to better treat their clients, but also individuals looking for better ways to live their life by exploring how Logotherapy can provide the tools for discovering meaning.

May you find the study of Logotherapy stimulating and noetically rewarding!

Cynthia Wimberly received her PhD in Counselor Education from Texas Tech University in Lubbock, Texas. She has over 40 years' experience in education and counseling working as a school counselor at all levels. She retired from the University of Texas Rio Grande Valley in 2018 where she served as Chair of the Department of Counseling. Currently, she works at the Noah Project, a shelter for individuals experiencing domestic violence, in Abilene Texas where she is director of primary prevention and coordinator of the Battering Intervention and Prevention Program. In addition, she serves as president of the Viktor Frankl Institute of Logotherapy. Her areas of research include school counseling, at risk students, domestic violence, and the application of Logotherapy in each of these areas.

Cynthia Wimberly, PhD, LPC-S, NCC, NCSC
Diplomate Clinician in Logotherapy
Contact: Cynthia.wimberlyphd@gmail.com
WEBSITE: Viktor Frankl Institute of Logotherapy
https://www.viktorfranklinstitute.org

REFERENCES

Batthyany, A. & Guttmann, D. (2006). Empirical research on logotherapy and meaning-oriented psychotherapy. Zeig, Tucker & Theisen, Inc.

Fabry, J. (First published in 1980, but recent editions available). The pursuit of meaning: Viktor Frankl, logotherapy and life. Harper & Row.

Frankl, V.K. (First published in1946, but any edition) Man's search for meaning, Washington Square Press.

Frankl, V.K. (First published in 1969, but recent editions available). The will to meaning. New American Library.

Lucid Dream Therapy

BILL OWENBY, EdD, MC, FAAETS, DAAETS, DCMHS, LPC, LAAC, NCC, CCMHC, ACS, DIPLOMATE, FELLOW

Lucid Dream Therapy (LDT) is a therapeutic approach that utilizes lucid dreaming—the ability to become aware that one is dreaming while still within the dream state—to address trauma, anxiety, nightmares, and personal growth. Emerging from a fusion of dream analysis, cognitive-behavioral therapy, mindfulness, and trauma recovery, LDT is gaining recognition as a promising intervention for individuals struggling with chronic nightmares, PTSD, and subconscious fears.

WHAT IS LUCID DREAM THERAPY?

Lucid Dream Therapy is based on the concept that within a dream state, individuals can become conscious of their surroundings, emotions, and thoughts, and actively participate in the dream's outcome. When trained effectively, clients can use this altered state of awareness to:

- Gain control over recurring nightmares
- Confront and integrate past traumas
- Resolve internal conflicts
- Explore subconscious fears and anxieties
- Enhance creativity and emotional regulation

Lucid dreaming has been studied extensively in neuroscience and psychology, showing measurable cognitive and emotional benefits (LaBerge, 1985; Dresler et al., 2014). Research suggests that training in lucid dreaming techniques can reduce nightmare frequency and intensity, increase emotional resilience, and improve mental clarity (Spoormaker & van den Bout, 2006).

THE SCIENCE BEHIND LUCID DREAMING

Neuroscientific research has identified distinct changes in brain activity during lucid dreaming, particularly in the prefrontal cortex, associated with metacognition, self-awareness, and executive functioning (Voss et al., 2009). This suggests that lucid dreaming engages cognitive processes similar to wakeful problem-solving, allowing individuals to process emotions, fears, and past traumas in a controlled manner (Hobson, 2009).

Therapeutically, lucid dreaming is considered an advanced form of exposure therapy, where individuals gradually expose themselves to distressing scenarios in a safe, dream-based environment (Harb et al., 2012).

1. Trauma and PTSD

- Many individuals suffering from PTSD experience repetitive, distressing nightmares related to traumatic events.
- Lucid dreaming provides a way to reframe, alter, and resolve these nightmares, reducing emotional reactivity and distress (Germain et al., 2013).

2. Nightmares and Sleep Disorders

- Lucid dreaming can be particularly useful for individuals with chronic nightmares, sleep paralysis, and night terrors.
- Studies indicate that learning to recognize and manipulate dream states helps reduce the frequency and severity of nightmares (Spoormaker et al., 2003).

3. Anxiety and Emotional Regulation

- Lucid dreaming allows individuals to explore anxiety-provoking situations in a controlled, subconscious space, leading to increased self-awareness and reduced daytime anxiety (Denis & Poerio, 2017).

4. Creative Problem-Solving

- Artists, writers, and scientists have historically used lucid dreams for creative insights and problem-solving (Barrett, 2001).
- Training individuals in lucid dreaming techniques can enhance cognitive flexibility, creativity, and emotional expression.

TECHNIQUES USED IN LUCID DREAM THERAPY

Several techniques are commonly employed in lucid dream training, each aimed at increasing dream recall, inducing lucidity, and enhancing dream control:

1. Reality Testing (RT):
   - Practicing self-awareness exercises during the day, such as questioning, "Am I dreaming?"
   - Helps individuals recognize dream inconsistencies and triggers lucidity in dreams.
2. Mnemonic Induction of Lucid Dreams (MILD):
   - Developed by Dr. Stephen LaBerge, this technique involves setting an intention before sleep to become aware within a dream (LaBerge, 1985).
3. Wake-Induced Lucid Dreaming (WILD):
   - A more advanced technique where individuals enter a lucid dream directly from wakefulness, bypassing unconscious sleep stages.
4. Dream Journaling:
   - Keeping a dream journal improves dream recall and strengthens self-awareness in the dream state.
5. Cognitive Reframing of Nightmares:
   - Individuals reinterpret distressing dream content, shifting fear-based scenarios into empowering experiences.
6. Guided Visualization and Meditation:
   - Meditation and progressive relaxation techniques increase dream control and awareness.

TRAINING AND CERTIFICATION IN LUCID DREAM THERAPY

Several organizations offer formal training and certification programs in Lucid Dream Therapy, dream-based interventions, and sleep psychology:

Lucid Dream Therapy Certification Programs

1. Introduction to Lucid Dreaming – Monroe Institute
   - A self-paced course focusing on lucid dream induction techniques, consciousness expansion, and dream exploration.
   - Website: MonroeInstitute.org
2. Mindful Lucid Dreaming Therapy – Foundations Series
   - A structured, step-by-step course in lucid dream therapy, mindfulness techniques, and dream journaling.
   - Website: MindfulLucidDreaming.com
3. Dream Yoga & Lucid Dream Therapy – The Shift Network
   - Focuses on spiritual and psychological applications of lucid dreaming in therapy and personal development.
   - Website: ShiftNetwork.com
4. CBT for Nightmares & Lucid Dream Therapy Training – The International Association for the Study of Dreams (IASD)
   - Offers a certification in CBT for nightmares and lucid dreaming interventions.
   - Website: ASDreams.org

CAUTIONS AND LIMITATIONS OF LUCID DREAM THERAPY

- Not a Standalone Treatment for PTSD: LDT should complement, not replace, evidence-based trauma therapies like EMDR, CBT, or prolonged exposure therapy (Germain et al., 2013).
- Risk of Sleep Disruptions: Some clients may experience insomnia, sleep paralysis, or dissociation if not properly guided.
- Not Suitable for All Clients: Individuals with schizophrenia, severe dissociation, or psychosis may experience increased derealization and distress.
- Requires Consistency: Learning lucid dreaming takes time, and results vary among individuals.

SUMMARY

Lucid Dream Therapy offers a fascinating, evidence-based approach to treating nightmares, trauma, and anxiety, utilizing dream awareness as a powerful psychological tool. With proper training, mental health professionals can integrate lucid dreaming techniques into clinical practice, empowering clients to transform distressing dreams, regulate emotions, and access deeper levels of healing.

For more information, visit:

- MonroeInstitute.org
- MindfulLucidDreaming.com

I hold two independent licenses in the states of Arizona and Ohio, supervisory status in Arizona, along with a substance abuse license in Arizona. I am board certified as a Diplomate and Clinical Mental Health Specialist, an Approved Clinical Supervisor, Nationally Certified Counselor, a Certified Clinical Mental Health Counselor, NeuroLinguistic Programming Practitioner, and a Clinical Trauma Specialist for Individuals and Family including EMDR Therapy and NET. I completed my training in Animal-Assisted Therapy and Pet Handlers certification in order to evaluate and incorporate the human-animal bond in therapy. I am the sole author and creator of the SxC Model of ESA Evaluation. My research interests surround post-traumatic growth, resiliency, strengths-based therapy, positive psychology, mindfulness, Animal-Assisted Therapy, Sandtray Therapy, Creative approaches in therapy, and martial arts in mental health. I have presented at local, state, regional, national, and international levels on various topics including personality traits, licensure reciprocity challenges, Sandtray and supervision, and Animal-Assisted Therapy within supervision. eonbllc@gmail.com

REFERENCES

LaBerge, S. (1985). Lucid Dreaming: The Power of Being Awake and Aware in Your Dreams. Ballantine Books.

Voss, U., Holzmann, R., Tuin, I., & Hobson, J. A. (2009). Lucid dreaming: A state of consciousness with features of both waking and dreaming. Sleep, 32(9), 1191-1200.

Spoormaker, V. I., & van den Bout, J. (2006). Lucid dreaming treatment for nightmares: A pilot study. Psychotherapy and Psychosomatics, 75(6), 389-394.

www.ingramcontent.com/pod-product-compliance
Lightning Source LLC
Chambersburg PA
CBHW080547270326
41929CB00019B/3217